DISINFORMATION, MISINFORMATION, AND DEMOCRACY

In today's digital age, the spread of dis- and misinformation across traditional and social media poses a significant threat to democracy. Yet repressing political speech in the name of truth can also undermine democratic values. This volume brings together prominent legal scholars from democracies worldwide to explore and evaluate different regulatory approaches for addressing this complex problem – all taking into account that the cure must not be worse than the disease. Using a comparative lens, the book offers important and novel insights into methods ranging from national regulation of politicians' speech to empowering civil-society groups that are well-positioned to blunt the effects of disinformation and misinformation. The book also provides solutions-oriented recommendations for policymakers, judges, legal practitioners, and scholars seeking to promote democratic values by encouraging free political speech while combatting disinformation and misinformation. This title is also available as Open Access on Cambridge Core.

Ronald J. Krotoszynski, Jr. is the John S. Stone Chair, Director of the Program in Constitutional Studies and Initiative for Civic Engagement. He is the author of numerous law review articles and several books, including *Free Speech as Civic Structure* (2024) and *The Disappearing First Amendment* (2019).

András Koltay is Research Professor at the Ludovika – University of Public Service (Budapest) and Professor of Law at Pázmány Péter Catholic University (Budapest). His principal research has been concerned with freedom of speech, personality rights, and media regulation. He is the author of *Media Freedom and the Law* (2024) and *New Media and Freedom of Expression* (2019).

Charlotte Garden is the Julius E. Davis Professor of Law at the University of Minnesota. Much of her scholarship and public commentary considers the relationship among the First Amendment, labor unions, and American democracy. She is a co-editor of *The Cambridge Handbook of U.S. Labor Law for the Twenty-First Century* (2019).

Disinformation, Misinformation, and Democracy

LEGAL APPROACHES IN COMPARATIVE CONTEXT

Edited by

RONALD J. KROTOSZYNSKI, JR.

University of Alabama

ANDRÁS KOLTAY

Ludovika – University of Public Service (Hungary)

CHARLOTTE GARDEN

University of Minnesota

CAMBRIDGE
UNIVERSITY PRESS

CAMBRIDGE
UNIVERSITY PRESS

Shaftesbury Road, Cambridge CB2 8EA, United Kingdom

One Liberty Plaza, 20th Floor, New York, NY 10006, USA

477 Williamstown Road, Port Melbourne, VIC 3207, Australia

314–321, 3rd Floor, Plot 3, Splendor Forum, Jasola District Centre, New Delhi – 110025, India

103 Penang Road, #05-06/07, Visioncrest Commercial, Singapore 238467

Cambridge University Press is part of Cambridge University Press & Assessment, a department of the University of Cambridge.

We share the University's mission to contribute to society through the pursuit of education, learning and research at the highest international levels of excellence.

www.cambridge.org
Information on this title: www.cambridge.org/9781009373289

DOI: 10.1017/9781009373272

First published 2024

A catalogue record for this publication is available from the British Library.

Library of Congress Cataloging-in-Publication Data
NAMES: Ronald J. Krotoszynski, Jr., 1967-editor. | Koltay, András, 1978-editor. | Garden, Charlotte, 1979-editor.
TITLE: Disinformation, misinformation, and democracy : legal approaches in comparative context / edited by Ronald J. Krotoszynski, Jr., András Koltay, Charlotte Garden.
DESCRIPTION: Cambridge, United Kingdom ; New York, NY : Cambridge University Press, 2024. | Includes bibliographical references and index.
IDENTIFIERS: LCCN 2024013567 (print) | LCCN 2024013568 (ebook) | ISBN 9781009373289 (hardback) | ISBN 9781009373302 (paperback) | ISBN 9781009373272 (epub)
SUBJECTS: LCSH: Freedom of speech. | Freedom of information. | Freedom of the press. | Freedom of expression. | Disinformation. | Misinformation. | Fake news. | Democracy.
CLASSIFICATION: LCC K3255 .D57 2024 (print) | LCC K3255 (ebook) | DDC 342.08/53–dc23/eng/20240412
LC record available at https://lccn.loc.gov/2024013567
LC ebook record available at https://lccn.loc.gov/2024013568

ISBN 978-1-009-37328-9 Hardback

Contents

Notes on Contributors

Eduardo Bertoni (PhD, Buenos Aires University) is the Director of the Center for Human Rights and Humanitarian Law at American University Washington College of Law, and was the first Director of the Access to Public Information Agency (AAIP), the Argentine Data Protection and Access to Information Authority. He was the Special Rapporteur for Freedom of Expression of the Inter-American Commission of Human Rights at the Organization of American States (2002–2005). He is an Argentinean lawyer and holds a Masters in International Policy and Practice from the Elliott School of International Affairs, George Washington University. He taught at Buenos Aires University School of Law and New York University School of Law (Global Clinical Professor), among others.

Gautam Bhatia is a practicing lawyer based in New Delhi, India, and an adjunct professor at the Jindal Global Law School. He is the author of *The Transformative Constitution: A Radical Biography in Nine Acts* (2019) and *Offend, Shock, or Disturb: Freedom of Speech under the Indian Constitution* (2015), among others. His work has been cited by the Supreme Court of India and various Indian High Courts. He was admitted as an *amicus curiae* before the Supreme Court of Kenya in its landmark *BBI* judgment. In his other life, he is a science fiction writer.

Vincent Blasi is the Corliss Lamont Professor of Civil Liberties at Columbia Law School. His undergraduate degree is from Northwestern University and his law degree is from the University of Chicago. He has served on the faculties of the University of Texas, the University of Michigan and the University of Virginia, as well as Columbia. He has published detailed accounts of the free speech theories of John Milton, John Stuart Mill, Learned Hand, Oliver Wendell Holmes and Louis Brandeis.

Joanna Botha is Professor of Public Law at Nelson Mandela University (South Africa) and served as Head of Department from 2016 to 2023. She holds BA and LLB degrees from Rhodes University and was awarded her LLD in 2016 by Nelson

Mandela University. She has authored many publications on freedom of expression. The South African Constitutional Court quoted her research with approval in its most important judgment on hate speech to date. She has represented Africa in expert panels convened by the United Nations to develop new global standards for the elimination of racial discrimination and hate speech.

John Charney is Professor of Law at Pontificia Universidad Católica de Valparaíso. He is the author of numerous publications on press freedom, including *The Illusion of the Free Press* (2018).

Charlotte Garden is the Julius E. Davis Professor at the University of Minnesota Law School. She specializes in constitutional law and the law of work, and her research interests include the intersection of workers' rights and the Constitution, and how law supports (or undermines) worker voice and power. She has authored various law review articles and casebooks; in 2019, Cambridge University Press published her edited volume *The Cambridge Handbook of U.S. Labor Law for the Twenty-First Century* (with Rick Bales).

Vicki C. Jackson is Laurence H. Tribe Professor of Constitutional Law Harvard Law School. She writes and teaches about comparative constitutional law, US constitutional law, and federal courts, and is the author of *Constitutional Engagement in a Transnational Era* (2010), and co-author, with Mark Tushnet, of *Comparative Constitutional Law* (3rd ed., 2014), and co-editor, with Yasmin Dawood, of *Constitutionalism and a Right to Effective Government?* (2022), among other works. Her recent writing concerns knowledge institutions in constitutional democracies, effective government and constitutionalism, judicial independence and restructuring the US Supreme Court, freedoms of expression, federalism, pro-constitutional representation, proportionality review, equality, unconstitutional constitutional amendments and standing.

Andrew T. Kenyon is Professor at the University of Melbourne and Associate Investigator in the Australian Research Council Centre of Excellence for Automated Decision-Making and Society. As well as legal doctrine, his research on comparative media law draws on media studies and political philosophy. He has been a visiting professor at the University of British Columbia, London School of Economics, Queen Mary University of London, and Université Paris 1 Panthéon-Sorbonne. He is joint editor of the *Journal of Media Law* and his most recent monograph is *Democracy of Expression: Positive Free Speech and Law* (2021).

András Koltay is Research Professor at the Ludovika – University of Public Service (Budapest) and Professor of Law at Pázmány Péter Catholic University (Budapest). From 2018 to 2021 he served as Rector of the University of Public Service. His most recent book is *Media Freedom and the Law* (2024). He is also the author of *New Media and Freedom of Expression* (2019). He is the co-editor of *Blasphemy and*

Freedom of Expression (2017, with Jeroen Temperman), *Comparative Privacy and Defamation* (2020, with Paul Wragg), and *Global Perspectives on Press Regulation, Vol.* 1 and *Vol.* 2 (2023 and 2024, with Paul Wragg).

Ronald J. Krotoszynski, Jr. is the John S. Stone Chair, Director of the Program in Constitutional Studies and Initiative for Civic Engagement. His scholarly research and teaching focus on constitutional law, First Amendment law, administrative law, telecommunications law and comparative constitutional law. His most recent book is *Free Speech as Civic Structure* (2024). He is also the author of *The Disappearing First Amendment* (2019), *Privacy Revisited: A Global Perspective on the Right to Be Left Alone* (2016) and the co-author of *First Amendment: Cases and Theory* (4th ed., 2022) (with Lyrissa Lidsky, Caroline Mala Corbin and Timothy Zick).

Victoria Miyandazi is Knight Fellow in Legal and Constitutional Research at the University of St. Andrews Institute of Legal and Constitutional Research. Previously, she was a lecturer at the University of Embu, researcher at the Oxford Human Rights Hub, and legal researcher at the Kenyan Judiciary Committee on Elections. She is an Advocate of the High Court of Kenya. She holds Doctor of Philosophy in Law, Master of Philosophy in Law, and Bachelor of Civil Law Degrees from the University of Oxford, where she studied as a Rhodes Scholar. She also holds a Bachelor of Laws (First Class Honours) degree from Kenyatta University.

Ahran Park is an associate professor in the School of Media and Communication at Korea University. Her main research interests are in media law and journalism, especially in relation to Internet law and regulation. She completed her MA from Seoul National University and PhD from the School of Journalism and Communication at the University of Oregon. She was a former news reporter for *Chosun Daily Newspaper* in Seoul. She has published several books and articles in international journals on Korean media law. Recently, she published the article "Digital Scarlet Letter on Journalists: Weaponized Harassment against Journalists in South Korea" in *Journalism Practice* (2023).

Robert C. Post is the Sterling Professor of Law at Yale Law School. From 2009 to 2017 he was the sixteenth Dean of Yale Law School. He writes frequently on issues of freedom of speech and is the author of, among other books, *Citizens Divided: Campaign Finance Reform and the Constitution* (2014); *Democracy, Expertise, Academic Freedom: A First Amendment Jurisprudence for the Modern State* (2012); and *Constitutional Domains: Democracy, Community, Management* (1995).

Indra Spiecker genannt Döhmann holds the Chair in Public Law, Law of Digitalisation, Environmental Law and Legal Theory at the University of Cologne. She heads the Center of Digitisation thereof and the Data Protection Research Institute at Goethe University Frankfurt. She has published numerous articles and books in the field of data protection, digitalisation and democracy, fragmentation and uncertainty and state communication. She is co-editor and co-author of the article-by-article-commentary on the GDPR.

Lucianna Thuo holds an LLM in Human Rights and Democratisation in Africa (University of Pretoria), a post-graduate diploma in Realising Human Rights through Criminal Law (Åbo Akademi University, Finland), an LLB from the University of Nairobi and a postgraduate diploma from the Kenya School of Law. She is an advocate of the High Court of Kenya. She has published widely in the area of elections and political inclusion. Having served as a visiting lecturer at the University of the Gambia, she is currently a lecturer and former associate Dean at Kabarak Law School, Kenya.

Ciara Torres-Spelliscy is Brennan Center Fellow and Professor of Law at Stetson University. She was counsel in the Brennan Center for Justice at NYU School of Law and an associate at Arnold & Porter. She is a graduate of Harvard and Columbia Law. She has testified before Congress as an expert on campaign finance, and has helped draft Supreme Court briefs. She is the author of the books *Corporate Citizen?* (2016) and *Political Brands* (2019). Her forthcoming book is Corporatocracy (New York University Press). She published over twenty law review articles and hundreds of legal op-eds.

Bernát Török is Associate Professor of Constitutional Law, and Director of the Institute of the Information Society at the Ludovika University of Public Service (Budapest). He worked as legal expert at the Hungarian media authority for seven years, then he was chief counsellor at the Constitutional Court of Hungary between 2010 and 2018. In 2016–17, he was visiting scholar at Yale Law School. He earned his PhD in 2018 with a thesis titled *To Speak Freely in a Democracy*. His research interests include freedom of speech, and fundamental rights in the information society.

Preface

The problem of disinformation needs no introduction for the readers of this book. It has been a topic of heightened public concern since the 2016 US presidential election at the latest, and since then we have seen and read about numerous legislative and self-regulatory initiatives, official positions taken by various public authorities, and a huge amount of academic analysis on the subject. We think that it is worth continuing to think together about how to tackle the problem, because we do not seem to be moving towards a satisfactory solution.

Of course, the problem of disinformation did not start in 2016. As long as there have been public debates, and especially since technology has made mass communication possible, disinformation has been present in the public sphere. It was therefore not the Internet that caused it; nevertheless, the interactive services made available on the Internet, especially social media platforms, have changed the structure of the public sphere and thus the phenomenon of disinformation. Since potentially everyone on the Internet can be a speaker, and since the loss of the former monopoly on disseminating information to the masses, which was primarily available to the media and the elites who were given the opportunity to speak through the media, the risk of disinformation has increased exponentially. Arguably, false information spreads much more widely, much faster, and much more effectively on the Internet. In addition, not only users who have not had access to the public sphere but also some governments and secret services have discovered the potential of this and are trying to influence public opinion or the outcome of an election through disinformation campaigns. And this carries serious dangers for the proper functioning of democracy, or even – especially in war zones, civil war zones, or in times of epidemics – for human lives.

The quality of public discourse is in all likelihood on the decline, although its overall opaque nature makes it difficult to say for sure. In any case, we may feel that the hopes, expressed at the dawn of the Internet in the 1990s, that internet communication would bring us closer to expanding democracy, broadening public debate and thus increasing the quality of joint decision-making are at least under threat. Internet content services destroy the cohesion between members of societies, trap users in filter bubbles, and ignore the aspects of public interest, or more precisely of democracy, in the interest of economic profit.

In principle, the range of tools for countering disinformation is very broad. The doctrine of freedom of expression allows legal systems, in principle, to prohibit untrue statements that cause harm but, in the age of global communication, national bans seem less effective. However, individual states' approaches to freedom of expression vary considerably and global agreement is unlikely (for example, the First Amendment to the US Constitution would only allow for a very narrow scope of action against false speech). Setting legal limits is difficult to imagine as an effective solution, since the law enforcement bodies (courts, authorities) would hardly be able to handle the huge number of potential disinformation cases spreading at an astonishing speed.

Indirect action against disinformation, which does not place the onus on the speakers but on the online platforms that make publishing the speech possible, is also feasible. This direction promises greater success, but also raises serious and difficult questions: putting the decision on which user content to delete in the hands of the platforms could harm freedom of expression. If we also accept that platforms define in their own private speech codes what they consider 'dangerous' speech (which does not necessarily mean that the content is illegal), then we are not only leaving the oversight but also the norm-setting to them. Some may argue that never before in the former media world has there been such a concentration of power, now in the hands of platforms, to influence the public sphere, and that in itself is dangerous.

Self-regulation by the industry also seems possible, but obviously only on a voluntary basis, and the technology market has not been very good at voluntarily reducing its own room for manoeuvre and handing over to an independent body decisions that directly affect its operations and thus its financial interests. The establishment of a co-regulatory system based on cooperation between public authorities (or even regional, supranational organisations, such as the European Union) and market players is also conceivable, and although this has already been initiated in the EU, its impact is not yet clear and will likely not be global.

We also have civil society and education, which are perhaps the best placed to mitigate the harmful effects of disinformation through awareness-raising without state coercion. These can be a valuable complement to public and industry efforts, but are unlikely to provide a comprehensive and definitive solution on their own.

Strengthening credible and reliable news sources is a vital interest in this situation. At the same time, the trust index of legacy media is deteriorating almost everywhere, with people less and less confident that the media can provide them with verified, accurate information and that they perform their duties impartially. The impact of internet communication, the weakening economic base of legacy media, the changing needs of audiences, and the polarisation of societies are also behind this phenomenon, making it difficult to imagine that the media can regain the role they once played in the public sphere.

It is not only the online debates of individual users that often present a disappointing picture, but the quality of public debate in the mainstream media is also in decline. It may seem that, in the age of the Internet, everyone has the right to their own truth. But 'someone's truth', or even 'alternative facts', are not 'the truth' and not 'the facts'. If the public is dominated by personal convictions as opposed to commonly agreed facts, and if the public at large is no longer interested in the latter, there is little chance of disinformation being countered.

Could there be no good solution to the problem of disinformation? At the moment, we cannot rule out this possibility either. Even so, for the time being, it is worth thinking about and fighting this phenomenon. This book was born out of that consideration. Its authors are lawyers, academics, and eminent representatives of their fields from all over the world. We, the editors, hope that their contributions will provide a broad picture of how disinformation is being tackled around the world. Apart from the introductory chapter, which sets out the basic issues in a common conceptual framework and describes the structure of the volume, the book largely refrains from describing the problem in detail, as we believe that it is well known to all interested parties and that it is similar in the various countries of the world.

We have tried to focus on the possible solutions that have emerged so far in different legal systems or regional organisations, and on the possible additional instruments suggested by our expert authors. The contributing authors approach the problem of disinformation and misinformation in different ways, but all working towards the same overall goals and objectives. Some propose new government regulations to combat the problem. Other contributing authors believe that the best solutions must involve better efforts at moderation and responsible journalism, with or without 'encouragement' from governmental authorities, so-called regulation by raised eyebrow. Finally, some believe that the best solutions must come from the bottom up rather than the top down; consistent with this approach, these contributing authors propose engaging non-governmental organisations and civil society entities to better inform voters and also empower citizens, through media literacy efforts and the like, to discern more reliably truth from fiction in the marketplace of political ideas. The editors believe that all of the reform proposals that follow have potential merit. Moreover, it seems very likely that all three general approaches, in combination, will prove necessary to identify, adopt, and then implement successfully reforms that can and will work (and, critically, that will do more good than harm).

We believe that the quality of public discourse determines the quality of democracy, and the quality of democracy determines the well-being of people. So the stakes are high. We hope that this volume will be a valuable contribution to the ongoing debate on its subject.

Acknowledgments

We are tremendously grateful to the Ludovika University of Public Service in Budapest (LUPS), whose financial support allowed this volume to be published in open-access format. In addition, the book benefitted immensely from a series of conferences at which contributing authors could meet in person to workshop drafts of their chapters. These workshops were hosted by the Columbia University Global Freedom of Expression Project with support from the University of Alabama School of Law; the Southeastern Association of Law Schools (SEALS) annual conference; and the LUPS's Information Society Project. For their logistical and moral support, we are especially grateful to Hawley Johnson, Associate Director of the Columbia University Global Freedom of Expression Project, Bernát Török, Director of the Institute of the Information Society at LUPS, and Russell L. Weaver, Executive Director of SEALS.

1

Disinformation, Misinformation, and Democracy

Defining the Problem, Identifying Potentially Effective Solutions, and the Merits of Using a Comparative Legal Approach

Ronald J. Krotoszynski, Jr.

1.1 INTRODUCTION: DISINFORMATION AND MISINFORMATION PRESENT A CLEAR AND PRESENT DANGER TO THE PROJECT OF DEMOCRATIC SELF-GOVERNMENT

The 2024 presidential election in the USA demonstrates, with unmistakable clarity, that disinformation (intentionally false information) and misinformation (unintentionally false information disseminated in good faith) pose a real and growing existential threat to democratic self-government in the United States – and elsewhere too. Powered by social media outlets like Facebook (Meta) and Twitter (X), it is now possible to propagate empirically false information to a vast potential audience at virtually no cost.[1] Coupled with the use of highly sophisticated algorithms that carefully target the recipients of disinformation and misinformation, voter manipulation is easier to accomplish than ever before – and frighteningly effective to boot.

Meanwhile, some social media companies, such as X (formerly Twitter), have shuttered efforts at meaningful moderation of disinformation and misinformation.[2] In the USA, conservative, mostly Republican, public officials attack social media companies for their moderation efforts and attempts to design and implement

[1] See Mark Scott, 'Why Western Democracy Faces a Nightmare Made Online', Politico, 3 October 2023, www.politico.eu/article/western-democracy-us-uk-eu-elections-2024-faces-nightmare-social-media-online (arguing that 'never before has the integrity of democracy been in so much danger, thanks to the transformation of political campaigning in recent years into a war waged largely online', observing that 'complex social media algorithms … heavily promote hateful content' thereby creating 'walled-off digital discussions, [in which] like-minded users reinforce their own opinions while demonizing their absent opponents', and placing 'at stake … the integrity of how much of the world is governed').

[2] Ibid. ('To make matters worse, social media giants are cutting back on their global election-monitoring teams to reduce costs amid falling advertising revenues. As politics increasingly shifts online, at stake is the integrity of how much of the world is governed.')

meaningful moderation policies to combat false information on their platforms.[3] Thus, even as the problem of disinformation and misinformation explodes, doing great damage to the process of democratic deliberation, to the electoral process, and to public confidence in the fairness of voting systems and the outcome of elections, and ultimately to democratic governing institutions, social media companies' efforts to arrest these trends are both more limited and under public attack.[4]

Nor are disinformation and misinformation uniquely US problems – they constitute *global* problems. For example, in a recent election in Chile associated with ratifying a new constitution, disinformation and misinformation circulated widely[5] – and could easily have affected the outcome (rejecting the proposed new Chilean constitution by a margin of 62 percent against and 38 percent in favor of ratification[6]). The same held true, in 2016, with the United Kingdom's Brexit vote – with both Boris Johnson, who would later become UK Prime Minister, and Nigel Farage, leader of the UK Independence Party (UKIP), intentionally disseminating vast quantities of false information (disinformation) to any and every British voter who would listen.[7] They did so with great alacrity and to good effect.[8] Indeed, one could cite examples of elections in which disinformation and misinformation might have turned the outcome one way or the other in virtually every democratic polity on Earth. When the margin of an election is razor thin – the final Brexit tally of 52 percent for Brexit to 48 percent against provides a salient example – the marginal voter who makes the majority might well be casting a vote in error.[9]

3 Naomi Nix, Cat Zakrzewski and Joseph Menn, 'Misinformation Research Is Buckling under GOP Legal Attacks', *The Washington Post*, 23 September 2023, www.washingtonpost.com/technology/2023/09/23/online-misinformation-jim-jordan ('Academics, universities and government agencies are overhauling or ending research programs designed to counter the spread of online misinformation amid a legal campaign from conservative politicians and activists who accuse them of colluding with tech companies to censor right-wing views. The escalating campaign – led by Rep. Jim Jordan (R-Ohio) and other Republicans in Congress and state government – has cast a pall over programs that study not just political falsehoods but also the quality of medical information online'.).

4 Ibid.

5 'Misinformation Spreads on Social Media in Chile ahead of Vote on New Constitution', NBC News, 31 August 2022, www.nbcnews.com/news/latino/misinformation-spreads-social-media-chile-ahead-vote-new-constitution-rcna45247 (noting that 'support is dropping amid a proliferation of "half truths" on social media about what's in the document, and voters are expected to reject it, say experts').

6 John Otis, 'Chile Rejects Its New Constitution', NPR, 5 September 2022, www.npr.org/2022/09/05/1121104531/chile-rejects-its-new-constitution.

7 Matt Kelly, 'Here's an A to Z of Brexit Lies', *British GQ*, www.gq-magazine.co.uk/article/list-of-brexit-lies.

8 Ibid.

9 By 'a vote in error' I do not mean to suggest that voting in favor of conservative or progressive candidates, in circumstances where a voter supports a candidate based on an accurate appraisal of the candidate's likely policies and beliefs is cast in error. Such a vote would directly advance a voter's moral, cultural, social, and economic preferences via the electoral process; perfectly rational voters can and will register varied views on these matters with their votes. See, e.g., Ben

The consequences of disinformation and misinformation also can be – and are – astonishingly high. Disinformation and misinformation about COVID vaccines, such as the ludicrous claims that they contained tracking chips designed by Bill Gates[10] and caused sterility in young women[11] created serious, and dangerous, headwinds for mass vaccination programs aimed at containing and controlling the spread of the virus. So, too, after the tragic events in Israel starting on 7 October 2023 and continuing thereafter, disinformation and misinformation spread like wildfire within both Israel and the Occupied Territories – creating even more fear, confusion, chaos and distress.[12] It is undeniable that disinformation and misinformation impose serious social costs on a mass scale, around the world, and do so with great regularity. The question is not whether a problem exists. Instead, the relevant question to be asked and answered is: What, if anything, is to be done about it?

As Judge Guido Calabresi has argued, 'At one time, America had a virtual monopoly on constitutional judicial review, and if a doctrine or approach was not tried out here, there was no place else to look' but '[t]hat situation no longer holds'.[13] If we cannot find solutions that work at home, there is certainly no harm in looking abroad to see if countries sharing a common set of core institutional and human rights values have found solutions to shared problems (such as disinformation and misinformation). Thus, a comparative legal analysis can and will yield important insights into what works and what does not.

Hubbard, Safak Timur and Elif Ince, 'The Women Are with You', *New York Times International Edition*, 1 June 2023, 1–2 (reporting that devout women voted in Turkey's May 2023 presidential election for incumbent Turkish President Recep Tayyip Erdogan by a very wide margin because his government loosened legal rules against public expressions of faith, such as head covering, that 'rankled many devout people, including women who felt that [Turkey's secularist policies] made them second-class citizens'). Instead, by 'vote in error', I mean circumstances in which a voter supports a candidate based on an objectively false fact related to that candidate, the candidate's opponent, or both.

[10] Jack Goodman and Flora Carmichael, 'Coronavirus: Bill Gates 'Microchip' Conspiracy Theory and Other Vaccine Claims Fact-Checked', BBC News, 30 May 2020, www.bbc.com/news/52847648.

[11] Adee Hassan, 'Covid Vaccine Misinformation Still Fuels Fears Surrounding Pregnancy, a New Study Finds', *The New York Times*, 3 June 2022, www.nytimes.com/2022/06/03/health/covid-vaccine-pregnancy-misinformation.html.

[12] See 'Misinformation about the Israel–Hamas War Is Flooding Social Media – Here Are the Facts', AP News, 24 October 2023, https://apnews.com/article/israel-hamas-gaza-misinformation-fact-check-e58f9ab8696309305c3ea2bfb269258e; Steven Lee Myers, 'Fact or Fiction? In This War, It Is Hard to Tell', *The New York Times*, 12 October 2023, www.nytimes.com/2023/10/13/business/israel-hamas-misinformation-social-media-x.html.

[13] *United States* v. *Then*, 56 F.3d 464, 469 (2d Cir. 1995) (Calabresi J, concurring); see *Printz* v. *United States*, 521 US 898, 977 (Breyer J, dissenting) (observing that 'we are interpreting our own Constitution, not those of other nations' yet the experience of other nations 'may nonetheless cast an empirical light on the consequences of different solutions to a common legal problem – in this case the problem of reconciling central authority with the need to preserve the liberty-enhancing autonomy of a smaller constituent governmental entity').

Because of the global nature of the problem, issues related to disinformation and misinformation would clearly benefit from a comparative legal analysis. What are the best ideas for addressing this problem? What are governments currently doing? How is the media within a given country trying to address these social phenomena? Are grass-roots organizations engaging in effective and broad-based voter education and media literacy campaigns? It would behoove both governments and voters around the world to learn from the experience of other democratic polities that have undertaken efforts to arrest the corrosive effects of disinformation and misinformation on the process of democratic deliberation, the perceived legitimacy of elections, and the health of democratic governing institutions.

By considering carefully and systematically how nations with a shared constitutional commitment to democratic self-government have attempted to address the growing problem of disinformation and misinformation being used successfully to manipulate electoral outcomes, it might be possible to identify the most (and least) promising responses. Again, these are common, or shared, social phenomena that do not respect any national borders. We can and should think globally about how best to reinforce democracy, the process of democratic deliberation that facilitates it, and democratic governing institutions. The chapters that follow will engage with precisely these themes.

To be sure, the problems presented by disinformation and misinformation today are not entirely new. After all, it has always been possible to trick voters into casting ballots based on false information. Throughout time and history, incumbent office holders routinely have sought to exploit voters' lack of access to full, complete, and truthful information in order to retain their grip on power. So what is different about the problem today? For starters, the scale of the problem and the efficacy of voter deception efforts vastly outstrip anything that democratic polities have seen before. Contemporary efforts at voter deception can be accomplished on a massive scale, at very low cost, with great precision, and with an astonishingly high success rate. All of that being said, however, the problems associated with the dissemination of false information have existed for as long as human societies have used elections to select their leaders.[14] Accordingly, it would be an overstatement to suggest that the problem itself is an entirely new one. The more plausible claim would be, and is,

[14] The Spanish–American War, in 1898, provides a salient example. Yellow-journalism czar William Randolph Hearst, using his national newspaper chain, propagated a false story about a Spanish attack on a US naval vessel, the *USS Maine*, in Havana Harbor. See Evan Thomas, *The War Lovers: Roosevelt, Lodge, Hearst, and the Rush to Empire, 1898* (Boston: Little Brown, 2010) (discussing how the press helped to instigate a war with Spain in order to help advance US dreams of a global empire). Indeed, Roman politicians, including Pompey the Great and Julius Caesar, routinely resorted to false speech and fake news in order to advance their electoral, and broader political, ambitions. See Elenora Zampieri, *Politics in the Monuments of Pompey the Great and Julius Caesar* (Abingdon: Routledge, 2023) pp. 9–22, 33–44 (discussing the use of propaganda, including intentional false speech, in the Roman Republic and early Roman Empire periods).

that the scale and scope of the social costs associated with disinformation and misinformation have increased concomitantly with the revolution – an explosion really – in the ability to disseminate a message to a mass audience instantly and at little to no cost.

Sometimes, it can be too easy to get lost in the weeds of the particular at the risk of losing sight of the bigger picture. For example, whether or not Cambridge Analytica actually manipulated voters by misusing Facebook data to dupe British voters,[15] a contested claim which the European Union's data protection commissioner has rejected,[16] statistical autopsies of the Brexit vote have found that Russian interference, including the active use of disinformation, probably did affect the outcome (which favored leaving the EU by a margin of 52 percent to 48 percent).[17] Russia, in particular, actively attempted to influence the vote in favor of the United Kingdom leaving the EU.[18] Thus, the outcomes of elections have been affected – and will be affected in future elections as well – by disinformation and misinformation campaigns. Of course, it bears noting that, with respect to the Brexit vote, Johnson and Farage probably disseminated more disinformation than all of Vladimir Putin's internet trolls combined. They were also highly credible purveyors of disinformation – which raises another problem with regulating it. How can you regulate disinformation being propagated by an elected head of government or the leader of a major political party?[19]

[15] See Jane Meyer, 'New Evidence Emerges of Steve Bannon and Cambridge Analytica's Role in Brexit', *The New Yorker*, 17 November 2018, www.newyorker.com/news/news-desk/new-evidence-emerges-of-steve-bannon-and-cambridge-analyticas-role-in-brexit. The available evidence suggests the use of likely illegal foreign campaign contributions and some clumsy, but ineffectual, efforts to mine the Facebook data.

[16] Jim Waterson, 'Cambridge Analytica Did Not Misuse Data in EU Referendum, Says Watchdog', *The Guardian*, 7 October 2020, www.theguardian.com/uk-news/2020/oct/07/cambridge-analytica-did-not-misuse-data-in-eu-referendum-says-watchdog ('The data watchdog has closed its investigation into Cambridge Analytica, concluding that the controversial data company did not directly misuse data to influence the Brexit referendum'.).

[17] See Clare Llewellyn et al., 'For Whom the Bell Trolls: Shifting Troll Behaviour in the Twitter Brexit Debate' (2019) 57(5) *Journal of Common Market Studies* 1148, at 1162 (concluding, based on a careful study of Brexit-related tweets on Twitter, that 'it appears that this was a part of a more widespread, centrally co-ordinated IRA [the Internet Research Agency, one of Russia's disinformation agencies] effort to influence international electoral processes, with troll activity temporarily diverted and repurposed to the Brexit case').

[18] See ibid. at 13–15.

[19] Robert Post's chapter (Chapter 2) goes into some detail regarding the problems associated with mass moderation of disinformation and misinformation on a major social media platform as well as the problems of moderating social media posts by high-level government and party officials. Simply put, neither task is easily accomplished. See ibid., Section 2.2 (observing that 'the immense scale of the internet' creates regulatory challenges because 'the internet is far too big to be policed through the exercise of human judgment' and '[a]lthough we can use AI to distinguish truth from falsity in the context of stereotypically false statements, which can be preprogrammed, AI is not a useful tool for distinguishing truth from falsity in the context of statements whose interpretation requires judgment').

This type of organized electoral fraud distorts the process of democratic deliberation and, ultimately, undermines the electoral process itself. At this point, it is clear that disinformation and misinformation both constitute a clear and present danger to the process of democratic deliberation and, more generally, to democratic self-government. The question, then, is not whether a problem exists – clearly it does – but rather what if anything can be done to address it more effectively.

In the age of metadata and microtargeting of voters, it has become rather obvious that John Milton, in his iconic *Areopagitica*,[20] might have been naïve to posit that Falsity invariably loses out to Truth in the marketplace of political ideas. Milton famously wrote that 'Let her [Truth] and Falsehood grapple; who ever knew Truth put to the worse, in a free and open encounter?'[21] He added, for emphasis, 'For who knows not that Truth is strong next to the Almighty?'[22] Milton arguably did not understand social psychology in an age of siloed voters in echo chamber environments.[23] It also bears noting that Milton's construction of 'truth' possessed a deeply religious connection that would seem to place it at some remove from Justice Oliver Wendell Holmes's equally famous argument that 'truth' constitutes the product of active and ongoing deliberation within a 'marketplace of ideas'.[24]

A long-held assumption has been that, if a nation creates the architecture of democracy, including regularly scheduled elections, rules for such elections, obtaining and using reliable voting machines and related technologies, creating and enforcing fair procedures for resolving electoral disputes, and the like, then

[20] John Milton, *Areopagitica* (ed. by J. W. Hales, Oxford: Clarendon, (1644) 1874).

[21] Ibid. pp. 51–52.

[22] Ibid. p. 52.

[23] See Martha Minow, *Saving the News: Why the Constitution Calls for Government Action to Preserve Freedom of Speech* (Oxford: Oxford University Press, 2021) pp. 3–4 (describing and discussing the problem of siloed voters in media echo chamber environments); Cass R. Sunstein, *#Republic: Divided Democracy in the Age of Social Media* (Princeton, NJ: Princeton University Press, 2018) pp. 7–12, 76–78 and 114–26 (same).

[24] Compare *Abrams* v. *United States*, 250 US 616, 630 (1919) (Holmes J, dissenting) ('But when men have realized that time has upset many fighting faiths, they may come to believe even more than they believe the very foundations of their own conduct that the ultimate good desired is better reached by free trade in ideas – that the best test of truth is the power of the thought to get itself accepted in the competition of the market, and that truth is the only ground upon which their wishes safely can be carried out. That at any rate is the theory of our Constitution. It is an experiment, as all life is an experiment'.). with Milton, *Areopagitica* (n 20) p. 54 (explaining that 'I mean not tolerated Popery, and open superstition, which as it extirpats all religions and civill supremacies, so it self should be extirpat, provided first that all charitable and compassionat means be us'd to win and regain the weak and the misled: that also which is impious or evil absolutely either against faith or maners no law can possibly permit, that intends not to unlaw itself'.). Thus, for Milton – unlike for Holmes – religious doctrines, and particularly those associated with the official Church of England, bounded 'truth'. Milton, then, did not really embrace a free and unregulated marketplace of ideas. Holmes, by way of contrast, claimed to believe 'that the best test of truth is the power of the thought to get itself accepted in the competition of the market, and that truth is the only ground upon which their wishes safely can be carried out'. *Abrams*, at 630 (Holmes J, dissenting).

democracy would thrive. This assumption is no longer tenable (if it ever really was). In reality, these are all necessary, but not sufficient, conditions for democracy to function (if not flourish).

How can democracy function and the democratic process reliably produce sound government if the marketplace of political ideas is filled with garbage? What is more, when traditional journalists try to correct these (often grotesque) factual errors, the people who inhabit the echo chambers will frequently fasten themselves more tightly to Falsity's mast.[25] As Cass Sunstein observes, '[e]cho chambers can lead people to believe in falsehoods, and it may be difficult or impossible to correct them'.[26] Social scientists have shown, convincingly, that traditional media sources cannot correct these false factual beliefs.[27] Can government or civil society entities do better? This question, and others like it, need to be investigated and answered.

It also bears noting that traditional journalists, and journalism, seem to be going the way of the dodo bird in today's increasingly balkanized media market. Rather than adopt a posture of strict editorial neutrality in the newsroom, media entities like Fox News and MSNBC instead lean into their viewers' political, economic, moral and even religious biases.[28] Media entities, such as CNN, that attempt to hew scrupulously to the line of editorial neutrality are losing their audiences. Even Fox News, whose infamous tagline is 'Fair and Balanced', is bleeding audience share to outlets like One America News Network (OAN) and Newsmax that feature an even stronger partisan and ideological edge to their 'reporting'.[29] Thus, at least some

[25] Sunstein, *#Republic* (n 23) pp. 93–97 (discussing how efforts to correct disinformation and misinformation can 'backfire', leaving voters believing false information even more intensely than before the effort to set the record straight).

[26] Ibid. p. 11; see ibid. p. 111 (noting that, with respect to disinformation and misinformation, 'correctives, even via the Internet may work too slowly or not at all, simply because people are not listening to one another' and warning about 'the (terrible) problem of the backfiring correction' which leads the recipient to believe a false statement even more intensely).

[27] See Minow, *Saving the News* (n 23) pp. 17–35. The problem is even deeper and broader than belief in false facts – many voters also inhabit information deserts in which computer-based algorithms select the content that they view. Minow notes that in today's media markets, '[a] majority of people in the United States now receive news selected for them by a computer-based mathematical formula derived from their past interests, producing echo chambers with few opportunities to learn, understand, or believe what others are hearing as news'. Ibid. pp. 3–4.

[28] See ibid. pp. 30–35; see also Sunstein, *#Republic* (n 23) pp. 59–75 (discussing the problem of polarized voters receiving news and information only from the same biased sources and neither seeking nor otherwise enjoying access to sources of news and information that would provide more diverse points of view).

[29] Jeremy Barr, 'Why These Fox News Loyalists Have Changed the Channel to Newsmax', *The Washington Post*, 27 December 2020, www.washingtonpost.com/media/2020/12/27/fox-news-viewers-switch-to-newsmax (discussing migration of Fox News viewers to Newsmax over Fox News calling the 2020 election for Joe Biden); Michael M. Grynbaum, 'Newsmax Ratings Climb after Tucker Carlson's Exit at Fox', *The New York Times*, 23 April 2023, www.nytimes.com/2023/04/27/business/media/newsmax-fox-ratings-tucker-carlson.html ('Viewership of Newsmax remains far below that of Fox News. But its audience at certain hours has doubled,

media entities that might once have been thought to be part of the solution are now part of the problem – and trap their readers/viewers/listeners in echo chambers. Indeed, the trend in the USA is particularly disheartening. Emerging media outlets that openly and shamelessly traffic in disinformation and misinformation, such as Newsmax and OAN, do not make even the pretense of observing a policy of editorial neutrality.[30]

Compounding the problem, the general public no longer trusts the traditional media – and this distrust is not limited to conservatives. A 2010 Gallup poll found that while 78 percent of conservatives believe the traditional news media are biased, 44 percent of progressives and 50 percent of moderates do too.[31] Only 36 percent of the overall survey respondents believe mass media reporting to be fair and reliable. A more recent poll produced equally dismal results. It found that most Americans believe the traditional media is untrustworthy and attempts to deliberately mislead the public.[32] Democrats, who traditionally placed more faith in the media, are growing more wary of it and its reporting. So too, mistrust of the media among independent voters has spiked in recent years.[33] Thus, what began as a phenomenon primarily affecting Republican, or Grand Old Party (GOP), voters in the USA now manifests across the political spectrum. A 2023 Gallup and Knight Foundation survey shows 'a low level of trust in the media to the startling point where many believe there is an intent to deceive'.[34] In other words, voters do not just think journalists get things wrong; they increasingly believe that journalists intend to deceive their viewers, listeners, and readers with disinformation.

What's more, social scientists have shown that even when traditional media sources attempt to correct widely believed false facts, these efforts fall short (that

and in some time slots tripled, in the immediate aftermath of Mr. Carlson's exit – an abrupt spike that has turned heads in conservative circles and the cable news industry'.).

30 David McKay, *American Politics and Society* (Oxford: Wiley Blackwell, 10th ed., 2022) p. 153 (observing that 'One American [sic] Newsnetwork (OAN) and Newmax … unashamedly advance a right-wing position' and noting that these media outlets, and others like them, constantly and consistently disseminate disinformation to their viewers). For a general discussion and careful empirical study of the problem of overtly biased media outlets in the contemporary United States and how they contribute to extremely high levels of polarization among voters, see Daniel F. Stone, *Undue Hate: A Behavioral Economic Analysis of Hostile Polarization in US Politics and Beyond* (Cambridge, MA: MIT Press, 2023) pp. 119–48.

31 Lymari Morales, 'Distrust in US Media Edges Up to Record High', Gallup, 29 September 2010, https://news.gallup.com/poll/143267/distrust-media-edges-record-high.aspx.

32 David Bauder, 'Trust in Media Is so Low that Half of Americans Now Believe that News Organizations Deliberately Mislead Them', Fortune, 15 February 2023, https://fortune.com/2023/02/15/trust-in-media-low-misinform-mislead-biased-republicans-democrats-poll-gallup ('Half of Americans in a recent survey indicated they believe national news organizations intend to mislead, misinform or persuade the public to adopt a particular point of view through their reporting'.).

33 Ibid.

34 Ibid.

is, they often do not work).[35] Sunstein hypothesizes that efforts at error correction not infrequently fail to work because, '[w]hen people start with strong convictions and really know what they think, they're a lot less likely to be moved by contrary arguments'.[36] Moreover, '[i]f you're strongly committed to a certain belief – say, that climate change is a serious problem – a contrary argument might do little to inform you'.[37]

Consider, for example, the broadly circulated, but patently false, claim, widely known as 'Pizzagate', during the 2016 US presidential election. On social media and other media outlets, stories claimed that the 2016 Democratic Party presidential candidate, Hillary Rodham Clinton, was operating a prostitution ring staffed with trafficked children in a Washington, DC, pizza joint (Comet Ping Pong). A great many media outlets, including both the *Wall Street Journal* and Fox News, repeatedly reported that the Pizzagate claim was completely false – a total and complete fabrication. Yet reliable polling data during fall 2016 showed that 46 percent of Trump voters believed that Clinton was personally involved in running a major child sex-trafficking operation at Comet Ping Pong.[38]

Such rumors not only distort the electoral process – they also put people's lives and safety at risk. A man from North Carolina fired a gun into Comet Ping Pong as part of an effort to rescue the (nonexistent) sex-trafficked kids.[39] Perhaps the most astonishing set of widely held beliefs relate to the QAnon conspiracy, which posits that the Democratic Party is merely a front organization for a large, well-organized pedophile ring.[40] At the same time, a 2018 Gallup poll found that almost 80 percent of Democratic Party voters believe, falsely, that Russia directly stuffed the ballot boxes in the 2016 presidential election to rig the outcome for Trump.[41] In point of

[35] See Sunstein, *#Republic* (n 23) pp. 93–97 (discussing how efforts to correct false statements of fact routinely fail to convince those who believe false information and actually can 'backfire' by leading persons to credit false information more intensely).

[36] Ibid. p. 96.

[37] Ibid.

[38] David A. Graham, 'The "Comet Pizza" Gunman Provides a Glimpse of a Frightening Future', *The Atlantic*, 5 December 2016, www.theatlantic.com/politics/archive/2016/12/the-inevitability-of-more-comet-pizza-incidents/509567.

[39] Ibid.

[40] Kevin Roose, 'What Is Q-Anon, the Viral Pro-Trump Conspiracy Theory?', *The New York Times*, 3 September 2021, www.nytimes.com/article/what-is-qanon.html ('QAnon is the umbrella term for a set of internet conspiracy theories that allege, falsely, that the world is run by a cabal of Satan-worshiping pedophiles'.).

[41] Jeffrey M. Jones, 'More in US Favor Diplomacy over Sanctions for Russia', Gallup, 20 August 2018, https://news.gallup.com/poll/241124/favor-diplomacy-sanctions-russia.aspx ('Democrats widely believe Russians interfered in the 2016 campaign and that it changed the outcome of the election (78 per cent say this), presumably by helping Trump defeat Hillary Clinton'.). A poll conducted by *The Economist*/YouGov from 4 to 6 November 2018 reported very similar results, finding that 67 percent of Democrats believe that 'Russia tampered with vote tallies in order to get Donald Trump elected President'. Question 26C, https://d25d2506sfb94s.cloudfront.net/cumulus_uploads/document/ylp5ygohjs/econTabReport.pdf.

fact, no credible evidence exists of any direct Russian tampering with the 2016 presidential vote totals.

The serious distortionary effects of disinformation and misinformation do not respect ideology or partisan identity. As the famous tagline from the X *Files* put it, '[t]he truth is out there'. But, even though it *is* out there, many voters resolutely refuse to credit it.[42] To state the matter simply, we face a serious problem with the operational mechanics of democracy that requires the formulation and implementation of an effective set of solutions – and this is a problem that does not respect national borders.

What, if anything, can be done to empower voters with the information that they require in order to cast prudent and well-informed ballots? To be clear, the coeditors and contributing authors do not take the position that only votes for the Democratic Party's (or other progressive political parties') candidates are rational. We do not have either a partisan or ideological ax to grind. Instead, we are deeply concerned about the marginal voter – meaning the voter who makes the majority – casting a well-informed ballot (meaning a ballot that does not rest on objectively false factual predicates). At the same time, however, the prospect of the government declaring 'truth' might make a great many people very nervous[43] – such a censorial power would present a serious risk of distortion to the process of democratic deliberation.[44] Moreover, free speech scholars and theorists routinely posit that the First Amendment should be understood primarily as a means of facilitating and safeguarding the process of democratic deliberation that informs the act of voting from government efforts to censor or distort it.[45]

In fact, one of the most difficult problems associated with formulating policy responses that would do more good than harm involves defining, in a fashion that would garner widespread acceptance across the ideological and partisan spectrum, what constitutes 'false' speech. To borrow Justice John Marshall Harlan II's

[42] Sunstein, *#Republic* (n 23) pp. 95–97.

[43] Ashutosh Bhagwat, *Our Democratic First Amendment* (Cambridge: Cambridge University Press, 2020) pp. 111–12 (arguing that empowering the government to declare 'truth' and punish false speech would run a serious risk of becoming 'a cure worse than the disease'); Minow, *Saving the News* (n 23) p. 131 ('Giving the government the job of removing misinformation and hateful comments would be giving it too much authority to suppress speech'); see Ronald J. Krotoszynski, Jr., *Privacy Revisited: A Global Perspective on the Right to Be Left Alone* (Oxford: Oxford University Press, 2016) p. 35 ('Even though no reasonable person disbelieves known historical facts, we nevertheless deny government the power to declare "truth", out of a fear that such a power would inevitably be used for crass partisan reasons; better to protect obvious falsehoods than to risk the suppression of inconvenient truths'.).

[44] See Lyrissa Barnett Lidsky, 'Where's the Harm? Free Speech and the Regulation of Lies' (2008) 65 *Washington and Lee Law Review* 1091, at 1097 ('Yet even if First Amendment theory's faith in the fundamental rationality of public discourse is misplaced, distrust of government still may be a strong enough basis, standing alone, to warrant declaring any attempt to punish Holocaust denial unconstitutional'.).

[45] Alexander Meiklejohn, *Free Speech and Its Relation to Self-Government* (New York: Harper & Brothers, 1948) pp. 25–27, 88–91.

wonderful turn of phrase, 'one man's vulgarity is another's lyric'.[46] In the context of disinformation and misinformation, one person's absurd and obvious falsehood is another's fundamental truth. To provide just one highly salient example, Donald Trump's oft-repeated 'Big Lie' about massive fraud in the 2020 presidential election is avidly believed as the gospel truth by an astonishing 71 percent of GOP voters.[47] What institutions – if any – can set the record straight for these badly informed voters? Certainly not *The New York Times*, CNN, or NPR.

Despite the real and serious problem with defining disinformation and misinformation in a way that enjoys broad acceptance, we have to make the effort.[48] After all, as Alexander Meiklejohn, generally regarded as one of the principal proponents of the democratic self-government theory of freedom of expression, strenuously argued, '[w]hen a free man is voting, it is not enough that the truth is known by someone else, by some scholar or administrator or legislator. The voters must have it, all of them'.[49] From this vantage point, '[t]he primary purpose of the First Amendment is, then, that all the citizens shall, so far as possible, understand the issues which American Individualism and the Constitution bear upon our common life'.[50]

Thus, the First Amendment's principal purpose arguably inheres in its role in facilitating democratic self-government.[51] In turn, the process of democratic deliberation that precedes an election, at least in theory, will equip voters with the information that they require to cast well-informed ballots on election day. Free speech must enjoy robust constitutional protection against government efforts to censor it because free and open debate among citizens constitutes an essential condition for democracy, which, after all, relies on free and fair elections to imbue governing institutions with legitimacy.[52] As Meiklejohn stated his case, '[w]hat is essential is not

46 *Cohen* v. *California*, 403 US 15, 25 (1971) ('For, while the particular four-letter word being litigated here is perhaps more distasteful than most others of its genre, it is nevertheless often true that one man's vulgarity is another's lyric. Indeed, we think it is largely because governmental officials cannot make principled distinctions in this area that the Constitution leaves matters of taste and style so largely to the individual'.).

47 Aaron Blake, 'Birtherism Paved the Way for the "Big Lie" – The Latter Is Proving more Pervasive and Stubborn', *The Washington Post*, 3 January 2022, www.washingtonpost.com/politics/2022/01/03/trump-voter-fraud-birtherism.

48 Vincent Blasi, in his 'Afterword' (Chapter 16), makes this precise point in a highly persuasive fashion.

49 Meiklejohn, *Free Speech* (n 45) p. 88.

50 Ibid.

51 This is not to say that freedom of speech does not also advance other important social values, such as the search for truth, the advancement of artistic, literary or scientific knowledge, and/or empowering and facilitating individual autonomy. See C. Edwin Baker, *Human Liberty and Freedom of Speech* (Oxford: Oxford University Press, 1989); Frederick Schauer, *Free Speech: A Philosophical Inquiry* (Cambridge: Cambridge University Press, 1982).

52 Meiklejohn, *Free Speech* (n 45) pp. 88–89 (arguing that '[t]he primary purpose of the First Amendment is, then, that all the citizens shall, so far as possible, understand the issues which bear upon our common life' and positing that freedom of speech is an essential condition in a polity where 'it is agreed that men shall not be governed by others' but rather 'shall govern themselves').

that everyone shall speak, but that everything worth saying shall be said'.[53] But how can these principles work in a society filled with siloed voters inhabiting media echo chambers? The very process of open debate and engagement that Meiklejohn argued is essential to making democratic self-government work is dying on the vine.

At the same time, however, using the metaphor of a New England town hall meeting for the ongoing process of democratic deliberation, Meiklejohn suggested that there might be a role for government to play, in the form of a 'chairman or moderator' who will call the meeting to order and enforce 'rules of order'.[54] Meiklejohn observed that '[h]is business on the negative side is to abridge speech'.[55] What if a person attempts to hijack the discussion with irrelevant materials? In such circumstances, the 'moderator' would have a duty to silence such a speaker:

> Anyone who would thus irresponsibly interrupt the activities of a lecture, a hospital, a concert hall, a church, a machine shop, a classroom, a football field, or a home, does not thereby exhibit his freedom. Rather, he shows himself to be a boor, a public nuisance, who must be abated, by force if necessary.[56]

In sum, '[t]he First Amendment, then, is not the guardian of unregulated talkativeness'.[57] However, discussing the abstract necessity of rules of order that structure collective democratic deliberation to facilitate rational decision making by voters is a very different project than actually drafting and then operationalizing such rules.

And, again, like language itself, which only has meaning within the context of particular interpretive communities,[58] arriving at a consensus about 'truth' in the marketplace of political ideas is much easier said than done. The devil lies in the details of any such undertaking – and, again, it is quite crucial that the cure not be worse than the disease; government interventions in the marketplace of political ideas to correct for disinformation and misinformation must not prove to be counterproductive. More specifically, if government regulations actually empower and enable the purveyors of disinformation and misinformation, it would be better for

[53] Ibid. p. 26.
[54] Ibid. pp. 22–23.
[55] Ibid. p. 23.
[56] Ibid. p. 24.
[57] Ibid.
[58] Stanley Fish, *Is There a Text in This Class? The Authority of Interpretive Communities* (Cambridge, MA: Harvard University Press, 1980) p. 14 ('Indeed, it is interpretive communities, rather than either text or the reader, that produce meanings and are responsible for the emergence of formal features'.). Fish explains that words only have meaning in the context of an interpretive community that imbues particular strings of symbols with meaning. See ibid. pp. 13–16 (describing and explaining how an interpretive community conveys meaning on language). Fish argues that the process of interpreting text involves both objective and subjective elements. Ibid. p. 14 ('An interpretive community is not objective because as a bundle of interests, of particular persons and goals, its perspective is interested rather than neutral; but by the very same reasoning, the meanings and texts produced by an interpretive community are not subjective because they do not proceed from an isolated individual but from a public and conventional point of view'.).

government to leave the marketplace of political ideas to operate on an unregulated basis.

With so many voters now inhabiting echo chambers on social media platforms, and engaging in siloing behavior, the process of democratic deliberation faces an existential threat: We the People no longer regularly and reliably interact with each other about candidates for public office or the issues of the day. Sunstein is surely correct to posit that, '[i]n a well-functioning democracy, people do not live in echo chambers or information cocoons' but, instead, seek to 'see and hear a wide range of topics and ideas'.[59] Alas, this is not how public debate works in the contemporary USA – or, for that matter, in most democracies across the globe.

Rather than seeking to engage those with whom they vehemently disagree, voters tend to seek out interactions with folks with whom they generally agree on issues ranging from the teaching of Critical Race Theory to whether immigration laws should be harsher or more welcoming to would-be immigrants.[60] One might ask, 'Well, why should this matter?' It matters a lot.

Perhaps most problematic: A great many people have and will cast ballots on election day that rest entirely on verifiably false factual premises. To be clear, by 'verifiably false premises' I do not mean mere disagreement about matters of public policy. For example, consider the claim that lower corporate taxes increase middle-class wages (maybe so, maybe not, one can argue the point). A claim of this sort cannot really be falsified. On the other hand, consider claims such as 'Donald Trump won the 2020 election' and 'ivermectin cures COVID-19 infections' (as well as being an effective treatment for worming horses). Both of these claims are verifiably *false*; they can be shown to be so using objective forms of proof; they are not matters about which reasonable people might plausibly disagree. Whether disseminated with knowledge of their falsity or in good faith, these statements can and will mislead voters into casting poorly informed ballots.

Even if reasonable minds might all readily agree that disinformation and misinformation constitute threats to democracy, finding agreement about the most promising solutions will prove a great deal more difficult than identifying the problem and its sources. Three general forms of intervention seem potentially available: (1) government regulation of speech markets to identify and eradicate disinformation and misinformation, (2) self-regulation by the press, including traditional print media, broadcasters, cablecasters and social media, or some combination of self-regulation augmented by government regulation by 'a raised eyebrow',[61] and (3) interventions by nongovernmental organizations (NGOs) and civil society

[59] Sunstein,*#Republic* (n 23) p. ix.

[60] Ibid. pp. 59–97; Minow, *Saving the News* (n 23) pp. 3–5.

[61] See David Zaring, 'Best Practices' (2006) 81 *NYU Law Review* 294, at 299–302, 309–18 (discussing the successful use of informal regulation via 'best practices' with the threat of more direct regulation providing the motivation for regulated entities to comply with an agency's 'soft' suggestion that, all things being equal, it might be best for the regulated entity to do

organizations. In the chapters that follow, authors will propose interventions that fall under each of these larger headings.

Moreover, by seeking solutions on both a local and a global scale, the coeditors and contributing authors hope that it might be possible to learn from reform efforts that already have been undertaken within one or more domestic legal systems. No one jurisdiction is likely to get the regulatory balance exactly right. Accordingly, by considering regulatory responses to disinformation and misinformation across jurisdictions, it should be possible to better understand what approaches present the most upside potential and the least downside risk.

Justice Louis Brandeis, commenting on the federal system in the United States, observed that '[i]t is one of the happy incidents of the federal system that a single courageous State may, if its citizens choose, serve as a laboratory; and try novel social and economic experiments without risk to the rest of the country'.[62] What is true of states or provinces in a federal system also holds true for nation-states in the global community. Although an attempted legal reform adopted in Chile or South Africa might or might not present a good fit for Germany or India, there surely is merit in at least considering whether a solution that works in one place might well work in another. And so too, the reverse also holds true – if a reform fails to do much good in one place, it would be prudent to consider whether local legal, social, and cultural conditions are sufficiently different in another to predict with any degree of confidence that the solution might work in one jurisdiction despite having failed in another.

1.2 NEW GOVERNMENT REGULATIONS THAT WOULD SAFEGUARD THE PROCESS OF DEMOCRATIC DELIBERATION

The first vector of potential intervention, new government regulations, is perhaps the most obvious. The government protects people against false claims in initial public stock offerings, in the promotion and sale of prescription drugs, and with respect to the terms of consumer credit. If the government can intervene in speech markets to protect consumers against financial fraud, it stands to reason that it could

business one way rather than another); see also Kimberly A. Zarkin and Michael J. Zarkin, *The Federal Communications Commission: Front Line in the Culture and Regulation Wars* (Westport, CT: Greenwood Press, 2006) pp. 146–47 (discussing the Federal Communications Commission's use of regulation by raised eyebrow, and 'voluntary' compliance by regulated entities, in lieu of direct command-and-control regulations that might have been subject to First Amendment objections). The FCC's power to withhold a license renewal for a broadcast station, although rarely used, enables the agency 'to achieve regulatory goals without actual regulations', also known as 'regulation by raised eyebrow', p. 146.

62 *New State Ice Co.* v. *Liebmann*, 285 US 262, 311 (1932) (Brandeis J, dissenting).

also adopt rules and regulations to protect We the People against forms of electoral fraud.[63] As Frederick Schauer correctly observes,

> 'distrust of government' theories, for example, cannot explain why that distrust has not been extended to the Securities and Exchange Commission (SEC), the Federal Trade Commission (FTC), the Food and Drug Administration (FDA), the Department of Justice, or judges managing a trial – all of which involve government officials making content-based decisions about speech and none of which is now covered by the First Amendment.[64]

Yet it is far from clear that government regulation can or will work in this context because of disagreement regarding what constitutes 'false speech'.

In the United States, of course, the conservative Supreme Court and the First Amendment's Free Speech Clause likely limit the ability of the federal or state governments to adopt direct regulations of speech markets.[65] Under current First Amendment precedents, even intentionally false speech enjoys constitutional protection absent a particularized showing of social harm resulting from the false speech.[66] The commitment to protecting speech and maintaining a largely unregulated marketplace of ideas even trumps efforts to protect children from potential harm associated with exposure to extreme forms of violence.[67] Thus, the prospects for government efforts to regulate disinformation and misinformation in the USA are, at best, bleak (and that assumes that Congress or state legislatures could muster the political courage to act in the first place). On the other hand, however, speech regulations do presently exist in the USA to protect consumers from fraud – for example in making credit offers, in issuing stocks for publicly traded companies, and for prescription medications.[68] In areas removed from the political process, anti-fraud speech regulations are commonplace.

It is also true that, in the wider world, government regulation of speech markets is not deemed presumptively suspect (or, more pejoratively, illegitimate). This book's

[63] Frederick Schauer, 'The Boundaries of the First Amendment: A Preliminary Exploration of Constitutional Salience' (2004) 117 *Harvard Law Review* 1765, at 1777–86 and 1806–07.

[64] Ibid. at 1786.

[65] See *Citizens United* v. *Federal Election Commission*, 558 US 310, 339–41 (2010) (invalidating on First Amendment grounds major provisions of the McCain–Feingold Campaign Reform Act which limited uncoordinated electoral campaign spending forty-five days before a primary election and sixty days before a general election); *Miami Herald* v. *Tornillo*, 418 US 241, 258 (1974) ('Even if a newspaper would face no additional costs to comply with a compulsory access law and would not be forced to forgo publication of news or opinion by the inclusion of a reply, the Florida statute fails to clear the barriers of the First Amendment because of its intrusion into the function of editors'.). see also *Arizona Free Enterprise Club's Freedom Club PAC* v. *Bennett*, 564 US 721 (2011) (invalidating an Arizona initiative to equalize candidate funding to make it more difficult for a wealthy candidate to buy a government office through unlimited self-funded campaign spending).

[66] *United States* v. *Alvarez*, 567 US 709 (2012).

[67] See *Brown* v. *Entertainment Merchants Association*, 564 US 786 (2011).

[68] See Schauer, 'The Boundaries of the First Amendment' (n 63), at 1786 and 1806–07.

global focus will feature sustained treatment of jurisdictions, such as Germany, that take the position that government regulation enhances rather than degrades the marketplace of political ideas. Potential regulatory responses might be related to deterring disinformation and misinformation, but they might also relate to better civics education and preparing young people for effective engaged citizenship.[69] Government efforts to promote media literacy also could comprise part of an effective regulatory program to check the corrosive effects of disinformation and misinformation.

Despite the US Supreme Court's assumption that government regulation of the marketplace of political ideas is invariably and inherently distortionary – a point of view that its *Citizens United* decision invalidating key provisions of federal campaign finance reform legislation best exemplifies[70] – in the global context, by way of contrast, government regulations of speech markets are not viewed as intrinsically harmful to the process of democratic deliberation. Showcasing this reality will be an important contribution to ongoing debates in both the United States and the wider world over the proper role of government in addressing the threat that disinformation and misinformation present to the electoral process and, ultimately, to the legitimacy of democratic governing institutions. It may be that mistrust of government makes regulatory solutions that work in the Chile or South Africa impossible

69 Finland, in particular, has adopted policies aimed at preparing its young adults for well-informed, active, and engaged citizenship through educational programs in civics and media literacy. Jenny Gross, 'How Finland Is Teaching a Generation to Spot Misinformation', *The New York Times*, 10 January 2023, www.nytimes.com/2023/01/10/world/europe/finland-misinformation-classes.html (discussing Finland's extensive efforts to inculcate media literacy, which begin in preschool and continue through high school); see Leticia Bodie and Emily K. Vraga, 'People-Powered Correction: Fixing Misinformation on Social Media' in Howard Tumber and Silvio Waisbord (eds.), *The Routledge Companion to Media Disinformation and Populism* (London: Routledge, 2021) pp. 498, 499 (observing that 'Finland's K-12 emphasis on media literacy, in which students are consistently encouraged to read information critically across all aspects of their curriculum, is often touted as a prominent success story' but cautioning 'that Finland may be the exception to the rule' because of its significant and consistent investments in media literacy education coupled with the presence of 'a highly literate and homogenous society' and 'top in the world in media trust'); Teemu Valtonen et al., 'Media Literacy Education in the Age of Machine Learning' (2019) 11 *Journal of Media Literacy Education* 20 (discussing Finland's extensive efforts to teach young citizens media literacy and observing that 'media literacy fostered with computing perspectives would provide students with deeper perspective of media, tools for critical analysis of modern media, and understanding of how and why certain contents are provided for them'). This approach makes sense; if effectively regulating disinformation and misinformation is a difficult, and perhaps impossible task, the next best solution would be efforts aimed at 'inoculating' voters. As with vaccines, such efforts will not work perfectly – but, in this context, we should not make the perfect the enemy of the good (or even the better).

70 See *Citizens United* v. *Federal Election Commission* at 339–41, 361, 365–66 (opining that the voters, not the government, get to decide what speakers, information, and ideas they wish to access, consider, and credit – and which they prefer to ignore). Thus, '[t]he government may not … deprive the public of the right and privilege to determine for itself what speech and speakers are worthy of consideration'. Ibid. at 341.

to implement in the USA, but considering examples of regulatory interventions in other democratic polities certainly would do no harm.

It is a bit puzzling to understand why government regulation produces so much push-back from at least some corners – not only in the USA but in other jurisdictions as well. For example, if a drug promoted as capable of curing pancreatic cancer simply does not work, most consumers would want to know that fact and, if told that human trials showed that the drug does not work, would not want to use it. By way of contrast, however, millions of Americans genuinely believe that Trump won the presidency in the 2020 general election – but had it stolen by corrupt state election officials (many of whom happen to be partisan Republicans, like Brad Raffensperger, Georgia's Secretary of State). Unlike a false claim associated with drug efficacy, those who believe the Big Lie are not much inclined to listen to or credit objectively true information showing that the 2020 general election in the USA was in fact free and fair.

At least in the USA, government efforts to address disinformation and misinformation have been weak and entirely ineffectual. For example, in April 2022, the Biden Administration briefly flirted with operating a 'Disinformation Governance Board' (DGB) within the Department of Homeland Security (DHS). Locating the DGB within the DHS probably did not constitute the most prudent approach to building widespread public support for either the board or its mission. Having a truth board located within DHS simply contributed to the narrative that the effort was a misguided and partisan effort to impose Orwellian 'Big Brother' controls over the democratic process. After opening up shop, on 27 April 2022,[71] the Biden Administration shuttered the DGB 'temporarily' three weeks later on 18 May 2022,[72] and finally, on 24 August 2022, converted this temporary pause into the permanent abolition of the DGB.[73] The DGB was well-intentioned but a complete and total public policy failure.

Clearly, something needs to be done to address efforts to propagate electoral frauds on the voters. However, some solutions, like the DGB, may actually exacerbate rather than mitigate the problems that disinformation and misinformation pose for democracy. A big part of the problem is that, in places with hyper-polarized electorates (the USA and Israel both provide salient examples), the government of

[71] Roger Koppl and Abigail Devereaux, 'Biden Establishes a Ministry of Truth', *The Wall Street Journal*, 1 May 2021, www.wsj.com/articles/biden-establishes-a-ministry-of-truth-disinformation-governance-board-partisan-11651432312 (reporting on the Biden Administration's creation of the DGB on 27 April 2023 and strongly criticizing the administration's efforts to use government power to check disinformation and misinformation).

[72] Taylor Lorenz, 'How the Biden Administration Let Right-Wing Attacks Derail Its Disinformation Efforts', *The Washington Post*, 18 May 2022, www.washingtonpost.com/technology/2022/05/18/disinformation-board-dhs-nina-jankowicz.

[73] Geneva Sands, 'DHS Shuts Down Disinformation Board Months after Its Efforts Were Paused', CNN News, 24 August 2022, www.cnn.com/2022/08/24/politics/dhs-disinformation-board-shut-down/index.html.

the day has little, if any, credibility with the opposition. Thus, in the USA, Republican voters are not much inclined to trust the Biden Administration or to assume that it is acting in good faith to advance the public good. The same held true with respect to Democratic Party voters under the Trump Administration. Accordingly, when an administration undertakes a reform initiative like the DGB, voters on one side or the other see an effort not to provide voters with truthful and accurate information related to the electoral process, but instead a nefarious scheme to silence the administration's most vociferous critics.

To be sure, one could take the view that both government *and* private regulation of truth would be intrinsically distortionary of the democratic process. Yet why could not government, rather than serving as a heavy-handed censor of disfavored political speech, be something more like South Africa's Truth and Reconciliation Commission? A kind of bipartisan, or better yet nonpartisan, fact-checking entity? Even if false information cannot be banned, why cannot government establish credible institutions that could help to identify and disseminate the truth? In the USA, for example, citizens trust the government, through an administrative agency (the FDA), to tell them that cigarettes cause lung cancer. And the federal courts have sustained compelled speech by entities that sell cigarettes; they literally must put warning labels on their own products.[74] If the First Amendment can tolerate compelled speech to promote the public's physical health, why cannot it also tolerate labeling efforts to protect its political health? The kinds of false facts circulating on the web are not any less objectively false than 'cigarettes promote lung health' or 'smoking will enhance your life span'. If it is possible to regulate – and effectively undermine through mandatory disclosures – these kinds of bogus health claims, then why could not it be equally possible to regulate objectively false political speech that contains empirically false assertions of fact that undermine the community's ability to be effectively self-governing?

If critics of new government regulations aimed at combating disinformation and misinformation are correct, and it is simply not possible to take any regulatory steps to address the corrosive effects of fake news, then the First Amendment will be doing as much, if not more, to kill democratic self-government than to sustain it. Such an

[74] See *Discount Tobacco City & Lottery, Inc.* v. *United States*, 674 F.3d 509, 530–31 (6th Cir. 2012) (upholding mandatory health warnings on cigarette packages); *United States* v. *Philip Morris USA, Inc.*, 566 F.3d 1095, 1138–45 (DC Cir. 2009) (upholding a district court's remedial order requiring the tobacco company defendants to disseminate 'corrective statements', including print and broadcast advertisements and inserts in tobacco product packaging, and finding the remedial order on these points constitutes 'a permissible restraint on Defendants' commercial speech'). But cf. *RJ Reynolds Tobacco Co.* v. *FDA*, 696 F.3d 1205, 1221–22 (DC Circ. 2012) (invalidating FDA-mandated graphic warnings about the adverse health effects of using tobacco products on First Amendment grounds because the regulations failed to directly advance the government's regulatory objectives but holding that properly drafted corrective advertising, despite being coerced or forced speech, would nevertheless constitute a constitutionally permissible burden on the defendants' First Amendment rights).

outcome would represent a total and complete inversion of Meiklejohn's normative claim that the First Amendment's principal and primary purpose is to facilitate the process of democratic self-government.[75]

If one embraces the democratic self-government rationale for protecting speech, then it becomes essential to keep an open mind on the question of the appropriate role of the state in the age of fake news. The First Amendment, as an enabler of democratic deliberation, arguably should be a basis for sustaining, not invalidating, government regulations that seek to ensure that voters are able to cast well-informed ballots.[76] Make no mistake, free speech potentially plays the role of the villain here. Of course, the cure must not be worse than the disease,[77] but we should not reflexively assume that government intervention invariably and inevitably would do more harm than good. In fact, thoughtful, well-designed regulatory responses might constitute the best response to the problem of disinformation and misinformation – and such regulations could conceivably be squared with commitments to the First Amendment project of viewpoint neutrality.[78]

What is more, we need to think systematically about how to regulate dominant social media entities, such as Meta (Facebook), X (Twitter), YouTube, and TikTok, as well as dominant internet search engines, such as Google and Bing. In times gone by, a private company could own a dominant voice within a particular community or perhaps have pronounced strength over one specific modality of speech more generally (such as William Randolph Hearst and newspapers). For example, owning the most watched television station in Dallas or the most listened-to radio station in

75 Meiklejohn, *Free Speech* (n 45) pp. 25–26, 88–89.

76 See Owen M. Fiss, 'Why the State?' (1987) 100 *Harvard Law Review* 781, at 788 ('The purpose of the state is not to supplant the market (as it would under a socialist theory), nor to perfect the market (as it would under a theory of market failure), but rather to supplement it. The state is to act as the corrective for the market'.). Fiss argues that '[t]he state must put on the agenda issues that are systematically ignored and slighted and allow us to hear voices and viewpoints that would otherwise be silenced or muffled', ibid.; see also Owen M. Fiss, 'Silence on the Streetcorner' (1992) 26 *Suffolk University Law Review* 1, at 19 ('A proper regard for democratic values requires easy access to all ideas, for without such exposure the public is not likely to know its options or the costs under the present arrangements under which it lives'.). see also Jerome A. Barron, 'Access to the Press: A New First Amendment Right' 80 (1967) *Harvard Law Review* 1641, at 1647 ('There is inequality in the power to communicate ideas just as there is inequality in economic bargaining power; to recognize the latter and deny the former is quixotic'.). Barron argues that the accident of ownership of a primary means of conducting democratic discourse should not be afforded controlling weight, see pp. 1653–56. In his view, private concentrated control of dominant forums for the communication of ideas and opinions itself constitutes a serious First Amendment problem in need of a regulatory solution, see at p. 1678 ('The changing nature of the communications process has made it imperative that the law show concern for the public interest in effective utilization of media for the expression of diverse points of view'.). If concentrated ownership was a problem in 1967, when Barron published his article, it has only grown worse in the intervening fifty-some years.

77 Bhagwat, *Our Democratic First Amendment* (n 43) pp. 112–13.

78 Ibid. pp. 112–18.

Los Angeles potentially would give the owner an outsized voice in local politics within those communities.

Today, dominant media companies do not just own a commanding presence within a particular media market – they essentially own *the entire medium of communication.* This reality makes the need for some form of government regulation pressing and substantial. Simply put, these entities constitute potential choke points to the on-ramps of today's information superhighways. It is difficult to understand, if private censorship of the marketplace of political ideas constitutes a social evil, why only government censorship presents a cause for collective concern – simply put, the dangers of private censorship support a credible argument in favor of collective action through democratic governing institutions.[79] As Owen Fiss cogently argued almost forty years ago, '[t]he state, like any other institution, can act either as a friend or enemy of speech and, without falling back on the libertarian presumption, we must learn to recognize when it is acting in one capacity rather than another'.[80]

1.3 SELF-REGULATION, REGULATION BY 'RAISED EYEBROW' AND THE ROLE OF THE TRADITIONAL PRESS, MASS MEDIA AND SOCIAL MEDIA IN SUCCESSFULLY COMBATING DISINFORMATION AND MISINFORMATION

Perhaps self-regulation by the media, of all stripes, would constitute a better approach than new government regulations for addressing the myriad problems associated with disinformation and misinformation. Alternatively, the government could regulate indirectly, by 'raised eyebrow',[81] by requiring media entities to address the problem of disinformation and misinformation effectively on their own or face the prospect of more direct, and invasive, government regulations of fake news. One or the other approach could work to mitigate the worst social effects of disinformation and misinformation.

In an ideal world, the traditional print press, mass media, and social media would all engage in self-regulation to combat the harms that disinformation and misinformation inflict on democratic deliberation and the electoral process. What 'best practices' might exist for content moderation for social media platforms like Meta

79 Fiss, 'Why the State?' (n 76), at 787–88 (arguing that highly concentrated media ownership puts the process of democratic deliberation at risk and arguing that 'the competition among these institutions is far from perfect, and some might argue for state intervention on a theory of market failure').

80 Ibid. at 787.

81 See Zarkin and Zarkin, *The Federal Communications Commission* (n 61) pp. 146–47 (explaining that '[r]egulation by raised eyebrow means that if the FCC suggests that it is unhappy with some situation, broadcasters will react as if a regulation has been handed down' because, if they do not, actual regulations will be forthcoming in short order and, thus, 'the FCC encourages without requiring, getting the industry to do what it wants without the messy business of regulation').

and X?[82] What kinds of internal and community-based controls might be adopted to combat disinformation and misinformation? What technological opportunities, and limits, exist with respect to algorithmic forms of content moderation? What kinds of self-regulation seem to work best – and which seem most ineffectual?

We know that, for better or worse, in today's world a great deal of democratic discourse will not take place in physical spaces, such as on public streets and sidewalks, in parks, or in traditional town squares. Instead, it will take place in virtual forums hosted by a handful of dominant social media companies. Again, for better or worse, and arguably for the worse, these companies enjoy a stranglehold over important aspects of the process of democratic deliberation and, hence, over the process of democratic self-government itself. Moreover, and as Ash Bhagwat has observed, in the age of new media, 'we are all the press now'.[83] Even so, he laments 'the collapse of even a basic factual consensus on what the world actually looks like'.[84] Bhagwat worries that if we are no longer able to engage in well-informed and reasoned political discourse, democratic deliberation will not effectively or reliably facilitate rational electoral decisions.[85]

As noted earlier, a quite logical response to the problem of the propagation of objectively false facts would be increased regulation of these modalities of communication – in the hope of exorcising disinformation and misinformation from our virtual public square. However, Bhagwat cautions, with good reason, that the Supreme Court would likely invalidate both new government regulatory controls over the internet and efforts to require dominant social media platforms to exercise more effective editorial control over false speech, 'because the Supreme Court (for better or worse) has interpreted [the First Amendment's Free Speech Clause] to protect even intentional falsehoods'.[86] More broadly, he argues that 'it seems a supremely bad idea in a democracy to permit the government to legislate truth or falsehood'.[87]

Bhagwat also rejects self-regulation by dominant media platforms because he is 'almost as unenthusiastic about having Mark Zuckerberg be my arbiter of truth as, say, Donald Trump'.[88] In sum, in his view, 'legislating the truth is a cure worse than the disease'.[89] His proposed solution would involve the adoption of government policies that encourage private associations to 'crowdsource' the truth.[90]

One might reasonably question the prospects for using crowdsourcing truth as an efficacious response to the problems associated with disinformation and

82 See Zaring, 'Best Practices' (n 61), at 299–318.
83 Bhagwat, *Our Democratic First Amendment* (n 43) p. 107.
84 Ibid.
85 Ibid. pp. 107–18.
86 Ibid. p. 111.
87 Ibid.
88 Ibid.
89 Ibid. p. 112.
90 See ibid. pp. 112–18.

misinformation. As Sunstein observes in *#Republic*,[91] the siloing of voters inside social media echo chambers makes correcting empirically false factual beliefs very difficult – perhaps even impossible. Unfortunately, the empirical evidence simply does not support the conclusion that crowdsourcing the truth would actually lead to more voters casting ballots based on accurate information – rather than patent falsehoods. The internet and virtual forums have greatly democratized the ability of ordinary citizens to reach a mass audience (at very little cost).[92] But these platforms also have greatly enabled and amplified disinformation and misinformation that plainly distorts the democratic process by deceiving voters into casting ballots based on false information.

Indeed, the lessons of the 2020 general election in the USA and Trump's Big Lie seem to teach us that Milton was just plain wrong. When Truth and Falsity wrestle in today's marketplace of political ideas, Falsity plays dirty and kicks Truth's ass. We have something like 50 million Americans who firmly believe former President Trump's Big Lie that he actually won both the popular and Electoral College votes in the 2020 general election. How can democracy function when the mechanism of conveying democratic legitimacy – the imprimatur of the people via their ballots – has been poisoned and rendered illegitimate by lies with widespread currency?

Simply put, monopoly private control over dominant forms of social media is not conducive to maintaining democratic deliberation. This was true even before Elon Musk bought Twitter, renamed it 'X', to better fit his corporate empire's branding practices, and turned it into his own personal free speech playground – and it is doubly true today. Comparing today's dominant social media companies to the newspapers or television stations of yesteryear constitutes a false equivalence. The degree of control that the owners of dominant social media platforms, such as Musk and Zuckerberg, enjoy over important forums for democratic discourse and the considerable influence it gives them to shape (if not control) public debate over critical questions of the day would have made William Randolph Hearst blush.

To be sure, legal scholars like Fiss and Jerome Barron sagely warned about the dangers of concentrated ownership of dominant media entities creating the power to censor the news and information available to the body politic – thereby distorting the process of democratic deliberation.[93] Prior to the internet era, television, radio,

91 Sunstein, *#Republic* (n 23) pp. 93–97.

92 Post, Chapter 2, Section 2.1.2(observing that 'digitized information spreads on the internet in a frictionless way that is virtually cost-free at the margin', '[t]he price of sending information to 1000 persons is no greater than sending it to 1 person', and that '[t]he price of sending information to someone on the other side of the globe is no greater than sending it to someone around the corner'). These realities of living in a post-web world mean that information spreads seamlessly across the globe and does so at great speed (what Post calls 'virality')

93 See Barron, 'Access to the Press' (n 76), at 1642–47; Fiss, 'Why the State?' (n 76), at 787–89. As Fiss states his case in chief, '[i]t is one thing to empower someone called a public official and to worry about whether the power entrusted is being used for public ends; it is another thing simply to leave that power in the hands of those who openly and unabashedly serve institutions

and newspapers did indeed rule the media roost – but this is no longer so. And even in times gone by, when there was the problem of unduly concentrated media ownership of over-the-air, analog broadcasting stations, considerable competition for an audience still existed. Today, that simply no longer holds true.

We will likely need new government regulations. Just as new regulations were necessary to prevent fraud on consumers, new regulations are plainly needed to prevent fraud on the voters. In the aftermath of 6 January 2021, the question we should be asking and seeking to answer is how might the power of the state be used to support, rather than to undermine, the kind of civic engagement essential to making elections work as a means of holding government accountable?

Meta (formerly Facebook) dominates social sharing among self-constituted groups. How should one reach a mass audience, reliably, via a short promotional burst (whether to promote a commercial product or a candidate for public office)? X (formerly Twitter). Web searches? Google or Bing. Media sharing? YouTube (which is Google/Alphabet, yet again). Twitter completely banished Trump from its platform after the 6 January 2021 assault on the US Capitol – before Musk welcomed The Donald back on to the platform on 19 November 2022.[94] One might posit that the company's action came too late and also constituted a gross overresponse. By the time Twitter acted, the damage of the Big Lie had already been done – something like 70 percent of GOP voters view President Joe Biden as an illegitimate president who lost the election but became president anyway.

Silencing Trump's tweets might have reduced the risk of another armed insurrectionist mob attacking the capitol – which is obviously to the good. But what about the weeks – more like months and years, actually – that Trump falsely claimed the nation's voting system was rigged and that if he lost an election, his loss simply served to prove that the election had been stolen from him? Those lies were propagated to millions of his followers, for years, without any regulatory response or reaction by Twitter. The situation is deeply depressing – but easy solutions do not seem to exist.

Of course, even 'responsible' media entities, like CNN, constitute part of the problem. For reasons that are far from self-evident, CNN decided it would be a good idea to host a Trump-free airtime campaign event, in the ostensible form of a 'town hall meeting', on 10 May 2023 – in terms of disinformation and misinformation, it constituted a superspreader event.[95] Despite repeated efforts by the host and moderator, Kaitlan Collins, to fact check The Donald in real time, the event descended

that rest on private capital and are subject to market pressures', ibid. at 789. He ultimately concludes that '[i]n another world things might be different, but in this one, we will need the state', ibid. at 794.

94 Shannon Bond, 'Elon Musk Allows Donald Trump Back on Twitter', NPR, 19 November 2022, www.npr.org/2022/11/19/1131351535/elon-musk-allows-donald-trump-back-on-twitter; Ryan Mac and Kellen Browning, 'Elon Musk Reinstates Trump's Twitter Account', *The New York Times*, 19 November 2022, www.nytimes.com/2022/11/19/technology/trump-twitter-musk.html.

95 Justin Peters, 'Donald Trump's CNN Town Hall Was a Disaster', Slate, 10 May 2023, https://slate.com/business/2023/05/trump-cnn-town-hall-kaitlan-collins-new-hampshire-disaster.html.

into a partisan campaign rally rather than a public affairs program. It proved completely impossible to fact check Trump in real time. No doubt thousands of voters who might have harbored doubts about the Big Lie became True Believers after watching Trump's astonishing, and likely highly effective, bravura performance. He also managed to turn a thirty-seven-count federal criminal indictment for stealing and then mishandling top secret government documents into a focal point for a campaign rally as well as a fundraising opportunity (raising $6.5 million in the first twenty-four hours after the indictment was issued[96]). Say what you will about The Donald – he knows how to market a product and the product he most excels at marketing is himself.

Attempts to correct the record by mainstream media entities, even those with a well-known conservative editorial bent, like the *Wall Street Journal*, do not work (at least reliably). In fact, because of siloing and echo chamber effects, the more that mainstream media entities such as CNN and the *Wall Street Journal* attempt to call out disinformation, the more strongly those who credit these falsehoods will cling to them.[97] As Professor Sunstein explains, efforts at error correction by the traditional press frequently 'backfire'[98] and '[t]he result of the correction is to increase polarization'.[99] Although some social scientists contest Sunstein's claim, good evidence suggests that siloing and echo chambers in social media outlets do make at least some voters less receptive to accepting empirical truths.

The ubiquity of disinformation and misinformation plainly distorts our electoral and governing processes. Again, there's nothing heroic about intentionally false speech that hoodwinks voters into casting misinformed ballots on election day. Rather than facilitating democratic self-government, this kind of speech disrupts and distorts it. But if these entities, at least to date, have proven incapable of reliable self-regulation, what, if anything, can be done? Sunstein questions why the fact of ownership of a principal means of democratic deliberation should imply a complete freedom from government regulation or the imposition of any public interest duties. He acknowledges that, '[i]f we believe that the Constitution gives all owners of speech outlets an unabridgeable right to decide what appears on "their" outlets, the answer is clear'[100] – namely, the government cannot require any mandatory moderation

96 Nick Robertson, 'Trump Campaign Says It Has Raised More Than $6.5M Since Federal Indictment', The Hill, 14 June 2023, https://thehill.com/blogs/blog-briefing-room/4050350-trump-campaign-says-it-has-raised-over-6-5m-since-federal-indictment.

97 See Sunstein, *#Republic* (n 23) pp. 93–97 and 109–11 (explaining that efforts by the mainstream media to correct disinformation and misinformation quite often do not work and, paradoxically, lead some people to believe false information even more intensely); see also Minow, *Saving the News* (n 23) pp. 21–33 (discussing in some detail the problem of false information being credited within siloed groups and the difficulties of successfully convincing people to believe what is actually true).

98 Sunstein, *#Republic* (n 23) p. 93.

99 Ibid. p. 94.

100 Ibid. p. 204.

to correct for disinformation or misinformation. Sunstein goes on to ask, 'But why should we believe that?'[101]

In my view, there must be First Amendment 'easements' on this private property, an AT&T-style 'breakup' of these companies to limit their reach by creating meaningful competition, or perhaps both. Indeed, the twentieth-century model of telephone regulation arguably fits pretty well.[102] So too the regulatory model that governs the once-dominant wireline cable system operators (CSOs).[103] The federal government treated both dominant telephone companies and CSOs as common carriers and imposed access requirements[104] – simply put, AT&T and Comcast cannot decide who can use their networks to communicate. They lack carte blanche authority to deny access to third parties to their modalities of speech.

If we think of Facebook not as a speaker, but as a means of speaking, the analogy to AT&T works pretty well. The telephone company, in the days of Ma Bell, permitted people to speak with each other over its network – AT&T itself never generated content. In other words, the telephone served as a conduit for the speech of others, rather than a conduit for the speech of AT&T. And, under the regulatory scheme Congress put in place in 1934, AT&T could operate as a monopoly, or near-monopoly, service provider *only* if it agreed to comprehensive regulation, including rate regulation, and a policy of serving any and all would-be customers who agree to pay the tariffed rates. These rules arguably should be applied to dominant social media companies.[105]

CSOs are a bit different, in that they quite often own cable stations that produce and distribute content – unlike the telephone company, they perform mixed functions as a means of transmitting the speech/content of third parties as well as their own content. And this is precisely why Congress, in 1992, required cable system operators to fill a minimum number of channels with nonaffiliated cable stations,[106] required them to carry broadcast stations,[107] and forced them to offer carriage on a 'leased-access' basis.[108] Because vertically integrated CSOs could and did use their dominant position to silence would-be competitors, it was necessary to regulate access to cable systems to ensure that they did not use their monopoly power over

[101] Ibid.

[102] Ibid. pp. 226–29; Minow, *Saving the News* (n 23) pp. 120–25; Eugene Volokh, 'Treating Social Media Platforms Like Common Carriers?' (2021) 1 *Journal of Free Speech Law* 377, at 383, 433–39.

[103] See Sunstein, *#Republic* (n 23) pp. 70–72.

[104] Cable Television Consumer Protection and Competition Act of 1992, Pub. L. 102-385, 106 Stat. 1460 (5 October 1992) (codified in various provisions of Title 47).

[105] Volokh, 'Treating Social Media Platforms' (n 102), at 454 ('For all these reasons, I think Congress could categorically treat platforms as common carriers, at least as to their hosting function'.).

[106] 47 U.S.C. § 533(f) (2018).

[107] 47 U.S.C. § 534(b) (2018).

[108] 47 U.S.C. § 532 (2018); see 47 CFR §§ 76.970–76.977 (defining and regulating CSO's leased access channel obligations under the Cable Act).

distribution of video content to achieve a monopoly over the creation and distribution of content.

Thus, government regulation of modalities of speech is, at least potentially, the solution, not the problem. Extreme concentration of ownership and the utter absence of competition is the problem. Unfortunately, however, too many legal scholars seem to assume that regulation of dominant social media outlets would necessarily involve content-based discrimination against disfavored speech. Some kinds of regulations would, indeed, likely involve content – the FDA, SEC, and FTC all enforce regulations that impose a variety of civil and criminal liabilities for false speech. But some of the problems relate to companies pursuing policies that promote profits rather than democracy and effective self-government. They are able to do this, at least in part, because of their monopoly positions.

This is not to say that self-regulation or regulation by raised eyebrow/best practices is hopeless. It could work. But failed efforts to make commercial television stations perform public interest duties, including producing and airing high quality public affairs, local, and children's educational programming, offer a strong cautionary note.[109] We should, of course, push privately owned media companies, including social media, to try harder and do better at moderation. But if those efforts fail, we must be open to the deployment of stronger regulatory medicine.[110] It bears noting that many dominant social media companies, such as X and Meta, are radically reducing the paid staff members charged with enforcing the platforms' terms of service (including their announced moderation policies).[111] This, of course, constitutes movement in exactly the wrong direction.

[109] Ronald J. Krotoszynski, Jr., 'The Irrelevant Wasteland: An Exploration of Why *Red Lion* Doesn't Matter (Much) in 2008, the Crucial Importance of the Information Revolution, and the Continuing Relevance of the Public Interest Standard in Regulating Access to Spectrum' (2008) 60 *Administrative Law Review* 911, at 913–15 (discussing the failure of the FCC's efforts to force commercial television stations to create and air high-quality educational children's programming); see Ronald J. Krotoszynski, Jr., 'The Inevitable Wasteland: Why the Public Trustee Model of Broadcast Television Regulation Must Fail' (1997) 95 *Michigan Law Review* 2101, at 2103 ('The sad truth, however, is that the Commission's attempts to implement the public interest standard, which Congress enshrined in the Communications Act of 1934 and the Telecommunications Act of 1996, are a portrait of regulatory failure, notwithstanding the good faith efforts of virtually every subsequent Chairman of the Commission. The Commission's efforts to enforce the public interest standard largely have failed to produce cognizable improvements in either the quality or scope of commercial broadcasters' discharge of their "public trustee" responsibilities'.). At bottom, the problem with the public trustee model for commercial broadcasters is that it constitutes 'a poor mechanism for protecting public values because those called to serve the public are not capable of acting as public servants', ibid. at 2110.

[110] See Scott 'Why Western Democracy' (n 1) (observing that '[y]et never before has the integrity of democracy been in so much danger, thanks to the transformation of political campaigning in recent years into a war waged largely online').

[111] Clothilde Goujard, 'Musk Ousts X Team Curbing Election Disinformation', Politico, 28 September 2023, www.politico.eu/article/musk-ousts-x-team-curbing-election-disinformation ('Elon Musk, the owner of X (formerly Twitter) said overnight that a global team working on

For example, we could imagine government regulations that would reduce, although not eliminate, the problems associated with both siloing and fake news. Make no mistake: these work together in a synergistic fashion to distort the marketplace of political ideas. It takes siloing to create a committed QAnon follower.[112] For example, until the 1980s, broadcasters had a regulatory obligation to provide a right of reply to people who were attacked (sustained against a First Amendment challenge in *Red Lion*[113]) and a concomitant duty to cover news in a balanced fashion (the 'fairness doctrine'). Why could not Facebook or Twitter operate under the exact same legal duty? (Better still, these companies could adopt moderation policies on a voluntary basis that incorporate these principles.) A personal attack rule, for example, would permit someone like Hillary Rodham Clinton to directly engage with QAnon groups on Facebook and Twitter. To be sure, such an approach might, on first blush, sound wild or hopelessly unrealistic or perhaps terminally naïve. And perhaps most QAnon devotees would tune out Clinton's exercise of a right of reply. But surely not all of them would. The problem is that these social media companies find it highly profitable to create intensely focused interest groups and then permit them to listen only to each other (in other words, social siloing within an echo chamber).[114]

Regardless of whether one finds my proposed reform proposals persuasive, if the First Amendment, including the Speech, Press, Assembly, and Petition Clauses, is at

curbing disinformation during elections had been dismissed – a mere two days after being singled out by the EU's digital chief as the online platform with the most falsehoods. Responding to reports about cuts, the tech mogul said on X, "Oh you mean the 'Election Integrity' Team that was undermining election integrity? Yeah, they're gone".). Nix, Zacrzeski and Menn, 'Misinformation Research' (n 3) ('Social media platforms have pulled back on moderating content even as evidence mounts that Russia and China have intensified covert influence campaigns; next week, the disinformation watchdog NewsGuard will release a study that found 12 major media accounts from Russia, China and Iran saw the number of likes and reposts on X nearly double after Musk removed labels calling them government-affiliated'.).

112 Donie O'Sullivan, 'Her Son Was an Accused Cult Leader – She Says He Was a Victim, Too', CNN.com, 23 September 2023, www.cnn.com/2023/09/23/us/qanon-trump-kennedy-protzman-cult-invs/index.html (discussing the mechanisms that lead people to join conspiracy groups and to support conspiracy theories with highly implausible, outlandish beliefs, such as QAnon, and noting that social science research establishes that '[t]he further one goes down the rabbit hole the more likely they are to encounter, and perhaps accept, racist and anti-Semitic hate').

113 *Red Lion Broadcasting Co., Inc.* v. *FCC*, 395 US 367, 388 (1969) ('Where there are substantially more individuals who want to broadcast than there are frequencies to allocate, it is idle to posit an unabridgeable First Amendment right to broadcast comparable to the right of every individual to speak, write, or publish'.). Writing for the *Red Lion* majority, Justice Byron White explained that '[t]here is no sanctuary in the First Amendment for unlimited private censorship operating in a medium not open to all. "Freedom of the press from governmental interference under the First Amendment does not sanction repression of that freedom by private interests". *Associated Press* v. *United States*, 326 US 1, 20 (1945)."').

114 Minow, *Saving the News* (n 23) pp. 125–29 (proposing the imposition of new fairness doctrine regulations for dominant social media platforms to ensure that platform users are exposed to different points of view about matters of public concern); Sunstein, *#Republic* (n 23) pp. 226–33 (same).

its essence about enabling democratic self-government, then we cannot continue to observe a simplistic public/private distinction that treats any government regulation of the principal modalities of democratic deliberation as an unacceptable betrayal of the First Amendment while permitting private companies to adopt and enforce policies that are increasingly rendering the USA entirely ungovernable. As Justice Robert Jackson once sagely observed, if at all possible, the US Constitution in general, and the First Amendment in particular, should not be construed in a way that renders either a 'suicide pact'.[115] Constitutional logic clearly points in the direction of a greater role for the state in creating the conditions necessary for We the People to deliberate collectively about what our government should, and should not, be doing.

Conceding the need for government regulation should not imply, however, that social media companies should not of their own volition make best efforts at devising and implementing moderation policies aimed at controlling and correcting widely circulating, empirically false information. The problem with self-regulation is that when socially responsible action comes into conflict with maximizing shareholder returns, corporate management almost invariably will put profits over the common good (or the production of public goods).[116] The US government's repeated, failed, efforts to force commercial broadcast networks to create and air high-quality children's educational television programming provides a telling example.[117]

We cannot realistically expect for-profit, publicly traded corporations to behave altruistically.[118] There is also nothing wrong with the management of publicly traded

[115] *Terminiello* v. *Chicago*, 337 US 1, 37 (1949) (Jackson J, dissenting) ('The choice is not between order and liberty. It is between liberty with order and anarchy without either. There is danger that, if the Court does not temper its doctrinaire logic with a little practical wisdom, it will convert the constitutional Bill of Rights into a suicide pact'.).

[116] Ronald J. Krotoszynski, Jr., 'Into the Woods: Broadcasters, Bureaucrats, and Children's Television Programming' (1996) 45 *Duke Law Journal* 1193, at 1239–46 (arguing that commercial television broadcasters will never produce and air high-quality children's educational programming because doing so would not be profitable and proposing the substitution of spectrum fees in lieu of imposing public trustee duties on commercial broadcast television and radio stations).

[117] See Krotoszynski, 'The Inevitable Wasteland' (n 109), at 2111–15 (providing an overview and critique of the FCC's failed efforts to make broadcasters produce and air high-quality children's educational programming); see also Krotoszynski, 'The Irrelevant Wasteland' (n 109), at 913–15 (arguing that 'if American children are to rely on the Fox Network to meet their educational programming needs, we are in deep trouble', noting that given the explosion of video content providers, 'parents need not rely on commercial television networks to provide educational programming', and positing that 'that the government should not seek public goods from entities (commercial broadcasters) with little or no interest in providing them').

[118] See Krotoszynski, 'The Inevitable Wasteland' (n 109), at 2109 ('The basic problem that must be overcome is that the public trustee model presumes that the "trustee" will act as a fiduciary for the benefit of the viewing public. Commercial broadcasters have established, however, that their primary motivation is the collection of rents from the sale of advertising time; they routinely avoid furnishing goods that benefit the public in order to maximize their rents'.). Krotoszynski, 'The Irrelevant Wasteland' (n 109), at 920 ('The larger problem with *Red Lion*,

corporations working diligently to improve a company's bottom line.[119] Because most corporations operate largely, if not exclusively, from a profit motive, government regulations probably will be needed to better align the bottom line with the common good. That said, the devil most certainly lies in the specific details of any particular set of regulatory interventions. For example, direct forms of government control, up to and including censorship of social media content, or efforts by the government to proclaim official truths, would almost certainly be met in the USA with widespread public opposition and derision. By way of contrast, less direct, 'soft' regulations – regulations by raised eyebrow or encouragement to 'voluntarily' adopt best practices – that create incentives for effective and reliable moderation by dominant social media companies might work. Taking this course also would plainly constitute a better regulatory approach than ham-fisted – and likely ineffective – efforts by the government to oversee social media content on a day-to-day basis (such as the Biden Administration's ill-fated DGB). Thus, self-regulation by the media, perhaps with a bit of government encouragement, might prove to be far more effective at countering disinformation and misinformation than more direct forms of government regulation.

1.4 THE POTENTIAL ROLE OF NONGOVERNMENTAL ACTORS AND CIVIL SOCIETY ORGANIZATIONS IN SAFEGUARDING DEMOCRACY AND THE DEMOCRATIC PROCESS

Civil society organizations and NGOs present yet another potentially fruitful source of solutions to the problems created by disinformation and misinformation. Both NGOs and civil society organizations, including, for example, educational institutions, civil rights organizations, labor unions, churches, civic groups, professional associations, and even social organizations might individually and collectively work both within their own memberships and within the larger community to combat the ill-effects of disinformation and misinformation. In the context of COVID-19 vaccinations, for example, the most credible advocates of vaccination within certain minority communities in the USA were medical professionals and clinics already working within these communities. In other words, NGOs and civil society

and indeed with the public interest standard itself, is that the policy presupposes the good faith production of public goods from commercial broadcasters with little, if any, economic incentive to provide them'.).

[119] See Krotoszynski, 'The Inevitable Wasteland' (n 109) at 2126–27 (proposing the use of spectrum fees in lieu of imposing public interest duties on commercial broadcasters because 'a direct spectrum fee is much more efficient at producing and providing public goods than the alternative – clunky regulatory command and control efforts, which are certain to be met with half-hearted attempts at compliance and routine backsliding'); see also ibid. at 2108 (arguing that 'the public interest standard conflicts squarely with the broadcasters' financial self-interest' and observing '[s]ince the earliest days of broadcasting, commercial broadcasters have relentlessly pursued profits at the expense of the public interest'.).

organizations possess credibility with their members – all potential voters – that the government and media might well lack.

How might these institutions, with their demonstrated ability to speak credibly to their memberships, be enlisted to help more voters cast well-informed ballots on election day? It may well be, because of pervasive mistrust of both the government and traditional media entities within some communities, that NGOs and civil society organizations present the most promising means of countering efforts to trick and deceive voters. Public polling data clearly establish that large swaths of the voting public deeply distrust both the government and media entities. By way of contrast, however, NGOs and civil society organizations might have the necessary credibility to check effectively disinformation and misinformation circulating within their memberships.

After all, if a person trusts an organization and voluntarily associates with it by joining it, that person is far more likely to trust information propagated by the organization. Because the source of voter education or media literacy efforts has credibility with those being targeted, the intervention stands a much better chance of success. As several of the chapters that follow demonstrate with convincing clarity,[120] good cause exists to believe that NGOs and civil society organizations could successfully engage their members with both voter education and media literacy efforts. The most obvious problem with this potential solution is the broad-based decline of voluntary membership organizations – in the USA and everywhere else too. Simply put, civil society organizations, including professional associations, churches, civic organizations, fraternal associations and clubs, as well as labor unions are all experiencing broad declines in both interest and membership.[121] These civil society organizations are suffering loss of membership and a concomitant loss of social visibility and cultural relevance. Once again, at least arguably, technology and the internet are to blame.[122]

Solutions rooted in NGOs and civil society organizations would require placing reliance on social organizations that, if not quite extinct, seem to be trending in that direction. Nevertheless, because these organizations enjoy the confidence of their (ever-dwindling) members, they could play a significant role in successfully combating the social ill-effects associated with disinformation and misinformation. And because these entities are almost invariably private and not directly connected to the

120 See Part V.

121 See Robert D. Putnam, *Bowling Alone: Revised and Updated: The Collapse and Revival of the American Community* (New York: Simon & Schuster, 2020).

122 See ibid. pp. 31–79 (describing and discussing the decline of civil society, community, recreational and professional organizations in the United States over time); see also ibid. pp. 277–86 (discussing and describing the contributing factors to the decline of civic, social and professional organizations in the United States). It bears noting that Putnam strongly believes the decline of in-person civic, social and professional organizations has contributed to a decline in the quality of democratic deliberation and, moreover, undermines our project of democratic self-government. See ibid. pp. 336–49.

government, their efforts to address disinformation and misinformation would not trigger any First Amendment problems. Simply put, NGOs and civil society organizations are not the state itself and are not bound by the same legal and constitutional constraints applicable to a legislature or a government administrative agency.

1.5 SEEKING WISDOM IN CROWDS: COMPARATIVE LAW CAN PROVIDE IMPORTANT INSIGHTS INTO HOW BEST TO ADDRESS DISINFORMATION AND MISINFORMATION

A common aphorism, rooted in Aristotle's *Politics*,[123] is the idea that there can be wisdom in crowds.[124] In other words, a group of individuals can sometimes better define and solve a problem than an individual working alone. It is our hope that *Disinformation, Misinformation and Democracy* will prove to be a useful resource for thinking about how best to safeguard the process of democratic deliberation, and ultimately democracy itself, from being subverted (or, worse yet, destroyed). In the chapters that follow, a highly talented group of leading scholars of free speech and the democratic process will attempt to address what might be done to make the world safe, or at least safer, for democracy and the process of democratic self-government. The contributing authors, sometimes focusing on a single jurisdiction and sometimes comparing approaches across several jurisdictions, will analyze and critique potential solutions rooted in government regulation, in the press/mass media/social media self-regulating or responding to limited government mandates to address disinformation and misinformation, and on the actions and activities of NGOs and civil society organizations to counteract disinformation and misinformation.

In Part I, Robert Post (Chapter 2) and Andrew Kenyon (Chapter 3) engage the theoretical and policy questions associated with efforts to curb the adverse social effects of disinformation and misinformation. Post focuses on the difficulties of moderation of false information on social media platforms whereas Kenyon addresses issues associated with arresting false information on social media, broadcast media, and in print media. The contributing authors in Part II, Indra Spiecker (Chapter 4) and Eduardo Bertoni (Chapter 5), tackle the issues and problems associated with the government itself as a purveyor of false information.

[123] Aristotle, *The Politics*, Book 3, ch. 11, line 1281b, p. 121 ('But the many, of whom each individual is but an ordinary person, when they meet together may very likely be better than the few good, if regarded not individually but collectively, just as a feast to which many contribute is better than a dinner provided out of single purse'.) (transl. by Benjamin Jowett, 1920).

[124] See ibid. pp. 121–22 (observing that '[f]or each individual among the many has a share of virtue and prudence, and when they meet together, they become in a manner one man, who has many feet, and hands, and senses' and positing that 'the many are better judges than a single man of music and poetry').

In Part III, András Koltay (Chapter 6) and Bernát Török (Chapter 7) address European regional approaches to regulating disinformation and misinformation that involve transnational regulatory efforts and mandates to member states to adopt regulations targeting the dissemination of false information. The contributing authors in Part IV all present jurisdiction-specific accounts of how governments are currently attempting to address false information. These chapters include Ciara Torres-Spelliscy's treatment of the US regulatory approach to false speech by political parties related to the 2020 general election (Chapter 8), John Charney's account of efforts in Chile to eradicate the dissemination of false information from the 1920s to the present (Chapter 9), Ahran Park's analysis of contemporary and historical efforts to regulate false information in South Korea (Chapter 10), Gautam Bhatia's treatment of India's regulatory efforts to prevent the circulation of socially harmful false information via both new media and traditional media outlets (Chapter 11), Joanna Botha's account of how South Africa is attempting, with at best mixed results, to address misinformation and disinformation (Chapter 12), and Victoria Miyandazi and Lucianna Thuo's thoughtful analysis and discussion of ongoing efforts by Kenya's government to prevent the dissemination of disinformation and misinformation both generally and more specifically in the electoral context (Chapter 13).

Part V's chapters focus on the potential role of NGOs and civil society organizations in addressing disinformation and misinformation. Vicki Jackson (Chapter 14) considers how 'knowledge institutions', such as universities and think tanks, could help reduce the potential social harms of false speech by helping to create better informed, more media literate, and hence more capable citizens. Charlotte Garden (Chapter 15) posits that labor unions can help media organizations better perform their critical Fourth Estate duties, which involve providing the voters with the accurate and truthful information that they need to cast well-informed ballots; Garden also argues that unions, more generally, can and should play an important role in promoting media literacy and voter education.

Finally, in the Afterword (Chapter 16), Vincent Blasi considers the social value of false speech and the legitimacy of government efforts to reduce the social costs of disinformation and misinformation. Blasi also posits that, in thinking about the value of freedom of speech and the legitimacy of government efforts to regulate the marketplace of political ideas, courts and legal academics alike should focus on the purpose of a constitutional free speech guarantee – namely, facilitating the process of democratic self-government.

Elections take place somewhere almost all the time, and the coeditors and contributing authors hope that the ideas set forth in this book might offer useful information about interventions that work well, interventions that do not work at all, and interventions whose outcomes might be unclear. As this book goes to press, the 2024 general election in the USA is shaping up to be a rematch of the 2020 general election and citizens of many of the world's leading democracies will be going to the polls in the near future. Accordingly, the implications of disinformation and misinformation to the global community could not be greater or more pressing.

Even if no single intervention promises to provide a quick, easy, and simple-to-implement solution to the problems associated with disinformation and misinformation, doing nothing and hoping that information markets will self-correct probably constitutes the worst possible approach. A potential reform must do more good than harm, but one cannot know whether a particular reform could meet this criterion without first asking and answering questions related to administrative feasibility and efficacy. The authors contributing to this book may not be able, individually or collectively, to solve the difficult and growing problems that disinformation and misinformation present to democracies around the world. However, they can help to shed important theoretical and empirical light on how best to begin the necessary public policy and constitutional conversations.

1.6 CONCLUSION: DISINFORMATION AND MISINFORMATION PRESENT CLEAR AND PRESENT DANGERS TO DEMOCRACY AND DEMOCRATIC SELF-GOVERNMENT THAT MUST BE ADDRESSED SUCCESSFULLY

The tsunami of disinformation and misinformation is poisoning – and, in the long run, threatens to kill off – ongoing experiments in democratic self-government. One can gladly and with alacrity affirm the global centrality of expressive freedoms to the process of democratic self-government. Even so, however, this concession does not mean, and must not mean, that we continue to inhabit the same First Amendment thought space that has existed since the Warren Court. Simply put, 6 January 2021's armed insurrection and attack on the Congress, fomented at a rally led by then-President Donald Trump, and fueled by Trump's Big Lie, should provoke a general rethink of how the First Amendment works – and should work – in the age of the virtual town square. It should also cause thoughtful citizens in other jurisdictions to consider systematically and carefully the potential social costs of disinformation and misinformation – as well as potential means of reducing these social costs.

The popular legitimacy of elections and democratic self-government are both under an existential threat. Indeed, in the USA, the legitimacy of the electoral process is itself already under direct assault. Trump's Big Lie regarding the outcome of the 2020 presidential election threatens to destroy public confidence in the American electoral process – and disinformation and misinformation rest at the very core of the noxious enterprise. Doing nothing simply will not work because doing nothing means that disinformation and misinformation will continue to degrade the process of democratic deliberation, contribute to the further erosion of public trust and confidence in both the electoral process and democratic governing institutions, and, in a worst-case scenario, empower would-be autocrats and tyrants to subvert self-government in favor of authoritarian and proto-fascist systems of government.

It seems unlikely that the contributing authors, individually or collectively, will be able to identify successfully a 'magic bullet' that will easily and quickly solve the problems associated with disinformation and misinformation in the marketplace of political ideas. The problems associated with successfully addressing disinformation and misinformation make a kind of regulatory vaccine a hollow hope. Even so, identifying potentially useful and effective responses would constitute an important contribution to ongoing public policy debates and, concurrently, help to sustain the project of democratic self-government (both in the USA and within the wider world).

Many, indeed probably most, freedom-of-expression scholars believe that constitutional free speech protections exist principally to facilitate democratic self-government. The question, after 6 January 2021, is whether and how that theoretical commitment should empower government to take a more active role in regulating the marketplace of political ideas. Disinformation and misinformation present a palpable threat to democracy, democratic deliberation, and democratic institutions not only in the USA but on a worldwide basis. Placing blind faith in unregulated speech markets will probably not lead to the best outcomes – in the United States or anywhere else.

We need to think carefully, thoughtfully and constructively about how the government, the media, and civil society institutions could work, both individually and collectively, to counter the threat that disinformation and misinformation present to the ongoing process of democratic self-government and, ultimately, to democratic governing institutions. This book represents an effort to make a constructive contribution to developing and deploying effective responses that will safeguard democracy from the potential damage that disinformation and misinformation seek to inflict on both the electoral process and democratic self-government itself. Efforts of this kind constitute first steps – but a long journey cannot be successfully completed without taking the first steps.

PART I

Theoretical Approaches to the Disinformation Problem

2

The Internet, Democracy, and Misinformation

Robert C. Post

The structure of society is heavily dependent upon its means of producing and distributing information. As its methods of communication change, so does a society. In Europe, for example, the invention of the printing press created what we now call the public sphere. The public sphere, in turn, facilitated the appearance of 'public opinion', which made possible wholly new forms of politics and governance, including the democracies we treasure today. Society is presently in the midst of an information revolution. It is shifting from analogue to digital information, and it has invented the Internet as a nearly universal means for distributing digital information. Taken together, these two changes are profoundly affecting the organization of our society. With frightening rapidity, these innovations have created a wholly new digital public sphere that is both virtual and pervasive.

Law is of course a lagging indicator. We typically call upon law only *after* our lives have been disrupted, when we turn to law to intervene and restore order. But law will prove a blunt and ineffective instrument unless we first identify with precision the causes of our discomfort. We have already witnessed too many incoherent legal interventions in the developing arena of the virtual public sphere.[1]

The theme of this volume is misinformation. This theme cannot be adequately understood unless it is theorized within the context of the new social structures everywhere emerging due to the Internet's distribution of digital information. In this chapter I shall discuss six unique and novel dangers that the Internet may pose to democratic forms of self-government. These threats stem from aspects of the Internet that are qualitatively different from all previous forms of mass communication. Each of these threats has important consequences for the problem of misinformation, but

[1] See, e.g., Robert Post, 'Privacy, Speech, and the Digital Imagination' in Susan J. Brison and Katharine Gelber (eds.), *Free Speech in the Digital Age* (Oxford: Oxford University Press, 2019); Robert Post, 'Data Privacy and Dignitary Privacy: *Google Spain*, the Right to Be Forgotten, and the Construction of the Public Sphere' (2018) 67 *Duke Law Journal* 981.

because these threats are fundamental new, we only dimly understand them. We cannot fashion adequate legal responses to the flood of misinformation that prompts this volume until we first theorize the nature of these threats.

2.1 HOW THE INTERNET DIFFERS FROM PAST MEDIA OF MASS COMMUNICATION

Without purporting to be comprehensive, there are (at least) three ways in which the Internet differs from all prior mass media: zero marginal information cost, integration with life tasks, and interactivity.

First, digitized information spreads on the Internet in a frictionless way that is virtually cost-free at the margin. The price of sending information to 1,000 persons is no greater than sending it to 1 person. The price of sending information to someone on the other side of the globe is no greater than sending it to someone around the corner. As a result, the Internet differs from prior mass media in three important ways:

- *Scale*: Information spreads on the Internet on a scale that is orders of magnitude greater than that attained by any prior medium of communication. Facebook, for example, had 2,989,000,000 monthly active users during the first quarter of 2023.[2]
- *Virality*: Not only is the *quantity* of information distributed on the Internet greater than that transmitted by prior media, but the *speed* of that distribution is far faster.[3] When we speak about the virality of information on the Internet, we refer to the almost unimaginably rapid pace at which information spreads from person to person in the virtual public sphere.
- *Cosmopolitanism*: The scale and virality with which information spreads on the Internet renders national borders almost irrelevant. This has put immense pressure on the integrity of national public spheres. In the past, we have conceptualized public spheres as tied to particular nation states. It used to make sense to speak of the German theater, of the English press, of the French novel, or of the American cinema. But the medium of the Internet is so cosmopolitan that we can now begin to glimpse the possibility of a virtual public sphere that is truly international. Although linguistic and legal barriers have so far prevented the realization of that

2 Stacy J. Dixon, 'Number of Monthly Active Facebook Users Worldwide as of 1st Quarter 2023', Statista, 9 May 2023, www.statista.com/statistics/264810/number-of-monthly-active-facebook-users-worldwide.

3 Mary Duffy, 'Internet Is the Fastest Mode of Information Dissemination' (2000) 15(4) *Health Promotion International* 350; Mistura A. Salaudeen and Ngozi Onyechi, 'Digital Media vs Mainstream Media: Exploring the Influences of Media Exposure and Information Preference as Correlates of Media Credibility' (2020) 7 *Cogent Arts & Humanities* 2.

possibility, it is easy to predict that in the not-so-distant future the Internet may foster a true and novel cosmopolitanism.

Second, the Internet is typically accessed through phones, which have become all-purpose tools for negotiating life tasks. We use phones to get directions, to order food, to contact friends, to monitor local news, to locate partners, to charge expenses, and so on. Traditional media did not permeate everyday life in this way. We may have watched a great deal of television, or spent every Sunday morning reading the newspaper, but the virtual public sphere is now integrated with everyday life in ways that dwarf our prior engagement with the traditional public sphere. Because the Internet is seamlessly integrated into our ordinary lives, its influence has become pervasive and inescapable. Our dependence on the communicative structure of the Internet for daily life practices is something entirely new in the world.

Third, the Internet differs from previous forms of mass communication because it is interactive. In traditional mass media, speakers unilaterally addressed large audiences. We ate popcorn while we watched movies in a theater; or we read what our daily newspaper had to tell us over brunch on Sunday mornings; or we listened to our favorite TV commentators over dinner. The Internet has rendered these isolated activities almost passé. It has given rise to wholly new social media like Facebook that are built on the principle of interactivity. Social media are constructed to sustain conversations in virtual space. This unique feature of the Internet has many profound social consequences, of which I shall focus on two: the loss of epistemological authority and polarization.

Traditional media featured professional gatekeepers who vouched for the authenticity and epistemological value of distributed information. The editors of newspapers and magazines staked their reputations on the quality of the product they published. Traditional mass media were controlled by elites who created structures of communication that were quintessentially top down. Social media like Facebook, by contrast, have no equivalent gatekeepers. Facebook may use algorithms to control feeds, but these algorithms do not guarantee the authenticity and epistemological value of the information they distribute.[4] They instead facilitate decentralized and dispersed conversations among users.[5] Those who participate in social media are thus less like the readers of a newspaper than they are like persons who gather to converse on a street corner or around the water cooler at work.

This has potentially important consequences for the creation of epistemological authority. In prior forms of mass communication, gatekeepers warranted the

[4] José Van Dijck, *The Culture of Connectivity: A Critical History of Social Media* (Oxford: Oxford University Press, 2013) p. 47. Cf. Claude Castelluccia and Daniel Le Métayer, *European Parliamentary Research Service. Understanding Algorithmic Decision-Making: Opportunities and Challenges* (Brussels: European Union, 2019).

[5] Beverly Skeggs and Simon Yuill, 'The Methodology of a Multi-model Project Examining How Facebook Infrastructures Social Relations' (2015) 19(10) *Information, Communication & Society* 1356.

epistemological authority of the news they conveyed. But Facebook features no such elite gatekeepers. The structure of epistemological authority produced on social media is more like that created in self-reinforcing circles of gossip. Some have celebrated traditional gossip because it created nodes of resistance to socially dominant ways of thinking. Gossip has this capacity because it is not just about the exchange of information. It is also about the creation of group solidarity and identity.[6] This solidarity underwrites self-validating forms of epistemological authority. The dynamics of a gossip circle become the measure of truth and falsity.

Traditional gossip is frequently dismissed as a premodern phenomenon. In contrast to mass media, gossip requires face-to-face interactions, which seems to render gossip irrelevant in the context of large nation states whose publics stretch over millions of persons. But the Internet creates, for the first time, the possibility of large, virtual gossip groups that are connected through the medium of the Internet. This has vast implications for the social construction of epistemological authority.[7] It fractures public epistemological authority and disperses it into competing circles of gossip. It democratizes truth.

The creation of gossip groups also has important implications for the phenomenon of polarization. Although traditional mass media often targeted discrete groups that were potentially at odds with each other, social media actually *create* such groups.[8] As social media increasingly integrate the virtual public sphere into the conduct of everyday life, so does its potential to create powerful groups whose influence permeates ordinary living. These groups can endow their members with identities that empower them to negotiate the tasks of everyday life. Such groups can acquire epistemological authority sustained by the social solidarity of the group itself. Because circles of gossip define themselves in terms of the distinction between those who are inside and those who are outside, interactive social media like Facebook can foster a terrifying tribalism, homologous to that which has come to dominate our public space. The combination of polarization and democratized epistemological authority creates a toxic brew.

2.2 DEMOCRACY AND THE PUBLIC SPHERE

Taken together, the three structural ways in which the Internet differs from all prior forms of mass communication may create new and fundamental threats to our democracy. I shall discuss six such threats. Each has important implications for how we should address the problem of misinformation. These threats are significant

6 Robin Dunbar, *Grooming, Gossip, and the Evolution of Language* (Cambridge, MA: Harvard University Press, 1996).

7 See, e.g., Neil F. Johnson et al., 'The Online Competition between Pro- and Anti-vaccination Views' (2020) 582 *Nature* 230.

8 Eli Pariser, *The Filter Bubble: How the New Personalized Web Is Changing What We Read and How We Think* (New York: Penguin, 2011).

insofar as we deem it imperative to defend democracy. Why might we deem that important? Democracy is the only modern form of government that instantiates the value of self-determination.[9] Democracy is therefore the only modern form of government that respects equally all persons who are subject to state authority. It is also the only form of government that seeks to reconcile the value of individual autonomy with the need for a state strong enough to perform the services required in the twenty-first century.

Freedom of speech is indispensable for democracy, because democracy consists of 'government by public opinion'.[10] Democracies were made possible when the invention of printing in the fifteenth century facilitated the emergence of the 'public sphere'[11] in the seventeenth and eighteenth centuries. What we now call the 'public'[12] emerged within the public sphere. It was created by 'the circulation of texts among strangers who become, by virtue of their reflexively circulating discourse, a social entity'.[13]

The public sphere, and its corresponding 'public', are presently maintained by an infrastructure of media, like newspapers or museums, which connect strangers to each other. To speak 'in public' is to speak to those whom one does not otherwise know, but whom one expects to reach through mass media that underwrite the public sphere. In our own time, social media and the Internet have created a new, vast, and comprehensive public sphere that is virtual.[14]

What we call 'public opinion' arises within the public sphere. The appearance of public opinion makes modern democracies possible. The public, in the words of

9 Robert Post, 'Between Democracy and Community: The Legal Constitution of Social Form' in John W. Chapman and Ian Shapiro (eds.), *NOMOS XXXV: Democratic Community* (New York: New York University Press, 1993) p. 163.

10 Carl Schmitt, *Constitutional Theory*, ed. and transl. by Jeffrey Seitzer (Durham, NC: Duke University Press, [1928] 2008) p. 275. Democracy is 'the organized sway of public opinion'; Charles Horton Cooley, *Social Organization: A Study of the Larger Mind* (New York: Charles Scribner's Sons, 1909) p. 118. For an account of the emergence of this concept of democracy, see Robert Post, *Citizens Divided: Campaign Finance Reform and the Constitution* (Cambridge, MA: Harvard University Press, 2014).

11 On the public sphere, see Jürgen Habermas, *The Structural Transformation of the Public Sphere: An Inquiry into a Category of Bourgeois Society*, transl. by Thomas Burger (Cambridge, MA: MIT Press, 1989); Charles Taylor, *Philosophical Arguments* (Cambridge, MA: Harvard University Press, 1995) pp. 257–87.

12 John B. Thompson, *The Media and Modernity: A Social Theory of the Media* (Stanford, CA: Stanford University Press, 1995) p. 126.

13 Michael Warner, *Publics and Counterpublics* (New York: Zone Books, 2002) pp. 11–12. Warner adds that 'one of the most striking features of publics, in the modern public sphere, is that they can in some contexts acquire agency ... They are said to rise up, to speak, to reject false promises, to demand answers, to change sovereigns, to support troops, to give mandates for change, to be satisfied, to scrutinize public conduct, to take role models, to deride counterfeits', ibid. pp. 122–23.

14 See Post, 'Data Privacy' (n 1).

Michael Schudson, is 'the fiction that brings self-government to life'.[15] All modern democracies must allow for the free formation of public opinion. If they do not, they no longer serve the value of self-determination and hence no longer deserve the appellation of democracy, whether liberal or illiberal. I shall use the term 'public discourse' to refer to the speech necessary for public opinion formation.

We can now ask whether the rise of the Internet and of the virtual public sphere poses distinctive threats to modern democracy. The Internet surely creates many dangers for democracy, but only some are truly novel. The widespread anonymity of the Internet, for example, can be disorienting. The possibilities of impersonation, of misattribution, of inauthenticity, are legion. But anonymity, with its accompanying dangers, was a phenomenon characteristic of the traditional public sphere, and law has had a few centuries to face down whatever issues it might pose. What I shall explore in this chapter are threats to democracy that *uniquely* arise from the digital circulation of information on the Internet. I shall discuss six such threats. Each will have important implications for the problem of misinformation.

2.3 THE INTERNET AND POTENTIAL THREATS TO DEMOCRACY

The first threat concerns the loss of epistemological authority. We know that every stable society requires a convincing form of epistemological authority. This is especially true for modern society, which depends so heavily on the authority of expertise. Division of labor has made expertise indispensable for nearly all aspects of modern life, from health to technology to energy to agriculture. But in recent decades this authority has come under sustained political assault from populist movements that reject the authority of expertise. Saliant examples include the contemporary attack on universities and the remarkable resistance to public health authorities during the COVID-19 pandemic.

Existing forms of epistemological authority have in the past been undermined by new structures of communication. The invention of printing in the fifteenth century had this effect. Prior to printing, bibles were hand-copied, and so were rare and expensive. Access to bibles was strictly controlled by the church, which prohibited lay persons from reading the words of the Gospel. Epistemological authority over salvation was monopolized by the church. The printing press, however, allowed the bible to be widely and cheaply disseminated. As people began to read the words of Jesus for themselves, the church began to lose control over theological knowledge. The upshot was the Reformation and two centuries of chaos, ranging from outright religious conflict to the English revolution to the Peasant's war in Germany. All

[15] Michael Schudson, 'Why Conservation Is Not the Soul of Democracy' (1997) 14 *Critical Studies in Mass Communication* 297, at 304–05. On the relationship between the development of printing and the creation of the nation state, see Benedict R. O'G. Anderson, *Imagined Communities: Reflections on the Origin and Spread of Nationalism*. Revised and extended ed. (London: Verso, 1991).

Europe struggled to contain the antinomian consequences of the communicative revolution produced by the printing press.

The widespread and virtually costless access to universal knowledge created by the Internet has had an analogous effect on today's society. Now everyone can be an expert on everything. They need only look up the relevant information on the Internet. If we go to the doctor, we research our symptoms and feel free to challenge the medical authority of our physician. I now see signs in doctors' waiting rooms to the effect: 'Your Google search is not equivalent to my medical degree.' The zero marginal information cost of the Internet, in other words, has potentially undermined the forms of epistemological authority by which modern society underwrites order and stability. The diminishment of epistemological authority is magnified by the existence of gossip groups, which construct their own epistemological authority based on the groups' needs for social solidarity.

The implications for democracy of these developments are obviously profound. As we lose the ability to identify figures of authority whom the public can trust to distinguish truth from fiction, we correspondingly lose the capacity to establish common facts. Hannah Arendt rightly observed that we cannot inhabit a common political world unless we acknowledge shared facts.[16] Democracy cannot survive in the absence of the epistemological authority necessary to create a shared political world. We need to be able to decide whether nicotine causes cancer, or whether climate change is produced by human action, or whether seat belts reduce the harms of automobile accidents. This can happen only if we are able to create authoritative disciplinary methods to underwrite our ability to answer such questions. By unleashing epistemological antinomianism, the Internet threatens the capacity of democracy for coherent self-governance.

It is in this context that the dangers of misinformation should be understood. It requires authority, which means it requires trust, to distinguish true information from false information. There was surely a great deal of untrue information distributed by traditional media. But misinformation has become a cardinal problem of the Internet age because zero marginal information has undermined the forms of authority society uses to distinguish falsity from truth. As Ross Douthat recently observed in the *New York Times* in the context of vaccine skepticism, the main theory of countering misinformation 'seems to be to enforce an intellectual quarantine, policed by media fact-checking and authoritative expert statements. And I'm sorry, but that's just a total flop. It depends on the very thing whose evaporation has made vaccine skepticism more popular – a basic trust in institutions, a deference to credentials, a willingness to accept judgments from on high'.[17]

[16] Hannah Arendt, *Between Past and Future* (New York: Viking, 1968) p. 238.

[17] Ross Douthat, 'Go Ahead: Debate Robert F. Kennedy Jr.', *The New York Times*, 24 June 2023, www.nytimes.com/2023/06/24/opinion/rfk-jr-joe-rogan-debate.html.

The social problem of misinformation, as distinguished from misinformation itself, concerns the loss of epistemological authority. The circulation of untrue information is a symptom of this underlying social dislocation. One can treat the symptom, of course, but the underlying disease will likely manifest itself in other ways. And if treating the symptom means using the state to suppress free participation in public discourse, it may well mean losing the patient in an effort to save it. Those who distrust 'trusted' flaggers or experts will distrust them even more if their objections are officially suppressed. In a democratic society, the revenge of the repressed can be a terrible thing.[18] In dealing with the undoubted problem of misinformation, we must negotiate between the Scylla of widely circulating falsehoods and the Charybdis of the loss of democratic participation. Under conditions of polarization, suppression that is experienced as illegitimate can easily lead to an existential opposition between friends and enemies that would undermine the very possibility of democratic politics.[19]

The second danger concerns the nature of a public in a democracy. At the turn of the twentieth century, sociological theorists such as Gabriel Tarde began to distinguish between a public and what they called a crowd or a mob.[20] Publics were created by mass communications like newspapers or magazines. Persons read these communications and then gathered in small groups to talk about them. The information contained in mass communications spread about as far and as fast as analogue communications could spread. This gave persons time to think about the information and to discuss its implications. Crowds or mobs, by contrast, are large groups of people created in the heat of a simultaneous exposure to common stimuli. Crowds interact immediately and in ways that are typically characterized as emotional.[21] We describe crowds using metaphors such as contagion or frenzy. We might today make the contrast between what Daniel Kahneman calls system 1 and system 2 thinking, the former being immediate and emotional, and the latter being slower and more reflective.[22]

A danger that the Internet poses to modern democracy is that the virality of information might convert the demos of a democracy from a public into a crowd.

[18] See, e.g., Robert Post, 'The Legality and Politics of Hatred' in Thomas Brudholm and Birgitte Schepelern Johansen (eds.), *Hate, Politics, Law: Critical Perspectives on Combating Hate* (Oxford: Oxford University Press, 2018).

[19] Compare Carl Schmitt, *The Concept of the Political*, transl. by George Schwab (Chicago: University of Chicago Press, 1996), with Chantal Mouffe, 'The "End of Politics" and the Challenge of Right-Wing Populism' in Francisco Panizza (ed.), *Populism and the Mirror of Democracy* (London: Verso, 2005) pp. 50–71. See Robert Post, 'Disagreement: Reconceiving the Relationship between Law and Politics' (2010) 98 *California Law Review* 1319.

[20] Gabriel Tarde, *L'opinion et la foule* (Paris: F. Alcan, 1901); cf. John S. McClelland: *The Crowd and the Mob: From Plato to Canetti* (London: Unwin Hyman, 1989) pp. 138–49.

[21] See, e.g., *Terminiello* v. *Chicago*, 337 US 1, 2–6 (1949) (invalidating on First Amendment grounds convictions for breach of the peace where right-wing speakers in Chicago deliberately and effectively provoked a large group of progressive demonstrators).

[22] Daniel Kahneman, *Thinking, Fast and Slow* (New York: Farrar, Straus and Giroux, 2013).

The flash mob is a physical representation of this social phenomenon. Mob thinking on the Internet is encouraged because the scarce resource in the virtual public sphere is not information, as we theorize in ordinary economic modeling, but instead attention. The Internet has accordingly developed methods to drive attention, which typically emphasize the arousal of emotional reactions like anger or affection. We thus slip from reflection into immediate and emotional reactions.

Democracy requires a public that thinks,[23] and thinking does not occur instantaneously. The virality and interactivity of the Internet, its integration in real time into the pressing tasks of everyday life, may well be inconsistent with necessary public reflection. As a medium, the Internet may privilege immediate reactions that marginalize self-conscious thoughtfulness and contemplation. The result is the production of a kind of mob mentality, characterized by rapid and instantaneous responses, that is inconsistent with democracy. The circulation of misinformation thus occurs in a context that is especially fertile for its uptake and use.

A third danger to democracy that might uniquely be posed by the Internet concerns issues of scale. The vast dimensions of the Internet frequently produce forms of harm that may best be characterized as stochastic. Previously we asked whether particular speech acts might *cause* particular harms. The Internet has rendered this kind of inquiry almost obsolete. Speech that is simultaneously distributed to millions of persons may produce harm in ways that cannot meaningfully be conceptualized through the discrete pathways of simple causality. We must instead think in terms of the statistical probabilities of harm. At present, however, we lack any legal framework capable of assessing stochastic harms in ways that will not drastically overregulate speech. If we were to suppress every form of communication that might cause harm if distributed in sufficiently large numbers, we would have precious little communication left unregulated.

This problem is particularly acute in the context of misinformation. No society punishes statements merely because they are false.[24] In traditional mass media, false information is regulated when it causes legally cognizable harm, such as loss of reputation or privacy. No epistemological authority has ever been strong enough to

[23] See William E. Hocking, *Freedom of the Press: A Framework of Principle. A Report from the Commission on Freedom of the Press* (Chicago: University of Chicago Press, 1947); Alexander Meiklejohn, *Free Speech and Its Relation to Self-Government* (New York: Harper & Bros, 1948) pp. 22–27, 89–91. See also John Dewey, *Democracy and Education: An Introduction to the Philosophy of Education* (New York: Macmillan, 1916) pp. 4–11, 23–24, 81–99. For a general overview of the integral relationship of education, informed engagement, and democratic self-government, see Diane Ravitch, 'Education and Democracy' in Diane Ravitch and Joseph P. Viteritti (eds.), *Making Good Citizens: Education and Civil Society* (New Haven, CT: Yale University Press, 2001) pp. 16–27.

[24] See generally *United States* v. *Alvarez*, 567 US 709, 718 (2012) ('Absent from those few categories where the law allows content-based regulation of speech is any general exception to the First Amendment for false statements. This comports with the common understanding that some false statements are inevitable if there is to be an open and vigorous expression of views in public and private conversation, expression the First Amendment seeks to guarantee').

sustain a state that might seek to suppress every false statement in traditional mass media. A fortiori this is true of the contemporary Internet. If the problem of misinformation is to be addressed, therefore, the concept of harm must be refined. But at present we lack the conceptual tools to distinguish among the kinds of stochastic harms that may be caused by the nearly infinite variety of false statements widely circulated on the Internet.

A fourth danger to democracy that might be uniquely caused by the Internet concerns the definition of the public sphere itself. Almost every sophisticated democratic legal system offers special protections to speech that is about public officials or public figures, or that is about matters of public concern.[25] Speech that is distributed to the public at large is often *ipso facto* accorded such protections, as can be seen in the unique privileges enjoyed by the press. The modern architecture of freedom of speech heavily depends upon the fundamental distinction between public and private speech. Public speech is protected insofar as modern legal systems seek to preserve the free development of public opinion that insures both public accountability and democratic legitimacy. Most states permit the circulation of a good deal more falsity in public discourse than, say, in commercial speech. Speech between private persons, by contrast, is more heavily regulated to sustain the community norms that define and maintain personal dignity and respect.

The Internet fundamentally threatens this essential legal architecture by blurring the distinction between public and private speech. Even the most personal communication on the Internet can be more widely circulated than an article of public concern in the largest newspapers. On the Internet the personal becomes public.[26] Yet so much about our understanding of how freedom of speech works depends upon a clear demarcation between public and private spheres of speech and action. As this demarcation is blurred by the Internet, so is our ability to conceptualize how speech on the Internet is to be categorized and regulated. This has major implications for the regulation of misinformation.

A fifth unique danger to democracy posed by the Internet concerns cosmopolitanism. All systems of freedom of speech in modern democracies aspire to subordinate political authority to national public opinion. But because the Internet produces opinion that may be cosmopolitan rather than national, it threatens to undermine

[25] *Grant* v. *Torstar Corp.*, [2009] 3 S.C.R. 640, 2009 SCC 61 (Can.) (holding protected under the Canadian Charter of Rights and Freedoms free expression guarantee false statements about matters of public interest published in good faith, and observing standards of responsible journalism); *Khumalo* v. *Holomisa*, CCT 53/01, 2002 (5) S.A. 401 (CC) (South Africa) (reaching the same conclusion under Section 16 of the Constitution of the Republic of South Africa, which safeguards the freedom of speech and press); *Jameel* v. *Wall Street Journal Europe*, [2007] 1 AC 359 (HL) (app. from Eng., reaching the same conclusion under the United Kingdom's Human Rights Act 1998).

[26] See, e.g., Liz Arcury, 'Here's What You Need to Know about the Backlash against Jonah Hill's Ex', *Huffpost*, 13 July 2023, www.huffpost.com/entry/jonah-hill-texts-emotional-abuse_n_64af22a3e4b033dd8e5d6f28?ncid=APPLENEWS00001.

this entire framework of analysis. It is not clear why the American government should hold itself accountable to Russian public opinion. That is why foreign actors spreading misinformation from abroad are accorded very different legal treatment than domestic actors who are accused of disseminating misinformation. Once the Internet transforms the public sphere into an international phenomenon, however, any such distinction will become problematic, and we shall have to develop entirely new paradigms to explain and justify our protections for freedom of speech.

I shall conclude by sketching a sixth and very subtle danger that the Internet may pose to modern democracies. This is a danger that derives from the immense scale of the Internet. That scale makes its regulation incompatible with law. The Internet is far too big to be policed through the exercise of human judgment. During the first quarter of 2022, for example, Facebook alone took down some 151,900,000 pieces of content. These removals resulted in some 2,614,400 appeals.[27] And these calculations do not even begin to account for the large number of communications that were *not* taken down but that should have been.

No court, no human legal institution, has the capacity to oversee this volume of business. Human judgment simply does not operate at this scale. Content moderation on the Internet therefore mostly does not operate through human decision-making, but instead through the application of Artificial Intelligence (AI). The upshot is that the free formation of public opinion on the Internet, which is the lifeblood of any democracy, has essentially been delegated to AI.

The problem is especially acute in the context of misinformation. It is necessary to understand facts about the world to know whether a statement is true or false. When certain falsehoods are frequently repeated and become stereotyped, it is possible to program AI to detect and remove them. But AI is a poor instrument for determining in the first instance whether statements are true or false. For such tasks we require human judgment, typically exercised in the form of law. Over the centuries, law has earned the political legitimacy and epistemological authority required to determine disputed facts about the world.

The implication of this analysis is that we may be facing a potential crisis insofar as democracy depends upon public speech, and insofar as public speech is controlled by an AI that lacks the political legitimacy and epistemological authority of law. We need, therefore, to theorize the relationship between AI and law so as to endow AI with the legitimacy and authority required to govern the Internet. How to accomplish this poses a profound puzzle.

Law carries authority because it instantiates the human capacity for judgment, which, as Immanuel Kant taught us in his third *Critique*, ultimately depends upon an appeal to the *sensus communis* of humanity. Judgment, including legal

[27] See Facebook's Community Standards Enforcement Report, https://transparency.fb.com/data/community-standards-enforcement.

judgment, depends upon our common participation in a shared community.[28] As we exercise judgment, we participate in and shape the nature of that community.[29] Judgments are validated by the reciprocal relationship between a community and its members,[30] which is why judges must be *representative* figures to pronounce law. Judges must *commit* to participating in the community that their judgments establish, which is one important reason why we trust their judgments and endow them with authority.[31]

AI cannot be a member of any human community. It cannot participate in, and hence construct a dialectical relationship with, any human community. AI therefore cannot pronounce law. At most AI can report factual determinations about the way that actual humans regard law. The decisions of AI are analogous to those of a jury that seeks to evade its responsibility to determine the 'reasonableness' of an action by taking an opinion poll of the ambient community. Juries are not permitted to act in this way because law is not a mere fact; it does not consist in mere information. Juries are required to exercise independent human judgment for the same reason as are judges. By exercising judgment, juries both participate in and define their community. This dialectical process is the essence of law.

It follows that AI cannot make content moderation decisions with the legitimacy or authority of law. The clear implication is that society will need to invent new ways to endow AI decisions with the kind of authority and legitimacy necessary to govern the Internet. One possibility is to take advantage of the fact that AI is not static. AI learns as it receives feedback about its decisions. Because AI algorithms learn through iterative training, politically appropriate participation in this training might offer the possibility of legitimating the decisions of AI. Whether or not these means are ultimately used, it is plain that the day-to-day governance of the Internet, which is of essential importance to the contemporary formation of public opinion, will remain estranged both from law and from political legitimation until we invent some mechanism to make AI accountable. The potential dangers to democracy are obvious.

2.4 CONCLUSION

I have identified six potentially unique threats that the Internet may pose to modern democracies: the loss of epistemological authority, the substitution of a crowd for a

[28] Ronald Beiner, *Political Judgment* (London: Routledge, 1983).

[29] Robert C. Post, 'The Constitutional Concept of Public Discourse: Outrageous Opinion, Democratic Deliberation, and *Hustler Magazine* v. *Falwell*' (1990) 103 *Harvard Law Review* 601.

[30] Robert C. Post, 'The Social Foundations of Privacy: Community and Self in the Common Law Tort' (1989) 77 *California Law Review* 957.

[31] Robert Cover, 'Foreword: Nomos and Narrative' (1983) 97 *Harvard Law Review* 4.

public, the creation of stochastic harm, the loss of the public/private distinction, the loss of the national public sphere, and the chasm between a regime of law and a regime of AI. The problem of misinformation is implicated in each of these threats. We cannot solve the problem of misinformation until we apprehend these dangers and develop strategies for their amelioration. That is the bad news. The good news is that there is much work for all of us to do.

3

Democratic Freedom of Expression and Disinformation

Andrew T. Kenyon

3.1 INTRODUCTION

When analysing disinformation, commentators often focus on major platforms and their influence on content circulation.[1] Some also examine institutional media, especially broadcasting. Platforms and media are both relevant; both are important in the communicative infrastructure underlying public speech. Whatever the focus, there is an almost endless examination of issues and suggestions regarding what to do about disinformation. Commentary defines false or misleading information in different ways,[2] compares it with historic practices of propaganda and persuasion, considers the emergence of large language models and content they could generate, documents varied legal responses, and considers what should be done. Here, I examine something that is relevant to that work but often not considered directly.

My interest is how democratic freedom of expression can be understood in quite different ways, and how this can affect legal responses to disinformation. This point

This research was partially funded through the Australian Research Council Centre of Excellence for Automated Decision-Making and Society (ADM+S) (CE200100005).

[1] There are three points of terminology to note: (1) Freedom of expression, expressive freedom, free speech, etc. are used interchangeably here; (2) 'Disinformation' is used expansively, encompassing false and misleading content. For a useful overview of its meanings in current EU approaches, see, e.g., Alexander Peukert, *The Regulation of Disinformation in the EU – Overview and Open Questions*. Research Paper of the Faculty of Law of Goethe University Frankfurt, 2023, https://ssrn.com/abstract=4496691; (3) While referring simply to 'platforms', multiple entities are involved in infrastructures underlying public speech, such as social media, search, data brokers, advertising intermediaries.

[2] See, e.g., Claire Wardle and Hossein Derakhshan, Information Disorder: Toward an Interdisciplinary Framework for Research and Policymaking. Council of Europe report DGI (2017)09; Edson C. Tandoc, Jr., Zheng Wei Lim and Richard Ling, 'Defining "Fake News": A Typology of Scholarly Definitions' (2017) 6 *Digital Journalism* 137–53.

may be recognised more outside the United States than within, in part because of the particular US understanding of freedom of expression. The currently dominant approach to the First Amendment limits what is possible when responding to disinformation. As communicative structures change, that is increasingly significant. Freedom of expression is arguably better protected in Europe than in the USA,[3] in ways that are becoming increasingly important for democratic opinion formation and a communicatively legitimate democracy. Freedom of expression is not a complete response to democracy's communicative needs, but it is important in supporting an infrastructure of communication sufficient for self-government. Alternatively, if the freedom is poorly understood it can obstruct that infrastructure. (Even in conditions that can be called post-democratic, freedom of expression can have a similar role supporting something closer to democratic opinion formation.[4])

This chapter considers some differences in how freedom of expression is understood in US and European law and scholarship.[5] The differences in understanding align with different responses to disinformation and help to clarify changes that will be needed for greater US responses to disinformation. It is not that European understandings of expressive freedom are ideal. As is common in Europe, there are multiple, overlapping and somewhat inconsistent ideas about free expression across the many settings involved, and at least parts of the European Union response are framed too closely to economic interests to meet the needs of democratic freedom of expression. Rather, the EU response can tend to protect 'market freedom against national democratic contestation' and enable platform business models.[6] However, the approach shows more of what may be useful overall and offers an interesting model. As all this suggests, my interest is less in the details of legal responses to disinformation than the conceptualisations of communicative freedom that frame them. That said, the analysis of communicative freedom that follows goes further than any existing legal position within Europe, whether in EU provisions, the European Convention of Human Rights (ECHR), or national laws. Rather, it draws from all these sources to suggest an approach to freedom of expression that is more than nascent in the existing European ideas and could be useful when considering disinformation or public speech more generally.

Section 3.2 below briefly examines the changed context of public speech. Structures underlying public communication have changed, they are no longer

[3] Thomas Hochmann, 'Why Freedom of Expression Is Better Protected in Europe than in the United States' (2022) 2 *Journal of Free Speech Law* 63–85.

[4] See, e.g., the role suggested for public media in Colin Crouch, *Post-Democracy* (Cambridge: Polity, 2004) pp. 46–51.

[5] One could also look to international material; e.g., United Nations Special Rapporteur et al., Joint Declaration on Media Freedom and Democracy (2023), www.ohchr.org/sites/default/files/documents/issues/expression/activities/2023-JD-Media-Freedom-and-Democracy.pdf, setting out positive obligations for states including online news and commentary.

[6] Rachel Griffin, 'Public and Private Power in Social Media Governance' (2023) 14 *Transnational Legal Theory* 46–89, 64.

dominated by mass media in the way they were in the twentieth century, and a broader range of actors is relevant. Distribution of expression is particularly important in the changes, along with the revenues that used to accompany it. Social media and search use commercially driven distribution very differently to what was imagined for past media distribution and commercial media financing. Section 3.3 moves to expressive freedom, focusing initially on US law and commentary. Debates about legal responses to disinformation resemble other content debates, such as whether vilification can be regulated in a communicatively legitimate democracy. The overlap is only partial, but examining the issue is instructive. It highlights differences in understanding freedom of expression and, perhaps especially, what freedom means within it. This helps to clarify what interpretations of expressive freedom support what legal approaches to regulation, including regulation relevant to disinformation. Section 3.4 draws out differences in European ideas of communicative freedom and takes their implications further. Then Section 3.5 examines some current EU measures relevant to disinformation, which have interest as a general model more than in the precise wording of their provisions or how they may operate in the short term. There are significant differences in how expressive freedom is understood which, as the chapter concludes, underline the value in reformulating the US understanding and in supporting a more comprehensive European interpretation of the freedom.

There are two further matters of introduction. First, while disinformation understandably receives attention, the term can clearly be misused. Johan Farkas and Jannick Schou have noted that post-truth is often 'a discourse crafted by those who benefit from the status quo'.[7] As they suggest, debates about disinformation can reduce the demos in democracy and focus on rational governance by experts over people's voices and agency.[8] The arguments can obscure a tension between democracy as representation and expertise on the one hand, and democracy as popular sovereignty on the other. That is not my intention. Those with political, financial and other power are always likely to have conflicts of interest about freedom of speech; that applies equally for disinformation. Even so, I think there *are* now differences in the way speech can reach and form publics and influence opinion formation that mean something is at stake beyond other longer-term changes in democratic practices.

Second, it is useful to consider at least two aspects of legal responses to disinformation. One concerns direct state *restrictions on expression* and whether accountability can be implemented for at least some disinformation. Another concerns

7 Johan Farkas and Jannick Schou, *Post-Truth, Fake News and Democracy* (New York: Routledge, 2020) p. 157.

8 See also, e.g., Ian Cram, 'Keeping the Demos out of Liberal Democracy? Participatory Politics, "Fake News" and the Online Speaker' (2019) 11 *Journal of Media Law* 113–41; Irini Katsirea, '"Fake News": Reconsidering the Value of Untruthful Expression in the Face of Regulatory Uncertainty' (2018) 10 *Journal of Media Law* 159–88.

structural or systemic responses to disinformation or *responses relevant to public debate* more widely. These might include state obligations to regulate private actors that affect public speech, support for communicative infrastructures more generally, and intervention in relevant actors' financial models. Particular structural or systemic responses might be hampered by freedom of expression, allowed by it, or required by it, depending on how communicative freedom is understood. And the responses can encompass institutional media as well as platforms. Both aspects – restrictions and structural or systemic responses – can be understood as falling within the freedom in freedom of expression. In simple terms, US law often says no both to restrictions and to structural interventions, while European law says yes, partly at least. In addition, beyond freedom of expression law, and beyond law more generally, a wide range of social practices is clearly significant. For news and commentary, the practice of journalism is one obvious example.[9] Public discourse has never required only law. Freedom of expression arises within social relations; it is nonsense to say the freedom only involves the absence of restraint or that law has no relevance to, and no effect on, those social relations.[10]

Current judicial interpretation of the First Amendment allows hardly any restriction of falsehoods in public discourse. Even deliberate lies are protected unless they fall into certain long-established categories. In addition, US free speech law does not require various state actions related to the infrastructures underlying public speech, such as actions supporting media pluralism and democratic opinion formation. On some analyses, the First Amendment does not even allow such structural or systemic action. At a minimum, it should. In Europe, things are different. Concerns exist about laws directly regulating disinformation, but more is possible than under US law. The second aspect, about state action, has clearer differences. For example, ECHR member states have positive obligations to make Convention rights effective.[11] This means states have obligations to regulate private actors where they threaten enjoyment of Convention rights, including expressive freedom for both speakers and recipients. And states may need to act in support of pluralism – they are its ultimate guarantors. This helps to explain why it can be said that freedom of expression is better protected than under the First Amendment. In Europe, positive dimensions of the freedom are legally recognised, not only negative ones.

9 I examine some implication of journalism's changed role in Andrew T. Kenyon, 'Regulating Opinion Power: Journalism, Platforms and Public Speech' in Martin Senftleben, Kristina Irion, Tarlach McGonagle and Joost Poort (eds.), *Cambridge Handbook of Media Law and Policy in Europe* (Cambridge: Cambridge University Press, forthcoming).

10 E.g., Thomas Streeter, 'Beyond Freedom of Speech and the Public Interest: The Relevance of Critical Legal Studies to Communications Policy' (1990) 40 *Journal of Communication* 43–63.

11 See, e.g., Andrew T. Kenyon, 'Sustained Plural Public Speech: Positive Obligations, Freedom of Expression and the European Court of Human Rights' in Charles Girard, Pierre Auriel and Andrew T. Kenyon (eds.), *The Cambridge Handbook of Freedom of Expression and Democracy: European Perspectives* (Cambridge: Cambridge University Press, forthcoming).

3.2 INFRASTRUCTURES OF PUBLIC SPEECH

That the infrastructures underlying public speech have changed is obvious. As one aspect, consider an individual's ability to reach a large audience when they believe an extreme political scandal has occurred that is not being publicly addressed. The belief is an 'outlandish fiction' in the example. It is false. Six decades ago, the possibilities for reaching people were limited:

> The only way to reach a large audience in 1965 would have been through one of the major metropolitan newspapers or the three [US] broadcast networks. But these prided themselves on practicing serious journalism. They . . . all were by and large determinedly centrist in orientation [in US terms], with high professional standards, and none would have aired this outlandish fiction.[12]

In the example, Larry Kramer notes US supermarket tabloids did publish outlandish fictions, but suggests they were not taken seriously by almost any readers so they did not change the overall possibilities for influencing public speech. The general situation was similar in other democratic jurisdictions, although often commercial broadcasting was far less dominant and public broadcasting more prominent than in the USA, newspaper–political party relations varied in multiple ways, and there were different habits of media reception and use.[13] But the basic point applied generally across established democracies. Reaching an audience required media.

Many challenges that are now raised about platform-distributed speech – the treatment of problematic content, where to focus attention, what to remove from circulation or limit in reach, questions of tone, and so forth – were formerly left to journalism or what can be called a journalistic-editorial function. This function was understood to have substantial, but not total, influence on content. Such an understanding was highly idealised, but it was the model at least. Journalists and editors made decisions about news and commentary (and broadly equivalent roles existed for entertainment and other genres). Of course, reality never matched the model, with media practices often including discrimination, elitism, or being subject to commercial or state domination.[14] 'Marginalized communities have long been "reduced" by the centrism and conservatism of traditional media.'[15]

Law attempted to deal with those challenges, again imperfectly. One set of legal responses was not focused on institutional media but was relevant to it. These were

[12] Larry Kramer, 'A Deliberate Leap in the Opposite Direction: The Need to Rethink Free Speech' in Geoffrey R. Stone and Lee C. Bollinger (eds.), *Social Media, Freedom of Speech, and the Future of our Democracy* (New York: Oxford University Press, 2022) pp. 17–39.

[13] See, e.g., Daniel C. Hallin and Paolo Mancini, *Comparing Media Systems: Three Models of Media and Politics* (Cambridge: Cambridge University Press, 2004); Jonathan Hardy, *Western Media Systems* (Abingdon: Routledge, 2008).

[14] See, e.g., John Charney, *The Illusion of the Free Press* (Oxford: Hart, 2018) ch. 1.

[15] Tarleton Gillespie, 'Do Not Recommend? Reduction as a Form of Content Moderation' (2022) 8(3) *Social Media and Society* 1–13, 9.

laws that limited certain content, such as defamation and copyright. Another set of responses involved structural measures aimed at promoting pluralism and independence across and within media organisations. (There were also content-related obligations in some jurisdictions – less so in the USA – about matters such as local content, children's content and election material.) The extent and style of the structural measures varied enormously across jurisdictions, but some responses at least aimed to lessen the marginalisation and centrism noted above.[16] Thus, some legal responses involved restrictions on expression; others were structural or systemic measures. Those responses still left a lot of room. Decisions about which issues received focus, which were ignored, what tone was used, and more were decisions for journalists and editors. The decisions were supposedly independent of financial and political domination. The media was responsible for publication and made choices about content that substantially influenced public speech. While law addressed issues related to content and structures, especially under some understandings of expressive freedom,[17] it also left a lot to journalism. Many challenges around content were left to speakers, and in a mass media context that meant they were left to a journalistic-editorial function.

To return to Kramer's example, things have changed. Today people and organisations can create professional-looking content (perhaps with explicit financial, political or geopolitical aims), promote its prominence in search results, and social media can 'spread the story' for its own commercial ends. Sufficient platform prominence can then 'make the story newsworthy in a way the fragmented, competitive world of mainstream media could not or would not ignore'.[18] As he states, '[current] technologies may not have created the problem, and they are not solely responsible for it, but they have *enabled* it – providing a necessary (indeed, indispensable) accelerant and catalyst for a change in degree so extreme as to amount to a change in kind'.[19] The greatly increased ability to find an audience helps socially beneficial speech too; the indispensable accelerant magnifies speech of many kinds. But if more speech was always to the good – as US law so often states and wider free speech analyses frequently suggest – many of the current challenges would not be emerging.[20]

[16] See Andrew T. Kenyon, *Democracy of Expression: Positive Free Speech and Law* (Cambridge: Cambridge University Press, 2021) for examples of more 'active' measures in some national laws and discussion of their implications.

[17] Including the US historically with measures such as the Fairness Doctrine and the decision in *Red Lion Broadcasting* v. *FCC*, 395 US 367 (1969).

[18] Kramer, 'Deliberate Leap' (n 12) 18.

[19] Ibid. 19 (emphasis in original).

[20] For another analysis that 'more speech is not always better', see Robert Post, 'The Unfortunate Consequences of a Misguided Free Speech Principle', *Daedalus* (special issue, 'The Future of Free Speech', in press) https://ssrn.com/abstract=4255938. Post focuses on social practices relevant to public discourse, leaving freedom of expression as a substantially negative freedom. See also Vincent Blasi's chapter in this book (Chapter 16).

To varying degrees, distribution of news and commentary is now separated from its producers, media are dependent on platform distribution, and commercial media have lost influence within advertising markets.[21] The degree of change varies globally and partly depends on people's habits of media and platform use but, overall, the change seems substantial. Even so, it is not that one form of distribution has replaced the other. Institutional media still produces content and makes it available directly to audiences, often doing so with less money and reshaping content for better reach in the varied distribution methods now used. If once media was imagined as a particularly dominant influence on public discourse, it now operates within wider infrastructures of public speech. And platform distribution's commercially driven moderation and amplification are far removed from journalism's public interest goals – even if those goals are highly idealised, never fully met, and have evolved across decades.[22] In simplified terms, the communicative structure underlying public speech has changed from a situation of journalistic-editorial gatekeepers and curators with distribution largely under media control. Now platforms have important roles in distribution. In some ways, platforms are like both (or lie between) content providers and conduits. They have similarities to both institutional media and telecommunications from decades past.[23] But platforms also have resources and powers that exceed those examples.

It is useful to think about two elements in the contemporary situation. First, there are complex interactions between institutional media and other speakers on the one hand, and platforms on the other. Content moderation and amplification overwhelmingly follow platform interests and problematic speech has gained far greater prominence – disinformation, vilification, trolling and more. Platform 'data harvesting and data-driven, programmatic advertising are astonishingly effective mechanisms for propagating disinformation, hate, and conspiracism'.[24] Second, institutional media continue to have influence, more successfully at national or transnational scales than for local news in many established democracies, although in notable

[21] See, e.g., James Meese, *Digital Platforms and the Press* (Bristol: Intellect, 2023); Tomás Dodds et al., 'Popularity-Driven Metrics: Audience Analytics and Shifting Opinion Power to Digital Platforms' (2023) 24 *Journalism Studies* 403–21.

[22] See, e.g., Michael Schudson, 'What Does "Trust in the Media" Mean?' (2022) 151(4) *Daedalus* 144–60, recounting two waves of change in twentieth-century journalism, the first in the 1970s and 1980s accompanied by a reduction in public trust: society became more questioning, journalism became more interpretive, and democracy became 'monitorial' or 'continuous'.

[23] Gregory P. Magarian, 'The Internet and Social Media' in Adrienne Stone and Frederick Schauer (eds.), *The Oxford Handbook of Freedom of Speech* (Oxford: Oxford University Press, 2021) pp. 350–68.

[24] Julie E. Cohen, 'Infrastructuring the Digital Public Sphere' (2023) 25 (special issue) *Yale Journal of Law and Technology* 1–40, 26.

instances institutional media also appear to promote disinformation due to the changes.[25]

All this means journalism does less in terms of public opinion formation and platforms do more. The degree of influence varies across different audiences and locations, but platforms now 'shape public communication and distribute attention' through their 'architectures, algorithmic amplification, and content moderation',[26] using very different values than the model of journalism. Platform interests have no clear relation to – they do not correspond with – the public opinion formation that is imagined as necessary in a communicatively legitimate democracy. Rather, platforms moderate content 'in order to sustain themselves',[27] and further their own position, not to create democratically legitimate structures of public communication.[28] Platforms' aims, along with changes to the scale and speed of expression, are fundamental challenges to past models of public discourse and democratic opinion formation. Automation at platform scale fits uneasily with those models.[29] The structural changes raise challenges about content, including disinformation. While not completely new, the challenges' form, distribution and effects are different with platform-based public speech. This means the understanding of freedom of expression has more significance and, particularly, the state's obligations regarding communicative freedom are more important. But how those obligations are understood is quite different in US and European contexts.

Before addressing that point, I want to clarify my use of journalism. The aim is not to recall some golden past – journalism's weaknesses have long been evident. Rather, the aim is to point out that a journalistic-editorial function was assumed, and relied on, in the public discourse imagined within law. Even the US First Amendment assumes 'a thriving press system'.[30] This has allowed law to defer many decisions about the content of public discourse to journalism. That role has been partially sidelined – it is less dominant but not completely removed – which makes it unsurprising that questions emerge about the content and curation of public speech. As Robert Post has suggested, a 'potential crisis is brewing insofar as democracy depends upon speech, and insofar as speech is controlled by politically

[25] See, e.g., Yochai Benkler, Robert Faris and Hal Roberts, *Network Propaganda: Manipulation, Disinformation, and Radicalization in American Politics* (New York: Oxford University Press, 2018).

[26] Seth Lazar, *Communicative Justice and the Distribution of Attention.* Tanner Lecture on AI and Human Values, University of Stanford, January 2023 (copy on file).

[27] Eugenia Siapera, 'Platform Governance and the "Infodemic"' (2022) 29 *Javnost – The Public* 197–214, 210.

[28] E.g. Martin Moore, 'Creating New Electoral Public Spheres' in Martin Moore and Damian Tambini (eds.), *Regulating Big Tech: Policy Responses to Digital Dominance* (Oxford: Oxford University Press, 2022) pp. 221–34.

[29] See, e.g., Mark Andrejevic, *Automated Media* (New York: Routledge, 2020).

[30] Victor Pickard, *Democracy without Journalism? Confronting the Misinformation Society* (New York: Oxford University Press, 2020) p. 175.

unaccountable algorithms'.[31] I agree that democracy depends in part on speech – a legitimate democracy *is* a democracy of expression, even if that is not its only requirement.[32] Further, the content of public spheres may well have always needed curation. Tarleton Gillespie states that 'it may not sit well with idealized notions' of free expression (I would say *some* idealised notions of free expression) but 'it may nevertheless be true that healthy public spheres actually require their information landscapes be curated'.[33] The need for curation is the interesting point here, rather than a deference to negative freedom under the First Amendment. In important ways, past curation of public debate was journalistic. 'Well before the digital age, institutions that curated content and made judgments about quality and civility were important elements of the public sphere.'[34] In the future, that sort of role could be supported by some approaches to freedom of expression.

3.3 EXPRESSIVE FREEDOM, ASCRIPTIONS AND FEAR

What is legally allowed or required by freedom of expression in established democracies differs enormously. In the US context, there is an argument that restricting objectionable expression would control the boundaries of public discourse in a manner that breaches the First Amendment. It is a well-rehearsed analysis, especially for hate speech.[35] As is also well known, the issues are understood differently in European law. Admittedly, some European writers take a broadly US-style approach – for example, against anti-vilification laws[36] – and some US scholarship has long called for a more active interpretation of the First Amendment.[37] But the basic position is that US law on freedom of expression forbids the control of hate speech within public discourse while European law requires it, at least for some forms of vilification. That characterisation might mislead in specific instances, but at a general level captures what freedom of expression means and the state's role. The issues are not identical in vilification and disinformation, but the point is significant

31 Robert Post, 'Democracy and the Internet' (28 January 2023), https://balkin.blogspot.com/2023/01/democracy-and-internet.html.

32 See Kenyon, *Democracy of Expression* (n 16).

33 Gillespie, 'Do Not Recommend' (n 15) 7.

34 Jack M. Balkin, 'To Reform Social Media, Reform Informational Capitalism' in Stone and Bollinger, *Future of Our Democracy*, pp. 233–54, at p. 240.

35 E.g., Ivan Hare and James Weinstein (eds.), *Extreme Speech and Democracy* (Oxford: Oxford University Press, 2009).

36 E.g., Eric Heinze, *Hate Speech and Democratic Citizenship* (Oxford: Oxford University Press, 2016).

37 E.g., Kenyon, *Democracy of Expression* (n 16) ch. 5; Pickard, *Democracy without Journalism* (n 30); Martha Minow, *Saving the News: Why the Constitution Calls for Government Action to Preserve Freedom of Speech* (New York: Oxford University Press, 2021); and in a somewhat similar vein focusing on diversity and dissent, Gregory P. Magarian, *Managed Speech: The Roberts Court's First Amendment* (New York: Oxford University Press, 2017).

for how the obligations on a democratic state arising from fundamental or constitutional rights are understood.

Arguments against vilification laws often emphasise that democratic legitimacy is lost where states regulate public discourse. It is said that, if states control speech about matters of public concern, citizens are not free to participate in self-government as they should be able to do. For example, Ash Bhagwat and James Weinstein write that, 'unless justified by extremely weighty reasons, rules forbidding the expression of particular viewpoints or perspectives on matters of public concern violate the basic democratic commitment to formal equality by selectively denying citizens their fundamental interest in equal political participation'.[38] The approach requires that public discourse, which includes much hate speech, is almost completely unrestricted. Greater restriction might be allowed within the 'election domain' of speech,[39] and is possible outside public discourse.[40]

In a key US decision for disinformation, *Alvarez*, the Supreme Court struck down a law against falsely claiming to have received military honours.[41] Lying about a miliary honour could not be penalised. The plurality opinion said the First Amendment means government has no general power 'to restrict expression because of its message, its ideas, its subject matter, or its content'. Instead, content-based restrictions are possible 'only when confined to the few historic and traditional categories of expression long familiar to the bar'.[42] The categories include defamation, obscenity, fraud and expression that is intended and likely to cause 'imminent lawless action'. Within those categories, false information can be controlled although there are still hurdles to meet, such as US defamation law's requirement of knowing or reckless falsity in speech about public officials or public figures.[43] Even those who support the general US approach can criticise the plurality's wording. For example, Weinstein would allow restriction of more falsehoods than the categories literally provide. He argues that knowing falsehoods outside public discourse should be open to restriction, and subject to less than strict scrutiny by courts. However, knowing falsehoods about 'government, science, and history'[44]

38 Ashutosh Bhagwat and James Weinstein, 'Freedom of Expression and Democracy' in Stone and Schauer, *Oxford Handbook* (n 23) pp. 82–105, at p. 93.

39 E.g., James Weinstein, 'Free Speech and Domain Allocation: A Suggested Framework for Analyzing the Constitutionality of Prohibition of Lies in Political Campaigns' (2018) 71 *Oklahoma Law Review* 167–236.

40 E.g., Robert C. Post, *Constitutional Domains: Democracy, Community, Management* (Cambridge, MA: Harvard University Press, 1995).

41 *United States* v. *Alvarez*, 567 US 709 (2012).

42 Ibid. at 716 and 717.

43 See, e.g., *New York Times* v. *Sullivan*, 376 US 254 (1964); *Gertz* v. *Robert Welch*, 418 US 323 (1974).

44 See James Weinstein, 'What Lies Ahead? The Marketplace of Ideas, *Alvarez v United States*, and First Amendment Protection of Knowing Falsehoods' (2020) 51 *Seton Hall Law Review* 135–67, 148 citing 'Brief of Eugene Volokh and James Weinstein as Amici Curiae in Support of Petitioner', 567 US 709 (2012) (No 11-210), 2011 WL 6179424, p. 2.

– lies within public discourse – would remain protected from general restriction. Public discourse, including much disinformation, would remain highly protected. For Weinstein, the plurality opinion did not match the public discourse focus that the First Amendment has or should have.

On this view, people have freedom to speak, judge public speech and form opinions relevant to their democratic role without (almost) any legal restrictions on public speech. Only restrictions within the few historic categories are possible, and then only if applicable tests are met. Similar to Post, Weinstein explains that the US constitution involves an ascription of rationality within public speech – an ascription of autonomy in Post's words – which prevents state control of public discourse.[45] In addition, there is a more empirical concern that 'government officials cannot be trusted to fairly and accurately identify and prosecute knowingly false statements in the often highly ideological context of public discourse'.[46] These two elements – constitutional ascription and fear of government action – explain a lot about US law relevant to public speech.[47]

I want to draw out something that can underly such analyses. At times, the ascribed rationality or autonomy amounts to, or at least suggests, a belief that democratic freedom exists without state action. Or it amounts to a belief that state action would only make matters worse. The analysis means government cannot set the boundaries of public discourse – the speech thought most relevant to self-government – because that would prejudge the domain of public discourse itself. Thus, government cannot limit hate speech unless it also falls into one of the historic categories. And, as Weinstein and all the Supreme Court explain in *Alvarez*, government cannot limit disinformation about matters of public discourse, again unless it falls into one of those historic categories.[48] Outside those categories, the agenda for public debate can only be set by its participants. Public discourse's boundaries – what is acceptable speech and what is not – should be formed through public discourse.

Various points might be raised about this understanding of democratic citizenship. I note two here. The first is whether vilification should be a category the First Amendment allows to be restricted, as allowed by free expression in Europe. The second point is slightly different, asking whether it is plausible to ascribe the autonomy needed for democratic opinion formation as existing without state action

45 Weinstein, 'What Lies Ahead?' (n 44) 166.

46 James Weinstein, 'Climate Change Disinformation, Citizen Competence and the First Amendment' (2018) 89 *University of Colorado Law Review* 341–76, 360.

47 US fear of government action limiting speech has probably increased over decades, but also become better recognised; e.g., cf. the two editions of Eric Barendt, *Freedom of Speech* (Oxford: Oxford University Press, 1985 and 2005). In 1985 (pp. 8–23) free speech rationales related to knowledge, self-fulfilment and democracy are examined. Twenty years later, the second edition adds a fourth rationale (pp. 21–23) – suspicion of government – and gives it substantive treatment.

48 See Weinstein, 'What Lies Ahead?' (n 44)

affecting speech. The action might involve limitations on speech, as in the first point, but it might also involve action against non-state entities that affect expression, and various structural or systemic supports for expression. This suggests several types of potential response *as part of* protecting free expression: content-related laws restricting some speech; state action against non-state entities that affect speech – here, think of platform regulation; and wider structural or systemic measures that affect the communicative environment. (There could also be positive content laws.[49]) The US approach is narrower: expressive freedom generally means freedom from state action that directly restricts speech. It is not that European approaches do not believe in autonomy or self-government, but there is a different understanding of what that needs. And the difference includes how expressive freedom is understood.

As all this suggests, freedom of expression can be understood in different ways. For example, if communicative freedom is interpreted in terms of non-domination – in any of the popular versions in the neo-republican literature[50] – then state action may be required in communicative environments that overwise involve domination.[51] Sufficient autonomy and freedom would not exist where there is only the absence of express state action. And if freedom is understood to have both negative and positive dimensions – to concern limitations on state interference with expression, and requirements for enablement and the effective protection and support of communicative rights – then again state action may be needed.[52] Such action is certainly not prohibited. European examples show freedom of expression can be understood that way, to entail limited direct restrictions on speech *and* enablement to make it a more effective freedom rather than only a formal one.[53]

First Amendment analyses often focus on the freedom's negative dimensions in line with much US law. But that focus can suggest, or be taken to mean, that the

49 See text near n 16.

50 See, e.g., Philip Pettit, *Just Freedom: A Moral Compass for a Complex World* (New York: Norton, 2014); Cécile Laborde, *Critical Republicanism: The Hijab Controversy and Political Philosophy* (Oxford: Oxford University Press, 2008); Cécile Laborde, 'Republicanism' in Michael Freeden and Marc Stears (eds.), *The Oxford Handbook of Political Ideologies* (Oxford: Oxford University Press, 2013) pp. 513–35.

51 E.g., Linnet Taylor, 'Public Actors without Public Values: Legitimacy, Domination and the Regulation of the Technology Sector' (2021) 34 *Philosophy and Technology* 897–922; Charney, *Illusion* (n 14).

52 Note this approach to communicative freedom's positive dimensions does not involve adopting Isaiah Berlin's ideas of monist perfection or self-mastery in positive freedom. His analysis is not relevant to speech and is distinct from much political philosophy on positive freedom which focuses on enablement. See Kenyon, *Democracy of Expression* (n 16) pp. 95–103.

53 I focus on positive dimensions rather than non-domination for broader reasons, although both approaches can lead to similar outcomes for free expression. E.g., John Charney in *Illusion* (n 14) uses a republican approach to make points very like the German Federal Constitutional Court, saying that 'Media regulation should prevent the possibility of *arbitrary interference* (or domination) from both government and markets' (p. 144, emphasis in original) and 'When the law is the expression of a self-governing society, it may interfere in the structure and functioning of media markets in order to reduce domination' (p. 150).

freedom has no important positive dimensions relevant to public discourse. Not even US law goes quite that far in relation to speech per se.[54] But it substantially does that for the structures underlying public debate. Thus, US writing commonly suggests a legitimate democratic state cannot restrict public discourse (outside the historic categories and the tests imposed within them) *and* that freedom of expression does not require the state to do anything supportive in relation to public discourse, such as regulating private entities or making wider structural or systemic interventions. I note again the continuing US scholarship that takes a fuller approach to what freedom in free speech requires, as well as work that allows a more active state as a political choice rather than a matter of free speech law.[55] While important, that work does not (yet) reflect much US law.

If communicative freedom has positive as well as negative dimensions, more is involved in democratically legitimate freedom of expression than the First Amendment currently provides. Rather, the approach should examine what environment of public speech is needed for people's democratic autonomy and what that entails for law. This is the point at which US law on free speech is highly atypical. If communicative freedom only concerns the absence of direct state interference with public speech, then much disinformation will not be responded to legally whether through restrictions or wider structural or systemic responses. Responses will be left to industry, which theoretically could do all that law might require, although history suggests it will not. Instead, people are said to be sufficiently free to participate, form opinions and act as democratic citizens where the state does not regulate the content and boundaries of public discourse. On this analysis, the overall communicative infrastructures that underlie public speech do not raise matters of free speech. Communicative structures are removed from questions of communicative freedom. As Thomas Streeter stated three decades ago, under a formalist approach to the First Amendment, 'free speech has come to mean freedom for private communicating entities (in practice, usually media businesses) against any sort of unwanted political interference, and *questions of media structure have become almost entirely disassociated from matters of free speech*'.[56] The approach is widely criticised. Perhaps increasingly so[57] because the 'communicating entities' now extend well beyond media organisations, and the commercial interests now involved appear far less suited to structuring a democratically legitimate public discourse.

54 US law has included (or still does) positive dimensions of free speech, see, e.g., Minow, *Saving the News* (n. 37), pp. 5–6; and cases such as *Hague* v. *Committee for Industrial Organization*, 307 US 496 (1939).

55 See n 37.

56 Thomas Streeter, *Selling the Air* (Chicago: University of Chicago Press, 1996) p. 192.

57 E.g., Minow, *Saving the News* (n. 37); Philip M. Napoli, *Social Media and the Public Interest* (New York: Columbia University Press, 2019).

3.4 EXPRESSIVE FREEDOM, STRUCTURES AND STATES

Things are different in Europe. There, the freedom's positive dimensions have many legal consequences.[58] Here I highlight two obligations they impose on states, which flow from a different understanding of what freedom involves in freedom of expression. The first is the indirect horizontal effect of rights. This justifies – and sometimes requires – that states regulate private parties who impede the effective enjoyment of rights,[59] including freedom of expression.[60] The approach encompasses the interests in expression of both speakers and audiences, or what are sometimes called the active and passive sides of free expression.

The second obligation is pluralism. While differing aspects are seen in different European jurisdictions, overall, democratic freedom of expression should aim for a situation of sustained plural public speech. This requires structural diversity, independence and transparency, all in support of individual and collective opinion formation. It should involve media with:

- *structural diversity* of organisations, people, funding and content, with
- *independence* from domination by political and economic interests, and
- *transparency* regarding ownership, control and content.[61]

As well as news and commentary, this pluralism would cover entertainment and wider cultural material.[62] Aspects of the approach are seen in German and French constitutional decisions, European Court of Human Rights (ECtHR) cases, and decades of academic scholarship, among other places. The case law and scholarship together suggest this sort of model for diversity, independence and transparency underlying public speech. Positive dimensions of communicative freedom involve choices; there is not only one way to meet positive rights. This differs from the freedom's negative dimensions where, in simple terms, the injunction is 'do not restrict expression' unless relevant legal tests are met. Here, it is whether the state has acted to support a sufficiently effective right, within the state's real but limited range of choice.

[58] E.g., Andrew T. Kenyon and Andrew Scott (eds.), *Positive Free Speech: Rationales, Methods and Implications* (Oxford: Hart, 2020).

[59] E.g., Jean-François Akandji-Kombe, *Positive Obligations under the European Convention on Human Rights* (Strasbourg: Council of Europe, 2007); Rory O'Connell, 'Realising Political Equality: The European Court of Human Rights and Positive Obligations in a Democracy' (2010) 61 *Northern Ireland Legal Quarterly* 263–79; Bruce Dickson, 'Positive Obligations and the European Court of Human Rights' (2010) 61 *Northern Ireland Legal Quarterly* 203–8.

[60] Thomas Hochmann in 'Better Protected in Europe' (n 3) provides a useful overview. See also Kenyon, 'Sustained Plural Public Speech' (n 11).

[61] See Kenyon, 'Regulating Opinion Power' (n 9); Kenyon, *Democracy of Expression* (n 16).

[62] E.g., Georgina Born et al., *Artificial Intelligence, Music Recommendation, and the Curation of Culture. White Paper* (Toronto: Schwartz Reisman Institute for Technology and Society, University of Toronto, 2021) https://srinstitute.utoronto.ca/s/Born-Morris-etal-AI_Music_Recommendation_Culture.pdf.

Both these aspects of communicative freedom – state regulation of private parties and structural or systemic actions, such as those aimed at supporting pluralism – can be seen in European initiatives relevant to disinformation, which I consider in the next section. Before doing that, it is worth noting these positive obligations align with calls to focus on infrastructures rather than instances of speech when considering disinformation. For example, Clare Wardle, who has been influential in recent disinformation scholarship, has argued against focusing on the truth or falsity of each item of speech.[63] She emphasises the issue is systemic and concerns the narratives that platforms enable. Similarly, Alicia Wanless draws on research into information conflicts and influence operations to suggest that focusing on disinformation 'is not useful' and leads 'democratic societies to miss larger problems'. It is not disinformation that needs regulating as much as 'the ecology of the information environment more generally'.[64] Moving attention to the wider context in this way can also be linked to greater recognition of the collective or institutional aspects of free expression (or recognition of the greater impact those aspects now have). It is not only a concern with particular items of speech that affect individuals or organisations; rather, the approach involves recognising free speech as 'a public good or value in a pluralist society'[65] and acting in support of it.

3.5 SOME EU MEASURES RELEVANT TO DISINFORMATION

The general understanding of free expression outlined above is relevant to many European actions about disinformation. As András Koltay shows in his chapter, there are multiple and partially overlapping initiatives at state and EU levels.[66] Some are directly relevant to disinformation; others encompass it in part while being aimed elsewhere. The measures include national laws against certain categories of speech, such as defamation and racist hate speech. The categories that can be regulated are wider than under US law, and the hurdles to limitation are lower. In addition, there is greater recourse to criminal penalties for some categories of speech, and more scope for states to extend the categories if social harm can be seen. But for these measures there is a family resemblance to the US approach. Speech within certain categories – none of which concern disinformation as such but can include disinformation – can be subject to legal control.

[63] Claire Wardle, 'Misunderstanding Misinformation' (2023) 39(3) *Issues in Science and Technology* 38–40, https://doi.org/10.58875/ZAUD1691.

[64] Alicia Wanless, 'There Is No Getting Ahead of Disinformation without Moving Past It', Lawfare Blog, 8 May 2023, www.lawfareblog.com/there-no-getting-ahead-disinformation-without-moving-past-it. For other systemic-related analyses, see, e.g., Evelyn Douek, 'Content Moderation as Systems Thinking' (2022) 136 *Harvard Law Review* 526–607; Kate Klonick, 'Of Systems Thinking and Straw Men' (2023) 136 *Harvard Law Review Forum* 339–62.

[65] Barendt, *Freedom of Speech* (2nd ed.) (n 47) p. 35.

[66] András Koltay, 'Freedom of Expression and the Regulation of Disinformation in the European Union' (Chapter 6 in this book).

As Koltay details, the EU is also developing multiple other measures.[67] For present purposes, this can be illustrated by the Strengthened Code of Practice on Disinformation,[68] the Digital Services Act (DSA)[69] and the proposed European Media Freedom Act (EMFA).[70] The measures together reflect positive and negative dimensions of democratic free speech, and they do things consistent with the positive dimensions of free expression in a way that is harder to imagine in the USA. The measures include indirect horizontal requirements on private actors, such as DSA obligations on platforms, and positive state actions, such as those supporting media pluralism in the EMFA. The emergence of this approach makes more sense 'when one recognises the broad European understanding of free expression. Together, the Code, the DSA and the EMFA suggest some ways in which freedom of expression may evolve in situations where control and curation are not dominated by a journalistic-editorial role.

How each of the three measures concerns disinformation could be analysed at length. Each is substantial; for example, the Code runs to 20,000 words and includes 44 commitments and more than 100 measures about how commitments will be met and reported. But outlining just some aspects suffices here. My interest is not so much the requirements' strengths and weaknesses – there are substantial doubts about how effective this iteration of measures will be. Rather, it is to understand the responses as a model that may well be consistent with freedom of expression, arguably one better suited to the current context than an overwhelming focus on negative dimensions of expressive freedom.

Some things needed for sustained plural public speech remain similar with changed communications. At the level of media organisations, this includes having multiple organisations with varied financial bases and missions, varied staffing, management and participation, independence from political and commercial domination, and transparency of ownership, control and content. The EMFA aims to support some of these needs uniformly across the EU. Among other things, the proposal addresses the rights and duties of media services and recipients, including 'the right to receive a plurality of news and current affairs content, produced with

67 Ibid., also noting general aspects of media regulation, such as the Audio-Visual Media Services Directive and other measures left aside here.

68 2022 Strengthened Code of Practice on Disinformation, https://digital-strategy.ec.europa.eu/en/library/2022-strengthened-code-practice-disinformation.

69 DSA: Regulation 2022/2065 of the European Parliament and of the Council of 19 October 2022 on a single market for digital services and amending Directive 2000/31/EC, OJ 2022 No. L277, 27 October 2022, p. 1.

70 Proposal for a Regulation of the European Parliament and of the Council establishing a common framework for media services in the internal market (European Media Freedom Act) and amending Directive 2010/13/EU, 16 September 2022, COM(2022) 457 final, 2022/0277 (COD). The DSA and proposed EMFA are EU regulations, which have direct application within member states as national legislation would. Other relevant measures include the Digital Markets Act, proposed Artificial Intelligence (AI) Act, the Democracy Action Plan, and multiple national provisions and statements of the Council of Europe.

respect for editorial freedom'.[71] It aims to safeguard the independence of public service media.[72] And it structures some interactions between very large online platforms and media services, including a requirement for good faith 'meaningful and effective dialogue' when an editorially independent media service considers a platform is frequently restricting or suspending its content.[73]

At the time of writing, the EMFA faces ongoing debate within the European legislative process,[74] and some strong criticism.[75] Here, I leave aside concerns about some aspects' plausibility and suitability,[76] and significant questions about its legal basis – the EMFA arguably covers matters within the powers of member states not the EU.[77] In addition, while trying to do more to support democratic needs the EMFA has a market focus. This is unsurprising given EU powers, but it is awkward given the aims for media freedom and does not sit easily with some member state approaches. Consider, for example, French and German judicial statements that the freedom should not be 'made the object of a market' and that 'Market opportunities may be a question of economic freedom, but not of freedom of opinion'.[78] However, whether taken at EU or member state level, my interest is the types of action and how they are understood as being consistent with freedom of expression. The EMFA illustrates a desire to reinforce important aspects of plural and independent media in the contemporary communications context as one part of protecting democratic freedom of expression, within a broader set of responses affecting disinformation.

Unlike the EMFA, the DSA has passed. It includes a range of obligations for platforms, and further requirements for very large online platforms and very large

[71] EMFA proposal, Art. 3.

[72] EMFA proposal, Art. 5.

[73] EMFA proposal, Art. 17; see also Art. 18.

[74] A European Parliament committee issued a draft report on EMFA in March 2023: see Sabine Verheyen, Draft Report on the proposal for a regulation of the European Parliament and of the Council establishing a common framework for media services in the internal market (European Media Freedom Act) and amending Directive 2010/13/EU (COM(2022)0457 – C9–0309/2022 – 2022/0277(COD)). See also, e.g., Mark D. Cole and Christina Etteldorf, Research for CULT Committee – European Media Freedom Act: Policy Recommendations (May 2023), www.europarl.europa.eu/supporting-analyses; Molly Killeen, 'EU Council Advances on Source Protection, Fund Transparency in Media Law', Euractiv, 26 May 2023.

[75] E.g., Joan Barata, 'Problematic Aspects of the European Media Freedom Act – Old and New' (LSE, 2 may 2023), https://blogs.lse.ac.uk/medialse/2023/05/02/problematic-aspects-of-the-european-media-freedom-act-old-and-new.

[76] E.g. Theresa Seipp, Ronan Ó Fathaigh and Max van Drunen, 'Defining the "Media" in Europe: Pitfalls of the Proposed European Media Freedom Act' (2023) 15 *Journal of Media Law* 39–51, examining EMFA's narrow approach to 'media' and challenges in assessing whether media is 'editorially independent'.

[77] E.g., Cole and Etteldorf, Research for CULT Committee; Christina Holtz-Bacha, 'Freedom of the Media, Pluralism, and Transparency: European Media Policy on New Paths?' (2023) 39(1) *European Journal of Communication*, online first, https://doi.org/10.1177/02673231231176966.

[78] Conseil constitutionnel 84-181 DC, 10–11 October 1984, *considérant* 38; 74 BVerfGE 297 (1987) (Fifth Broadcasting/Baden-Württemberg case).

online search engines (often labelled VLOPs and VLOSEs).[79] Among other things, these very large actors need to assess and mitigate systemic risks posed by their systems. The DSA does not explicitly mention disinformation in its Articles – the term appears repeatedly in the Recitals – but disinformation is clearly intended to come within systemic risks. Under Article 34, risk assessment needs to be proportionate to the severity and probability of systemic risks, and include these systemic risks:

(a) the *dissemination of illegal content* through their services;
(b) *any actual or foreseeable negative effects for the exercise of fundamental rights*, in particular the fundamental rights to human dignity, … to respect for private and family life … to the protection of personal data, … *to freedom of expression and information, including the freedom and pluralism of the media* …
(c) any *actual or foreseeable negative effects on civic discourse and electoral processes*, and *public security*;
(d) any *actual or foreseeable negative effects* in relation to *gender-based violence*, the *protection of public health and minors* and serious negative consequences to the person's *physical and mental well-being*.[80]

So systemic risks related to illegal content, fundamental rights, civic discourse and electoral processes, public security, gender-based violence, public health and more need to be assessed. Assessments need to consider the effects of services' recommender systems (and other algorithmic systems), content moderation systems, advertising systems, data practices, and terms and conditions.[81] Article 34's wording was strengthened during the legislative process so media pluralism is now explicitly mentioned, and negative effects on civic discourse and electoral processes need not be linked to intentional manipulation of services.[82] While the words look powerful in some ways, there are many doubts about their application in practice.[83]

79 The DSA also contains measures applicable to platforms more generally, separate provisions empowering the European Commission in 'crisis' situations, and provisions providing liability for specific items of content after notification and failure to remove the content. See, e.g., Martin Husovec, *Principles of the Digital Services Act* (Oxford: Oxford University Press, in press); Antje von Ungern-Sternberg (ed.), *Content Regulation in the European Union: The Digital Services Act* (Trier: Verein für Recht und Digitalisierung – Institute for Digital Law Trier, 2023); Peukert, 'The Regulation of Disinformation in the EU' (n 1).

80 DSA, Art. 34(1) (emphasis added).

81 DSA, Art. 34(2).

82 In the initial DSA proposal, 'pluralism' appeared only once in relation to the Charter of Fundamental Rights in proposed Recital 105. The proposed Article 26 (which became Article 34 in the enacted DSA) had the following paragraph (c): 'intentional manipulation of their service, including by means of inauthentic use or automated exploitation of the service, with an actual or foreseeable negative effect on the protection of public health, minors, civic discourse, or actual or foreseeable effects related to electoral processes and public security'.

83 E.g., Cohen, 'Infrastructuring' (n 24) 34–35, expected limited success of DSA; Rachel Griffin, 'Rethinking Rights in Social Media Governance: Human Rights, Ideology and Inequality' (2023) 2 *European Law Open* 30–56, 44–46, offering useful overview of expected weaknesses in

As well as assessing systemic risks, very large actors need to mitigate them by putting 'in place *reasonable, proportionate and effective mitigation measures*, tailored to the specific systemic risks identified … *with particular consideration to the impacts of such measures on fundamental rights*'.[84] Article 35 sets out a large list of possible mitigations, including making changes to services' design, features or functioning, terms and conditions and their enforcement, content moderation, recommender systems and advertising systems. Very large actors are also subject to regular independent audit (which may end up focusing on compliance with obligations to conduct assessments rather than assessments' validity).[85]

Direct state action against disinformation is not being taken here. Rather, influential private entities need to assess and mitigate systemic risks posed by their systems. The requirements go beyond illegal content.[86] They seek to regulate aspects of content curation. Of course, very large actors are likely to use restricted interpretations of risks and mitigation, subject to regulators, courts or legislatures demanding more.[87] But my point is that the model appears broadly consistent with European ideas of free expression. Or, at least, it is seeking to find a way to deal with harmful but legal content that furthers the multiple interests of multiple actors in freedom of expression. Clearly, many of the challenges linked to communicative freedom are hidden within Article 35's brief reference to mitigating systemic risks while also considering the effects on fundamental rights. Multiple parties are affected in terms of freedom of expression, and it is far from clear how 'particular consideration' will occur. That is just one reason to expect future legal disputes drawing on free speech arguments about exactly what the provisions mean, how platforms apply them, how regulators enforce them, and whether regulators are sufficiently independent. There are also challenges posed by individual entities assessing and mitigating risks which may be broader than the risks seen by any one very large actor. And the approach does not challenge platform business models.

implementation, even if the provisions' aim is understood to include the collective, structural aspects that should be significant parts of free expression. Also note that the proposed AI Act may make very large online platforms' recommender systems high-risk and subject them to various requirements in support of the DSA; see, e.g., Draft Compromise Amendments on the Draft Report, Proposal for a Regulation of the European Parliament and of the Council on Harmonised Rules on Artificial Intelligence (Artificial Intelligence Act) and amending certain Union Legislative Acts (COM(2021)0206 – C9 0146/2021 – 2021/0106(COD)) (9 May 2023) Recital 40b and Annex III (8(ab)) which proposes to add as high-risk: 'AI systems intended to be used by social media platforms that have been designated as very large online platforms within the meaning of [the DSA], in their recommender systems to recommend to the recipient of the service user-generated content available on the platform.'

84 DSA, Art. 35(1) (emphasis added).

85 DSA, Art. 37; see, e.g., Anna-Katharina Meßmer and Martin Degeling, *Auditing Recommender Systems: Putting the DSA into Practice with a Risk-Scenario-Based Approach* (Berlin: Stiftung Neue Verantwortung, 2023) pp. 1–60, p. 21.

86 Peukert, 'The Regulation of Disinformation in the EU' (n 1), at 25.

87 E.g., Griffin, 'Rethinking Rights' (n 83), at 45; Martin Husovec, 'The Digital Services Act's Red Line' (2024) 16 Journal of Media Law, in press.

This is unsurprising given the EU's internal market powers, but the problematic effects of platforms' data-based business models have been raised repeatedly in commentary. If freedom of expression includes freedom from market domination of public expression – a clear element of European approaches in general – it is not obvious how that is possible if commercially driven platforms come to dominate public speech. Indeed, this appears to be a central weakness in the approach in terms of democratic freedom of expression.[88] I would agree with Rachel Griffin that European traditions of public service media are based on the judgment that 'wholly privatised broadcast media systems cannot serve the public interest even if they are well-regulated', which makes it 'inherently problematic that online media are governed by profit-driven conglomerates, even if they are subject to human rights obligations'.[89] However, the general idea of requiring private actors to do things related to the content they distribute is important. In some ways, it is seeking to model the curation of public speech once provided, in theory at least, by a diverse media environment and its journalistic-editorial function. Doing something like that – even if doing it better than this initial attempt – appears to be part of the future of democratic freedom of expression.

The Code is a more detailed catalogue of what platforms (and others such as advertising brokers) might do about disinformation, particularly electoral and issue-based political advertising. A handful of commitments illustrate the Code's approach. These include:

- defunding the dissemination of disinformation and improving policies, systems and controls over content monetisation;
- preventing the use of advertising systems to disseminate disinformation in the form of advertisements; and
- adopting a common definition of 'political and issue advertising', clearly labelling it as paid content and providing 'clear, comprehensible, comprehensive information about why' it is shown to users.[90]

There are also system design commitments to minimise the viral spread of disinformation, which might include recommender systems improving 'the prominence of authoritative information' and reducing disinformation's prominence 'based on clear and transparent methods and approaches for defining the criteria for authoritative information'.[91] The Code does not specify those criteria, although it includes

88 E.g., Mattias Wendel, 'Taking or Escaping Legislative Responsibility? EU Fundamental Rights and Content Regulation under the DSA' in Ungern-Sternberg, *Content Regulation* (n 79) p. 82, 'the DSA effectively amounts to an escape from legislative responsibility as far as the protection of EU fundamental rights is concerned'.

89 Griffin, 'Rethinking Rights' (n 83), at 55–56.

90 See Code, commitments 1–9.

91 Code, commitment 18 and measure 18.1.

commitments to work with fact-checking organisations.[92] The Code is intended to be recognised under the DSA, so complying with it could be relevant for very large actors showing they have made appropriate mitigation efforts. While the Code is sometimes seen as a form of co-regulation or partially enforced self-regulation – with the European Commission influencing its development and revision[93] – membership is entirely voluntary, and the Code is not directly enforceable. For example, when Twitter since renamed X) withdrew from the Code in 2023 reports suggested this could end 'a headache for the Commission, given the platform's lack of compliance' with the Code and the Commission's lack of power to 'force them out'.[94] Overall, the Code sets varied objectives, with their meaning and implementation substantially left to platforms, alongside continuing involvement of various EU-linked organisations, and undertakings about reporting and research. In comparison, the DSA could have greater influence if it is strongly applied, but all three initiatives are useful to understand the multifaceted EU approach.

A related matter is how truth is determined in these measures. The Code and DSA leave platforms to determine what amounts to disinformation, in the first instance at least. DSA powers of regulators and courts may lead to those determinations being overruled. But what was once deferred to journalism is now in part deferred to platforms and fact-checkers (suggesting the value in examining the fact-checking organisations).[95] Of course, platforms cannot perform that public speech role in the same way as journalism, whether journalism's actual practice or its idealised role. As well as platforms' data- and attention-centred commercial focus, the speed and scale of platform-distributed speech means content decisions cannot be made as they are for journalistic content in institutional media.

Paolo Cavaliere has examined legal standards used to assess truth,[96] comparing ECtHR decisions involving journalism and EU advertising rules. While the ECtHR is not an arbiter of truth in general, it distinguishes truth and opinion in journalism cases. When assessing public interest expression, it uses a journalistic or process-based understanding of truth. It is not that a particular fact has necessarily been proved true; rather, appropriate journalistic practices provided sufficient certainty about the material before publication. In effect, the ECtHR relies on a journalistic-editorial function for truth. In contrast, advertising laws focus on a publication's misleading quality, which need not necessarily involve falsity. While 'respect for

92 See Code, Part VII.

93 E.g., Paolo Cavaliere, 'The Truth in Fake News: How Disinformation Laws Are Reframing the Concepts of Truth and Accuracy on Digital Platforms' (2022) 3 *European Convention on Human Rights Law Review* 481–523; Koltay, 'Regulation of Disinformation' (n 66).

94 Luca Bertuzzi, 'Twitter Set to Exit EU Code of Practice on Disinformation, Sources Say', Euractiv, 26 May 2023, www.euractiv.com/section/digital/news/twitter-set-to-exit-eu-code-of-practice-on-disinformation-sources-say.

95 E.g., Paolo Cavaliere, 'From Journalistic Ethics to Fact-Checking Practices' (2020) 12 *Journal of Media Law* 133–65.

96 Cavaliere, 'Truth in Fake News' (n 93).

appropriate procedures can exonerate even factually false statements' in journalism, the CJEU 'has ruled out ... a professional diligence defence for misleading advertising'.[97] Cavaliere suggests the DSA and the Code lean more towards an advertising standard, but the ECtHR requires political and public interest content (whether paid or unpaid) to be assessed on a journalistic standard.[98] Perhaps the outcome of this apparent conflict will depend on the approaches of fact-checking organisations, which might mirror traditional journalistic aims in some ways at least. If so, that would lessen a conflict between the EU provisions and ECHR protections for freedom of expression (with which European Charter provisions should be consistent). If not, EU aims could be frustrated because platform 'content moderation decisions will ... be assessed for their compliance with the level of protection of freedom of expression required by the ECHR'.[99]

3.6 DISCUSSION AND CONCLUSION

Analyses of the First Amendment and disinformation can emphasise two points – a constitutional ascription of autonomy existing without state action and a fear of state action. Other approaches to democratic free speech do not follow the first point in the same way. To me, they are more attuned to the reality of democratic choice. They see state action as ubiquitous – the state is always involved in one way or another in ordering, enforcing or tolerating private actors that affect speech.[100] And this links to the state's positive obligations to protect freedom of expression, to attempt to make the freedom real and effective.

However, the second point about fearing government action is relevant beyond the USA. In Europe, there is clearly not the *same* fear of government action as in US law. That would be impossible given the understanding of freedom of expression, but at the same time there is understandably no great appetite for state determinations of truth. This can be seen in the reluctance of the ECtHR to support limits on false speech, and the way in which measures like the DSA and the Code mean that states – whether executives, parliaments or courts – are not determining truth directly. The EU responses to disinformation involve legislating 'for more societal responsibility for very large online platforms' while leaving platforms to decide 'if and how to deal with any systemic risks to freedom of expression'.[101] The European measures do not outlaw false facts as such. For example, only Holocaust denial is clearly established as a false fact that receives judicial protection in ECtHR decisions.[102] Other historical debates are allowed. This leads Irina Katsirea to suggest the

97 Ibid. 510.
98 Ibid. 521.
99 Ibid. 522.
100 E.g., discussion in Hochmann, 'Better Protected in Europe' (n 3) 77–81.
101 Koltay, 'Regulation of Disinformation' (n 66).
102 Katsirea, 'Fake News' (n 8).

ECtHR would not act as arbiter of truth in general, and criminalising disinformation in news appears problematic under Article 10 of the ECHR.[103]

In a mass media context, there were important ways in which the legal approach to freedom of expression relied on journalism. The journalistic-editorial function decided much about the content of public speech, and where and how public attention would be focused. Those decisions were made at a particular scale and speed, with the relevant actors considering individual pieces of content. Now, legal and regulatory approaches seek to deal with significant changes, and freedom of expression is highly relevant to what can and should be done. Admittedly, the versions of freedom of expression outlined above are somewhat exaggerated, and the European model goes further than existing law. However, the law and ideas about expressive freedom seen in Europe suggest the model that I have sketched. The idea of positive obligations flowing from fundamental rights is clearly established and it suggests how current European initiatives have consistencies with important aspects of free expression. The EU measures are not as explicit as they should be in relation to the multifaceted quality of freedom of expression – ways in which interests are held individually and collectively across speakers and recipients. And much of the complexity is submerged in the current approaches, such as the DSA's requirements for very large actors to mitigate systemic risks with due regard to fundamental rights. How to do both those things at once – mitigate risks and pay regard to fundamental rights – involves subtle evaluations. Whether platforms can do that is questionable, perhaps especially for platforms imbued with US ideas of rights and the broader scope that is needed here for rights moving beyond individual interests. It may mean that very little is done. As well as the very large actors, the European Commission, with 'relatively little institutional experience in freedom of expression principles',[104] faces regulatory challenges.

However, the *models* of communicative freedom and the *illustrative responses* to disinformation in Europe suggest how different dimensions of freedom of expression might be supported in a changed context of public communication. Details of the Code, the DSA and the proposed EMFA are less significant than the ideas they illustrate. US analysis, in comparison, is left looking for technical arguments to adapt earlier regulatory approaches, such as cable access provisions or telecommunications regulation, or sidestep the First Amendment, or remain reliant on platforms' leeway under US law to moderate content almost without restraint.

That free speech law has long relied on journalism reflects longstanding practices of who decided about content and the scale and speed of decision-making. Platform moderation is not the same. It applies complex, networked decision processes at a scale and speed far removed from what has often been imagined for rights such as expression. It is systemic, and so are many current legal responses. But in being

[103] Ibid.

[104] Seipp et al., 'Defining the "Media" in Europe' (n 76).

systemic, measures like the DSA still leave a lot of discretion to platforms. They face challenges in mass moderation,[105] including how, if at all, public values can be included in recommender systems.[106] As Gillespie has observed, 'platforms now function at a scale and under a set of expectations that increasingly demands automation. Yet the kinds of decisions that platforms must make, especially in content moderation, are precisely the kinds of decisions that should not be automated'.[107] While that raises conceptual questions for freedom of expression, a fuller approach to freedom – one that understands its positive as well as negative dimensions – can go some way towards accommodating the changes.

My aim has been to explain something about why US approaches take the form they often do, and to highlight how different approaches to freedom of expression are possible. Much comes down to an understanding of freedom, which in turn relates to the state's role. The differences are not minor. The 'conceptual and normative differences between a US-oriented, First Amendment tradition and a positive rights, European and international human rights perspective'[108] should not be underestimated, with 'differences in underlying expectations on governmental involvement in speech regulation' being 'fundamental'.[109] While some past commentators have found the differences problematic, they now appear increasingly problematic for democratic freedom of expression. Communicative freedom has positive and not only negative dimensions. This means there are obligations on states, which can include measures to tackle disinformation, though not necessarily by direct prohibition. The state obligations are challenging to implement and may be abused. But believing in a purely negative freedom without support or enablement seems at least as problematic or, given current infrastructures of public speech, more so.

[105] See Robert Post's chapter in this book (Chapter 2).

[106] E.g., Jonathan Stray et al., 'Building Human Values into Recommender Systems: An Interdisciplinary Synthesis' (2022) arXiv:2207.10192 [cs.IR].

[107] Tarleton Gillespie, *Custodians of the Internet* (New Haven, CT: Yale University Press, 2018) p. 206.

[108] Damian Tambini, 'Reconceptualizing Media Freedom' in Moore and Tambini, *Regulating Big Tech* (n 28) pp. 299–322, p. 300.

[109] Jan Oster, 'Which Limits on Freedom of Expression Are Legitimate? Divergence of Free Speech Values in Europe and the United States' in Uta Kohl (ed.), *The Net and the Nation State* (Cambridge: Cambridge University Press, 2017) pp. 39–47, p. 39.

PART II

The Case of Government Disinformation

4

Communication of State Authorities

The Power of the Office

Indra Spiecker genannt Döhmann

4.1 INTRODUCTION

During the Trump presidency in the United States of America, the social media network Twitter (now known as X) became a new, unofficial media channel through which the former president issued many political statements and informed the public about planned activities and new decisions. At the same time, however, he also continued to use this venue for more personal information, most frequently somehow connected to his office, for example on the size of his 'nuclear button' in comparison to that assumed to be the North Korean leader's one after a news report. This type of communication was until then unknown as a general communication strategy at least for most public officials. Press conferences and bulletins were the typical means of informing the public and professionally interested parties about the standpoints of the government, its actions and its plans. Also, government information was typically delivered in a rather neutral and down-to-earth tone and was carefully drafted and revised, rather than being spur-of-the-moment ideas frequently dismissing other ideas using direct, sometimes offensive language. It is obvious that the statements of the president of a leading nation and the largest democracy in the world will attract attention. However, the Twitter postings under the Trump presidency attracted more attention than the usual; Trump's tweets reached millions of followers and generated countless clicks. The criminal proceedings and the impeachment process following the storming of the Capitol in January 2021 were based on the realization and consequently the recognition of the impact of those communicative acts on Trump's followers.[1]

I am very grateful to Lilly Schroeder, research assistant at the Chair, for her resourceful and persistent search for even better footnotes and for taking care of the formalities.

[1] E.g., Nicholas Fandos, 'Trump Impeached for Inciting Insurrection', *The New York Times*, 13 January 2021, www.nytimes.com/2021/01/13/us/politics/trump-impeached.html.

A contrasting picture can be found across the Atlantic in Germany. There, Chancellor Angela Merkel also contributed to a Twitter channel throughout most of her chancellorship.[2] It was – unlike that of the US President during his term of office – officially handled by Merkel's spokesperson, and it included no personal information or personal statements, let alone commenting on news coverage, current affairs or giving imprudent, discriminatory or abusive assessments. However, German history knows well how heads of state may misuse and mislead the media and abuse the attention given to them due to their office in order to manipulate an entire people, even into the worst atrocities and a catastrophic world war.

Therefore, the question of the legal boundaries of state communication is not only of historical importance but is a cornerstone of the relationship between a state and its citizens, and, at the same time, part of a democracy-enabling and -defending communication relationship. States need to communicate their doings and decisions to the public in order for society to be informed and to prepare the people for participation and elections as the core instrument of control.[3] The use of digitalized formats of communication of (not so) 'new' media is something democratic states urgently needed to integrate into their communication strategy in order to stay in touch with their sovereign and to shape the constitutional and administrative space.[4] Transparency laws or rights to freedom of information requests complement this as active tools of citizens.[5] At the same time, however, not only the content but also the format, mediator and tone of the communication influence the resulting perception of the state, and may also contributing to forming the opinions of the constituency.[6] Thus, not only does access to information need to be legally established to ensure a solid and resilient democracy but also the means of communication. This can only be done if not only the protagonists at the top of the government – the heads of state and ministries – but also the state officials act within a predetermined and controllable legal framework.

2 https://twitter.com/RegSprecherStS.

3 Konrad Hesse (ed.), *Grundzüge des Verfassungsrechts der Bundesrepublik Deutschland* (Heidelberg: C. F. Müller, 1995) para. 152; Felix Drefs, *Die Öffentlichkeitsarbeit des Staates und die Akzeptanz seiner Entscheidungen* (Baden-Baden: Nomos, 2019) p. 52; Tobias Hinderks, 'Staatliche Kommunikation in den neuen Medien' (2023) 67(1) *Zeitschrift für Urheber- und Medienrecht* 26, at 29.

4 Utz Schliesky, 'Digitalisierung – Herausforderung für den demokratischen Verfassungsstaat. Ein Beitrag zur Zukunftsfähigkeit des Grundgesetzes am Vorabend des 70. Geburtstags' (2019) 38 *Neue Zeitschrift für Verwaltungsrecht* 693; Sophie Tschorr, 'Wenn der Staat Fake News verbreitet' (2021) 60 *Zeitschrift für Digitalisierung und Recht* 381, at 384.

5 BVerfGE 105, 279, at 302; annotated by Marion Albers, 'Rethinking the Doctrinal System of Fundamental Rights: New Decisions of the Federal Constitutional Court' (2002) 3(11) *German Law Journal*; BVerfGE 105, 252, at 269, English version: www.bundesverfassungsgericht.de/SharedDocs/Entscheidungen/EN/2002/06/rs20020626_1bvr055891en.html.

6 Tobias Mast, 'Gute Öffentlichkeitsarbeit und die Europäische Union' (2021) 81(2) *Zeitschrift für ausländisches öffentliches Recht und Völkerrecht* 443, at 458.

Section 4.2 analyses the actors and different means or formats in which government communication can take place, focusing on executive communication. It examines non-individualized communication in which state officials issue statements to a general public. Thus, other typical communicative acts between the state and its citizens such as individualized requests for information by a regulatory agency or the processing of data by the intelligence services are not part of the scope of this chapter, although many of its findings also apply to those individual interactions. In Section 4.3, the problem will be outlined: There are hardly any legal rules which cover this field. Section 4.4 will describe the special characteristics of information and perceptions of it. Section 4.5 then explores the existing legal setting from a legal theory perspective, with reference to German law. At the bottom of any regulation, there is an understanding of the conflict between the private and the public person (Section 4.6). The chapter concentrates on the constitutional perspectives for solving this problem, first by establishing the core framework in Section 4.7, then by dealing with more specific aspects connected to the principle of proportionality or the balancing of interests in Section 4.8. A short analysis of the right to counterattack and the changes in the previously developed principles follows in Section 4.9. A conclusion and outlook round off the findings.

4.2 ACTORS AND FORMATS

A large number of executive state actors communicate with the public, and the informative content they convey differs greatly. Also, the format and the media used vary. Some examples: The United States Environmental Protection Agency (EPA), an independent agency, informs the public about July being Ocean Month,[7] or publishes information on how to apply for or manage an EPA grant through its homepage on the Internet. A European data protection authority issues a statement through a written press release which is then distributed to the press, declaring that it finds the use of Microsoft Office 365 to be in violation of the General Data Protection Regulation.[8] The German Financial Regulation Agency (BaFin) publishes a guideline on securities supervision or cross-sectoral issues to the subscribers of its email lists.[9] The US Federal Drug Agency (FDA) warns professionals about the use of a certain medicine by sending out letters to pharmacists and medical doctors.[10]

[7] www.epa.gov, 3 July 2023.

[8] For example, https://www.edps.europa.eu/press-publications/press-news/press-releases/2024/european-commissions-use-microsoft-365-infringes-data-protection-law-eu-institutions-and-bodies_en Regulation (EU) 2016/679 of the European Parliament and of the Council of 27 April 2016 on the protection of natural persons with regard to the processing of personal data and on the free movement of such data, and repealing Directive 95/46/EC (General Data Protection Regulation) (Text with EEA relevance).

[9] www.bafin.de/EN/DieBaFin/Service/Newsletter/newsletter_node_en.html.

[10] www.fda.gov/drugs/enforcement-activities-fda/warning-letters-and-notice-violation-letters-pharmaceutical-companies.

Vaccinations against measles are recommended by the Centers for Disease Control and Prevention in the USA.[11] A municipality displays an organization diagram on its webpage.[12] The German consumer protection agency outlines the choices available in disability insurance and advises on the most important aspects to consider.[13] The US Department of the Treasury publishes press releases on various topics on its website.[14] A publicly funded research institute issues a printed activity report. The Irish Data Protection Commission publishes information about the amount of a fine it has imposed on Meta.[15] During a public session, a German regulatory authority shows pictures of violations of hygiene and food regulations in individual restaurants two years ago to demonstrate its level of activities.[16] A secretary of state gives an interview to a radio station on the political status quo and her opinion on the Ukraine War.[17] The head of the antitrust agency holds, as an adjunct professor of a state university, a competition law seminar on the recent case law of his agency. A prosecutor informs the press about the allegations made against a famous TV moderator by his former girlfriend,[18] or demands that a famous politician is forced into a perp walk because of the allegations of a prostitute.[19]

4.3 THE PROBLEM: WHERE ARE THE RULES?

These examples illustrate the diversity of messages and information conveyed by official bodies and their representatives. They can range from offers of advice and consultation to general information on organizational structures, to declarations of activity, to clear warnings and orders. The information can be directed at the general public with low barriers of access, such as information shared on the Internet, or be passed on through individualized communication such as email. Social media interaction has become a common tool in recent years.[20] Even at first glance, the

[11] www.cdc.gov/vaccines/vpd/mmr/public/index.html#:~:text=CDC%20recommends%20that%20people%20get,date%20on%20their%20MMR%20vaccination.

[12] www.stadt-koeln.de/politik-und-verwaltung/dezernate/index.html (the website is available in English, the diagram is not).

[13] www.verbraucherzentrale.de/wissen/geld-versicherungen/weitere-versicherungen/berufsunfaehigkeit-wie-sie-sich-gegen-verlust-des-einkommens-absichern-13931.

[14] https://home.treasury.gov/news/press-releases.

[15] www.dataprotection.ie/en/news-media/press-releases/data-protection-commission-announces-decision-in-facebook-data-scraping-inquiry.

[16] www.berlin.de/ba-pankow/politik-und-verwaltung/aemter/ordnungsamt/veterinaer-und-lebensmittelaufsicht/downloadservice/artikel.240708.php.

[17] www.zdf.de/nachrichten/politik/baerbock-waffenlieferung-mehr-hilfe-ukraine-krieg-100.html.

[18] https://de.wikipedia.org/wiki/Kachelmann-Prozess.

[19] On the criticalities of perp walks, Clyde Haberman, 'For Shame: A Brief History of the Perp Walk', *The New York Times*, 2 December 2018, www.nytimes.com/2018/12/02/us/perp-walk.html.

[20] See also the overview at Indra Spiecker genannt Döhmann, '§ 23 Informationsverwaltung' in Wolfgang Kahl and Markus Ludwigs (eds.), *Handbuch des Verwaltungsrechts* (Heidelberg: C. F. Müller, 2021) Vol. I, para. 71 et seq.

wide variety of these measures and the different impacts they have on individuals is obvious. The depiction of hygiene deficits at a restaurant two years previously interferes with the rights of the new restaurant owner. The recommendation of a particular product changes the competitive setting.[21] Making public the information about investigations may violate the integrity of the individual, and hampers the guarantees of 'innocent-until-proven-guilty'.[22]

This also includes the communication of public officials in political offices. Hardly anyone would deny that a statement made by public authorities, let alone the head of state, has a special impact on and influences public opinion.[23] Does it make a significant difference whether John Doe in a pub near his home or the President of the United States comments on social media about the House of Representative's bill for tax regulation? Who expresses what through which means may influence elections and thus impede individuals' rights, considering both the individual voter and the individual candidates. It shapes the democratic state, and reinforces the principles of the rule of law.

Interestingly, hardly any written legal rules exist as to what types of information may be distributed, by whom and under what conditions or in which format. Even fewer rules do so on a differentiated basis which reflects the differences in format, the potential impact of communication and the actors. Mostly, a rugged set of legal boundaries have been set by – typically few – court decisions which may not serve as a comprehensive and conclusive framework.[24] Both freedom of information laws and transparency laws typically address adverse situations, where individuals are interested in information within the realm of the state which the state does not freely distribute and perhaps even restricts access to. This type of regulation covers the passive distribution of information by the state – passive because the state responds to a request rather than initiating communicative procedures. This chapter, in contrast, discusses the kinds of proactive communication and distribution described above.

4.4 INFORMATION DOES NOT HURT AND NEEDS NO REGULATION

One reason for the silence of the law on the distribution of public information may be that a general understanding exists that in a democracy, the public as the sovereign needs to know what its officials are doing.[25] Freedom of information laws

[21] Christoph Gusy, 'Verwaltung durch Information – Empfehlungen und Warnungen als Mittel des Verwaltungshandelns' (2000) 53(14) *Neue Juristische Wochenschrift* 977, at 986.

[22] Anne-Sophie Landwers, *Behördliche Öffentlichkeitsarbeit im Recht* (Baden-Baden: Nomos, 2019) p. 93 et seq.

[23] BVerfGE 154, 320, para. 50; Sebastian Nellesen, *Äußerungsrechte staatlicher Funktionsträger* (Tübingen: Mohr Siebeck, 2018) p. 21.

[24] Friedrich Schoch, 'Die Schwierigkeiten des BVerfG mit der Bewältigung staatlichen Informationshandelns' (2011) 30 *Neue Zeitschrift für Verwaltungsrecht* 193, at 193.

[25] BVerfGE 40, 296, at 327.

are part of a reconstruction of this understanding in terms of rights and interests.[26] This approach also includes some active informational measures by the state itself,[27] typically if the state expects increased interest in particular information. In such cases, the state shall present the information proactively.[28] This is, for example, the rationale behind rules like Article 552(a)(2)(D)(ii)(I) and (II) of the US Freedom of Information Act (FOIA), which allows and even requires public agencies to distribute information under certain circumstances. This, however, is no less than a proactive means of reducing the resources spent on both sides of the information request. A freedom-of-information perspective allows any statement and distribution of information by officials to seem to be part of a desirable transparency of the state, enabling its control. Therefore, no regulation seems necessary.

The second, and most probably more forceful, reason for the silence of the law on the active communication of the state may lie within the common misunderstanding that informational measures are non-intrusive, and thus have little impact on individuals' rights.[29] Unlike law-and-order approaches, informational measures are frequently considered to be less infringing than other approaches to regulation.[30] If one believes this then, even under a strict rule of law (such as Article 20 (3) of the German Constitution (*Grundgesetz*)), no active entitlement is necessary for the state to issue communicative acts. Where infringements are impossible, no legal framework is required. Both arguments, however, are critical and short-sighted from all perspectives.

First of all, the assumption that the availability of information has no legal impact has long been proven wrong. Freedom of speech and communication take place within the private sphere, a non-state-influenced realm. As a starting point of the analysis, there is no place for the state to participate in communication as such. The state itself has no 'freedom of speech', it is not a legally valid participant in a private activity. However, it has long been acknowledged that communication about

26 For example, the explanatory memorandum to the German Freedom of Information Act (*Informationsfreiheitsgesetz*) states that it is intended to promote the democratic formation of opinion, see BT-Drs. 15/4493, at 6; Matthias Hong, 'Das Recht auf Informationszugang nach dem Informationsfreiheitsgesetz als Recht zur Mobilisierung der demokratischen Freiheit' (2016) 35 *Neue Zeitschrift für Verwaltungsrecht* 953, at 945; for the US Freedom of Information Act (FOIA), see Daniel Solove and Paul Schwartz, *Information Privacy Law* 7th ed. (Los Angeles: Aspen, 2021) p. 630.

27 Landwers, *Behördliche Öffentlichkeitsarbeit* (n 22) pp. 46 and 56.

28 BVerfGE 44, 125, at 147; Hinderks, 'Staatliche Kommunikation' (n 3), at 28.

29 OVG Münster, 5 June 1987 – 13 A 1273/86, LMRR 1987, at 35; Dietrich Murswiek, 'Das Bundesverfassungsgericht und die Dogmatik mittelbarer Grundrechtseingriffe' (2003) 22 *Neue Zeitschrift für Verwaltungsrecht* 1, at 4; Gertrude Lübbe-Wolff, 'Rechtsprobleme der behördlichen Umweltberatung' (1987) 40 *Neue Juristische Wochenschrift* 2705, at 2711.

30 OVG Münster, judgment of 5 June 1987 – 13 A 1273/86, LMRR 1987, at 35; of the opinion that correct information is not an infringement, see Gabriele Britz, Martin Eifert and Thomas Groß, 'Verwaltungsinformation und Informationsrichtigkeit – Pflichten und Ansprüche nach dem Umweltinformations- und dem Informationsfreiheitsgesetz' (2007) 60 *Die öffentliche Verwaltung* 717, at 721.

activities of the state is a part of the self-serving purposes of the state. A democratic institution needs to exchange information with its constituents: the citizens need to know what their state is doing, why and how. This opens the door to communication that potentially influences the discourse on matters of state: if a state authority warns people about a product, this has a significant impact on the competitive value of that product. The use of certain products or even a recommendation by official authorities creates interest in these products. A visit by the head of state during a municipal election campaign typically increases the likelihood of a win for the candidate backed by that individual. Information released by the government is usually considered more 'correct', more authentic and more reliable than other types of information. The publication of a suspect's photograph on a police Facebook page[31] increases the likelihood of that suspect being turned in.[32] Examples like these illustrate that state communication does take place and that it does change the framework within which private communication and private action happens, and under which private rights are enacted.

Secondly, it is often assumed that informational measures have little potential for severe infringements in comparison to other measures, in particular law-and-order measures. Information is considered to be at best part of soft – non-legally binding – law, to have little impact, to be of little power.[33] A principle of proportionality test, it is assumed, would therefore typically allow informational measures as there would be no other, less infringing means.

Thirdly, and closely connected to this argumentation, is the consideration that due to the weak power for infringement of information and communication, the interest of the public would justify any potential infringement of rights. This again employs the argument that a democratic state needs transparency in regard to state actors, thus allowing for only limited and diffuse regulation of information activities as the interests of transparency, open communication and freedom of information would override any private interest. The only exception that is typically addressed is a potential violation of business and trade secrets, or sometimes also of private

[31] On the serious doubts of the legality of the use of Facebook pages through the press office of the federal government, see the order of the Federal Data Protection Authority, www.bfdi.bund.de/SharedDocs/Pressemitteilungen/DE/2023/06-Untersagung-Betrieb-Fanpage-BReg.html?nn=251944.

[32] On the legal problems of such measures Sönke F. Gerhold, *Münchener Kommentar zur Strafprozessordnung* 2nd ed. (München: C. H. Beck, 2023) § 131 para. 1 et seq. with further references.

[33] See Lübbe-Wolff, 'Rechtsprobleme' (n 29), at 2711 et seq.; see also Dietrich Murswiek, 'Staatliche Warnungen, Wertungen, Kritik als Grundrechtseingriffe – Zur Wirtschafts- und Meinungslenkung durch staatliches Informationshandeln' (1997) 112 *Deutsches Verwaltungsblatt* 1021; Lars Bechler, *Informationseingriffe durch intransparenten Umgang mit personenbezogenen Daten* (Halle-Wittenberg: Univ.-Verlag Halle-Wittenberg, 2010) p. 162 et seq. Compare also the analysis on infringement by information by Spiecker genannt Döhmann, '§ 23: Informationsverwaltungsrecht' (n 20), at 109 et. seq.

secrets.[34] It neglects, however, to consider that even if transparency is the driving force, the matter of when, why, how and by whom (that is, format, style, timing and framing) is left open for regulation.

Even from a historical standpoint, it is surprising that an understanding that communicative measures need little regulation is upheld: evidence from the dictatorial episodes in the histories of modern democracies illustrate the fatal impact of communication.[35] This directly relates to the latest developments where impulsive, intrusive and often even targeted wrongful statements by state officials are being used to influence public opinion in a so far unknown manner. Such influence is wielded by unfair means, undermines democratic standards, violates tolerance and the freedom of opinion, and challenges the acceptance of the democratic, rule-of-law state as such.[36]

4.5 THE STATUS QUO: THE CASES BEFORE THE GERMAN CONSTITUTIONAL COURT

In the past seventy years, Germany's Constitutional Court has ruled on only a few cases relating to communication acts by state authorities. They illustrate well the status quo of the legal framework, in particular, since in most cases no regulatory measures have followed. Despite some of the attention these cases have garnered – especially on warnings about religious groups and on the consumption of particular wines – the practical results remain opaque and do little to answer the questions arising from recent developments surrounding state officials' communicative acts. Nevertheless, the German jurisprudential experience may shed some light on core issues and suggest legal answers to the questions posed. It illustrates the scope of the field. Most importantly, the court's decisions help us to understand and analyse the core guidelines on state communication beyond the German Constitution for any democratic, rule-of-law-based state.

34 The explanatory memorandum to the German Freedom of Information Act (Informationsfreiheitsgesetz) that public information shall be as transparent as possible and provide as much protection of secrets as necessary, see BT-Drs. 15/4493, at 6; Gerhard Wiebe, 'Der Geschäftsgeheimnisschutz im Informationsfreiheitsrecht' (2019) 28 *Neue Zeitschrift für Verwaltungsrecht* 1705; Rainer Wolf, 'Grundrechtseingriff durch Information? Der steinige Weg zu einer ökologischen Kommunikationsverfassung' (1995) 28(3) *Kritische Justiz* 341, at 349.

35 So common understanding goes, for example, on the rise of the Nazis in Germany due to the impact of communication, www.nzz.ch/ueber-hitlers-sprache-ld.808406?reduced=true; see the motivation of the project on editing Hitler's speeches, www.ifz-muenchen.de/en/research/ea/research/collection-of-adolf-hitlers-speeches-1933-1945, doubted recently by Peter Selb and Simon Munzert, 'Examining a Most Likely Case for Strong Campaign Effects: Hitler's Speeches and the Rise of the Nazi Party, 1927–1933' (2018) 112(4) *American Political Science Review* 1050–1066.

36 Tschorr, 'Wenn der Staat Fake News verbreitet' (n 4), at 382 et seq. and 389.

4.5.1 *Government Public Relations: Transparency and Part of State Action, No Legal Justification Necessary*

That the topic of information has not been at the core of constitutionally charged conflicts can be illustrated easily by the fact that the first decision of the German Constitutional Court dealing with it was only in 1977.[37] It took roughly thirty years after the constitution was enacted for the Court to deal with state communication for the first time. In this case, the governing parties had used a variety of communication options, some of them quite cost-intensive, to draw attention to their achievements and thus to campaign for re-election. The opposition filed a complaint against this. The Court established the principle that state officials and state institutions of the government of Germany, representing the most prominent executive institution, may distribute general information. It argued along the lines of transparency and found that no special legal ground for this action was needed as it is included in the general task of 'state action' (*Staatshandeln*). It even stressed – again in line with the argument for transparency – that there even existed a duty to inform the public about its decisions and the background of its actions. The legal consequence of this is that public informative statements are allowed, but their limits are where election advertising begins.

4.5.2 *Warning–Religious Freedom–Governing Sufficient*

The second case followed almost fifteen years later: Various members of the federal and state (*Länder*) governments mentioned and provided information about a particular religious organization. This group organized popular clubs for young people. Their members were, due to their peculiar attire and active missionary activities, quite visible in larger cities. The Federal Secretary of Youth, Family and Health warned the public in a press conference about this organization, labelling it as a sect; the federal government officially called the group 'destructive' and 'pseudo-religious'.[38] The Constitutional Court concentrated on potential infringements of religious freedom, and established the interpretation that information can be an infringing means only to a limited extent.[39] It found that a right to publicity (and thus to providing such information) can be derived from the federal government's general task of governing the state (*Staatsleitung*). However, this would not cover measures that are a substitute for interventionist means such as orders or prohibitions. In the end, the description of the group as a 'sect' was considered to be constitutionally acceptable because it was factual while the description as

[37] BVerfGE 44, at 125.
[38] BT-Drucks 8/2790.
[39] BVerfGE 105, 279.

'destructive' and 'pseudo-religious' was held to be unconstitutional because it was considered to be defamatory.

4.5.3 *(Commercial) Side Effects of Warning of Dangerous Goods*

The Court issued on the same date another decision on state warnings, this time one that was somewhat more difficult and legally challenging. A scandal had rocked the German wine industry in the 1980s; in many vineyards illegal and even unhealthy additives had been added to give wine extra taste and sweetness. The ministry of one of the *Länder* issued a list of such wines in order to warn consumers. The rationale behind this activity was the fact that wineries did not keep records of all the bottles sold in their business-to-company dealings, and as many bottles were traditionally sold locally, it was impossible to reach ordinary customers and warn them.

The Constitutional Court addressed the problem from a strictly dogmatic point of view.[40] It stressed that while the warning about the wines mentioned was legal (as they were indeed dangerous), the side effects of this announcement led to severe economic consequences for the vineyards involved: customers would not only avoid buying and consuming the contaminated sorts but would in general refrain from doing any business with the wineries on the list, thus also not buying non-affected sorts. Here, the Court found that under certain circumstances, those informational measures could constitute an infringement of the commercial rights of the wineries (and of the resellers, but that was not discussed), if the side effects were not accidental and the state act was intended to regulate business. This took care of the common understanding that informational measures were irrelevant and needed no legal framework. Only in these cases, however, did the Constitutional Court consider that there was a legal requirement for the legitimation of the informational measure, while in general they were devoid of legal boundaries.

4.5.4 *Deemed 'Nutcases' by the President*

In the first of several cases where prominent members of government voiced opinions, the President of Germany had, in response to questions from students, referred to members, activists and supporters of a right-wing party as 'nutcases'. The Constitutional Court held that this was lawful,[41] from the starting point that it is a requirement of the President to observe the right of the parties to free and equal participation in the formation of the political will of the people in the political discourse. However, the Court accepted different rules for the President in

40 Ibid. at 252, English version: www.bundesverfassungsgericht.de/SharedDocs/Entscheidungen/EN/2002/06/rs20020626_1bvr055891en.html.

41 BVerfGE 136, at 323, English version: www.bundesverfassungsgericht.de/SharedDocs/Entscheidungen/EN/2014/06/es20140610_2bve000413en.html.

comparison to government politicians due to his special position, as he is not part of the elected government and does not allocate resources for a campaign, thus referring explicitly to the 1977 judgment. In particular reference to his position, the Court clarified that the President is in general obliged to safeguard and promote the common good and a free society; hence limits to statements exist, but only in the case of an evident neglect of his integration task as a president and if thus the statement became arbitrary and unrelated to his professional task.

4.5.5 *Relevance to Political Party: Statement 'Red Flag'*

A later decision covered the case in which the Federal Minister of Education and Research mimicked the slogan ('red flag') of a right-wing party's event on the webpage of the ministry she headed, and clearly stated her belief that the positions of this party were not in accordance with democratic values and that they promoted neo-Fascist thinking and action. The Constitutional Court found this to be a violation of the right-wing party's right to fair elections since the minister had violated a duty of neutrality.[42] The Court in general acknowledged that the government's authority affects its actions, even if not in direct connection to an election campaign. Therefore, the government must not identify with individual parties and use state resources for their own ends. This established a substantive standard, that a duty to neutrality exists in general and at all times.

4.5.6 *Relevance to Political Party: Interview*

In another very similar case discussed by the Constitutional Court, a minister, this time the Federal Minister of Interior, had expressed disparaging assessments about the same right-wing party in an interview.[43] Again, this touched upon the fairness of elections, but the court only found it to be in violation of the duty of neutrality because this interview was posted on the webpage of the ministry and as such combined his position with his personal opinion. Although it was not quite clear whether this would also have been a violation if the interview had been published independently, it was clear that the combination of office and official means of distributing this opinion triggered the courts' sanctions.

4.5.7 *Head of State Comment on Election Result*

In a dramatic vote, the same right-wing party as in the other cases seemed to have enabled a liberal to become president of one of the *Länder*, which caused a public

[42] BVerfGE 148, 11, English version: www.bundesverfassungsgericht.de/SharedDocs/Entscheidungen/EN/2018/02/es20180227_2bve000116en.html.

[43] BVerfGE 154, 320.

outcry. The Chancellor commented, in a statement given during a press conference held far from Germany (in South Africa), that his election ought to be reversed. The Court found that the constitutionally guaranteed competences within the Federal Government give the Chancellor an extended right to issue political statements.[44] Nevertheless, this statement violated the fair election rights of this party because neutrality and objectivity had to be adhered to by all those in all public positions.

4.5.8 *Twitter Chancellor*

Two more instances have prompted lawyers to discuss the legality of statesmen's (and stateswomen's) expressions in public: the most prominent one, and shadowed by the President of the United States' actions, was the German Chancellor's official Twitter account. This channel was in her name, but it was administered by her press officer. When she left office, she offered to turn her Twitter account over to her successor. However, due to Twitter's terms and conditions, this would have meant that all her and her press officer's statements would now be attributed to the new Chancellor and his press officer. Therefore, the account remained in her name and under her supervision, but has been dormant since her departure from office.[45]

4.5.9 *The Berlin Pankower List of Disgust ('Ekelliste')*

Another instance has been publicized among lawyers,[46] but has not been in the public eye to the same degree. In this case from the 2000s, a Berlin hygiene control unit of the municipal administration published a list of findings of hygiene deficiencies in restaurants, together with the names of the restaurants and pictures, for example of mice excrement in a storage room, rotten chicken breasts or other

44 BVerfG, judgment of 15 June 2022 – 2 BvE 4/20, 2 BvE 5/20, English version: www.bundesverfassungsgericht.de/SharedDocs/Entscheidungen/EN/2022/06/es20220615_2bve000420en.html.

45 'Twitterkonto von Steffen Seibert wird archiviert', *Spiegel*, 12 March 2021, www.spiegel.de/netzwelt/web/steffen-seibert-twitter-konto-des-regierungssprechers-wird-archiviert-a-a8a2a07d-0a56-4dd4-95c8-b00647f79a5f.

46 For example, Thomas Holzner, 'Die "Pankower Ekelliste" – Zukunftsweisendes Modell des Verbraucherschutzes oder rechtswidriger Pranger?' (2010) 29 *Neue Zeitschrift für Verwaltungsrecht* 489; Ferdinand Wollenschläger, 'Staatliche Verbraucherinformation als neues Instrument des Verbraucherschutzes' (2011) 102(1) *Verwaltungsarchiv* 20; Elke Gurlit, 'Zeitwert von Verbraucherinformation und Rechtsschutzanforderungen' (2011) 30 *Neue Zeitschrift für Verwaltungsrecht* 1052; Friedrich Schoch, 'Neuere Entwicklungen im Verbraucherinformationsrecht' (2010) 63 *Neue Juristische Wochenschrift* 2241, at 2246; Fritz Ossenbühl, 'Verbraucherschutz durch Information' (2011) 30 *Neue Zeitschrift für Verwaltungsrecht* 1357; Alexander Schink, 'Smileys in der Lebensmittelkontrolle – Verfassungsrechtliche Zulässigkeit einer amtlichen Information der Öffentlichkeit über die Ergebnisse der amtlichen Lebensmittelkontrolle' (2011) 126 *Deutsches Verwaltungsblatt* 253.

disgusting evidence.[47] The reason why this information was shared with the public was not clearly stated, but at least one potential reason was a demonstration of the hygiene department's efficiency and activities, including shaming of the individual restaurants and as warnings to the public. The problem, however, was that some of the violations of the law had been committed quite some time before, and it was unclear whether the owners were still the same (and whether the wrongdoings were continuing). Moreover, there was no mechanism for taking the information down, requiring correction or checking the veracity of its content.

The case never went to court, but it led to the relevant law being altered to include a passage stating that under certain circumstances, and taking into consideration the principle of proportionality, publication of such warnings was – to a limited extent – possible. This was upheld by the Constitutional Court.[48] Here, the common understanding was that the administration must have legal grounds, according to the rule of law, on which it could act and that there need to be certain minimum standards of control, accuracy, monitoring and take-down procedures which could in individual cases supersede the competitive interests of the company.

4.6 GOVERNING THE CONFLICT BETWEEN OFFICE AND POLITICAL OPINION

Behind most of these problems lies a conflict between different interests rooted in the actions of a single person acting in different roles: A secretary of interior is a political person in a political office serving particular goals. As such, the person represents certain interests, that of their office, or maybe that of the democratic government as such. Already here, interests may collide as the government's interests may not align with the interests of the department. At the same time, this is a private person with political opinions.[49] They may not agree with the general position of the government or indeed that of the department. Finally, every politician is interested in remaining in office, in being re-elected and in creating their own legacy, according to public choice theory.[50] Thus, statements may serve any of these

[47] Thomas Heinicke, in Olaf Sosnitza and Andreas Meisterernst (eds.), *Lebensmittelrecht* (Munich: C. H. Beck, 2023) p. 185; EL Dezember 2022, VIG, § 6 para. 11; see www.berlin.de/ba-pankow/politik-und-verwaltung/aemter/ordnungsamt/veterinaer-und-lebensmittelaufsicht/downloadservice/artikel.240708.php.

[48] BVerfG, Order of 21 March 2018 – 1 BvF 1/13, English version: www.bundesverfassungsgericht.de/SharedDocs/Entscheidungen/EN/2018/03/fs20180321_1bvf000113en.html.

[49] See dissenting opinion in *Rottmann*, BVerfGE 44, 125, at 186.

[50] Emanuel Towfigh, 'Rational Choice and Its Limits' (2016) 17(5) *German Law Journal* 763, at 769; see also Emanuel Towfigh and Niels Petersen, '§ 6: Public and Social Choice Theory' in Emanuel Towfigh and Niels Petersen (eds.), *Ökonomische Methoden im Recht* 3rd ed. (Tübingen: Mohr Siebeck, 2023) para. 333; The first edition is available in English, Emanuel Towfigh and Niels Petersen (eds.), Economic Methods for Lawyers (Cambridge: Cambridge University Press, 2017).

different roles and conflict with the interests of the other role. Government politicians are, therefore, typically in at least a double position.[51]

This is usually unproblematic if all three (or four) roles are in synchronization, if the private person agrees with the political person interested in re-election, with the statesperson and with the general government political line. This is probably frequently the case and may be considered to be the norm. After all, a politician chooses a particular party because of their general concordance with the party's positions, and the defending and upholding of those positions while in office will be in line with the government's positions, of which the party is part.

However, more prominent, socially discussed and legally interesting situations are those involving conflicting opinions. A parliamentary representative may issue unfair, non-substantial, potentially pejorative and derogatory statements about political opponents or other political ideas in order to further their chances of re-election: The individual in this case trumps the democratically elected representative of the entire people. A head of state may misinform others about a political situation in order to avoid impeachment: the private person who is afraid of public shame and degradation trumps the commitment of the statesman to truth and honesty.

These examples illustrate that the communication of people in public service and of state authorities is potentially conflict-laden and as such calls for both socially and legally binding norms to keep this conflict in check. To reveal how this can be achieved requires us to take a closer look at the legally recognized interests which can be affected by public communication. The above-mentioned examples, which have illustrated the reasons for defining public and private interests that may be potentially infringed by state communication, may serve as a background for a more general understanding of the situation.

4.7 THE CONSTITUTIONAL PERSPECTIVE: CONFLICT OF INTERESTS AND ROLES

Taking into account that most of the cases involving administrative communication – or at least those which the German Constitutional Court decided on – have involved the heads of departments and thus members of the governing authority and designated representatives of the government, a first analysis needs to consider constitutional aspects. It should be noted at this stage that a large proportion of public communication also takes place at lower levels of government and with less nationwide attention – although perhaps with just as many consequences for the individuals and institutions about and to which information is distributed. Nevertheless, the statements of (directly) elected officials, namely heads of state or leaders of departments or public agencies can have a severe impact on the political

[51] BVerfG, 2 BvE 4/20, 2 BvE 5/20 [77].

discourse, the fairness of elections and democratic values and practices per se. Consequently, they need to be in accord with the constitutional structure.

4.7.1 *The Dominance of the Public Office*

All individuals are protected by constitutionally granted human rights. This is true also for persons performing tasks in the executive branch. In general, holding public office does not completely preclude the application of constitutional rights, whether in an elevated position such as head of state or fulfilling a rather down-to-earth function as an accountant in a small municipality. States and branches of the state power, such as the executive, individual state institutions, departments and agencies, typically do not have constitutional rights, as human rights protect the individual of the state and not the state itself. Therefore, constitutional rights of the municipality – not of the restaurant owners – are not affected directly if an agency, department or institution publishes statements that do not show any personal linkage, but which clearly represent the opinion of the state, of the administrative agency or of the institution. Thus, the distribution of pictures portraying hygiene deficiencies in restaurants by the competent regulatory agency does not fall under the protection of any individual constitutional right of the municipality or the person acting on its behalf. It is a different matter if the person behind the agency is clearly visible, for instance, if a head of state, the head of a department or an individual officer issues a statement or declares a position. This is certainly the case if a communication occurs under the name of the private person, not of their office.

Freedom of speech is the constitutional right which typically protects communication. Although this freedom exists in very many different manifestations depending on its exact constitutional understanding, it is everywhere considered to be one of the essential human rights for any free and democratic society.[52] Freedom of speech as such is an important backbone of any democratic society:[53] Only the continuous enjoyment of this constitutional right enables citizens to form an opinion, to weigh arguments, to accept different opinions and to express convictions of their own. In this way, freedom of speech promotes democratic self-governance.[54] Consequently, the existence and use of freedom of speech prepares citizens to become empowered citizens, to form their own political convictions, to

[52] Déclaration des droits de l'homme et du citoyen (Declaration of the Rights of Man, 1789), Art. 11: 'The free communication of ideas and opinions is one of the most precious of the rights of man'; 'freedom of thought and speech … is the matrix, the indispensable condition, of nearly every other form of freedom', Benjamin Cardozo in *Palko* v. *Connecticut*, 302 US 319 (1937), para. 10. Also BVerfGE 7, 198, [31], English abstract: www.bundesverfassungsgericht.de/SharedDocs/Entscheidungen/EN/1958/01/rs19580115_1bvr040051en.html.

[53] BVerfGE 7, 198, [31].

[54] Ian Curie, 'Freedom of Expression and Association' in Mark Tushnet, Thomas Fleiner and Cheryl Saunders (eds.), *Routledge Handbook of Constitutional Law* (Abingdon: Routledge, 2012) p. 235.

judge candidates and political parties and to use their voting rights in a free and autonomous way, so the common understanding goes.[55]

Thus, any legal framework which regulates the communication by a person might be understood to threaten the infringement or even a violation of the freedom of speech. Any such infringement must be justified for a higher good. Nevertheless, no constitutional rights exist without restrictions: Where the practice of a constitutional right violates those of others, a balancing of both rights has to take place, and thus restrictions of the exercise of a human right may be justified. This may lead to the possibility of restrictions on issuing statements or on realising individual freedom of speech under particular circumstances and in particular positions such as statements in relation to one's role as part of state administration.

A person does not forfeit their constitutional status and rights by assuming public office or starting to work for the executive;[56] justification is also required for the regulation of their communication in office. Therefore, the human right of freedom of speech remains an especially important factor in determining where the potential boundaries of state action lie and how a legal framework for legitimate communication of the state can be construed. On the other hand, the fact that someone speaks in relation to their executive function in general allows a restriction of this particular area of freedom of speech.

This framework of state communication includes the determination of where the public and the private person are legally separated as well as whether potential spheres of legal friction may exist between those two (and more) roles.[57] Nobody would consider it to be legally problematic, for the colleague or for the democratic system, for a police officer to tell his wife that his colleague is an idiot. However, this evaluation would change if the police officer issued that statement at an official press conference on the quality of police service in a municipality. It is highly questionable whether such a statement could be legally assessed without taking into account the potential effects on the general political atmosphere, the acceptance of police measures and even the support of the state monopoly of use of force let alone the special circumstances of the statement.

55 Ibid.; Anna-Bettina Kaiser, 'Art. 5' in Horst Dreier and Frauke Brosius-Gersdorf (eds.), *Grundgesetz-Kommentar* 4th ed. (Tübingen: Mohr Siebeck, 2023) s. 1 para. 41.

56 BVerfG, 2 BvE 4/20, 2 BvE 5/20, [76]; see also Thomas Kliegel, 'Freedom of Speech for Public Officials vs. the Political Parties' Right to Equal Opportunity: The German Constitutional Court's Recent Rulings Involving the NPD and the AfD' (2017) (18)1 *German Law Journal* 189, at 201, who says that the government is composed of party members and therefore the party's agenda also influences the government's decisions. A similar finding was also reached by Janet McLean and Mark Tushnet, 'Administrative Bureaucracy' in Tushnet, Fleiner and Saunders, *Routledge Handbook of Constitutional Law* (n 54) p. 124.

57 RhPfVerfGH, Order of 21 May 2014 – VGH A 39/14, NVwZ-RR 2014, 665, at 667; BVerfG, judgment of 16 December 2014 – 2 BvE 2/14, [56]–[58], English abstract: www.bundesverfassungsgericht.de/SharedDocs/Entscheidungen/EN/2014/12/es20141216_2bve000214en.html; Kliegel, 'Freedom of Speech' (n 56), at 202.

A decisive factor is that any person working for a state authority in a free state is there by their own free will. Thus, any restrictions due to the office are part of the autonomous decision of the individual to prefer the advantages of this office over avoiding potential restrictions. The circumstances of the state authority for which a person works determine the boundaries and burdens on their freedom of speech in a publicly relevant manner. The impact of this distinction between the private person and the administrative person becomes quite clear if we contrast the two ends of the spectrum: a conversation at a private dinner table between family and friends is typically a private issue where freedom of speech is unaffected by the office one holds (see also Section 4.7.3.3).[58] However, a discussion of current issues as a background interview in a café constitutes an official communicative act, even though only two persons are present in a relatively private environment.

The private person merges with the public person when performing a public administrative function. This leads, on the one hand, to the protection of the private person: It is not the private person who acts, but the holder of the position; errors are attributed to the office or the agency, not the private person; damages are paid by the state. On the other hand, this may be viewed as a restriction, as the actions of the private person may not collide with the functions of the office. Thus, considerations of the public office override individual rights in matters concerning the non-private communication of a state official. This indeed leads to a restriction of constitutional rights, in particular of the freedom of speech, in all but exclusively private communications. The exact boundaries and the exact design of a framework for public communication will be described on the basis of the following analysis of competing interests.

4.7.2 *Constitutional Conflicting Interests*

A dominance of the public office over the private person exists when a communicative act is closely linked or directly attributed to that office.[59] This boundary between the two fluctuates, however, and this depends on a number of factors that will be further developed in the course of this chapter. There are two groups of constitutional interests which trigger restrictions on a state authority officer's freedom of speech: first, individual rights exist which can be affected by public communication. Second, there are more generalized, common-good interests which may

[58] However, this is different if those considered to be family and friends themselves work for public authorities, the press or may use these private communications, as this is then not a solely private matter. A helpful distinction can be the definition of 'personal use' as applied in the GDPR in order to set a border between GDPR-relevant data processing, and those, solely private, not under GDPR restrictions, see Vagelis Papakonstantinou and Paul De Hert, 'Art. 2' in Indra Spiecker genannt Döhmann et al. (eds.), *General Data Protection Regulation. Article-by-Article Commentary* (Hart, Beck and Nomos, 2023) n. 54 et. seq.

[59] Thomas Spitzlei, 'Die politische Äußerungsbefugnis staatlicher Organe' (2018) 58(9) *Juristische Schulung* 856, at 857.

potentially be infringed by public communication. These latter constitutional interests are especially likely to influence the position of the individual in general because they constitute minimum standards of neutrality, fairness, correctness and disinterestedness of communication, to name just a few (see Section 4.7.3.2 and following).

4.7.2.1 Individualized Interests

A wide variety of individual constitutional rights may potentially be infringed. Almost any individual right may be affected directly or indirectly by state communication. The cases from the German Constitutional Court discussed in Section 4.5 display an impressive range of those rights: While rights connected to commercial interests, fair elections, personality or ensuring free competition are easily identified, freedom of religious expression would not necessarily come to mind at first glance as potentially suffering from the negative consequences of state communication. Almost all the individual rights which may be affected by public speech may thereby justify restrictions on a public official's freedom of speech in fields such as schooling and education, property, press, assembly, labour, informational self-determination, telecommunications – to name just the obvious. The German Constitutional Court has also stressed the rights of political parties to a fair election several times. It has thus extended the set of counterbalancing rights also to the political sphere.[60]

4.7.2.2 Common Good Interests: Democracy, Rule of Law, Fairness of Elections

Any official who acts in the course of a public office fulfils public duties beyond their individual official tasks. They represent the state in general, and this means also representing the idea of the democratic state, based on the rule of law. Any action by the executive is attributed to 'the' state and to 'the' democratic system as such.[61] The quality, content, style and format of statements are interpreted as representing the status of democracy. The interaction between any citizen and any state official is directly linked to larger concepts such as the acceptance of the state–government relationship and thus the democratic system.[62] Therefore, actions of a public official may also violate these general common interests of the democratic state, which means that its personnel represent the state per se.

[60] Equal chances of the political parties: BVerfGE 14, 121 (133); BVerfGE 6, 84 (90); Rudolf Streinz, 'Art. 21' in Hermann von Mangoldt, Friedrich Klein and Christian Starck (eds.), *Grundgesetz-Kommentar* 7th ed. (Munich: C. H. Beck, 2018) para. 123.

[61] This is true also for the legislature and judiciary, but due to the focus of this chapter, this is not further developed.

[62] Drefs, *Die Öffentlichkeitsarbeit des Staates* (n 3) p. 187 et seq.

A number of common goods are integrated into any constitution. They typically depend on the history and cultural background of the given state and may vary substantially from one state to another. For the purposes of this chapter, only the two most dominant interests will be explicitly taken into account: democracy and the rule of law. Both are essential pillars of a free society and the essence of state organizations, enabling far-reaching individual freedom and autonomy.[63] Thus, the democratic, rule-of-law-based state has a legitimate interest in self-preservation.[64]

Democracy establishes, among other things, the rule of the many over the few, while also including the protection of minority rights. As the minority of today can in theory become the majority of tomorrow, a democracy must protect minority groups within the population.[65] Human rights are an expression of this. Therefore, democracy and human rights are intertwined.[66] Democracy also installs the personnel of the state in a non-permanent way: Although civil servants may serve over the long term in order to assure a high professional quality of administrative decisions, the leaders of democratic institutions must be politically responsible – their positions are non-permanent and they must win elections on a regular basis, which serves as an instrument of control for the people.[67]

The other aspect which influences the actions of persons in official functions is the rule of law. Although the concept is fuzzy and is differently understood in different jurisdictions, the core concept is that of legality: the state is legally responsible for its actions and has to base its actions on legal grounds.[68] This is also closely connected to democratic values: while individuals may act freely and even arbitrarily, the democratic state has to act in accordance with the will of the people as expressed by the vote of the electorate and the institutions formed on this basis. Thus, the state may not act arbitrarily but is required to adhere to a minimum of rationalizability, if not rationality. Indra Spiecker genannt Döhmann, Staatliche Entscheidungen unter Unsicherheit (Tübingen: Mohr Siebeck, 2025, in print).

In addition, any democratic system depends on the freedom of elections. Elections are one of the main instruments by which the sovereign, the people,

[63] For democracy, see Horst Dreier, 'Art. 20 (Demokratie)' in Horst Dreier (ed.), *Grundgesetz-Kommentar* 3rd ed. (Tübigen: Mohr Siebeck, 2015) [Verfassungsprinzipien; Widerstandsrecht] para. 61; for the rule of law, see BVerfGE 144, 20 para. 547, and Hans Jarass, 'Art. 20' in Hans Jarass and Bodo Pieroth, *Grundgesetz für die Bundesrepublik Deutschland* 17th ed. (Munich: C. H. Beck, 2022) para. 37.

[64] See, in general, Helmut Rumpf, 'Die Staatsräson im demokratischen Rechtsstaat' (1980) 19(2) *Der Staat* 273.

[65] Indra Spiecker genannt Döhmann, 'Kontexte der Demokratie: Parteien – Medien – Sozialstrukturen' in *Fragmentierungen, 77 Veröffentlichungen der Vereinigung der Deutschen Staatsrechtslehrer* (Berlin: Walter de Gruyter, 2018) 9, at 24.

[66] Horst Dreier, *Dimensionen der Grundrechte: Von der Wertordnungsjudikatur zu den objektiv-rechtlichen Grundrechtsgehalten* (Hannover: Hennies & Zinkeisen, 1993) p. 54.

[67] Spiecker genannt Döhmann, 'Kontexte der Demokratie' (n 65), at 22 et seq.

[68] Very clearly so, see Grundgesetz (German Basic Law), Art. 20 s. 3.

and those enacting state power, the administration, are linked.[69] Every act of state power must be traceable to the will of the people and the government is answerable to them.[70] This requires fair elections, including both fairness during the campaign prior to the actual election and during the term of office.[71]

4.7.3 *Core Constitutional Requirements: Neutrality, Self-Restriction and Competence of Office as Balancing of Interests*

Both democracy and the rule of law affect the behaviour of persons acting in an official function, and they therefore also affect the informational output of state authorities and the means by which state authorities may communicate.

4.7.3.1 Competence and Self-Restriction

The most straightforward consequence of the rule of law is a requirement of competence: in a public function, state officials may only communicate with the public or selected people in their official function if they are competent to do so in regard to territory and content-wise.[72] A police officer in Minnesota may not, as a Minnesota police officer, criticize the actions of colleagues in Florida, not being competent to do so while fulfilling a public position in a different state. A New York hygiene law enforcement agency may not issue pictures of violations of hygiene laws in Vermont. This extends to substantial competence, not just territorial competence: a French police officer may not comment on the actions of the building authorities in the municipality as this is not the officer's material area of competence.

Democratic communication also includes elements of control, and communications about the actions of state authorities form an important part of this. Therefore, the matter of competence may allow for statements on comparable actions – for instance, whether a similar action as those of colleagues in Florida or Italy was legal under Minnesota or French law. However, such statements may not violate competence, so they must not give the impression that the authority which issues a statement is actively commenting on actions within the competence of another authority.

Also, there has to be a certain amount of self-restriction which goes back to the differentiation between the private and the public position, since even a statement

69 Paul Kirchhof and Josef Isensee, *Handbuch des Staatsrechts der Bundesrepublik Deutschland II* 3rd ed. (Heidelberg: C. F. Müller, 2003) § 24 para. 11; BVerfGE 83, 60, at 71 et seq.; Christoph Degenhart, *Staatsrecht I, Staatsorganisationsrecht* 38th ed. (Heidelberg: C. F. Müller, 2022) para. 28.

70 BVerfGE 83, 60, at 71 et seq.

71 BVerfGE 44, 125, at 152.

72 BVerfGE 44, 125, at 149; Tristan Barczak, 'Die parteipolitische Äußerungsbefugnis von Amtsträgern' 34 (2015) *Neue Zeitschrift für Verwaltungsrecht* 1014, at 1016 et seq.

made by a person working for a state authority who is obviously not competent in that field may, in the context of this authority be accorded special status because it derives from a state authority. As such, any public servant has a heightened responsibility not to abuse this natural authority of state officials.

The line may be fine when judging exact practical statements. However, in abstract terms, this line can be clearly construed: where an informative act exceeds the legal borders of the competence of the issuing state authority, be it territorial or substantial in nature, the statement is illegal regardless of its content. The principle of self-restriction is useful in doubtful cases: if in doubt, a state official should remain silent. Consequently, any communicative act crossing this line has to be recalled and any consequences addressed.

4.7.3.2 Duty to Rightful Information Responsibly Researched and Properly Monitored

A core element of state communication and information concerns the truth of the information to be distributed.[73] Again, the people can legitimately expect that when state officials claim a special authority in their field of expertise this is indeed the case. Democratic communication should be free of manipulation. In consequence, it can be expected that the executive only issues statements which are thoroughly researched, properly checked and are to the best of its knowledge 'right' and 'truthful',[74] or actually 'true'.[75] What is currently being discussed under headings such as 'fake news' or 'alternative news' is not a means of communication appropriate for the state or any of its officials.[76]

This does not require state authorities to only distribute information that is absolutely certain and undisputed, but in cases of uncertainty, reasonable doubts and at least an overview of the reasons for and sources of those doubts must be

[73] BVerfGE 105, 252 [57].

[74] Ibid. [58]; see also OVG Bremen, Order of 31 May 2021 – 1 B 150/21, NVwZ-RR 2021, 886 [15].

[75] The exact meaning of the word has been disputed: Plato in *Cratylus* already addressed the question whether there is a natural meaning of words, or the meaning of words is created by convention, see https://plato.stanford.edu/entries/word-meaning, s. 2.1. For further references to what truth is, see Rob Cover, Ashleigh Haw and Jay Daniel Thompson, 'What Is Fake News? Defining Truth, Fake News' in Rob Cover, Ashleigh Haw and Jay Daniel Thompson, *Digital Cultures: Technology, Populism and Digital Misinformation* (Bingley: Emerald, 2022) p. 18 et seq.

[76] For the purposes of this chapter and its character as an overview, the discussion on when fake news is fake will not be described further; see, e.g., Tschorr, 'Wenn der Staat Fake News verbreitet' (n 4), at 382 and 388 et seq.; Bernd Holznagel, 'Phänomen "Fake News" – Was ist zu tun?' (2018) 21 *Multimedia und Recht* 18; Thorsten Quandt et al., 'Fake News' in *The International Encyclopedia of Journalism Studies* (Hoboken: John Wiley & Sons, 2019) p. 1; Jessica Pepp, Eliot Michaelson and Rachel Katharine Sterken, 'What's New about Fake News' (2019) 16(2) *Journal of Ethics and Social Philosophy* 67; Cover, Haw and Thompson, 'What Is Fake News?' (n 76)

shared. Therefore, a European head of state could only claim that a national holiday ceremony attracted more people under their term of office than any other national holiday ceremony had to date if that claim was previously checked by accepted independent means, for example with pictures or police reports.

A further consequence of this is that the validity of informational statements has to be continuously monitored, as otherwise the information distributed would violate these standards. Even if a statement may be correct at the time of publication, as long as it is part of the official communication channels its ongoing correctness needs to be monitored and, if later found to be wrong or disputed, it must be corrected.[77] Information that is no longer accurate, because it is outdated for instance, may not be distributed except for historical or archival reasons. This increases the authority of the state and the quality of the information which it distributes to the public. For instance, a report on the hygiene standards of restaurants[78] in New York City's Theatre District in January 2022 displaying pictures of particular restaurants with their names would be a violation, as the city of New York's hygiene executive body could not claim that these were still true in July 2023 and thus there is no reason to continue to share that information. Similarly, if the above-mentioned head of state's claims about the unprecedented size of a ceremony on a national holiday were found to be inaccurate, they would have to inform the public about this, and certainly not repeat it – and ensure that others do not repeat it either.

4.7.3.3 Office, Not Person in Communication

The dominance of the public office (see Section 4.7.1) due to the democratic and rule-of-law impact on state communication also has consequences for the communicative power of the individual who holds an office in administration. As the office and the private person are intertwined,[79] the office may not be damaged by the actions of the individual. This is closely linked to the requirement of self-restraint mentioned above (Section 4.7.3.1).

Legal rules reducing the impact of the individual, private person and thus concentrating on the duties and responsibilities of the office exist in different manifestations throughout the entire law. Civil servants are restricted when undertaking commercial enterprises in order for them to concentrate on their public duties; any personal interest in a decision leads to the exclusion of officials from that

[77] Tobias Mast, *Staatsinformationsqualität* (Berlin: Duncker & Humblot, 2020) p. 270; for differentiating regarding warnings, see Bernd Tremml, 'Amtshaftung wegen behördlicher Warnungen nach dem Produktsicherheitsgesetz' (1997) 50 *Neue Juristische Wochenschrift* 2265, at 2271.

[78] For example, health inspection results for New York City's 27,000 restaurants can be found on ABCEats, www.nyc.gov/site/doh/services/restaurant-grades.page.

[79] BVerfG, 2 BvE 4/20, 2 BvE 5/20 [77].

decision; there are duties to act rationally and to present justifications for official decisions to avoid decisions driven by personal reasons. The personal interest – which can be financial, but which may also be otherwise motivated – shall not compromise the fairness of the procedure, so that there is a fair decision.[80] Behind all of these restrictions is the motive to restrict the impact of the private in the office and thus to require the individual to be subordinate to the public duty. Thus, trust in the democratic, rule-of-law-based, objectively and neutrally deciding state is fostered and the integrating and legitimizing function of the law is strengthened.[81]

In communication, the dominance of the office requires the private person to be separated from the official person. As a consequence, the general rule is that private communication with any impact on or relation to the administrative position has to remain private. In general, private communication with the public is not allowed, in order to avoid anything that the private person states being attributed to the office and the public service. This rule is applied in a flexible way depending on several factors, among them the significance, the likely level of public attention and the current relevance of the subject, as well as the importance of the office holder and the content and political charisma of the position. Thus, a head of state or the head of the migration office during a migration crisis is bound to a stricter division of private and public speech than a janitor in a public school or a clerk in a social security office, and an autobiographical recounting of one's time as the head of the Environmental Agency during an energy crisis may take place years after.

Thus, social media accounts in particular have to be restricted in their accessibility and moderated with clear and enforced rules not to transfer any of the contents of these private communications to anybody outside the private group. A secretary of state may have a private social media account, but may not use it as a public forum, even less announce the government's policy on the Ukraine war through it. Moreover, the secretary may subscribe to other – private or official – sites but may not comment on them because of their position. This restriction means that only an exclusive and select group of people who are in a private relationship with an official may have access to their private opinions. Confidentiality is thus obligatory for officials both as a sender and a receiver of messages.

Of course, officials are not completely restricted in their private communication because freedom of speech remains an important human right, as are similar rights such as the rights to assemble or to demonstrate. However, the content, the format or the style of their public intercourse may not interfere with their role as a civil servant or as part of the democratic establishment. Accordingly, it is possible to test whether interest in this communication would also exist if the person had no public position.

80 See Sophie Boyron and Wendy Lacey, 'Procedural Fairness Generally' in Tushnet, Fleiner and Saunders, *Routledge Handbook of Constitutional Law* (n 54) p. 267.

81 See Margarethe Schuler-Harms in Friedrich Schoch and Jens-Peter Schneider (eds.), *Verwaltungsrecht – Verwaltungsverfahrensgesetz* 3rd ed. (Munich: C. H. Beck, 2022) § 21 VwVfG mn. 2.

In one of the German Constitutional Court cases related to this issue, the secretary of interior gave an interview in which his stance towards a right-wing party was of special interest because as secretary of interior he also headed the police and security force as well as the secret service and the office for protection of the constitution. A light background biographical article ('homestory' in German) on a rancher running for governor is of public interest because of the insights into his personality and thus his eligibility for office (so some say). In the first example, the content is political in nature, and the person interviewed discusses another party while acting and speaking his official capacity. In the second case, the content is clearly private; therefore a 'homestory' fluff piece would only be possible to the extent that it introduces certain values to the public which will play a role in the position, otherwise it would be illegal.

Such boundaries exist not only during an official's term of office but also for period of time after leaving office – for instance, a politician being voted out or retiring – in order not to interfere with their successor's position. Again, it is the office that binds, and this binding power does not end immediately on leaving office, although this, of course, depends on the office. A head of state's assessment of decisions will be of common historical interest even years after their retirement while the common interest in a janitor's assessment of an office building ends shortly after his change of jobs.

4.7.3.4 Objectivity

Similarly, a mixture of rule of law and democratic principles requires that officials do not exploit the power of their office and the easy access they enjoy to the public. Objectivity and calmness are thus deemed fitting for this style of communication. This derives from the democratic feature of equal access to information and the requirement of a fair democratic discourse. The fact that an official takes part in the democratic exchange has to be diminished in its effects, and objectivity is one important tool to achieve this. A person in a public office typically has advantages in communication for at least two reasons: for one, they speak with the power of the office.[82] Therefore, it can be expected that anyone hearing or reading those statements will pay special attention to the information.[83]

82 'Authority of the Office', see BVerfG, Judgment of 27 February 2018 – 2 BvE 1/16, [39]; 52, English version: www.bundesverfassungsgericht.de/SharedDocs/Entscheidungen/EN/2018/02/es20180227_2bve000116en.html; Hans-Jürgen Papier and Meinhard Schröder, 'Verfassungsrechtliche Grenzen kommunaler Publikationen' 132 (2017) *Deutsches Verwaltungsblatt* 1, at 5. Compare Hinderks, 'Staatliche Kommunikation' (n 3), at 35, who criticizes this as a 'blanket insinuation', citing further references.

83 BVerfG, 2 BvE 1/16 [64]–[66]; Sebastian Nellesen, *Äußerungsrechte staatlicher Funktionsträger* (Tübingen: Mohr Siebeck, 2019) p. 21.

The second advantage worth examining for the purposes of this chapter derives from the competitive situation in a state just prior to elections: the incumbent has advantages over any competitor, being able to demonstrate practical ability and suitability for the official position. The incumbent is much more prominent in the public discussion because of the office, which enables more frequent and effective communication with the public. State resources in terms of personnel, technology, media and finance are available and can have a lasting impact on the formation of the political will – this involves the risk of distorting the competition between the political parties.[84] The incumbent can also act and publicize strategically.[85] Thus, communication by a person in office should be performed in a manner that lets the office, not the person speak. Self-promotion has to be avoided; objectivity ought to be the typical style of communication.

4.7.3.5 Neutrality

Democracy enables continuous change in personnel *and* in political positions. This hinders the accumulation of power over time and to certain persons as well as helping to avoid irreversible decisions.[86] It thus demands restrictions on the actions of persons in office in order to ensure the change in persons, thoughts and positions. In principle, such a change is only possible if those in charge and who work in the executive branch actively contribute to the possibility of their own disengagement. This is – from an individual perspective, in particular from a rational choice theory point of view – against the individual's best interest, which is to remain in the position. Therefore, a law that enables and sustains the democratic state needs to create institutional arrangements to allow for such smooth transitions. Continuous financial contributions for politicians after their removal from office is one instrument, along with their status as a civil servant, which enables individual security while at the same time requiring high flexibility. Civil service systems in particular are designed to promote independence.[87]

In more general terms, the institutional arrangement has to be one that hinders the incumbent from using their position to actively restrict competitors. State authorities and their officials may not use the power and position of their office to improve their own political situation, the situation of a candidate of their party or their interests in general.[88] Any activity by which office holders exploit their position

[84] BVerfG, 2 BvE 2/14 [46].

[85] Hinderks, 'Staatliche Kommunikation' (n 3), at 36; Mast, *Staatsinformationsqualität* (n 78) p. 102.

[86] Democracy also means ruling for a certain time, see Dreier in Dreier, *Grundgesetz-Kommentar* (n 63) para. 73; Bodo Pieroth, 'Das Demokratieprinzip des Grundgesetzes' (2010) *Juristische Schulung* 473, at 479; Spiecker genannt Döhmann, 'Kontexte der Demokratie' (n 65) at 18 et seq.

[87] See McLean and Tushnet, 'Administrative Bureaucracy' (n 56), at 125.

[88] BVerfG, 2 BvE 4/20, 2 BvE 5/20 [73] and [74].

in the administration must be avoided. Rules against corruption and beyond, especially against partiality, are a typical set of instruments to achieve this, which can also be interpreted as a means to protect the personal integrity of the person in the position and thus may also be in their best interests. In regard to communication, this means that officials must refrain from any direct evaluation of their competitor's practices, such as commenting actively on the campaigns of other parties. The examples within some of the German Constitutional Court decisions illustrate this: a secretary of interior is first and foremost the secretary of interior. They may not use the power of their office to denounce a political party on the department's official webpage, in an interview or through their private, but widely accessible social media account.

4.7.3.6 No Direct Influence of Administrative Staff in Electoral Campaigns

Officials are often connected and intertwined with political parties: the likelihood of being selected to many positions, especially political ones, is influenced by the party affiliation of the candidates, and success in elections often depends on party affiliation. Parties, as the mediators between the public and the state,[89] frequently influence the selection process, sometimes even directly determining the candidates and office holders, certainly when appointing people to leading positions. Thus, any election leads to a change in personnel. Even if a governing party remains in office, elections typically trigger a round of new appointments, changes to positions, retirements and removals from office. Such changes in personnel may often have already started prior to an election because those who foresee changes and thus fear the loss of their positions protect their own interests by securing an alternative professional future for themselves.[90]

Any administration relies on competent staff to produce high-quality decisions. Competency, among other factors, grows with education, specific knowledge and experience. Networks and connections play a role in the success of projects. Thus, the highest and most exposed positions in the administration, especially in government, are typically considered to be 'political' positions prone to political change. This is usually legally and factually enabled through non-permanent civil servant status, straightforward procedures for the dissolution of contracts and the retraction of positions. To counterbalance the resulting personal instability in leading administrative positions, salaries are high and the positions promise power, a leadership

[89] So explicitly the German Constitution, see Jarass, 'Art. 21' in Jarass and Pieroth, *Grundgesetz für die Bundesrepublik Deutschland* (n 63) s. 1; the German Constitutional court stated that political parties are 'intermediaries between individuals and state authorities' in BVerfGE 44, 125, at 145; Spiecker genannt Döhmann, 'Kontexte der Demokratie' (n 65), at 25 et. seq.

[90] Emanuel Towfigh and Niels Petersen, '§ 6: Public Choice Theory' in Towfigh and Petersen, *Ökonomische Methoden im Recht* (n 50) para. 333.

position and the potential of influence on government decisions, including agenda-setting power.

Even though most administrative systems in democracies establish only a very limited number of political positions that are prone to change due to elections, this nevertheless also influences lower positions: During their time in office, politically unproblematic or aligned persons usually have easier access to career positions and thus rise in the hierarchy, drawing with them other, lower positions. As the head of a department, an agency or any administrative body drafts the guidelines of this institution and defines its core focus, the selection of personnel as well as the content and the direction of impact of the administration's decisions is potentially influenced by political interests, typically party positions and party networks.

This political dimension of the administration and thus the potential conflicts need to be reflected in the boundaries set for statements by state authorities. The functionalities of democracy – especially the potential for change – demand this. Any person working in the executive branch has to be aware that any statement in the course and competence of their office will not only be attributed to the democratic state as such, but also reflect the status of fairness among the political parties. This connection is heightened the more exposed within a political party or a political office someone is and the closer an election is. Again, position (both in the administration and a political party), timing, content, context and exposure matter. Thus, a head of state must refrain from actions and statements which may have a direct impact on an election and a direct connection to their party's campaign, while the head of an environmental municipal department does not have to be so careful. A secretary of state who is also the head of a political party has to restrict their statements close to the elections in one of the states in a federal state.

4.7.4 *Intermediate Conclusion*

The Constitutional Perspective shows that a framework for state authority communication exists: The public office overrides the private person in public communication; this condition demands a balancing of the freedom of speech of the official with the individual rights that may potentially be infringed as well as the requirements of fostering democracy and the rule of law as the most prominent and pressing state-preserving common interests.

4.8 THE CONSTITUTIONAL PERSPECTIVE: THE PRINCIPLE OF PROPORTIONALITY AND ITS SPECIFICATIONS

These general guidelines, however, can be defined even more specifically when taking into account further constitutional requirements, first and foremost the principle of proportionality.

4.8.1 *General Understanding of Balancing of Interests or Principle of Proportionality*

Most democratic, rule-of-law-based constitutional regimes involve something similar to the principle of proportionality. It is typically part of any constitutional testing of state measures. The principle of proportionality, in all its variations, provides an additional barrier for justified infringements of human rights and constitutional principles. In the final analysis, it provides for a standard test for the instruments the state uses to achieve a particular legally valid goal.

The modern form of the principle probably originates from German law. There, it has blossomed since the early twentieth century, with its legal foundation as early as the late eighteenth century in Prussian police law.[91] By now it has been developed into a four-step test[92] which assesses the legality of the means and the goals of a law or an administrative action and tests, in its fourth step, the relationship between them. This fourth step is in essence a balancing-of-interests test, in which the legal weight of the state's goal is evaluated in the light of the infringements and legal consequences for individual interests. In the course of extensive practice of this test in the courts, a fine-tuned assessment of the balance between goals and means has been established, including procedural safeguards.[93]

Within the EU, the principle was first applied as a test of approximation. The European Court of Justice (ECJ) in particular typically only tested whether the goal of the common good and the infringements arising from applying the legal instrument were not completely disproportionate.[94] Only in the more recent past has the

[91] Michael Sachs, 'Art. 20', in Michael Sachs (ed.), *Grundgesetz – Kommentar* 9th ed. (Munich: C. H. Beck, 2021), para. 145; Andreas Voßkuhle, 'Grundwissen – Öffentliches Recht: Der Grundsatz der Verhältnismäßigkeit' (2007) *Juristische Schulung* 429; Moshe Cohen-Eliya and Iddo Porat, *Proportionality and Constitutional Culture* (Cambridge: Cambridge University Press, 2013) p. 24 et seq. Often, the Magna Charta Libertatum of 1215 is cited as the first written source, and also that the ancient Greeks were familiar with the principle, see, e.g., Karl-Peter Sommermann, 'Art. 20', in Mangoldt, Klein and Starck, *Grundgesetz-Kommentar* (n 60) para. 309; Eric Engle, 'The History of the General Principle of Proportionality: An Overview' (2012) 10(1) *Dartmouth Law Journal* 1, at 2; Bartosz Makowicz, 'Das Prinzip der Verhältnismäßigkeit – ein Strukturvergleich zwischen deutschem und polnischem Recht' (2010) 56 *Osteuropa-Recht* 167, at 168.

[92] For German law, see Sachs, *Grundgesetz – Kommentar* (n 92), at 149; for a more general perspective, see Cohen-Eliya and Porat, *Proportionality* (n 92) p. 17.

[93] See Andrej Lang, 'Der Verhältnismäßigkeitsgrundsatz in der Rechtsprechung des Bundesverfassungsgerichts – Eine rechtsempirische Untersuchung mit rechtsvergleichenden Perspektiven' (2020) 145 *Archiv des öffentlichen Rechts* 75 (the article includes an English summary); Mathias Dumbs, 'Der Grundsatz der Verhältnismäßigkeit in der Rechtsprechung des Bundesverfassungsgerichts' (2016) 131 *Deutsches Verwaltungsblatt* 691.

[94] For example, in Case 104-75, *Adriaan de Peijper*, preliminary ruling, judgment of 20 May 1976; see Tor-Inge Harbo, 'The Function of the Proportionality Principle in EU Law' (2010) 16 *European Law Journal* 158, at 174; Bernhard Oreschnik, *Verhältnismäßigkeit und Kontrolldichte: Eine Analyse der Rechtsprechung des EuGH zu den Grundrechten und Grundfreiheiten* (Wiesbaden: Springer, 2019) p. 79.

ECJ sharpened the standard in a more complex way to increase its resemblance to the German dogmatic approach, in particular by assessing more closely the exact configuration of infringements and thus establishing more refined tests of the balancing of interests.[95]

Although the US law explicitly addresses the principle of proportionality only infrequently, many of the judicial standards by which infringements caused by law or administrative action are tested show great similarities to the European understanding of the principle of proportionality.[96] Although the standards may differ, the general idea of a refined requirement for the balancing of interests that is enforced by a court is present in US law, as it also is in many other jurisdictions. Consequently, the principle of proportionality needs to be adhered to when the state authorities communicate with the public or others. Of course, considering the breadth of state communication and its different formats, styles, framing, context, history and content (see Section 4.2), each test carried out according to the principle of proportionality will produce different results depending on the individual constitutional and legal setting. Therefore, the following individualized manifestations are naturally approximations of what the exact framework could be. They cannot take into account the particular characteristics of a specific constitutional regime. However, they do drive stakes into the ground which democratic, rule-of-law-based nations would generally agree on and which thus constitute a common ground to start from.

The following remarks take into account the core elements of the matrix regarding the person communicating, the office or position held by the person, the format, the time frame, the specific characteristics of the information and the consequences of releasing it. With these cornerstones, the principle of proportionality or any balancing-of-interest test can be brought to life and tailor-made for the individual circumstances.

4.8.2 *Inability to Retract Information or Irreversibility of Disclosure*

Information is a special good. Among other features, it can be classified as a common good in the economic sense – that is, a good that does not involve competition for resources and which it is also difficult to restrict access to.[97] Although this is not always the case – for example, it is not true of secrets – it is

[95] Oreschnik, *Verhältnismäßigkeit* (n 95) p. 80; Eckhard Pache, 'Der Grundsatz der Verhältnismäßigkeit in der Rechtsprechung der Gerichte der Europäischen Gemeinschaften' (1999) 18 *Neue Zeitschrift für Verwaltungsrecht* 1033, at 1034. For a more general overview see Engle, 'The History' (n 92), at 8.

[96] The similar doctrine used in US law is 'balancing'. Balancing can be found to be similar to the principle of proportionality. Cohen-Eliya and Porat, *Proportionality* (n 92) p. 17 et seq., show similarities and analytical differences.

[97] For example, Spiecker genannt Döhmann, '§ 23: Informationsverwaltungsrecht' (n 20) para. 31; Roger A. McCain, 'Information as Property and as a Public Good: Perspectives from the

useful to understand that once information is 'out' it can hardly be retrieved and reversed. A scandal cannot be erased from the public memory once the information it was based on is found out. Once information is saved in a person's memory it cannot easily be unlearned. While the – wrong – information about a lioness walking through a European capital, supposedly captured on amateur video footage, may attract many reactions on social and classical media, the information that the animal in question was probably a boar is viewed and digested much less often. Thus, wrong information is frequently not retracted and remains believed by many earlier recipients, especially when conveyed in a sensational way. The impact factor of information is thus uncontrollable and needs to be generally considered as high.

As state information and state communication typically has a special impact and authority (see at Section 4.3), any information released by the state consequently needs to be especially carefully researched and tested before being distributed (see also Section 4.7.3.2): its authenticity and source, as well as its fact-oriented and science-based nature are core requirements prior to its disclosure in order to minimize the risk of infringement of those who are impacted by it. Beyond this, however, the special qualities of information – and consequently of communication – also require officials to consider the far-reaching consequences of information distribution: As retraction is hardly possible and immaterial damages are the only feasible recompense, following the release of wrong information, the use of the wrong style or wrongful communication one can never fully re-establish the status quo ante. This additionally strengthens the duties to maintain neutrality, objectivity and self-restraint (see Sections 4.7.3.1, 4.7.3.4 and 4.7.3.5).

4.8.3 *Procedural Safeguards: Right to Hearing*

Proportionality often requires countermeasures to restrict the legal impact of a measure. Procedure is often used to diminish the weight of infringements at the substantive law level. It can also be employed in communicative settings. One core element of procedure is the right to a hearing. The following remarks concentrate on this procedural element because it is little recognized when discussing the boundaries of state communication. In some legal regimes this right has a constitutional rank, for example as part of the due-process clause of the US Constitution[98] or as part of the rule of law under the German Constitution.[99] However, even without any constitutional foundation of its own, the potential impact of informational measures on individuals is such that it typically requires an executive body

Economic Theory of Property Rights' (1988) 58(3) *The Library Quarterly: Information, Community, Policy* 265, at 271 and 278.

98 In the recent past, this started with *Goldberg* v. *Kelly*, 397 US 254 (1970); see Henry J. Friendly, 'Some Kind of Hearing' (1975) 123 *University of Pennsylvania Law Review* 1265, at 1267.

99 BVerfGE 9, 89, at 95; Sachs, *Grundgesetz – Kommentar* (n 92) 163.

to grant a legal hearing to those who would be affected by the planned release of information to the public.

A legal hearing often constitutes a less infringing means in comparison to informing the public right away. This, of course, depends greatly on the goal which is pursued by the information and the exact context. If the information aims at inciting a particular action from individuals, it might be similarly effective to inform those individuals themselves rather than the general public. This is particularly true in cases of "shaming" (see Section 4.8.4). However, a right to a hearing may also have the desired effect in other areas. For example, in competition law cases, informing the public that a particular market situation is now officially being observed because there are grounds for investigating potential violations of the law would not be necessary if the competition agency informed the relevant actors that their behaviour is being scrutinized and this causes reactions to their commercial behaviour.

This again underlines how volatile state information can be and how strictly it must be checked and evaluated before being published (see Section 4.7.3): even the fact of being named in an investigation might influence public opinion about those named, with potentially severe consequences, such as loss of reputation or loss of business. This also has consequences for the right to a hearing: being informed about the intention of the state to name a person or company may make them refrain from activities that, were they taken to court, would be considered to be legal. The mere threat of publicity takes its toll on private action.

In any case, legal hearings allow the private entity or person to participate in the state communication themselves. It gives them the chance to interact with the officials and to influence the state authority's decision to communicate with the public. It might also bring to light additional information that was not available to the administration, which may influence its further actions. In addition, it allows the private entity or person to deploy countermeasures – for example, to prepare for the expected attention being drawn to them. If a warning is issued about particular products, the producer may take measures to communicate itself, or to recall those products from the market on a large scale, even prior to the announcement by the authorities. Thus, the – unwanted – effects on the market of business-related state information may be levelled out and potential dangers better assessed and counteracted, which is in the best interests of all. Exceptions to a procedural safeguard of the right to hearing exist, of course. This may especially be the case if prior information would hinder the successful achievement of the goals of releasing the information (for example, in a search), or if a rapid reaction (for instance, fake news going viral) is necessary.

4.8.4 *Reduction of Content*

Often, public statements include information about private persons or institutions. One way to lessen the risk of infringing is typically to exclude this particular piece of information, to anonymize the person or to generalize the details so that identification of the individual is more difficult or even impossible. Thus, the negative side effects of an informational measure might be avoided. Typical public relations or transparency measures which aim at informing the public about the activities of the administration fall into this category.

This, of course, would only be employed if the information about the exact situation and private persons and institutions is not vital to the goal of publication. This requires a careful assessment of what the goal behind a communication measure involving an official truly is. Therefore, the communicative measures of officials have to be judged while bearing in mind the potential private interests that could interfere with democratic and public interests: only a public goal may justify infringements on third-party interests, and thus the requirements may only be suspended after full consideration. An example of this is the interview situation: it is expected that a politician will declare their political ambitions and convictions. An interview is a legitimate means to fulfil this – private – goal. It is also a legitimate – public – goal to inform the public about the measures their department has taken and the results which the strategy pursued by the office has had. In general, however, a 'homestory' involves too much – private – information.

The exact circumstances such as the context and content and the position of the speaker have to be taken into account: for anyone who is in a non-elected position in the government, no reason exists why the public would need to know this information. However, for a person in an office that is closely linked to elections, a certain amount of knowledge about the person might be appropriate to help inform the public about their qualities. However, an interview or biographical piece set in a person's home, concentrating on creating an image of a sympathetic individual would go too far and disclose too much – private – information about the person behind the office. This, again, reflects the fine line between desirable transparency and non-legal display of the private which requires close consideration of what is being published. There may be a legal interest in giving citizens easy access to those serving the state and allowing them to easily monitor them, but it may not be used to display the private as a private goal hidden behind the state communication.

4.8.5 *Shaming and Purposeful Public Disclosure*

Aspects of the disclosure of information in general, such as transparency or monitoring, have to be distinguished from cases where information is disclosed with the intention of putting social pressure on a person or institution, by so-called shaming.[100] Information released by one public official about another public official

[100] See David A. Skeel, Jr., 'Shaming in Corporate Law' (2001) 149 *University of Pennsylvania Law Review* 1811; Sharon Yadin, 'Regulatory Shaming' (2019) 49(2) *Environmental Law* 407; Judith van Erp, 'Shaming and Compliance' in Benjamin van Rooij and D. Daniel Sokol (eds.), *The Cambridge Handbook on Compliance* (Cambridge: Cambridge University Press, 2021) ch. 30, pp. 438–50.

may also fall into this category, especially in times of election campaigns where one competitor or one party tries to discredit their opponent or another party.

First, when describing the legal framework for such state communications, the boundaries (such as objectivity, neutrality, and so on; see Sections 4.7.3.4. and 4.7.3.5) are fully binding. Second, the principle of proportionality additionally governs the use of the release of specific information which informs the public about wrongdoing by private persons or companies: as information is not retrievable, especially given the functionalities of the Internet ('the Internet never forgets'), the social stigma a person or institution receives through this directed negative public attention should not be underestimated. The principle of 'innocent until proven guilty' also puts additional pressure on the state to justify why public shaming is still a permissible means of administrative action in the twenty-first century prior to adjudicated convictions.

4.8.6 *The Format*

Surprisingly little attention has been paid to the effects of different formats of communication, despite it having immediate consequences for the exact balance between the legal interests involved. A press communique released to media professionals differs greatly in its effects from an interview to a broadcaster lasting a maximum of three minutes. An advisory opinion issued by a specified agency authored by leading scientists after a months-long process may claim to have higher relevance, thoroughness and validity than a 120-character post on social media. Information provided by the EPA on an altered process to calculate the impact of certain chemicals addresses (and reaches) a different clientele than a report about the president 'pardoning' a turkey at Thanksgiving. A warning about an imminent thunderstorm on the radio has to be analysed by different standards of format (and context and content) than the information that the president will be serving Moselle Riesling 'Piesporter Goldtröpfchen' (Golden Drop of Piesport) wine from a particular vineyard, as printed on the menu card of a state dinner.

This is not the place to analyse the different means by which state authorities may communicate with the public and how information that is aimed at certain groups (for example, professionals, the guest at a state dinner, students) may be framed. The examples merely illustrate that different aspects must be considered when judging the impact of how the state authorities release information and the varying effects of their use of certain media. Publication theory and communication theory need to assist the law to find the relevant standards; the law, even if clear standards are yet to be finalized, nevertheless has to address this.

4.8.7 *Equality of Information Access*

One distinct aspect is the use of various media outlets, or, if viewed from another perspective, the requirement of public officials to make information accessible to all media on equal terms. This means that although state authorities may prefer specific formats, they have to ensure that all the media has access and that no particular private media outlet is considered to be the dominant source of information. A typical format, therefore, should be publication of information by the executive through its own channels – that is, via press conferences (post-COVID also in a hybrid format) or press statements, as well as information on official webpages. Interviews may be selective, but may not be given exclusively to certain journalists. The use of social media has to be legal and open to everyone (which excludes some platforms that violate data protection laws through micro-targeting or which are not accessible if a reader is not registered).

4.8.8 *The Timing*

The proximity of elections heightens the requirements on the principle of proportionality as the need to ensure the fairness of elections comes into effect. Issuing potentially misleading information, which at any time is difficult to justify, must be avoided even more at such times.[101] Defamatory judgements by high-ranking politicians about their opponents are particularly harmful, as are false or misleading news stories. Photographs of a meeting between two high officials of the Secretary of Treasury with a leading bank's officials during a financial crisis may have a different impact on the public prior to an election than the same people meeting in a period of financial stability. It may then be imperative not only to publish the photograph, which would leave ample room for speculation, but to explain the content and results of this meeting.

4.8.9 *Intermediate Conclusion*

The principle of proportionality sharpens the general balancing of interests. Due to its different manifestations under different legislation, the exact weighing of interests may lead to different results. Procedural safeguards, restrictions on the distribution of information due to the irreversibility of information release, care when providing direct information about private persons and companies, and a more informed approach to the various media outlets of public communication are some of the outcomes of using this test.

4.9 COMMUNICATION AS A PROCESS: THE RIGHT TO COUNTERATTACK

In theory, administration typically initiates active communication. In practice, executive bodies are constantly reacting to societal discussions and political

[101] BVerfGE 44, 125, at 151 and 153.

currents.[102] Society and administration are in a continuous relationship. The executive is not, however, faced by one people with one voice and one opinion in one format. While some citizens may send emails and post individualized statements on the Internet, others use simpler means of expressing their opinion, such as 'like buttons' or clicks or sharing links and reposting on social media. All of these expressions form part of a digitalized democratic exchange of information and opinions and thus lead to a renewed relationship between the administration and the people.

While the rules for neutrality, objectivity, disinterestedness, and so on, of political bodies have in general been well established (see Sections 4.7.3.4 and 4.7.3.5), the debate on what constitutes private rules of public communication is presently still raging. The most hotly discussed topics in this debate include whether hate speech can be banned in the light of freedom of speech and how a civilized discourse can proceed in an era of digitalized communication. Moreover, the regulation of private information intermediaries, in particular on the Internet, is still incomplete. In the EU, important legal rules have been established, among them the Network Enforcement Act (*Netzwerkdurchsetzungsgesetz*) in Germany or the Digital Services Act of the EU. These regulatory impulses have been shadowed by rising right-wing and populist movements, which have had surprising success on both sides of the Atlantic despite historical experiences, in particular in Europe, with extremist and fascist parties.

These developments influence public discourse not only between individuals and private entities, but also between the state authorities and the public. The increase in potentially offensive language and the speed of communication and unforgiving nature of the Internet, best represented by 'shitstorms', are also used to judge and comment on administrative action. On the other hand, political activists and state officials have been interacting in a wider variety of formats; one of the most highlighted effects of the Internet and social media is the direct access of the people to their representatives in administration.[103]

It is thus an important question whether the framework of state communication as described undergoes changes if we are evaluating official statements as part of a communication process rather than one singular act. An example where the analysis of state action covers a process would be when a member of a political party aggressively comments on the decision of an administrative agency using untrue facts to smear it ('fake news'). Another example would be offensive speech used in an anonymous post on a social media network directed against the head of an administrative agency which attracts thousands of 'likes' or other agreeing posts and clicks over several hours. In both instances, the framework thus created would require

[102] For example, the statement of the Federal Minister of Education and Research (see Section 4.5.5) was a reaction to an assembly of the 'red-wing' party, using the same expression towards the then chancellor ('Rote Karte für Merkel' – 'red flag for Merkel'), see BVerfGE 148, 11.

[103] See Spiecker genannt Döhmann, 'Kontexte der Demokratie' (n 65), at 28, for political parties, see also p. 39 with further references.

neutrality, objectivity and self-restraint – which would restrict the response of the authorities. Considering a statement as an answer or a direct response might, however, change the binding elements of the framework.

An administrative agency in this situation could post correcting statements. It could also issue a statement on netiquette and on the inappropriateness of the original postings. However, the effort would most probably not be very successful, and not gain much attention. The administration could look weak, while the response would be seen as inadequate. Would a post on behalf of the agency ridiculing the language of the author of the post together with a correcting message on the wrong content be appropriate? Could the agency make – albeit to a lesser degree than the aggressor – pointed remarks? According to the principle of objectivity and self-restraint, this would hardly seem appropriate. However, one could argue that the democratic exchange of arguments needs to take into account that the relationship is not determined by one side only and that the history of a communicative relationship influences the standard of neutrality, self-restriction and so on.

Without applying to this problem the in-depth analysis it would need, as a starting point this chapter argues that communication functions in a sender–receiver process, especially when it is individualized. Thus, state authorities act on the basis of this relationship. If the state initiates the communication, thus acting first, then the communication has to adhere strictly to all the criteria described earlier. If, however, there is an individualized communicative process, some of the standards may undergo modifications to reflect the relationship and the process in order to communicate authentically. If the private sender acts in a fair, friendly, rational, non-discriminatory and non-defamatory manner, the state is strictly bound. If, however, the private actor has previously and blatantly violated the rules of fair conduct first, that is, by distributing inaccurate information, using hate speech or aggressive speech against the state, threatening or incriminating core democratic and human rights values and the like, then the framework alters because the balancing of interests alters. The decisive legal factors in this respect are the common good interests in democracy and the rule of law that any state official is bound by. State officials are required to protect those values and must become active defenders of democracy not only in their actions (such as by defending the parliament against violators) but more frequently in words. An ironic or even sarcastic response that discredits the private offender may then be in order.[104] Other relevant

[104] The German Constitutional Court changed its opinion on this matter: in an earlier decision, the Court agreed (BVerfGE 40, 287 (293 f)), however, in the 'red-flag' decision the Court explicitly rejected a right to counterattack, see BVerfGE 148, 11 para. 60. See, as here, but with a different argument, Christoph Degenhart, 'Der Staat im freiheitlichen Kommunikationsprozess: Funktionsträgerschaft, Funktionsschutz und Funktionsbegrenzung' 41 (2010) *Archiv für Presserecht* 324, at 331. On the latest Constitutional Court decision, see Mast, *Staatsinformationsqualität* (n 78) p. 215 et seq; Matthias Friehe, 'Anmerkung zu BVerfG, Urt. v. 27.2.2018, 2 BvE 1/16' (2018) 11 *Neue Juristische Wochenschrift* 928.

circumstances, however, such as timing, opaqueness, publicity, speed of distribution and position, would also have to be considered.

4.10 CONCLUSION AND OUTLOOK

As always, a right without sanctions and enforcement is of little value and is a 'toothless tiger'. Not only does state communication need a legal framework; it must also be one that is enforceable and will thus be adhered to. Otherwise, the incentives to violate neutrality, objectivity and fairness and to let the conflict between office and person work to the advantage of the person and the detriment of the office would be too strong. At the risk of being repetitive, it is important to stress that information can rarely be retrieved, and that a violation of privacy or wrongful dissemination of information can hardly ever be fully compensated for. Therefore, damages and other sanctions post-violation are of scarcely any use. Information is a powerful tool of the state, and it is also a powerful tool for private interests hidden behind the public face of those in office and serving the state.

Therefore, a democratic society, based on rule of law needs to clearly define the standards of communication by state authorities in all its facets. Despite the many distinctive characteristics of and differences between different jurisdictions and legal regimes, the common impetus of democracy and the rule of law, of fairness of elections and protection of human rights leads to the emergence of a general framework. The dominance of the public over the private, which requires private interests of public officials to be subordinated to the public good is an important consequence of this. Requirements of competence, impartiality and self-restraint should be taken into consideration in a general balancing of interests. The principle of proportionality, in its essence, requires procedural safeguards, reduction of the scope of content and individualization, care in sharing direct personal information, distinguishing between media outlets and treating them equally, and attention to framing, context and timing.

What is also needed is a change in the juridical system in order to ensure that these legal requirements are not futile. The procedural problem is a common obstacle to this. Violations of the established requirements can be brought before courts only if there is an interested party that has full standing. This is typically the case if individual rights are violated, but that is often difficult to prove, for example in hate speech or in the discriminatory impact of state communication on groups. Violations of the neutrality of media are hard to identify. These violations, as has been shown, nevertheless have severe effects on the democratic, respectful, civil discourse and thus on the acceptance and health of democracy. Therefore, informational misconduct needs procedural systems to move beyond the traditional comprehension of status in order to restrict the power of those in office and in charge of state action.

In addition to procedural problems, clear sanctions must be spelled out on both the institutional and individual levels. If in a conflict between the office and the person the person prevails despite all the other legal requirements, then not only the office but also the person has to be held responsible for any wrongdoing. Damages and sanctions must be regulated accordingly, including in special situations where information incites third parties. This will help us to understand and establish that information is not per se less infringing or that it typically has little power. The opposite is true: information is surprisingly powerful, and one of the reasons is that the power of information is hard to establish beforehand. What messages the public may assimilate from state communication and what it may not is often unpredictable. This unpredictability demands particularly careful and cautious acts on the part of the state authorities, and particular self-restraint from all those in a political or public office. Only thus can democratic values survive, one of the most important of which seeks to enable the fair representation of all opinions regardless of whether or not they are stated by those with access to power.

5

Public Officials' Lies and Their Effects on the Proliferation of Disinformation

Another Way to Approach the Crisis

Eduardo Bertoni

5.1 INTRODUCTION

State responses to the recent 'crisis' caused by misinformation in social media have mainly aimed to impose liability on those who facilitate its dissemination.[1] Internet companies, especially large platforms, have deployed numerous techniques, measures and instruments to address the phenomenon.[2] However, little has been done to assess the importance of who originates disinformation and, in particular, whether some originators of misinformation are acting contrary to their preexisting obligations to the public.[3] My view is that it would be wrong to attribute only to social

The research for this chapter began in 2021 under the coordination of Agustina del Campo, Director of the Centro de Estudios en Libertad de Expresión y Acceso a la Información of University of Palermo. A different version was then drafted and published in Spanish. See 'La mentira de los funcionarios, ¿tiene patas cortas o efectos largos?', https://dspace.palermo.edu/dspace/bitstream/handle/10226/2337/Desinformacion-y-funcionarios-publicos.pdf?sequence=1&isAllowed=y. This chapter is a new and revised version that includes the feedback and comments provided during the workshop organized by the Global Freedom Program of Columbia University on 27 April 2023, and during the workshop hosted by the National Public Service University's Information Society Project, in Budapest, on 9 June 2023. Special thanks to my colleagues Charlotte J. Garden, Ronald Krotoszynski and András Koltay for their comments.

1 See Agustina Del Campo, *¿La desinformación en democracia o la democracia de la desinformación?* CELE, 2020, www.palermo.edu/Archivos_content/2021/cele/papers/Disinformation-in-democracy%20(2).pdf.

2 See, for example, Carlos Cortes and Luisa Isaza, *Noticias falsas en Internet: la estrategia para combatir la desinformación*, CELE, 2017, www.palermo.edu/cele/pdf/FakeNews.pdf; see also Carlos Cortes and Luisa Isaza, *¿La nueva normalidad? Desinformación y control de contenidos en las redes sociales con ocasión del covid-19*, CELE, 2021, www.palermo.edu/Archivos_content/2021/cele/papers/Moderacion-Covid-19.pdf; Álvarez Ugarte and Agustina Del Campo, *Noticias falsas en Internet: acciones y reacciones de tres plataformas*, CELE, 2021, www.palermo.edu/Archivos_content/2021/cele/papers/Desinformacion-y-acciones-de-plataformas-2021.pdf.

3 Among the few initiatives in this regard, in 2018 a bill was presented in the Chilean Congress aimed at incorporating a reform to Arts. 27, 60 and 15 of the Chilean National Constitution to

media a central or exclusive role in the new disinformation crisis that impacts the information ecosystem.[4] I also believe that disinformation has different effects depending on who promotes it – particularly whether it is promoted by a person with a public role. Importantly, the law of many countries already reflects this distinction – across a variety of contexts, public officials are obligated both to affirmatively provide certain types of information, and to take steps to ensure that information is true. In contrast, private individuals rarely bear analogous obligations; instead, law often protects their misstatements, in order to prevent censorship and promote public discourse.

This chapter analyzes the obligations of public officials and electoral candidates to refrain from spreading disinformation and misinformation, in light of the legal obligations that loom over officials expressing themselves in the exercise of their office. To this end, Section 5.2 reviews Cass Sunstein's 'taxonomy' of falsehoods, a useful tool for research on this topic. Section 5.3 draws on moral philosophy to discuss the particular harms that misstatements cause when the speaker is a public official. Then, the chapter turns to the Inter-American System, showing how that system, like the laws of various Latin American countries, already distinguishes between public officials and private citizens in criminal and administrative law, and codes of public ethics. Finally, I call for approaches to the problem of misinformation that focus on its origins, highlighting the obligations of public officials and emphasizing the role and duty of the government to avoid the proliferation of disinformation.

determine the cessation of the office of president, parliamentarians and other officials (respectively) when they have been convicted as perpetrators, accomplices or abettors in the dissemination, promotion or financing of false news about their electoral opponents during the campaign from the moment of the final judgment of the electoral court that decides in this regard. The clauses of the law establish the principles of freedom of expression concerning public officials and candidates in electoral periods, and provide real malice as the applicable standard in the case, https://observatoriolegislativocele.com/chile-proyecto-de-ley-cesacion-de-cargo-por-difusion-de-noticias-falsas-2018

4 In a recent work, Yochai Benkler, Robert Faris and Hal Roberts studied the actual influence of false claims that circulated on social media during the electoral campaign that ended with the election of former President Donald Trump. Starting with the hypothesis that technology is the main cause of the current crisis in the information ecosystem, the authors conclude that: 'These putative risks are, for the near future, not the major causes of disruption. We have argued throughout this book that none of these actors – Russians, fake news entrepreneurs, Cambridge Analytica, Facebook itself, or symmetric partisan echo chambers – were the major cause of the epistemic crisis experienced within the U.S. media ecosystem during the 2016 election or since. Instead of these technologically driven dynamics, which are novel but ultimately less important, we see longer-term dynamics of political economy: ideology and institutions interacting with technological adoption as the primary drivers of the present epistemic crisis.' See Yochai Benkler, Robert Faris and Hal Roberts, *Network Propaganda: Manipulation, Disinformation, and Radicalization in American Politics* (Oxford: Oxford University Press, 2018) p. 351. Though I do not deny the impact of fake news on the democratic process and other aspects of social life, in this chapter I suggest an approach to the problem from a different point of view.

5.2 'TAXONOMY' OF 'FALSE EXPRESSIONS' TO JUSTIFY THEIR REJECTION

I adopt the conceptual framework presented by Yochai Benkler, Robert Faris and Hal Roberts in their book *Network Propaganda*.[5] Their classification is important because, '[t]here is no universally accepted definition of disinformation. While the lack of agreement makes a global response challenging, the lack of consensus underlines the complex, intrinsically political and contested nature of the concept'.[6] False statements may be (a) socially accepted; (b) socially rejected; (c) deemed harmful (anti-value) but deserving only of moral reproach; or (d) deemed harmful and deserving of legal consequences. But what considerations bear on the seriousness of a particular instance of false expression? Following Sunstein's recent work, I agree that four factors bear on this question, though I would also add a fifth factor.[7]

Sunstein's four relevant factors are:

- The state of mind of the person who is expressing themselves: are they (a) lying; (b) reckless; (c) negligent; or (d) mistaken, but reasonably so.
- The magnitude of the harm caused by their false expression: (a) grave; (b) moderate; (c) minor; (d) nonexistent. Grave harms would include wars begun under false pretenses, or excess pandemic deaths; importantly, harms at this scale are more often attributable to governments than to private citizens. But public officials can also cause moderate or minor harms, such as the termination of a beneficial (but not lifesaving) program, or the unjustified firing of a public employee, through their misstatements.

5 Ibid. 'Propaganda' and 'disinformation': manipulating and misleading people intentionally to achieve political ends. 'Network propaganda': how the architecture of a media ecosystem makes it more or less susceptible to disseminating these kinds of manipulations and lies. 'Bullshit': communications of outlets that don't care whether their statements are true or false, and usually not what their political effect is, as long as they make money. 'Misinformation': publishing wrong information without meaning to be wrong or having a political purpose in communicating false information. 'Disorientation': a condition that some propaganda seeks to induce, in which the target population simply loses the ability to tell truth from falsehood or where to go for help in distinguishing between the two.

6 Irene Khan, 'Disinformation and Freedom of Opinion and Expression', A/HRC/47/25, 13 April 2021, https://digitallibrary.un.org/record/3925306/files/A_HRC_47_25-EN.pdf.

7 Cass Sunstein, *Liars: Falsehoods and Free Speech in an Age of Deception* (Oxford: Oxford University Press, 2021). In this chapter, I am adopting Sunstein's explanation unchanged, although I would add as a fifth factor the 'speaker's level of obligation', which relates to the speaker's professional position. For example, professional speech – such as doctors' diagnoses or lawyers' advice to clients and representations to courts – often must comply with ethical guidelines, and can also give rise to malpractice liability. General obligations can be established about speech (of public officials); specific obligations according to professions (such as lawyers, doctors); ethical obligations (citizenship). In other words, the 'fifth element' would tend to focus on assessing who is issuing the expression and what obligations they have. In addition to the subject matter of the speech, a speaker's position can also matter.

- The likelihood that the harm will take place: (a) certain; (b) probable; (c) improbable; (d) highly improbable. Here, the position and credibility of the public official will again be relevant. A minister of health stating that drinking water with chlorine derivatives cures COVID-19 is not the same as that statement being spread on social media by an unknown person, or an advertiser that obviously has a vested interest in promoting their product.[8]
- How soon the harm will take place: (a) imminently; (b) in the near future; (c) reasonably soon; (d) in the distant future.

Sunstein summarizes this taxonomy in a useful table:

Relevant factors	A	B	C	D
1. State of mind	Lie	Reckless	Negligent	Reasonable
2. Magnitude of harm	Grave	Moderate	Minor	Nonexistent
3. Likelihood of harm	Certain	Probable	Improbable	Highly improbable
4. Timing of harm	Imminent	Near future	Reasonably soon	Distant future

Readers might have an intuition that false statements in column 'A' deserve harsh sanction, and statements in column 'D' deserve little or no sanction. But what about false statements that draw from both columns 'A' and 'D'? Should a case of intentional lying that causes no harm be punished? What about an intentional lie that will cause grave harm to future generations, but little or no harm in the immediate future?

My focus is on expression by public officials, whether that expression occurs in the course of carrying out an official obligation or in a less formal setting. The speaker's role and the setting of the speech might affect the likelihood and severity of the harm that results from a false statement, and therefore also the appropriate consequence – whether moral condemnation, official sanction imposed by the state, or sanctions imposed by private third parties such as contracting partners[9] or social media platforms.[10] So far, I have assumed an unstated premise: that lying is always or

[8] This example is not simply a hypothetical case, to the point that the Pan-American Health Organization had to publicly clarify the situation. See 'La OPS advierte contra el uso de productos de cloro como tratamientos para COVID-19', PAHO, 5 August 2020, www.paho.org/es/noticias/5-8-2020-ops-advierte-contra-uso-productos-cloro-como-tratamientos-para-covid-19.

[9] Contracts may contain binding obligations regarding confidentiality among other limitations.

[10] In addition, a public official might be subject to concrete sanctions from a private entity with which the official has a contractual relationship, such as when a politician is barred from posting on a social media platform because of a statement that violates the platform's terms of service. The most obvious example is Facebook's recent decision regarding former President Donald Trump. Nick Clegg, Vice President of Global Affairs at Facebook, said Trump's actions 'constituted a serious violation of our rules that deserve the highest penalty available under the new protocols'. For this reason, the account was suspended for two years. See 'Facebook anuncia que suspensión a Donald Trump será de dos años', France 24, 4 June 2021, www.france24.com/es/minuto-a-minuto/20210604-facebook-anuncia-que-suspensi%C3%B3n-a-donald-trump-ser%C3%A1-de-dos-a%C3%B1os.

nearly always a moral wrong. But in the next section, I turn to the harms that can result when public officials lie.

5.3 THE SOCIAL AND MORAL CONSEQUENCES OF LIES

Consider the following statement by a teacher to her six-year-old students: 'Students with good behavior in my class will surely receive a gift from an alien that will arrive from the planet Mars at the end of the year.' One can probably agree that this expression falls within taxonomy category 1(a) (intention to lie). Now, will it cause harm? Or, in truth, does it produce nonexistent harm 2(d), or at most, minor harm 2 (c) if, for example, one believes that it may have some psychological consequence on those who receive that information? (Especially if at the end of the year they do not receive any gifts). Assuming that this lie leads to better behavior in that class, is it still worthy of informal or official condemnation? Could it instead be considered to be praiseworthy? This section considers that question from the perspectives of the Utilitarian and Kantian schools of thought.

The father of utilitarianism, Jeremy Bentham, argued that lies should not be objectionable if they maximize the utility – happiness – of society: 'Falsehood, taken by itself, consider it as not being accompanied by any other material circumstances, can never, upon the principle of utility, constitute any offense at all.'[11] This is not to say that Utilitarians approve of lying. On the contrary: human relationships are based on communicative interactions, which can be degraded by lies. In other words, Utilitarians see lying as wrong because of the harmful consequences for interpersonal or social trust.

The moral obligation to communicate truthfully was approached in a similar way by Günter Jakobs in a work that is already several decades old.[12] Breaking with the statement that honor is protected insofar as it is necessary to protect the dignity of people, he argued that 'offenses of libel can no longer be conceived exclusively as crimes against persons, but must also be defined as crimes against public interests'. Jakobs's reasoning was as follows: first, he rightly understood that criminal law is not the only method of social control. In addition, institutions such as family, school, religion, associations and unions mete out various kinds of sanctions against members who violate community norms. But this works only in an environment where there is regular, truthful expression about norms and violations – that is, where true expression about a violation of a norm or rule is not suppressed, and untrue expression can be sanctioned in a formal or informal way. Still, Jakobs correctly says that there is no 'broad' right to hear the truth – the need for truth is greater in some settings than others; hence lying in court is a criminal violation, but

[11] Jeremy Bentham, *The Principles of Morals and Legislation* (1789), cited by Sunstein, *Liars* (n 7) p. 26.

[12] Günter Jakobs, *La Misión de la protección jurídico-penal del honor* (Madrid: Civitas, 1997), Vol. I, pp. 627–43.

lying in most other settings will give rise only to civil liability or informal social sanction.

Let us now briefly turn to our analysis of a Kantian view of ethical duty. If one agrees with Kant that human beings should be respected for their inherent dignity, then false expression is always to be condemned, even if it does not cause other harm. It matters only that a person has been treated without respect. Therefore, from a Kantian perspective, a public officer who lies about their opponent to win an election has been disrespectful and has affected the autonomy of the public. Similarly, Sunstein argues that political candidates who lie 'deny the central premise of democracy: the sovereignty of the citizenry' and that politicians who lie, 'act as if citizens are merely instruments for their own use.' From a Utilitarian perspective, Sunstein remarks that when citizens realize that politicians are lying, many are outraged, and after a while they become indifferent and may even stop listening.[13]

In sum, various philosophical traditions agree that lying is morally reprehensible, though they may differ about the appropriate response. But of course only some lies are actionable in civil or criminal legal systems, raising the question of when it is appropriate to regulate lies. The answer takes us back to the first column of Sunstein's taxonomy: lies in contexts such as political elections or public health can cause enormous and readily identifiable harms. Therefore, we would expect to see legal obligations to tell the truth in these and similar contexts. Before delving into these two fields, I will first analyze the Inter-American human rights system's guidelines on public officials' ethics and expression.

5.4 THE INTER-AMERICAN HUMAN RIGHTS SYSTEM AND FALSE EXPRESSIONS FROM THE GOVERNMENT AND PUBLIC OFFICIALS

In this section I include two distinct, though well-connected, ideas. I start with some general background standards coming from the Inter-American Court of Human Rights (IACHR) that protect freedom of expression, including the limits for lies. Then I highlight special obligations for public officials when they publicly inform people on public or general interest issues.

5.4.1 *General Freedom of Expression Standards and the Limits for Lies*

Advisory Opinion No. 5 (AO-5/85), issued by the IACHR in 1985 offered the Court's first analysis of false expressions and their protection under Article 13 of the

[13] Sunstein, *Liars* (n 7), p. 33.

American Convention on Human Rights (ACHR)[14]. In this Opinion, the Court considered whether a Costa Rican law that required journalists to belong to a professional association was consistent with Articles 13 and 29 of the ACHR. AO-5/85 had the virtue of responding far beyond the query that Costa Rica had submitted to the IACHR.[15] The outcome is very well known: the IACHR determined that these laws violated freedom of expression. But to arrive at that answer, the Court left for posterity a complete analysis of Article 13, to be taken up by both the IACHR and the Inter-American Commission on Human Rights directly or indirectly when they had to resolve possible violations of Article 13 of the ACHR.[16] Importantly, the IACHR stated that false expressions were protected, mainly because of the risk of censorship if government was free to decide whether a statement was true or false.

Fifteen years after this Advisory Opinion, the IACHR approved the Declaration of Principles of Freedom of Expression.[17] In interpreting this principle, the IACHR Office of the Special Rapporteur for Freedom of Expression explained that false expressions cannot be sanctioned unless 'actual malice' is demonstrated: knowing or reckless disregard of the truth. It is important to mention that the actual malice doctrine taken by the Special Rapporteur has its origin in the US Supreme Court case law: false statements can also give rise to other kinds of liability, such as in tort cases. Under this

[14] ACHR, Art. 13. [Freedom of Thought and Expression]:

1. Everyone has the right to freedom of thought and expression.
   This right includes the freedom to seek, receive and disseminate information and ideas of all kinds, regardless of frontiers, either orally, in writing or in printed or artistic form, or by any other procedure of their choice.
2. The exercise of the right set forth in the preceding paragraph cannot be subject to prior censorship but to subsequent liabilities, which must be expressly established by law and be necessary to ensure:
   a) respect for the rights or reputation of others, or
   b) the protection of national security, public order or public health or morals.
3. The right of expression cannot be restricted by indirect means, such as the abuse of official or private controls of newsprint, radio frequencies, or of appliances and devices used in the dissemination of information or by any other means aimed at preventing communication and the circulation of ideas and opinions.
4. Public shows may be subject by law to prior censorship for the sole purpose of regulating access to them for the moral protection of childhood and adolescence, without prejudice to the provisions of subsection 2.
5. Any propaganda in favor of war and any defense of national, racial or religious hatred that constitutes incitement to violence or any other similar illegal action against any person or group of persons, for any reason, including those of race, color, religion, language or national origin are prohibited.

[15] In the inter-American system, the Inter-American Court can exercise its advisory jurisdiction so that the states can ask it questions, such as the one formulated by Costa Rica regarding the compatibility of its legislation with the American Convention.

[16] For those interested in the history and contents of AO-5/85, see *Libertad de expresión:* A *30 años de la Opinión Consultiva sobre la colegiación obligatoria de periodistas* (Bogotá: Trust for the Americas, 2017), www.oas.org/es/cidh/expresion/docs/publicaciones/OC5_ESP.PDF.

[17] Declaración de Principios sobre Libertad de Expresión, Principle 7, www.cidh.oas.org/basicos/basicos13.htm.

standard announced by the Supreme Court of the United States in *The New York Times* v. *Sullivan*,[18] which has been incorporated to some degree into the law of free expression in various countries and, as I mentioned, in the Inter-American human rights system, a false statement about a public official or other person in the public eye can give rise to defamation liability only if the plaintiff can prove the false statement was made with actual malice. The actual malice standard encompasses statements that were knowingly false, or that were made with reckless disregard for the truth.

The doctrine of 'actual malice' allows legislatures to negatively value false claims made intentionally or with reckless disregard for the truth. This standard reflects a balance between competing values: concern for how lies can damage individual reputations and the public trust, and an interest in protecting speakers who make reasonable mistakes while participating in public discourse. Thus, the actual malice standard means speakers have more 'breathing space' to discuss matters of importance to the public than when they are discussing mere private individuals or concerns. As one can see, at the dawn of the twenty-first century in the Inter-American Human Rights System (IAHRS), the so-called moral taboo prevailed regarding lies: intentionally false statements deserve reproach. But, as Catalina Botero Marino explains:

> it is possible to argue that Inter-American jurisprudence offers at least two important standards applicable to any state effort aimed at prohibiting or regulating so-called 'fake news'. In the first place, the simple objective falsehood of an expression cannot be object of prohibition or state sanction . . . Second, based on the decisions of the Inter-American Court, it is possible to argue that restricting freedom of expression is only justified as a means to protect the rights of third parties or public order understood from a narrowly defined democratic perspective.[19]

So far, the interpretation of the IAHRS fits quite well with the proposed taxonomy: if the expression is knowingly false and it causes harm (column 'A' of the table above), it could deserve state sanctions.

The Joint Declaration on Freedom of Expression and 'Fake News', Disinformation and Propaganda draws a similar distinction between knowing and accidental falsehoods.[20] It urges the 'abolition' of '[g]eneral prohibitions on the dissemination of information based on vague and ambiguous ideas, including "false

[18] *The New York Times Co.* v. *Sullivan*, 376 US 254 (1964). For those interested in a detailed history of the case, see Eduardo Bertoni, *La Libertad de Expresión en el Estado de Derecho* 2nd ed. (Buenos Aires: Editores Del Puerto, 2000), ch. 'New York Times vs. Sullivan y la malicia real de la doctrina'; Anthony Lewis, *Make No Law: The Sullivan Case and the First Amendment* (New York: Vintage Books, 1992).

[19] Catalina Botero Marino, 'La regulación estatal de las llamadas "noticias falsas" desde la perspectiva del derecho a la libertad de expresión' in *Libertad de Expresión* (n 16).

[20] Joint Declaration on Freedom of Expression and 'Fake News', Disinformation and Propaganda (2017), www.osce.org/files/f/documents/6/8/302796.pdf. This document was signed by the United Nations Special Rapporteur for Freedom of Opinion and Expression, the Representative for Freedom of the Media of the Organization for Security and Co-operation in Europe, the OAS Special Rapporteur for Freedom of Expression and the Special Rapporteur

news" or "non-objective information"' (Article 2(a)), but also notes that 'State actors should not make, sponsor, encourage or further disseminate statements which they know or reasonably should know to be false (disinformation) or which demonstrate a reckless disregard for verifiable information (propaganda)' (Article 2(c)). The Declaration also contemplates harms of different magnitudes, stating that public officials should particularly 'take care to ensure that they disseminate reliable and trustworthy information, including about matters of public interest, such as the economy, public health, security and the environment' (Article 2(d)).

5.4.2 *Freedom of Expression and Special Obligations of Public Officials*

In 2009, the IAHRS, considered Advisory Opinion No. 5's postulates in the context of criticism of certain media by private individuals, other media outlets and public officials. In *Ríos* v. *Venezuela*[21] and *Perozo* v. *Venezuela*,[22] the Inter-American Court wrote that while public officials have a 'duty' of expression under certain circumstances, they also have a special duty of care to make 'reasonable' efforts to tell the truth, especially during times of high conflict. That obligation is necessary both because of the 'wide scope and eventual effects on certain sectors of the population' of official statements, and to prevent citizens from 'receiving a manipulated version of certain events'.[23] These ideas were again expressed by the IACHR in Resolution 1/2020 'Pandemia y Derechos Humanos en las Américas'.[24] The Court reiterated that government officials 'should take special care' when discussing the pandemic, including by 'counter[ing]' misinformation spread by private individuals.

In conclusion, the 'moral taboo' – lying is wrong – is limitedly compatible with the IAHRS. A statement's falsity does not exclude it from the protection of Article

for Freedom of Expression and Access to Information of the African Commission on Human and People's Rights.

21 *Ríos and Others* v. *Venezuela*, Series C no. 194, Preliminary exceptions, Merits, Reparations and Costs, judgment of 28 January 2009.

22 *Perozo and Others* v. *Venezuela*, Series C no. 195, Preliminary exceptions, Merits, Reparations and Costs, judgment of 28 January 2009.

23 The main facts in *Rios*, relevant for this chapter, were that 'several people linked to the television channel Radio Caracas Televisión (RCTV) suffered a series of acts of harassment, persecution and physical and verbal attacks between 2001 and 2005 for exercising their freedom of expression. Additionally, several Venezuelan government officials made intimidating statements about these people and the television station's journalistic activities. The Inter-American Court heard the case and determined that the totality of these acts constituted ways of obstructing, interfering and intimidating the exercise of the professional activities of RCTV journalists. It also noted that, due to the context in which the senior officials' statements were issued, the individuals connected RCTV were put in more vulnerable circumstances and, further, the lack of diligence in the investigations constituted a breach of the state's obligation to prevent and investigate the facts. It should be noted that this decision is very similar to *Perozo et al.* v. *Venezuela*', https://globalfreedomofexpression.columbia.edu/cases/rios-v-venezuela.

24 Resolution 1/2020, Pandemia y Derechos Humanos en las Américas, IACHR, April 2020, www.oas.org/es/cidh/decisiones/pdf/Resolucion-1-20-es.pdf.

13 of the ACHR. But public officials' freedom of expression is distinct: for them, lying about important matters is reprehensible, and the obligation not to do so can be regulated, especially to prevent grave harms. The following are provisions of domestic law of administrative, criminal and ethical nature that explain the foundations and justification given in domestic law to public officials' obligation to tell the truth.

5.5 CRIMINAL LAW AND ADMINISTRATIVE LAW APPROACH: MUST PUBLIC OFFICIALS TELL THE TRUTH?

5.5.1 *Criminal Law in the Face of a Dishonest Act of a Public Official*

Imagine the following scenario: a high-ranking official is in charge of recording statistical data about criminal cases. To this end, they must fact-check that information against source documents. After some time, it becomes known that the official has entered false information, creating a problem for the statistical monitoring of the penal system. What is their responsibility? This case is not merely hypothetical. The Criminal Cassation Chamber of the Supreme Court of Justice of Colombia recently handled a similar situation.[25] The Court described the crime of 'ideological falsehood in a public document', which is committed 'by a public official who in the exercise of their duties, by issuing a public document that can serve as proof, expresses a falsehood or totally or partially conceals the truth'.[26]

This case is illustrative of the approach taken in many Latin American countries.[27] It shows that some lies by public officials are sanctioned in the orbit of punitive law,[28] because of the public's need to have faith and trust in documents

[25] Supreme Court of Justice of Colombia, Criminal Cassation Court, SP154-2020 Filing 49523 (Passed Record No. 017), 29 January 2020. These types of rulings abound in Latin America.

[26] It is worth clarifying that the interpretation made by the Court of the crime of 'ideological falsehood in a public document' imposes a general obligation to tell the truth in public documents, and it is not limited to fraud cases.

[27] The Argentine Criminal Code includes the crime of ideological falsehood of a public instrument in its Art. 293. In Brazil the crime 'ideological falsehood' is provided for in the penal code in Art. 299. In Chile, Art. 193 refers to a special crime, committed by public officials, with various behaviors that involve falsehoods in an official document. In Costa Rica, the Penal Code includes the crime of ideological falsehood in Art. 360. The Guatemalan Penal Code includes the crime of ideological falsehood of a document in its Art. 322; in Mexico, the crime of ideological falsification is included in Art. 243 of the Federal Criminal Code. The Panamanian Penal Code contains in its Title XI on 'Crimes against the Public Trust' the crime of falsifying documents in general, specifically in Art. 366. Drafting unauthentic public documents in Paraguay is penalized in the Penal Code with law 1,160/97 in Title V of the 'Punishable Acts' against legal relationships. In Peru, Art. 428 of the Penal Code regulates the crime of ideological falsehood.

[28] Not all acts of public officials establish public trust. Acts of officials concerning their specific functions do establish public trust.

within the legal system. To be clear, criminal law may or may not be the right way to address these false public statements by public officials. My point is only to demonstrate the reasoning in support of this approach, which shows the high value placed on truthfulness when public officials are carrying out their mandate. What if a high-ranking public official's false claims are expressed on social media rather than in a document? Would the main argument justifying reproach change? I contend that it would not. In the same way that false expressions in a public document destroy public trust, so can public officials' false statements made in other circumstances.

It may be that a falsehood embodied in a public document can cause more damage than the same expression posted on a widely disseminated social media platform. But this is not necessarily the case. For example, imagine that a public official registers the wrong place of birth for a person. Suppose that same official lies about that person's birthplace on social media. Let us now add two facts: the person about whom the public official is lying is a presidential candidate, and the place falsely declared is a foreign state. Finally, assume that the statements on social media are made during an electoral campaign. Would anyone assert that the damage is greater in the case of the false written inscription than in the case of posting on social media?

In summary, punitive law recognizes an anti-value in falsehood in certain circumstances, especially in the case of public officials with a duty to tell the truth. The law of many Latin American countries reflects concern and protection for the 'public trust'. In addition to the ideological falsehood laws discussed above, countries in the region punish forgery and even in some cases malicious omissions of true data in public documents. The penalty increases when it is a public official who perpetrates such falsehoods. This increase seems to correlate to the public trust granted to public officials in the exercise of their functions.

5.5.2 *Administrative Law in the Face of a Dishonest Act of a Public Official*

Criminal law usually requires intentionality, and therefore is most likely to apply in cases that fall under column 'A' of the taxonomy. But administrative law and public ethics could have a broader scope. Parallel to the discussion in the previous section, administrative law specialists see harms to public trust – sometimes called 'legitimate trust'[29] – when public officials make decisions affecting groups or individuals based

[29] See Pedro J. J. Coviello, *La Protección de la Confianza del Administrado, Derecho Argentino y Derecho Comparado* (Buenos Aires: LexisNexis – Abeledo Perrot, 2004), p. 462.

on untrue information. These authors are referring to cases where administrative acts are signed with 'false pretenses and legal ruses' that can be misleading, in writing or orally in some cases.[30] In Latin America, for example, some laws and regulations allow the invalidation of administrative acts that are not truthful.[31]

A prestigious Latin American scholar, Agustín Gordillo,[32] explains there is administrative liability:

> If the person due to their work has access to public power [and] uses it in bad faith, through gimmicks or tricks – by action or omission, including silence – to carry out deceit or induce error; this type of conduct is certainly incompatible with the correct exercise of the administrative function. It is illegitimate even if the power exercised in the case was discretionary; in some of the rulings it is linked to the doctrine of personal acts and the prohibition of self-contradiction.

In the rule of law there is value when the public officer does not mislead citizens. Gordillo says that this is 'incompatible' with the public office. Thus, in administrative law there is also a particularly negative assessment regarding the falsehoods of public officials in the exercise of their functions, which extends, according to experts in the matter, not only to public documents but also to expressions, acts and other manifestations that may create rights and obligations or harm those who trusted them.

5.6 CONCLUSIONS

Criminal and administrative law of several Latin American countries establishes consequences when public officials lie, at least in some contexts. Moreover, there

[30] These authors are referring to acts carried out in writing, or in some cases orally. But if it is not appropriate to deceive citizens in writing, nor is it appropriate to deceive them orally or on social media. As discussed, the requirement of public officials to tell the truth in certain circumstances in the exercise of their functions cannot be different if it is expressed in a written act than if it is done *en masse* in a social media platform.

[31] In Argentina, law 19,549 of administrative procedure establishes in its Art. 14 that the administrative act is null and void when the act is issued with 'lack of cause due to the facts or the right invoked are false or non-existent'. In Colombia, the wording of Art. 88 of the Code of Administrative Procedure and Contentious Administrative Matters implies a presumption of veracity of administrative acts. In Costa Rica, the General Law of Public Administration expresses in its Art. 132: '1) The content must be lawful, possible, clear and precise and cover all questions of fact and law arising from the motive, even if they have not been debated by the interested parties.' In Peru, one of the guiding principles of the Peruvian General Administrative Procedure is the presumption of veracity in all actions of the administrative procedure, regulated in Art. 51 of the General Administrative Procedure Law. In the Dominican Republic, Law No. 107 of 2013 describes the presumption of validity of administrative acts in Arts. 9 and 10.

[32] Agustín Gordillo, *Tratado de Derecho Administrativo y obras selectas* (Buenos Aires: Fundación de Derecho Administrativo, 2017), Vol. 1, Parte General, 15.4. X-30.

exists a duty or obligation to tell the truth, which is reflected in some countries' codes of ethics.[33] Public officials who intentionally lie may face personal or professional sanctions, or their official decisions and the consequences of those decisions may be annulled.

The law reflects a highly contextual analysis that either implicitly or explicitly accounts for the various dimensions in Sunstein's taxonomy. In contrast, analysis that is focused narrowly on social media platforms sometimes fails to draw these distinctions. These initiatives do not always address the origin of false statements, or the specific obligations that certain people have due to their position or activity in a democratic society. I believe we should develop more context- and speaker-dependent approaches to regulating misinformation. In addition to delving into the study of our new media ecosystem, including social media, their business models, their scope and their potential liability (when appropriate), attention should be paid to the other actors who participate in the public debate and who have long had specific responsibilities regarding their speech.

The basic pillars of the rule of law, democracy and the republic are both the publicity of government acts and access to public information. The duty of truthfulness is a consequence of these rights, and it applies regardless of public officials' manner of expression.[34] Although there is a heated discussion in case law and academic discourse regarding the nature of the social media accounts of public officials, political parties and even public institutions, much of the information that

[33] According to these codes, in general, they consider the characteristics that should govern the public office include the qualities of probity, rectitude, integrity and honesty. These qualifications mean something simple: they are qualities of a person who can be trusted. And whoever lies cannot be trusted. Therefore we believe that all these regulations, demanding honesty, trustworthiness, probity or integrity, require from the public official that they be truthful in their statements. For examples of codes of ethics in the region see Argentina, Ley de Ética en el Ejercicio de la Función Pública, No. 25,188, www.argentina.gob.ar/normativa/nacional/ley-25188-60847/actualizacion; Uruguay, Declaración de interés general del Código de Ética en la función pública, www.impo.com.uy/bases/leyes/19823-2019; Chile, Law No. 20,880 on probity in public office and prevention of conflicts of interest, www.cmfchile.cl/portal/principal/613/articles-27838_doc_pdf.pdf; Colombia, Código de Integridad del Servicio Público Colombiano, www.funcionpublica.gov.co/documents/28587425/34877072/2019-08-21_Codigo_integridad.pdf/da1a074a-8309-a46e-11a5-cfff0a3279e9?t=1566404916392; Mexico, Código de Ética de las Personas Servidoras Públicas del Gobierno Federal, www.gob.mx/asa/acciones-y-programas/codigo-de-etica-de-los-servidores-publicos; Panamá, Código de Conducta de los Servidores Públicos de la Contraloría General, www.oas.org/juridico/PDFs/mesicic4_pan_cod_cond.pdf; Perú, Ley del Código de Ética en la Función Pública, No. 27,815, www.mimp.gob.pe/files/transparencia/CET/ley27815.pdf.

[34] It is relevant at this point, for example, to name the lawsuit of the Knight Center of Columbia University against former President Donald Trump to request that the President be banned from blocking followers on his Twitter account. The Knight Center argued and the court agreed that the President disseminated public and government information and thus the account constituted a public forum. See *Knight First Amendment Institute at Columbia University* v. *Trump*, No. 1:17-cv-5205 (S.D.N.Y.), No. 18-1691 (2d Cir.), No. 20-197 (Supreme Court).

the government disseminates today comes from official accounts on social media and other digital media, with an increasing number of people who are informed by these means.[35]

This chapter began with a conceptual classification of false claims. I focused on the intent of the author and the possible harm in order to evaluate the cases where they deserve a reproach and what type of reproach they deserve. The first conclusion was that, despite the existence of what I, along with Sunstein, call the 'moral taboo' of lies, there may be cases that do not deserve any consequence. However, neither the IAHRS nor the regulations in force in the countries of the region ignore false statements by public officials, or allow them to exist without consequences. The study described a mandate and an expectation – explicit in some cases and tacit in others – that officials must take special care to ensure (within reason) that their statements are true, at least when they fall into certain categories. Failure to do so in certain circumstances can have consequences ranging from criminal to ethical. On the other hand, other categories of false speech – including many unintentionally false statements – are protected under Article 13 of the ACHR, and law that incorporates a version of the 'actual malice' standard.

Many false claims circulated on social media platforms have a wide reach in the population. But there is no consensus on the effect that social media alone has in these types of cases. Expressions do not happen in a vacuum; when public officials misspeak on social media, it is often then amplified in traditional media outlets. When that happens, it is extremely difficult to tease apart the effects of one versus the other – but the potential for amplification (and therefore likely amplified harm) is another reason to more closely regulate statements by public officials than private citizens.

It is important to mention that the UN Secretary-General submitted to the UN General Assembly the report 'Countering Disinformation for the Promotion and Protection of Human Rights and Fundamental Freedoms'.[36] In it, the Secretary-General notes that countering the different manifestations of disinformation requires addressing underlying societal tensions, fostering respect for human rights, online and offline, and supporting a plural civic space and media landscape. Among the recommendations to the states, the Secretary-General makes the following recommendations:

> Discourage public officials from disseminating disinformation through measures such as professional codes of conduct, and adopt measures aimed at holding them accountable for expressions amounting to advocacy of national, racial or religious

[35] See Ines Mergel, 'Implementing Social Media in the Public Sector' (2013) (Fall) *State & Local Energy Report* 16–23,: 'It is therefore not surprising that according to a recent Fels Institute report, 90% of all local government organizations are using Facebook and 94% have set up a Twitter account', ibid. at 16.

[36] A/77/287, 12 August 2022.

hatred that constitute incitement to discrimination, hostility or violence, as prohibited under international human rights law, in line with the United Nations Strategy and Plan of Action on Hate Speech. Public officials should never denigrate, intimidate or threaten the media.

However, taking seriously the above conclusions – such as that the duty of truthfulness is a consequence of fundamental rights and it applies regardless of public officials' manner of expression, but, at the same time, some lies are insignificant – one might object that my approach is not realistic: laws and rules mentioned here will never be enforced against powerful public officials, because judges will not be willing to do so.[37] Or worse: the necessity to adapt and reform those laws and regulations will never happen because policymakers want to protect the scope of their own speech. This might be true. But many proposals to regulate misinformation are subject to the same critique; for example, social media platforms may be unwilling to police the false speech of powerful individuals or prominent companies.[38] For that reason, this chapter urges that we look beyond the messenger and focus on the substance and context of misinformation, and the speakers who disseminate it. This targeted approach is better suited to dealing with the grave threats posed by certain kinds of misinformation.

[37] However, former Brazilian President Jair Bolsonaro was convicted in June 2023 and banned from running as a candidate because a panel of judges at Brazil's electoral court voted to bar him from office until 2030 because of his conduct during the previous year's presidential election campaign. Five of the court's seven judges ruled that Bolsonaro abused his power and misused the media on 18 July 2022 when he used government staff members, the state television channel and the presidential palace in Brazil for a meeting in which he insisted to foreign ambassadors that the country's election system was rigged, the Associated Press reported. My point is that he was convicted because he lied using state resources. And this is just an example that regulation could be used against powerful people.

[38] I would like to thank Agustina Del Campo for this observation.

PART III

Regional Regulatory Approach to Disinformation: Europe

6

Freedom of Expression and the Regulation of Disinformation in the European Union

András Koltay

6.1 INTRODUCTION

The issue of mass disinformation on the Internet is a long-standing concern for policymakers, legislators, academics and the wider public. Disinformation is believed to have had a significant impact on the outcome of the 2016 US presidential election.[1] Concern about the threat of foreign – mainly Russian – interference in the democratic process is also growing.[2] The COVID-19 pandemic, which reached global proportions in 2020, gave new impetus to the spread of disinformation, which even put lives at risk.[3] The problem is real and serious enough to force all parties concerned to reassess the previous European understanding of the proper regulation of freedom of expression.

The author would like to thank all those who read and commented on earlier versions of the manuscript at various conferences and workshops, especially Eduardo Bertoni, Joanna Botha, John Charney, Mark Cole, Michael Epstein, Domingos Farinho, Andrew Kenyon, Ron Krotoszynski, Michael Losavio, Péter Nádori, Bernát Török, Louis Virelli, Russell Weaver, Cristopher Yoo, Vincenzo Zeno-Zencovich and Zsolt Ződi.

1 Alexandre Bovet and Hernán A. Makse, 'Influence of Fake News in Twitter during the 2016 US Presidential Election' (2019) 10(7) *Nature Communications*, https://doi.org/10.1038/s41467-018-07761-2.

2 See, e.g., Richard Sakwa, *The Russia Scare: Fake News and Genuine Threat* (Abingdon: Routledge, 2022); Foreign Threats to the 2020 U.S. Federal Elections. Intelligence Community Assessment ICA 2020-00078D. National Intelligence Council, 10 March 2021, www.dni.gov/files/ODNI/documents/assessments/ICA-declass-16MAR21.pdf; Christopher Paul and Miriam Matthews, 'The Russian "Firehose of Falsehood" Propaganda Model: Why It Might Work and Options to Counter It', RAND, 2016, www.rand.org/pubs/perspectives/PE198.html.

3 Hendrik Bruns, François J. Dessart and Myrto Pantazi, 'Covid-19 Misinformation: Preparing for Future Crises' EUR 31139 EN, Luxembourg, Publications Office of the European Union, 2022, https://publications.jrc.ec.europa.eu/repository/handle/JRC130111.

This chapter reviews the measures taken by the European Union and its Member States to limit disinformation, mainly through regulatory instruments. After a clarification of the concepts involved (Section 6.2), I will review the options for restricting false statements which are compatible with the European concept of freedom of expression (Section 6.3), and then examine the related tools of media regulation (Section 6.4). This will be followed by a discussion of the regulation of online platforms in the EU (Section 6.5), and by a presentation of EU (Section 6.6) and national (Section 6.7) measures which specifically address disinformation. Finally, I will attempt to draw some conclusions with regard to possible future regulatory responses (Section 6.8).

6.2 DEFINITIONAL ISSUES

Not only are the categories of fake news, disinformation and misinformation not precisely defined in law, but their exact meaning is also disputed in academia. Since the 2016 US presidential election campaign, the use of the term 'fake news' has spread worldwide. It is usually applied to news published on a public platform, in particular on the Internet, that is untrue in content or misleading as to the true facts, and which is not published with the intention of revealing the truth but with the aim of deliberately distorting a democratic process or the informed resolution of a public debate.[4] According to Hunt Allcott and Matthew Gentzkow, fake news is news that is 'intentionally and verifiably false, and could mislead readers',[5] meaning that intentionality and verifiable falsehood are important elements of it. However, in principle, fake news could also include content that is specifically protected by freedom of expression, such as political satire, parody and subjective opinions, a definition which would certainly be undesirable in terms of the protection of freedom of expression.[6] Since President Trump, after his successful campaign in 2016, mostly applied the term to legacy media that was critical of him, it has gradually lost its original meaning and has fallen out of favor in legal documents.[7]

The EU has for some time preferred the term 'disinformation' to describe the phenomenon. Of course, fake news and disinformation are in fact two categories with a significant overlap, and as Björnstjern Baade points out, the former will not disappear from the public sphere either, so legislators, law enforcers and public

[4] Alessio Sardo, 'Categories, Balancing, and Fake News: The Jurisprudence of the European Court of Human Rights' (2020) 33(2) *Canadian Journal of Law & Jurisprudence* 435–60, 451.

[5] Hunt Allcott and Matthew Gentzkow, 'Social Media and Fake News in the 2016 Election' (2017) 31(2) *Journal of Economic Perspectives* 211–36, 213.

[6] Rachael Craufurd Smith, 'Fake News, French Law and Democratic Legitimacy: Lessons for the United Kingdom?' (2019) 11(1) *Journal of Media Law* 52–81, 57.

[7] Irini Katsirea, '"Fake News": Reconsidering the Value of Untruthful Expression in the Face of Regulatory Uncertainty' (2019) 10(2) *Journal of Media Law* 159–88, 162.

policymakers will have to continue dealing with it.[8] Tarlach McGonagle cuts the Gordian knot by defining fake news as content that is 'disinformation that is presented as, or is likely to be perceived as, news'.[9] The Code of Practice on Disinformation, in line with several EU documents, defines disinformation as 'false or misleading content that is spread with an intention to deceive or secure economic or political gain and which may cause public harm'.[10] Thus, intentional deception and the undue gain accrued or harm it causes are also conceptual elements here. By comparison, misinformation is 'false or misleading content shared without harmful intent though the effects can still be harmful, e.g. when people share false information with friends and family in good faith'.[11] However, the inclusion of intentionality as an essential characteristic of disinformation may also raise concerns. It is inherently problematic to limit speech on the basis of a speaker's intent, and not merely on the basis of the effect achieved. Furthermore, while there is a consensus that satire and parody, being protected opinions, cannot be considered disinformation, they can also be published in bad faith, distorting the true facts, which can have an effect similar to that which attempts to suppress disinformation seek to prevent.[12]

The Code of Practice approved by the EU focuses primarily on curbing disinformation in political advertising, which, according to the European Council and Parliament's proposal for a regulation, 'means the preparation, placement, promotion, publication or dissemination, by any means, of a message: (a) by, for or on behalf of a political actor, unless it is of a purely private or a purely commercial nature; or (b) which is liable to influence the outcome of an election or referendum, a legislative or regulatory process or voting behavior' (on the Code, see Section 6.6.1).

The distinction between disinformation and misinformation, or in other words, the difference between falsehoods made with the intent to harm and untruths that are communicated in good faith but are likely to cause harm, is indeed important and each problem warrants different levels of action and intervention. Prosecuting both disinformation and misinformation with equal force might lead to an

8 Björnstjern Baade, 'Don't Call a Spade a Shovel: Crucial Subtleties in the Definition of Fake News and Disinformation', Verfassungsblog, 14 April 2020, https://verfassungsblog.de/dont-call-a-spade-a-shovel.

9 Tarlach McGonagle, '"Fake News": False Fears or Real Concerns?' (2017) 35(4) *Netherlands Quarterly of Human Rights* 203–9, 203.

10 2022 Strengthened Code of Practice on Disinformation, I. Preamble, https://digital-strategy.ec.europa.eu/en/library/2022-strengthened-code-practice-disinformation. See also Communication from the Commission to the European Parliament, the Council, the European Economic and Social Committee and the Committee of the Regions – On the European Democracy Action Plan. Brussels, 3.12.2020, COM(2020)790 final, Art. 17(4).

11 Ibid.

12 Maria L. Stasi and Pier L. Parcu, 'Disinformation and Misinformation: The EU Response' in Pier L. Parcu and Elda Brogi (eds.), *Research Handbook on EU Media Law and Policy* (Cheltenham: Edward Elgar, 2021) pp. 407–26, p. 408.

unfortunate situation in which citizens who wish to participate in the debate on public affairs, but who do not have the means to verify the truth of a piece of information or communication, who have no malicious intent and seek no direct personal gain, would suffer a disproportionate restriction on their freedom of expression. The most dangerous form of disinformation is that which comes from governments and public bodies. Tackling this is a separate issue, which allows for the use of more robust instruments.[13] For example, in March 2022, the Council of the EU banned certain Russian television broadcasters on that basis following the outbreak of the Russian–Ukrainian war.[14]

To summarize the above brief conceptual overview, the current approach in the EU is to consider as disinformation content that: (a) is untrue or misleading; (b) is published intentionally; (c) is intended to cause harm or undue gain; (d) causes harm to the public; (e) is widely disseminated, typically on a mass scale and (f) is disseminated through an internet content service. Points € and (f) are not conceptual elements but refer to the usual characteristics of disinformation. Consequently, distorted information resulting from possible bias in the traditional media is not considered disinformation, nor is the publication of protected opinions (satire, parody). Since a specific characteristic of disinformation is that it is spread mainly on the Internet, in particular on social media platforms, attempts at preventing it focus especially on these services.

6.3 THE RESTRICTION OF FALSE STATEMENTS IN THE EUROPEAN FREE SPEECH DOCTRINE

The European approach to disinformation, unlike that of the United States, allows for a broad restriction of certain false statements. The US Supreme Court in *United States* v. *Alvarez* held that the falsity of an allegation alone is not sufficient to exclude it from First Amendment protection,[15] but that does not mean that untrue statements of fact, if they cause harm, cannot be restricted, albeit within a narrower range than that of the EU.[16] While the extent to which and under what circumstances disinformation is restricted in Europe is a matter for national law, normative considerations generally take into account the following three requirements when assessing a restriction on speech: the principle of legality (that the restriction is

[13] See Katie Pentney, 'Tinker, Tailor, Twitter, Lie: Government Disinformation and Freedom of Expression in a Post-Truth Era' (2022) 22(2) *Human Rights Law Review* 1–29.

[14] Council Regulation (EU) 2022/350 of 1 March 2022 amending Regulation (EU) No 833/2014 Concerning Restrictive Measures in View of Russia's Actions Destabilising the Situation in Ukraine. See also Section 6.6.1.

[15] *United States* v. *Alvarez*, 567 US 709 (2012).

[16] See Leslie Gielow Jacobs, 'Freedom of Speech and Regulation of Fake News' (2022) 70(1) *American Journal of Comparative Law* 278–311.

provided for by an appropriate rule, preferably codified law), the principle of necessity (that the restriction is justified in a democratic society) and the principle of proportionality (that the restriction does not go beyond the legitimate aim pursued).[17]

Within the framework of the protection of freedom of expression in Europe, according to the current doctrine, deliberate lies (intentional publication of untruthful information) may not be subject to a general prohibition. This does not mean that it is not permissible in certain circumstances to prohibit false factual statements but that a general prohibition is usually understood to be incompatible with the doctrine of freedom of speech. The special circumstances in which speech may be prohibited can be grouped into several areas.

First, defamation law and the legal protection of reputation and honor seek to prevent unfavorable and unjust changes being made to an individual's image and evaluation by society. These regulations aim to prevent an opinion published in the public sphere concerning an individual from tarnishing the 'image' of an individual without proper grounds, especially when it is based upon false statements. The approaches taken by individual states to this question differ noticeably, but their common point of departure is the strong protection afforded to debates on public affairs and the correspondingly weaker protection of the personality rights of public figures compared to the protection of freedom of speech.[18]

Second, the EU Council's Framework Decision on combating racism and xenophobia in the Member States of the EU[19] places a universal prohibition on the denial of crimes against humanity, war crimes and genocide. Most Member States of the EU have laws prohibiting the denial of the crimes against humanity committed by the Nazis before and during World War II, or the questioning of those crimes or watering down their importance.[20]

Third, a number of specific rules apply to false statements made during election campaigns. These can serve two purposes. On the one hand, communication in the campaign period enjoys robust protection: political speech is the most closely guarded core of freedom of expression, and what is spoken during a campaign is as closely linked to the functioning of democracy and democratic procedures as any

[17] Rebecca H. Helm and Hitoshi Nasu, 'Regulatory Responses to "Fake News" and Freedom of Expression: Normative and Empirical Evaluation' (2021) 21(2) *Human Rights Law Review* 302–28, 308.

[18] See *Lingens* v. *Austria*, app. no. 9815/82, decision of 8 July 1986, and the many cases decided by the ECtHR, www.echr.coe.int/Documents/FS_Reputation_ENG.pdf.

[19] Council Framework Decision 2008/913/JHA of 28 November 2008 on combating certain forms and expressions of racism and xenophobia by means of criminal law.

[20] See the French 'Gayssot Act' (Loi no. 90-615 du 13 juillet 1990 tendant à réprimer tout acte raciste, antisémite ou xénophobe, amending the Law on the Freedom of the Press of 1881, by adding a new Article 24) and the German Criminal Code (Strafgesetzbuch), Art. 130(3).

speech can be. On the other hand, these procedures must also be protected so that no candidate or community party distorts the democratic decision-making process and ultimately damages the democratic order.[21]

Fourth, commercial communication can be regulated in order to protect consumers from false (misleading) statements. The European Court of Human Rights (ECtHR), in *Markt Intern and Beerman* v. *Germany*,[22] declared that advertisements serving purely commercial interests, rather than contributing to debates in the public sphere, are also to be awarded the protection of the freedom of speech.[23] Nevertheless, this protection is of a lower order than that granted to 'political speech'.

Fifth, in some jurisdictions, 'scaremongering' – that is, the dissemination of false information that disturbs or threatens to disturb public order or peace – may also be punishable.[24]

Another example of an indirect ban on untrue statements is tobacco advertising. The EU has a broad ban on the subject,[25] which may be further strengthened by national regulations. The advertising ban includes, by definition, the positive portrayal of tobacco, while the publication of opinions other than advertising arguing for the potential positive effects of tobacco is obviously not banned from the public discourse.

6.4 EUROPEAN AND NATIONAL MEDIA REGULATION

Hate speech can also be tackled through media regulation. The Audiovisual Media Services Directive requires Member States to prohibit incitement to violence or hatred directed against a group of persons or a member of a group on the grounds of race, sex, religion or nationality as well as public provocation to commit terrorist offences in linear and nonlinear, television and other audiovisual media services (Article 6). Member States have transposed these provisions into their national legal systems. Under the Directive, only the authority of the state in which the media service provider is broadcasting has jurisdiction to verify whether the conduct in question constitutes hate speech, and to ensure that the broadcasts of the media

[21] See, e.g., the UK's Representation of the People Act 1983, s. 106 (False statements as to candidates); Austrian Penal Code (Strafgesetzbuch), § 264 ('Spreading fake news during an election or referendum').

[22] *Markt Intern and Beerman* v. *Germany*, app. no. 10572/83, judgment of 20 November 1989.

[23] Ibid. [36].

[24] This is the case in Hungary (2012 Criminal Code, s. 337); see András Koltay, 'On the Constitutionality of the Punishment of Scaremongering in the Hungarian Legal System' in *Hungarian Yearbook of International Law and European Law* (The Hague: Eleven Publishing, 2021) pp. 23–42.

[25] Directive 2003/33/EC of the European Parliament and of the Council of 26 May 2003 on the approximation of the laws, regulations and administrative provisions of the Member States relating to the advertising and sponsorship of tobacco products (Text with EEA relevance).

service provider do not contain incitement to hatred or violence. If a media service provider is not established in an EU Member State, it is not subject to the provisions of the Directive, and the national authorities can take action against it under their own legal systems. According to the well-established case law of the Court of Justice of the EU and the ECtHR, a television broadcaster which incites terrorist violence cannot itself claim freedom of expression.[26]

Other (indirect) measures can also be applied against disinformation in media regulation. Access to the content of a media service provider is granted by the legislator based not on an external condition but on the right of reply, in response to content published previously by the service provider. The Audiovisual Media Services Directive prescribes that EU Member States should introduce national legal regulations with regard to television broadcasting that ensure adequate legal remedies for individuals whose personality rights have been infringed through false statements.[27] Such regulations are applied throughout Europe and typically impose obligations not only on audiovisual media but also on both printed and online press,[28] and the granting of the right of reply is also suggested in the EU High Level Expert Group's report on disinformation (see Section 6.6.1) as a possible tool to combat disinformation.[29] The promotion of media pluralism may involve a requirement for impartial news coverage, on the basis of which public affairs must be reported impartially in programs which provide information on them. Regulation may apply to television and radio broadcasters, and it has been implemented in several states in Europe.[30]

In July 2022, the British media regulator Ofcom published its decisions on twenty-nine programs that were broadcast on Russia Today (RT) between 27 February 2022 and 2 March 2022. The licence for the RT service was, at the time of broadcast, held by Autonomous Non-Profit Organization TV-Novosti. The programs had raised

26 Cases C-244/10 and C-245/10 *Mesopotamia Broadcast A/S and Roj TV A/S* v. *Bundesrepublik Deutschland*, judgment of the Court (Third Chamber) of 22 September 2011; *Roj TV A/S* v. *Denmark*, app. no. 24683/14, judgment of 17 April 2018.

27 Directive 2010/13/EU on the coordination of certain provisions laid down by law, regulation or administrative action in Member States concerning the provision of audiovisual media services ('AVMS Directive'), Art. 28.

28 Kyu Ho Youm, 'The Right of Reply and Freedom of the Press: An International and Comparative Perspective' (2008) 76(4) *George Washington Law Review* 1017–64; Andrei Richter, 'Fake News and Freedom of the Media' (2018–19) 8(2) *Journal of International Media & Entertainment Law* 1–34, 14–19; András Koltay, 'The Right of Reply in a European Comparative Perspective' (2013) 54(1) *Hungarian Journal of Legal Studies – Acta Juridica Hungarica* 73–89.

29 Final Report of the High Level Expert Group on Fake News and Online Disinformation (2018), https://ec.europa.eu/digital-single-market/en/news/final-report-high-level-expert-group-fake-news-and-online-disinformation, pp. 15–16.

30 See, e.g., the German regulations (Rundfunkstaatsvertrag, ss. 25–34) and the UK regulation (ss. 319(2)(c) and 319(2)(d), 319(8) and 320 of the Communications Act 2003, and s. 5 of the Broadcasting Code).

issues warranting investigation under the due impartiality rules.[31] Under Section 3(3) of the Broadcasting Act 1990 and of the Broadcasting Act 1996, Ofcom 'shall not grant a licence to any person unless satisfied that the person is a fit and proper person to hold it' and 'shall do all that they can to secure that, if they cease to be so satisfied in the case of any person holding a license, that person does not remain the holder of the license'. Taking into account a series of breaches by RT of the British broadcasting legislation concerning the due impartiality and accuracy rules, Ofcom revoked these licences.[32]

The 1936 International Convention on the Use of Broadcasting in the Cause of Peace and the 1953 Convention on the International Right of Correction would also provide for action against communications from state bodies that have a detrimental effect on international relations, but they are hardly applicable generally to disinformation or misinformation.[33]

6.5 PLATFORM REGULATION IN THE EUROPEAN UNION

False claims are spreading across different online platforms at an unprecedented rate and at the same time to a massive extent. In particular, disinformation is being distributed on social media platforms which consciously focuses on electoral campaigning, for political reasons (involving political parties with conflicting interests, other states acting against a particular state and so on). Initially, the platforms defended themselves by claiming that they were neutral players in this communication.[34] It became increasingly obvious, however, that the platforms themselves are actively able to shape the communication on their services, and that they have an economic interest in its vigor and intensity, and hence that the spread of false news is not necessarily contrary to their interests.[35] Under EU law, online platforms are considered a type of host providers, whose liability for infringing content which appears in their services is limited, but by no means excluded.

6.5.1 *Directive on Electronic Commerce*

According to the Directive on Electronic Commerce, if these platforms provide only technical services when they make available, store or transmit the content of others

[31] Ofcom Broadcasting Code, s. 5.

[32] Notice of a decision under s. 3(3) of the Broadcasting Act 1990 and s. 3(3) of the Broadcasting Act 1996 in Respect of Licences TLCS 000881, TLCS 001686 and DTPS 000072 held by ANO TV Novosti, www.ofcom.org.uk/__data/assets/pdf_file/0014/234023/revocation-notice-ano-tv-novosti.pdf.

[33] See Björnstjern Baade, 'Fake News and International Law' (2019) 29 *European Journal of International Law* 1357–76.

[34] Andrew Marantz, 'Facebook and the "Free Speech" Excuse', *The New Yorker*, 31 October 2019, www.newyorker.com/news/daily-comment/facebook-and-the-free-speech-excuse.

[35] According to George Soros, Facebook was working directly to re-elect President Trump. See George Soros, 'Remove Zuckerberg and Sandberg from Their Posts', *Financial Times*, 18 February 2020, www.ft.com/content/88f6875a-519d-11ea-90ad-25e377c0ee1f.

(much like a printing house or a newspaper stand), then it would seem unjustified to hold them liable for the violations of others ('illegal activity or information'), as long as they are unaware that such violations have occurred. However, in the European approach, gatekeepers may be held liable for their own failure to act after becoming aware of a violation (if they fail to remove the infringing material).[36] The Directive requires all types of intermediaries to remove such materials after they become aware of their infringing nature (Articles 12–14). In addition, the Directive stipulates that intermediaries may not be subject to a general monitoring obligation to identify illegal activities (Article 15).

While this system of legal responsibility should not necessarily be considered outdated, things have certainly changed since 2000, when the Directive was enacted: there are fewer reasons to believe that today's online platforms remain passive with regard to content and do nothing more than store and transmit information. While content is still produced by users or other independent actors, the services of gatekeepers select from and organize, promote or reduce the ranking of such content, and may even delete it or make it unavailable within the system. This notice and takedown procedure applies to the disinformation that appears on the platforms, but resorting to the actual removal of content is reserved for disinformation that is unlawful under the legal system of the state in question (slander, terrorist propaganda, denials of genocide and so on). Generally speaking, false claims are not subject to the removal obligation as they are not illegal. Similarly, even if a piece of content is infringing, but no one reports it to the platform, there is no obligation to remove it.

The notion of 'illegal activity or information' raises an important issue, as the obligation to remove offending content is independent of the outcome of any possible court or official procedure that may establish that a violation has been committed, and the host provider is required to take action before a decision is passed (provided that a legal procedure is actually initiated). This means that the provider has to decide on the illegality of content on its own, and its decision is free from any legal guarantee (even though it may have an impact on the freedom of expression). This rule may encourage providers to remove content to escape possible liability, even in highly questionable situations. It would be comforting (but probably inadequate, considering the speed of communication) if the liability of an intermediary could not be established unless the illegal nature of the content it has not removed is established by a court.[37]

Although continuous, proactive monitoring of infringing content is not mandatory for platforms, the European Court of Justice opened up a loophole for it well

[36] Directive 2000/31/EC of the European Parliament and of the Council of 8 June 2000 on Certain Legal Aspects of Information Society Services, in Particular Electronic Commerce, in the Internal Market ('Directive on Electronic Commerce'), Art. 14.

[37] Christina M. Mulligan, 'Technological Intermediaries and Freedom of the Press' (2013) 66 *SMU Law Review* 157–88, 175.

before the recent Regulation banning Russian media outlets, in 2019, in *Glawischnig-Piesczek* v. *Facebook Ireland*.[38] The decision in that case required the platform to delete defamatory statements that had been reported once and removed but which had subsequently reappeared. Likewise, the hosting provider may be obliged to 'remove information which it stores, the content of which is identical to the content of information that was previously declared to be unlawful, or to block access to that'. This is only possible through the use of artificial intelligence, which is encouraged by this decision and even implicitly made mandatory. Putting that decision in a broader context, it seems that platforms are required to act proactively against unlawful disinformation (or any unlawful content), even given the purported continued exclusion of monitoring obligations. The legality of the content is determined by algorithms, which seems quite risky for freedom of speech.[39]

6.5.2 *Digital Services Act*

The EU's Digital Services Act (DSA),[40] which aims to regulate online platforms in a more detailed and nuanced way, and is applicable from 2023 and 2024, respectively, keeps the most important foundations of European regulation of online platforms in place. The response of the EU to the problem of disinformation is to legislate for more societal responsibility for very large online platforms, while still leaving it to the discretion of the platforms themselves to decide if and how to deal with any systemic risks to freedom of expression.

The DSA retains the essence of the notice and takedown procedure, and platforms still cannot be obliged to monitor user content (Articles 6 and 8), but if they receive a notification that a certain piece of content is illegal, they will be obliged to remove it (Article 6), as set out also in the Directive on Electronic Commerce. The DSA will also seek to protect users' freedom of expression. It requires users to be informed of the content removed by platforms and gives them the possibility to have recourse to dispute resolution mechanisms in their own country, as well as to the competent authorities or courts if the platform has infringed the provisions of the DSA. These provisions seek to strengthen the position of users, in particular by providing procedural guarantees (most importantly through greater transparency,

38 Case C-18/18 *Eva Glawischnig-Piesczek* v. *Facebook Ireland Ltd.*, judgment of the CJEU of 3 October 2019, https://curia.europa.eu/juris/document/document.jsf?text=&docid=218621&pageIndex=0&doclang=EN&mode=lst&dir=&occ=first&part=1&cid=7924.

39 Elda Brogi and Marta Maroni, '*Eva Glawischnig-Piesczek v Facebook Ireland Limited*: A New Layer of Neutrality', CMPF, 17 October 2019, https://cmpf.eui.eu/eva-glawischnig-piesczek-v-facebook-ireland-limited-a-new-layer-of-neutrality.

40 Regulation (EU) 2022/2065 of the European Parliament and of the Council of 19 October 2022 on a Single Market For Digital Services and Amending Directive 2000/31/EC (Digital Services Act) (Text with EEA relevance).

the obligation to give reasons for deletion of a piece of content or for the suspension of an account, and the right of independent review).[41]

The democratic public sphere is protected by the DSA (Article 14(4)), which states that the restrictions in contractual clauses (Article 14(1)) must take into account freedom of expression and media pluralism. Article 14(4) states that:

> Providers of intermediary services shall act in a diligent, objective and proportionate manner in applying and enforcing the restrictions ... with due regard to the rights and legitimate interests of all parties involved, including the fundamental rights of the recipients of the service, such as the freedom of expression, freedom and pluralism of the media, and other fundamental rights and freedoms as enshrined in [the Charter of Fundamental Rights of the European Union].

Where platforms do not act with due care, objectivity and proportionality in applying and enforcing restrictions when deleting user content, taking due account of the rights and legitimate interests of all interested parties, including the fundamental rights of the users of the service, such as to freedom of expression, freedom and pluralism of the media, and other fundamental rights and freedoms as set out in the Charter of Fundamental Rights of the European Union (CFR), the user may have recourse to the public authorities. In regard to very large online platforms in Europe, this will most often be the designated Irish authority, to which other national authorities must also refer complaints they receive concerning these platforms, for which the European Commission has also reserved certain powers (it is for the Commission to decide whether to act itself or to delegate this power to the Irish authority).

Under the DSA, the authorities do not explicitly take action against disinformation, only doing so if it constitutes an infringement (war propaganda, which can be conducted through disinformation, can of course constitute an infringement). However, since disinformation alone does not constitute an infringement in national jurisdictions, the DSA does not introduce any substantive change in this respect. Furthermore, very large online platforms and very large online search engines must identify and analyze the potential negative effects of their operations (in particular their algorithms and recommendation systems) on freedom of expression and on 'civil discourse and electoral processes',[42] and must then take appropriate and effective measures to mitigate these risks (Article 35). In addition, the DSA's rules on codes of conduct also encourage the management of such risks and promote the enforcement of codes (including, for example, the Code of Practice on Disinformation, which predates the DSA). These tools also provide an indirect means of tackling disinformation. One of the main purposes of the DSA is to protect users' freedom of speech, but users' speech can also contain dis- or misinformation.

[41] Ibid. Arts. 17, 21 and 24.

[42] Ibid. Arts. 34(1)(b) and 34(1)(c).

It will be difficult to reconcile these conflicting interests when applying the regulation.

Article 36 of the DSA introduces a new 'crisis response mechanism'. Crisis in this legislation means 'extraordinary circumstances' that 'lead to a serious threat to public security or public health in the Union or in significant parts of it' (Article 36(2)). Very large online platforms will need to assess to what extent and how the functioning and use of their services significantly contribute to a serious threat, or are likely to do so and then to identify and apply specific, effective and proportionate measures, to prevent, eliminate or limit any such contribution to the serious threat identified (Article 36(1)).

6.6 THE EUROPEAN UNION'S EFFORTS TO CURB DISINFORMATION ON ONLINE PLATFORMS

European jurisdictions allow actions against disinformation, defined as action on the grounds of defamation or the violation of the prohibition of hate speech or scaremongering, while platforms, being 'host providers', can be required to remove infringing content. However, these measures in and of themselves seem inadequate to deal with such threats in a reassuring manner. Concerns of this nature have been addressed by the EU in various documents it has produced since 2017.

6.6.1 *Communications, Recommendations and Co-Regulation*

The first relevant EU Communication, issued in 2017,[43] concerns tackling illegal content, so it only indirectly addresses the issue of disinformation. It mentions that '[t]here are undoubtedly public interest concerns around content which is not necessarily illegal but potentially harmful, such as fake news or content that is harmful for minors. However, the focus of this Communication is on the detection and removal of illegal content.'[44] The Communication introduced a requirement for platforms to take action against violations in a proactive manner and even in the absence of a notice, even though the platforms are still exempted from liability.[45] The Recommendation that followed the Communication reaffirmed the requirement to apply proportionate proactive measures in appropriate cases, which thus permits the use of automated tools to identify illegal content.[46]

43 Communication on Tackling Illegal Content Online: Towards an Enhanced Responsibility of Online Platforms, 28 September 2017, COM(2017) 555 final.

44 Ibid. s. 2.

45 Ibid. s. 3.3.1.

46 Commission Recommendation of 1.3.2018 on Measures to Effectively Tackle Illegal Content Online, C(2018) 1177 final, ss. 12 and 18.

The High Level Expert Group on Fake News and Online Disinformation published a report in 2018.[47] The report defines disinformation as 'false, inaccurate, or misleading information designed, presented and promoted for profit or to intentionally cause public harm'.[48] While this definition might be accurate, the report refrains from raising the issue of government regulation or co-regulation, and is limited to providing a review of the resources and measures that are available to social media platforms and which they may apply voluntarily. The Communication[49] issued following the report of the High Level Expert Group already recognized the need for more concrete action, not only by online platforms but also by the European Commission and Member States. The document called for a more transparent, trustworthy and accountable online ecosystem. It foresaw the reinforcement of the EU bodies concerned and the creation of a rapid alert system that would identify in real time, through an appropriate technical infrastructure, any disinformation campaign.

Later in 2018, online platforms, leading technology companies and advertising industry players agreed, under pressure from the European Commission, on a code of conduct to tackle the spread of online disinformation. The 2018 Code of Practice on Disinformation was designed to set out commitments in areas ranging from transparency in political advertising to the demonetization of disinformation spreaders. The Code may appear to be voluntary in form – that is, a self-regulatory instrument – but it is in fact a co-regulatory solution that was clearly imposed on the industry players by the European Commission. Its primary objectives are to deprive disseminators of disinformation of advertising revenue from that activity, to make it easy to identify publishers of political advertising, to protect the integrity of the platform's services (steps against fake accounts and bots) and to support researchers and fact-checkers working on the subject. The Code actually further exacerbates the well-known problem of private censorship (the recognition of the right of platforms to restrict the freedom of expression of their users through rules of their own making),[50] by putting decisions on individual content in the hands of the platforms, which raises freedom of expression issues.[51]

47 Final Report of the High Level Expert Group on Fake News and Online Disinformation (2018), https://ec.europa.eu/digital-single-market/en/news/final-report-high-level-expert-group-fake-news-and-online-disinformation.

48 Ibid. p. 10.

49 Communication from the Commission to the European Parliament, the Council, the European Economic and Social Committee and the Committee of the Regions – Tackling Online Disinformation: A European Approach, 26 April 2018, COM(2018) 236 final.

50 See András Koltay, 'Private Censorship of Internet Gatekeepers' (2020–2021) 59(2) *Louisville Law Review* 255–304; András Koltay, 'The Protection of Freedom of Expression from Social Media Platforms' (2022) 73(2) *Mercer Law Review* 523–89.

51 Matteo Monti, 'The EU Code of Practice on Disinformation and the Risk of the Privatisation of Censorship' in Serena Giusti and Elisa Piras (eds.), *Democracy and Fake News: Information Manipulation and Post-Truth Politics* (Abingdon: Routledge, 2016) pp. 214–25, 220–21.

The Code of Practice was signed in October 2018 by online platforms such as Facebook, Google, Twitter and Mozilla, as well as advertisers and other players in the advertising industry, and was later joined by Microsoft and TikTok. The online platforms and trade associations representing the advertising industry submitted a report in early 2019 setting out the progress they had made in meeting their commitments under the Code of Practice on Disinformation. In the first half of 2019, the European Commission carried out targeted monitoring of the implementation of the commitments by Facebook, Google and Twitter, with a particular focus on the integrity of the European Parliament elections. The Commission published its evaluation of the Code in September 2020, which found that the Code provided a valuable framework for structured dialogue between online platforms, and ensured greater transparency and accountability for their disinformation policies. It also led to concrete actions and policy changes by relevant stakeholders to help combat disinformation.[52]

The Joint Communication of the European Parliament and of the Council on an Action Plan against Disinformation foresees the same measures as in the previous Communication in 2018.[53] The Communication called upon all signatories of the Code of Practice to implement the actions and procedures identified in the Code swiftly and effectively on an EU-wide basis. It also encouraged the Member States to launch awareness-raising initiatives and support fact-checking organizations. While this document reaffirms the primacy of means that are applied voluntarily by platform providers, it also displays restraint when it comes to compelling the service providers concerned to cooperate (in a forum convened by the European Commission). If the impact of voluntary undertakings falls short of the expected level, the necessity of action of a regulatory nature might arise.[54]

The arrival of the COVID pandemic in Europe in early 2020 gave a new impetus to the mass spread of disinformation, this time directly threatening human lives. Therefore, the EU bodies issued a new document proposing specific measures to be taken by platforms to counter disinformation about the epidemic, but did not actually broaden the scope of the general measures on disinformation previously set out.[55] Section 4 of the European Democracy Action Plan also specifically addresses the fight against disinformation and foresees the reinforcement of the

[52] Code of Practice on Disinformation (2018), https://ec.europa.eu/newsroom/dae/redirection/document/87534.

[53] Joint Communication to the European Parliament, the European Council, the Council, the European Economic and Social Committee and the Committee of the Regions, Action Plan against Disinformation. Brussels, 5.12.2018, Join(2018) 36 final.

[54] Ibid. 9, Action 6.

[55] Joint Communication to the European Parliament, the European Council, the Council, the European Economic and Social Committee and the Committee of the Regions, Tackling COVID-19 Disinformation – Getting the Facts Right. Brussels, 10.6.2020, Join (2020) 8 final.

2018 Code of Practice, the addition of further commitments and the establishment of a monitoring mechanism.[56]

In 2021, EU bodies issued a new Communication,[57] which foreshadowed the content of the updated Code of Practice. Subsequently, a review of the Code was launched, leading to the signing of the Strengthened Code of Practice on Disinformation by thirty-four signatories in June 2022.[58] The updated and strengthened Code aims to deliver on the objectives of the Commission's guidance,[59] presented in May 2021, by setting out a broader range of commitments and measures to combat online disinformation. While the Code has not been officially endorsed by the Commission, the Commission set out its expectations in its Communication, and has indicated that it considers that the Code meets these expectations overall. Since this guidance sets out the Commission's expectations in imperative terms ('the Code should', 'the signatories should', and so on), it is not an exaggeration to say that the fulfilment of the commitments is seen as an obligation for the platforms, which, if fulfilled, could avoid the imposition of strict legal regulation. Consequently, it is correct to consider the Code not as a self-regulatory instrument, but as a co-regulatory mechanism, which is not created and operated purely by the free will of industry actors but by a public body (in this case, the EU Commission) working in cooperation with industry players.

The Strengthened Code of Practice on Disinformation includes 44 commitments and 128 concrete measures in the areas of demonetization (reducing financial incentives for the disseminators of disinformation), transparency of political advertising (provisions to allow users to better identify political ads through better labelling), ensuring the integrity of services (steps against manipulative behavior such as the use of spam or disinformation), and the protection of the integrity of services (for example, measures to curb manipulative actions such as fake accounts, bot-driven amplification, impersonation and malicious deep spoofing), empowering users through media literacy initiatives, ensuring greater transparency for platforms' recommendation systems, supporting research into disinformation, and strengthening the fact-checking community. These measures will be supported by an enhanced monitoring framework, including service-level indicators to measure the implementation of the Code at EU and Member State level. Signatories submitted their first reports on the implementation of the Code to the Commission in early 2023. Thereafter, very large online platforms (as defined in the DSA) will report every

[56] Communication from the Commission on the European Democracy Action Plan.

[57] Communication from the Commission to the European Parliament, the Council, the European Economic and Social Committee and the Committee of the Regions; European Commission Guidance on Strengthening the Code of Practice on Disinformation. Brussels, 26.5.2021, COM(2021) 262 final.

[58] 2022 Strengthened Code of Practice on Disinformation.

[59] Communication from the Commission; Guidance on Strengthening the Code of Practice on Disinformation.

six months, while other signatories will report annually. The Strengthened Code also includes a clear commitment to work towards the establishment of structural indicators to measure the overall impact of the Code's requirements. The 2022 Strengthened Code focuses on political advertising, but also refers to other 'malicious actors' beyond those who commission political campaigns containing disinformation.[60] However, it only covers other speakers beyond the political sphere (citizens interested in public affairs and participating in debates) and misinformation without malicious intent more narrowly. Moreover, as with previous documents, it leaves the most important question open: who decides what constitutes disinformation? More precisely, it leaves the decision to the platform moderators and, to a lesser extent, to the fact-checkers.

The first baseline reports on the implementation of the Code were published in February 2023.[61] According to their reports, the service providers that signed the Code have taken a number of measures: for example, Google deprived disseminators of disinformation of €13 million in advertising revenue in the third quarter of 2022, while TikTok removed 800,000 fake user accounts, followed by a total of 18 million users during the same period and, on Facebook, 28 million fact-checking tags were added to different posts.

An ongoing legislative procedure is also worth noting in this regard. In 2021, the European Parliament and the Council proposed a regulation on the transparency and targeting of political advertising.[62] The regulation, if adopted, would be uniformly binding on all Member States, covering the identification of the customers of political advertising, their recognizability, measures against illegal political advertising and the requirements for targeting specific users.

The EU's approaches are in many respects forward-looking and can help to achieve several objectives, although they have also faced a number of criticisms. We may perceive a certain lack of sincerity on the part of both Member States and the EU when it comes to disinformation. All the related documents avoid a clear assessment of the question of whether the dissemination of disinformation falls within the scope of freedom of expression. Following the prevailing European doctrine, one cannot but conclude that a significant proportion of communications containing disinformation is content protected by freedom of expression, so their restriction by instruments with a not entirely clear legal status, such as a co-regulatory code of practice, may be cause for concern. These communications relate to matters of public interest and are therefore subject to the strongest

[60] 2022 Strengthened Code of Practice on Disinformation, pp. 8–9, 15–16, 19 and 37.

[61] European Commission, 'Signatories of the Code of Practice on Disinformation Deliver Their First Baseline Reports in the Transparency Centre', 9 February 2023, https://digital-strategy.ec.europa.eu/en/news/signatories-code-practice-disinformation-deliver-their-first-baseline-reports-transparency-centre; for the reports, see https://disinfocode.eu/reports-archive/?years=2023.

[62] Proposal for a Regulation of the European Parliament and of the Council on the Transparency and Targeting of Political Advertising. Brussels, 25.11.2021, COM(2021) 731 final.

protection of freedom of expression, with the exception of unlawful content, the publication of which is prohibited by specific rules (see Section 6.3). This also applies to content generated or sponsored by governments. However, communications involving untrue statements of fact may not be considered particularly valuable in the European approach, and could actually be restricted by the imposition of further prohibitions. In other words, Member States are free to introduce prohibitions against intentional disinformation that harms society, if this is necessary and proportionate, as this is not within the EU's competence.[63] Member States must take the ECtHR's case law into account when restricting freedom of expression, and this applies equally to disinformation.[64] Even so, the production and transmission of disinformation can justify restrictions on freedom of expression. However, other content beyond the sufficiently narrow prohibitions thus defined may still claim protection of freedom of expression, so measures taken against them by online platforms – based either on voluntary commitments or on the co-regulatory Code of Practice, but which are not based on the law as it stands – may be unjustified or disproportionate.[65]

The EU approach also reveals a kind of hidden elitism. While the EU focuses on political advertising and intentional disinformation campaigns, some of the measures it enforces on platforms also cover misinformation and communications by citizens. Ian Cram argues that the ECtHR's jurisprudence privileges traditional (institutional) media over citizen journalists, imposing standards of 'responsible journalism' on the latter.[66] It follows from this that the obligations of the media and other speakers are, where conceptually possible, the same. According to Cram, this is a kind of elitist approach, linked to a – democratically contradictory – perception of media freedom that seeks to create an 'enlightened public opinion' even vis-á-vis 'the people' (that is, individual speakers, who may be unbridled, perhaps foul-mouthed, and may lack the resources of the institutional media to uncover reality or create informed opinions).[67] The same is true for the obligations

[63] Donato Vese, 'Governing Fake News: The Regulation of Social Media and the Right to Freedom of Expression in the Era of Emergency' (2022) 13 *European Journal of Risk Regulation* 477–513.

[64] Sardo, 'Categories, Balancing, and Fake News'; Ethan Shattock, 'Fake News in Strasbourg: Electoral Disinformation and Freedom of Expression in the European Court of Human Rights (ECtHR)' (2022) 13(1) *European Journal of Law and Technology* 1–25; Paolo Cavaliere, 'The Truth in Fake News: How Disinformation Laws are Reframing the Concepts of Truth and Accuracy on Digital Platforms' (2022) 3(4) *European Convention on Human Rights Law Review* 481–523.

[65] Paolo Cavaliere also draws attention to the threat to freedom of expression, see Cavaliere, 'The Truth in Fake News' (n 64) 520–21.

[66] Ian Cram, *Citizen Journalists: Newer Media, Republican Moments and the Constitution* (Cheltenham: Edward Elgar, 2015) pp. 112–43; Ian Cram, *Liberal Democracy, Law and the Citizen Speaker: Regulating Online Speech* (Oxford: Hart, 2022) pp. 30–37, 144–86.

[67] Cram, *Liberal Democracy* (n 66) p. 30. Jacob Rowbottom points to a similar problem, arguing that the ECtHR 'tends to protect speech that is deemed to be of "high value", and therefore

imposed on platforms, which ultimately also restrict this kind of citizen participation in the public sphere. The EU thus turns to the 'elite' of the public arena, namely to the traditional media and fact-checking organizations, for help in judging disinformation.

The lack of honesty is also reflected in the interpretation of the Code of Practice, a formally self-regulatory instrument, which in reality is co-regulation imposed by the EU,[68] where coercion is not based on legislation but on informal agreements, and accompanied by concerns on the part of service providers about the risk of stricter regulation in the future. This co-regulatory nature is recognized by the reference in the Preamble of the Code: 'This Code of Practice aims to become a Code of Conduct under Article 35 of the DSA'[69] (in this section, the DSA itself advocates the creation of codes of conduct that set out the various obligations of platforms). Of course, the concerns of service providers are not necessarily justified, given their economic interest in the spread of disinformation, as the 2021 leak by a former Facebook employee, Francis Haugen, starkly highlighted.[70] Disinformation, unfortunately, tends to attract users, who readily consume such content and interact with it heavily, which in turn generates financial benefits for the platforms. It is therefore also difficult to believe that the transparency required by the EU and committed to by the service providers in relation to the spread of disinformation – covering decision-making and all relevant information – will actually be achieved, and it is very difficult for an actor outside the platform to verify whether it has been.

Twitter announced in May 2023, under the leadership of Elon Musk, that it would leave the Code. Because of its formally self-regulatory nature, this was, of course, within its rights. In any case, Thierry Breton, a senior official of the European Commission, announced immediately after the decision that the Code would nevertheless be enforced, including against Twitter.[71] This will be possible indirectly, if the Code becomes a kind of industry standard, and thus effectively binding, by applying Section 35 of the DSA.

A problem that goes hand in hand with the spread of disinformation is the breakdown of traditional media. The media are gradually losing the trust of the public,[72] but their economic foundations and, in turn, their professionalism are also

does little to protect much internet content'. See Jacob Rowbottom, 'To Rant, Vent and Converse: Protecting Low Level Digital Speech' (2012) 71(2) *Cambridge Law Journal* 355–83.

68 Cavaliere, 'The Truth in Fake News' (n 64) 490.

69 2022 Strengthened Code of Practice on Disinformation, I. Preamble, para. (i).

70 Scott Pelley, 'Whistleblower: Facebook Is Misleading the Public on Progress against Hate Speech, Violence, Misinformation', CBS News, 4 October 2021, www.cbsnews.com/news/facebook-whistleblower-frances-haugen-misinformation-public-60-minutes-2021-10-03; Stasi and Parcu, 'Disinformation and Misinformation' (n 12) p. 410.

71 'Twitter Withdraws from EU Disinformation Code, Commissioner Says', *Time*, 27 May 2023, https://time.com/6283183/twitter-withdraws-from-eu-disinformation-code-commissioner-says.

72 Megan Brenan, 'Americans' Trust in Media Remains Near Record Low', Gallup, 18 October 2022, https://news.gallup.com/poll/403166/americans-trust-media-remains-near-record-low.aspx.

under threat, not least because of the proliferation of internet services. Some EU documents mention the role and importance of the traditional media, although they can hardly offer solutions to these problems. Similarly, only at the level of a mere mention does the EU, including the DSA, address the issue of filter bubbles,[73] which reinforce social fragmentation, such as the '*Daily Me*' content offer,[74] customized for each user, which contributes significantly to the spread of disinformation among susceptible users.[75] It would not be inconceivable to adopt some of the approaches taken in the regulation of traditional media, such as the right of reply, which would allow disinformation to be accompanied immediately by a reaction containing true facts, or an appropriate adaptation of the obligation of balanced coverage, which would allow a controversial issue to be presented in several readings, immediately visible to the user. This is also hinted at in the Code of Practice, which seeks to steer users towards reliable sources. Measure 22 (7) of the Code states that 'Relevant Signatories will design and apply products and features (for instance, information panels, banners, pop-ups, maps and prompts, trustworthiness indicators) that lead users to authoritative sources on topics of particular public and societal interest or in crisis situations.' The right to information from multiple sources is the objective of both the right of reply and the obligation to provide balanced information, meaning that even if the means differ, the objectives may be similar in the regulation of traditional media and platforms.

Finally, another problem with the EU's approach that has been identified is that it is up to platforms and fact-checkers to judge content in the fight against disinformation. This is understandable, since the EU did not want to set up a kind of Orwellian Ministry of Truth, as it would consider it incompatible with freedom of expression for state bodies, courts and authorities to decide on the veracity of a claim. However, it is also doubtful whether leaving such decisions up to private individuals is capable of facilitating informed, fair and unbiased decision-making and whether it does not itself pose a threat to freedom of expression. The very term 'fact-checking' is unfortunately Orwellian, and the fact-checkers – and the platform moderators – can themselves be biased, as well as wrong.[76] Human cognitive mechanisms themselves make fact-checking difficult,[77] and its credibility is easily

[73] Eli Pariser, *The Filter Bubble: How the New Personalized Web Is Changing What We Read and How We Think* (London: Penguin, 2011).

[74] Nicholas Negroponte, *Being Digital* (New York: Alfred A. Knopf, 1995).

[75] The 2022 Code of Practice only requires platforms to provide information on recommendation systems, although, under the DSA, users will be able to prohibit the operation of recommendation systems based on profiling by changing their settings (see Section 6.5.2).

[76] Otávio Vinhas and Marco T. Bastos, 'Fact-Checking Misinformation: Eight Notes on Consensus Reality' (2022) 23(4) *Journalism Studies* 448–68; '6 Ways Fact Checkers Are Biased', AllSides, 23 February 2022, www.allsides.com/blog/6-ways-fact-checkers-are-biased.

[77] Sungkyu Park et al., 'The Presence of Unexpected Biases in Online Fact-Checking' (2021) 2(1) *Harvard Kennedy School Misinformation Review*, https://misinforeview.hks.harvard.edu/wp-content/uploads/2021/01/park_unexpected_biases_online_fact_checking_20210127.pdf.

undermined, as 'fact-checkers ... disagree more often than one might suppose, particularly when politicians craft language to be ambiguous'.[78] An empirical study found that 'fact-checkers are both less likely to fact-check ideologically close entities and more likely to agree with them'.[79] Fact-checkers are not accountable to society, even less so than the traditional media (through legal regulation or ethics-based self-regulation). Their activities are neither necessarily transparent, nor do they have guarantees of independence. In many cases, such as EU-funded organizations, they operate using public money, which makes these shortcomings problematic. If the traditional media are increasingly losing people's trust, what reason would people have to trust fact-checking organizations, which face similar credibility problems? While fact-checkers share similar problems with traditional media, their emergence is an interesting development and, if they can bridge the institutional problems, it is not inconceivable that they could be a useful contributor to the public sphere.[80] It is noteworthy that those fact-checkers who work on behalf of or with the approval or support of social media platforms, and who check the veracity of users' posts on those sites, bring social media closer to traditional media in terms of the way they operate, as these verifiers have a specific editorial role.

6.6.2 *Banning Russian Media Outlets in the Context of the Russian–Ukrainian War*

Shortly after the outbreak of the Russian–Ukrainian war, on 1 March 2022, the Council of the EU adopted a Decision[81] pursuant to Article 29 of the Treaty of the European Union (TEU) and a Regulation[82] pursuant to Article 215 of the Treaty on the Functioning of the European Union (TFEU) under which it is prohibited for:

> operators to broadcast or to enable, facilitate or otherwise contribute to broadcast, any content by the legal persons, entities or bodies listed in Annex XV [RT – Russia Today English, RT – Russia Today UK, RT – Russia Today Germany, RT – Russia Today France, RT – Russia Today Spanish, and Sputnik news agency], including through transmission or distribution by any means such as cable, satellite, IP-TV, internet service providers, internet video-sharing platforms or applications, whether new or pre-installed.
>
> (Article 1(1))

78 Chloe Lim, 'Checking How Fact-Checkers Check' (2018) 5(3) *Research & Politics* 1–7.

79 Charles Louis-Sidois, 'Both Judge and Party? An Analysis of the Political Leaning of Fact-Checkers' (2022), https://papers.ssrn.com/sol3/papers.cfm?abstract_id=4030887.

80 See Michael M. Epstein, 'Sustaining Country-Specific Fact-Checking Remedies, the Sierra Leone Experience' (manuscript, on file with author).

81 Council Decision (CFSP) 2022/351 of 1 March 2022 Amending Decision 2014/512/CFSP Concerning Restrictive Measures in View of Russia's Actions Destabilising the Situation in Ukraine.

82 Council Regulation (EU) 2022/350 of 1 March 2022.

All broadcasting licences or authorization, transmission and distribution arrangements with RT and Sputnik were suspended. (Later, these measures were extended to other Russian media outlets.) These sanctioning rules derive directly from the TEU. The Council of the EU used the prerogatives under Title V of the TEU concerning the general provisions on the EU's External Action and the specific provisions on the Common Foreign and Security Policy.[83] According to a leaked letter, the Regulation should be applied to any links to the internet sites of the media outlets, as well as to their social media accounts.[84] As a result, the ban is a departure from the general monitoring ban in Article 15 of the E-Commerce Directive.[85] This provision makes it clear that any state-imposed orders on social media platforms (referred to in the Directive as host services) to monitor users' content are not compatible with European law. Later, a lawsuit was initiated by RT France against the Regulation, but the Court of Justice of the EU dismissed RT France's application.[86]

According to the Recitals of the Decision and the Regulation, the Russian Federation 'has engaged in a systematic, international campaign of media manipulation and distortion of facts in order to enhance its strategy of destabilization of its neighboring countries and of the Union and its Member States'.[87] The recitals indicate two reasons for the ban: disinformation and propaganda.[88] Under Article 52 (1) of the CFR, any such interference must pursue 'objectives of general interest recognized by the Union'. Considering this, the restriction targeting disinformation and propaganda might be in line with the CFR.[89] However, according to Baade, the EU should not invoke the prohibition of disinformation or propaganda as a legitimate aim, as they may be protected expressions. An alternative aim would be to stop propaganda for war specifically.[90] The prohibition of propaganda for war is enshrined in Article 20 of the International Covenant on Civil and Political Rights. As all the EU Member States have ratified the Covenant, this prohibition

[83] Francisco J. Cabrera Blázquez, *The Implementation of EU Sanctions against RT and Sputnik* (Strasbourg: European Audiovisual Observatory, 2022), https://rm.coe.int/note-rt-sputnik/1680a5dd5d.

[84] A letter from the European Council to undisclosed recipients, see https://lumendatabase.org/file_uploads/files/5061360/005/061/360/original/6-9267000032260.pdf?1646430529&access_token=w6YC_Vjutt85UvZMLExMag, p. 2.

[85] Directive 2000/31/EC on Electronic Commerce.

[86] Case T-125/22, *RT France* v. *Council of the European Union*, judgment of the General Court (Grand Chamber) on 27 July 2022,

[87] Council Regulation (EU) 2022/350 of 1 March 2022, Recital 6; Council Decision (CFSP) 2022/351 of 1 March 2022 Recital 6.

[88] Council Regulation (EU) 2022/350 of 1 March 2022, Recitals 3–10; Council Decision (CFSP) 2022/351 of 1 March 2022, Recitals 4–6 and 10.

[89] Igor Popović, 'The EU Ban of RT and Sputnik: Concerns Regarding Freedom of Expression', EJIL: Talk!, 30 March 2022, www.ejiltalk.org/the-eu-ban-of-rt-and-sputnik-concerns-regarding-freedom-of-expression.

[90] Baade, 'Don't Call a Spade a Shovel' (n 8).

can also be considered a generally accepted principle of EU law. As Baade notes, the justification for the ban imposed on RT and Sputnik in the current situation cannot be based solely on the character of their content as 'propaganda' and not even as disinformation.[91] As already mentioned, propaganda and disinformation are generally protected by the freedom of expression, with certain exceptions.

After the Regulation came into force, the largest social media companies relaxed the enforcement of their rules involving threats against Russian military personnel in Ukraine.[92] According to a leaked internal letter, Meta allowed Facebook and Instagram users to call for violence against the Russian and Belarusian leaders, Vladimir Putin and Alexander Lukashenko, so long as the violence was nonspecific (without referring to an actual plot), as well as violence against Russian soldiers (except prisoners of war) in the context of the Ukraine invasion, which involves a limited and temporary change to its hate speech policy.[93] Twitter also announced some changes in its policies related to the war, although the company did not amend its generally applicable hate speech policies.[94]

The right of platforms to change the boundaries of free speech at will, without any constitutional guarantee or supervision, is an extremely dangerous development. Their propensity to make changes in a less transparent way, avoiding any meaningful public debate on the proposed changes, only increases the risk to freedom of expression.

6.7 ATTEMPTS TO REGULATE DISINFORMATION AT THE NATIONAL LEVEL

In order to strengthen the obligations of online platforms, some European countries have adopted rules, in line with common European law, to compel platforms to remove illegal content more quickly and effectively. The corresponding Act in German law (effective as of 1 January 2018) is a paramount example of this trend.[95] According to the applicable provisions, all platform providers within the scope of the Act (that is, platform providers with over 2 million users from Germany) must

[91] Björnstjern Baade, 'The EU's "Ban" of RT and Sputnik: A Lawful Measure against Propaganda for War', Verfassungsblog, 8 March 2022, https://verfassungsblog.de/the-eus-ban-of-rt-and-sputnik.

[92] Munsif Vengattil and Elizabeth Culliford, 'Facebook Allows War Posts Urging Violence against Russian Invaders', Reuters, 10 March 2022, www.reuters.com/world/europe/exclusive-facebook-instagram-temporarily-allow-calls-violence-against-russians-2022-03-10.

[93] Emerson T. Brooking, 'Meta Meets the Reality of War', SLATE, 17 March 2022, https://slate.com/technology/2022/03/meta-facebook-calls-violence-invading-russians.html.

[94] Sinéad McSweeney, 'Our Ongoing Approach to the War in Ukraine', Twitter, 16 March 2022, https://blog.twitter.com/en_us/topics/company/2022/our-ongoing-approach-to-the-war-in-ukraine.

[95] Act to Improve Enforcement of the Law in Social Networks 2017 (Gesetz zur Verbesserung der Rechtsdurchsetzung in sozialen Netzwerken (Netzwerkdurchsetzungsgesetz)), Art. 1 G. v 01.09.2017 BGBl. I S. 3352 (Nr. 61).

remove all user content that commits certain criminal offences specified by the Act. Such offences include defamation, incitement to hatred, denial of the Holocaust and the spreading of scaremongering news stories.[96] Manifestly unlawful pieces of content must be removed within twenty-four hours after receipt of a notice, while any 'ordinary' unlawful content must be removed within seven days.[97] If a platform fails to remove a given piece of content, it may be subject to a fine of up to €50 million (theoretically, in cases of severe and multiple violations).[98] The German legislation does not go much further than the E-commerce Directive itself, or its successor, the DSA; it simply refines the provisions of the Directive, lays down the applicable procedural rules and sets harsh sanctions for platforms which violate them. Nonetheless, the rules are followed in practice, and Facebook seems eager to perform its obligation to remove objectionable content.[99] The German regulation shows how difficult it is to apply general pieces of legislation and platform-specific rules simultaneously, and it demonstrates how governments prefer to have social media platforms act as the judges of user-generated content.

Subsequently, France[100] and Austria[101] adopted similar rules, although the French law ('Avia law') was annulled by the Constitutional Council because some of its provisions did not meet the constitutional requirements.[102] France had introduced transparency and reporting obligations for platforms in a law adopted in 2018, prior to the Avia law, along with a fast-track judicial procedure to remove content disseminated during election campaigns and deemed misleading or inaccurate.[103] The law confers new powers on the Media Council (Conseil Superieur de l'Audiovisuel), such as the ability to suspend or withdraw the licence of certain media services if, for example, a service under the control or influence of a foreign company is endangering France's fundamental interests, including the proper functioning of its institutions, by transmitting false information.[104] Under an amendment to the 1986 Freedom of Communication Act,[105] the Media Council can order

[96] Ibid. s. 1.

[97] Ibid. s. 3.

[98] Ibid. s. 4.

[99] 'Facebook Deletes Hundreds of Posts under German Hate-Speech Law', Reuters, 27 July 2018, www.reuters.com/article/us-facebook-germany-idUSKBN1KH21L.

[100] Law to Combat Hateful Content on the Internet (Loi no. 2020–766 du 24 juin 2020 visant à lutter contre les contenus haineux sur internet, JORF no. 0156 du 25 juin 2020 ('Avia Law')).

[101] Federal Law on Measures for the Protection of Users on Communication Platforms (Bundesgesetz über Maßnahmen zum Schutz der Nutzer auf Kommunikationsplattformen (Kommunikationsplattformen-Gesetz–KoPl-G)).

[102] Décision no. 2020-801 DC du 18 juin 2020, see www.conseil-constitutionnel.fr/decision/2020/2020801DC.htm.

[103] Law on the Fight against the Manipulation of Information (Loi no. 2018-1202 du 22 décembre 2018 relative à la lutte contre la manipulation de l'information, JORF no. 0297 du 23 décembre 2018); Craufurd Smith, 'Fake News, French Law and Democratic Legitimacy'.

[104] Law on the Fight against the Manipulation of Information, Art. 8.

[105] Law on Freedom of Communication (Loi no. 86-1067 du 30 septembre 1986 relative à la liberté de communication ('Léotard Law')).

the suspension of the electronic distribution of a television or radio service owned or controlled by a foreign state if the company deliberately transmits false information that could call into question the integrity of an election.[106] These powers may be exercised from the beginning of the three months preceding the first day of the month in which the presidential, general or European Parliamentary elections or referendums are held. The Constitutional Council found this law constitutional.[107]

The German and French attempts to regulate disinformation have introduced rules imposing obligations on platforms to remove certain content quickly. At the same time, German legislation only imposes obligations on content that is in breach of the Criminal Code, hence it is only the 2018 French law that regulates disinformation that is not in any case illegal, during election campaigns. However, these approaches still leave the decision on content in the hands of the platforms, and do not attempt to limit the spread of disinformation in general.[108] In Germany, another important piece of legislation has been passed, which also addresses the issue of disinformation. In 2020, the Interstate Treaty on Media Services (Medienstaatsvertrag, MStV) was adopted, which provides for the transparency of algorithms, the proper labelling of bots and the easy findability of public service media content on the platforms on which it is available. The MStV obliges social media platforms, video-sharing platforms and search engines to be nondiscriminatory in terms of content and to prioritize public service content, while not restricting user preferences. On video-sharing platforms, available public broadcasting content should be especially highlighted and made easy to find. These intermediaries may not unfairly disadvantage (directly or indirectly) or treat differently providers of journalistic editorial content to the extent that the intermediary may potentially have a significant influence on their visibility.[109] These rules only indirectly limit the spread of disinformation, but they provide a good example of how regulation can try to steer users towards credible content, in line with the traditional approach to media regulation.[110]

In the fight against the COVID pandemic and the disinformation related to it, several European countries tried to curb the spread of false and dangerous information by tightening criminal laws. Hungary, for example, tightened its rules on scaremongering,[111] and Greece extended the scope of the existing offence of

[106] Ibid. Art. 33-1-1.
[107] Conseil Constitutionnel, Décision no. 2018-773 dc du 20 décembre 2018.
[108] Licia Cianci and Davide Zecca, 'Polluting the Political Discourse. What Remedies to Political Microtargeting and Disinformation in the European Constitutional Framework?' (2023) 10 *European Journal of Comparative Law and Governance* 1–46, 1.
[109] Interstate Media Treaty (Medienstaatsvertrag), especially § 18 Abs. 3; § 19; § 84; §§ 93 and 94.
[110] On the national measures against disinformation, see Giovanni Pitruzella and Oreste Pollicino, *Disinformation and Hate Speech: A European Comparative Perspective* (Milan: Bocconi University Press, 2020) pp. 94–126.
[111] 2012 Criminal Code of Hungary, s. 337 (see Section 6.3).

dissemination of false information and introduced a prison sentence for those who spread disinformation on the Internet.[112]

8. ON THE POSSIBLE FUTURE SOLUTIONS: SOME CONCLUSIONS

The European states and the EU clearly assign primary responsibility for addressing disinformation issues to the platforms. Of course, the national governments and the European institutions have made a number of commitments themselves, but they leave it to the platforms to sort out the substantive issues, including compliance with their commitments under the Code. However, this is not a reason to give up on introducing further restrictions on free speech, as allowed by the European concept of freedom of expression. Even in the context of the US legal system, Cass Sunstein argues that intentional lies, if they cause at least moderate harm, may be constitutionally prohibited – and even negligent or mistaken misrepresentations can be restricted, if the harm incurred by them is serious.[113] It is still better – at least in Europe, we typically think so – that the line between forbidden and permissible speech is drawn by the legislature and the courts, constrained by strict constitutional guarantees, rather than by private organizations (in this case, mainly social media platforms) operating without such guarantees. But each and every social media post of concern cannot be taken to court, because nowhere could the judicial system cope with such a workload. Therefore, the right of platforms to decide on user content is likely to remain necessary in the long-term future. However, the protection of content that is *not* prohibited under the regime of freedom of expression is an important consideration, even if it contains untruths.

Although the European approach is wary of considering the communication of untrue statements of fact to be of high value, freedom of expression, at least according to the traditional approach, is in a sense a 'black and white' issue. Either a particular piece of content falls within the scope of freedom of expression or it does not. In other words, once the sometimes-difficult question of whether a particular piece of content constitutes defamation, invasion of privacy, hate speech and so on has been successfully answered, the consequences are self-evident: the content will either be protected or it will not. 'Pizzagate',[114] for example, could in

[112] Law 4855/2021: Amendments to the Penal Code, the Code of Criminal Procedure and other urgent provisions (Τροποποιήσεις του Ποινικού Κώδικα, του Κώδικα Ποινικής Δικονομίας και λοιπές επείγουσες διατάξεις του Υπουργείου Δικαιοσύνης), Art. 36.

[113] Cass R. Sunstein, *Liars: Falsehoods and Free Speech in an Age of Deception* (Oxford: Oxford University Press, 2021) pp. 12–18, 128–30.

[114] Amanda Robb, 'Anatomy of a Fake News Scandal', *Rolling Stone*, 16 November 2017, www.rollingstone.com/feature/anatomy-of-a-fake-news-scandal-125877.

principle have been dealt with under defamation law (at least if it would have happened in Europe, as under US defamation law it is more difficult to protect the reputation of a specific person against false allegations), and the false allegations made in the Brexit campaign[115] could in principle also have been prohibited under the rules governing fair election or referendum campaigns. Of course, even in these cases, the permissibility of restricting speech is not clear-cut and requires a nuanced decision by a court. Furthermore, an otherwise patently untrue statement – for example, how much more money will be available for the National Health Service in the United Kingdom if the country leaves the EU – may not necessarily be clearly refutable in a legal proceeding. But the main point is that many untrue statements are actually protected by freedom of speech. This does not mean that the protected content has the right to reach an audience or to have its volume amplified by a particular service (for example, through the media), but rather that its restriction is not allowed. This traditional approach is being disrupted by online platforms, which, as is their general practice, also restrict content that is not legally prohibited, according to their own intentions and contractual terms. The same problem dogs the fight against (not legally prohibited) disinformation: the EU also encourages restrictions on content that is otherwise protected by freedom of expression, and the relevant documents do not attempt to resolve this contradiction.

It is also important to make a clear distinction between disinformation originating from governments and dis- or misinformation that comes from members of society, whether deliberate or in good faith, but in this respect the EU documents currently available are not fully consistent. Members of society should not be disproportionately restricted in their freedom of expression, even if they approach public debate with malicious intent, and certainly not if they are unaware of the falsity or potential for damage of the news they are spreading (the good faith transmission of government disinformation also falls into this category). Private speech controlled or promoted by the government should be taken into account and only the freedom of honest citizens' speech who are otherwise wrong should be strongly protected. The question is whether this separation is even possible. And if so, whose job is it, the legal regulators or purely the platforms? We do not have good answers to this dilemma at the moment.

Nor would it be inconceivable to regulate platforms more strictly, setting out their obligations vis-à-vis content not protected by freedom of expression, not in self- or co-regulatory instruments but in clearly prescribed legal rules. This would of course require close cooperation between Member States and the EU, as speech bans can only be imposed at Member State level, while platform regulation can only be effective at EU level.

115 Hannah Marshall and Alena Drieschova, 'Post-Truth Politics in the UK's Brexit Referendum' (2018) 26(3) *New Perspectives* 89–106.

Users need to be led out of the filter bubble imposed on them by the platforms, which would fundamentally affect their business model. In this regard, the provision of the option prescribed by the DSA to opt out of content recommendation based on profiling is a step in the right direction, but not big enough, because it puts the decision in the hands of the users, and it is questionable how many will take advantage of it, and that particular bubble can also be produced by means other than profiling. Data protection regulations can also be called upon to help in the fight, in particular by tightening up data-processing actions by platforms.[116]

It would be worth considering making the transmission of substantiated statements and opinions on public affairs to users mandatory, or providing easy access to divergent and dissenting views on specific issues, while maintaining the choice for users who do not wish to hear them, as exemplified by the regulation of traditional media. Such instruments include, in respect of television and radio, the right of reply and the obligation to provide balanced (impartial) news coverage, the mandatory publication of local or national content or the mandatory transmission of certain content of public interest by broadcasters. These duties could also be applied to social media, with some adaptation. In principle, social media could be required to make available, alongside a post on a contentious issue, posts that present the dissenting views on that issue. Algorithms might be able to do this, although the business model of the platforms might be adversely affected. Such a rule would be similar to the right-of-reply and impartial information obligations known from media regulation, except that it could be done automatically without a specific request. Strengthening nonlegislative approaches, raising awareness and supporting traditional media are also necessary tools – within the competence of Member States.

The fight against disinformation is a seemingly open-ended task that poses particular challenges for policymakers, both in terms of protecting freedom of expression and in defining new obligations for members of the public. It has become clear that traditional legal instruments, legislation and the imposition and enforcement of obligations by the relevant authorities can only partially address the problems it raises, and that the cooperation of all stakeholders is necessary. However, this should not lead to the 'outsourcing' of decisions by putting them fully in the hands of private companies. Member States and the EU must continue to play a leading role in shaping the rules. The EU has taken a number of important measures, and some Member States are trying to address some of the issues, but it is reasonable to fear that we are only at the beginning of the journey and that further technological

116 Joris van Hoboken and Ronan Ó Fathaigh, 'Regulating Disinformation in Europe: Implications for Speech and Privacy' (2021) 6(9) *UC Irvine Journal of International, Transnational, and Comparative Law* 9–36.

developments will bring new risks. Disinformation, as Paul Bernal has so eloquently demonstrated,[117] is essentially the same age as public communication; there is nothing new under the sun, but we must be able to formulate new answers to old questions all the time. But the end result of any struggle of legal systems in this regard will be that responsible, informed participation in public debates will remain primarily the responsibility of the individual concerned, just as it has been in past centuries.

[117] Paul Bernal, *The Internet, Warts and All: Free Speech, Privacy and Truth* (Cambridge: Cambridge University Press, 2018) pp. 230–34; Paul Bernal, 'Fakebook: Why Facebook Makes the Fake News Problem Inevitable' (2018) 69(4) *North Ireland Legal Quarterly* 513–30, 516–19.

7

The Fight against Disinformation in the Council of Europe, and the Relevant Case Law of the European Court of Human Rights

Bernát Török

7.1 INTRODUCTION

A broad consensus has emerged in recent years that although rumours, conspiracy theories and fabricated information are far from new,[1] in the changed structure and operating mechanisms of the public sphere today we are faced with something much more challenging than anything to date,[2] and the massive scale of this disinformation can even pose a threat to the foundations of democracy.[3] However, the consensus extends only to this statement, and opinions differ considerably about the causes of the increased threat of disinformation, whom to blame for it, and the most effective means to counter it. From the perspective of freedom of speech, the picture is not uniform either, and there has been much debate about the most appropriate remedies. It is commonly argued, for example, that the free speech doctrine of the United States does not allow for effective legal action against disinformation, while in Europe there is much more room for manoeuvre at the disposal of the legislator.

This chapter presents an example of European thinking: the search for answers to the problem of disinformation within the Council of Europe (CoE). For several reasons, the CoE provides an excellent opportunity to examine this quest as a joint European journey. The organization, that comprises forty-seven Member States, truly represents the vast majority of Europe, and thanks to the diversity of the work within its institutions, it has a complex impact on the legal development and public policy of the continent. The bodies of the CoE, with their sometimes harder,

[1] Cass R. Sunstein and Adrian Vermeule, 'Conspiracy Theories: Causes and Cures' (2009) 17(2) *Journal of Political Philosophy* 202.

[2] Claire Wardle and Hossein Derakhshan, *Information Disorder: Toward an Interdisciplinary Framework for Research and Policy Making*. Council of Europe report DGI(2017)09, Council of Europe, 2nd revised ed., August 2018, p. 4.

[3] The European Democracy Action Plan launched by the European Commission expressly addresses disinformation as a challenge for democracy in its Section 4.

sometimes softer tools – binding international court rulings, opinions on national legislation, public policy recommendations, various reports and analyses – always seek the common European denominator that can provide a solid basis for identifying the peculiarities of the continent's joint approach.

In this chapter, I will examine the practice of three institutions of the CoE (the European Court of Human Rights, the Committee of Ministers and, to a lesser extent, the Venice Commission) which have had a great impact on the development of Member States' legislative and judicial processes. The problem of disinformation has not been directly addressed by a specific policy document, either in the decisions of the European Court of Human Rights (ECtHR) or in the recommendations of the Council of Europe's Committee of Ministers, or among the documents of the Venice Commission. However, the key points that can serve as guidelines for a European approach can be identified from the practice of the three bodies. First, I will outline the common conceptual frameworks in the relevant practice of the three institutions, with special regard to the fundamentals of the doctrine of freedom of speech (Section 7.2). After that, I will analyse the decisions of the ECtHR that can be considered relevant to the question of disinformation, especially those involving the possibility of restrictive legal means against it (Section 7.3). Finally, through the recommendations of the Ministerial Committee, I will examine what public policy solutions the CoE recommends for dealing with disinformation (Section 7.4). My three main sources are: the decisions of the ECtHR (the implementation of which is a fundamental obligation for all Member States), the recommendations of the Committee of Ministers (which provide guidelines for the legislators and political decision-makers), and the relevant documents of the Venice Commission, the advisory body on constitutional matters (which comments on the constitutional processes of the Member States).

The chapter will focus chiefly on the role of the state in the fight against disinformation, so other issues that might be extremely important for the topic – for instance, the complex question of self-regulation – are discussed only tangentially. I hope that by the end of the chapter it will be clear that – although European law undoubtedly seeks answers based on different constitutional doctrines compared to the United States, and this leads to significantly different legal practices on important social issues (especially in the area of hate speech) – the problem of disinformation represents a challenge that even on the old continent cannot be effectively answered by restrictive legal means.

7.2 THE LEGAL FRAMEWORK OF THE FIGHT AGAINST DISINFORMATION IN THE COUNCIL OF EUROPE

Although the CoE has not issued any decision or recommendation specifically aimed at combating disinformation, the outlines of how to deal with the issue can be clearly drawn from the relevant documents. The present problem of disinformation did not materialize in a vacuum, as clear principles and a system of criteria for the regulation of public discourse have been developed in recent decades. There is no doubt that the challenge posed by disinformation lies precisely in the fact that digital technologies, platforms and social media have significantly subverted the previous operating mechanisms of the public sphere. However, the response to it needs to be situated among established constitutional principles. We must confront the accepted doctrine with the new phenomenon: we must determine whether new approaches are needed at some point and we must also make it clear where it is not possible to compromise on the principles that have been followed so far.

The Council of Europe has been at the forefront of analysing the social issue of disinformation from the beginning. It was one of the first bodies to recognize the gravity of the phenomenon while trying to clear up the increasingly confusing picture. Between the rampant use of the label 'fake news', on the one hand, and the demands for immediate and decisive interventions against misleading information, on the other, a comprehensive study carried out in 2017 for the CoE was pioneering in its emphasis on the importance of taking a calm, analytical approach. The significance of the paper for us is that – examining the intensifying information disturbances in a nuanced manner – it has provided a new conceptual framework for the analysis of the issue. The authors of the study successfully proposed a threefold conceptual categorization to describe information disorders, which until then had been mostly associated with the vague concept of 'fake news'.[4]

In this model, misinformation is when false information is shared, but no harm is meant. Disinformation, meanwhile, is when false information is knowingly shared to cause harm. A further category, mal-information, is when genuine information is shared with the intent to cause harm, often by bringing information designed to remain private into the public sphere. In this section, I will consider this conceptual framework to be authoritative while dealing primarily with the response to disinformation – that is, knowingly and harmfully spreading untruths. The starting points for the regulatory treatment of social information disturbances, including the intensification of attempts at disinformation, are provided by the legal framework of public communication. The most important points of this framework in the work of the bodies of the CoE are summarized below.

[4] It underlines: 'In this report, we refrain from using the term "fake news", for two reasons. First, it is woefully inadequate to describe the complex phenomena of information pollution. The term has also begun to be appropriated by politicians around the world to describe news organisations whose coverage they find disagreeable. In this way, it is becoming a mechanism by which the powerful can clamp down upon, restrict, undermine and circumvent the free press.' Wardle and Derakhshan, *Information Disorder* (n 2), 5.

7.2.1 *The Participatory Model of Free Speech and the Democratic Public Opinion*

The question that defines the entire doctrine of freedom of speech concerns which theoretical justification that right relies on, or to put it more accurately: which aspects each justification prioritizes. The concept of 'speech' has a normative nature that is defined by each constitutional doctrine based on which justification(s) it emphasizes.[5] These justifications have already been systematized by others.[6] Essentially, communications represent three types of value: they can contribute to the discovery of truth we seek together,[7] they can be manifestations of the free fulfilment of our personality (the individualist approach),[8] and they can ensure our participation in democratic social life (democratic theories).[9] Despite the fact that it is neither possible nor necessary to insist on exclusivity among the justifications, the primary basis the European doctrine rests on can be clearly established.[10]

From the very beginning, the ECtHR has focused on the democratic justification of freedom of expression. According to the reasoning it has consistently ascribed to, 'freedom of expression constitutes one of the essential foundations of a democratic society and one of the basic conditions for its progress and for each individual's self-fulfilment'.[11] Considering the practice as a whole, it is clear that, despite the mention of individual fulfilment, the legal interpretations are not primarily based upon the individualistic justification, although it plays an important role within the democratic approach. Democratic justifications are not completely uniform in all details, and the two main models focus on somewhat different elements in important legal interpretation situations – and the issue of disinformation is one such situation.

One democratic theory sees the value of freedom of speech in that it is essential for the common, informed decision-making which is the essence of democracy, and

5 Frederick Schauer, 'Categories and the First Amendment: A Play in Three Acts' (1981) 34 *Vanderbilt Law Review* 265, at 272–73.

6 E.g., Eric Barendt, *Freedom of Speech* (Oxford: Oxford University Press, 2005) pp. 1–39.

7 William P. Marshall, 'The Truth Justifications for Freedom of Speech' in Adrienne Stone and Frederick Schauer (eds.), *The Oxford Handbook of Freedom of Speech* (Oxford: Oxford University Press, 2021) pp. 44–60.

8 Martin H. Redish, 'The Value of Free Speech' (1982) 130 *University of Pennsylvania Law Review* 591; Ronald Dworkin, *Freedom's Law. The Moral Reading of the American Constitution* (Oxford: Oxford University Press, 1996) pp. 199–202.

9 For the origin of the democratic theories, see Alexander Meiklejohn, *Free Speech and Its Relation to Self-Government* (New York: Harper & Brothers, 1948).

10 See Robert Post on the 'lexical priority' of the justifications, Robert Post, 'Participatory Democracy as a Theory of Free Speech' (2011) 97(3) *Virginia Law Review* 617, at 618.

11 See, e.g., in the latest case law with several references to previous decisions, *Sanchez* v. *France*, app. no. 45581/15, judgment of 15 May 2023, [145].

which places the audience's need for information at the centre.[12] The other theory sees the value of free speech above all in that it ensures that everyone has the opportunity to become involved in the life of the democratic community. In this model, participation is at the centre of the concept of democracy and democratic public opinion,[13] and freedom of speech focuses much more strongly on the speaker and their intention to communicate.[14] The practice of the ECtHR draws on both approaches, but it is chiefly based on the participation model in the sense that the central issue of legal interpretations is the protection of the speaker's right to personal expression.

The aspects of participatory democracy are also emphasized in the documents of other bodies of the Council of Europe. As a recommendation of the Committee of Ministers on the new notion of media highlights, freedom of expression is indispensable for a genuine democracy and for democratic processes. 'In a democratic society, people must be able to contribute to and participate in the decision-making processes which concern them.'[15] The internet-related recommendations of the Committee of Ministers – as will be shown below – also recognize the revolutionary importance of the digital age for freedom of speech in the expansion of opportunities for personal participation. In addition, the democracy-based approach is most evident in the concrete interpretation of the law, in which, although the scope of freedom of speech is broader than that of political communication, significantly stronger protection is afforded to political speech. The ECtHR consistently emphasizes that 'the promotion of free political debate is a very important feature of a democratic society and the Court attaches the highest importance to freedom of expression in the context of such debate'.[16] The importance of this approach is particularly highlighted by the practice of the ECtHR on artistic expressions, which grants strong protection to works of art only if they form part of the public debate.[17]

Both the ECtHR and other bodies of the CoE therefore attach special importance to the democratic formation of public opinion, to which they attribute specific characteristics. On the one hand, democratic public opinion means a lively discourse that embraces as many points of view as possible, and develops according to

[12] Alexander Meiklejohn, 'The First Amendment Is an Absolute' (1961) 25 *Supreme Court Review* 245; Owen M. Fiss, *Liberalism Divided: Freedom of Speech and the Many Uses of State Power* (Boulder, CO: Westview, 1996); Robert H. Bork, 'Neutral Principles and Some First Amendment Problems' (1971) 47(1) *Indiana Law Journal* 1, at 20.

[13] Post, 'Participatory Democracy' (n 10) 618.

[14] Robert C. Post, 'Meiklejohn's Mistake: Individual Autonomy and the Reform of Public Discourse' (1993) 64 *University of Colorado Law Review* 1109.

[15] Recommendation CM/Rec(2011)7 of the Committee of Ministers to member states on a new notion of media (Adopted by the Committee of Ministers on 21 September 2011 at the 1121st meeting of the Ministers' Deputies), s. 2.

[16] E.g., *Sanchez* v. *France*, [146].

[17] See *Müller and Others* v. *Switzerland*, app. no. 10737/84, judgment of 24 May 1988; *Wingrove* v. *United Kingdom*, app. no. 17419/90, judgment of 25 November 1996; *Vereinigung Bildender Künstler* v. *Austria*, app. no. 68354/01, judgment of 25 January 2007.

its own logic and under its own rules in a lively discussion of opinions and counter-opinions. As the Venice Commission emphasizes, open and robust public debate is the cornerstone of democracy: 'A democracy should not fear debate, even on the most shocking or anti-democratic ideas. It is through open discussion that these ideas should be countered and the supremacy of democratic values be demonstrated ... Persuasion through open public debate, as opposed to ban or repression, is the most democratic means of preserving fundamental values.'[18] On the other hand, although this does not appear *expressis verbis* in the documents, the legal interpretation of the public debate starts from a specific anthropological view.

The decisions of the ECtHR on the restriction of commercial communication can be usefully contrasted with its decisions on communication deemed to be part of the public debate. The court has consistently held that although the freedom of speech extends to commercial advertisements, their publication can be widely restricted. In order to ensure that consumers receive accurate information about the specific features of goods and services, restrictions may be imposed especially in the case of misleading or untrue information. The ECtHR therefore considers the consumer as a player that is vulnerable to the manufacturer, and needs to be protected.[19] As we will see in the democratic public debate, even in the case of untrue information, the Court does not admit the possibility of such a general restriction, and considers citizens participating in the formation of public opinion as autonomous (rather than vulnerable) actors.[20]

It should also be mentioned that, in the European doctrine, the press is an actor in the public sphere with distinct rights and obligations. As multiple recommendations of the CoE function, namely scrutiny of public and political affairs and private or business-related matters of public interest, contributes to justify media's broad freedom; however, it is counterpoised by a requirement of greater diligence in respect of factual information. Regarding the reliability of information, 'professionalism requires verifying information and assessing credibility'.[21]

In the ECtHR's view, electoral campaigns have their own significance for the formation of democratic public opinion. The Court reiterated several times that free

[18] Compilation of Venice Commission Opinions and Reports Concerning Freedom of Expression and Media, CDL-PI(2016)011, 19 September 2016, s. 1.1.

[19] *Casado Coca* v. *Spain*, app. no. 15450/89, judgment of 24 February 1994, [51]; *Stambuk* v. *Germany*, app. no. 37928/97, judgment of 17 October 2002, [39].

[20] A clear framing of this anthropology can be found in the case law of the Hungarian Constitutional Court that closely follows the Strasbourg jurisprudence in the field of political debates: 'The approach of the constitutional evaluation is determined by the consideration that during the democratic discussion of public affairs participants of the debate are the citizens who interpret political events in their complexity, being aware of the special characteristics of partizan political opinions, especially during electoral campaigns that tend to exaggerate in order to attract voters' attention.' Decision No. 3107/2018. (IV. 9.) AB, [28].

[21] Recommendation CM/Rec(2011)7, s. 85.

elections and freedom of expression, particularly freedom of political debate, together form the bedrock of any democratic system.

> For this reason, it is particularly important in the period preceding an election that opinions and information of all kinds are permitted to circulate freely ... At the same time the Court recognises the importance of protecting the integrity of the electoral process from false information that affect voting results, and the need to put in place the procedures to effectively protect the reputation of candidates.[22]

We will see below in the relevant case law (Section 7.3) that the ECtHR has so far always put the reputation of candidates concerned in the focus.

7.2.2 *The Internet and Freedom of Speech*

To discuss the issue of disinformation, it is important and instructive to examine more closely how the documents of the CoE view the Internet. A wealth of material is available in this regard, as the Ministerial Committee has dealt with the issues raised by the Internet in many of its recommendations – even mentioning disinformation among these problems – and, of course, cases related to the role of the Internet have also been raised before the ECtHR.

It is clear from the documents that the CoE has taken into account new dangers arising from the functioning of the Internet since the very beginning, but in the first place it still welcomes it as a tool that can radically expand the possibilities for democratic participation. The recommendation of the Committee of Ministers on measures to promote the public service value of the Internet notes that while digital tools can significantly enhance the exercise of human rights and fundamental freedoms, such as freedom of expression, it admits that they may adversely affect these and other rights. Still, the Committee recommends that, in order to promote democracy, Member States should strengthen the participation and involvement of their citizens in public debate through the Internet, and encourage the use of infocommunication services, including online forums, weblogs, political chats, instant messaging and other forms of citizen-to-citizen communication. The recommendation strongly supports citizens' engagement with the public through user-generated communities rather than official websites.[23]

The ECtHR also approaches the Internet as one of the principal means of providing essential tools for the participation in discussions concerning political issues, highlighting that the possibility for user-generated expressive activity on the Internet provides an 'unprecedented platform for the exercise of freedom of

[22] *Staniszewski* v. *Poland*, app. no. 20422/15, judgment of 14 October 2021, [47].

[23] Recommendation CM/Rec(2007)16 of the Committee of Ministers to Member States on measures to promote the public service value of the Internet (Adopted by the Committee of Ministers on 7 November 2007 at the 1010th meeting of the Ministers' Deputies), Section III.

expression'.[24] The Court welcomes the fact that the Internet has fostered the 'emergence of citizen journalism', as political content ignored by the traditional media is often disseminated via websites to a large number of users, who are then able to view, share and comment upon the information.[25] However, the bodies of the CoE have also identified the dangers that making use of the new opportunities provided by the Internet entails. Defamatory and other types of clearly unlawful speech, including hate speech and speech inciting violence, can be disseminated as never before, in a matter of seconds.[26] Digital transformation and the shift towards an increasingly digital, mobile and social media environment have profoundly changed the dynamics of production, dissemination and consumption of news.[27] Newer materials also mention the problem of disinformation among its dangers: 'Targeted disinformation campaigns online, designed specifically to sow mistrust and confusion and to sharpen existing divisions in society, may also have destabilizing effects on democratic processes.'[28] Meanwhile, '[d]emocracies have experienced growing threats posed by the spread of disinformation and online propaganda campaigns, including as part of large-scale co-ordinated efforts to subvert democratic processes'.[29]

It is worth briefly mentioning the CoE bodies' main approach to responsibility for internet content. The central concept of the documents is 'shared liability'. According to this, 'a wide, diverse and rapidly evolving range of players facilitate interactions on the Internet between natural and legal persons by offering and performing a variety of functions and services',[30] and the responsibility for content must be adapted to this multi-player approach. According to the Ministerial Committee, instead of summary solutions, a fine-tuned approach is needed that elaborates and delineates the boundaries of the roles and responsibilities of all key stakeholders within a clear legal framework, using complementary regulatory

[24] See, e.g., *Vladimir Kharitonov* v. *Russia*, app. no. 10795/14, judgment of 23 June 2020, [33]; *Melike* v. *Turkey*, app. no. 35786/19, judgment of 15 June 2021, [44]; *Times Newspapers Ltd* v. *United Kingdom (No. 1 and No. 2)*, app. nos. 3002/03 and 23676/03, judgment of 10 March 2009, [27].

[25] *Cengiz and Others* v. *Turkey*, app. nos. 48226/10 and 14027/11, judgment of 1 December 2015, [52].

[26] *Sanchez* v. *France*, [161] and [162].

[27] Recommendation CM/Rec(2022)4 of the Committee of Ministers to member States on promoting a favourable environment for quality journalism in the digital age (Adopted by the Committee of Ministers on 17 March 2022 at the 1429 meeting of the Ministers' Deputies), Preamble.

[28] Recommendation CM/Rec(2018)2 of the Committee of Ministers to Member States on the roles and responsibilities of internet intermediaries (Adopted by the Committee of Ministers on 7 March 2018 at the 1309th meeting of the Ministers' Deputies), Recital (3).

[29] Recommendation CM/Rec(2022)4, s. A(6).

[30] Recommendation CM/Rec(2018)2, Recital (4).

frameworks.[31] The ECtHR also focuses on 'a context of shared liability between various actors'.[32]

An important starting point for the CoE's approach to responsibility is that providers of intermediary services – which contribute to the functioning or accessing of media and content, but do not themselves exercise editorial control – should not be regarded as media. However, their activity is certainly relevant in the media context and for the formation of democratic public opinion.[33] The CoE agrees with the view that state authorities should not impose a general obligation on intermediaries to monitor content which they merely provide access to, and recommends that they should ensure that intermediaries are not held liable for such third-party content. Intermediaries may be liable if they do not act expeditiously to restrict access to content or services as soon as they become aware of their illegal nature.[34] As the ECtHR emphasized: 'to exempt these services from all liability might facilitate or encourage abuse and misuse, including hate speech and calls to violence, but also manipulation, lies and disinformation'.[35]

7.2.3 *Competing Values and Their Power against Free Speech*

Before examining the concrete decisions of the ECtHR in Section 3, it is also worth establishing in principle the methodology with which the jurisprudence evaluates the values and interests that may compete with the interest of freedom of speech. It is clear what these values and interests are under the European Convention on Human Rights. Article 10(2) of the Convention, on freedom of expression, lists the reasons that may serve as a basis for restricting freedom of expression. According to this part of the text, freedom of expression can be limited in the interests of national security, territorial integrity or public safety, for the prevention of disorder or crime, for the protection of health or morals, for the protection of the reputation or rights of others, for preventing the disclosure of information received in confidence, or for maintaining the authority and impartiality of the judiciary. It is well established in the jurisprudence of the ECtHR and the CoE documents that the list provided in the Convention is exhaustive: any restrictions of the right to free speech must pursue a legitimate aim as exhaustively enumerated in Article 10.[36]

The further question of what power these specific reasons for restriction represent against freedom of speech is connected to a dilemma that is also known from the

[31] Recommendation CM/Rec(2007)16.
[32] *Sanchez* v. *France*, [183].
[33] Recommendation CM/Rec(2011)7, s. 36.
[34] Recommendation CM/Rec(2018)2, s. 1.3.7.
[35] *Sanchez* v. *France*, [185].
[36] Recommendation CM/Rec(2016)5 of the Committee of Ministers to Member States on Internet Freedom (Adopted by the Committee of Ministers on 13 April 2016 at the 1253rd meeting of the Ministers' Deputies), s. 2.4.1.

academic discourse: whether freedom of speech should be protected with a categorical or a balancing approach,[37] or – to adapt this question to the more recent American terminology – whether strict or intermediate scrutiny should be the main method.[38] At one end of the scale of theoretically possible answers is the position that grants constitutional protection to communications in all circumstances, while the other end of the scale is represented by the view that conflicts of relevant constitutional values can only be resolved by considering the special circumstances of specific cases. According to the most common view, which rather oversimplifies the picture, while the categorical approach prevails in the USA, in Europe balancing interests is more typical. However, the situation is more complex than this: although the absolutist understanding of freedom of speech is undoubtedly quite different from the European doctrine, the jurisprudence of the ECtHR strives to combine both the categorical and the balancing approaches in its practice.[39]

On the one hand, the Court must take into account the reasons for restriction listed in the Convention that compete against freedom of speech, which is itself protected by it.[40] On the other hand, with regard to political speech, the jurisprudence applies a more categorical understanding of protection. According to the consistently emphasized thesis, there is little scope under Article 10(2) for restrictions on freedom of expression in the field of political speech, and the authorities' margin of appreciation in assessing competing interests against freedom of expression in this context is particularly narrow.[41] The Recommendation of the Committee of Ministers concerning internet freedom also points out that restrictions on freedom of speech based on legitimate aims, including defamation laws, hate speech laws or laws protecting public order should be specific and narrowly defined in their application so that they do not inhibit public debate.[42] Although included in the above-mentioned list, hate speech is something of an exception to the more categorical approach, as its restriction is accepted by the CoE's bodies, including the Court, with an increasingly permissive attitude. In general, however, it remains true that the

[37] Laurent B. Frantz, 'The First Amendment in the Balance' (1961–1962) 71(8) *Yale Law Journal* 1424, 1432; Wallace Mendelson, 'On the Meaning of the First Amendment: Absolutes in the Balance' (1962) 50(5) *California Law Review* 821, 821; Steven Shiffrin, 'Defamatory Non-media Speech and First Amendment Methodology' (1977–1978) 25 *UCLA Law Review* 915, 955.

[38] T. Alexander Aleinikoff, 'Constitutional Law in the Age of Balancing' (1986–1987) 96(5) *Yale Law Journal* 943, 946; Ashutosh Bhagwhat, 'The Test That Ate Everything: Intermediate Scrutiny in First Amendment Jurisprudence' (2007) (3) *University of Illinois Law Review* 783, 785.

[39] Alessio Sardo, 'Categories, Balancing, and Fake News: The Jurisprudence of the European Court of Human Rights (2020) 33(2) *Canadian Journal of Law and Jurisprudence* 439.

[40] European Convention on Human Rights, Art. 10(2).

[41] See, among others, *Tête* v. *France*, app. no. 59636/16, judgment of 26 March 2020, [63]; *Lingens* v. *Austria*, app. no. 9815/82, judgment of 8 July 1986, [42]; *Sanchez* v. *France*, [146].

[42] Recommendation CM/Rec(2016)5 s. 2.4.2.

ECtHR's approach to political speech departs from case-by-case consideration and tends towards a more categorical protection.[43]

7.2.4 *The Role of the State*

In the practice of the CoE concerning freedom of speech, the peculiarities of the European approach to fundamental rights can be clearly identified when considering the role of the state in the enforcement of those rights. Their starting point differs little from the US doctrine: the purpose of the constitution and fundamental rights is, above all, to limit state power, thus ensuring the exercise of civil liberties. The primary obligation of the state is therefore to refrain from violating these freedoms. Regarding freedom of speech, the key point is that the state should not interfere in the formation of public opinion. However, the European approach goes beyond this starting point in two important ways.

On the one hand, the documents of the CoE consistently emphasize that the state has not only negative but also positive obligations in connection with the protection of freedom of speech.[44] The state is obliged not only to refrain from restricting expression but also to actively contribute to the creation of an environment that supports the exercise of freedom of speech.[45] In line with this, states also have a positive obligation in the digital environment, 'to create a safe and enabling environment for everyone to participate in public debate and to express opinions and ideas without fear, including those that offend, shock or disturb State officials or any sector of the population'.[46] The state must not only protect the individual exercise of rights, but also promote the fulfilment of freedom of opinion as a social value and institution based on its obligation to ensure an 'objective institutional protection'. This obligation allows broader scope than the US doctrine to regulate social relations related to the fundamental right. The state's obligation to act in support of the formation of democratic public opinion – as we will see in Section 7.3 analysing the practice of the ECtHR – justifies only a very narrow range of substantive intervention in the content of social communication.

Jurisprudence considers only the 'gravest forms of hate speech' to be inherently incompatible with the basic values of democracy, so they can be excluded from the

43 Somewhat similar to what Melville Nimmer describes as definitional balancing, Melville B. Nimmer, 'The Right to Speak from Times to Time: First Amendment Theory Applied to Libel and Misapplied to Privacy' (1968) 56(4) *California Law Review* 935, 942.

44 Recommendation CM/Rec(2016)5, s. 1.

45 For the doctrine and practice of the positive obligation of states, see Andrew T. Kenyon, *Democracy of Expression: Positive Free Speech and Law* (Cambridge: Cambridge University Press, 2001); Andrew T. Kenyon and Andrew Scott (eds.), *Positive Free Speech: Rationales, Methods and Implications* (Oxford: Hart, 2020).

46 Recommendation CM/Rec(2018)2, Recital (6).

scope of freedom of speech without further consideration.[47] Beyond that, however, the protection of democracy does not justify substantive intervention in the formation of public opinion but serves as a basis for the state to contribute through regulation to the proper framework and structure of the democratic public sphere. Among other things, this consideration creates a solid basis for European media regulations, the development of which is strongly supported by the CoE. According to its Recommendation on media pluralism, the states are the 'ultimate guarantors' of the democratic, plural functioning of the social public domain and have a positive obligation to put in place an appropriate legislative and policy framework to ensure the proper flow of views and information.[48]

On the other hand, the role of the state is fundamentally influenced because, according to the European doctrine, the protection of fundamental rights can not only be relevant between citizens and states. An integral tenet of European constitutional law for decades is that in some cases, when private actors find themselves in a situation that significantly affects the enforcement of the fundamental rights of others, constitutional values also impose requirements on them.[49] States have a 'positive obligation to ensure the exercise and enjoyment of rights and freedoms (which) includes, due to the horizontal effects of human rights, the protection of individuals from actions of private parties by ensuring compliance with relevant legislative and regulatory frameworks'.[50] Recently, the thesis of the horizontal scope of fundamental rights has gained traction in the field of freedom of speech, especially in the relationship between social media platforms and their users.[51] According to this argument, platforms cannot shape and apply their community rules at their own discretion, but must pay attention to the rights of their users, above all their freedom of speech. In terms of content moderation, for instance, the hands of the service providers are therefore tied to a certain extent by the requirements arising from the freedom of speech. As a consequence, while the recommendation

47 See Section 7.3.7 of this chapter about the application of the 'abuse clause' (Article 17) of the Convention on Human Rights. The Venice Commission also highlights this: 'in a true democracy imposing limitations on freedom of expression should not be used as a means of preserving society from dissenting views, even if they are extreme … It is only the publication or utterance of those ideas which are fundamentally incompatible with a democratic regime because they incite to hatred that should be prohibited.' CDL-AD(2008)026, Report on the relationship between freedom of expression and freedom of religion: the issue of regulation and prosecution of blasphemy, religious insult and incitement to religious hatred, para. 46.

48 Recommendation CM/Rec(2018)1 of the Committee of Ministers to Member States on media pluralism and transparency of media ownership (Adopted by the Committee of Ministers on 7 March 2018 at the 1309 meeting of the Ministers' Deputies), s. 2.1.

49 Eleni Frantziou, *The Horizontal Effect of Fundamental Rights in the European Union* (Oxford: Oxford University Press, 2019); Hans-Wolfgang Micklitz et al. (eds.), *Constitutional Challenges in the Algorithmic Society* (Cambridge: Cambridge University Press, 2022).

50 Recommendation CM/Rec(2018)2, Recital (6).

51 The profound change in relations regarding free speech certainly appears also in the US literature, but in a different conceptualization, see Jack M. Balkin: 'Free Speech is a Triangle' (2018) 118(7) *Columbia Law Review* 2011.

of the CoE welcomes that 'some online platforms have made considerable efforts to prevent the use of their networks as conduits for large-scale disinformation and manipulation of public opinion', it also warns that 'the impact of these measures on the free flow of information and ideas in democratic societies must be studied carefully'.[52]

7.3 FALSE AND HARMFUL INFORMATION IN THE JURISPRUDENCE OF THE ECTHR

According to the previously cited definition from the analysis of the CoE, disinformation is when false information is knowingly shared in order to cause harm. Although, with the exception of a single stray mention, the ECtHR has not yet addressed disinformation in its decisions,[53] it has a remarkable body of practice regarding the untruthfulness of communications and the harm caused by it. By analysing this practice, I will take into account the aspects that play an important role in the Court's consideration when clarifying the conceptual elements of disinformation (falsity, intent and harm).

7.3.1 *Statements of Facts and Value Judgements*

One of the most important guiding threads of the ECtHR's decisions reveals the difficulty of distinguishing between factual statements and value judgements. According to the Court's general practice, the protection of freedom of speech applies differently to statements of facts and value judgements. The Court distinguishes between the two categories on the ground that 'while the existence of facts can be demonstrated, the truth of value judgments is not susceptible of proof', and 'the requirement to prove the truth of a value judgment is impossible to fulfil and infringe freedom of opinion itself'.[54] The two categories cannot be completely separated, however. First, statements of facts are an integral part of the formation of present or future value judgements, and this must also be taken into account when determining the standards of their protection. Second, the ECtHR reiterates that where a statement amounts to a value judgement, 'the proportionality of an interference may depend on whether there exists a sufficient factual basis for the impugned statement, since even a value judgment without any factual basis to support it may be excessive'.[55]

52 Recommendation CM/Rec(2022)4, s. A.6.

53 For the only exception, see *Sanchez* v. *France*, [185].

54 E.g. *Feldek* v. *Slovakia*, app. no. 29032/95, judgment of 12 July 2001, [75]; *Lingens* v. *Austria*, app. no. 9815/82, judgment of 8 July 1986, [46]; and *Oberschlick* v. *Austria (No. 1)*, app. no. 11662/85, judgment of 23 May 1991, [63].

55 *De Haes and Gijsels* v. *Belgium*, app. no. 19983/92, judgment of 24 February 1997, [47]; *Jerusalem* v. *Austria*, app. no. 26958/95, judgment of 27 February 2001, [43].

From the perspective of the legal prosecution of disinformation, an important question is how strictly the categories of facts and value judgements are regarded as separable. If we rigidly insist on the truthfulness of each element of an expression, then the possibility of restriction opens up greatly, while if we place the emphasis on judging the expression of opinion as a whole, the participation of the speaker in the democratic dialogue becomes much more protected. In the practice of the ECtHR, the latter approach clearly follows from the fundamental aspects of freedom of speech. This is well illustrated by the Polish cases described below, that dealt with the application of a provision of the local election law that prosecutes falsity.[56]

In *Kita* v. *Poland*, a decision had to be made on the legality of leaflets distributed in a local election campaign, which drew the voters' attention to financial abuses. The ECtHR disallowed the summary classification of the Polish courts, since in the course of the categorization of the statements in question they unreservedly qualified all of them as statements which lacked any factual basis without examining the question of whether they could be considered to be value judgements. While the ECtHR recognized that some of the statements could be considered lacking a sufficient factual basis, it based its decision on the fact that 'the thrust of the applicant's article was to cast doubt on the suitability of the local politicians for public office' related to issues of public interest. According to the *ratio decedendi* of the Strasbourg judgment, 'the distinction between statements of fact and value judgments is of less significance in a case where the impugned statements were made in the course of a lively political debate, even where the statements made may lack a clear basis in fact'.[57]

In *Kwiecien* v. *Poland*, the question was again the interpretation of the Polish election law. In this case, an open letter attacked one of the candidates, and the ECtHR assumed again that the purpose of the speech published in the campaign was to dispute the candidate's suitability for public office. As a general rule of interpretation, the court establishes a presumption for expressions belonging to the campaign that 'opinions and information ... should be considered as forming part of a debate on questions of public interest' in the case of campaign communications. The judgment did not dispute the assertion that certain elements of the open letter lacked sufficient factual basis, but overall it considered that 'its thrust was

[56] The relevant provision of the Act reads as follows: 'If posters, slogans, leaflets, statements or other forms of propaganda and campaigning contain untrue data and information, a candidate standing for local election or a representative of an electoral committee has the right to make an application asking the Regional Court to: 1) order the confiscation of such materials, 2) issue an injunction restraining [the defendant] from publishing such data and information, 3) order the information to be corrected, 4) order [the defendant] to apologise to the aggrieved party, 5) order [the defendant] to pay to a charity up to PLN 10,000, 6) order [the defendant] to pay to the claimant up to PLN 10,000 in damages.'

[57] *Kita* v. *Poland*, app. no. 57659, judgment of 8 July 2008, [45] and [46]; *Lombardo and Others* v. *Malta*, app. no. 7333/06, judgment of 24 April 2007, [60].

to cast doubt on the candidate's suitability for local public office, based on the applicant's long experience with him'.[58]

7.3.2 *Good Faith or Bad Faith*

In both *Kita* and *Kwiecien*, the ECtHR also referred to the fact that nothing in the circumstances of the case indicated that the speakers had acted in bad faith. As we have seen, the fact that certain elements of the expressions did not have an adequate factual basis was not enough to establish bad faith. Proving bad faith means rebutting the presumption that the speaker acted with the intention of participating in democratic political debate. If it emerges from the circumstances of the case that the author of the opinion was no longer motivated by the shaping of the debate on public affairs, but by the goal of an unfounded personal attack, then their expression of opinion is not entitled to the same protection.[59]

Salov v. *Ukraine* sheds light on the same consideration in a true 'conspiracy theory case'. One of the candidates in the Ukrainian presidential election campaign was held responsible by the Ukrainian courts for disseminating the false information that the incumbent (and running for re-election) president was actually already dead and was being replaced by a stuntman during his public appearances. However, the ECtHR emphasized in its decision that the original source and publisher of the untrue information was not the convicted presidential candidate, but that he had only dealt in good faith with information that had already emerged during the campaign. The judgment points out that the sharing or discussion of the received information cannot be prohibited in itself, 'even if it is strongly suspected that this information might not be truthful. To suggest otherwise would deprive persons of the right to express their views and opinions about statements made in the media'. The Court considered that the presidential candidate had acted in good faith because he emphasized that he had not known whether this information was true or false while he was discussing it with others, having alleged that he was trying to verify it.[60]

At the same time, the standard of good faith is not uniform, but may vary according to the position of the speaker. In *Medzlis Islamske Zadnice Brcko*, religious and ethnic civil organizations appealed to the competent authorities of an administrative district in Bosnia and Herzegovina and criticized a person they considered to be unsuitable for the post of director of the district's multi-ethnic public radio station by making a number of incriminating allegations. Some of the claims came from other people's reports, while others were presented to the authorities without sources. The ECtHR started from the fact that, in the eyes of society,

58 *Kwiecien* v. *Poland*, app. no. 51744/99, judgment of 9 January 2007, [51], [54].
59 Ibid. [54]; *Kita* v. *Poland*, [45].
60 *Salov* v. *Ukraine*, app. no. 65518/01, judgment of 6 September 2005, [113] and [114].

reputable non-governmental organizations (NGOs) have an increased responsibility for disseminating factual statements. According to the Code of Ethics and Conduct for NGOs adopted by the World Association of Non-Governmental Organizations, they were bound by the requirement to verify the veracity of allegations submitted. In contrast, those involved in the case made statements based on guesswork and rumour without making any serious efforts to verify the authenticity of the non-governmental organizations.[61]

7.3.3 *Journalistic Ethics*

The standard of good faith and careful conduct is always stricter when it applies to the press. The ECtHR attributes a particularly important and prominent role in the functioning of democracy to the press as an institution that professionally informs the public.[62] This role does not mean that the press should not respect the rights of others, but the aspects of information dissemination are given special weight, since its basic task is to present information and opinions related to public affairs.[63]

However, according to the practice of the court, the press is entitled to enhanced protection in its informative activities only when it acts in good faith – that is, when it acts in accordance with the tenets of 'responsible journalism'.[64] The standard of good faith is acting according to journalistic ethics, which sets expectations for journalists in order to provide the public with accurate and reliable information.[65] Based on journalistic ethics, it is the basic task of the press to take steps before publication to verify the accuracy of the information it receives.[66] However, the fulfilment of this obligation is, by definition, adjusted to the circumstances of the given case. When covering communication by others, for example in an interview, the general requirement for journalists to distance themselves systematically and formally from the content of a quotation that might insult or provoke others or damage their reputation is not reconcilable with the press's role of providing information on current events, opinions and ideas. 'Punishment of a journalist for assisting in the dissemination of statements made by another person in an interview would seriously hamper the contribution of the press to discussion of matters of

[61] *Medzlis Islamske Zajednice Brcko and Others* v. *Bosnia and Herzegovina*, app. no. 17224/11, judgment of 27 June 2017, [114] and [115].

[62] It is worth noting that the mainstream doctrine about the special duties of the press in the formation of public opinion has recently been debated in the academic discourse, see Paul Wragg, *A Free and Regulated Press: Defending Coercive Independent Press Regulation* (Oxford: Hart, 2020).

[63] *Jersild* v. *Denmark*, app. no. 15890/89, judgment of 23 September 1994, [31]; *De Haes and Gijsels* v. *Belgium*, [37].

[64] *Bédat* v. *Switzerland*, app. no. 56925/08, judgment of 29 March 2016, [50].

[65] *Staniszewski* v. *Poland*, [48]; *Goodwin* v. *United Kingdom*, app. no. 17488/90, judgment of 27 March 1996, [39]; *Bladet Tromsø and Stensaas* v. *Norway*, app. no. 21980/93, judgment of 20 May 1999, [65].

[66] *Sallusti* v. *Italy*, app. no. 22350/13, judgment of 7 March 2019, [56].

public interest.'[67] In addition, it should always be taken into account that journalistic freedom also covers possible recourse to a degree of exaggeration, or even provocation.[68]

It is very instructive, however, that in *Staniszewski*, the ECtHR saw no reason for protecting the free flow of information when the editor of a monthly newsletter completely failed to indicate the sources of his information. Without any indication of sources, we are probably facing a case of fabrication rather than dissemination of news, which the Court considered as clear proof of acting in bad faith.[69] In the Court's approach, in today's ever more effervescent information whirlwind, the importance of journalistic ethics has not diminished at all, in fact it is becoming more and more important: 'In a world in which the individual is confronted with vast quantities of information circulated via traditional and electronic media and involving an ever-growing number of players, monitoring compliance with journalistic ethics takes on added importance.'[70] The ECtHR quite accurately and tellingly identifies that one of the main reasons why disinformation is felt to be overwhelming in our public discourse is that partisan and activist journalism is increasingly trumping standards of responsible journalism.

7.3.4 *The Impact of Speech*

The Strasbourg Court considers the influencing power of speech to be a factor to be taken into account even in the case of harmful communications, including untrue statements of fact. In the above-mentioned *Salov* case, for example, an important circumstance was that the convicted presidential candidate shared untrue information from a small newspaper reporting fabricated news with a limited number of people.[71] When assessing information published in the legacy media, the ECtHR traditionally takes into account the differences between the influencing powers of different media. 'In considering the duties and responsibilities of a journalist, the potential impact of the medium concerned is an important factor and it is commonly acknowledged that the audio-visual media often have a much more immediate and powerful effect than the print media.'[72]

There may also be large variations in the potential impact of different expressions given the extremely wide range of types of communication on the Internet.

67 *Ólaffson* v. *Iceland*, app. no. 8493/13, judgment of 16 March 2017, [56]; *Jersild* v. *Denmark*, [35]; *Delfi AS* v. *Estonia*, app. no. 64569/09, judgment of 16 June 2015, [135].
68 *Dalban* v. *Romania*, app. no. 28114/95, judgment of 28 September 1999, [49].
69 *Staniszewski* v. *Poland*.
70 *NIT S.R.L.* v. *The Republic of Moldova*, app. no. 28470/12, judgment of 5 April 2022, [181]; *Stoll* v. *Switzerland*, app. no. 69698/01, judgment of 10 December 2007, [104].
71 *Salov* v. *Ukraine*, [114].
72 *Delfi AS* v. *Estonia*, [134].

> It is clear that the reach and thus potential impact of a statement released online with a small readership is certainly not the same as that of a statement published on mainstream or highly visited web pages. It is therefore essential for the assessment of a potential influence of an online publication to determine the scope of its reach to the public.[73]

Likewise in connection with the potential influence of speech, it is worth mentioning the thread of interpretation which – primarily in cases related to hate speech – also attributes importance to the person of the speaker. In certain positions, according to the Court, more attention is paid to a speaker's opinion, so its impact can be more significant. In *Sanchez* v. *France*, the ECtHR emphasized that with politicians, the degree of notoriety and representativeness necessarily lend a certain resonance and authority to a person's words or deeds. Owing to politicians' particular status and position in society, they are more likely to influence people.[74] In terms of communication on the Internet, a similarly enhanced impact can be presumed if the speaker is a well-known blogger or a popular contributor to social media.[75]

The Court always evaluates the social and political context of the expression of an opinion as an important or, in some cases, decisive factor in the impact of the communication. When a statement is made against a tense political or social background, the presence of such a background generally leads the Court to accept that some form of interference is justified.[76] In contrast, if there was no indication that a sensitive social or political background existed, the Court was reluctant to admit the necessity of restriction.[77]

7.3.5 *The Use of Internet Sources*

The line of interpretation developed by the ECtHR regarding the use of internet sources in the press has significance beyond the media. The study prepared for the CoE also emphasizes the importance of the fact that 'in the age of disinformation' people are increasingly seeing information created by unofficial sources (from social media accounts, or websites which have only recently appeared), and there is 'a need to be doing source-checking as well as fact-checking'. This is partly because of the fact that the nature of the source which originally created the content or which first shared it can provide the strongest evidence about whether the information is accurate.[78]

At the same time, the practice of the court does not accept objective responsibility for the dissemination of information, even by the press, which is charged with a strict

[73] *Savva Terentyev* v. *Russia*, app. no. 10692/09, judgment of 28 August 2018, [79].
[74] *Sanchez* v. *France*, [150] and [187].
[75] *Savva Terentyev* v. *Russia*, [81].
[76] *Perincek* v. *Switzerland*, app. no. 27510/08, judgment of 15 October 2015, [205].
[77] *Kilin* v. *Russia*, app. no. 0271/12, judgment of 11 May 2021, [92].
[78] Wardle and Derakhshan, *Information Disorder* (n 2), p. 18.

duty of care. In *Editorial Board of Pravoye Delo and Shtekel* v. *Ukraine*,[79] the ECtHR held accountable the Ukrainian regulation since, although the Press Act exempts journalists from civil liability for verbatim reproduction of material published in the press, no such immunity existed for journalists reproducing material from internet sources not qualified as press. The Court admitted that the risk of certain forms of harm posed by content and communications on the Internet is higher than that posed by the press, therefore the policies governing the reproduction of material from the printed media and the Internet may differ. Even so, considering the importance of the Internet for the exercise of the right to freedom of expression, the Court ruled that 'the absence of a sufficient legal framework allowing journalists to use information obtained from the Internet without fear of incurring sanctions seriously hinders the exercise of the vital function of the press as a public watchdog'.[80]

Similarly, the ECtHR considered the practice of the Hungarian Constitutional Court, which only exempted journalists from responsibility for the coverage of official press conferences, to be insufficient. In the case of *Magyar Jeti Zrt.* v. *Hungary*,[81] the Court considered it necessary to enforce such immunity on a much wider scale. In the specific case, in connection with the distribution of hyperlinks, the reasoning explained that their very purpose, by directing internet users to other pages and web resources, is to allow them to navigate to and from material in a network characterized by the availability of an immense amount of information. Hyperlinks, as a technique of reporting, are essentially different from traditional acts of publication in many senses, including that the person offering information through a hyperlink does not exercise control over the content of the website to which the hyperlink enables access. Consequently, the Court could not agree with the approach equating the mere posting of a hyperlink with the dissemination of defamatory information, thus automatically entailing liability for the content itself.[82] Of course, the consideration of other factors also played a role in the decision, especially that the press organ acted in good faith, in the service of the discussion of public affairs.

In another Hungarian case, the ECtHR explained in connection with the comments section of an internet portal that providing a platform for third parties to exercise their freedom of expression by posting comments is a journalistic activity of a particular nature. Therefore, the question of liability for defamatory statements posted there should always be considered on the grounds that 'the punishment of a journalist for assisting in the dissemination of statements made by another person in an interview would seriously hamper the contribution of the press to discussion of

[79] *Editorial Board of Pravoye Delo and Shtekel* v. *Ukraine* No. 33014/05, judgment of 5 August 2011.

[80] Ibid. [61]–[64].

[81] *Magyar Jeti Zrt* v. *Hungary*, no. 11257/16, judgment of 4 December 2018.

[82] Ibid. [74]–[77].

matters of public interest'.[83] Although the above theses regarding the use of internet resources were elaborated by the ECtHR in cases related to the press, they are deeply rooted in its general approach to internet communication and are thus also applicable to other speakers.

7.3.6 *The Harm of Speech*

It is also worth briefly considering what in the ECtHR's case law the legal basis for action against false information may be. In other words, what kind of grievances can justify legal restrictions that respond to disinformation? As has already been discussed, the limitation of freedom of speech must be traceable to one of the grounds for limitation listed in Article 10(2) of the Convention. Those decisions of the ECtHR which considered that it was permissible to limit the freedom of expression due to the dissemination of false information accepted such restrictions in order to protect the rights of others. In terms of the legal response to disinformation, the 'protection of the rights of others' can be interpreted in two ways, however. When a restriction is imposed in order to protect the rights of a specific person, typically their reputation, this has long been considered a traditional intervention in line with the doctrine of freedom of speech. In such cases, the ECtHR considers in each situation how much the person affected by the opinion is obliged to tolerate in the interest of the free discussion of public affairs. On the other hand, the 'rights of others' can also be interpreted in a more abstract way if it is understood as the legitimate interests of certain groups or even of the entire society. While the protection of social groups, especially minorities in a sensitive situation, is an obvious consideration in cases related to hate speech, the ECtHR has so far considered the protection of the rights of specific individuals as the appropriate goal in decisions related to the dissemination of false statements.

Although the Court – considering the legitimate aim of the interference – has already referred to the more abstract ways in which disinformation may cause harm in two election-related cases, in both cases the individual candidates concerned were actually affected by the false statements. According to the summarizing statement of the *Salov* judgment, the Court agreed with the government that the interference at issue was intended to pursue the legitimate aim of providing the voters with true information in the course of the presidential campaign.[84] However, the submission of the government was based on the argument that the dissemination of false information about a presidential candidate could have a damaging effect on

[83] *Magyar Tartalomszolgáltatók Egyesülete and Index.hu Zrt.* v. *Hungary*, app. no. 22947/13, judgment of 2 February 2016, [79]; see also, *Jersild* v. *Denmark*, [35]; *Delfi AS* v. *Estonia*, [135].

[84] *Salov* v. *Ukraine*, [110].

their reputation and effectively prevent them from conducting an effective electoral campaign.[85]

The rights of the voters therefore only arose indirectly in the case. In *Staniszewski*, the ECtHR similarly indicated that the interference had served to protect the integrity of the electoral process and thus the rights of the voters, but in the first place the Court emphasized that the legitimate aim of the restriction was to protect the reputation of one of the candidates in the local elections.[86] The ECtHR thus considers it relevant to refer to the rights of the voters and the integrity of the election as a more abstract value to be protected in the case of disinformation published in an election campaign, but the restrictions on the freedom of speech that have been deemed legal until now have always been imposed to protect the rights of a specific person, even in the context of an election.

At the same time, the right to adequate information can also be a valid reason for intervention in the field of media law in a more abstract form. The practice of the bodies of the CoE, including the Court, regards the audiovisual media as an actor with particularly strong power to influence others, thus it has developed specific standards of intervention, which are now applied as a matter of convention. The misleading information containing untruths in *NIT* v. *Moldova* was found to be a suitable legal basis even for revoking the right to broadcast, as the measure was intended to ensure the audience's right to a balanced and unbiased coverage of matters of public interest in news programmes.[87]

In principle, 'prevention of disorder' could also be grounds for the limitation of free speech, based on the list in Article 10(2) in the field of disinformation. It may not be a coincidence that the title of the report of the CoE on disinformation is 'Information Disorder'.[88] It can be argued that, within the changed framework of the public sphere, disinformation, especially in relation to election campaigns, disrupts democratic conditions and causes hard-to-repair damage to the smooth functioning of public discourse and democratic elections. However, the case law of the ECtHR does not support that 'prevention of disorder' becomes another legal basis for restricting freedom of speech in the fight against disinformation.

In the Court's approach, given that the Convention serves to protect individual freedoms, the legal grounds for limiting rights must always be interpreted restrictively. The meaning of 'prevention of disorder' was interpreted by the ECtHR together with the term 'protection of public order' used elsewhere in the Convention. Accordingly, while 'public order' appears to bear a wider meaning, referring to the body of political, economic and moral principles essential to the maintenance of the social structure, the notion of 'disorder' 'conveys a narrower

85 Ibid. [101].
86 *Staniszewski* v. *Poland*, [44].
87 *NIT S.R.L.* v. *The Republic of Moldova*, [174].
88 See note 4.

idea, understood in essence in cases of this type as riots or other forms of public disturbance'.[89] This means that the 'prevention of disorder' can serve as a legitimate aim for restricting free speech in case of disinformation only when the communication in question can trigger riots or other forms of violent public disturbance. This cannot be ruled out, but it is certain that disinformation – even if it clearly disturbs the debate on public affairs – has such an effect only in very special circumstances.

Interventions for the sake of public health have recently come into focus in the wake of the COVID-19 pandemic. The convention mentions public health as one of the reasons for restrictions, and although such a case has yet to be brought before the ECtHR, it may well be relevant in the field of disinformation. It is clear from *Hertel* v. *Switzerland* that when a public health issue – in this specific case, the effect of microwave ovens on health – is the subject of social debate, the state has only a very narrow margin to limit the viewpoints expressed.[90] However, this room for manoeuvre increases according to how solid the (European) consensus is on a given health issue. In the event of such a consensus, fundamental considerations of public health could prevail even over fundamental rights such as freedom of expression.[91]

7.3.7 *Article 17: Abuses of Freedom of Expression*

Due to their significance, I will separately examine the types of harms in which Article 17 of the Convention, the so-called abuse clause, is referred to by the Court. Article 17 of the Convention is a provision on the prohibition of the abuse of rights. It reads as follows: 'Nothing in this Convention may be interpreted as implying for any State, group or person any right to engage in any activity or perform any act aimed at the destruction of any of the rights and freedoms set forth herein or at their limitation to a greater extent than is provided for in the Convention.' The methodological significance of Article 17 lies in the fact that, when applied, the ECtHR treats the expression in question as speech outside the scope of freedom of speech, and does not even conduct a strict examination of the legality of the restriction.[92]

Article 17 is the ultimate tool for the protection of human rights and democracy, the application of which is reserved by the ECtHR for cases that deny democratic values and principles.[93] It is only applicable on an exceptional basis and in extreme

89 *Perincek* v. *Switzerland*, [146] and [151].

90 *Hertel* v. *Switzerland*, app. no. 25181/94, judgment of 25 August 1998, [47].

91 *Société de conception de presse et d'édition and Ponson* v. *France*, app. no. 26935/05, judgment of 5 March 2009, [56].

92 For the key distinction between the scope of the freedom of speech and the protection provided by it, see especially, Schauer, 'Categories and the First Amendment'; Barendt, *Freedom of Speech*, 74–78, Robert C. Post, 'Recuperating First Amendment Doctrine' (1994–1995) 47(6) *Stanford Law Review* 1249, 1250.

93 Hannes Cannie and Dirk Voorhoof, 'The Abuse Clause and Freedom of Expression: An Added Value for Democracy and Human Rights Protection?' (2011) 29(1) *Netherland Quarterly of Human Rights* 54.

situations, and in cases concerning freedom of expression it should only be resorted to in situations where it is immediately clear that the impugned statements involve this right for ends clearly contrary to the values of the Convention.[94] Given that, according to general opinion, the increasing prevalence of disinformation ultimately undermines democracy, and in its radical sense disinformation is per se contrary to all the values that the Convention promotes and protects, the possibility of applying Article 17 can also be raised.[95] The validity of this suggestion seems to be strengthened by the fact that the ECtHR saw the possibility of its application in several cases in connection with the denial of true facts or untrue statements of facts. However, it is clear from the following relevant cases that Article 17 is actually applied in practice as a means of action against special forms of hateful and discriminatory speech.

The book that is the subject of *Garaudy* v. *France*[96] analysed in detail a number of historical events relating to the Second World War, such as the persecution of the Jews, the Holocaust and the Nuremberg Trials, questioning the reality, extent and seriousness of these historical events. The Court emphasized that this opinion is far from political or ideological criticism, or one calling for 'a public and academic debate' on the historical events.

> There can be no doubt that denying the reality of clearly established historical facts, such as the Holocaust, does not constitute historical research akin to a quest for the truth. The aim and the result of that approach are completely different, the real purpose being to rehabilitate the National-Socialist regime and, as a consequence, accuse the victims themselves of falsifying history. Denying crimes against humanity is therefore one of the most serious forms of racial defamation of Jews and of incitement to hatred of them.

The Court therefore found that the denial or rewriting of this type of historical facts undermines basic values and is incompatible with democracy and human rights.

In relation to the prohibition of an association in *W.P. and Others* v. *Poland*,[97] the subject of the case was not the denial of historical facts, but the assertion of untrue historical claims. The association of 'Polish Victims of Bolshevism and Zionism' proclaimed, among other things, that the persecution of Poles was a crime perpetrated by the Jewish minority, and one of the main points of its programme was to eliminate the inequality oppressing the Polish majority in favour of the Jewish

[94] *Perincek* v. *Switzerland*, [114]; *Hizb ut-Tahrir and Others* v. *Germany*, app. no. 31098/08, judgment of 12 June 2012, [73], [74] and [78].

[95] Davor Derencinovic, 'Freedom of Expression and its Restrictions in Europe: On the Applicability of Article 17 of the European Convention of Human Rights to Disinformation (Fake New)' (2021) 2 *Law, Identity and Values* 7; Ethan Shattock, 'Fake News in Strasbourg: Electoral Disinformation and Freedom of Expression in the European Court of Human Rights' (2022) 13(1) *European Journal of Law and Technology*.

[96] *Garaudy* v. *France*, app. no. 65831/01, decision of 24 June 2003.

[97] *W.P. and Others* v. *Poland*, app. no. 42264/98, decision of 2 September 2004.

minority. The Court observed that the general purpose of Article 17 is to prevent totalitarian groups from exploiting in their own interests the principles enunciated by the Convention, and the anti-Semitic activities of the association hence clearly met this standard. The ECtHR also closed the case by applying Article 17 when the applicant did not deny the Holocaust as such, but 'denied an equally significant and established circumstance of the Holocaust considering it false and historically unsustainable that Hitler and the NSDAP had planned, initiated and organized the mass killing of Jews'. The Court found again that these views ran counter to the text and the spirit of the Convention.[98]

Regarding historical facts beyond the Nazi atrocities, a decision of great importance was made in *Perincek* v. *Switzerland*. The essential question in this case was whether the criminal conviction for the opinion that 'the allegations of the "Armenian genocide" are an international lie' is lawful. The ECtHR found that the decisive point under Article 17 – whether the applicant's statements sought to stir up hatred or violence, and whether by making them he attempted to rely on the Convention to engage in an activity or to perform acts aimed at the denial of the rights and freedoms laid down in it – is not immediately clear, thus the question of the applicability of Article 17 must also involve consideration of the merit. First and foremost, the Court admitted that its assessment of the necessity of interference with statements relating to historical events has been quite case-specific.

Taking into account a plethora of aspects – that the applicant's statements related to a matter of public interest and did not amount to a call for hatred or intolerance, that the context in which they were made was not marked by heightened tensions or special historical overtones in Switzerland, that the statements cannot be regarded as affecting the dignity of the members of the Armenian community to the point of requiring a criminal-law response in Switzerland, that there is no international-law obligation for Switzerland to criminalize such statements, that the Swiss courts appear to have censured the applicant for voicing an opinion that diverged from the established opinion in Switzerland, and that the interference took the serious form of a criminal conviction – the Court concluded that the criminal conviction violated the Convention.[99] However, as the remarkable dissenting opinion of four Judges shows, despite all the efforts of the majority's reasoning and the many factors put forward for the sake of distinction, one of the most controversial points of the decision remained the question of the application of Article 17.[100] The debate of the judges clearly points out that the standard used in the context of the abuse clause regarding the denial of historical facts has become unpredictable.

[98] *Witzsch* v. *Germany (No. 2)*, app. no. 7485/03, decision of 13 December 2005.
[99] *Perincek* v. *Switzerland*, [208].
[100] See the additional dissenting opinion of Judge Silvis, joined by Judges Casadevall, Berro and Kuris.

Although they are not directly related to the veracity of factual statements, it is instructive to look at two additional cases regarding the application of Article 17. *Norwood* v. *United Kingdom*[101] concerned a poster that depicted a photograph of the Twin Towers in flames, with the words 'Islam out of Britain – Protect the British People' and a symbol of a crescent and star in a prohibition sign. The Court noted that the words and images on the poster amounted to a public expression of attack on all Muslims in the United Kingdom. Such a general, vehement attack against a religious group, linking the group as a whole with a grave act of terrorism, was found to be incompatible with the values proclaimed and guaranteed by the Convention, thus Article 17 was applied.

In *Lillendahl* v. *Iceland*,[102] however, the Court did not find the abuse clause applicable in connection with statements describing homosexual people as disgusting sexual deviants. Trying to clarify its case law, the ECtHR explained that hate speech falls into two categories. The first category is composed of the gravest forms of hate speech which the Court regards as falling under Article 17. The second category includes less grave forms of hate speech which the Court does not consider to fall entirely outside the scope of Article 10, but which it is permissible to restrict.

> Into this second category, the Court has not only put speech which explicitly calls for violence or other criminal acts, but has held that attacks on persons committed by insulting, holding up to ridicule or slandering specific groups of the population can be sufficient for allowing the authorities to favour combating prejudicial speech within the context of permitted restrictions on freedom of expression.[103]

In relation to the discussion about the fight against disinformation, the following conclusions can be drawn from the judicial application of Article 17. The abuse clause has been applied in practice as a tool for handling the gravest forms of hate speech. Cases of disinformation (denial of true facts or untrue statements of facts) may fall within the scope of Article 17 if the Court can establish that they are manifestations of racial discrimination and incitement to hatred. In addition, the conditions for the application of Article 17 are not objective and predictable but were based on complex consideration of the special circumstances of socially sensitive cases. In such circumstances, it is theoretically not desirable to make a decision without applying the strict methodology of restricting freedom of speech, that is, for it to expand the range of cases that can be handled under Article 17. Finally, it is particularly undesirable to circumvent investigation methods in relation to disinformation, the limitation of which is always decided on by the Court, as we have seen, by taking into account a complex set of criteria. The threat posed by disinformation to the sustainable functioning of elections and democracy in general by no means constitutes a sufficient reason for the use of the abuse clause.

[101] *Norwood* v. *United Kingdom*, app. no. 23131/03, decision of 16 November 2004.

[102] *Lillendahl* v. *Iceland*, app. no. 29297/18, decision of 1 May 2020,

[103] Ibid. [33]–[36].

7.3.8 *Restrictive Legal Means against Disinformation*

After Sections 7.2 and 7.3 of this chapter, the main conclusions can already be drawn, based on the doctrine shared by the CoE, on the extent to which the challenge posed by disinformation can be answered by legal means that limit the freedom of speech. The key finding is that there is no justification for general action against speech that can be classified as disinformation, and that restrictive intervention can only take place in rare, exceptional cases. The basic principles and aspects of the democratic participatory concept of free speech bind the legal interpretation of the conceptual elements of disinformation (untrue statement of facts, intent to deceive and causing harm) in such a way that restrictive mechanisms can only be justified within a narrow range of misleading (and socially otherwise problematic) cases. In the following section, I will first summarize the most important arguments against restrictive interventions, and then I will identify the scope in which restrictive measures can still be justified.

7.3.8.1 Arguments against Restrictive Legal Means

Among the theoretical obstacles that stand in the way of imposing legal restrictions on disinformation, the first is the basic approach of the participatory model of free speech, according to which the active involvement of as many people as possible in the discussion of public affairs is not a circumstance that causes risks but a value to be supported. In the logic of democratic public opinion, the answer to the undoubtedly existing risk that anyone can shape public opinion is not the limitation of participation but the corrective power of a robust debate. This represents more than an abstract doctrine: this argument is also based on the fact that where a pathological social weakness of corrective factors exists, legal restrictions are actually unsuitable tools for improving the situation. The findings of the CoE presented in Section 7.4 are telling. Restrictive legal instruments are hardly suited for remedying the problems of the lack of sources of information worthy of public trust, the shrinking of the ethos of quality journalism, and the increasingly irrational tribalism prevailing in public discussions. They can, however, further increase distrust in the institutional system at any time.

Second, under the auspices of democratic public opinion, the European doctrine (also) regards the speaker and their audience first and foremost as autonomous citizens who interpret information and context in their complexity, and who then jointly bear the result of the exchange of opinions. Democratic public opinion emerges from the dialogue of the members of the community that organizes itself democratically regarding how to self-govern. All this supports the rejection of any intervention that would steer the development of public opinion in the 'right' direction and protect the audience in a paternalistic way. In the field of disinformation (and without specific additional circumstances), the many restrictions applied to commercial communication cannot be taken as an example to be followed,[104] because their anthropological approach sees the consumer as vulnerable to the manufacturer and distributor, whose position must be protected by the state, above all for the sake of their health and safety.

Third, for the doctrine of freedom of speech, statements that can be considered troubling in the informational sense are in many cases not untrue statements of fact, but political opinions in whole or in part, with which the participant in the public debate explains reality. Conspiracy theories, misinterpretations or distortions are traditional elements of the public discourse, which must also be reckoned with in the altered circumstances of the public sphere today.

Fourth, in line with this, in the evaluation of the motivation of the speaker, harmful intent can only be interpreted narrowly. Influencing the plural political public is often accompanied by one-sided communications, thus carrying the possibility of misrepresentation, even without the speaker being guided by the intention to harm. In a public life that is based on political competition, the discrediting of an opponent's ability or policies are parts of participation in the public debate, even if they are based on arbitrary highlighting, exaggeration of certain factors, or subjective and baseless assumptions.

Fifth, in order to promote participation and avoid excessive interventions, the doctrine of freedom of speech also limits the legal consideration of grievances. In the case of public figures, jurisprudence often decides in favour of freedom of speech, even when specific personal rights are involved, and the abstract interest of informing society or the electorate can be used to justify restrictions even more narrowly.

7.3.8.2 Possible Legal Restrictions

While the allegation of untruthfulness alone is not a sufficient reason for intervention, in the case of expressly fabricated news, there is room for limitation under the Strasbourg jurisprudence. This requires both for the intention of the communicator to be clearly and directly aimed at publishing untrue and harmful information, and for this information to have an independent significance and weight (that is, the speech cannot be evaluated as a political expression of opinion as a whole). When these conditions exist, the scope of the restriction is determined by the nature of the harm: the rights of a specific person are more broadly protected, while more abstract social interests (for example, public health) can only be protected at the cost of free speech in special cases, when they are especially endangered. In particular, there is room for intervention in the case of information sources (for example, social media

[104] Paolo Cavaliere, 'The Truth in Fake News: How Disinformation Laws Are Reframing the Concepts of Truth and Accuracy on Digital Platforms' (2022) 3(4) *European Convention on Human Rights Law Review* 523.

profiles) that are created and operated in order to systematically fabricate and spread falsity.

In the field of shaping public opinion, even within the new framework of the public, stricter rules apply to journalists, who have a privileged role, which also carries responsibilities in that they are liable for violating journalistic ethics, especially for untruths reported without a good-faith attempt to check the veracity of the information. This obligation may also apply to other actors (for example, to NGOs) that participate in the discourse with a 'public watchdog' function. In addition, the media law can impose the obligation to provide factual and objective information on the audiovisual media with greater influence as a specific obligation limiting their editorial freedom.

The increased responsibility in the field of shaping the political aspects of the public sphere seems to appear in the practice of the ECtHR in cases where the speaker is an active politician. However, for the time being, the case law has established a higher-level standard only in the field of hate speech, and there are strong arguments against the development of a similar interpretation in the field of disinformation. The arguments for politicians having to accept even the harshest criticism and personal attacks are also valid in the other direction: in their case, the correction of inaccuracies can best be entrusted to the public exchange of ideas. The attention paid to politicians' statements is especially multidirectional, and their misleading statements are attacked by many other speakers in public. Moreover, in the conditions of the democratic, pluralistic, multi-party public sphere, the audience may be aware of the often exaggerated and even manipulative nature of political communication. On the basis of the state's obligation to support the proper structure of democratic public opinion, special requirements supporting the dissemination of quality information can be imposed on the operation of social platforms that do not qualify as media. However, since these requirements are different in nature from the classic restrictive state interventions discussed so far, they will be discussed separately in Section 7.4.1.

Overall, the documents of the CoE and the practice of the ECtHR suggest that measures restricting communication in the fight against disinformation can only play a more significant role than at present if the basic principles of freedom of speech are set aside. The prospect of overruling the aspects that have defined the doctrine of freedom of speech to date can definitely be considered an open question. It can be argued that these aspects were tailored to circumstances in which there were fewer speakers, a slower flow of communication, and more rational expressions of public life. In the new, altered circumstances, new standards must be established and used as tools for effective interventions. However, these constitutional aspects of freedom of speech doctrine were actually not tailored to certain circumstances but to a general principle of the democratic formation of public opinion. It is an undoubted fact that social relations in today's society and the conditions for democratic exchange of ideas are significantly different now than they were decades ago.

Even so, the aforementioned starting points stem from the essence of democracy; hence, as long as there is a shared belief that we want to manage our public affairs democratically, our social practices must be adapted to them, and not the other way around. However, the limitations this responsibility places on the use of restrictive legal instruments does not mean that we are helpless. What is more, deeper reasons for the growth of disinformation can be found in social phenomena against which the state can successfully act primarily not with restrictive measures but through other means. The next section will describe what other tools the regulator has at its disposal in the fight against disinformation.

7.4 POLICY MEANS AGAINST DISINFORMATION

It is clear from the materials of the CoE that the institution is aware that solving the aggravating problem of disinformation cannot be achieved by means of restricting public discourse. It is difficult to imagine such wide-scale interventions without violating the democratic principles of freedom of speech, and the problem in any case has deeper roots than could be successfully countered by enforcing new prohibitions. The common understanding within the CoE is that 'our problem isn't "fake news". Our problem is trust.'[105] A large part of the disinformation problem stems from the phenomenon that trust in mainstream media has been falling for decades, as has trust in other public institutions.[106] In other words, there is a serious problem with sources in the sense that people trust neither traditional nor the new sources of the widened information ecosystem.[107] As the Committee of Ministers has summarized it, in the present environment of intensified political partisanship and an increasingly polarized information ecosystem, 'individuals' trust in media, as well as trust in politics, institutions and expertise, has in many States declined to a worryingly low level'.[108]

Several documents produced by the CoE outline a multifaceted action plan for the actors involved, adapted to the complexity of the problem. It is clear that both the old and new players in the digital ecosystem have a lot to do to improve the quality of the public discourse. In accordance with the focus of this chapter, I will now consider the main proposals that identify the areas in which the state can take action. Three such areas stand out in terms of their importance: (1) the state's

[105] Jeff Jarvis, 'Our Problem Isn't "Fake News". Our Problems Are Trust and Manipulation', Medium, 12 June 2017, https://medium.com/whither-news/our-problem-isnt-fake-news-our-problems-are-trust-and-manipulation-5bfbcd716440.

[106] Matthew Harrington, 'Survey: People's Trust Has Declined in Business, Media, Government, and NGOs', *Harvard Business Review*, 16 January 2017, https://hbr.org/2017/01/survey-peoples-trust-has-declined-in-business-media-government-and-ngos.

[107] A Hungarian survey conducted by the Institute of the Information Society at University of Public Service (Budapest) – among others – clearly demonstrates this at the national level, https://iis.uni-nke.hu/hirek/2020/07/15/trust-awareness-and-alarm-on-the-internet.

[108] Recommendation CM/Rec(2022)4, s. A.7.

participation in the regulation of newer actors; (2) the promotion of quality journalism, and (3) the development of media and information literacy skills. The latter two areas are considered soft actions relegated to the background in traditional regulatory logic, but actually represent the best hope for progress in the field of disinformation. The proposals formulated by the Council fit well into the European approach, according to which the state also has a positive obligation to create a regulatory and social environment that best serves the enforcement of free speech. The state has a constitutional responsibility to play its part in forming an appropriate framework for democratic public opinion.

7.4.1 *Regulation of Intermediaries*

7.4.1.1 Content Moderation

Self-regulation is not a subject of this paper for several reasons. First, the role of the state is not a major focus in self-regulation, and second, the importance and complexity of the topic requires a separate analysis.[109] However, it is necessary to consider self-regulation from the point of view that the materials of the CoE also emphasize constitutional reasons why the state cannot leave self-regulation systems completely alone. At certain points, the European doctrine of the horizontal effect of freedom of speech limits the room for manoeuvre of the major actors of digital communication, and compliance with these boundaries must ultimately be guaranteed by the state.

This dichotomy can be observed in every mention of self-regulation in the CoE's documents. On the one hand, the Ministerial Committee also emphasizes that states should encourage the establishment and maintenance of appropriate self-regulatory frameworks or the development of co-regulatory mechanisms. On the other hand, these mechanisms must take due account of the role of intermediaries in providing services of public value and in facilitating public discourse and democratic debate as protected by Article 10 of the Convention. More specifically, and in connection with one of the most pressing issues in this regard, during their content moderation efforts 'Internet intermediaries should respect the rights of users to receive, produce and impart information, opinions and ideas'.[110]

When restricting access to content in line with their own community standards and policies, intermediaries should do so in a transparent and non-discriminatory manner. In addition, the providers must pay attention to users' right to freedom of speech. This is not to say that the system of requirements placed upon states should

[109] See András Koltay, 'Freedom of Expression and the Regulation of Disinformation in the European Union' (Chapter 6 in this book) on the self-regulation of online platforms in the EU.

[110] Recommendation CM/Rec(2018)2, s. 2.3.1.

be transferred wholesale to social media platforms. First, the bearer of obligations with regard to fundamental rights remains primarily the state, so it follows that it is states which are most restricted by precepts arising from freedom of expression. Second, the enforcement of constitutional rights against private actors always takes into account the specific, legitimate interests of the obliged party. In spite of this, the emergence of a fundamental rights aspect hinges precisely on the fact that these interests cannot be invoked without restriction

Although platform providers may, on the basis of the objectives of the social network operator, impose special restrictions, they must respect the essential aspects of the fundamental rights thus affected. One such criterion, which follows from the principle of freedom of expression, is that everyone should be free, above all, to express and publish their views in the debate on public affairs. The more current and legitimate the debate on social issues, the narrower the opportunity for the owners of platforms to intervene with regard to the expression of opinion, and the less the service provider can deviate from the consideration of the key constitutional standards.

Based on all of this, in connection with disinformation there are strong arguments against platforms restricting the content of individual communications that are considered worrisome but are not illegal. Where the criteria for the free discussion of public affairs protect speakers against the state, there is a chance that they can also be invoked against the major social media service providers. Platforms can refer to their own legitimate interests under the doctrine of the horizontal effect of free speech, but they are much more limited in current social debates. On the other hand, considering how difficult it is to judge disinformation, it does not seem reasonable for private companies to be granted the right to decide instead of state authorities, especially courts. In the area of self-regulation, the situation is therefore just the opposite to the usual, and in constitutional terms there is a narrower scope for intervention in Europe. The hands of service providers are tied by the requirements of freedom of speech, and the courts must be careful to develop a corresponding practice.

7.4.1.2 The Regulation of Algorithmic Navigation

The nature of the algorithmic recommendation systems used by platforms seems to be particularly important for state policymaking. The fundamental controlling factor of the communication taking place on social media is algorithmic navigation: an algorithm decides what content it draws the attention of users to, and the content it selects has an incomparably greater chance of enjoying widespread dissemination. It is certainly worrisome that, in the current state of affairs, we can only catch a glimpse of the workings of this influence on the social dialogue through the arbitrarily dripped data of the service providers or the subsequent (self-)critical testimony of their former employees. Particularly strong arguments in favour of ensuring transparency have resulted from the information that has been made public so far, which mostly points to the deliberate neglect by social media firms of the harmful effects of algorithms.[111]

At the same time, this issue concerns more than just increasing transparency. Navigation can play an important role in alleviating some of the public's problems, which can justify the formulation of meaningful expectations. Either we also regulate algorithms, or they alone will regulate us.[112] It would be a valuable contribution to the further development of public debate, for example, if the platforms used their algorithms to shape the structure of the discourse in their domain in such a way that the masses of users encounter more diverse content – instead of further deepening the gap between echo chambers. In the fight against disinformation, making reliable news sources more accessible could bring substantial progress. Similar to the algorithms they have used so far for their various business goals, the platforms could develop a methodology of navigation that tries to respond to these problems. Ultimately, the state can also oblige them to do so in the context of regulating the structure of the democratic public sphere. However, such an obligation can of course only be meaningful and workable if there are credible news sources that are deserving of public trust, so that their positioning in the digital environment can contribute – across political tribes – to clearing up the information chaos. I am convinced that we have just arrived at key areas of state involvement.

7.4.2 *Promoting Quality Journalism*

The importance of quality journalism is clearly demonstrated by the fact that the CoE dedicated a separate document to the topic among its recommendations discussing the problems of the digital media environment. The Ministerial Committee identifies the shift towards an increasingly digital, mobile and social media environment as posing fundamental challenges that have profoundly changed the dynamics of the production, dissemination and consumption of news and other media content. Resultantly, quality journalism needs to compete for audience attention with other types of content that are not subject to the same legal, regulatory or ethical frameworks. A number of media outlets that have traditionally been committed to producing reliable information now find themselves unable to counteract these processes due to a declining reader or viewer base. They are struggling to adapt their operations to a digital environment and to stay connected to the communities they serve.

[111] The Facebook Files, *The Wall Street Journal*, www.wsj.com/articles/the-facebook-files-11631713039.

[112] See the keynote speech of Lawrence Lessig on the conference titled 'Society of Internet Platforms' at the University of Public Service, Hungary (Budapest, 29 October 2021): www.youtube.com/watch?v=Ucym9AlXr1k&t=84s.

An important question, of course, is what we consider to be quality journalism. According to the definition provided in the recommendation, quality journalism is characterized by a firm commitment to the search for truth, correctness, credibility and independence, as well as the enforcement of social responsibility in the public interest. It is important to note that, in terms of the general picture of the media situation, the task is twofold: it is necessary to work not only on positioning quality journalism in a new environment but also even on recreating it. One of the explanations for the weakening of trust in the media is the participation of a critical mass of activist journalists in the intensified partisanship in the political sphere.

The Council of Europe basically advocates a significant role for the state in two areas: financing and education. States are encouraged to ensure the financial sustainability of quality journalism, which is one of the most formidable challenges facing them. 'Traditional, advertising-based media business models have been disrupted, while the transformation of major online platforms, in many respects, into publishing organizations has separated news production from news dissemination.' State actions should include, in a viewpoint-neutral manner:

- granting tax relief for media organizations;
- making public funds available for community and local media;
- removing any regulatory obstacles to the operation of not-for-profit journalism with new forms of donation;
- providing funds, grants or other targeted assistance to investigative journalism;
- financing self-regulatory press councils and mechanisms.

As for education, the state must help journalists to regularly update their skills and knowledge, specifically in relation to their duties and responsibilities in the digital environment, through fellowship programmes and financial support. In addition, specific education curricula and professional training courses should be made available in the fields of science, health, environment, engineering, law and other specialized subjects of public interest, which would ideally motivate journalism students to acquire the practical skills and theoretical background needed to cover such fields.

Due to its importance, the issue of maintaining public service media should be highlighted separately. The CoE believes that public service media are a key stabilizing actor in the media sector if they function as an authentic and reliable source of information independent from political and commercial interests. Public service media could and should play a special role in setting quality standards.

> States should ensure stable and sufficient funding for public service media in order to guarantee their editorial and institutional independence, their capacity to innovate, high standards of professional integrity, and to enable them to properly fulfil their remit and deliver quality journalism.

The recommendation emphasizes that public service media should be at the forefront of the fight against disinformation and should mobilize the actors of quality journalism to develop and share good practices of fact-checking and credible reporting.

When addressing the issue of the proper financing of quality journalism, the question of the transparency of advertising mechanisms should also be discussed. In light of the dominance of the major online platforms in the online advertising market, measures should be undertaken to improve the transparency of their advertising systems and practices, underpinned by legal obligations and independent oversight mechanisms. States should intervene 'to avoid the diversion of advertising revenues from accurate and reliable news sources to sources of disinformation and blatantly false content, and instead seek to reward reliable sources of news.'

7.4.3 *Media and Information Literacy*

Another crucial field for policy-based state actions is the development of the media and information literacy (MIL) skills of society. A well-informed and media-literate society (including journalists, the media, online platforms, non-governmental organizations and individuals) is an essential part of the defence against information manipulation in democratic societies. States have a responsibility for creating and promoting MIL initiatives to help citizens recognize and develop resilience to disinformation. The aim is 'to encourage a media- and information-literate public that is empowered to make informed and autonomous decisions about its media use, that is able and willing to critically engage with the media, that appreciates quality journalism and that trusts credible news sources'.[113] The skills that are required to understand information disorders should be developed as part of more general MIL skills for accessing and managing the digital space, including the ability to deal with an information and communications environment that provides access to degrading content of a sexual or violent nature.[114]

The Council of Europe lists the following actions that states should take in terms of MIL skills:

- provide maximum support for the development of MIL initiatives that illustrate the benefits of quality journalism to various audiences and help them engage with such content in new ways and on new platforms;
- support MIL programmes and activities, which should help users to better understand how online infrastructure and economy are operated and regulated and how technology can influence choice in relation to media;

[113] Recommendation CM/Rec(2022)4, Recital.
[114] Recommendation CM/Rec(2018)2, Recital 8.

- define the promotion of MIL as an explicit common aim of media, information and education policies;
- invest adequate resources in MIL and in developing strategies for collaboration, communication and education;
- integrate MIL measures in the education of all age groups, as an essential part of school curricula from primary school onwards;
- fund independent MIL initiatives by media organizations, public service media, community media, independent regulatory bodies, civil society actors and other relevant actors;
- promote specific media literacy programmes for newsrooms, in particular to promote newsroom collaboration, community building and participatory audience engagement.
- assist in the development of MIL initiatives that help individuals become more aware of how online advertising works.

7.5 CONCLUSION

Having searched for European answers to the problem of disinformation, this chapter examined the practice of three institutions of the CoE which have had a great impact on the development of Member States' legislative and judicial processes. Overall, the practice of the ECtHR, and the documents of the Committee of Ministers and of the Venice Commission suggest that solving the aggravating problem of disinformation cannot be achieved by means of restricting public discourse. It is difficult to imagine such wide-scale interventions without violating the basic principles of the democratic formation of public opinion, and the problem in any case has deeper roots than could be successfully countered by enforcing new prohibitions.

However, the limitations on the use of restrictive legal instruments does not mean that there is no way to address the challenges of disinformation. Indeed, the deeper reasons for the growth of disinformation can be found in social phenomena against which the state can successfully act primarily not by means of restrictive measures, but through other instruments. The common understanding within the CoE is that the problem of disinformation largely stems from a situation where – in the present environment of intensified political partisanship and an increasingly polarized information ecosystem – people trust neither traditional media nor the new online sources of information. According to the European approach, states also have a positive obligation to create a regulatory and social environment that best serves the enforcement of free speech. The state has a constitutional responsibility to play its part in forming an appropriate framework for democratic public opinion. The materials of the CoE identify important areas in which the state can take action. Through the promotion of quality journalism, or the development of media and literacy skills, or the regulation of newer actors in the public, states can seek ways of fostering the creation or the positioning of credible news sources that are deserving of public trust across the political spectrum. Make no mistake: if we are to see any positive development in this field, clearing up the information chaos needs to be a joint effort by the whole of society.

PART IV

National Approaches to Disinformation

8

The Perils of Fundraising Using the Disinformation of the Big Lie

Ciara Torres-Spelliscy

8.1 INTRODUCTION

Many legal and political commentators dubbed Donald Trump's false claim that he was the actual victor of the 2020 American presidential election, 'the Big Lie'.[1] No matter how he complained and dissembled, he lost. After losing the 2020 election, Trump went on a fundraising binge, asking his supporters to give to his legal defense fund so that he could litigate the results of the 2020 election, which he fraudulently claimed he had won.[2] According to the House of Representatives' January 6 Select Committee, this fund did not exist.[3] As Select Committee member Congresswoman Zoe Lofgren put it, 'the Big Lie was also a big rip-off'.[4] Because the 2020 presidential election was not stolen,[5] and the legal defense fund he touted was

The author would like to thank her research assistants Rebecca Doloski, Jeremy Haas, Hannah Klonowski, Sierra Luther and Colin Sullivan, as well as Stetson Librarians Sally Waters and Kristen Moore, for their help in researching this chapter.

1 Melissa Block, 'The Clear and Present Danger of Trump's Enduring "Big Lie"', NPR, 23 December 2021, www.npr.org/2021/12/23/1065277246/trump-big-lie-jan-6-election.

2 Shanna Ports, 'Trump's Abuse of Recount Funds Shows the Need for Clear Regulations', Campaign Legal Center, 31 January 2023, https://campaignlegal.org/update/trumps-abuse-recount-funds-shows-need-clear-regulations.

3 Final Report before the Select Committee to Investigate the January 6th Attack on the United States Capitol of the House of Representatives One Hundred Seventeenth Congress Second Session, H.R. Rep. No. 117-663, 117th Cong. (2023) [hereinafter Final Report], www.govinfo.gov/content/pkg/GPO-J6-REPORT/pdf/GPO-J6-REPORT.pdf, at 770.

4 'Big Lie "Big Rip-Off"', Marketplace, 13 June 2022, www.marketplace.org/shows/make-me-smart/big-lie-big-rip-off.

5 John Danforth et al., 'Lost, Not Stolen: The Conservative Case That Trump Lost and Biden Won the 2020 Presidential Election', July 2022, https://drive.google.com/file/d/1aqorZ61AYFqZU-EDQBBzjqfvAoC5nKcB/view, at 1–67.

nonexistent, Trump's post-2020 election fundraising was a fraud within a fraud[6] – giving rise to a reasonable argument that it violated the federal wire fraud statute and also constituted common law fraud.[7]

Wire fraud involves 'any scheme to defraud another person that uses electronic communications, either across state lines or internationally'.[8] Since most solicitations for funds in the digital age are done with email or texts to mobile phones using telecommunications infrastructure, the federal wire fraud statute is triggered when such solicitations contain fraud. As Tyler Yeargain once described wire fraud, '[p]ut simply, lies were communicated over the Internet in an attempt to yield a financial return for the liars.'[9] Common law fraud includes that the 'main purpose of fraud is to gain something of value by misleading or deceiving someone into thinking something which the fraud perpetrator knows to be false. Criminal fraud requires criminal intent on the part of the perpetrator, and is punishable by fines or imprisonment'.[10]

Legal accountability for the attempts to overturn the 2020 election is finally coming home to roost with an indictment for federal crimes from Special Counsel Jack Smith against ex-President Trump and an indictment for Georgia crimes against Trump and eighteen co-conspirators from Fulton County District Attorney.[11] Both indictments cover expansive ground, ranging from the crimes of pressuring state officials to illegally overturn the 2020 election, to fabricating fake electors, to interfering with Congress's electoral count. But one charge seemed to be conspicuously absent from both indictments: any charge of fraud for fundraising from the Big Lie (that Trump was the true victor of the 2020 election) and for the Big Rip Off (raising money for an election defense fund which did not exist).

6 Ed Pilkington, 'The "Big Rip-Off": How Trump Exploited His Fans with "Election Defense" Fund. The Former President Used Donations to a Nonexistent Legal Defense Fund for His Hotels and the January 6 Ellipse Rally', *The Guardian*, 18 June 2022, www.theguardian.com/us-news/2022/jun/18/donald-trump-election-defense-fundraising-defrauded-fans.

7 Jordan Rubin, 'Why Jack Smith's Reported Wire Fraud Probe into Trump Campaign Could Be a Big Deal', MSNBC, 14 April 2023, www.msnbc.com/deadline-white-house/deadline-legal-blog/trump-wire-fraud-probe-2020-election-rcna79620.

8 Wire Fraud Law, Justia, www.justia.com/criminal/offenses/white-collar-crimes/wire-fraud; 18 U.S.C. 1343; but see *Neder* v. *United States*, 527 US 1, 4 (1999) ('We also hold that materiality is an element of the federal mail fraud, wire fraud, and bank fraud').

9 Tyler Yeargain, 'Fake Polls, Real Consequences: The Rise of Fake Polls and the Case for Criminal Liability' (2020) 85 *Missouri Law Review* 129, at 168.

10 Fraud, Civil or Criminal, Florida Bar, 12 December 2022, www.floridabar.org/practice-areas/fraud-civil-or-criminal/; see also Fraud, Legal Information Institute Cornell Law School, www.law.cornell.edu/wex/fraud.

11 *United States of America* v. *Trump*, Case No. 1:23-cr-00257-TSC (1 August 2023), https://int.nyt.com/data/documenttools/trump-jan-6-indictment-2020-election/1f1c76972b25c802/full.pdf, Indictment; *The State of Georgia* v. *Trump and Others*, No. 23SC188947 EJ15 McAffee (14 August 2023), https://s3.documentcloud.org/documents/23909543/23sc188947-criminal-indictment.pdf, Indictment.

The question of whether to prosecute Trump, his campaign, or his fundraising team for pushing this aspect of the Big Lie is up to Special Counsel Smith, who was assigned by US Attorney General Merrick Garland to look into Trump's handling of classified and military documents at Mar-a-Lago as well Trump's actions related to January 6.[12] The Special Counsel may not pursue these charges because there are easier cases to make, including violations related to conspiracy to have fake electors submit paperwork purporting to be real electors.[13] But this chapter argues that there were real violations of federal wire fraud statutes surrounding the fundraising after the 3 November 2020 election by Trump and his fundraisers, who were trafficking in disinformation about the outcome of the 2020 election as well as the uses of the money. (Another possible source of accountability is state prosecutors in Fulton County, Georgia, who could prosecute this as common law fraud.) In this chapter, I will outline why Trump's deceptive fundraising after the 2020 election (including some fundraising that is ongoing while this chapter was written in 2024), is legally fraught.[14]

The chapter argues that when Trump (and his allies) used the Big Lie after the 2020 election to raise money from unsuspecting supporters who trusted him, he (and his allies) likely stepped across the line from protected free speech into criminal fraud, which enjoys no First Amendment protection.[15] It will proceed as follows: Section 8.2 will explain why this Big Lie that Trump was the true victor of the 2020 election was disinformation. Section 8.3 will demonstrate how federal courts, including the Supreme Court conceptualize fraud as being outside the protection of the First Amendment. Section 8.4 will show that the Department of Justice (DOJ) often uses wire fraud as a charge in cases involving campaign funds. Section 8.5 will argue that Trump, the head of his political action committees (PACs), and even the Republican Party – all of whom used the Big Lie to fundraise – have exposed themselves to possible prosecution for wire fraud. Finally Section 8.6 will follow the money trail, showing where money from the Big Lie was used.

12 Appointment of a Special Counsel, DOJ, 18 November 2022, www.justice.gov/opa/pr/appointment-special-counsel-0 (announcing the appointment of Jack Smith).

13 See 18 U.S.C. § 1001; Diamond Brown, 'What Trump's Federal Indictment for Attacks on the 2020 Election Could Look Like', Citizens for Responsibility and Ethics in Washington, 17 July 2023, www.citizensforethics.org/reports-investigations/crew-reports/what-trumps-federal-indictment-for-attacks-on-the-2020-election-could-look-like.

14 Alex Woodward, 'Trump's Campaign Is Selling $47 T-Shirts Commemorating His Latest Indictment', *The Independent*, 2 August 2023, www.independent.co.uk/news/world/americas/us-politics/trump-indictment-shirts-campaign-donations-b2386497.html; Betsy Woodruff Swan and Kyle Cheney, 'Special Counsel Still Scrutinizing Finances of Trump's PAC', *Politico*, 8 August 2023, www.politico.com/news/2023/08/08/jack-smith-donald-trump-pac-00110279.

15 *Illinois ex rel. Madigan* v. *Telemarketing Associates, Inc.*, 538 US 600, 612 (2003) ('the First Amendment does not shield fraud'); *United States* v. *Hansen*, 143 S.Ct. 1932, 1939 (2023) (same).

8.2 THE BIG LIE WAS DISINFORMATION

After Trump lost the 2020 election, he, some of his lawyers and certain members of his campaign staff all pushed the disinformation known as the 'Big Lie' that Trump was the true victor of the 2020 election.[16] He was not.[17] This Big Lie was deployed unsuccessfully in over sixty lawsuits that challenged the legitimacy of the 2020 election in court.[18] The lawyers who brought these frivolous suits have been subject to sanctions,[19] calls for disbarment,[20] as well as withering disapproval from fellow lawyers.[21] As I explained in a law review article, happily the American judiciary

[16] Eric Lutz, 'Lindsey Graham Takes His Trump Fealty to a New Level', *Vanity Fair*, 17 November 2020, www.vanityfair.com/news/2020/11/lindsey-graham-throw-out-ballots-georgia; David Landau, Hannah J. Wiseman and Samuel Wiseman, 'Federalism, Democracy, and the 2020 Election' (2020–2021) 99 *Texas Law Review*, online ed., 96, at 99 ('in the wake of former President Trump's determined effort to refute the election, experts have described recent events as "one of the gravest threats to democracy", noting that they "never would have imagined seeing something like this in America"').

[17] Official 2020 Presidential General Election Results, Federal Election Commission, www.fec.gov/resources/cms-content/documents/2020presgeresults.pdf.

[18] 'Here's Every Word of the First Jan. 6 Committee Hearing on Its Investigation', NPR, 10 June 2022, www.npr.org/2022/06/10/1104156949/jan-6-committee-hearing-transcript (quoting Liz Cheney: 'the President had every right to litigate his campaign claims, but he ultimately lost more than 60 cases in state and federal courts. The President's claims in the election cases were so frivolous and unsupported that the President's lead lawyer, Rudy Giuliani, not only lost the lawsuits, his license to practice law was suspended').

[19] *King* v. *Whitmer*, No. 20-13134, 2021 WL 3771875, at *1 (E.D. Mich. 25 August 2021) (sanctioning the 'Kraken' lawyers); David Eggert, 'Lawyers Allied with Trump Ordered to Pay $175K in Sanctions', Associated Press, 2 December 2021, https://apnews.com/article/donald-trump-joe-biden-michigan-detroit-election-2020-4fd2ba9b84e9d9a6bcddd51872ba3f97.

[20] Matter of *Giuliani*, No. 2021-00506, at *30–31 (N.Y. App. Div. 3 May 2021) (suspending Rudolph W. Giuliani's ability to practice law in New York).

[21] '25 Former D.C. Bar Presidents: Lawyers should Not Be Complicit in Trump's Attack on Democracy', *The Washington Post*, 1 December 2020, www.washingtonpost.com/opinions/2020/12/01/dc-bar-presidents-lawyers-trump-election ('that these lawsuits were filed on behalf of the incumbent president … makes matters even worse. Here, lawyers have willingly agreed to become the instruments of a wholesale attack on the integrity of the democratic process, which is the framework for binding together a peaceful, civil society under law'); Mary Papenfuss, '1,500 Attorneys Call on Bar Associations to Condemn Trump Campaign Lawyers', *HuffPost*, 8 December 2020, www.huffpost.com/entry/lawyers-condemn-trump-campaign-lawsuits_n_5fcef25fc5b626e08a2c7d4e ('"Our profession needs to affirm that this behavior grossly deviates from the bar's deep commitment to democratic institutions and the fact-based processes that maintain our democracy's vitality", the letter concludes'); Matt Naham, 'Former American Bar Association Presidents, 1,000-Plus Lawyers Call for Bar Investigations of Trump Campaign Attorneys', *Law & Crime*, 7 December 2020, https://lawandcrime.com/2020-election/former-american-bar-association-presidents-1000-plus-lawyers-call-for-bar-investigations-of-trump-campaign-attorneys ('Former ABA President Bellows, also a former president of the Chicago Bar Association, said that bar associations should "disavow" Trump campaign lawyers').

was not deceived by the Big Lie.[22] But tragically, thousands of Republican donors, including many small donors, did fall for the Big Lie.[23]

While most campaign fundraising activities are enrobed in a thick blanket of First Amendment protections,[24] the fundraising by Trump and his allies that relied on the Big Lie arguably falls outside of the free speech protections, landing squarely in the category of both common law fraud and federal wire fraud.[25] While no one has yet been prosecuted for this activity, there are hints in press reporting that Special Counsel Smith may be investigating this aspect of the run-up to January 6.[26] And press reports indicate that he is looking not just at Trump, but at the Save America PAC, the Make America Great Again PAC, as well as other campaign finance entities such as a Trump lawyer and Georgia co-defendant named Sidney Powell's group Defend Our Republic.[27] In Trump's federal indictment regarding January 6,

[22] Ciara Torres-Spelliscy, 'The Political Branding of the Big Lie' (2022) (5) *University of Illinois Law Review* 1711.

[23] Philip Bump, 'More than Half the Money Given to Trump's PAC Was from Retirees', *The Washington Post*, 14 June 2022, www.washingtonpost.com/politics/2022/06/14/more-than-half-money-given-trumps-pac-was-retirees.

[24] *Buckley* v. *Valeo*, 424 US 1, 48–49 (1976) ('the concept that government may restrict the speech of some elements of our society in order to enhance the relative voice of others is wholly foreign to the First Amendment'); *Davis* v. *Federal Election Commission*, 128 S.Ct. 2759, 2770 (2008) (the so-called Millionaire's Amendment was held to violate the First Amendment); *Citizens United* v. *Federal Election Commission*, 130 S.Ct. 876, 913 (2010) (striking down restrictions on corporate independent expenditures and electioneering communications on First Amendment grounds); *McCutcheon* v. *Federal Election Commission*, 572 US 185, 191 (2014) ('The right to participate in democracy through political contributions is protected by the First Amendment'); *Williams-Yulee* v. *Florida Bar*, 575 US 433, 443 (2015) ('As we have long recognized, speech about public issues and the qualifications of candidates for elected office commands the highest level of First Amendment protection'; ibid. at 446: 'nobody argues that solicitation of campaign funds by judicial candidates is a category of unprotected speech'); but see the *Federal Election Commission* v. *Beaumont*, 539 US 146 (2003) (direct contribution ban from nonprofit corporation is consistent with the First Amendment).

[25] *Barr* v. *American Association of Political Consultants*, 140 S.Ct. 2335, 2381 (2020) ('The Court has held that entire categories are speech – for example, obscenity, fraud, and speech integral to criminal conduct – are generally unprotected by the First Amendment entirely because of their content'); Alan Feuer, Maggie Haberman and Jonathan Swan, 'Prosecutors in Jan. 6 Case Step up Inquiry into Trump Fund-Raising', *The New York Times*, 28 April 2023, www.nytimes.com/2023/04/28/us/politics/jan-6-prosecutors-trump-fund-raising.html ('prosecutors are trying to determine whether Mr. Trump … violated federal wire fraud statutes as they raised as much as $250 million through a political action committee by saying they needed the money to fight to reverse election fraud even though … there was no evidence to back up those fraud claims').

[26] Alan Feuer et al., 'Trump's Post-Election Fund-Raising Comes under Scrutiny by Justice Dept.', *The New York Times*, 8 September 2022, www.nytimes.com/2022/09/08/us/politics/trump-save-america-pac-subpoenas.html ('According to subpoenas issued by the grand jury, the contents of which were described to *The New York Times*, the Justice Department is interested in the inner workings of Save America PAC, Mr. Trump's main fund-raising vehicle after the election').

[27] Josh Dawsey, Devlin Barrett and Rosalind S. Helderman, 'Trump Campaign Officials Got Subpoena Asking New Questions about Jan. 6', *The Washington Post*, 11 January 2023, www

there are no charges related to fundraising,[28] but there could yet be a superseding indictment that adds such charges, just as happened in the Mar-a-Lago documents case where additional criminal charges were added later.[29]

Here I use Andrew Guess' and Benjamin Lyons' definitions of misinformation and disinformation. Misinformation is false information that 'contradicts or distorts common understandings of verifiable facts'.[30] Meanwhile, 'disinformation is the subset of misinformation that is deliberately propagated. This is a question of intent: Disinformation is meant to deceive, while misinformation may be inadvertent or unintentional.'[31] The Big Lie as propagated by Trump, his lawyers and his political committees was not just misinformation, rather the Big Lie was a particularly potent and virulent form of disinformation. As scholars and advocates have found, such disinformation can be particularly corrosive in a democracy.[32]

The Special Counsel's 1 August 2023 indictment against Trump focused on his actions leading up to and on January 6, and mentioned six unindicted co-conspirators, five of whom were lawyers. As the indictment recited:

> The Defendant [Trump] lost the 2020 presidential election . . . Despite having lost, the Defendant was determined to remain in power. So for more than two months following election day on November 3, 2020, the Defendant spread lies that there

.washingtonpost.com/national-security/2023/01/11/trump-subpoena-jan6-campaign-officials ('The subpoena shows the Justice Department is interested in other Trump entities besides the Save America PAC . . . It seeks "all documents and communications" related to a panoply of other Trump-affiliated groups, including the Make America Great Again PAC, the Save America Joint Fundraising Committee and the Trump Make America Great Again Committee'); Zachary Cohen and Paula Reid, 'CNN Exclusive: Special Counsel Election Probe Continues with Focus on Fundraising, Voting Equipment Breaches', CNN, 5 September 2023, www.cnn.com/2023/09/05/politics/special-counsel-election-probe-continues-fundraising-voting-equipment-breaches-sidney-powell/index.html.

28 *United States of America* v. *Trump and Others*, Indictment.

29 *United States of America* v. *Trump*, Case No. 9:23-cr-80101-AMC (8 June 2023), https://storage.courtlistener.com/recap/gov.uscourts.flsd.648653/gov.uscourts.flsd.648653.3.0_2.pdf, Indictment; *United States of America* v. *Trump and Others*, Case No. 23-CR-80101-CANNON (27 July 2023), www.justice.gov/storage/US-v-Trump-Nauta-De-Oliveira-23-80101.pdf, Superseding Indictment.

30 Andrew M. Guess and Benjamin A. Lyons, 'Misinformation, Disinformation, and Online Propaganda' in Nathaniel Persily and Joshua A. Tucker (eds.), *Social Media and Democracy: The State of the Field and Prospects for Reform* (Cambridge: Cambridge University Press, 2020) p. 10.

31 Ibid. p. 11.

32 Katie Couric, Chris Krebs and Rashad Robinson, 'Commission on Information Disorder Final Report', Aspen Institute, 15 November 2021, www.aspeninstitute.org/publications/commission-on-information-disorder-final-report (at 1: 'Information disorder . . . undermines democracy'); Martin H. Redish and Juilo Pereyra, 'Resolving the First Amendment's Civil War: Political Fraud and the Democratic Goals of Free Expression' (2020) 62 *Arizona Law Review* 451, at 453–54 ('extending First Amendment protection to false speech in the political process may also encourage those who are intent on distorting the democratic process to defraud the voters into making misguided choices on the basis of factually inaccurate information').

> had been outcome-determinative fraud in the election and that he had actually won. These claims were false, and the Defendant knew that they were false.[33]

The Big Lie was condemned in real time, in November 2020, in '[a]n open letter signed by retired federal and state judges, former state attorneys general who served under Republican and Democratic governors, and law professors condemned Trump's claims of fraud as being presented "without evidence and false", singling out Republican officials who have publicly supported the president's efforts to have thousands of ballots thrown out.'[34] And in 2023 the former assistant director of the FBI Frank Figliuzzi asserted about Trump's fundraising that '[w]hen you raise millions based on a fraudulent claim, you've committed a crime. And, you just might have to give those millions back.'[35] Meanwhile former federal prosecutor Andrew Weissmann indicated that he anticipates 'a criminal case about the Trump PAC and forfeiture allegations/seizures'.[36] In other words, if the Special Counsel alleges that the money in Trump PAC(s) are the fruit of a crime, then he could move for pre-trial seizure of those funds.[37]

8.3 THE COURTS' VIEWS OF FRAUD

Trump's criminal lawyers are already relying heavily on the First Amendment as defense for his actions that are charged in the Special Counsel's 1 August 2023 indictment about January 6.[38] But although the Supreme Court has been very lenient on liars, even in the context of elections,[39] it still maintains that fraud is

[33] *United States of America* v. *Trump and Others*, Indictment, at 1.

[34] Julia Conley, '1,000 Legal Experts Sign Letter Condemning "Shameful Attack" on Democracy as Trump Continues Baseless Election Lies', *Common Dreams*, 13 November 2020, www.commondreams.org/news/2020/11/13/1000-legal-experts-sign-letter-condemning-shameful-attack-democracy-trump-continues.

[35] Shweta Sharma, 'Jack Smith May Force Trump to Pay Back Millions in Donations, Ex-FBI Official Says', *The Independent*, 9 August 2023, www.the-independent.com/news/world/americas/us-politics/trump-jack-smith-donations-election-campaign-b2389994.html.

[36] Gabriella Ferrigine, '"Might Have to Give Those Millions Back": Legal Experts Say Jack Smith could "Seize" Trump PAC Cash', Salon, 9 August 2023, www.salon.com/2023/08/09/might-have-to-give-those-millions-back-legal-experts-say-jack-smith-could-seize-pac-cash.

[37] Vance Cariaga, 'Donald Trump's Election Money to Be Seized "If Obtained by Fraud" – Where Do Frozen Campaign Funds Go?', Yahoo Finance, 10 September 2023, https://finance.yahoo.com/news/donald-trump-election-money-seized-115856785.html.

[38] Elena Burnett, Tinbete Ermyas and Ailsa Chang, 'Trump's Legal Defense Focuses on Free Speech – Will That Strategy Hold Up in Court?', All Things Considered, 3 August 2023, www.npr.org/2023/08/03/1191972821/trump-s-legal-defense-focuses-on-free-speech-will-that-strategy-hold-up-in-court; Susan Milligan, 'Trump's Fine Legal Line on Free Speech', US News & World Report, 7 August 2023, www.usnews.com/news/politics/articles/2023-08-07/trumps-fine-legal-line-speaking-for-the-courtroom-and-the-campaign-trail.

[39] *United States* v. *Alvarez*, 567 US 709, 720–21 (2012); *Susan B. Anthony List* v. *Driehaus*, 573 US 149, 153 (2014); Alan K. Chen and Justin Marceau, 'Developing a Taxonomy of Lies under the First Amendment' (2018) 89 *University of Colorado Law Review* 655, at 663 ('Instead of a

outside of the ambit of First Amendment protections.[40] The argument I am advancing here is that just as common law fraud (and wire fraud) is not protected by the First Amendment, raising money for Trump's Save America PAC (and other political committees) with the Big Lie is not covered by the First Amendment either.

The Supreme Court has long been hostile to individuals who have defrauded others. Dating back to 1820 the Court stated, 'the first principles of the common law [is that] fraud [is] the object of its peculiar abhorrence, and [fraud] contaminat[es] every act'.[41] The Court has defined common law fraud as including 'a scheme to deprive a victim of his entitlement to money'.[42] In 1976, the Supreme Court concluded in *Virginia Board of Pharmacy* v. *Virginia Citizens Consumer Council, Inc.* about commercial advertisements that '[u]ntruthful speech, commercial or otherwise, has never been protected for its own sake.'[43] And in another case the Supreme Court added to this definition, 'common-law fraud has long encompassed certain misrepresentations by omission, "false or fraudulent claims" include more than just claims containing express falsehoods. The parties and the Government agree that misrepresentations by omission can give rise to liability.'[44] Thus, according to the Supreme Court, fraud can be both express lies as well as failures to tell key truths. In Trump's case the express lie was the Big Lie that he won the 2020 election, and the failure to tell the truth was omitting where the money raised by his PACs would really be used.

In a case decided in 2023, *United States* v. *Hansen*,[45] the Supreme Court considered a First Amendment defense raised by an individual who induced immigrants to break US immigration and naturalization laws through fraudulent promises of an easy path to US citizenship. As the Supreme Court explained 'federal law prohibits "encourag[ing] or induc[ing]" illegal immigration. 8 U.S.C. § 1324(a)(1)(A)(iv) . . . Properly interpreted, this provision forbids only the intentional solicitation or facilitation of certain unlawful acts. It does not "prohibi[t] a substantial amount of protected speech".'[46] Defendant Helaman Hansen sold immigrants the false hope of becoming US citizens through 'adult adoption'. This path to

general rule against speech protection for lies, *Alvarez* suggests a presumption that lies are covered by the First Amendment').

40 *Illinois ex rel. Madigan* v. *Telemarketing Associates, Inc.*, at 612.

41 *Polk's Lessee* v. *Wendell*, 18 US 293, 296–97 (1820).

42 *Pasquantino* v. *United States*, 544 US 349, 356 (2005).

43 *Virginia Board of Pharmacy* v. *Virginia Citizens Consumer Council, Inc.*, 425 US 748, 771 (1976).

44 *Universal Health Services* v. *United States*, 579 US 176, 187 (2016); *Illinois ex rel. Madigan* v. *Telemarketing Associates, Inc.*, at 606 ('While bare failure to disclose that information directly to potential donors does not suffice to establish fraud, when nondisclosure is accompanied by intentionally misleading statements designed to deceive the listener, the First Amendment leaves room for a fraud claim').

45 *United States* v. *Hansen*, 143 S.Ct. 1932.

46 Ibid. at 1937.

citizenship is nonexistent. This grifter charged desperate immigrants who wanted to stay in the USA thousands of dollars, making $2 million in the illegal scheme.[47]

When the federal government prosecuted Hansen for this fraud, he defended himself by claiming that the immigration law that was being used against him was constitutionally overbroad and violated his free speech rights.[48] The Ninth Circuit had agreed with him.[49] The Supreme Court disagreed in a seven-to-two decision, quoting *Illinois ex rel. Madigan* v. *Telemarketing Associates, Inc.*, a case about charitable fraud, for the proposition that 'the First Amendment does not shield fraud'.[50] In *Hansen*, the Court explained what counted as criminal solicitation:

> Criminal solicitation is the intentional encouragement of an unlawful act. Facilitation – also called aiding and abetting – is the provision of assistance to a wrongdoer with the intent to further an offense's commission. While the crime of solicitation is complete as soon as the encouragement occurs, liability for aiding and abetting requires that a wrongful act be carried out. Neither solicitation nor facilitation requires lending physical aid; for both, words may be enough.[51]

Hansen's lawyers argued that criminalizing speech that only induced an immigrant to break a civil law violated the First Amendment (as many violations of immigration law are handled as civil not criminal matters).[52] But the Supreme Court rejected this distinction, and upheld the challenged law as being constitutional under the First Amendment.[53] While *Hansen* is of course focused on immigration law, nonetheless its principles would apply in prosecutions of fraud in other contexts like raising

47 Adam Shaw, 'Supreme Court Upholds Law Barring Encouraging Illegal Immigration', Fox News, 23 June 2023, www.foxnews.com/politics/supreme-court-upholds-law-barring-encouraging-illegal-immigration.

48 Court Cases: *United States* v. *Helaman Hansen*, ACLU, 17 February 2023, www.aclu.org/cases/united-states-v-helaman-hansen ('This case is about whether the First Amendment permits criminal punishment of speech that merely encourages a noncitizen to remain in the United States, without any requirement of intent to further illegal conduct, and when remaining in the United States unlawfully is itself not a crime').

49 *United States* v. *Hansen*, 25 F.4th 1103, 1106 (9th Cir. 2022) ('we hold that subsection (iv) is facially overbroad').

50 *United States* v. *Hansen*, 143 S.Ct. 1932 at 1939 (quoting *Madigan Illinois ex rel. Madigan* v. *Telemarketing Associates, Inc.*, at 612; ibid. at 1952 (Justices Jackson and Sotomayor dissented); *Madigan Illinois ex rel. Madigan* v. *Telemarketing Associates, Inc.*, at 623–24, citing *Riley* v. *National Federation of the Blind of North Carolina*, 487 US 781, 800 (1988) ('Just as government may seek to inform the public and prevent fraud through such disclosure requirements, so it may vigorously enforce its antifraud laws to prohibit professional fundraisers form obtaining money on false pretenses of by making false statements').

51 *United States* v. *Hansen*, 143 S.Ct. 1932 (internal citations omitted).

52 Ibid. at 1947–48 (Hansen 'resists the idea that the First Amendment permits Congress to criminalize speech that solicits or facilitates a civil violation – and some immigration violations are only civil . . . [And] generally does not carry a criminal sentence. See *Arizona* v. *United States*, 567 US 387, 407, 132 S.Ct. 2492, 183 L.Ed.2d 351 (2012)').

53 *United States* v. *Hansen*, 143 S.Ct. 1932 at 1948 ('As we have discussed, the provision has a wide legitimate reach insofar as it applies to non-expressive conduct and speech soliciting or facilitating criminal violations of immigration law').

money for an election defense fund which, like 'adult adoption citizenship', did not exist.

In 2010 in *United States* v. *Stevens* the Supreme Court infamously said that 'crush videos' are protected by the First Amendment; nonetheless, in that same case the Court noted that '[f]rom 1791 to the present . . . the First Amendment has permitted restrictions upon the content of speech in a few limited areas . . . [The punishment of these] historic and traditional categories long familiar to the bar[,] including . . . fraud . . . and speech integral to criminal conduct . . . have never been thought to raise any Constitutional problem.'[54] The Supreme Court came to a similar conclusion in *United States* v. *Alvarez* (better known as the stolen valor case) in 2012, that '[w]here false claims are made to effect a fraud or secure moneys or other valuable considerations, say offers of employment, it is well established that the Government may restrict speech without affronting the First Amendment.'[55]

In *United States* v. *Smith*, Malcom Smith, a New York Democratic State Senator, and Vincent Tabone, the Queens County Republican Party Vice Chairman, entered into a complicated scheme to allow Democrat Smith to run for the Mayor of New York City as a Republican. They were both convicted of bribery and honest services wire fraud, and Tabone raised First Amendment defenses during his prosecution. The Southern District of New York Judge Kenneth Karas rejected this argument:

> [If] Tabone is attempting to raise an as-applied or facial First Amendment challenge to the statute, he fundamentally misconstrues the statute's thrust. The statute does not criminalize mere association with a political party, or advocacy for certain political candidates. In fact, in this case, the statute is being applied to alleged bribes offered and received in return for certain conduct. Just because this alleged quid pro quo arrangement involved political-party officials, they are not entitled to immunity for their actions under the guise of protected speech.[56]

These appeals failed and both men went to prison.[57]

A 2023 federal district court case reached a similar result in a case involving a scheme to defraud voters. In *United States* v. *Mackey*, a man was charged with tricking voters who supported Hillary Clinton to vote online (a voting method which

[54] *United States* v. *Stevens*, 559 US 460, 468–69 (2010) (citations and internal quotation marks omitted).

[55] *United States* v. *Alvarez* at 723 (citing *Virginia Board of Pharmacy* v. *Virginia Citizens Consumer Council, Inc.*, at 771 (noting that fraudulent speech generally falls outside the protections of the First Amendment)); see also *United States* v. *Alvarez* at 718 (quoting *Brown* v. *Hartlage*, 456 US 45, 60–61 (1982): 'False statements "are not protected by the First Amendment in the same manner as truthful statements"').

[56] *United States* v. *Smith*, 985 F.Supp.2d 547, 605–6 (S.D.N.Y. 2014).

[57] Luca Marzorati, 'Former State Senator Malcolm Smith Sentenced to 7 Years', Politico, 1 July 2015, www.politico.com/states/new-york/albany/story/2015/07/former-state-senator-malcolm-smith-sentenced-to-7-years-090717.

does not exist in the USA).[58] This is sometimes referred to as the 'vote by Tweet' case.[59] Defendant Douglass Mackey, as known as 'Ricky Vaughn', argued that he had the free speech right to say what he said on social media to Clinton supporters. The federal district court in his case rejected this argument, stating: '[t]his case is about conspiracy and injury, not speech … [T]he language [Defendant Mackey] used is akin to verbal acts, which fall outside the scope of the First Amendment, rather than protected' speech.[60] Mackey was sentenced to seven months incarceration for his crime.[61] As the Southern Poverty Law Center, which tracks right-wing hate groups, said of the *Mackey* verdict that it 'set more clearly visible boundaries around what is legal when sowing disinformation online, prosecutors may have also created inroads to bring about charges similar to those filed against other radical-right activists who engaged in coordinated efforts to shape the outcome of elections'.[62] Defendant Mackey has appealed his conviction using the argument that his actions in the 2016 election are protected by the First Amendment.[63] These cases, *Hansen*, *Stevens* and *Alvarez*, at the Supreme Court level and *Mackey* and *Smith* at the district court level, all indicate that defrauding individuals is not going to enjoy First Amendment protections.

8.4 DEPARTMENT OF JUSTICE FREQUENTLY USES WIRE FRAUD CHARGES IN CAMPAIGN FINANCE CASES

The Department of Justice has frequently used wire fraud to charge crimes that involve campaign funds. In 2023 alone, the DOJ alleged wire fraud violations in a case 'charging the [Republican] Sheriff of Culpepper County, Virginia, and three … men with a conspiracy to exchange bribes for law enforcement badges

58 *United States* v. *Mackey*, Memorandum and Order, United States District Court Eastern District of New York, Document 54 (23 January 2023), 1, at 5, https://storage.courtlistener.com/recap/gov.uscourts.nyed.459733/gov.uscourts.nyed.459733.54.0.pdf ('The scheme, as alleged, aimed to cause [Hillary] Clinton supporters to believe they could cast their ballots by sending a text message or posting on social media and, as a result, fail to cast their vote for [Hillary Clinton] in the Election in a legally valid manner').

59 Eugene Volokh, 'Douglass Mackey Convicted for Vote-by-Tweet Meme', *Reason*, 31 March 2023, https://reason.com/volokh/2023/03/31/douglass-mackey-convicted-for-vote-by-tweet-meme-prosecution.

60 *United States* v. *Mackey*, Memorandum and Order at 39 (internal quotation marks removed).

61 'Social Media Influencer Douglass Mackey Sentenced after Conviction for Election Interference in 2016 Presidential Race,' DOJ, 18 October 2023, www.justice.gov/usao-edny/pr/social-media-influencer-douglass-mackey-sentenced-after-conviction-election.

62 Michael Edison Hayden, 'Douglass Mackey Verdict Sinks "Shitposting" Defense', Southern Poverty Law Center, 4 April 2023, www.splcenter.org/hatewatch/2023/04/04/douglass-mackey-verdict-sinks-shitposting-defense.

63 Nika Schoonover, '"On Trial for Memes": Man Asks Second Circuit to Overturn Conviction over Election Day Shenanigans', Court House News, 5 April 2024, www.courthousenews.com/on-trial-for-memes-man-asks-second-circuit-to-overturn-conviction-over-election-day-shenanigans.

and credentials. According to court documents, from at least April 2019 … Sheriff Scott Howard Jenkins, … accepted cash bribes in the form of campaign contributions totaling … $72,500.'[64] Additionally, on 9 May 2023, sitting Republican Congressman George Santos was indicted by the DOJ. He was charged with seven counts of wire fraud, three counts of money laundering, one count of theft of public funds, and two counts of making materially false statements to the House of Representatives.[65] Santos was expelled from the House of Representatives after the House Ethic Committee 'unanimously concluded that there was substantial evidence that Representative George Santos: knowingly caused his campaign committee to file false or incomplete reports with the Federal Election Commission; used campaign funds for personal purposes; [and] engaged in fraudulent conduct'.[66]

In 2022, a Democratic ex-Congressman was hit with wire fraud charges. As a press release from DOJ stated, a '28-count indictment was unsealed … charging a former member of Congress with multiple fraud schemes and campaign contribution fraud. Terrance John "TJ" Cox … is charged with 15 counts of wire fraud, … and one count of campaign contribution fraud.'[67] The DOJ leveled similar charges against a former Republican Governor of Puerto Rico, Wanda Vázquez Garced.[68]

There have been guilty pleas in cases where defendants have been charged with wire fraud in campaign finance cases. A former Republican congressional candidate, Nicholas Jones, pleaded guilty to wire fraud 'for falsifying records to conceal thousands of dollars of in-kind contributions by employees in a report to the Federal Elections Commission (FEC)'.[69] In 2023, the Chair of the Louisiana Democratic

64 'Sheriff and Three Men Charged with Bribery Scheme Involving Purchase of Law-Enforcement Badges and Credentials', DOJ, 29 June 2023, www.justice.gov/opa/pr/sheriff-and-three-men-charged-bribery-scheme-involving-purchase-law-enforcement-badges-and.

65 'Congressman George Santos Charged with Fraud, Money Laundering, Theft of Public Funds, and False Statements', DOJ, 10 May 2023, www.justice.gov/usao-edny/pr/congressman-george-santos-charged-fraud-money-laundering-theft-public-funds-and-false.

66 'Statement of the Chairman and Ranking Member of the Committee on Ethics Regarding Representative George Santos', House Committee on Ethics, 16 November 2023, https://ethics.house.gov/press-releases/statement-chairman-and-ranking-member-committee-ethics-regarding-representative-76; Kevin Freking, 'The House Expels Rep. George Santos. An Ethics Report Had Accused Him of Breaking Federal Law', Associated Press, 1 December 2023, https://apnews.com/article/george-santos-expulsion-vote-ethics-investigation-fd0f15240658830c6b2fe3e6f9afd84db.

67 'Former Member of Congress Charged with Multiple Fraud Schemes', DOJ, 16 August 2022, www.justice.gov/opa/pr/former-member-congress-charged-multiple-fraud-schemes.

68 'Former Governor of Puerto Rico Arrested in Bribery Scheme', DOJ, 4 August 2022, www.justice.gov/opa/pr/former-governor-puerto-rico-arrested-bribery-scheme ('A former governor of Puerto Rico was arrested today on bribery charges related to the financing of her 2020 campaign').

69 'Congressional Candidate Pleads Guilty to Wire Fraud and Falsification of Records', DOJ, 1 June 2022, www.justice.gov/opa/pr/former-congressional-candidate-pleads-guilty-wire-fraud-and-falsification-records.

Party, Karen Carter Peterson, pled guilty to wire fraud in a case that accused her of defrauding the party and political donors.[70] Republican ex-Arkansas State Senator Jeremy Hutchinson pled guilty to taking bribes as an elected official to move legislation for a business.[71] In 2020, Republican then-Member of Congress Duncan Hunter and his wife were accused of wire fraud for the personal use of campaign funds.[72] Congressman Hunter pled guilty,[73] and was sentenced to eleven months in prison.[74] But the Congressman never served jail time because President Trump pardoned him.[75]

Individuals running so-called Scam PACs have also been convicted of wire fraud violations. An example of this from 2020 is a 'Maryland political consultant [who] was sentenced to three years in prison … for fraudulently soliciting hundreds of thousands of dollars in political contributions through several scam political actions committees (PACs) that he founded and advertised as supporting candidate for office and other political causes'.[76] In another example, in 2022, a 'California man pleaded guilty … to conspiracy to solicit millions of dollars in contributions to two political action committees based on false and misleading representation that the funds would be used to support presidential candidates during and after the 2016 election cycle'.[77] A former Republican candidate for the US House of Representatives, Robert Cannon Hayes, pled guilty and was sentenced for 'wire fraud and willfully violating the Federal Election Campaign Act (FECA) by

70 'Former Louisiana State Senator and Chair of State Political Party, Sentenced to 22 Months Imprisonment for Role in Nearly Seven-Year Scheme to Defraud Campaign Entity, Donors, and Political Party Organization', DOJ, 11 January 2023, www.justice.gov/usao-edla/pr/former-louisiana-state-senator-and-chair-state-political-party-sentenced-22-months.

71 'Former Arkansas State Senator Jeremy Hutchinson Pleads Guilty to Bribery and Tax Fraud Charges in Multi-District Investigation', DOJ, 25 June 2019, www.justice.gov/opa/pr/former-arkansas-state-senator-jeremy-hutchinson-pleads-guilty-bribery-and-tax-fraud-charges.

72 'Rep. Duncan D. Hunter and Wife Indicted for Converting Hundreds of Thousands of Dollars in Campaign Funds and Falsifying Campaign Finance Records', DOJ, 21 August 2018, www.justice.gov/usao-sdca/pr/rep-duncan-d-hunter-and-wife-indicted-converting-hundreds-thousands-dollars-campaign.

73 'Congressman Duncan D. Hunter Pleads Guilty to Stealing Campaign Funds', DOJ, 3 December 2019, www.justice.gov/usao-sdca/pr/congressman-duncan-d-hunter-pleads-guilty-stealing-campaign-funds.

74 'Former Congressman Duncan D. Hunter Sentenced to 11 Months in Prison for Stealing Campaign Funds', DOJ, 17 March 2020, www.justice.gov/usao-sdca/pr/former-congressman-duncan-d-hunter-sentenced-11-months-prison-stealing-campaign-funds.

75 'Pardons Granted by President Donald J. Trump (2017–2021)', DOJ, 2021, www.justice.gov/pardon/pardons-granted-president-donald-j-trump-2017-2021.

76 'Maryland Man Sentenced to Prison for Fraudulent Scheme to Solicit Hundreds of Thousands of Dollars in Contributions to Scam-PACs', DOJ, 17 January 2020, www.justice.gov/opa/pr/maryland-man-sentenced-prison-fraudulent-scheme-solicit-hundreds-thousands-dollars.

77 'California Man Pleads Guilty to $3.5 Million Scam-PAC Fraud', DOJ, 9 August 2022, www.justice.gov/opa/pr/california-man-pleads-guilty-35-million-scam-pac-fraud.

operating fraudulent and unregistered political action committees'.[78] And in 2023, Jack Daly and Nathanael Pendley 'pled guilty to conspiring to (i) commit mail fraud and (ii) lie to the Federal Election Commission' because of their actions related to a scam PAC called the Draft PAC.[79]

The Department of Justice has also chalked up wins in front of juries in cases about campaign funds that charged wire fraud. For instance, in 2020, Greg Lindberg and John Gray were convicted in a case of bribing the North Carolina Insurance Commissioner. As Acting Assistant Attorney General Brian Rabbitt said, '[w]hen Greg Lindberg and John Gray offered millions of dollars in bribes to the North Carolina Insurance Commissioner, they referred to their elaborately corrupt scheme as a "win–win" – unaware that the FBI was watching and listening'.[80] In another case, a jury convicted 'former [Republican] US Representative Stephen E. Stockman for orchestrating a scheme to steal hundreds of thousands of dollars from charitable foundations and the individuals who ran those foundations to illegally finance Stockman's campaigns for public office and to pay for his and others' personal expenses'.[81]

All of this is evidence that if the DOJ wants to charge Trump, his PACs or his campaign with wire fraud for defrauding donors of money using the Big Lie, this prosecutorial tool is available.[82] Another thing to note is that these listed prosecutions have been against both Republicans and Democrats. Moreover, the Trump Administration prosecuted Republicans and the Joe Biden Administration has prosecuted Democrats. So this does not fall into the lazy and inaccurate trope of criminalizing politics, or of an administration going after its political enemies.

78 'Former Candidate for the U.S. House of Representatives Sentenced After Conviction for Fraud and Campaign Finance Violations', DOJ, 24 July 2019, www.justice.gov/opa/pr/former-candidate-us-house-representatives-sentenced-after-conviction-fraud-and-campaign.

79 'Two North Carolina Lawyers Plead Guilty to Conspiracy Involving Scam Political Action Committee', DOJ, 12 June 2023, www.justice.gov/usao-edwi/pr/two-north-carolina-lawyers-plead-guilty-conspiracy-involving-scam-political-action-0.

80 'Founder and Chairman of a Multinational Investment Company and a Company Consultant Convicted of Bribery and Public Corruption Are Sentenced to Prison', DOJ, 19 August 2020, www.justice.gov/opa/pr/founder-and-chairman-multinational-investment-company-and-company-consultant-convicted ('The founder and chairman of a multinational investment company and a company consultant were sentenced to prison today for orchestrating a bribery scheme involving independent expenditure accounts and improper campaign contributions').

81 'Former US Congressman Convicted of Mail and Wire Fraud, Campaign Finance Violations, Money Laundering and Filing a False Tax Return', DOJ, 12 April 2018, www.justice.gov/opa/pr/former-us-congressman-convicted-mail-and-wire-fraud-campaign-finance-violations-money.

82 Sami Azhari and Sergio Lopez, 'Guilty until Proven Guilty: The Prosecution of Public Corruption and White Collar Crime' (2021) *The Champion* 32, at 35, www.federalcriminallawyer.us/wp-content/uploads/2021/06/Bridgegate.Final-copy.pdf ('Notwithstanding the highest court's limitation in the prosecution of public officials for "honest services", prosecutors have recently been able to successfully utilize the honest services fraud statute for the prosecution of self-benefiting individuals').

8.5 LEGAL PERIL FOR TRUMP, TRUMP FUNDRAISERS AND THE REPUBLICAN NATIONAL COMMITTEE

Two investigations have focused on the post-2020 fundraising by team Trump: one by Congress and one by the Special Counsel Smith.[83] The Save America PAC was created on 9 November 2020, just days after Trump lost the 2020 election.[84] Trump's Save America PAC was the primary vehicle for his post-election fundraising.[85] Super PACs that are nominally independent of Trump have also fundraised on the basis of the Big Lie.[86] The Select Committee found that Save America PAC along with the Trump campaign raised a quarter of a billion dollars.[87] Many of its fundraising emails and texts featured the Big Lie prominently.[88] As the Select Committee detailed:

> Evidence gathered by the Committee indicates that President Trump raised roughly one quarter of a billion dollars in fundraising efforts between the [2020] election and January 6th [footnote omitted]. Those solicitations persistently claimed and referred to election fraud that did not exist. For example, the Trump Campaign, along with the Republican National Committee, sent millions of emails

[83] Kenichi Serino, 'Jan. 6 Committee Alleges Funds Raised by Trump to Overturn 2020 Election Used to Sway Witness Testimonies', Associated Press, 19 December 2022, www.pbs.org/newshour/politics/jan-6-committee-alleges-funds-raised-by-trump-to-overturn-2020-election-used-to-sway-witness-testimonies; Feuer, Haberman and Swan, 'Prosecutors in Jan. 6 Case'; Rubin, 'Why Jack Smith's Reported Wire Fraud Probe'.

[84] 'Save America', Ballotpedia, https://ballotpedia.org/Save_America.

[85] Feuer et al., 'Trump's Post-Election Fund-Raising' ('Save America was officially registered with the Federal Election Commission on Nov. 9, 2020 – two days after news organizations declared Mr. Biden's victory over Mr. Trump').

[86] Super PACs are committees that make 'independent expenditures' in federal elections, which means they do not coordinate with candidates or political parties. Super PACs are allowed to accept unlimited amounts of money from US individuals and corporations because the DC Circuit has found after Citizens United that 'the government has no anti-corruption interest in limiting contributions to an independent expenditure group'; *SpeechNow.org* v. *Federal Election Commission*, 599 F.3d 686, 695 (D.C. Cir. 2010), cert. denied sub nom. *Keating* v. *Federal Election Commission*, __ S.Ct. __, 2010 WL 4272775 (1 November 2010).

[87] Final Report at 770 ('the Big Lie helped President Trump and the Republican National Committee (RNC) raise more than $250 million after the election, much of it from small-dollar donors who were promised their money would "Stop the Steal"'); Feuer et al., 'Trump's Post-Election Fund-Raising Comes under Scrutiny by Justice Dept.' ('At a committee hearing in June, Representative Zoe Lofgren, Democrat of California, laid out the panel's account of how Save America PAC and Mr. Trump's campaign raised $250 million after the election by claiming they were fighting widespread fraud when they knew there was none').

[88] Jill Colvin, Brian Slodysko and Eric Tucker, 'Trump's PAC Faces Scrutiny amid Intensifying Legal Probes', Associated Press News, 13 September 2022, https://apnews.com/article/2022-midterm-elections-russia-ukraine-donald-trump-presidential-campaigns-4ce3a13c3fe27255210adc0c83a80da1 ('Much of the money Trump has amassed was raised in the days and weeks after the 2020 election, which he lost to Democrat Joe Biden. That's when Trump supporters were bombarded with a nonstop stream of emails and texts, many containing all-caps lettering and blatant lies about a stolen 2020 election, soliciting cash for an "election defense fund"').

to their supporters, with messaging claiming that the election was 'rigged', that their donations could stop Democrats from 'trying to steal the election', and that Vice President Biden would be an 'illegitimate president' if he took office.[89]

As the Select Committee also documented, none of this was true, and multiple people told Trump in real time that there was 'no there, there' when it came to massive election fraud in the 2020 election.[90] The fact that multiple individuals told Trump he was completely wrong about the existence of election fraud featured prominently in his third indictment by Special Counsel Smith for his actions surrounding January 6.[91] Moreover, some of the post-2020-election Trump fundraising emails indicated that the money would be used for an election defense fund related to the 2020 election litigation for the sixty-plus litigations that he would eventually lose.[92] The Select Committee investigated the fundraising by Save America PAC and other Trump fundraising entities and discovered that the election defense fund did not exist.[93] Rather, as the Select Committee explained: 'Despite what they told their supporters, however, most of their money was not used to stop any purported steal – it was diverted to accomplish the Big Rip-off. Millions of dollars that were raised ostensibly for "election defense" and "fighting voter fraud" were not spent that way at all.'[94]

Finally, in an indication of how bizarre the post-2020 election period has become, there is also potential for wire fraud charges against the Republican National Committee (RNC) itself. Key events happened at RNC headquarters. For example, the following incidents are detailed in Fulton County, Georgia's indictment of Trump and eighteen co-conspirators to overturn Georgia's election:

[89] Final Report at 27–28.

[90] Barack Obama, Keynote Address at the Challenges to Democracy in the Digital Information Realm Symposium: Disinformation Is a Threat to our Democracy, Stanford University, 21 April 2022 ('I already mentioned the 2020 presidential election. President Trump's own attorney general has said that the Justice Department uncovered no evidence of widespread voter fraud . . . A review of the ballots in Arizona's largest county, the results of which were endorsed by some pretty courageous local Republicans, because many of them were harassed and received death threats, actually more votes for President Biden and fewer votes for President Trump').

[91] *United States of America* v. *Trump and Others*, Indictment.

[92] Final Report at 784 ('The false claims of election fraud and the "Official Election Defense Fund" were so successful President Trump and his allies raised more than $250 million after the election.[footnote omitted] . . . The Trump Campaign continued to publicly state the election had been stolen by "the Left", while behind closed doors they prepared a new plan to spend their supporters' money').

[93] Dawsey, Devlin and Helderman, 'Trump Campaign Officials Got Subpoena Asking New Questions about Jan. 6' ('Recipients [a federal subpoena] were . . . asked for documents related to the genesis of an "Election Defense Fund", an entity that Trump officials created to raise money from grass-roots donors. . . . Officials later testified to the House committee investigating the events of Jan. 6, 2021, that such a fund never technically existed').

[94] Final Report at 770.

> On or about the 19th day of November 2020, Rudolph William Louis Giuliani, Jenna Lynn Ellis, Sidney Katherine Powell, and unindicted co-conspirator Individual 3, whose identity is known to the Grand Jury, appeared at a press conference at the Republican National Committee Headquarters on behalf of Donald John Trump and Donald J. Trump for President, Inc. (the 'Trump Campaign') and made false statements concerning fraud in the November 3, 2020 presidential election in Georgia and elsewhere. These were overt acts in furtherance of the conspiracy.[95]

And as the Select Committee found:

> Moreover, the Select Committee's investigation shows that the RNC knew that President Trump's claims about winning the election were baseless and that post-election donations would not help him secure an additional term in office. Yet, both the Trump Campaign and the RNC decided to continue fundraising after the election, a decision that would have come from President Trump himself.[96]

Thus, if Trump is culpable for defrauding donors by fundraising on the basis of the Big Lie, then so too are the upper echelons of the RNC who did the same thing.

There should be legal consequences for defrauding donors with the Big Lie. The brutal repetition of the Big Lie for years warped Republicans' and especially Trump supporters' views of the 2020 election. Years later, many still think there was voter fraud.[97] And many are still forking out their hard-earned dollars because of the Big Lie.[98] Incidentally, the RNC is also implicated in a completely different crime of Trump's fake elector scheme. As the Special Counsel detailed in his 1 August 2023 indictment of Trump:

> On December 6 [2020], the Defendant [Donald Trump] and Co-Conspirator 2 [John Eastman] called the Chairwoman of the Republican National Committee to ensure that the plan was in motion. During the call, Co-

[95] *The State of Georgia* v. *Trump and Others*, Indictment, at 20.

[96] Final Report at 770.

[97] Obama, Keynote Address ('And yet today, as we speak, a majority of Republicans still insist that President Biden's victory was not legitimate. That's a lot of people'); see also Glenn Kessler, Scott Clement and Emily Guskin, 'Which Trump Lies Stick? Republicans Believe Some Falsehoods more than They Did Six Years Ago, Our Poll Finds,' *The Washington Post*, 9 April 2024, www.washingtonpost.com/politics/2024/04/09/some-trump-falsehoods-stick-more-than-others-fact-checker-poll-finds/ ('Trump has made significant inroads in convincing Republicans that his lies are the truth. That applies to election integrity especially – the basis of Trump's "big lie."… Trump has convinced 70 percent of Republicans – and 81 percent of his strong supporters – that Biden won the 2020 election because of voter fraud, though not a single allegation has been proven. Slightly more than one-third of Americans overall believe this').

[98] Stephen Collinson, 'New Signs Trump's Campaign Is Designed to Bankroll His Legal Defense', CNN, 31 July 2023, www.cnn.com/2023/07/31/politics/donald-trump-campaign-legal-defense-2024/index.html; Jeffrey M. Berry, '"Stop the Steal" Is about Trump. It's Also about Lots and Lots of Money', WBUR, 11 January 2022, www.wbur.org/cognoscenti/2022/01/11/trump-2020-election-big-lie-jeffrey-berry.

> Conspirator 2 told the Chairwoman that it was important for the RNC to help the Defendant's Campaign gather electors in targeted states, and falsely represented to her that such electors' votes would be used only if ongoing litigation in one of the states changed the results in the Defendant's favor. After the RNC Chairwoman consulted the Campaign and heard that work on gathering electors was underway, she called and reported this information to the Defendant, who responded approvingly.[99]

And then, a week later, the Chairwoman of the RNC sent the names of fake electors who had pretended to vote for him to Trump. As detailed in the indictment, this is what happened:

> That evening [14 December 2020], at 6:26 p.m., the RNC Chairwoman forwarded to the Defendant [Trump], through his executive assistant, an email titled, 'Electors Recap Final' which represented that in 'Six Contested States', Georgia, Michigan, Nevada, Pennsylvania and Wisconsin the Defendant's electors had voted in parallel to Biden's electors. The Defendant's executive assistant responded, 'It's in front of him!'

This behavior was also noted in the Fulton County indictment, which stated:

> On or about the 8th day of December 2020, Donald John Trump and John Charles Eastman placed a telephone call to Republican National Committee Chairwoman Ronna McDaniel to request her assistance gathering certain individuals to meet and cast electoral votes for Donald John Trump on December 14, 2020, in certain states despite the fact that Donald John Trump lost the November 3, 2020, presidential election in those states. This was an overt act in furtherance of the conspiracy.[100]

At this point, neither the RNC nor its Chairwoman have been charged with any crimes in any venue.

Though the Fulton County Prosecutor did note that one of the overt acts in the overall conspiracy to overthrow the 2020 election in Georgia included:

> On or about the 27th day of December 2020, Mark Randall Meadows sent a text message to Office of the Georgia Secretary of State Chief Investigator Frances Watson that stated in part, 'Is there a way to speed up Fulton county signature verification in order to have results before Jan. 6 if the trump campaign assist financially.' This was an overt act in furtherance of the conspiracy.[101]

Put another way, the sitting Chief of Staff to the president was offering Trump campaign funds to speed up the vote count in Georgia as part of the alleged criminal conspiracy to overturn the lawful 2020 election. A federal judge has already found that these actions were beyond Meadows' powers as a federal official because the Hatch Act bars executive officers from interfering or intervening in an

[99] *United States of America* v. *Trump and Others*, Indictment, at 23.
[100] *The State of Georgia* v. *Trump and Others*, Indictment, at 30.
[101] Ibid. at 45.

election.[102] Nonetheless, there are thirty unindicted co-conspirators in the Fulton County indictment that could face future prosecution, including for fraudulent fundraising, so this story is still unfurling.

8.6 WHERE DID THE MONEY RAISED USING THE BIG LIE GO?

Some of the fundraising after the 2020 election using the Big Lie was done through Donald J. Trump for President, Inc. – that is, the Trump 2020 campaign. Even before the physical insurrection at the Capitol, the Select Committee found that Trump and certain of his lawyers and his supporters waged a campaign to get state election officials to overturn the results of the 2020 election. The Select Committee further found that President Trump had approved funding of ads that badgered state lawmakers to overturn the election, including in Arizona:

> President Trump personally approved a series of advertisements that the Campaign ran on cable television and social media in several important States. One advertisement in Arizona called for pressure on Governor Ducey . . . alleging, 'The evidence is overwhelming. Call Governor Ducey and your legislators. Demand they inspect the machines and hear the evidence.' . . . Stand up for President Trump. Call today. Paid for by Donald J. Trump for President, Inc.[103]

Top Trump advisors, including his son-in-law Jared Kushner, were involved in approving the ad campaign to pressure state lawmakers to overturn the results of the 2020 election. As the Select Committee noted:

> Trump Campaign Senior Advisor Jason Miller . . . wrote that 'the President and Mayor Giuliani want to get back up on TV ASAP, and Jared [Kushner] has approved in budgetary concept, so here's the gameplan' in order to 'motivate the GOP base to put pressure on the Republican Governors of Georgia and Arizona and the Republican-controlled State legislatures in Wisconsin and Michigan to hear evidence of voter fraud before January 6th.' Miller anticipated a budget of $5 million . . . On December 22nd, Jason Miller texted Jared Kushner that 'POTUS has approved the buy'.[104]

This places President Trump, Donald J. Trump for President, Inc., and his key advisors at the center of the effort to illegitimately overturn a democratic election at the state level.

The Select Committee found that the Save America PAC, in turn, gave funds to former White House Chief of Staff Mark Meadows' charity the Conservative

[102] *State of Georgia* v. *Meadows*, Case 1:23-cv-03621-SCJ (8 September 2023), www.documentcloud.org/documents/23945268-meadowsord090823, Order at 33.

[103] Final Report at 300 (internal citation omitted).

[104] Ibid. at 300–1 (internal citation omitted).

Partnership Institute (CPI).[105] The CPI then gave $1 million to another group called American Voting Rights Foundation,[106] which was created two days after the CPI got money from Save America PAC.[107] Through this daisy-chain of donations, which occurred in 2021, Save America PAC helped fund the bogus effort to audit the 2020 vote in Arizona – which the press derisively called the Cyber Ninjas' 'fraudit', a portmanteau of 'fraudulent' and 'audit'.[108] As criminal investigations around Trump heated up in 2022 and 2023, Save America PAC spent tens of millions on criminal defense lawyers for Trump and witnesses around him.[109]

Money was diverted from the 2020 Trump Campaign to the Save America PAC. And much of this money went to Trump-affiliated companies. As the Select Committee noted when following the money:

> The Trump Campaign spent the money on President Trump, giving donations to his associates, and keeping it for himself in Save America. Hundreds of millions of dollars that were raised to go towards 'election defense' and 'fighting voter fraud' were not spent that way at all. To the contrary, most of the funds remain unspent, and millions have been paid to companies that are known affiliates of President Trump, or payments to entities associated with former Trump administration officials. Since the election, former Trump officials who are still working for President Trump's PACs and are publicly receiving salaries as FEC-reported 'payroll', are also associated with these companies.[110]

Another entity to consider is American Made Media Consultants, an LLC to which the Trump campaign paid millions throughout the 2020 re-election campaign. This LLC spent hundreds of thousands of dollars on messaging about January 6.[111] According to the Campaign Legal Center, 'reporting shows that Jared Kushner

[105] Brendan Fischer and Ed Pilkington, 'Revealed: Trump Secretly Donated $1M to Discredited Arizona Election "Audit"', *The Guardian*, 27 January 2023, www.theguardian.com/us-news/2023/jan/27/trump-secretly-donated-1m-arizona-election-audit ('In its final report released in December, the bipartisan January 6 committee investigating the insurrection at the US Capitol highlighted how Save America Pac gave $1m to the Conservative Partnership Institute (CPI). Top CPI officials include Mark Meadows, Trump's former chief of staff, along with other senior Trump insiders after they left the White House').

[106] Ibid. ('Tax filings obtained recently show that CPI in turn gave $1m to AVRF in 2021 – the only known donation that the group has ever received').

[107] Ibid. ('Ten days later, on 26 July 2021, Trump's Save America Pac made its $1m transfer to CPI, according to Federal Election Commission records. Two days after that, on 28 July, a new group called the American Voting Rights Foundation (AVRF) was registered as a corporation in Delaware').

[108] Ibid. ('An analysis by the watchdog group Documented has traced [$1 million in] funding for the Arizona audit back to Trump's Save America Pac').

[109] Maggie Haberman and Shane Goldmacher, '$60 Million Refund Request Shows Financial Pressure on Trump from Legal Fees', *The New York Times*, 29 July 2023 ('That $40 million was in addition to $16 million that Save America spent in the previous two years on legal fees').

[110] Final Report at 784–85.

[111] Anna Massoglia, 'Details of the Money behind Jan. 6 Protests Continue to Emerge', Open Secrets, 25 October 2021, www.opensecrets.org/news/2021/10/details-of-the-money-behind-jan-6-protests-continue-to-emerge.

approved AMMC's [American Made Media Consultants'] formation and that its board initially included members of the former president's and former vice president's families who also held senior roles with the Trump campaign.'[112] The Select Committee summed up: 'After raising $250 million dollars on false voter fraud claims, mostly from small-dollar donors, President Trump did not spend it on fighting an election he knew he lost. Instead, … President Trump got a war chest with millions of dollars, and the American people were left with the U.S. Capitol under attack.'[113] If any of money raised by the Big Lie ended up in Trump's hands, that could be a key element in proving wire fraud in a federal criminal case or common law fraud in a state criminal case. In other words, Trump was not lying about the outcome of the 2020 election only to puff up his own ego – he was lying for monetary gain, which is a factor that triggers criminal liability.

8.7 CONCLUSION

Within weeks of the Select Committee making criminal referrals to the DOJ, Attorney General Merrick Garland appointed Jack Smith Special Counsel to investigate (1) Trump's alleged retention of classified documents at Mar-a-Lago after he was president and (2) crimes that may have been committed during the events leading up to and on 6 January 2021.[114] As Jack Smith's office became a subpoena factory, the Save America PAC funded lawyers for witnesses close to Trump.[115] And press reports indicate that the Special Counsel's office is investigating the Save America PAC.[116]

The Special Counsel's investigations go directly into the inner circle running Trump's 2024 election campaign. Presently, instead of having a traditional 'campaign manager', the Trump 2024 campaign has four senior advisors: Brian Jack, Chris LaCivita, Jason Miller and Susie Wiles, who is also the CEO of the Save America PAC.[117] Wiles is a key witness in Trump's federal criminal case about

[112] 'Supplemental FEC Complaint: Trump Payments to American Made Media Consultants', Campaign Legal Center, 28 January 2021, https://campaignlegal.org/document/supplemental-fec-complaint-trump-payments-american-made-media-consultants.

[113] Final Report at 789.

[114] 'Appointment of a Special Counsel', DOJ, 18 November 2022, www.justice.gov/opa/pr/appointment-special-counsel-0.

[115] Devlin Barrett, Josh Dawsey and Isaac Stanley-Becker, 'Trump's Committee Paying for Lawyers of Key Mar-a-Lago Witnesses', *The Washington Post*, 5 December 2022, www.washingtonpost.com/national-security/2022/12/05/trump-witnesses-legal-bills-pac ('Former president Donald Trump's political action committee is paying legal bills for some key witnesses involved in the Justice Department investigation into whether Trump mishandled classified documents').

[116] Ibid. ('The [Save America] PAC is the subject of a federal investigation for its fundraising tactics around false claims that the election was stolen').

[117] 'Donald Trump Presidential Campaign Staff, 2024', Ballotpedia, 19 June 2023, https://ballotpedia.org/Donald_Trump_presidential_campaign_staff,_2024; Matt Flegenheimer, Maggie Haberman and Michael C. Bender, 'DeSantis Tried to Bury Her: Now She's Helping Trump Try to Bury Him', *The New York Times*, 18 April 2023, www.nytimes.com/2023/04/18/us/politics/susie-wiles-trump-desantis.html ('Ms. Wiles brought in an ally, Brian

classified documents.[118] She is apparently referred to as 'PAC Representative' in Trump's Mar-a-Lago indictment, and Trump allegedly showed her a classified map even though she did not have the security clearance to see it.[119] She worked on Trump's 2016 election as its Florida chair, and she also worked on his 2020 election until being fired in September 2020.[120] But she is back for round three with Trump's 2024 campaign.[121] For the past few years, Wiles worked out of both of Trump's resorts, Bedminster and Mar-a-Lago.[122] At present, Wiles has been accused of no wrongdoing by prosecutors, though it is possible that prosecutors are considering charges related to how the Save America PAC acted while she ran it.[123] She has been interviewed by the Special Counsel's office several times.[124]

When this chapter was written, Special Counsel Smith had not charged any actions related to fundraising using the Big Lie or its closely related problem of the

Jack, to oversee the campaign with her alongside Chris LaCivita, a longtime Republican strategist').

[118] Areeba Shah, '"She Is a Potential Government Witness": Top Trump Campaign Official Cited in Indictment Revealed', Salon, 29 June 2023, www.salon.com/2023/06/29/she-is-a-potential-government-witness-top-campaign-official-cited-in-indictment-revealed.

[119] *United States* v. *Trump and Others*, Case 9:23-cr-80101-AMC (8 June 2023), https://d3i6fh83elv35t.cloudfront.net/static/2023/06/trump-indictment.pdf.

[120] Maggie Haberman, 'Donald Trump's Florida Effort Relied on Veteran of Gov. Rick Scott's Campaign', *The New York Times*, 15 March 2016, https://archive.nytimes.com/www.nytimes.com/politics/first-draft/2016/03/15/donald-trumps-florida-effort-relied-on-veteran-of-gov-rick-scotts-campaign ('Donald J. Trump . . . will have to thank . . . Susie Wiles [for electoral success in Florida]'); Alex Isenstadt and Matt Dixon, 'Trump Campaign Cuts Ties with Top Adviser in Florida', Politico, 17 September 2019, www.politico.com/states/florida/story/2019/09/17/trump-campaign-cuts-ties-with-top-adviser-in-florida-1189767 ('President Donald Trump's campaign has severed ties with Florida adviser Susie Wiles').

[121] Gabby Orr and Steve Contorno, 'She Helped Trump Win Florida Twice. Now She Could Lead His Expected 2024 Campaign', CNN, 8 August 2022, www.cnn.com/2022/08/08/politics/susie-wiles-donald-trump-2024-campaign/index.html ('Susie Wiles was searching for her next act when Donald Trump came knocking last spring [in 2021]').

[122] Ibid. ('Wiles spends most of her time with Trump huddling in offices at his Bedminster, New Jersey, golf club or Mar-a-Lago resort [in the summer of 2022], . . . Wiles was seated to the right of Trump during a meeting at Bedminster with Hungarian Prime Minister Viktor Orban, according to a photo posted by Orban's spokesman').

[123] Feuer et al., 'Trump's Post-Election Fund-Raising Comes under Scrutiny by Justice Dept.' ('A federal grand jury . . . is examining the formation of – and spending by – a fund-raising operation created by Donald J. Trump after his loss in the 2020 election as he was soliciting millions of dollars by baselessly asserting that the results had been marred by widespread voting fraud').

[124] Kaitlan Collins et al., 'Top Trump Campaign Aide Susie Wiles Met Numerous Times with Special Counsel Investigators in Documents Probe', CNN, 29 June 2023, www.cnn.com/2023/06/29/politics/susie-wiles-special-counsel-investigation-documents-trump/index.html ('A senior campaign official for Donald Trump was allegedly shown a classified map by the former president during a meeting at his New Jersey golf club . . . The campaign adviser, Susie Wiles, has spoken to federal investigators numerous times'); Isaac Arnsdorf and Josh Dawsey, 'Awkwardness in Trump's Circle: Top Aides Could Be Trial Witnesses', *The Washington Post*, 5 August 2023, www.washingtonpost.com/national-security/2023/08/05/trump-trial-witnesses-2020-election-charges.

Big Rip Off.[125] Nor had the Fulton County District Attorney. Smith's indictment has been analogized to a rifle shot, while the Fulton County indictment was compared to a shotgun blast.[126] But the lack of fundraising-related charges is not because these avenues are legally foreclosed. Indeed, as this chapter has demonstrated, the DOJ frequently charges similar campaign finance cases with wire fraud. With four charges already pending against ex-President Trump for his actions surrounding January 6, it is possible that viable charges about wire fraud were left out just to streamline the Special Counsel's case against Trump.[127] Additionally, the Fulton County Prosecutor did not focus on the fundraising in her sprawling Racketeer Influenced and Corrupt Organizations Act indictment of ex-President Trump and his eighteen co-conspirators.[128] It is still possible that the Fulton County District Attorney could charge common law fraud offenses related to Save America PAC's fundraising that defrauded residents of Fulton County, Georgia, of their hard-earned money.[129] Prosecuting these crimes would be better for future elections as it would disincentivize other politicians from copying Trump's fundraising using disinformation.

[125] *United States of America* v. *Trump and Others*, Indictment (listing six co-conspirators none of whom appear to be fundraisers with the possible exception of the yet unnamed co-conspirator 6); *United States of America* v. *Trump and Others*, Superseding Indictment (against Trump and co-conspirators Waltine Nauta and Carlos De Oliveira).

[126] Glenn Thrush and Danny Hakim, 'Court Skirmishes Show Divergent Strategies by Prosecutors in Trump Cases', *The New York Times*, 29 August 2023, www.nytimes.com/2023/08/29/us/politics/trump-prosecutors-strategy.html.

[127] *United States of America* v. *Trump and Others*, Indictment, at 1 (charging Count 1 18 U.S.C. 371 (Conspiracy to Defraud the United States); Count 2 18 U.S.C. 1512(k) (Conspiracy to Obstruct an Official Proceeding); Count 3: 18 U.S.C. §§ 1512(c)(2) (Obstruction of and Attempt to Obstruct an Official Proceeding); Count 4 18 U.S.C. 241 (Conspiracy against Rights)).

[128] *The State of Georgia* v. *Trump and Others*, Indictment.

[129] Charles Bethea, 'Georgia's Broad Racketeering Law May Now Ensnare Donald Trump', *The New Yorker*, 31 July 2023, www.newyorker.com/news/letter-from-the-south/georgias-broad-racketeering-law-may-now-ensnare-donald-trump.

9

Fake News under Siege

A Century of Regulation in Chile

John Charney

9.1 INTRODUCTION

Chile's regulation of fake news dates back nearly a century. The initial instance occurred in 1925 during a constitutional crisis that resulted in the drafting of a new constitution. At that time, a de facto government issued a decree making it illegal to publish and distribute fake news. The second regulatory milestone occurred during the dictatorship of General Augusto Pinochet with the inclusion of provisions related to defamation in the 1980 constitution. Defamation involved spreading false information through mass media to unjustly tarnish someone's reputation.[1] Upon the restoration of democracy in Chile in 1990, these stipulations were permanently abolished from the legal system.[2] Since 2001, the judicial pursuit of disinformation in Chile has been limited to exceptional means such as the State Security Law or, indirectly, through the right to rectification.[3]

Nearly a century after the initial criminalization of fake news in Chile's history, the discussion has resurfaced. In recent years, several bills have been proposed to penalize the dissemination and propagation of fake news. The current government has set up a commission against disinformation to, among other objectives, evaluate the impact of disinformation on democracy and contribute to the design of a policy against it.[4] As in the past, the drive to regulate comes at a time of constitutional crisis

This contribution forms part of Fondecyt Research Project No. 1231034 whose main researcher is the author. The author is grateful to Fabiana Casali and Matías Schäfer for providing brilliant work as research assistants.

1 Constitution, Art. 19(4).

2 The constitutional provision was abolished through a constitutional amendment in 2005, while the offence of spreading fake news was removed from the legal system by the Press Act 2001.

3 See notes 48–50.

4 See Decreto No. 12 of the Ministerio de Ciencia, Tecnología, Conocimiento e Innovación in 'Comisión contra la desinformación', *Diario Oficial de la República de Chile*, No. 43.582, 20 June 2023, www.diariooficial.interior.gob.cl/publicaciones/2023/06/20/43582/01/2331911.pdf.

with a high degree of political tension and instability. As with prior instances, the drive towards regulation could be perceived as an authoritarian endeavour to suppress political dissent. Nevertheless, in contrast to previous contexts, the current regulatory drive is occurring within a democratic framework.

Moreover, the phenomenon of fake news has assumed global dimensions – prompting the present volume – and responds to technological transformations that have accelerated its production and dissemination. In Chile, these shifts have not just influenced the dynamics of shaping public opinion but also destabilized the system of fundamental rights where the right to freedom of expression and information lie. This disruption is due to the fact that the authority to define the scope of online freedom of expression, its boundaries (including false or incorrect information), and the power to penalize transgressors increasingly rests in the hands of major internet corporations and progressively less within the constitutional framework protecting these rights.

This chapter addresses the phenomenon of fake news through the lens of its regulatory history in Chile. The analysis not only elucidates the factors that prompted its regulation but also examines the array of techniques employed to prevent the propagation of disinformation. From this analysis, it will be possible to conclude that although some of the causes that motivated the regulation of fake news in the past coincide with those of the present, persuasive reasons underscore the renewed interest in their criminalization that were absent in the past. These reasons explain the significance that disinformation has acquired in the present and that motivates the publication of this book. The chapter is divided into four sections. Section 9.2 examines the history of fake news regulation in Chile between 1925 and 1973, which corresponds to the period when the 1925 Constitution was in force. Section 9.3 analyses the constitutionalization of fake news during Augusto Pinochet's dictatorship. Section 9.4 looks at the criminalization of disinformation in State Security Law. Section 9.5 delves into the prosecution of fake news once democracy was restored in the country and the offences of disseminating fake news and defamation were repealed. Within this section, it will be demonstrated that the lack of regulation resulted in the procedural redirection of the phenomenon through alternative avenues, such as the right to rectification and the so-called Amparo remedy against injury to individuals' reputation. While these tools have, to a certain extent, facilitated the judicial redirection of prosecuting fake news when disseminated through traditional mass media channels (press, radio and television), the same cannot be stated for those circulating online for reasons to be mentioned here. This brings us to Section 9.6, where the intricacies of fake news in the digital era are examined, along with the impacts they have had on shaping public opinion and the protection of fundamental rights in Chile.

9.2 A CONCISE HISTORY OF DISINFORMATION REGULATION IN CHILE (1925–1973)

The regulation of fake news in Chile has been initiated by de facto governments, in times of great political instability and polarization, as well as during constituent processes or constitutional crises. The first of these instances occurred in late 1924, amidst a severe political crisis that pitted the Chilean army against the President of the Republic, Arturo Alessandri Palma. The catalyst for this conflict was the processing of a legislative bill aimed at establishing parliamentary allowances.[5] This was a significant project as it aimed to ensure parliamentary participation regardless of the economic capacity of the representatives. However, its development sparked substantial tension as lawmakers were determining their own remuneration during an economically difficult period for the country, while failing to enact a set of long-demanded social laws. Among the affected groups was the army, which was lobbying for an adjustment of its wages. During the advancement of the project, a cohort of 200 officers gathered at the premises of the National Congress to express their dissatisfaction. Days following this, the faction issued a series of demands to President Alessandri, which included vetoing the parliamentary allowance, accelerating the process of implementing social laws, replacing specific state ministers and instituting a constitutional reform to establish a presidential regime.[6] At this point, and despite many of the demands being met, the army no longer responded to constitutional authority. After appealing unsuccessfully to President Alessandri to dissolve the Congress, he ultimately resigned and went into exile in Italy.[7]

On 11 September 1924, a governing junta commanded by the military's highest-ranking official seized power. This effectively suspended President Alessandri's constitutional mandate. He would return to the country six months later to lead the constitutional process that resulted in the formulation of the 1925 Constitution.[8] This period was marked by a high degree of political instability and conflict for the control of power. Moreover, it was characterized by a severe crackdown on the media.[9] During this period, the junta shut down opposition newspapers, and censorship became a frequently employed weapon for managing political dissent. The justification for censorship was public safety, and it was enacted through the declaration of constitutional states of exception.[10]

5 Sofía Correa et al., *Historia del siglo XX chileno* (Santiago: Editorial Sudamericana, 2001) p. 94.

6 Fernando Muñoz, *Introducción a la historia del derecho chileno* (Santiago: Der Ediciones, 2021) p. 131.

7 Mario Góngora, *Ensayo histórico sobre la noción de Estado en Chile en los siglos XIX y XX* (Santiago: Editorial Universitaria, 2006) pp. 172–84.

8 Fernando Silva, 'Expansión y crisis nacional' in Sergio Villalobos et al., *Historia de Chile* (Santiago: Editorial Universitaria, 1975) pp. 818–24.

9 Fernando Silva, 'Un contrapunto de medio siglo: Democracia liberal y estatismo burocrático 1924–1970' in Villalobos et al., *Historia de Chile*, pp. 905–6.

10 Ibid.

In this context, during the final days of the junta's rule (prior to President Alessandri's return), Decree Law 425 of 1925, labelled 'Regarding Abuses of Publicity', was enacted. This decree replaced the Press Act of 1873, which had a distinctly liberal bent and codified what had been specific harassment and press censorship measures during this time period.[11] The 1925 decree brought significant alterations to Chilean press regulation.[12] Notable among them was the abolition of trial by jury for press abuses, as established by the 1833 Constitution. The decree also broadened the scope of offences committable via print or other publication types. Particularly noteworthy is the establishment of the offence of incitement to commit other felonies, such as homicide, robbery, or arson, which is punishable even if the offences are not committed.[13]

This decree introduced the offence of disseminating fake news into the Chilean legal system for the first time. Article 17 imposes custodial sentences and fines for 'the publication or reproduction of fake news, alleged documents, adulterated materials, or inaccurately attributed documents to another individual'.[14] For distribution or reproduction to constitute an offence, it must occur orally in public places or through radio broadcasting, or via written materials sold, disseminated, or displayed at public venues or events.[15] In addition, the provision requires malice to be proven for the execution of such actions and the production of illegal results. Additionally, the decree assigns responsibility not only to the authors of the fake news publication but also to the media outlet's director. In the director's absence, liability is transferred to the publisher, and in the absence of the publisher, it falls upon those selling or disseminating the newspapers carrying the news.[16]

[11] Since the late nineteenth century, both conservatives and liberals exhibited a growing hostility towards the press as a consequence of the expansion of the workers' press. Both sides were insistent on amending the Press Act of 1873 to increase penalties for abuses by the press. See Julio Heise, *Historia de Chile, El periodo parlamentario 1861–1925* (Santiago: Andrés Bello, 1974); Karen Donoso Fritz, 'Las mordazas a la prensa obrera: Los mecanismos de la censura política en Chile 1919–1925' (2016) 28 *Izquierdas* 211.

[12] See Heise, *Historia de Chile*, pp. 336–56.

[13] Many of these rules were supported by conservative and nationalist sectors during the parliamentary period in order to reform the Press Act of 1873. See ibid. pp. 336–39.

[14] Decreto Ley 425, 'Sobre abusos de la publicidad', Art. 17, www.bcn.cl/leychile/navegar?idNorma=6073.

[15] Ibid., Art. 12.

[16] Decreto Ley 425, 1925, Art. 32. This criterion changes radically over time. In one of the latest rulings on fake news, the Supreme Court states that the director of a newspaper cannot be held liable for the publication of fake news because 'it was beyond his reasonable capabilities to personally verify the truth of the published news, a task that corresponds to an investigative function assigned to a journalist . . . in whom the director of the newspaper had to put his trust'. Corte Suprema, January 1998, Rol No. 4.406-97.

The prohibition on disseminating fake news experienced several amendments during its history.[17] The most notable was introduced in 1967 under President Eduardo Frei Montalva's government through the new Press Act. Most of its modifications involved limiting the circumstances under which its publication could be prosecuted criminally, extending the accused's defence opportunities and mitigating the repercussions of its commission.[18] The first of these amendments eliminated imprisonment for the dissemination of false information, leaving only fines as penalties. A subsequent set of amendments sought to increase the standards for liability enforcement. In this context, the law adds a new element to the definition of the criminal offence, requiring that the falsity communicated be substantive. This implies that the false information must be of significant magnitude to alter the essence of the content constituting the information's core. Furthermore, the law specifies that the dissemination of fake news must have the potential to *seriously harm* various public interests enumerated within the provision. These encompass public safety, order, administration, health and the economy, in addition to individual interests such as the dignity, credit or reputation of persons, as well as the interests of legal entities. Additionally, the law affords the defendant, particularly in cases involving mass media outlets, ample opportunities for a robust defence. Notably, the defendant may be exempt from criminal liability if they promptly and exhaustively rectify the falsehood in the disseminated information. Rectification involves a complete acknowledgement of the falsity of the news realized through a publication in the same media outlet, maintaining identical characteristics to the initial publication containing the false information.[19]

These amendments diminished the incentives for judicial prosecution regarding the dissemination of fake news. Nevertheless, such incentives were practically unnecessary, as this offence was scarcely subjected to judicial prosecution between 1925 and 1967. This phenomenon can be attributed to the presence of alternative and more efficient procedural mechanisms. As will be further examined, the State Security Law also regulated fake news. This legislation imposed considerably harsher penalties not only on the individuals responsible for its creation, but also on directors and even media proprietors involved in its dissemination or reproduction.[20] In comparison to the Press Act 1967, which imposed fines for the dissemination of false news, the State Security Law carries the penalty of imprisonment for a maximum of five years.

Furthermore, Decree Law 425 introduced the right to rectification. This provision obligated mass media outlets to disseminate, free of charge, clarifications or

[17] In 1964, Decree Law 425 was amended by Law 15,476; these amendments were subsequently incorporated into the 1967 Press Act. This law instituted only a fine as a penalty (eliminating the penalty of incarceration) and added requirements for the prosecution of the offence.

[18] Ley 16643 de abusos de publicidad, Art. 19.

[19] Ley 16643, Arts. 11–15.

[20] See Ley 12927, Arts. 17(b) and 17(c).

rectifications of information that might have caused offence or made unjustifiable insinuations about an individual. When faced with such material, it became the responsibility of the media outlet to promptly publish clarifications or rectifications upon receiving appropriate notification. Failure to comply with this requirement resulted in penalties such as imprisonment and fines for contempt of court.[21] This was an easier and faster route to obtain redress from the publication of fake news than judicial actions.

9.3 THE OFFENCE OF DEFAMATION SINCE THE 1980 CONSTITUTION

On 11 September 1973, another *coup d'état* shook the nation. On this occasion, the armed forces overthrew President Salvador Allende and established a brutal military dictatorship that, under the command of Army General Augusto Pinochet Ugarte, remained in power for seventeen years. The dictatorship radically transformed the country's institutional order and began doing so from the very moment it assumed power. Just days after the coup, the junta entrusted a group of lawyers with drafting a constitutional proposal. In 1978, this Commission concluded its work with what would become the preliminary draft of the 1980 Constitution. The final text was approved through a plebiscite conducted without the existence of electoral records, political parties and a free and independent press.[22] In terms of freedom of expression and the press, the constitutional text reflected the dynamics that characterized the dictatorship's relationship with the media throughout its tenure in power.[23]

The boldest stride in the regulation of fake news in the nation's history took place within the 1980 Constitution, which included an express constitutional provision addressing this issue. This was done in the chapter on fundamental rights, specifically within the provision safeguarding the right to private and public life and reputation. In the relevant part, the provision stipulated that 'the infringement of this precept', meaning the violation of these rights, 'committed through a mass media, and consisting of the imputation of a false fact or act, *or* that unjustifiably

21 See Decreto Ley 425, Art. 8.

22 See Robert Barros, *La junta militar: Pinochet y la constitución de 1980* (Santiago: Sudamericana, 2005).

23 During the dictatorship, there was no free and independent press. On 11 September 1973, the military junta ordered 'the press, radio broadcasters and television channels loyal to the Unidad Popular' to 'cease all informational activities … or face air and ground retaliation'. Multiple media entities were shut down, their assets were confiscated and their employees were detained and exiled. During the dictatorship, critical media that managed to survive did so clandestinely or under constant intimidation, censorship and threats from state agents. See 'Periodismo de Oposición (1976–1989)', Memoria Chilena, Biblioteca Nacional de Chile, www.memoriachilena.gob.cl.

inflicts harm or discredit to an individual or their family, shall constitute an offence and shall be subject to the penalty determined by law'.[24]

The constitutional provision was ambiguous. Not only did it safeguard a broad array of legal interests, including public life – conceptually challenging and of questionable normative value – but also because the criminal offences it encompassed were not precisely defined in either the 1980 Constitution or elsewhere in Chilean law. At first glance, it appeared to include a single offence (referred to as defamation by Chilean legal scholars), yet in truth it contained – at the very least – two distinct offences that are classified as offences against reputation.

The disjunctive conjunction 'or' (highlighted above in italics) separated the first from the second. Both were violations of a person's private or public life or reputation and could only be perpetrated 'through mass media'. The first consisted of attributing a false fact or act, whereas the second referred to any attribution (false or true) that unjustifiably causes damage or discredit to a person or their family.[25] Although the latter was equivalent to libel expressed through mass media outlets (enforced at the time by the 1967 Press Act), the former was similar to spreading fake news (also covered by the 1967 Press Act), with the distinction that the criminal offence in the constitutional provision seemed not to require malice from the party making the imputation. In fact, it is only in the second offence that the inflicted harm is required to be *unjustified*. In other words, what this particular offence seemed to pursue was an objective liability for the attribution of false facts or acts that harm the protected constitutional interests in question.

During the dictatorship, the ambiguities of the constitutional provision were only partially addressed by a law that shaped and established penalties for these criminal offences. This law included two different offences based on the protected constitutional interests. The first of these protects people's private lives and is not relevant for the purposes of this chapter. The second relates to the protection of people's public lives and states that 'anyone who, without intent to libel, maliciously attributes a false fact related to their public life to a person' through a mass media outlet 'that causes or could cause material or moral harm' will face imprisonment and fines as indicated in the provision. This provision establishes a distinct offence against reputation that protects a person's public life, penalizing the deliberate attribution of a false fact via a mass media source. As mentioned earlier, Chilean legal scholars commonly refer to this offence as defamation.

[24] Constitution of 1980, Art. 19(4)(2) (emphasis added).

[25] This is the only way to understand that this same provision explicitly excludes proof of truth when the imputation itself constitutes 'the crime of libel against individuals', as defined by the constitutional provision. In the case of libel, falsity is not a necessary element of the offence. Therefore, it is entirely conceivable for truthful statements to constitute defamation. What is at stake in these cases is not the integrity of the discourse: whether the truth was told or not. What matters is restoring the aggrieved party's honour. Consequently, the old English proverb asserts 'the greater the truth, the greater the libel'.

Even though the repressive political landscape made this provision practically unnecessary, the offence of defamation offered authorities substantial advantages in prosecuting critical publications compared to other press law offences, such as libel and publication of fake news. There were two advantages regarding libel. The first relates to the protected constitutional interest. Libel protects a person's reputation, which is a legally established concept with a long historical tradition and substantial doctrinal development that help define its scope and facilitate its judicial application. On the other hand, 'public life' lacks these traits and is basically ambiguous, allowing it to be infused with any meaning the judge decides to attribute to it. Furthermore, safeguarding public life as a fundamental right is a reversal of the logic of fundamental rights, which protect individual rights against state authority. In this case, it is the political authority that is shielded from the scrutiny by the press and from the right of every citizen to be well informed, particularly about how the authorities wield power.

Another benefit of defamation over libel is malice. Libel requires the complainant to prove not merely that the defendant acted with malice, that is, with an intention to harm the offended party through illegal behaviour. According to well-established precedent, the complainant in a libel case must also demonstrate that the defendant had a specific intent, frequently referred to by legal scholars and case law as *animus injuriandi*: the intent to offend.[26] In this regard, the Supreme Court in a relatively recent judicial decision has indicated that the *animus injuriandi* is a 'distinct subjective element from malice, revealing a direct predisposition to harm one's reputation, and without which sanctioning for said offence is not possible'.[27]

The key issue here is not just that the absence of *animus injuriandi* precludes criminal liability, but that the presence of other types of motivations, such as the purpose to inform, precludes *animus injuriandi* as well. As a result, courts have historically been reluctant to convict mass media outlets of libel in circumstances involving publications that, while insulting to an individual, serve informative purposes. This is what motivated Enrique Ortúzar, the President of the Commission (bearing his name) that drafted the preliminary proposal for the 1980 Constitution during the dictatorship, to advocate for the inclusion of the offence of defamation within the constitutional framework.[28] In a session of the Commission, Ortúzar argued that in cases of libel 'judges considered the presence of *animus injuriandi* as a condition for the existence of the criminal offence, and there was no professional libeller who, when brought to court, would not claim that

[26] Jaime Vera, 'Delitos contra el honor' in Luis R. Collao (ed.), *Derecho Penal, Parte Especial* (Valencia: Derecho PUCV/ Tirant lo Blanch, 2022) pp. 562–63.

[27] Case No. 5935/2015, Corte Suprema, 11 June 2015.

[28] Enrique Ortzar was historically an unwavering advocate of highly restrictive measures on press freedom. In 1964, as Minister of Justice under then-President Jorge Alessandri Rodríguez, he defended the creation of the defamation offence before the parliament, a law that was enacted, but only in effect for three months.

there was no *animus injuriandi* in their conduct, thus largely avoiding any criminal liability'.[29] The provision of defamation explicitly excluded this intent by stating that the law applied to 'anyone who, without intent to injure, maliciously attributes a false fact related to their public life to a person'. This granted defamation significant procedural advantages over libel.

Defamation also offered more advantages for criminal prosecution than the offence of publishing fake news. In fact, it is important to recall that while the Press Act of 1967 kept this offence (which originated from Decree Law 425 of 1925), it introduced significant modifications to make judicial prosecution of the crime more demanding. The first of these is that the falsehood of the news must be substantive and significantly harm a public right or interest as specified by the law. The second is that the defendant may avoid criminal liability by admitting the falsehood and rectifying the information promptly and completely.[30] None of these limitations applied to the offence of defamation. On one hand, the law made no mention of the quality of falsehood, merely criminalizing the attribution of a false fact concerning a person's public life. On the other hand, the provision did not allow rectification of the information in order to avoid criminal liability. In contrast to the imposition of fines for the publication of false news, defamation was subject to penalties potentially resulting in up to five years of imprisonment. The aforementioned characteristics have endowed defamation with significant efficacy in maintaining the existing status quo, while simultaneously posing a formidable threat to democratic principles and freedom of speech. It is not surprising, as we will see later, that upon the restoration of democracy in Chile this offence was swiftly removed from the legal system.

9.4 FAKE NEWS AS A THREAT TO STATE SECURITY

Before analysing the regulation of false news in Chile following the restoration of democracy, it is necessary to provide a concise overview of the State Security Law, which also criminalizes the dissemination of fake news. This is the only law that remains in force to sanction such dissemination. It establishes that individuals commit crimes against the security of the state if they, among other things:

> propagate verbally or in writing or through any other means, or send abroad, tendentious or fake news information intended to destroy the republican and democratic regime of government, or to disrupt the constitutional order, the country's security, the economic or monetary system, price normalcy, stability of

[29] Actas de la Comisión de Estudios de la Nueva Constitución, Sesión No. 129 del 12 de junio de 1975, Historia de la Constitución Política, Art. 19(4), p. 23.

[30] See n. 19.

values and public assets, and the supply of populations, and Chileans who, while outside the country, disseminate such news abroad.[31]

This provision extends back to another dictatorship, which lasted from 1927 to 1931 and was led by General Carlos Ibáñez del Campo. Towards the end of this period, during a moment of high political tension that eventually forced Ibáñez to resign from power and go into exile in Argentina, he issued a decree that contained the initial version of the aforementioned provision.[32]

In its current form, the offence of disseminating deceptive or fake news, as outlined in the State Security Law, constitutes an offence of endangerment. What is pursued is disinformation that could be detrimental to state security or economic public order, without the need for actual harm or a specific threat to legally protected interests.[33] During Pinochet's dictatorship, individuals were convicted of this offence under these terms. For instance, a woman was convicted of transporting anti-government documents on a flight to Europe, despite the fact that these documents never reached the people they were intended for. The lower court judge was incapable of distinguishing the political nature of the information and ruled that 'labelling the military government as a "dictatorship" or using similar terms constitutes a false statement because our country has both a democratic and a republican system of government'.[34]

Notably, prior to 2001, the law allowed the courts to suspend media outlets for up to ten days if they committed an offence sanctioned by this law, such as the dissemination of false news, and to confiscate immediately any editions in which the commission of these offences is evident.[35] In addition to the authors, the directors of the media outlet where they were published and potentially their owners and even printers if the latter did not exist were also criminally liable.[36] Ultimately, the penalties associated with these offences have historically been much more severe than those related to the Press Act-regulated dissemination of fake news.[37]

[31] Ley 12,927, Art. 4(g).

[32] The provision is contained in DFL 143 of 5 May 1931.

[33] See Carlos Künsemüller Loebenfelder, *Estudio de los delitos atentatorios de la seguridad interior del Estado contenido en leyes penales especiales* (Santiago: Jurídica de Chile, 1970) p. 16.

[34] Corte de Apelaciones de Santiago, Rol 6-1983.

[35] Ley 12,927, Art. 16.

[36] Ibid., Art. 17. Under this rule, in June 1999, two executives of Planeta Publishing were apprehended for their involvement in the publication of *El libro negro de la justicia chilena* by Alejandra Matus. This case ultimately reached the Inter-American Commission on Human Rights, which issued recommendations for the State of Chile to redress the harm inflicted upon the author due to the violation of her freedom of expression. See Case 12,142, *Alejandra Matus y otros* v. *Chile*, Informe No. 90/05, 24 October 2005.

[37] In its latest version (2001), the Press Act established only fines and civil sanctions for this offence, whereas the State Security Law stipulates imprisonment for up to five years.

9.5 THE RETURN TO DEMOCRACY AND THE END OF FAKE NEWS REGULATION

Upon the restoration of democracy in Chile, the government led by President Patricio Aylwin made the normal operation of the mass media a top priority. This endeavour required a substantial transformation of the legal framework governing the press, which was accomplished in two legislative stages. The first step consisted of an urgent measure to align existing legislation with the democratic reality, in which freedom of expression would play an important role. The second stage, which spanned a significant amount of time, involved the drafting of a new Press Act designed to effectively protect the freedom of the press and strengthen the media's contribution to the democratic process.

On 17 April 1990, less than a month after assuming the presidency of the Republic, Patricio Aylwin submitted to the National Congress a bill intended to adapt press legislation to the country's new political and institutional realities. The purpose of the bill was to eliminate all restrictions imposed by the law that impeded the free exercise of speech.[38] This law introduced two significant amendments that are especially relevant to this chapter. First, it repealed the criminal offence of defamation, which was introduced to the Press Act by the ruling junta in 1985. A broad spectrum of political parties agreed that the regulation of defamation enacted during the dictatorship severely impeded the exercise of free speech, and that the legal interests it protected were already covered by the slander and libel laws. In contrast to the brief duration of legal defamation, the constitutional provision lasted longer, as it was not until 2005 that the necessary political support was gathered to implement one of the most extensive and significant reforms to the 1980 Constitution. This reform included the elimination of defamation from the Constitution, as well as numerous other modifications.[39]

The second relevant amendment pertains to the offence of disseminating false news under the Press Act 1967. Although retaining the core elements of its regulation, it modified the liability of mass media outlet owners, editors and directors. Prior to the reform, they were all jointly responsible for false information spread through their media. In three instances, the reform absolved them of liability. First, when it involves the simple reproduction of information or news from news agencies or information provided by public authorities on matters within their jurisdiction, or

[38] Mensaje presidencial, Sesión 5, Legislatura 319, 17 April 1990, Historia de la Ley 19,048, www.bcn.cl/historiadelaley/nc/historia-de-la-ley/7421.

[39] The reform dismantled the authoritarian legacy of the 1980 Constitution. It achieved this by transforming the Senate into a fully democratically elected chamber, placing the army under the authority of the President of the Republic and abolishing the political influence of the National Security Council. Additionally, the reform bolstered the Deputy Chamber's political oversight of the government, removed the binominal electoral system from the constitution and enhanced the role of the Constitutional Court. See Francisco Zúñiga (ed.), *Reforma Constitutucional* (Santiago: LexisNexis, 2005).

from individuals or institutions that, in the court's opinion, are reasonably reliable or appropriate in relation to the subject. The second scenario is in the case of live radio or television broadcasts, assuming the media outlet exercised reasonable care to prevent their dissemination. Lastly, they are exempt from liability in the event that fake news is disseminated in programmes or sections that are accessible to the public, with an explicit statement that what is broadcast there does not bind the media entity.[40]

The second legislative effort, related to the democratization of mass media, was a lengthy endeavour initiated by President Aylwin during the return to democracy. In July 1993, the president sent a bill to Congress, and eight years later, in May 2001, the 'new' Press Act went into effect. Some of the objectives of this law were to democratize the mass media and consolidate of a set of issues that were scattered across various legal statutes. Despite the fact that the contents of the new law were not radically changed from those of the 1967 Press Act, there are some significant differences. Among them, the principle of pluralism was incorporated for the first time in the history of press regulation in Chile. This was intended to promote the expansion of mass media outlets and to encourage the diversification of informational content.[41]

Significant modifications were also made from the perspective of reducing punitive measures. First, the legislation repealed the so-called offence of contempt under the State Security Law. This offence included libel, slander and defamation directed at the President of the Republic, ministers, parliamentarians, members of higher courts of justice and other important authorities. It was essentially a form of seditious libel aimed at preventing hostile attack against government and preserving public order. During the dictatorship, the government made extensive use of this provision and its application continued during the transition to democracy. Indeed, its use eclipsed reliance on other, related offences (such as disseminating fake news).[42] At that time, many international human rights organizations severely criticized the existence of the offence of contempt.[43] With its repeal, Chile made a significant step towards democratization and the expansion of freedom of speech. As previously explained, a second substantial change to the State Security Law was the elimination of the provision that authorized courts to suspend media outlets and confiscate their publications in connection with convictions for violations of the law. In the same vein, the strict liability of directors and owners of media outlets was eliminated

[40] Ley 19,048.

[41] John Charney, 'Media Regulation in Chile: Authority and Liberty Compounded' in Paul Wragg and András Koltay (eds.), *Global Perspectives on Press Regulation* (Oxford: Hart, 2024), Vol. II.

[42] See Felipe González, 'Hacia la derogación de las normas de desacato en Chile' in *Libertad de expresión en Chile* (Santiago: Universidad Diego Portales, 2006) pp. 199—241.

[43] See Informe Anual Comisión Interamericana de Derechos Humanos 1994, www.cidh.oas.org/annualrep/94span/indice.htm.

and a common procedure for adjudicating criminal and civil liability for offences committed through a mass media outlet was established.

A number of long-standing criminal offences contained in the Press Act 1967 were also repealed by the Press Act 2001. For the purposes of this chapter, the dissemination of fake news was the most relevant one. Undoubtedly, its repeal was a significant historical event, as it signalled the end of a provision that had been in effect in Chile for an important portion of the twentieth century. However, despite its long existence, this offence had a limited impact in judicial practice. Very few cases exist in which the courts actually applied this provision, and even fewer cases in which they used it to convict someone of spreading fake news.[44] Numerous reasons explain why this was so. First, fake news was not only governed by the Press Act, but also by the State Security Law. This law provided more favourable conditions for criminally prosecuting the dissemination of fake news than the Press Act did.[45]

As a result of the 2001 repeal of the fake news law, alternative measures have been taken to redirect its prosecution. The right to rectification and clarification was one of them. The Decree Law 425 of 1925 first granted this power, which the Press Act of 1967 subsequently reaffirmed, and which the Press Act of 2001 again reaffirmed. The right to rectification and clarification holds constitutional status in the Chilean legal system. Incorporated initially in 1970 as an amendment to the 1925 constitution, it was also enshrined in the 1980 Constitution and is still in effect today.[46] This right allows any person who has been unfairly mentioned or offended by a mass media outlet to demand that the outlet publish a clarification or retraction. The responsible media outlets are required to publish it, and if they fail to do so, the offended party may pursue legal action.[47] The courts have used the right to rectification in various ways in relation to disinformation and misinformation. For example, courts have recently indicated that the rectification procedure is appropriate for challenging the dissemination of false news,[48] and have ordered media outlets to correct any such news and imposed fines for failing to do so.[49] On the other hand, courts have occasionally considered the rectification by media outlets regarding the

[44] One of those cases is *Staub Jacqueline con Pinto Marco*, Supreme Court, 1 June 1993, where the director of the *Diario Austral* was sentenced for disseminating fake news.

[45] See notes 35 and 36.

[46] Its constitutional origins date back to 1970, when a set of reforms to the 1925 Constitution were introduced as a prerequisite for the centre political forces in parliament to support Salvador Allende's bid for the presidency of the Republic. This constitutional amendment, like other processes examined in this chapter that led to the regulation of fake news, was the result of a highly polarized political environment. See Arturo Valenzuela, *The Breakdown of Democratic Regime: Chile* (Baltimore: Johns Hopkins University Press, 1978).

[47] Constitution, Art. 19(12); Press Act of 2001, Arts. 16–20.

[48] See Corte de Apelaciones de Santiago, Rol 35815-2022.

[49] C-3069-2014, 28° Juzgado Civil de Santiago; C-8146-2021, 17° Juzgado Civil de Santiago.

dissemination of false news as pertinent evidence to exempt them from civil liability for damages or constitutional liability for the violation of fundamental rights.[50]

Lastly, false news has also been pursued through constitutional measures that protect fundamental rights. This is the Amparo remedy, which offers a rapid procedure and grants courts broad powers in the face of violations of constitutional rights, whether they originate from a state entity or even from a private entity (such as a media outlet). Although some courts have been reluctant to grant these remedies,[51] arguing that there are legal avenues to resolve such disputes, a significant number of cases have seen these remedies granted. They mainly involve situations where the dissemination of false news harms a person's reputation. As reputation is a constitutionally enshrined right and is safeguarded by the Amparo remedy, the courts have accepted these actions and ordered media outlets to rectify false information they have published.[52]

9.6 THE REGULATION OF DISINFORMATION IN THE DIGITAL CONTEXT

Over two decades after the repeal of the offence of dissemination of fake news from the Press Act, a new regulatory drive has emerged in Chile. In June 2023, the government established a commission against disinformation, responsible for analysing the phenomenon and its implications for democracy. Among its primary responsibilities is the provision of recommendations to the relevant authorities regarding the steps necessary to develop a comprehensive public policy to address the challenges posed by disinformation and its detrimental impact on democratic processes.[53] Furthermore, beginning in 2020 and continuing onward, no fewer than six bills have been presented in the National Congress aimed at criminally penalizing the dissemination of false news in the country. These bills have garnered support from parliamentarians from across the political spectrum, reflecting a broad consensus regarding the urgent need to address the proliferation of false information, particularly on digital platforms and during electoral cycles.

[50] See C-3151-2010, 17° Juzgado Civil de Santiago. For identical reasons, constitutional actions for the dissemination of information affecting the right to honour have been rejected when the media has corrected false information, see Corte de Apelaciones de Valdivia, Recurso de Protección 196-2017. Likewise, it has been pointed out that the refusal by a social media company to rectify is an illegal act that constitutes the basis for a constitutional action against the media company for misinforming the population. See Corte Suprema, 150.450-2020.

[51] Corte de Apelaciones de Santiago, Recurso de Protección 46752-2019; Corte de Apelaciones de Santiago, Recurso de Protección 35815-2022.

[52] Corte Suprema, *Berríos González con revista Qúe Pasa*, 19 March 1991; Corte Suprema, *Contreras López Feliciano y otros con El Mercurio de Antofagasta*, 2 November 1982; Corte de Apelaciones de Santiago, Rol 84116-2018; Corte de Apelaciones de Talca, Rol 3779-2019.

[53] Decreto No. 12 of 2023 of the Ministerio de Ciencia, Tecnología, Conocimiento e Innovación, published in *Diario Oficial*, No. 43.582, 20 June 2023.

Does this renewed desire to regulate the dissemination of false news correspond to a similar motivation that led to its regulation in the past? Fake news has historically been regulated in Chile by de facto administrations and during periods of high political polarization. Moreover, regulation has occurred during constitutional processes,[54] as a result of those processes,[55] or immediately following the ratification of a new constitution.[56] Since October 2019, Chile experienced a constitutional crisis triggered by a massive popular uprising that engaged millions of people nationwide. In response to this pervasive discontent among citizens, a political consensus was reached to initiate a constitutional process aimed at addressing these issues through institutional means.[57] Two attempts were made to replace the constitution through democratically elected conventions.[58] Both failed as the public rejected the constitutional proposals in a referendum held in October 2022 and then in December 2023.[59] Unquestionably, this process has occurred in an atmosphere of high tension and political polarization, similar to the political climate that characterized different historical periods in which Chile has regulated fake news. Despite these similarities, there is a significant difference between the political conditions motivating the current regulatory interest, as Chile is presently governed under a democratic system.

Despite the political parallels between the contemporary interest in regulating false news and its regulation in the past, significant differences exist that distinguish contemporary efforts to combat disinformation and misinformation from those of the past. All of them can be attributed to the technological transformations that have reconfigured the public opinion formation process in the modern world.

The transition to digital technologies has significantly altered what Jack Balkin refers to as the 'infrastructure of freedom of expression' – that is, the technologies and institutions that people use and trust to inform and communicate.[60] Today, our ability to inform and communicate depends significantly on large private companies

[54] This is the case with the regulation of fake news in Decree Law 425 of 1925, which was a precursor to the process that led to the Constitution of 1925.

[55] It is the case of the defamation clause included in the original text of the 1980 Constitution.

[56] It is the case of DFL 143 of 1931, which criminalizes fake news as a state security offence.

[57] See John Charney, Pablo Marshall and Emilios Christodoulidis, '"It Is not 30 Pesos, It Is 30 Years": Reflections on the Chilean Crisis' (2021) 30(4) *Social & Legal Studies* 627–68, for an analysis of the causes that prompted the constitutional process.

[58] See Diego Gil, Guillermo Jiménez and Pablo Marshall (eds.), *El dilema constitucional: Una aproximación institucional al proceso constituyente* (Santiago: Fondo de Cultura Económica, 2023), for a critical analysis of the first constituent process.

[59] The initial process led by a majority of radical left-wing social movements lacking prior political experience ended in a dramatic failure, as their proposal was rejected by 68 per cent of the population in a referendum held in October 2022. The second constituent process was spearheaded by a radical right-wing majority which proposed a Constitution that was rejected by 56 per cent of the population.

[60] Jack M. Balkin, 'Old School/New School Speech Regulation' (2014) 127(8) *Harvard Law Review* 2296.

such as Google, X (Twitter), Meta (Facebook), YouTube and TikTok. These companies have created enormous user communities worldwide, so much so that in January 2023, the latter three combined had more than 6 billion active users.[61] The phenomenon of disinformation and misinformation has evolved significantly within this framework. The legal regulatory structure in Chile has, to date, not been updated to address the new challenges that these technologies have created.

Pivotal events like the 2016 UK referendum on exiting the European Union and the election of Donald Trump as President of the United States of America during the same year were early indicators of the vast scale and scope of the new issues associated with disinformation and misinformation. These events underscored the digital infrastructure's capability to generate and disseminate false information, on a vast scale, carrying profound implications for electoral processes and the overall democratic system. Although an in-depth exploration of the structural factors contributing to the expansion of false news in the digital realm is beyond the scope of this chapter, certain aspects warrant elucidation to grasp its distinctive nature and differentiate the current regulatory efforts against false news in Chile from past initiatives.

The first point underscores the remarkable level of user concentration that prominent internet corporations have achieved in recent years.[62] Initially conceived as a realm promoting freedom and democratization in communication, the Internet represented a shift away from the vertically centralized content production model dominated by major media corporations. It embraced a decentralized model, allowing individual users to create and distribute content under conditions resembling those of traditional media outlets.[63] However, this ideal was overshadowed by the explosive growth of major internet companies, which solidified their dominance by expanding their global user bases. Billions of users now converge on a single network, effectively competing with established news publishers for attention. Unlike these publishers, who generate their content – requiring careful curation to retain audience trust and avoid legal liabilities – major internet firms and platforms serve as intermediaries, organizing or disseminating content produced by third parties, generally lacking editorial control over it.[64]

[61] 'Most Popular Social Networks Worldwide as of January 2023', Statista, www.statista.com/statistics/272014/global-social-networks-ranked-by-number-of-users.

[62] See Martin Moore and Damian Tambini (eds.), *Digital Dominance: The Power of Google, Amazon, Facebook and Apple* (Oxford: Oxford University Press, 2018).

[63] Yochai Benkler, *The Wealth of Networks: How Social Production Transforms Markets and Freedom* (New Haven, CT: Yale University Press, 2006); Eben Moglen, 'The Invisible Barbecue' (1997) 97 *Columbia Law Review* 945.

[64] This is changing, and for economic and legal reasons, as will be demonstrated, they are increasingly participating actively in content moderation; see specifically Kate Klonick, 'Inside the Making of Facebook's Supreme Court', *The New Yorker*, 12 February 2021, www.newyorker.com/tech/annals-of-technology/inside-the-making-of-facebooks-supreme-court.

The primary challenge stems from the business model employed by these companies, which depends on retaining users' attention for extended durations, and evidence suggests that sensational content tends to attract more attention.[65] In essence, major internet corporations possess incentives for the widespread dissemination of false news that traditional media outlets either lack or possess to a lesser degree. Furthermore, users receive this content as a result of potent algorithms that determine their political preferences based on their online searches and likes.[66] These users then become potential conduits for propagating this information across highly concentrated networks that facilitate rapid and extensive dissemination. The combination of these factors has produced an unprecedented capacity to disseminate false or misleading information at an unprecedented rate and to an audience unparalleled in human history.

Section 230 of the Communications Decency Act is a second important legal factor that further explains the ease with which fake news spreads on the Internet. Except in cases involving federal offences or violations of intellectual property rights, this provision provides internet intermediaries with complete immunity regarding illicit content posted on their platforms or services. One of its primary goals was to eradicate the ambiguity created by precedents that determined intermediary liability based on the amount of editorial control they exercised over content.[67] If intermediaries exercised editorial control, they were considered *publishers* and held liable for illegal content; otherwise, they were regarded as distributors and were exempt from liability for the same content. The issue was that courts frequently struggled with these classifications, causing uncertainty for intermediaries regarding potential legal actions and discouraging self-regulation through content moderation on their platforms due to the elevated risk of being classified as *publishers*.[68]

Section 230 of the Communications Decency Act eliminates the ambiguity surrounding intermediary liability by granting them complete immunity with respect to illegal content circulating on their platforms or services. Internet intermediaries in the United States that host or transmit third-party content are therefore exempt from a set of laws that would otherwise hold them accountable. This provision is frequently praised as the most important rule protecting freedom of expression on the Internet and a driving force behind its current form.[69] Some

[65] See Craig Silverman, 'This Analysis Shows How Viral Fake Election News Stories Outperformed Real News on Facebook', BuzzFeed News, 16 November 2016, www.buzzfeednews.com/article/craigsilverman/viral-fake-election-news-outperformed-real-news-on-facebook.

[66] Eli Pariser, *The Filter Bubble: What the Internet Is Hiding from You* (London: Penguin, 2011) p. 9.

[67] Kate Klonick, 'The New Governors: The People, Rules and Processes Governing Online Speech' (2018) 131 *Harvard Law Review* 1604.

[68] Ibid.

[69] Emily Bazelon, 'How to Unmask the Internet's Vilest Characters', *The New York Times Magazine*, 22 April 2011, www.nytimes.com/2011/04/24/magazine/mag-24lede-t.html.

scholarly literature has even described it as a mechanism intended to foster the economic growth of internet companies, aligning with the principles of the First Amendment of the United States Constitution by preventing any state interference in the exercise of their freedom of expression.[70]

The immunity rule of Section 230 of the Communications Decency Act (CDA) has an impact on the current interest in regulating the dissemination of false news in Chile. In fact, the Chilean Press Act 2001 targets media outlets. They are the entities that will be held accountable for the offences or abuses, specified by the law. Although this law abolished the crime of disseminating fake news, the right to clarification and rectification has been used to address these issues since its repeal.[71] In certain cases, media-based libel and slander have also been used for the same purpose. The problem is that the law is not clear about the legal status of internet intermediaries and digital platforms, such as Meta, X or YouTube.

Courts have occasionally categorized these services as media outlets, but this has not always been the case, and they have never held them liable for the crimes outlined in the law. Furthermore, because many of these companies are headquartered in the United States, they are not subject to the jurisdiction of Chilean courts, remaining entirely subject to Section 230 of the CDA. The immunity rule means that the limited legal options that the Chilean legal system currently provides for the prosecution of false news do not apply to the platforms that most vigorously disseminate such news at present.

Another significant effect of Section 230 of the Communications Decency Act is relevant to Chile's ongoing efforts to regulate false news. This provision not only absolves intermediary services of liability for illegal content posted on their platforms, but also grants them broad authority to define the scope of acceptable expressions within their domains. Remarkably, it grants them immunity for actions taken in good faith to restrict access or availability of offensive material. This has prompted self-regulation among digital platforms and contributed to the development of sophisticated content moderation systems. These systems frequently involve centralized regulatory bodies responsible for formulating moderation policies, establishing rule-based frameworks delineating the boundaries of freedom of expression and creating adjudicatory entities tasked with resolving user disputes using procedures they independently devised.[72] In both their operational principles and organizational structure, these systems bear striking similarities to legal systems, particularly the model of the First Amendment of the US Constitution. Notable is the fact that those responsible for designing these moderation systems, shaping their procedures and training individuals engaged in content moderation are frequently US legal

70 Anupam Chander, 'How Law Made Silicon Valley' (2014) 63(3) *Emory Law Journal* 639.

71 See notes 48–50.

72 Klonick, 'The New Governors', at 1630–62.

professionals educated in First Amendment doctrine and rooted in a legal and political culture they export to global user communities.[73]

These systems have effectively transformed major digital platforms into influential governance structures that not only define the fundamental rules of communication within the digital domain but also enforce these rules through intricate moderation mechanisms.[74] The magnitude of the power amassed by these major digital platforms is such that, particularly in the Chilean context, it poses a potential threat to the established framework of fundamental rights that underpins the right to information and freedom of expression. This framework is enshrined in the Constitution, and the regulation of these rights is delegated to legislative acts. It operates under the supervision of a Constitutional Court, which examines whether legal provisions regulating freedom of expression are consistent with the Constitution. In contrast, conflicts involving an individual's freedom of expression are resolved by the courts, which can directly invoke the Constitution to protect these rights or, when necessary, employ legal provisions to assess and penalize unlawful or abusive expressions.[75]

In sum, major digital platforms pose a direct threat to the principles of the Chilean constitutional system. By autonomously defining the limits of acceptable speech on their platforms, they affect the basic principle according to which any restriction or limitation on the right to information and freedom of expression must be derived from statutory law. Moreover, because decisions made by these platforms in this context are beyond the jurisdiction of the Constitutional Court, judicial review is undermined. Furthermore, since major digital platforms fall outside the jurisdiction of Chilean courts, illegal content posted on them may remain immune, leaving the fundamental rights of their users inadequately protected under the Chilean legal system. This is why the current interest in regulating false news must also be understood as an effort to regain control over the basic rules governing the scope of freedom of expression within the basic system of fundamental rights. These factors represent novel variables that were absent from the equation that prompted the regulation of fake news in the past, and they are essential to understanding the impetus behind the current drive for regulation.

9.7 CONCLUSION

The Chilean history of regulating fake news demystifies the notion that disinformation is a contemporary phenomenon. A century-old regulation reveals historical patterns that can offer insights into current approaches. One such pattern is the

[73] Ibid. at 1621.

[74] Ibid.

[75] John Charney and Pable Marshall, 'Libertad de expresion' in Pablo Contreras and Constanza Salgado (eds.), *Curso de Derechos Fundamentales* (Valencia: Tirant lo Blanch, 2021).

tendency to introduce regulations during periods of heightened political instability, often in the wake of constitutional processes or immediately thereafter. These regulations typically emerge under de facto governments. Conversely, they tend to be relaxed or abolished during democratic periods. This historical trend suggests that the regulation of fake news in Chile has been employed as a tool to quell political criticism, a stance at odds with the principles of free speech.

The current impulse to regulate fake news in Chile, much like previous instances, arises against the backdrop of a constitutional process marked by intense political polarization and instability. However, the present situation is unique in that it unfolds within a democratic government framework. Of greater significance, fake news has evolved into a global threat to democracy, primarily due to the ease with which disinformation and misinformation can spread in today's digital public sphere. These circumstances introduce new arguments in favour of regulating fake news. Another pertinent argument applies specifically to Chile's situation. As digital platforms assume increasingly influential roles of governance in digital communication, wielding the power to establish and enforce intricate systems of communication norms, they have begun to impact the fundamental rights framework, including free speech and the right to information. Concurrently, basic constitutional principles such as the rule of law, due process and transparency are now compromised.

Rather than serving as a tool to suppress political dissent, fake news regulation could be an appropriate means of tackling these issues. When tailored to address the regulatory challenges posed by digital infrastructure to free speech, it must be designed within a framework that upholds fundamental rights and aims to prevent significant threats to democracy. Lessons from past regulatory experience can offer valuable guidance in this endeavour.

10

The Battle against Disinformation

Legislative Challenges in South Korea

Ahran Park

10.1 INTRODUCTION

In the digital age, the landscape of information dissemination has undergone a profound transformation. The traditional boundaries between information and news have become increasingly blurred as technology allows anyone to create and share content online. The once-excusive realm of authoritative media outlets and professional journalists has given way to a decentralized public square, where individuals can voice their opinions and reach vast audiences regardless of mainstream coverage. The evolution of the digital age has dismantled the conventional notions of journalism and reshaped how news is obtained and interpreted. This shift has paved the way for the proliferation of fake news and online disinformation. The ease with which false information can be fabricated, packaged convincingly and rapidly disseminated to a wide audience has contributed to the rise of fake news. This phenomenon gained global attention during the 2016 US presidential election, prompting nations worldwide to seek strategies for tackling this issue.

In South Korea, the regulation of disinformation has emerged as a significant concern, particularly during election periods, and the impact of disinformation intensified amidst the backdrop of the COVID-19 pandemic. The extent of disinformation's influence has prompted considerable attention. According to a 2023 global survey conducted by the Reuters Institute for Journalism at Oxford University,[1] 66 percent of Korean respondents expressed concern about disinformation. This places South Korea as the ninth highest among the forty-six countries surveyed, underscoring a significant degree of concern within the population. Notable is the focus on disinformation in the political sphere. Among Korean respondents, 40 percent identified politics as a prime target of disinformation, which

[1] Reuters Digital News Report 2023, Reuters Institute for Journalism, https://reutersinstitute.politics.ox.ac.uk/digital-news-report/2023.

is twice the percentage for disinformation concerning the economy (21 percent) or COVID-19 (21 percent). This emphasis on political disinformation suggests a considerable weariness among the public and a heightened sense of apprehension regarding the potential repercussions of disinformation on democratic processes and values.

The increasing need to address disinformation has led to a call for the regulation of media platforms. The Korean National Assembly has proposed more than forty bills aimed at regulating disinformation since 2017, but those bills faced challenges in passing due to various reasons. This chapter delves into the legislative struggle aimed at regulating disinformation in South Korea. Commencing with a historical overview of disinformation regulation, the chapter proceeds to scrutinize the existing legal framework employed to counter disinformation. It further categorizes the fake news bills introduced since 2017. Subsequently, it investigates the delegation of responsibility to digital platforms for regulating disinformation, evaluating the current state of self-regulation and potential avenues for enhancement.

10.2 HISTORY OF REGULATING ONLINE FALSE EXPRESSIONS

The Constitution of Korea has consistently enshrined the principle of freedom of expression. However, this freedom has undergone revisions to different degrees during the nine instances of constitutional amendment. On occasion, the scope of freedom of expression was subject to qualifications, contingent upon the inclusion of the phrase 'except as specified by law' within the constitutional text.[2] In the context of this constitutional history, efforts to fight against disinformation have been underway since the 1970s.

The most notable historical attempts to regulate disinformation occurred during the dictatorship in the 1970s. On 17 October 1972, President Park Chung Hee issued a special presidential declaration, which dissolved the National Assembly and suspended the constitution. This proclamation effectively established a long-term dictatorship. The regime, concerned about the dangers of free speech and a free press to its stability, adopted a series of emergency measures, with the first being Emergency Measure No. 1 in 1974. This measure explicitly forbade the 'fabrication or dissemination of rumors' (Article 3) and also prohibited the act of 'broadcasting, reporting, publishing, or otherwise communicating rumors to others' (Article 4). The autocratic government, under Emergency Measure No. 1, utilized its provisions to arrest and punish critics of the regime who were accused of spreading rumors. Similarly, Emergency Measure No. 9, enacted in 1975, criminalized the act of 'fabrication and disseminating rumors or distorting facts'.

[2] Ahran Park and Kyu Ho Youm, 'Freedom versus Regulation: An Evolving Free Press in South Korea' in Paul Wragg and András Koltay (eds.), *Global Perspectives on Press Regulation*, Vol. 2 (Oxford: Hart, 2024).

These Emergency Measures were primarily aimed at restricting criticisms of the president and the government through regulating rumors. They also provided a convenient means of stifling dissent and punishing dissenters. In addition, the Emergency Measures went as far as prohibiting any debate of constitutional revision, effectively suppressing citizens' expression of political views and infringing upon their fundamental rights. The enforcement of the Emergency Measures led to the prosecution of over 1,100 people, primarily consisting of those who expressed dissent against the dictator and the government. For instance, a man who criticized President Park Chung Hee was subject to a seven-year term of imprisonment on charges of fabricating rumors.

More than thirty years later, the South Korean Supreme Court made significant rulings declaring the Emergency Measures, which severely restricted people's freedom of expression, unlawful. In a retrial held in 2010, the Supreme Court acquitted a defendant who had previously been sentenced for spreading falsehoods. The court ruled that Emergency Measure No. 1 was unconstitutional and invalid due to its excessive restriction on an individual's freedom of expression and physical integrity.[3]

After the Supreme Court's ruling, the Constitutional Court further solidified its stance in 2013 by declaring Emergency Measures Nos. 1, 2 and 9 unconstitutional, citing the same constitutional concerns the Supreme Court identified when it invalidated Emergency Measure No. 1.[4] The Constitutional Court's decision stemmed from its assessment that the provisions punishing rumor-mongering were not only abstract and vague in their criminal elements but also exhibited an excessively broad scope of application. As a result, the Court elucidated, this provision made it challenging for citizens to anticipate which conduct would be deemed prohibited under the law. These historical instances illustrate how the criminalization of disseminating falsehoods can be wielded to stifle dissenting voices critical of the government. In reaction to this, the Korean courts have held that laws seeking to curb freedom of expression through the criminalization of falsehood dissemination must be narrowly drawn to be constitutional.

Although the prohibition on spreading rumors was limited to a specific period through the Emergency Measures, under normal circumstances the spreading of falsehoods could fall under the purview of regulation through the Basic Telecommunications Act. Article 47(1) of the Act states that 'any person who issues a false communication through telecommunications facilities with the intention of harming the public interest shall be subject to punishment, including imprisonment for up to 5 years or a fine up to 50 million Won (approximately $37,600)'. Initially, this provision was crafted to penalize individuals who used landline phones by adopting a fabricated identity or using another person's name.

[3] Supreme Court, decided on 16 December 2010, 2010Do5986, en banc.

[4] Constitutional Court, 21 March 2013, 2010HunBa70.

Since its enactment in 1961, Article 47(1) of the Basic Telecommunications Act had remained inactive for over forty years, with no recorded instances of its application for actual penalties. This inactivity can be attributed to the absence of documented cases involving deceptive communications using someone else's identity. Nonetheless, the emergence of the Internet in the 2000s revitalized this provision, reinstating its significance in overseeing online communications. Article 47(1) of the Act was employed to punish online users who propagated false information.[5]

An illustrative case highlighting the implementation of Article 47(1) was the notable *Minerva* case. The individual behind the username 'Minerva' gained online prominence for astute predictions and insightful economic analyses. However, Minerva found himself facing charges subsequent to posting on a popular portal site that the government's foreign exchange reserves had been depleted, and currency exchange had been prohibited. These posts incited panic among online users and triggered a decline in stock prices. In the aftermath, the finance minister accused Minerva of spreading falsehoods regarding financial policies, leading to Minerva's arrest. The charges against Minerva were based on the alleged spread of falsehoods that were deemed harmful to the public interest, as stipulated under Article 47(1) of the Basic Telecommunications Act.

The Constitutional Court, however, ruled that Article 47(1) was unconstitutional.[6] The Court held that this clause, as it restricts freedom of expression and imposes criminal penalties, must adhere to a rigorous standard of protecting free expression. This includes a requirement that it must be narrowly drawn to address potentially serious social harms. Although the provision prohibited misleading communication with the intention of 'harming the public interest', the Constitutional Court found that the definition of 'public interest' was too ambiguous and imprecise, making it challenging for even legal experts to determine whether particular speech activity harms the 'public interest' or not. The Court noted that such judgments of 'public interest' are likely to vary significantly based on the individual values and ethics of each person. Consequently, the Constitutional Court concluded that the provisions failed to inform the accused which purposes of communication were prohibited among the generally allowed online communications. This lack of clarity violated the requirement for clear guidance demanded by free expression and the principle of clarity in criminal justice.

The Justices expounded on the legality of spreading falsehoods as follows:

> The evolution of Internet communication into the 'most participatory marketplace' and a 'medium for fostering expression' empowers recipients of information to access a diverse array of sources, while also facilitating real-time challenges or rebuttals to certain assertions. It proves arduous to assume that the aforementioned

5 Ahran Park, 'A Critical Perspective on Regulating "Fake News" and Disinformation' (2021) 56 (2) *Press Information Research* 113–55 (in Korean).

6 Constitutional Court, decided on 28 December 2010, 2008HunBa157.

> possibilities will be entirely obstructed by the inherent attributes of communication, encompassing elements such as anonymity and indiscriminate dissemination. Therefore, it cannot be conclusively asserted that there exists a distinct risk of encroaching upon the public's entitlement to accurate information of fomenting criminal activities or disturbances in the national order solely due to the dissemination of false facts.[7]

The Justices pointed out that false information does not inherently jeopardize the public interest or undermine the advancement of democracy. It also serves the additional function of directing societal attention towards pertinent matters and encouraging public engagement. Even if false communication itself does not inherently inflict societal damage, according to the Court, the state's broad and paternalistic intervention, employing vague criteria such as 'for the purpose of harming the public interest', lacks sufficient justification. The Justices emphatically elucidated in their supplementary opinion that assessing the value and detriment of expression or information 'ought not to be initially determined by the state; instead, it should be entrusted to the self-correcting dynamics of civil society and the competitive interplay of ideas and viewpoints'.[8]

Following the Constitutional Court's ruling that Article 47(1) was invalid, the clause lost its effectiveness and Minerva was finally acquitted. However, a significant concern arose from the absence of a comprehensive rule that had formerly penalized online dissemination of falsehood jeopardizing public safety. To rectify this legal loophole, several amendments have been put forth in the National Assembly but the provision remains unmodified as of now.

Article 47(1) of the Basic Telecommunications Law necessitates a more precise and constitutionally sound amendment, particularly in light of the absence of adequate regulation over disinformation that jeopardizes societal security or impairs the public interest. A more meticulous and constitutionally grounded amendment to Article 47(1) is imperative, one that mandates penalties solely when specific harm is inflicted, rather than merely targeting those who disseminate false information. Nevertheless, considering the legislative backdrop of the Act, it is prudent to address disinformation through other pertinent internet-related legislation. In the subsequent sections, we will delve into the various legal frameworks within South Korea that hold potential for regulating disinformation.

10.3 REGULATING DISINFORMATION UNDER THE CURRENT LAW

In South Korea, intentional dissemination of falsehood is rigorously prohibited across a range of statutes. Three primary categories of current laws are commonly used to regulate various forms of disinformation. First, there are laws targeting

[7] Ibid.
[8] Ibid.

disinformation specifically related to elections. The Public Official Election Act governs the dissemination of false information about political candidates and their families. Those who publish such incorrect information may face penalties, including imprisonment with labor or fines, under Article 250 of the Public Official Election Act. Similarly, the Political Parties Act penalizes individuals who publish or distribute falsehoods about candidates or their families in connection with an intraparty competitive election for selecting a political party representative (Article 52), as well as false registration applications of a party (Article 59).

Second, there are laws that counter disinformation that poses a threat to the security and stability of the nation. Given South Korea's divided status and its ongoing situation with North Korea, the imperative to combat disinformation that threatens national security is of paramount importance. The National Security Act imposes punishments on members of anti-state organizations or persons under their command who fabricate or disseminate a false statement likely to disrupt social order (Article 4). In a similar vein, the Act penalizes members of anti-state organizations who fabricate or disseminate false statements concerning a matter that is likely to disrupt social order (Article 7).

Third, defamation laws can be employed to combat disinformation that harms the reputation of others. Defamation in South Korea falls under the purview of both criminal and civil law. Consequently, individuals who spread defamatory disinformation may face penalties under both legal systems. The Criminal Act addresses defamation in Article 307, distinguishing between penalties for 'stating the truth' (Article 307(1)) and 'stating a falsehood' (Article 307(2)). Additionally, those who publish false facts to defame the deceased are subject to punishment under Article 308. When defamatory disinformation is disseminated through mass media such as newspapers, magazines or radio with an intent to harm someone's reputation, Article 309 of the Criminal Act prescribes even more severe punishment. Beyond criminal consequences, defamation is recognized as a tort under the Civil Act.

Especially within the context of internet defamation, the Information and Communications Network Act imposes enhanced penalties (Article 70).[9] Article 44-7 specifically addresses the dissemination of unlawful information, encompassing defamatory online content that is intended to tarnish the reputation of others.

[9] Article 70(1) of the Act provides: (1) A person who commits defamation of another person by disclosing a (true) fact to the public through an information and communications network purposely to disparage his/her reputation shall be punished by imprisonment with labor for up to three years or by a fine not exceeding ~~KRW~~ 30 million Won.

(2) A person who commits defamation of another person by disclosing a false fact to the public through an information and communications network purposely to disparage his/her reputation shall be punished by imprisonment with labor for up to seven years, by suspension of qualification for up to ten years, or by a fine not exceeding ~~KRW~~ 50 million Won.

(3) The public prosecutor may not prosecute a defamer against the victim's will.

Defamation is granted immunity if the statement accused of being libelous is proven to be true and serves the public interest. Article 310 of the Criminal Act outlines that if the facts presented are verified as true and solely intended to serve the public interest, they shall not be subject to punishment. This truth-based defense does not necessitate absolute accuracy; it may encompass inaccuracies or hyperbolic expressions to afford greater leeway for freedom of speech and the press. In determining whether a statement of fact is false, the Supreme Court clarified that (1) it should be considered in its entirety and (2) if the statement aligns with objective facts in significant aspects, even if it contains minor discrepancies or slight exaggerations in detail, it should not be deemed a false statement of fact.[10] In addition, if a defamatory statement involves only opinion, it cannot be actionable.[11]

When a speaker genuinely held a belief in the truth of their statement, even if later proven false, the speaker may be granted immunity if their belief was grounded in a 'reasonable belief' in the accuracy of the statement.[12] Hence, a statement made in the public interest, based on a reasonable belief in its truthfulness at the time of utterance, can still be shielded under the 'reasonable belief' standard. This standard strongly safeguards freedom of expression by affording protection to statements that, although ultimately proven false, were made with a genuine belief in their accuracy.[13] The standard of 'reasonable belief' applies to the media domain as well. In one case where a journalist was sued for defamation, the Supreme Court ruled that the journalist should be exempt from liability for defamation because he had 'reasonable belief' in his report as he tried to verify all the facts and contact witnesses in a criminal case.[14] Conversely, in another case, where a journalist conveyed a conviction without engaging in additional interviews with relevant people, the court denied his reasonable belief in the news report.[15]

As the severity of penalties depends on the veracity of the statement, it is critical for the court to assess whether a statement is true or false in defamation cases. The Supreme Court has established that if the primary essence of an expression aligns with the objective facts, even minor discrepancies or slight exaggerations in the details do not render it false.[16] As long as the key element of the expression is true, any minor exaggerations or differences in how the factual relationship is portrayed should not lead to severe penalties for false expression.[17] The Supreme Court has ruled that when determining falsity, the overall impression should serve as the standard.

[10] Supreme Court, decided on 25 February 2000, 99Do4757.
[11] Supreme Court, decided on 9 February 1999, 98Da31356.
[12] Supreme Court, decided on 11 October 1988, 85DaKa29.
[13] Yongsang Park, *Freedom of Expression* (Seoul: Hyunamsa, 2002; in Korean).
[14] Supreme Court, decided on 23 August 1996, 94Do3191.
[15] Supreme Court, decided on 28 May 1996, 94Da33828.
[16] Supreme Court, decided on 19 January 2001, 2000Da10208.
[17] Supreme Court, decided on 27 February 2004, 2001Da53387.

These criteria for evaluating truth are crucial when considering authenticity in the context of disinformation. In order for someone to be subject to penalties for disseminating false information, a significant portion of the content must be proven to be factually inaccurate, rather than merely constituting a minor error or exaggeration. Furthermore, even if the content is proven to be untrue, it may not lead to punishment if the person had a 'reasonable belief' in truth and the content is determined to contribute to the public interest.

In a case where several people were indicted for spreading false rumors about allegations of bribery and fraud involving competing candidates, the Court was tasked with determining whether they held a reasonable belief in the truthfulness of these rumors. The Seoul High Court emphasized the importance of fair elections through democratic procedures, which 'establish the legitimacy of state power and foster the development of democratic politics'. The Court further emphasized that the propagation of 'fake news' that undermines these principles requires utmost attention.[18] Its judgment delineated that the defendants systemically and intentionally propagated 'fake news' through widely circulated media channels shortly prior to the election, with the aim of misleading voters regarding their choice of candidates. Given the gravity of their actions, the Court held that the defendants lacked a reasonable belief in the truth of their claims and must face severe punishment for defaming the victim. This case illustrates how spreading disinformation that tarnishes someone's reputation can lead to serious legal consequences.

10.4 MAKING NEW LAWS AGAINST DISINFORMATION

The debate on regulating 'fake news' began in South Korea in early 2017, ahead of the nineteenth Korean presidential election. The fake news controversy surrounding the US presidential election in 2016 raised concerns that fake news could become prevalent in Korean presidential elections as well. In fact, former UN Secretary-General Ban Ki-moon, a prominent conservative presidential candidate at that time, announced his withdrawal from the race in February 2017, citing damage caused by fake news. During a subsequent meeting with the National Assembly, Ban highlighted his fake news cases to advocate for government regulation and legislation against fake news.

Since 2017, the National Assembly has introduced dozens of bills aimed at regulating fake news. There are three main types of legislation that have been proposed to regulate fake news. First, standalone bills have been put forward, focusing solely on the regulation of fake news. An example of such a bill is the Act on the Composition and Operation of the Fake News Countermeasures Committee.[19] This proposal suggests the establishment of such a committee under

[18] Seoul High Court, decided on 12 August 2022, 2022No594.

[19] Bill No. 2013495 (9 May 2018).

the Prime Minister's authority to oversee fake news regulation. Additionally, it suggests designating the Ministry of Culture, Sports and Tourism as the primary agency responsible for preventing the dissemination of fake news in print and online newspapers, while assigning the Communications Commission with similar responsibilities for broadcasting and digital networks. The bill, aimed at tacking the problem of fake news, provides a definition for it as follows: 'Fake news refers to information, whether distributed via print media, online newspapers, broadcasts, or communication networks, that is deliberately fabricated or manipulated for political or economic purposes, with the deliberate aim of misleading the public into believing it to be genuine news'.

Second, legislative efforts against disinformation have been made by proposing amendments to the Information and Communication Network Act, which serves as the overarching law governing online communication and safeguarding online users. Several proposed amendments to this Act assign responsibilities to platform operators.[20] These proposals involve monitoring disinformation, along with the requirement to promptly remove or temporarily take down such content. Penalty surcharges are also proposed to be levied upon platform operators in case of failure to fulfill these obligations. For instance, a bill from 2018[21] proposed that platform operators must undertake 'necessary measures' to remove or block fake news that harm others' privacy and reputation. A bill from 2022[22] specified that in case an online content is requested to be removed, the platform operator has the option to request a review by the Online Dispute Resolution Committee.

Third, bills have been proposed to amend the Press Arbitration Act, aiming to establish heightened accountability for inaccurate reporting.[23] These bills are designed to ensure that traditional media outlets are held responsible for disseminating disinformation. Notably, some of these bills propose the imposition of punitive damages on media entities for the publication of false information. These bills to amend the Press Arbitration Act sparked considerable opposition from media companies and organizations, triggering social controversies.[24]

The Press Arbitration Act stands out among press statutes worldwide.[25] This legislation, applied to news reports in print, broadcasting and on the Internet, affords individuals the right to request the correction of inaccuracies in factual news and to reply to factual claims within a news article if they have suffered harm due to such

[20] See, e.g., Bill No. 2100815 (22 June 2020); Bill No. 2107093 (31 December 2020); Bill No. 2107285 (11 January 2021).

[21] Bill No. 2013251 (25 April 2018).

[22] Bill No. 2115428 (27 April 2022).

[23] See, e.g., Bill No. 2102829 (7 August 2020); Bill No. 2107949 (4 February 2021); Bill No. 2110702 (9 June 2021); Bill No. 2111047 (23 June 2021).

[24] Soyoung Cho, 'Issue of Legislative Process and Contents of the Revision: Bill of Act on Press Arbitration and Remedies Etc. for Damage Caused by Press Reports' (2021) 20(3) *Press and the Law* 157–88, doi:10.26542/JML.2021.12.20.3.157 (in Korean).

[25] See note 2 above.

allegations. Furthermore, the law mandates the right to demand a follow-up story following a previous report about an individual involved in criminal proceedings, especially when the individual has been acquitted of criminal charges. Operating as a distinct form of media regulation, the Press Arbitration Act serves as an effective remedial system, facilitating the delicate balance between safeguarding press freedom and upholding an individual's right to reputation and privacy.

The distinctive feature of the Press Arbitration Act lies in its provision for expedient and cost-effective redress for those who have suffered harm due to media content, enabling them to pursue resolution through press arbitration prior to resorting to the legal system. However, endeavors to regulate disinformation via the press arbitration mechanism underscore a prevailing societal distrust toward the Korean press. A longstanding history of ideological confrontations between conservative and liberal factions have given rise to a media landscape that is similarly divided along these lines. This polarization has bred a deep-seated skepticism regarding media coverage, especially when politicians, often engaged in fierce political struggles, denounce critical media as purveyors of fake news. The media itself is not safe from criticism for occasionally intervening in political battles through biased reporting.

Amidst this deeply divided context, the suggested revision to the Press Arbitration Act has emerged, aiming to establish punitive penalties for media outlets disseminating falsehoods. For instance, a bill proposed in February 2021[26] seeks to address false news content by categorizing it as fake news. Notably, Article 30(2) of this amendment introduces the concept of punitive damages, specifying that the amount of compensation should surpass the actual damage incurred if such damage stems from the public dissemination of erroneous or manipulated information through media reports, with the intention of defaming others. Moreover, the amendment incorporates a presumption of malicious intent on the part of the press.

Another bill[27] introduces the provision that if a media entity inflicts harm upon an individual through the dissemination of false facts leading to defamation, the court holds the authority to grant damages up to three times the actual amount of harm incurred. The bill's objective revolves around preventing the media from propagating fake news.

A proposed bill in June 2021[28] exhibits increased stringency compared to earlier amendments. Article 2(17) delineates 'false or manipulative reporting' as 'the act of disseminating or conveying false facts or information manipulated to appear as facts through media outlets, Internet news services, or online multimedia broadcasts'. This definition has garnered criticism due to its exclusion of disinformation propagated on social media and platforms like YouTube. The amendment also provides

[26] Bill No. 2107949 (4 February 2021).
[27] Bill No. 2110702 (9 June 2021).
[28] Bill No. 2111047 (23 June 2021).

for the victims to seek compensation ranging from no less than three times to no more than five times the amount of damage resulting from false reports by the news media (Article 30-2).

In sum, despite the introduction of numerous anti-fake news bills since 2017, none of the bills have successfully passed through the National Assembly. Many of these bills had to encounter challenges in defining the elusive concept of 'fake news', while others faced backlash for potentially infringing the freedom of expression online. The proposed amendments to the Press Arbitration Act were met with significant opposition from the media industry, as they appeared to target media outlets as primary purveyors of fake news. While the impact of fake news remains a concern, particularly with the advancement of artificial intelligence, the failure of fake news bills indicates that the task of regulating disinformation with legislation will likely continue to pose challenges in the future.

10.5 DIGITAL PLATFORMS AS GATEKEEPERS AGAINST DISINFORMATION

With the evolution of the Internet, various challenges have emerged in the realm of online communication. Digital platforms, which serve as intermediaries for online expression, have assumed the role of digital gatekeepers, entrusted with the duty and responsibility to address these issues. In the dynamic landscape of the digital world, these platforms have increasingly shouldered a rage of obligations.

The Information and Communication Network Act, serving as a fundamental statute governing internet regulation, is designed to offer online users an effective means of safeguarding their privacy and reputation. Article 44-2 of the Act mandates that the information service provider, when it receives a request from the alleged victim, must expeditiously delete or block the harmful contents and subsequently notify both the requester and the poster about the actions taken. Should the information service provider fail to remove harmful content from its platform, it can potentially face liability for defamation or invasion of privacy, in conjunction with the original poster. However, in cases where the information service provider can demonstrate a sincere effort to remove or block injurious content, the provider may be eligible for a reduction or even exemption from liability for damages arising from such content (Article 44-2(6)). Hence, this law creates a robust incentive for digital platforms to promptly remove harmful content.

In cases where digital platforms encounter challenges in ascertaining whether the information in question infringes upon the right of others, they are empowered to exercise discretion to restrict access to the information for a period of thirty days. The question of whether such takedown decisions by platforms may encroach upon freedom of online expression has been raised. Nonetheless, the Constitutional Court ruled that the temporary takedown process did not infringe upon online users' freedom of expression.[29] The Court's rationale for this decision was based on the rapid and extensive dissemination of harmful expression, where a temporary takedown was deemed the most effective means to prevent the propagation of defamatory content. The Constitutional Court further asserted that the significance of safeguarding reputation and privacy outweighed the complainant's freedom of expression. In the Court's view, the thirty-day period of temporary takedown was an appropriate means of protecting the reputation of a potential victim.

Moreover, the Supreme Court rendered a landmark decision regarding the liability of digital platforms in 2009. In the case of *Kim* v. *NHN Corp.*,[30] the Supreme Court established a key precedent by holding that digital intermediaries may be held liable even in instances where they had not been notified by the plaintiff about the existence of defamatory content. The case revolved around a plaintiff, Kim, who took legal action against three major Korean internet platforms on grounds of online defamation. Kim contended that these intermediaries had disseminated news articles alleging his betrayal of a pregnant ex-girlfriend. Additionally, Kim asserted that these intermediaries had facilitated various individual blogs where users disclosed his workplace and phone number, leading to relentless harassment. The intermediaries countered by asserting that they had simply distributed news articles originally published by legacy news media, and that they were bound by legal agreement with these media outlets not to modify news stories at their discretion.

The Supreme Court, however, rejected the intermediaries' argument. It clarified that these intermediaries were more than mere search engines; they received news articles from various sources, stored this news in their database, curated stories for online publication, and ultimately shared these stories with the public. In light of their role as news aggregators, the Court held that these intermediaries should be held accountable akin to offline news media that had initially published the contentious articles.[31]

In the current legal landscape, as shown above, existing Korean laws and precedents establish the legal responsibility of digital platforms for online content. This led to a heightened emphasis on platform operators to take on the role of regulating disinformation. An illustrative example is the proposed amendment to the Information and Communications Network Act on 22 June 2020.[32] The amendment provides a definition of disinformation as 'false information presented in the guise of a journalistic report, crafted with the intent to mislead recipients through a communication network'. In line with this amendment, platform providers are bound by an obligation to promptly remove such disinformation. Failure to fulfill this duty may

29 Constitutional Court, decided on 31 May 2012, 2010Hun-Ma88.
30 Supreme Court, decided on 16 April 2009, 2008Da53812.
31 Ibid.
32 Bill No. 2100815 (22 June 2020).

result in a penalty of up to 30 million Won. This legal framework signifies a robust effort to empower operators with the responsibility to curtail the spread of disinformation, underscoring the importance of accountability and accuracy in online communication.

Another proposed amendment[33] to the Information and Communications Network Act incorporates the term 'fake news'. According to this amendment, fake news constitutes 'false or distorted information with the aim of achieving political or economic gains and presented in a manner that resembles a news report'. This definition underscores the deceptive nature of such content, highlighting its potential to mislead the public while masquerading as legitimate news coverage. Under this provision, if adopted, platform providers must continuously monitor content to identify instances of fake news. Upon receiving a request to remove fake news or identifying it through monitoring, the proposed statute would obligate platform providers to remove such false information. The amendment further establishes penalties for noncompliance with the obligation of continuous monitoring. Should platform providers fail to fulfill this obligation, their employees and corporate officers would potentially be subject to imprisonment for up to one year or a fine of up to 10 million Won.

There are several other amendments, but they all suffer from a similar set of challenges. First, the proposed amendments lack clarity regarding their definition of 'fake news' or 'disinformation'. In order to comply fully with the governing Constitutional Court precedents on freedom of expression and the press, legislation aimed at penalizing publishers and disseminators of fake news must provide explicit and specific guidelines, allowing citizens and platform providers alike to anticipate which actions are potentially unlawful. However, most bills create ambiguity that hinders individuals from comprehending the boundaries of prohibited conduct. Particularly concerning is the difficulty in determining the threshold for categorizing information as 'false'. Indeed, court precedents have illustrated that the concept of truth encompasses even minor inaccuracies and nuances, making it complicated for the general public to gauge the threshold at which misinformation state authorities would deem to be 'false'. Consequently, defining the precise boundaries of 'fake news' and 'disinformation' within the framework of the law becomes a formidable challenge, as attempting to encompass all forms of erroneous information under the label of fake news is impractical.

Second, obligating platform providers to monitor and take down fake news raises concerns about potential encroachments on online freedom of expression. Granting platform providers unchecked authority for private censorship, devoid of clear guidelines, jeopardizes the integrity of the online environment. Many of these legislative proposals entail substantial fines for platforms failing to remove flagged false posts swiftly. Consequently, platform providers may opt for a conservative

[33] Bill No. 2107093 (31 December 2020).

approach by removing or blocking flagged content without comprehensive verification, thereby posing a substantial risk to online freedom of expression. To mitigate this, it is imperative that the law not only authorize platforms to engage in monitoring but also establishes a structured framework encompassing criteria and protocols for identifying disinformation. Procedural guidelines would also be necessary to permit someone accused of posting disinformation or misinformation to contest this characterization meaningfully. Further, ensuring transparency in the determination of disinformation is essential to strike a balance between combating fake news and protecting freedom of expression (as well as other forms of expressive freedom).

Third, excessively stringent penalties for fake news creators and disseminators also present a constitutional problem. Several legislative proposals punish people for generating or spreading fake news, but this potentially infringes upon the 'principle of proportionality'.[34] As previously explained, the propagation of falsehoods is subject to aggravated punishment within the confines of defamation laws or the Information and Communication Network Act. Under these laws, the imposition of sanctions for falsehood should be limited to cases where tangible rights such as reputation or privacy have been violated. Therefore, it is inappropriate to impose penalties solely on the grounds of crafting and then disseminating false information. Instead, to avoid potential constitutional objections, a regulation that levies sanctions or imposes financial liability for damages may constitutionally do so only when the intentional creation or dissemination of falsehood actually results in demonstrable harm to others.

10.6 LIMITATIONS OF SELF-REGULATION

Pure self-regulation, which grants operators autonomy at all stages from rule-making to post-management, remains an ideal model but faces challenges in practical implementation. The European Union has introduced a 'regulated self-regulation' or 'co-regulation' approach that enhances the efficacy of self-regulation. This is achieved by providing a foundational framework for platform operators' self-regulation through legal and institutional mechanisms, as exemplified by the enactment of digital-related laws like the Digital Service Act.[35] These legislative measures render self-regulation more enforceable. The Information and Communication Network Act mandates that platform operators establish codes of conduct and self-regulatory guidelines to ensure user protection and provide safe and reliable

[34] The 'principle of proportionality' is a constitutional principle. Under this principle, any laws that limit the rights of citizens (1) must be suitable to achieve the desired end, (2) must be necessary to achieve the desired end, (3) must not impose a burden on the individual that is excessive in relation to the objective sought to be achieved.

[35] Regulation (EU) 2022/2065 of the European Parliament and of the Council of 19 October 2022 on a Single Market for Digital Services and amending Directive 2000/31/EC (Digital Services Act) (Text with EEA relevance).

communication service (Article 44-4). In accordance with this law, self-regulation is mainly overseen by the Korea Internet Self-Governance Organization (KISO), a consortium consisting of sixteen platform companies, including major players such as Naver and Kakao.

In 2018, the KISO introduced a self-regulatory policy targeting 'fake news presented in the format of news reports', known as 'False Posting Policy in the Form of Media Reports'.[36] Amidst the COVID-19 pandemic, the KISO also devised and put into action a policy aimed at addressing misleading information related to the treatment and prevention of and vaccination against COVID-19.[37] This policy involves appropriate actions, including content removal, in cases where posts are definitely identified as false and manipulative information based on official announcements from authoritative bodies such as the World Health Organization or the Center for Disease Control and Prevention. Nevertheless, due to the fact that the KISO's activities are initiated based on requests from its member platform companies, the scope of posts subject to moderation remains limited. Consequently, although the KISO operates effectively as a self-regulatory mechanism, its impact in countering disinformation is somewhat limited. Overseas platforms such as Google, Meta and TikTok have not joined the KISO, preventing a collective effort to combat disinformation on YouTube and Facebook and further limiting the efficacy of KISO's self-regulation efforts.

Under existing legislation, platform operators bear the responsibility of independently blocking illicit posts. Article 44-3 of the Information and Communications Network Act provides platform operators with the discretion to temporarily block posts for a maximum of thirty days. Platform operators may employ this measure when they determine that the information being disseminated on their platforms violates the rights of others, such as privacy infringement or defamation. However, in practice, this provision is infrequently invoked due to the considerable difficulty faced by platform operators in discerning whether a post genuinely infringes upon those rights. Although platform operators possess the technical and economic capacity to function as administrators of internet communication, imposing the exclusive duty of moderation upon them could potentially result in an excessive number of takedowns or disregard for harmful content. Although promoting platform operators' self-regulation constitutes a laudable policy, the devil lies in the detail. Establishing clearer legal norms would provide more effective protection against the social harms caused by disinformation and misinformation. Moreover, better and more transparent fundamental regulatory frameworks and procedures would also help to ensure the effective implementation of these mandatory moderation policies.

[36] KISO Fake News Report Center, https://report.kiso.or.kr/fakenews.

[37] COVID-19 False Information Policy (terminated on 31 March 2023).

10.7 CONCLUSION

Disinformation that is skillfully crafted to appear authentic can have dire consequences for democracy. It can infringe upon individual rights and cloud the rational judgment of citizens on crucial political matters as well. Furthermore, the term 'fake news' has cast a shadow on media credibility by associating it with 'news', thereby eroding trust in traditional journalism and undermining its very foundation. These issues have fueled the call for regulating fake news – that is, disinformation – promoting global efforts to devise legal remedies. South Korea also has been attacked by fake news, which raised concerns during the presidential election and escalated in severity during the COVID-19 pandemic.

In South Korea, where freedom of speech does not hold the same prominent position as it does in the United States,[38] a range of bills aimed at amending defamation law, internet law and press arbitration law have been employed to combat the dissemination of disinformation. However, South Korea's endeavors to combat fake news through legislative means have proven to be less effective than anticipated, leading to increased social controversy. This highlights that the creation of new laws targeting fake news may not be the optimal solution. Instead of attempting to delineate a clear boundary between truth and falsehood under the banner of 'fake news', it is crucial to establish a transparent and inclusive mechanism for discerning authenticity. Strengthening the self-regulation of platform operators and providing a structured framework for self-regulation by government are pivotal steps in this direction. As digital technology and artificial intelligence continue to advance, the demand for regulation becomes even more pronounced.

[38] Ahran Park and Kyu Ho Youm, 'Fake News from a Legal Perspective: The United States and South Korea Compared' (2019) 25(1) *Southwestern Journal of International Law* 100–19.

11

Disinformation, Misinformation and Democracy

An Indian Constitutional Perspective

Gautam Bhatia

11.1 INTRODUCTION

In April 2023, the Government of India amended a set of regulations called the Information Technology Rules, which primarily dealt with issues around online intermediary liability and safe harbour.[1] Until 2023, these rules required online intermediaries to take all reasonable efforts to ensure that 'fake, false or misleading' information was not published on their platforms.[2] Previous iterations of these rules had already been challenged before the Indian courts for imposing a disproportionate burden on intermediaries, and having the effect of chilling online speech.[3] Now, the 2023 Amendment went even further: it introduced an entity called a 'Fact Check Unit', to be created by the government. This government-created unit would flag information that – in its view – was 'fake, false or misleading' *with respect to* 'the business of the central government'.[4] Online intermediaries were then obligated to make reasonable efforts to ensure that any such flagged information would not be on their platforms. In practical terms, what this meant was that if intermediaries did not

The author is one of the counsels appearing in the constitutional challenge to the Information Technology Rules 2023, which are discussed in some detail in this chapter. The author has drawn upon his access to the case files, and to his experience arguing the case, in shaping the arguments in this chapter; at the same time, readers may therefore filter these views for bias.

1 Information Technology (Intermediary Guidelines and Digital Media Ethics Code) Amendment Rules 2023, G.S.R. 275(E), 6 April 2023.

2 See Information Technology (Intermediary Guidelines and Digital Media Ethics Code) Amendment Rules 2022, G.S.R. 794(E), 28 October 2022.

3 See Information Technology (Intermediary Guidelines and Digital Media Ethics Code) Amendment Rules 2021, G.S.R. 131(E), 25 February 2021; *Nikhil Wagle* v. *Union of India* Public Interest Litigation (L) No. 14204 of 2021, order dated 14 August 2021 (High Court of Bombay).

4 Information Technology Amendment Rules 2023 (n 2).

take down flagged speech, they risked losing their safe harbour (guaranteed under the Information Technology Act[5]).

The 2023 Amendment was immediately challenged before the High Court of Bombay, and at the time of writing, hearings were in progress. A perusal of the pleadings in the case reveals that the state's defence of the 2023 Amendment rested on a few important aspects.[6] *First*, the state highlighted the dangers of online 'fake news', its threat to public order, and that the 'virality' of the Internet made counter-speech an unviable solution. *Second*, as a matter of constitutional law, the state argued that 'fake' or 'false' news was unprotected by the constitutional guarantee of freedom of speech and expression.[7] Citing US Supreme Court judgments such as *Hustler Magazine* v. *Falwell*, it noted that fake news had no 'constitutional value', and therefore did not deserve constitutional protection. And *third*, it argued that the spread of fake news undermined other constitutional rights, such as the right to information[8] and – by extension – the right to vote (which the state read as a right to vote based on true and accurate information). This, in turn, allowed the regulation of online fake news in order to preserve other equally important constitutional rights.

The state's arguments in the IT Rules challenge reveal an inherent tension within Indian free speech jurisprudence. In this chapter, and keeping the IT Rules challenge as the background framework, I will excavate this tension, and tease out its implications for the regulation of misinformation and disinformation in the contemporary context. Broadly, this tension is manifested in two lines of jurisprudence. The first line can be broadly characterised as the 'autonomy' approach to free speech. Classically liberal in orientation – and drawing from US First Amendment jurisprudence, although not as expansive as in the USA – the 'autonomy' approach advocates for a degree of content-neutrality in restrictions to free speech. Its underlying principle is that autonomous individuals decide for themselves how to receive and respond to speech. The second line can be called the 'perfectionist' approach to free speech (I use 'perfectionist' in the sense that it is used by political philosophers, such as Joseph Raz[9]). The perfectionist approach as it appears in Indian jurisprudence eschews content neutrality, links the degree and nature of constitutional protection that speech has to its 'value', and is comfortable with the state being the arbiter of value. While these two lines of jurisprudence have proceeded on an

5 Information Technology Act 2000, s. 79. The safe harbour provision, which is discussed in more detail in Section 11.4, protects intermediaries that comply with certain due diligence requirements.

6 See Affidavit-in-Response, filed by the Respondent Union of India in *Kunal Kamra* v. *Union of India*, on file with the author.

7 Ibid.

8 The right to information was 'read into' the right to free speech and expression by the Supreme Court of India in the mid-1970s.

9 Steven Wall, 'Perfectionism in Moral and Political Philosophy', *Stanford Encyclopedia of Philosophy*, 15 December 2017, https://plato.stanford.edu/entries/perfectionism-moral.

almost parallel track in the seven decades of constitutional history, it is in cases such as the IT Rules challenge – I will argue – that they come to a head; and it is in contexts such as that of contemporary online disinformation that both lines reveal their limitations, and demonstrate the need for a new way of thinking about the relationship between speech, misinformation and the Constitution.

11.2 THE AUTONOMY LINE

Article 19(1)(a) of the Indian Constitution guarantees to all citizens the right to freedom of speech and expression. Article 19(2) authorises the state to make, by law, 'reasonable restrictions' upon the exercise of this freedom, 'in the interests' of eight different categories. These include, for example, 'public order', 'defamation', 'incitement to an offence' and so on.[10] The structure of India's free speech clause largely resembles the familiar, two-tiered structures that we see in many constitutions: the declaration of the right, followed by an exhaustive list of circumstances under which it may be restricted.[11] This approach precludes 'content neutrality' in the US First Amendment sense, as Article 19(2) itself authorises the restriction of speech on the basis of its content. The proof of the pudding, however, is in the interpretation.

The debates of the Constituent Assembly reveal the tension underlying the free speech clause right from the outset: liberal arguments in favour of minimising the restrictions clause were met with perfectionist arguments extoling the expertise and legitimacy of the newly elected government.[12] This internal tension has then spilled over into the judicial interpretation of the free speech clause.

Right from the beginning, a set of Indian judgments cited classic liberal arguments – from John Stuart Mill to Oliver Wendell Holmes' 'marketplace of ideas' – as the underlying foundation of the free speech clause. This is most clearly visible in the evolution of Supreme Court jurisprudence on socially subversive, or dissident, speech. In 1960, the Supreme Court set aside the criminal conviction of a politician who had been prosecuted for exhorting citizens not to pay a tax that he considered unjust.[13] Responding to the state's arguments that incitement to disobedience of a law could spark a general revolution, the Court insisted on a 'proximate link' between speech and the feared public disorder before it could be restricted or criminalised.[14] A few years later, the Court used the colourful analogy of a 'spark in a powder keg' to describe the degree of proximity that was required between

10 Constitution of India 1949, Art. 19.
11 See, e.g., Constitution of South Africa 1996, s. 16.
12 See Gautam Bhatia, 'The Conservative Constitution: Freedom of Speech and the Constituent Assembly Debates' in Udit Bhatia (ed.), *The Indian Constituent Assembly: Deliberations on Democracy* (Abingdon: Routledge, 2017).
13 Superintendent, Central Prison, *Fatehgarh* v. *Ram Manohar Lohia* 1960 SCR (2) 821 (Supreme Court of India).
14 Ibid.

speech and public disorder.[15] Most recently, while considering certain broadly worded provisions of the Information Technology Act, the Court drew a distinction between 'advocacy' and 'incitement', holding that only the latter could be criminalised consistent with the free speech clause of the Constitution.[16]

The distinction between 'advocacy' and 'incitement', in particular, is a clear statement of the autonomy approach to free speech. It brings to mind Justice Brandeis' famous observation that as long as there is *time* to respond, the remedy to subversive speech is counter-speech, and not censorship.[17] The idea underlying this is that the default presumption is that the autonomous listener is responsible for choosing how to take – and respond – to speech, *except* in narrowly defined cases of diminished autonomy.[18] The classic example given is of shouting 'fire' in a crowded theatre, a situation where the listeners have no time to evaluate the truth of the speech but must act immediately. The requirement of imminence – the *Brandenburg* test, as it is known under First Amendment jurisprudence[19] – broadly tracks this underlying theory, limiting itself to situations (for example) such as inciting an already enraged mob to commit acts of direct violence.[20]

The autonomy approach to free speech is also evident in other aspects of Indian free speech jurisprudence: in particular, in cases dealing with the question of whether some forms of speech are inherently more 'valuable' than others. In a series of early cases, for example, the Supreme Court beat back the government's attempts to curtail the volume of advertisements in newspapers by drawing a direct link between advertisements, income flow, volume of circulation and – thereby – the newspapers' right to free speech.[21] Another example is that of the 'commercial speech doctrine' issue, where the Court departed from earlier jurisprudence to hold

[15] *S. Rangarajan* v. *P. Jagjivan Ram* 1989 (2) SCC 574 (Supreme Court of India).

[16] *Shreya Singhal* v. *Union of India* AIR 2015 SC 1523 (Supreme Court of India).

[17] *Whitney* v. *California* 274 US 357 (concurring opinion of Brandeis J) (Supreme Court of the United States): 'If there be time to expose through discussion the falsehood and fallacies, to avert the evil by the processes of education, the remedy to be applied is more speech, not enforced silence.'

[18] See the discussion in Gautam Bhatia, *Offend, Shock, or Disturb: Freedom of Speech under the Indian Constitution* (Oxford: Oxford University Press, 2015), Ch. 3.

[19] *Brandenburg* v. *Ohio* 395 US 444 (196) (Supreme Court of the United States), which laid down the 'incitement to imminent lawless action test', and overruled the previous – and more restrictive 'clear and present danger' test.

[20] It must be noted, however, that the Indian Supreme Court has been inconsistent on this point; it has, for example, upheld the constitutionality of sedition law on the basis of a vague 'tendency towards public disorder' test (see *Kedar Nath Singh* v. *State of Bihar* 1962 SCR Supl (2) 769) (Supreme Court of India), and reversed its own judgment that sought to apply the *Brandenburg* incitement standard to the interpretation of anti-terrorism legislation (see *Arup Bhuyan* v. *State of Assam* CA No. 889/2007 (24 March 2023) (Supreme Court of India), reversing *Arup Bhuyan* v. *State of Assam* 2011 (3) SCC 377 (Supreme Court of India).

[21] *Sakal Papers* v. *Union of India* 1962 SCR (3) 842 (Supreme Court of India); this case is also famous for affirming the proposition that the restrictions under Art. 19(2) were exhaustive, and fresh restrictions could not be smuggled in under the guise of public interest – a holding that has been honoured more in the breach than in the observance, even by subsequent Supreme

that commercial speech was as much protected by Article 19(1)(a) as any other form of speech.[22]

This vein of Supreme Court jurisprudence is what the petitioners in the *IT Rules* case tapped into in order to rebut the state's argument that 'fake' or 'false' speech is excluded from Article 19(1)(a) protection *altogether*, because it possesses low or no value.[23] The autonomy approach to free speech – which regards listeners as autonomous individuals, responsible for their own choices – precludes a priori assessments of value, and any attempt to link constitutional protection to the value of speech, other than that which is already in the Constitution. The basic idea is that judgements of value are to be made by the listeners and not by the state. The structure of Article 19(1)(a) and (2), which specifically sets out the kinds of content that can be regulated, appears to support arguments against additional value judgements being made by the state: after all, the argument goes, those value judgements have *already* been made – exhaustively – within the Constitution itself. And false speech – for both principled and pragmatic reasons – is not one of the categories under Article 19 (2).

11.3 THE PERFECTIONIST LINE

However, even as early Supreme Court judgments were entrenching the autonomy approach to free speech, there were other judgments that took another line, and accentuated the tension inherent within the interpretation of Articles 19(1)(a) and 19 (2). Early on, when considering a ban on misleading medicinal advertisements under a law evocatively titled the Drugs and Magical Remedies Act, the Supreme Court upheld the ban by noting that advertisements for magical remedies were unprotected by the free speech guarantee because they made no contribution to the exchange of ideas – political, economic or cultural – that constituted the basis for *why* there existed a free speech guarantee in the first place.[24] Here, the Supreme Court constructed a hierarchy between kinds of speech, assigning them relative value based on their 'contribution' to the democratic public sphere, and linking the degree or nature of constitutional protection with the value they had. Other than this, an unarticulated major premise of the judgment, of course, was that the target audience of misleading information would *not* be in a position to sift the wheat from

Court judgments. See also, for a related point, *Bennett Coleman* v. *Union of India* 1973 (2) SCR 757 (Supreme Court of India).

[22] *Tata Press* v. *MTNL* 1995 (5) SCC 139.

[23] Written Submissions in *Association of Indian Magazines* v. *Union of India* (*IT Rules* case), on file with the author.

[24] *Hamdard Dawakhana* v. *Union of India* 1960 (2) SCR 671 (Supreme Court of India); arguably, the underlying rationale of this judgment has been eroded with the passage of time. See, e.g., *Tata Press* v. *MTNL*.

the chaff, or be able to identify the misleading content in medicinal advertisements[25] – something that justified state intervention in this domain.

Similar reasoning can be glimpsed in the evolution of the Court's jurisprudence on obscenity. In its early days, the Court adopted the Victorian British '*Hicklin* test', which asked whether speech had the tendency to 'deprave or corrupt' the minds of those into whose hands it might fall.[26] Over the course of time, this test was gradually liberalised, until in 2011, the Court replaced it with the US *Miller* test, where the focus is on whether the offending work appeals solely to the 'prurient interest'.[27] However, whether the more strait-laced *Hicklin* or the more liberal *Miller*, what unites them both is the belief that certain kinds of speech are inherently *valueless*. This is made clear by the fact that both judgments – as well as the obscenity provision in India's Penal Code[28] – have exceptions for works with genuine 'literary' or 'cultural' value.[29] Once again, therefore, in the realms of obscenity jurisprudence, we have a judgement – made by the state, and subject to judicial review by the Courts – about the value of forms of speech, and linking up perceived value with constitutional protection.

The perfectionist impulse is most strikingly visible in a judgment called *Union of India* v. *Motion Picture Association*, where the Court was considering a state requirement for cinemas to show short 'educational' or 'cultural' documentaries before the start of the film.[30] This was challenged on grounds of being akin to a 'must-carry' provision, tantamount to compelled speech. The Supreme Court's response is instructive, and merits quoting in some detail:

> However, whether compelled speech will or will not amount to a violation of the freedom of speech and expression, will depend on the nature of a 'must carry' provision. If a 'must carry' provision furthers informed decision-making which is the essence of the fight to free speech and expression, it will not amount to any violation of the fundamental freedom of speech and expression. *If, however, such a provision compels a person to carry out propaganda or project a partisan or distorted point of view, contrary to his wish, it may amount to a restraint on his freedom of speech and expression.* To give an example, at times a statute imposes an obligation to print certain information in public interest. Any food product must

[25] It should be noted, however, that the specific facts of *Hamdard Dawakhana* were not particularly off-the-wall: the law in question could have easily been recast as a basic regulation preventing consumer fraud, which is found in most countries. It is widely accepted that consumer fraud legislation *generally* does not raise free speech concerns, as its target is not the content, but the effect. Of course, the line between the two is blurry at the best of times.

[26] *Ranjit Udeshi* v. *State of Maharasthra* 1965 SCR (1) 65 (Supreme Court of India), relying upon *R* v. *Hicklin* L.R. 3 Q.B. 360 (1868) (Court of the Queen's Bench).

[27] *Aveek Sarkar* v. *State of West Bengal* (2014) 4 SCC 257 (Supreme Court of India), relying on *Miller* v. *California* 413 US 15 (1973) (Supreme Court of India).

[28] Indian Penal Code 1860, s 295A.

[29] Interestingly, this required the Court to hold, in 1965, that *Lady Chatterley's Lover* had no redeeming literary or cultural value, a judgment that has perhaps not aged all that well.

[30] *Union of India* v. *Motion Picture Association* 1999 (3) SCR 875.

> carry on its package the list of ingredients used in its preparation, or must print its weight. These are beneficial 'must carry' provisions meant to inform the public about the correct quantity and contents of the product it buys. It enables the public to decide on a correct basis whether a particular product should or should not be used. Cigarette cartons are required to carry a statutory warning that cigarette smoking is harmful to health. This is undoubtedly a 'must carry' provision or compelled speech. *Nevertheless, it is meant to further the basic purpose of imparting relevant information which will enable a user to make a correct decision as to whether he should smoke a cigarette or not, such mandatory provisions, although they compel speech, cannot be viewed as a restraint on the freedom of speech and expression.*[31]

And:

> We have to examine whether the purpose of compulsory speech in the impugned provisions is to promote the fundamental freedom of speech and expression and dissemination of ideas, or whether it is to restrain this freedom, the social context of any such legislation cannot be ignored. *When a substantially significant population body is illiterate or does not have easy access to ideas or information, it is important that all available means of communication*, particularly audiovisual communication, are utilised not just for entertainment but also for education, information, propagation of scientific ideas and the like. The best way by which ideas can reach this large body of uneducated people is through the entertainment channel which is watched by all – literate and illiterate alike; to earmark a small portion of time of this entertainment medium for the purpose of showing scientific, educational or documentary films, or for showing news films has to be looked at in this context of promoting dissemination of ideas, information and knowledge to the masses so that there may be an informed debate and decision making on public issues. Clearly, the impugned provisions are designed to further free speech and expression and not to curtail it.[32]

The excerpted passages are important because they go to the heart of the perfectionist approach to free speech. The Court here drew a clear-cut distinction between 'propaganda' or 'partisan speech' or a 'distorted point of view' and (presumably accurate) information that 'furthered informed decision-making'. A must-carry rule that required compulsory broadcasting of the former would violate the right to freedom of speech and expression, but a requirement of carrying the latter would not, since its net effect was to further the right by providing information to all, rather than curtailing it.

It is particularly instructive that the Court drew a link between consumer warnings on cigarette packs (a classic example, as indicated above, in the consumer fraud domain, where concerns of autonomy are thought to be of relatively low intensity), with the domain of political speech, where the concerns of autonomy are believed

[31] Ibid. (emphasis added).
[32] Ibid. (emphasis added).

to be at their highest. The overarching theme, then, cuts across domains of speech: the perfectionist approach to free speech, which sees the role of free speech in a democracy as performing a very specific function, and accords constitutional protection to only that kind of speech that is consistent with this function. This necessarily requires the state – and the courts – to construct an internal content-based hierarchy within speech, and to assign social value to forms or kinds of speech.

This, it must be noted, is distinct from a free speech jurisprudence where regulations or restrictions are justified not on the basis of the value of the speech in question but by virtue of its impact on other constitutional principles. Hate speech jurisprudence, for example, is based not on the premise that hate speech is low or no-value speech, but that it is destructive of the constitutional principles of equality and equal protection.[33] This jurisprudence is also at odds with a strict articulation of the autonomy approach to free speech.[34] But at the same time, liberal democracies have been broadly able to reconcile the existence of hate speech laws with a general autonomy-based approach to free speech: there is an understanding that the principles underlying the free speech guarantee need to be balanced against the maintenance of other constitutional principles, which – in turn – will require overriding autonomy in select domains, without conceding its own importance as a constitutional principle.[35]

What is crucial to note is that such arguments do not depend – as already pointed out – on assigning values to forms of speech. The criminalisation or penalisation of 'misinformation' or 'disinformation' *simpliciter*, however, raises different concerns. For instance, in the *IT Rules* case, had the clause referred to 'fake or false speech' that 'incites public disorder', or 'fake or false speech' that 'vilifies a community of people', different constitutional questions would have arisen. By contrast, penalising misinformation or disinformation *simpliciter* is – in effect – penalising bare falsehood. To defend such a provision – which, on its face, falls outside the eight sub-clauses of Article 19(2) – would require the state to construct an argument along the lines of low- and high-value speech, as the only other option is to argue that false speech falls out of the ambit of the free speech clause altogether. As we have seen, this is indeed what the state did, and how it chose to defend the constitutionality of the 2023 IT Rules Amendment when it was challenged in court.

And it is this defence that lays bare the tension between the autonomy and perfectionist approaches to free speech, which have pulled Indian free speech jurisprudence in different directions from the inception of the Indian

[33] See, e.g., *Pravasi Bhalai Sangathan* v. *Union of India* AIR 2014 SC 1591 (Supreme Court of India); Jeremy Waldron, *The Harm in Hate Speech* (Cambridge, MA: Harvard University Press, 2012).

[34] For an example of a judgment accepting the premise of such laws but *also* holding them to be inconsistent with the autonomy approach to free speech, see *American Booksellers* v. *Hudnut* 771 F.2d 323 (7th Cir. 1985), considering Indianapolis' anti-pornography ordinance.

[35] See, e.g., *R* v. *Keegstra* [1990] 3 SCR 697.

Constitution. As we have seen, it is in the context of contemporary online misinformation and disinformation – with its virality, and its admittedly corrosive effects on democracy – that these tensions become particularly stark. And in the final section, we shall examine how these tensions play out in this context.

11.4 MISINFORMATION AND DISINFORMATION IN CONTEMPORARY CONTEXTS

As pointed out, the state's core argument in the *IT Rules* case was that outright falsehoods are unprotected by the constitutional guarantee of free speech, as false speech has no constitutional value. On the flip side, the state argued that citizens have a right to receive true and accurate information, a right that is frustrated in an online environment awash with falsehoods. In particular, the state linked this right to the right to vote: it argued that false or fake news distorted the voting process – and thereby democracy – by distorting the base of information upon which voters made their decisions.[36] (This last argument, one will notice, specifically takes issue with the autonomy approach to free speech.) And finally, it flagged the specific character of the Internet and online speech: in particular, virality, which makes it difficult for false speech to be 'countered' with facts.

Taken on their own, these arguments do not necessarily sound unreasonable. The constitutional issue, however, lies in the regulatory mechanism that the state devised to deal with the problem: a regulatory mechanism that involved a government-mandated fact-check unit 'checking' speech about the government, and backing it up with the coercive consequences of losing safe harbour. To elaborate, safe harbour – recognised by Section 79 of the Indian Information Technology Act – refers to the legal position where intermediaries cannot be held liable for the content that is posted or disseminated on their platforms. Safe harbour is normally a qualified right, imposing certain obligations of due diligence upon the intermediary. In India, this takes the form of 'actual knowledge' – that is, the intermediary needs to be notified, either by a court order or a government notice, that it is hosting unlawful content. If, on receiving such knowledge, the intermediary refuses to act, it then 'loses' safe harbour, and is open to lawsuits seeking to hold it liable of the offending speech.

Deprivation of safe harbour is therefore not direct censorship, such as a book ban or the blocking of a website. Theoretically, an intermediary can disagree with the government on the issue of whether flagged content is actually lawful or unlawful, defend its assessment in court, and even possibly win. Practically, however, safe

[36] It is important to note that this argument is not restricted to false speech that actually prevents a voter from exercising their right to vote (such as, for example, incorrect news that an election has been postponed, or that the location of the polling booths has been shifted); but rather, false speech or a broader kind, such as mischaracterisation of government policy.

harbour is a vital safeguard that allows intermediaries to perform their functions without the constant threat of multiple lawsuits hanging over their heads. An intermediary will – in its own interests – prefer to comply with a government directive rather than lose safe harbour. The coercion is therefore indirect – a threat of the loss of safe harbour and the consequences that follow – and the free speech implications lie in accompanying self-censorship and the chilling effect.

This detour is important, as it was the basis of the petitioners' argument that the language of the 2023 IT Amendment creates a slippage between regulating misinformation and making the state the arbiter of truth. The possibility of such a slippage is always present in state efforts to tackle misinformation, and – the petitioners argued – the 2023 Amendment reveals how it actually happens. If the consequence of an intermediary not complying with the government Fact Check Unit is the loss of safe harbour, then – as far as the intermediaries are concerned (and by extension, the users of the platform, both the speaker and the recipient of the speech) – the government Fact Check Unit's assessment of what is true or false is effectively determinative.

This leads to a few problems. The most obvious one, of course, is whether a free speech guarantee is consistent with allowing the state to act as an effective arbiter of truth, even if one were to accept the proposition that false speech is outside the pale of constitutional protection. It is, after all, one thing to say that false speech should be regulated, and another thing to say that the state (and in this case, specifically, the political executive) should be the body that has control over regulation. While the perfectionist line of free speech jurisprudence in India might well support the first proposition, the second presents a greater challenge. The autonomy approach, on the other hand, would reject out of hand the regulation of bare falsehood altogether, as – in the absence of any legally cognisable harm traceable to Article 19(2) of the Constitution – its rationale can be nothing other than an internal hierarchy within Article 19(1)(a).

Secondly – as petitioners' counsel pointed out – there is a range of statements and forms of speech where the question is not merely whether something is true or false, but whether it falls within the true/false binary at all. For example, consider the judgment of the South African Constitutional Court in *DA* v. *ANC*. The case involved a bulk SMS sent by the main opposition party, the Democratic Alliance, which stated that an impartial report 'shows how [President] Zuma *stole* your money' to build his home, whereas the report had not made any finding of 'theft' against President Zuma.[37] Justices of the constitutional court split over the exact meaning of the phrases 'shows how' and 'stole', with some judges holding that it was an allegation of theft (and therefore, false), while others held that it was an accusation of unethical behaviour (and therefore neither true nor false, only

[37] *Democratic Alliance* v. *African National Congress* (2015) 3 BCLR 298 (Constitutional Court of South Africa).

convincing or unconvincing). As the case reveals, therefore, there is a subjectivity underlying not merely whether a claim is true or false, but the nature of the claim itself.[38]

Although this issue would dog any regulatory attempt to curtail misinformation or disinformation online, it acquired a particular salience in the *IT Rules* case, as the regulatory form was one that proposed to give the executive the effectively determinative power of settling such questions. But although the issues and arguments arose in a specific context, it is evident that they need to be considered by regulators grappling with these questions across the board.

The *IT Rules* case is complicated by the tensions between the autonomy approach and the perfectionist approach within Indian free speech jurisprudence (by now, it should be obvious that this tension exists in the constitutional jurisprudence of most liberal democracies). It does appear – for the reasons pointed out above – that the IT Rules, in their specific form, go even beyond what is permitted by the perfectionist approach.

At the same time, it also appears that a strict application of the autonomy approach is not entirely appropriate to the era of mass online misinformation, with its well-known corrosive effects on democracy. As the scholarship around hate speech has taught us, it is not *only* in the Brandeis-type situations of incitement, or shouting 'fire' in a crowded theatre, that the remedy of counter-speech fails. There are other reasons – and other contexts in which – counter-speech can fail. This is especially true when one accounts for – in the words of Jack Balkin – the 'infrastructure' of free speech, and recognises the fact of unequal access to infrastructure determining who can speak, how much and to what extent.[39] The question of virality on the Internet – and specifically virality of misinformation on the Internet – often tracks inequalities of power and resources in the offline world, which are transplanted into the online domain.

Thus, neither the autonomy approach nor the perfectionist approach – the two strands of Indian free speech jurisprudence – might give us all the adjudicatory resources we need to fit the regulation of online disinformation and misinformation within the contours of constitutional jurisprudence. However, there are other, promising avenues: for example, in a one-off judgment, the Supreme Court has recognised a right of reply as forming a part of the right to free speech;[40] another has recognised the importance of access to the infrastructure of speech.[41] How this might work in the online domain remains an open question – for instance, the success of Twitter (now X) 'Community Notes' – as a community-moderated

[38] Of course, this is not new to law, lawyers or judges: defamation law, in large part, consists of arguments over whether an allegedly defamatory statement is a statement of fact (and therefore must be demonstrated to be true), or whether it is a *comment* (which must only be 'fair').

[39] Jack Balkin, 'The First Amendment Is an Information Policy' (2012) 41(1) *Hofstra Law Review* 1.

[40] *LIC* v. *Manubhai D. Shah* (1992) 3 SCC 637.

[41] *Bennett Coleman* v. *Union of India*.

reply – is much debated. What is clear, however, is that any attempt must draw both from the autonomy-respecting strand of Indian free speech jurisprudence, while also taking seriously the problem of online misinformation, in shaping the nature and the form of regulatory remedies. The IT Rules perhaps are an example of how not to do it: that is, by eschewing autonomy entirely, taking the perfectionist approach to its extreme, and opting to combat misinformation by making the state the arbiter of what is misinformation and what is not.

12

Disinformation and Democracy in Africa and South Africa

Joanna Botha

12.1 INTRODUCTION AND THE AFRICAN CONTEXT

This chapter reviews the regulation of disinformation from an African human rights' law perspective, focusing on the right to freedom of expression and the right to vote. It provides an overview of the African regional law framework, specifically the African Charter on Human and Peoples Rights of 1981 (the African Charter)[1] and corresponding jurisprudence.[2] The chapter also analyses the way in which freedom of expression and disinformation laws have been applied in African countries, the aim being to contextualize and illustrate how African regional law plays out at the domestic level, but with an emphasis on the position in South Africa.

The African treatment of disinformation makes a valuable contribution to a book addressing the relationship between the regulation of freedom of expression, specifically disinformation, and the promotion of the democratic state. There are two key reasons. Firstly, most research on the impact of 'fake news' incidents on democracies has been conducted in the Global North, with few case studies considering the situation in countries positioned in the Global South. This is so, even though (a) disinformation as a concept has existed for years in the Global South and (b) credit was taken by former United States' president, Donald Trump, for coining the term 'fake news'.[3]

[1] [Banjul] Charter on Human and Peoples' Rights, adopted by the Assembly of Heads of State and Government (AHSG) of the Organization of African Union (OAU), now the African Union, at its meeting in Nairobi, Kenya on 26 June 1981.

[2] Whilst mention is made of sub-regional developments, it is not possible here to provide a detailed analysis of the regulation of freedom of expression, specifically disinformation, at the sub-regional level.

[3] Vincent Chenzi, 'Fake News, Social Media and Xenophobia in South Africa' (2021) 19(4) *African Identities* 502; 'Domestic Disinformation on the Rise in Africa', African Center for Strategic Studies, 2021, https://africacenter.org/spotlight/mapping-disinformation-in-africa; Martin Pengelly, 'Trump Accuses CNN of Fake News over Reported Celebrity Apprentice

Secondly, many African democracies are in a precarious position, with some governments implementing multifaceted strategies to silence their political opponents or critics, especially during elections. These include laws criminalizing the publication of false news, the filtering of online content and internet shutdowns.[4] The consequences of such strategies for democracies are dire: they undermine the rule of law, transparency, accountability, the right of citizens to receive information and the electoral processes.

Thirdly, and in juxtaposition to the use of censorship to undermine the spread of information, political campaigners in numerous African states have discovered how the freedom of the Internet can be used to create and disseminate false news and divisive digital content (through inter alia algorithms, bots, fake social media accounts, image manipulation and even the broadcast of fake information designed to appear as emanating from legitimate and reputable service broadcasters, such as the BBC).[5] Such disinformation is usually intended to distort political debate, silence opponents and win votes.[6]

The South African regulation of disinformation is also insightful. South Africa's political history makes for a fascinating country study, given its negotiated transition from a colonized and racist state, with strict censorship laws, to a constitutional democracy, based on human dignity, equality and freedom. The Bill of Rights in

Plans', *The Guardian*, 10 December 2016, www.theguardian.com/us-news/2016/dec/10/trump-celebrity-apprentice-cnn-fake-news.

4 See Marystella A. Simiyu, 'Freedom of Expression and African Elections: Mitigating the Insidious Effect of Emerging Approaches to Addressing the False News Threat' (2022) 22(2) *African Human Rights Law Journal* 76; Herman Wasserman and Dani Madrid-Morales, 'An Exploratory Study of "Fake News" and Media Trust in Kenya, Nigeria and South Africa' (2019) 40(1) *African Journalism Studies* 107, at 109–10, quoting Anne Fleischmann and Viola Stefanello, 'African Governments Use Internet Shutdowns to Silence Opposition More and More', *Euronews*, 26 January 2019, www.euronews.com/2019/01/26/african-governments-use-internet-shutdowns-to-silence-opposition-more-and-more-what-can-pe.

5 As occurred in Kenya in the 2017 presidential elections, and in Nigeria in 2015. See 'The Reality of Fake News in Kenya', *Portland Communications*, 2017, https://portland-communications.com/publications/reality-fake-news-kenya; Nanjira Sambuli, 'How Kenya Became the Latest Victim of Fake News', *Al Jazeera*, 17 August 2017, www.aljazeera.com/indepth/opinion/2017/08/kenya-latest-victim-fake-news-170816121455181.html; Brian Ekdale and Melissa Tully, 'African Elections as a Testing Ground: Comparing Coverage of Cambridge Analytica in Nigerian and Kenyan Newspapers' (2019) 40(4) *African Journalism Studies* 27.

6 Kate Jones, 'Online Disinformation and Political Discourse: Applying a Human Rights Framework', Policy Commons, 6 November 2019, https://policycommons.net/artifacts/1423530/online-disinformation-and-political-discourse/2037807; Herman Wasserman, 'The State of South African Media: A Space to Contest Democracy' (2020) 65 *Publizistik* 451. Misinformation in African countries includes vitriolic speech that can incite violence and group-based hatred. Messages containing racist, misogynistic and xenophobic content are also common.

South Africa's Constitution[7] protects both the right to freedom of expression[8] and the right to access information.[9] Political rights are entrenched in Section 19 of the Constitution, giving every citizen the freedom to make political choices and the right to free, fair and regular elections. Section 19 should be read with Section 1 of the Constitution,[10] which provides that South Africa is 'one, sovereign, democratic state' founded upon listed constitutional values, with Section 1(d) recording that the constitutional democracy is based on 'universal adult suffrage, a national common voters roll, regular elections and a multi-party system of democratic government, to ensure accountability, responsiveness and openness'.[11] This means that, in the South African context, where the spread of disinformation is often linked to political control, a delicate balancing of competing rights is required to ensure that the regulation of disinformation does not unjustifiably violate the right to freedom of expression.

The stability of the South African democracy and a concomitant free press and media, which have been instrumental in uncovering widespread state corruption,[12] have however been undermined by challenges aimed at stifling freedom of expression.[13] Examples include a state-proposed Media Appeals Tribunal,[14] stricter state control over the flow of information through a proposed Bill on the Protection of State Information,[15] the spreading of false information and propaganda whilst

[7] The Constitution of the Republic of South Africa, 1996.

[8] Section 16(1) of the Constitution protects freedom of expression. Four forms of expression are listed in the ambit of the right. These include freedom of the press and other media in s. 16(1)(a) and the right to receive information and ideas in s. 16(1)(b).

[9] Constitution, s. 32. The Promotion of Access to Information Act (PAIA), Act 3 of 2000, was enacted to give effect to the constitutional right of access to information. It provides a right to receive information from public and private bodies.

[10] This is the most entrenched provision in the Constitution.

[11] The Preamble to the Constitution is also important. It upholds democratic principles, stating that a government acquires legitimacy through 'the will of the people' and records that '[w]e, the people of South Africa, ... through our freely elected representatives, adopt this Constitution as the supreme law of the Republic so as to ... [l]ay the foundations for a democratic and open society in which government is based on the will of the people and every citizen is equally protected by law ... [and b]uild a united and democratic South Africa able to take its rightful place as a sovereign state in the family of nations'.

[12] Helge Rønning, 'The Politics of Corruption and the Media in Africa' (2009) 1(1) *Journal of African Media Studies* 155.

[13] See *Print Media SA* v. *Films and Publications Board* 2012 (6) SA 443 (CC); S v. *Mamabolo (E-tv Intervening)* 2001 (3) SA 409 (CC).

[14] See Lianne van Leeuwen, 'The Recent Decline in Press Freedom in South Africa' 2012 6(1) *Global Media Journal Africa Edition* 67; Alicestine October, 'Report Raises Concern over Diminishing Press Freedom in SA', News 24, 30 April 2015, www.news24.com/SouthAfrica/News/Report-raises-concern-over-diminishing-press-freedom-in-SA-20150430. The African National Congress (ANC), the ruling party in South Africa, first introduced a Media Appeals Tribunal, with state officials presiding, to replace the self-regulation of the press in 2007. The plan has resurfaced regularly.

[15] B-6 [2010]. There were many objections to the Bill, which was never enacted into law.

electioneering,[16] and threats and attacks on journalists during election campaigns.[17] Additionally, incidents of extensive media censorship were exposed in the Judicial Commission of Inquiry into allegations of state capture, corruption and fraud in the public sector including organs of state (the 'Zondo Commission'), convened at huge state expense between 2018 and 2022.[18]

Even more intriguing is that one of the most prominent global examples of the spread of false information, the 'Bell Pottinger affair', occurred in South Africa in 2016.[19] It involved a British public relations firm in a 'large-scale fake news propaganda war',[20] designed as a clandestine campaign to perpetuate racial polarisation in South Africa. It was really aimed, however, at influencing public opinion and discrediting detractors of former South African President Jacob Zuma, threatening to expose his corrupt relationship with the Gupta family (the instigators of state capture).[21] Disinformation was spread through media outlets owned by the Guptas,[22] fake blogs and tweets (amplified by the use of bots which generated automated retweets),[23] catchphrase hashtags designed to undermine critics (such as #PravinMustGo and #WhiteMonopolyCapital),[24] and the manipulation of social media sites, including Facebook and Wikipedia. Journalists who exposed the

[16] Chenzi, 'Fake News' (n 3), at 504–5.

[17] Wasserman and Madrid-Morales, 'Exploratory Study' (n 4), at 111.

[18] The Judicial enquiry into State Capture in South Africa, the so-called Zondo Report, was published in 2022, see www.thepresidency.gov.za/report-type/judicial-commission-inquiry-state-capture-report. Raymond Zondo is the current Chief Justice and chaired the Commission.

[19] Albert Wöcke, Morris Mthombeni and Alvaro Cuervo-Cazurro, 'Reputations and Corruption: Bell Pottinger in South Africa' (2020) 10(4) *Emerald Emerging Markets Case Studies* 1.

[20] Julie Posetti and Alice Matthews, *A Short Guide to the History of 'Fake News' and Disinformation*, International Center for Journalists, 2018, www.icfj.org/sites/default/files/2018-07/A%20Short%20Guide%20to%20History%20of%20Fake%20News%20and%20Disinformation_ICFJ%20Final.pdf.

[21] The Gupta family arrived in South Africa in 1993. Initially small business owners, they grew a vast business empire, owning Sahara Computers and Oakbay Investments Pty (Ltd), consisting of subsidiaries in inter alia the mining, media, leisure, firearms and real estate sectors. They built strong networks in the African National Congress from the 1990s, and used their power to win tenders, influence the Treasury, engage in controversial business deals and create strategies to enable politicians to exploit the resources of state-owned entities, such as SAA, Eskom, Telkom and others. See Wöcke, Mthombeni and Cuervo-Cazurro, 'Reputations and Corruption', at 4–6.

[22] The *New Age Newspaper* and television channel ANN7.

[23] Sonja Verwey and Clarissa Muir, 'Bell Pottinger and the Dark Art of Public Relations: Ethics of Individuality *versus* Ethics of Communality' (2019) 38(1) *Communicare: Journal for Communication Sciences in Southern Africa* 96.

[24] Pravin Gordham was then minister of finance. He launched an application to confirm that he had no authority to intervene in banking relations between clients and their banks, as was alleged. This occurred after four prominent banks closed the Gupta family accounts. Gordham was later fired by Zuma, and replaced by a puppet minister of finance. See ibid. at 104–6.

corrupt relationship between Zuma and the Guptas were accused of being lackeys of 'white monopoly capital' and were repeatedly threatened.[25]

Having sketched this contextual background, the chapter commences with a brief description of the definitional terms used and then links the regulation of misinformation to the rationales for the protection of freedom of expression. Thereafter, the way in which African regional law protects freedom of expression and access to information is examined, including recent developments by institutions operating at the African regional level. This is followed by examples of reported incidents of the spread of disinformation and censorship in African countries, usually occurring during election time, and a description of the type of false news laws applying in Africa. Finally, the South African approach to the promotion of freedom of expression is analysed, focusing on disinformation, which is illustrated through the normative human rights lens of freedom of expression, free and fair elections, government accountability and the promotion of democratic values.

12.2 DEFINITIONAL CONCEPTS

Any chapter in a book dedicated to the protection of freedom of expression and disinformation should use the correct nomenclature. So, whilst the chapter refers occasionally to the catchphrases 'false news' and 'fake news', the term 'disinformation' is preferred. Disinformation is defined as information that is verifiably false or misleading and is created and disseminated with the intention of causing public harm.[26] In the African context, public harm constitutes mainly threats to democratic principles, the undermining of free and fair elections, plus political and policy-making processes.[27] It also includes the undermining of pluralism and

[25] Herman Wasserman, 'Fake News from Africa: Panics, Politics and Paradigm' (2020) (21)1 *Journalism* 3, at 4. For example, the editor of a prominent newspaper was targeted in a campaign of online harassment designed to silence her exposure of state capture. Other targets included journalists working for amaBhungane, an independent newsroom, at the forefront of investigative journalism in South Africa, who were subjected to harassment and intimidation. See Ferial Haffejee, *Days of Zondo: The Fight for Freedom from Corruption* (Cape Town: Vendor, 2022); and *Sole* v. *Black First Land First; In re: South African Editors Forum* v. *Black First Land First* (23897/2017) [2017] ZAGPJHC 299 (17 October 2017). The journalists were involved in the so-called Gupta leaks, see https://amabhungane.org/stories/special-report-the-guptaleaks-and-more-all-our-stories-on-state-capture-2.

[26] Claire Wardle and Hossein Derakhshan, 'Information Disorder: Toward an Interdisciplinary Framework for Research and Policymaking', Council of Europe Report, 2017, https://edoc.coe.int/en/module/ec_addformat/download?cle=5905aa3361a00b7d9356fa6cf222396d&k=1349852033253 43f5703e874bed476e2, at 5; 'Tackling Online Disinformation: A European Approach', European Commission, 2018 COM/2018/236, para 2.1.

[27] 'Tackling Online Disinformation' (n 26) para 2.1.

diversity in democratic societies, usually through the spread of vitriolic messages intended to exploit divisions in society and to subordinate vulnerable groups, based inter alia on race, ethnicity, social origin and religion.[28]

'Disinformation' does not include information that is false, but which was not created and distributed with the intention of causing harm. Instead, this type of information is usually labelled 'misinformation' and includes reporting errors or news and commentary that is identified as being partisan to a particular viewpoint or political party.[29] Although there is no consensus on the correct legal meaning of fake or false news,[30] the terms refer 'to false information that mimics news media content in order to deceive so as to influence various reactions from the public'.[31] The terms are broadly used and include hoaxes, the manipulation of photos, clickbait campaigns, deliberate political disinformation campaigns, propaganda and even genuine political satire and parodies.[32]

The discussion now moves to the traditional rationales justifying the protection of freedom of expression and whether they permit the regulation of 'false news' and/or disinformation. It will be shown that African countries tend to regulate the dissemination of false news in overly broad terms, including the media and misinformation within their ambit. These laws impact negatively on the protection of freedom of expression and democratic principles.

[28] Simiyu, 'Freedom of Expression', at 83; Wasserman, 'Fake News from Africa' (n 4), at 5–7.

[29] 'Tackling Online Disinformation' (n 26) para. 2.1.

[30] Wasserman and Madrid-Morales, 'Exploratory Study' (n 4), at 108, citing, among others, Santanu Chakrabarti, Claire Rooney and Minnie Kweo, 'Verification, Duty, Credibility: Fake News and Ordinary Citizens in Kenya and Nigeria', BBC News, 2018, https://downloads.bbc.co.uk/mediacentre/bbc-fake-news-research-paper-nigeria-kenya.pdf; Oliver Boyd-Barrett, 'Fake News and "RussiaGate" Discourses: Propaganda in the Post-Truth Era' (2019) 20(1) *Journalism* 87; Aljosha K. Schapals, 'Fake News: Australian and British Journalists' Role Perceptions in an Era of "Alternative Facts"' (2018) 12(8) *Journalism: Theory, Practice & Criticism* 108.

[31] Wasserman and Madrid-Morales, 'Exploratory Study' (n 4), at 108; Sandra L. Borden and Chad Tew, 'The Role of Journalist and the Performance of Journalism: Ethical Lessons From "Fake" News (Seriously)' (2007) 22(4) *Journal of Mass Media Ethics* 300; Edson C. Tandoc, Jr., Zheng W. Lim and Richard Ling, 'Defining "Fake News"' 2018 6(2) *Digital Journalism* 137.

[32] Note that in South Africa, the right to expression includes artistic creativity and is interpreted broadly at threshold level. The right can be limited using s. 36, the general limitation clause, which permits the justifiable and proportionate limitation of rights. See *Laugh It Off Promotions CC* v. *South African Breweries International* 2006 (1) SA 144 (CC), [85]–[88], dealing with commercial parody. The court *a quo* held that the racial parody printed on the Carling Black Label t-shirts (the 'Black Label' trademark was replaced with 'Black Labour' and the 'Carling Beer' mark was substituted with 'White Guilt') was unprotected speech. But the Constitutional Court (at [98]) did not agree, holding that the expression was protected – parody being a valuable form of speech.

12.3 THE RELATIONSHIP BETWEEN DISINFORMATION AND THE RATIONALES FOR FREEDOM OF EXPRESSION IN THE AFRICAN CONTEXT

The earlier contextual background confirmed that, in most African states, the public harm that disinformation causes is the spread of false information aimed at influencing public opinion during elections, silencing opposing views and undermining groups of persons perceived to have power (whether economic or political).[33] Often, the purpose of the dissemination is to gain or retain power and to control public revenues (which could potentially be misused through corruption).[34] The African context therefore demonstrates the strong connection between freedom of expression and its most commonly advanced rationale, namely that free speech is an integral component of the proper functioning of a democracy and helps to promote democratic self-government by the people. This is true both for the formation of a democracy and the strengthening of a developing or fragile democracy.[35]

The democratic rationale for freedom of expression, which has influenced the development of free speech jurisprudence worldwide (including in South Africa),[36] is based on the premise that speech enables people to participate in political and social debate, to have access to governmental policies and to make informed decisions about how they are governed.[37] In sum, free expression is vital in a democracy for three reasons. Firstly, in a democracy, the people are assumed to be sovereign and should play a significant role in decision-making. Freedom of expression ensures that they receive relevant information to enable the exercise of democratic self-governance and to ensure 'wise decisions by wise voters'.[38] Both censorship of information and the spread of disinformation can distort the thinking capacity of the community and undermine a democracy.[39] Those in power should

[33] 'Domestic Disinformation on the Rise in Africa' (n 3), at 1–8; Simiyu, 'Freedom of Expression' (n 4), at 79–80.

[34] Wasserman, 'Fake News from Africa' (n 25), at 7.

[35] Raymond Suttner, 'Freedom of Speech' (1990) 6 *South African Journal of Human Rights* 372, at 378.

[36] Eric Barendt, *Freedom of Speech* (Oxford: Oxford University Press, 2007) p. 20; Joanna Botha, 'Towards a South African Free Speech Model' (2017) 134(4) *South African Law Journal* 778.

[37] Derek Spitz, 'Eschewing Silence Coerced by Law: The Political Core and Periphery of Freedom of Expression' (1994) 10(3) *South African Journal of Human Rights* 301, at 306.

[38] Frederick Schauer, *Free Speech: A Philosophical Enquiry* (Cambridge: Cambridge University Press, 1982) p. 38; Alexander Meiklejohn, *Political Freedom: The Constitutional Powers of the People* (Oxford: Oxford University Press, 1960) p. 27; Robert Post, 'Participatory Democracy and Free Speech' (2011) 97(3) *Virginia law Review* 477, at 482.

[39] See Shauer, *Free Speech*, pp. 37–39; Richard Moon, *The Constitutional Protection of Freedom of Expression* (Toronto: University of Toronto Press, 2000) pp. 14–17; Steven Shiffrin, 'Dissent, Democratic Participation, and First Amendment Methodology' (2011) 97(3) *Virginia Law Review* 559, at 560–61.

thus not be able to manipulate the flow of public information and withhold public debate.[40]

Secondly, freedom of expression acts as a check and balance against the abuse of power and promotes governmental accountability and transparency. A democratic government should be regarded as the 'servant' of the people, entitling the latter to criticize their leaders, government officials and implemented policy, where necessary.[41] Here, the role of the media as public watchdog is critical.[42] So, any law that stifles a free media under the guise of false news regulation should be closely scrutinized to ensure that it does not encroach unduly upon freedom of expression.

Thirdly, free speech promotes social stability by allowing everyone to participate in public speech, resulting in the expression of diverse views and an informed and sovereign electorate.[43] Ironically, as has been shown, both disinformation and its regulation have the potential to undermine the democracy rationale. To ensure the integrity of freedom of expression, a balance must be struck between the two opposing interests so that only disinformation which causes public harm (as described earlier) is restricted.

For the regulation of disinformation, another three interconnected rationales – namely the truth rationale (the 'marketplace of ideas' metaphor),[44] the 'fear of government suppression' rationale and the 'checking valve' theory – are also important.[45] It is arguable that false information is incapable of advancing the truth, justifying the need for disinformation laws.[46] At face value this claim appears to have merit, but it fails to consider that the underlying basis of the rationale, as formulated by John Stuart Mill, is that views censored because of their supposed

40 Meiklejohn, *Political Freedom*, p. 79 [n38]; Jeremy Waldron, *The Harm in Hate Speech* (Cambridge, MA: Harvard University Press, 2012) p. 4; Shiffrin, 'Consent, Democratic Participation', at 560–61; Stephen M. Feldman, 'Hate Speech and Democracy' (2013) 32(1) *Criminal Justice Ethics* 78, at 87; Robert Post, 'Hate Speech' in Ivan Hare and James Weinstein (eds.), *Extreme Speech and Democracy* (Oxford: Oxford University Press, 2011) 128, p. 287.

41 Meiklejohn, *Political Freedom*, p. 79.

42 See *Print Media SA* v. *Films and Publications Board*; *S* v. *Mamabolo (E-tv Intervening)*.

43 James Weinstein, 'Extreme Speech, Public Order and Democracy: Lesson from the Masses' in Hare and Weinstein, *Extreme Speech*, p. 23; James Weinstein, 'An Overview of American Free Speech Doctrine and its Application to Extreme Speech' in Hare and Weinstein, *Extreme Speech* (n 40) p. 81.

44 See generally Frederick Schauer, 'The First Amendment as Ideology' (1992) 33(3) *William and Mary Law Review* 853, at 866; Robert Post, 'Reconciling Theory and Doctrine in First Amendment Jurisprudence' (2000) 88(6) *California Law Review* 2353.

45 Barendt, *Freedom of Speech*, p. 21 [n36]; Vincent Blasi, 'The First Amendment and the Ideal of Civic Courage: The Brandeis Opinion in *Whitney* v. *California*' (1988) 29(4) *William and Mary Law Review* 653, referred to with approval by Ngcobo J, in the South African case of *The Citizen 1978 (Pty) Ltd* v. *McBride* 2011 (4) SA 191 (CC), [142].

46 Schauer, *Free Speech*, pp. 7–10 [n38]; *R* v. *Keegstra* 1990 3 SCR 697, [87] (untrue statements cast as hate speech are unlikely to further knowledge or 'lead to a better world', and cannot be justified by the truth rationale). In South Africa, see *Khumalo* v. *Holomisa* 2002 (5) SA 401 (CC), [35]; Judge Cameron, in *The Citizen 1978 (Pty) Ltd* v. *McBride* [78], holding that 'truth-telling' is a tenet of the transition from the injustices of the past to democracy.

falsity may in fact be true and that their elimination increases the possibility of 'exchanging error for truth'.[47] The public are more likely to learn the truth if exposed to varied views. Plus the suppression of information, even if potentially false, undermines the attainment of human knowledge, because censors are not infallible.[48] The banning of perceived false beliefs can be dangerous because it may suppress some true beliefs, impeding the search for the truth[49] and, in turn, permitting undue censorship.[50] This is especially problematic in the African context where false news laws are introduced to censor the media expressing views critical of those in power. The reality is that the impact is oppressive governments which usually retain power.[51]

The fear of government suppression theory adds weight to the argument. Its proponent, Frederick Schauer, explains that '[f]reedom of speech is based ... on a distrust of the ability of government to make the necessary distinctions, a distrust of governmental determinations of truth and falsity, an appreciation of the fallibility of political leaders, and a somewhat deeper distrust of governmental power'.[52] Governments are considered 'particularly bad' at regulating speech, with ample historical evidence of censorship gone wrong.[53] Factually, censorship of public

47 John Stuart Mill, *On Liberty* (London: John W. Parker & Son, 1859) p. 33. For a development of Mill's work, see Leonard W. Sumner, *The Hateful and the Obscene: Studies in the Limits of Free Expression* (Toronto: University of Toronto Press, 2004). In the South African context, see Joanna Botha, '"Swartman": Racial Descriptor or Racial Slur? *Rustenburg Platinum Mine* v. *SAEWA obo Bester* [2018] ZACC 13; 2018 (5) SA 78 (CC)' (2020) 10(1) *Constitutional Court Review* 353.

48 Mill, *On Liberty* (n 47) pp. 33–34; Schauer, 'The First Amendment as Ideology' (n 44), at 866.

49 A fair argument is that obviously false, irrational or objectionable opinions could be excluded from public discourse without impacting on the truth. For, as Post states, '[t]he creation of knowledge ... depends upon practices that continually separate the true from the false, the better from the worse'. This, however, justifies tightly drafted disinformation laws only. See Robert Post, 'Participatory Democracy and Free Speech' (2011) 97(3) *Virginia Law Review* 477, at 479. See too *R* v. *Zundel* [1992] 2 SCR 73 – the Canadian Court declared the false news provision in the Criminal Code unconstitutional. The majority reasoned that even deliberate lies had value and serve a useful social purpose, promoting political participation and self-fulfilment. The Court thus held that false statements were a form of protected expression in terms of s. 2(b) of the Canadian Charter and that the false news provision, as a limitation thereto, had to be justified by s. 1 of the Charter. Ultimately, the provision was considered overly broad as an offence punishing the dissemination of false and mischievous statements.

50 Barendt, *Freedom of Speech* (n 36) pp. 8–9.

51 See generally, Agnès Callamard, 'Accountability, Transparency, and Freedom of Expression in Africa' (2010) 77(4) *Social Research: An International Quarterly* 1211, at 1244; Statement by the Special Rapporteur on Freedom of Expression and Access to Information in Africa on the Occasion of the International Day for Universal Access to Information, 28 September 2023, African Commission, https://achpr.au.int/index.php/en/news/press-releases/2023-09-28/statement-special-rapporteur-freedom-expression-and-access-infor.

52 Schauer, *Free Speech* (n 38) p. 86 (noting that the theory is not conceived as a 'naïve conspiracy theory').

53 He refers, for example, on p. 81, to the condemnation of Galileo, prosecutions for seditious libel and treason when persons publicly expressed views contrary to government policy in both the USA and the United Kingdom, and the banning of works of art and literature.

speech is usually entrusted to government officials, who are inclined to be biased and may suppress speech critical of government in order to retain power.[54] The African regional and sub-regional courts have regularly used this rationale to declare overly broad speech restrictions illegitimate.

The 'government suppression' rationale is closely linked to the 'checking valve' theory, proposed as a 'vital' supplement to the traditional free speech values.[55] Noting the abuse of government power as 'an especially serious evil', the claim is that free speech, in conjunction with a free press, provides an important check on government authority through exposure and deterrence.[56] The scrutiny and exposure of government activities by organized, well-financed and professional critics (the press) ensures that corrective action can be taken when an abuse of power occurs and, if aware of public scrutiny, officials are less likely 'to yield to the inevitable temptation presented to those with power to act in corrupt and arbitrary ways'.[57] The distrust of government censorship rationale resonates in South African jurisprudence, with the judgment in S v. *Mamabolo (E-tv Intervening)*[58] serving as the best example. Here, it was held that '[h]aving regard to our recent past of thought control, censorship and enforced conformity to governmental theories ... we should be particularly astute to outlaw any form of thought-control, however respectably dressed'.[59]

Insofar as the regulation of disinformation is concerned, care must be taken to ensure that robust (but fair) criticism of politicians and government officials is not misconstrued as false or fake news and suppressed as such. For African states, tightly drafted laws are crucial to ensure the promotion of accountability, transparency, good governance and democratic values and principles.[60] As noted by Robert Keohane: 'rulers generally dislike being held accountable. Yet they often have reasons to submit to accountability mechanisms. In a democratic ... system, accountability may be essential to maintaining public confidence ... But we can expect power holders to seek to avoid accountability when they can do so without jeopardizing other goals'.[61] When it comes to elections, accountability is even more pressing, because as Agnès Callamard has observed, state accountability is

[54] Schauer, *Free Speech* (n 38) pp. 81–82.

[55] Vincent Blasi, 'The Checking Value in First Amendment Theory' (1977) 2(3) *American Bar Foundation Research Journal* 521, at 527–28; Vincent Blasi, 'The First Amendment and the Ideal of Civic Courage: The Brandeis Opinion in *Whitney* v. *California*' (1988) 29(4) *William and Mary Law Review* 653, referred to with approval by Ngcobo J, in *The Citizen 1978 (Pty) Ltd* v. *McBride* [142].

[56] Blasi's article, 'The Checking Value in First Amendment Theory', written in 1977, refers to incidents like Watergate and the Vietnam War.

[57] Kent Greenawalt, 'Free Speech Justifications' (1989) 89(1) *Columbia Law Review* 119, at 142.

[58] S v. *Mamabolo (E-tv Intervening)*.

[59] Ibid. [37].

[60] Callamard, 'Accountability' (n 51), at 1212.

[61] Robert O. Keohane, 'Abuse of Power, Assessing Accountability in World Politics' 2005 (27) *Harvard International Review* 48–53, quoted by Callamard, 'Accountability' (n 51), at 1213.

impossible 'without a fully functioning parliament and free and fair elections, all of which require respect for freedom of ... expression, transparency, [and] freedom of information'.[62] A free and robust media is an added safeguard for state accountability. False news laws which include the media in their ambit have a chilling effect on freedom of expression and the ability of the media to report and investigate freely and without fear of sanction. Similarly, they hamper the capacity of citizens to participate democratically, contribute to decision-making and enrich democratic pluralism.[63]

It is now necessary to move to African regional law, noting upfront that the African Commission on Human and Peoples Rights (the African Commission) has repeatedly stressed the importance of freedom of expression and the role of the media, both as a human right and to achieve state accountability. Indeed, it has also emphasized that freedom of expression and the right of access to information held by public bodies promotes public transparency, accountability, good governance and the strengthening of democracy.[64]

12.4 FREEDOM OF EXPRESSION AND DEMOCRATIC PRINCIPLES IN AFRICAN REGIONAL LAW

This section commences with an explanation of how the African Charter protects the free flow of information and freedom of expression. The textual limitations to the rights are also addressed. It then moves to the work done by the African Commission and the African Court on Human and Peoples' Rights (the African Court), including sub-regional courts, to advance the right to freedom of expression and a free media, focusing on the link between expression and the advancement of democratic governance.

12.4.1 *The African Charter*

Article 9(1) of the African Charter[65] provides that every individual has the right to receive information.[66] Article 9(2) goes on to provide every individual with the right

[62] Callamard, 'Accountability' (n 51), at 1214. See too, more recently, Agnès Callamard, 'Challenges to, and Manifesto for, Fact-Finding in a Time of Disinformation' (2020) 10(2) *Notre Dame Journal of International Comparative Law* 128; Wasserman, 'Fake News from Africa' (n 25), at 8–9.

[63] See, *Print Media SA* v. *Films and Publications Board* [23]; *S* v. *Mamabolo (E-tv Intervening)* [70]; *R* v. *Keegstra* [105], [293], [301] and [322] (a criminal sanction for hate speech would have a chilling effect on expression in Canada).

[64] The African Commission was established in terms of Article 30 of the African Charter. Its mandate is to promote human and peoples rights and to advance their protection in Africa. Complaints (or communications) may be submitted by individuals, NGOs or states parties to the Charter.

[65] South Africa ratified the Charter on 9 June 1996.

[66] The African Commission on Human and Peoples' Rights released a Model Law on Access to Information for Africa on 12 April 2013, https://achpr.au.int/en/node/873.

to express and disseminate opinions within the constraints of the law. Whilst Article 9(2) recognizes that the right to freedom of expression can be limited, the 'within the constraints of the law clause' has caused difficulty. It has, however, been interpreted to mean that only domestic restrictions consistent with state parties' international and Charter obligations are permissible.[67] This means that laws enacted to regulate disinformation must comply with the standard legitimacy and proportionality tests for limitations to freedom of expression in international law, both offline and on digital platforms.[68]

The African Charter, however, does not contain limitation clauses as in most international human rights law instruments.[69] Nevertheless, Article 9 of the Charter must be read with Article 27(2), which provides that all rights and freedoms are to be exercised with due regard for the 'rights of others, collective security, morality and common interest'. This is a general limitation clause.[70] Arguably, false news laws could be introduced to protect the rights of others, the collective security, morality and the common interest, although, as mentioned, any restrictions to Charter rights must also comply with binding international law.[71]

Article 29 of the African Charter, known as the 'duty clause', can also limit freedom of expression. Article 29(4) is the most relevant and places a duty on individuals to conserve and enforce national harmony. Article 29(3) imposes a duty on individuals not to compromise state security, and Article 29(7) provides that individuals should respect African cultural values in their interactions. The totality of these duties entails that individuals should contribute towards the integrity of society and respect diversity and tolerance. To the extent that the dissemination of false news does not further these goals, it could conceivably be prohibited by Article 29, but within the parameters of relevant international law.[72]

67 Sometimes called the 'claw-back clause', see *Constitutional Rights Project and Civil Liberties Organisation* v. *Nigeria, African Commission on Human and Peoples' Rights* Comm. No. 102/93 (1998); *Article 19* v. *the State of Eritrea, African Commission on Human and Peoples' Rights* Comm No. 275/ 2003 (2007).

68 See, generally, the law that has developed under the International Convention on the Elimination of All Forms of Racial Discrimination (ICERD), adopted and opened for signature and ratification by UN General Assembly Resolution 2106 (XX) of 21 December 1965, entered into force in 1969 and the International Covenant on Civil and Political Rights (ICCPR), adopted by the UN General Assembly Resolution 2200A (XXI) of 6 December 1966 and entered into force in 1976.

69 ICCPR, Arts. 19 and 20; ICERD, Art. 4.

70 Christof Heyns, 'Civil and Political Rights in the African Charter' in Malcolm D. Evans and Rachel Murray (eds.), *The African Charter on Human and Peoples' Rights: The System in Practice*, 1986–2000 (Cambridge: Cambridge University Press, 2004) p. 140.

71 But see *Scanlen and Holderness* v. *Zimbabwe* Comm. 297/2005, African Court (3 April 2009) – a false news law was declared invalid. See the discussion in Section 12.4.3.

72 Ibid. The ICCPR requires that restrictions must: (a) be 'provided by law'; (b) serve a narrow, specified list of 'legitimate aims' and (c) be proportionate and 'necessary'. The last requirement means that interferences with expression must be proportionate to the legitimate aim pursued and that there must be no less intrusive measure available.

12.4.2 *The Normative Framework Created by the African Commission*

Despite these potential limitations to freedom of expression in the Charter, the Commission has repeatedly emphasized that freedom of expression advances democratic principles. For example, in 1989, in one of its earliest Communications, the Commission stated that expression is a fundamental human right, vital for an individual's self-development, political consciousness and participation in public affairs.[73] In its 2002 Declaration of Principles on Freedom of Expression in Africa, which developed the scope and content of Article 9, the Commission affirmed that freedom of expression is a 'fundamental and inalienable human right and an indispensable component of a democracy', and that any interference with freedom of expression 'must not be arbitrary, must be provided for by law, must serve a legitimate interest and be necessary in a democratic society'.[74]

The Declaration treats press and media freedom as vital and recommends self-regulation as the best system for promoting high media standards (Principle IX). The broadcast media may be more strictly regulated than print media,[75] but such regulation must comply with the legitimate restrictions for freedom of expression in international law. Thus, Principle V of the Declaration stresses that '[s]tates shall encourage a diverse, independent private broadcasting sector. A State monopoly over broadcasting is not compatible with the right to freedom of expression'. Where self-regulation has been futile, Principle VII permits public authorities to exercise limited media regulation, if they do not operate in a quasi-judicial manner and remain independent of state control.[76]

In 2004, at its thirty-sixth Ordinary Session in Senegal, the Commission established a Special Rapporteur of Freedom of Expression in Africa.[77] The Commission has constantly renewed the mandate of the Special Rapporteur and extended it to include 'Access to Information'.[78] Since then, the Rapporteur has played a

[73] *Media Rights Agenda* v. *Nigeria* Comm. Nos. 105/93, 130/94, 128/94 and 152/96 (31 October 1998), [52].

[74] Declaration of Principles on Freedom of Expression in Africa, African Commission of Human and Peoples Rights, 32nd Session, 17–23 October 2002, Banjul, the Gambia, www1.umn.edu/humanrts/achpr/expressionfreedomdec.html. Freedom of expression and press freedom also features in the New Partnership for Africa's Development (NEPAD) Declaration on Democracy. Signed in Nigeria in 2003, the Declaration provides that African states must 'ensure responsible freedom of expression, inclusive of freedom of the press'.

[75] Given the limited available radio spectrums in Africa at the time.

[76] Callamard, 'Accountability' (n 51) at 1219.

[77] https://achpr.au.int/en/mechanisms/special-rapporteur-freedom-expression-and-access-information.

[78] At the 42nd Ordinary Session of the Commission. The mandate of the Special Rapporteur was extended in 2022; see African Commission Res. 528 (LXXIII) 2022.

prominent role in advancing the soft law normative standards for the protection of freedom of expression and access to information in Africa. For example, in 2012 and in 2016 the Commission modified the 2002 Declaration to address the right of access to information and freedom of expression in the digital age. It also adopted a Model Law on Access to Information for Africa, plus Guidelines on Access to Information and Elections in Africa, in 2013 and 2017, respectively.[79]

In 2019, again led by the Rapporteur, the Commission adopted a revised Declaration of Principles on Freedom of Expression and Access to Information in Africa.[80] The aim was to consolidate the developments on freedom of expression and access to information, guided by African and international human rights standards, including the jurisprudence of African judicial bodies.[81] The revised Declaration has five parts, which include general principles and specific principles on freedom of expression and access to information respectively. The Preamble notes that the protection of freedom of expression and the free flow of information and ideas, especially through print, broadcast media and the Internet, is directly linked to facilitating and strengthening democracy. In turn, a strong democracy fosters transparency and efficiency. States parties must also create a framework which promotes freedom of expression and the right of access to information. This includes reviewing criminal restrictions on expression so that they are justified and aligned with international human rights law standards by, inter alia, amending overly broad criminal laws on sedition, insult and the publication of false news. The Commission has also specifically called for the abolition of domestic criminal defamation laws,[82] especially those that target journalists and permit detention as a sanction.

12.4.3 *African Jurisprudence Addressing Speech Restrictions*

The legitimacy of domestic speech restrictions has been addressed head-on by the African Court on Human and Peoples' Rights (the African Court)[83] and the African

[79] Declaration of Principles on Freedom of Expression and Access to Information in Africa 2019, https://achpr.au.int/en/node/902; Model Law on Access to Information for Africa 2013, https://achpr.au.int/en/node/873; Guidelines on Access to Information and Elections in Africa, https://achpr.au.int/en/node/894.

[80] Declaration of Principles on Freedom of Expression and Access to Information in Africa 2019 (n 79).

[81] Simiyu, 'Freedom of Expression' (n 4), at 87.

[82] African Commission, Res. 169 (XLVIII) 2010, Resolution on Repealing Criminal Defamation Laws in Africa (24 November 2010).

[83] See, for example, *Kenneth Good* v. *the Republic of Botswana* 313/05 African Court (26 May 2010). The victim was expelled from Botswana after publishing an academic paper criticizing the respondent's government. The African Court confirmed the decision of the African Commission in *Amnesty International* v. *Zambia* (2000) AHRLR 325 (ACHPR 1999), [54] and the European Court of Human Rights in *Handyside* v. *United Kingdom* (1976) 1 EHRR 737, at 754, where it was held that freedom of expression is a fundamental human right and necessary for a democracy. The African Court held further that in an open and

Commission in two important cases, namely *Scanlen and Holderness* v. *Zimbabwe*[84] and *Konaté* v. *Burkina Faso*.[85] The complainants in *Scanlen* alleged that Zimbabwe's Access to Information and Protection of Privacy Act, 2003[86] infringed Article 9(2) of the African Charter, because it required the accreditation of journalists and created the offence of 'publication of falsehoods'. Referring to the 2002 Declaration, the African Court held that whilst freedom of expression may be limited by domestic laws aimed at protecting individuals and the public from journalistic practices deviating from legitimate interests in a democracy, such laws must conform to international law standards.[87] Zimbabwe's contention that the registration of journalists and the criminalization of falsehoods were justified on the grounds of public order, safety and the protection of the rights and reputation of others was rejected and held to be an unjustified restriction of freedom of expression.[88]

In *Konaté*,[89] the applicant, a newspaper editor, was charged with criminal defamation. The applicant had published articles in which he accused the Prosecutor of Burkina Faso of corruption and criminal activity. The applicant was convicted on all charges and sentenced to twelve months' imprisonment, plus a hefty fine.[90] After analysing Burkina Faso's criminal defamation laws, the African Court declared that the domestic law criminalizing defamation with a custodial sentence violated Article 9 of the Charter, Article 19 of the International Covenant on Civil and Political Rights (ICCPR) and Article 66(2) of the Revised Treaty of the Economic Community of West African States (ECOWAS).[91] The Court found that Burkina Faso had not demonstrated that imprisonment was a necessary limitation to freedom of expression to protect the reputation of legal officers. It also held that apart from 'serious and very exceptional circumstances' involving incitement to crimes or hate speech, 'violations of laws on freedom of speech and the press cannot be sanctioned by custodial sentences'.[92] Burkina Faso's legislation[93] thus constituted

democratic society, such as that in Botswana, dissenting and potential offensive views must be 'allowed to flourish'. Botswana had accordingly infringed Article 9(2), see [197]–[199].

84 *Scanlen and Holderness* v. *Zimbabwe*.

85 *Konaté* v. *Burkina Faso* Comm. 004/2013 African Court (5 December 2014). See also ACHPR Resolution 169 on Repealing Criminal Defamation Laws in Africa, adopted by the African Commission on Human and Peoples' Rights, 48th Session (10–24 November 2010) Banjul, the Gambia.

86 Sections 79 and 80.

87 *Scanlen and Holderness* v. *Zimbabwe* [107] and [116].

88 Ibid. [117].

89 *Konaté* v. *Burkina Faso* [164].

90 Ibid. [3]–[8].

91 Revised Treaty of the Economic Community of West African States, 24 July 1993, www.refworld.org/docid/492182d92.html.

92 *Konaté* v. *Burkina Faso* [136]–[137].

93 The Information Code of Burkina Faso of 1993, the Penal Code of Burkina Faso of 1996. See *Konaté* v. *Burkina Faso* [120].

a disproportionate interference with a journalist's right to freedom of expression.[94] This decision illustrates that criminal prosecution and imprisonment for alleged defamation of public officials is neither a 'necessary' nor 'proportionate' state interference with freedom of expression, because less intrusive measures are available for remedying injuries to individual reputation, namely civil defamation remedies.[95] The same principles apply to false news laws, as held in *Scanlen*.

More recently, in 2018, the Community Court of Justice of the Economic Community of West African States (the ECOWAS Court) decided *Federation of African Journalists* v. *The Gambia*.[96] The case was launched by the Federation (representing Gambian journalists broadly) and four Gambian journalists (forced into exile).[97] The journalists had been prosecuted and tortured whilst in custody for violating the Gambia's press laws, specifically speech criticizing the President and officials. The applicants asked for a declaration that the criminal offences of sedition, false news and defamation in the Gambian Criminal Code[98] violated the right to freedom of expression in Article 9 of the African Charter, Article 19 of the ICCPR and the rights of journalists under Article 66(2) of the Revised ECOWAS Treaty.[99] The basis of the journalists' complaint was that the Gambian laws had made it impossible for them to disseminate information in the public interest freely.[100] They claimed that the laws had a chilling effect on press freedom by creating a fear of potential arrest and prosecution for publishing information critiquing the government. Whilst acknowledging that limitations to freedom of expression are permissible, the journalists also argued that the laws were imprecise and overly

94 *Konaté* v. *Burkina Faso* [136]–[137] and [164]. In 2010, the African Commission published a resolution that criminal defamation laws should be repealed. See Resolution 169: On Repealing Criminal Defamation Laws in Africa, adopted by the Commission at its 48th Session, November 2010, Banjul, the Gambia.

95 See generally Hawley Johnson, 'Lohé Issa Konaté v. Burkina Faso: A Tipping Point for Decriminalization of Defamation in Africa' in Lee C. Bollinger and Agnès Callamard (eds.), *Regardless of Frontiers: Global Freedom of Expression in a Troubled World* (New York: Columbia University Press, 2021) 357.

96 *Federation of African Journalists* v. *The Gambia* ECW/CCJ/JUD/04/18. See also *Hydara* v. *The Gambia* ECW/CCJ/APP/30/11 where the ECOWAS Court held that states must 'protect media practitioners including those critical of the regime', as freedom of expression includes criticism of the government.

97 An international coalition comprising Amnesty International, Article 19 and others filed an intervention, as did the Redress Trust and the UN Special Rapporteur on the Freedom of Opinion and Expression.

98 Gambian Criminal Code 2009, ss. 51, 52, 52A, 59, 173A, 179, 180, 181 and 181A.

99 They also argued that the detention and torture they experienced infringed their right to liberty and security under Art. 6 of the African Charter and Art. 9 of the ICCPR. An order was sought order compelling the Gambia to repeal the impugned laws or to amend them to comply with its international obligations. The journalists also asked for reparations and relief for the torture experienced in custody.

100 They also submitted that 'the fear of being re-arrested, prosecuted and tortured . . . forced them to remain in exile', *Federation of African Journalists* v. *The Gambia*, p. 32.

broad.[101] Regarding the false news offence specifically, the journalists accepted that journalistic errors can occur, but claimed that the imposition of criminal liability for such errors infringed the right to freedom of expression[102] and that the law did not serve a legitimate purpose.[103]

The ECOWAS Court analysed comparative international and foreign law on the right to freedom of expression and freedom of the press, stressing that vague criminal offences undermine the enjoyment of the right.[104] It used this jurisprudence to hold that narrowly drafted criminal offences were needed to regulate free speech because of the 'chilling effect' created by wide and vague censorship restrictions. Holding that erroneous statements are inevitable in free debate, the Court relied on *Konaté* to find that individuals in 'highly visible public roles must necessarily face a higher degree of criticism than private citizens; otherwise public debate may be stifled altogether'.[105] The Court concluded that the criminal laws of the Gambia, which included a false news offence, did not guarantee a free press in accordance with the African Charter and international law. The laws had a chilling effect, unduly restricted expression and the press and were disproportionate and unnecessary 'in a democratic society where freedom of speech is a guaranteed right'.[106] The Court thus ordered that the impugned laws be reviewed and decriminalized to conform with freedom of expression.[107]

The decisions in *Federation of African Journalists* and *Konaté* were confirmed in 2020 by the ECOWAS Court in *Incorporated Trustees of Laws and Rights Awareness*

[101] Specifically, sedition which assessed subjective reactions and the broad definition of defamatory material.

[102] See *Federation of African Journalists* v. *The Gambia*, pp. 33–34.

[103] The journalists pointed to the definitions of 'seditious intent' (s. 51), 'defamatory material' (s. 179), 'publication for purposes of criminal libel' (s. 180(2)) and 'false news publication' (s. 59) as being vague, too broad and illegitimate. See ibid. pp. 34 and 38–39.

[104] It referred to General Comment No. 34 published by the UNHRC, which describes a free and uncensored media as the 'bedrock of a democratic society'; *Ramlila Maidan Incident* v. *Home Secretary Union of India* (2012) S SCC 1, the Indian Court calling freedom of expression 'the mother of all liberties'; and the European Court of Human Rights decisions in *Castells* v. *Spain*, app. no. 11798/85 (1992); *Lingens* v. *Austria*, app. no. 9815/82 (1986); *Altuğ Taner Akçam* v. *Turkey*, app. no. 27520/07 (2011) and *Otegi Mondragon* v. *Spain*, app. no. 2034/07 (2018). Regard was also had to *New York Times* v. *Sullivan* 376 US 254, the Zimbabwean case of *Madanhire* v. *Attorney General* Judgment No. CCZ 2/14 (an overly broad criminal defamation offence, which stifled the free flow of information in the public domain) and the judgment in *Konaté*.

[105] *Federation of African Journalists* v. *The Gambia*, p. 46.

[106] Ibid. pp. 47–48.

[107] Ibid. p. 48. Note that UNESCO and the ECOWAS Court signed a Memorandum of Understanding to strengthen freedom of expression, press freedom and safety of journalists in West Africa in 2019. There have been ongoing attempts in the region to promote press freedom and democratic governance. See 'MFWA Engages ECOWAS on Press Freedom, Media Development in West Africa', www.mfwa.org/issues-in-focus/mfwa-engages-ecowas-on-press-freedom-media-development-in-west-africa.

Initiatives v. *The Federal Republic of Nigeria*.[108] Here, the Court held that a criminal sanction in the Nigerian Cybercrime Act 2015, penalizing expression offensive to 'honour', reputation and morals, violated the African Charter as being a disproportionate restriction to freedom of expression.[109]

12.4.4 *The Relationship between Freedom of Expression and Democratic Governance*

The most recent development emanating from the African Commission on the link between media freedom and democratic principles is a September 2023 statement by the Special Rapporteur that '[t]he right to access information is … a key component of democracy, … when people are able to access information about how their Government is performing, they can exercise their right to freedom of expression more meaningfully. Individuals need to have access to reliable sources … to form an accurate opinion'. The Rapporteur added that the information right is both a human right and an indispensable tool empowering citizens to participate publicly and demand state accountability. The role of the media is essential. Accordingly, the Rapporteur recommends that states adopt laws guaranteeing the right of every individual 'to receive information' as per the African Charter, because despite efforts to protect the expression and information rights, African domestic law does not facilitate such rights.[110]

Non-compliance at domestic level occurs even though Article 13 of the African Charter provides that every citizen shall have the right to participate freely in the government of their country, either directly or through freely chosen representatives in accordance with the law. Moreover, the African Charter on Democracy, Elections and Governance declares that regular, free and fair elections are the basis of a legitimate government.[111] The Democracy Charter specifically emphasises the link between the promotion of democracy, the rule of law and human rights, including free expression.[112] The rationale of the Guidelines on Access to

[108] *Incorporated Trustees of Laws and Rights Awareness Initiatives* v. *The Federal Republic of Nigeria* [2020] ECOWASCJ 6.

[109] Ibid. [163] and [164].

[110] See https://achpr.au.int/index.php/en/news/press-releases/2023-09-28/statement-special-rapporteur-freedom-expression-and-access-infor. See also African Union Convention on Cyber Security and Personal Data Protection, 27 June 2014 (Ex.CL/846(XXV), https://au.int/en/treaties/african-union-convention-cyber-security-and-personal-data-protection. Chapter 3 of the so-called Malabo Convention deals with cyber security and cybercrime. South Africa has not ratified the Convention because of clashes between it and the Protection of Personal Information Act; however, it implemented many of its aspects by regulating electronic communications and cybercrimes.

[111] See https://au.int/en/treaties/african-charter-democracy-elections-and-governance.

[112] Guarantees for freedom of expression are also provided in the African Democracy Charter. These call for the necessary conditions to ensure participation, transparency, access to information, freedom of the press and accountability in public affairs.

Information and Elections in Africa, published by the African Commission in 2017, states the need to ensure freedom of expression and access to information during elections.[113] Including within their ambit a wide range of public bodies, such as political parties, election observers, the media and internet intermediaries, the Guidelines record that disclosure of information enabling the public to participate actively in public affairs is needed, plus transparency and accountability.[114] The Preface notes the importance of 'access to accurate, credible and reliable information'. This is reinforced by Section 25 which provides that regulatory bodies must enact regulations to promote 'fair and balanced coverage of the electoral process', whether offline or in the digital space. Internet shutdowns are also addressed, with the Guidelines calling on states not to block the Internet or restrict media freedom during elections.[115] Should restrictions be needed, their legitimacy will be tested against the international standard of legality, legitimacy, necessity and proportionality for the limitations of rights.[116]

12.5 INSTANCES OF FALSE NEWS DISSEMINATION AND ITS REGULATION IN DOMESTIC AFRICAN STATES

Despite the strong normative framework for the protection of freedom of expression and the press at regional level, most African states continue to regulate false news, mainly through criminal sanctions. Internet shutdowns are also frequently implemented. Another reality is the repeated political manipulation of information, often with the assistance of powerful actors, aimed at retaining power and control of public finances.[117] These campaigns make it increasingly difficult for the public to discern the truth, which undermines the ability to make decisions (whether personally or in relation to public matters) and to participate in democratic processes in an informed manner.[118]

Research conducted by the African Centre for Strategic Studies from 2020 to 2022 has revealed a vast array of disinformation schemes in African states, especially on digital and social media platforms.[119] Those responsible for the dissemination of this 'information' include political parties, individual politicians and state and non-state

[113] Guidelines on Access to Information and Elections in Africa (n 79).

[114] Ibid. 'Objectives and Rationales'. See for detail, Simiyu, 'Freedom of Expression' (n 4), at 89.

[115] Guidelines on Access to Information and Elections in Africa (n 79) s. 26.

[116] Ibid. ss. 27 and 28.

[117] Jean-Claude Kouladoum, 'The Role of Freedom of Communication in Modulating the Effect of Political Participation on Electoral Outcome in Africa' (2023) 51(4) *Politics & Policy* 588.

[118] Scott Timcke, Liz Orembo and Hanani Hlomani, 'Information Disorders in Africa: An Annotated Bibliography of Selected Countries', Research ICT Africa, 2023, https://researchictafrica.net/publication/information-disorders-in-africa-an-annotated-bibliography-of-selected-countries.

[119] See 'Mapping Disinformation in Africa', African Centre for Strategic Studies, April 2022, https://africacenter.org/spotlight/mapping-disinformation-in-africa. See too Jan Rydzak, Moses Karanja and Nicholas Opiyo, 'Dissent Does Not Die in Darkness: Network Shutdowns and

actors from beyond Africa (who create, inter alia, fake social media accounts, hashtags and messages designed to boost the support of leaders sympathetic and amenable to the actor or state's particular cause).[120] This research and many other studies show that the target countries include Nigeria,[121] Kenya,[122] Ghana, Mali, Cameroon,[123] Tanzania, Ethiopia,[124] Guinea[125] and Sudan,[126] amongst others.[127]

It is therefore not surprising that many African states have either enacted false news laws or made use of the existing common law colonial-era crimes of

Collective Action in African Countries' (2020) 14 *International Journal of Communication* 4264; Tina Freyburg and Lisa Garbe, 'Blocking the Bottleneck: Internet Shutdowns and Ownership at Election Times in Sub-Saharan Africa' (2018) 12 *International Journal of Communication* 3896; Lisa Garbe, Lisa-Marie Selvik and Pauline Lemaire, 'How African Countries Respond to Fake News and Hate Speech' (2021) 26(1) *Information, Communication & Society* 86. The authors report that fake news and hate speech is highly regulated in African countries (forty-seven African countries were included in the study), and conclude that the state is the main driver of content creation.

120 'Mapping Disinformation in Africa' (n 119).

121 Charles M. Fombad, 'Democracy and Fake News in Africa' (2022) 9(1) *Journal of International and Comparative Law* 131, at 142, stating that the British firm Cambridge Analytica has 'gained notoriety in Africa for their dubious campaign practices during elections using social media platforms in Kenya and Nigeria'.

122 See Ekdale and Tully 'African Elections' (n 5). The study reveals interference by Cambridge Analytica in the Kenyan and Nigerian elections. Conclusions reached are that African elections create platforms for proxy wars between global interests and that whilst both countries have passed data protection laws, they do not regulate the interference of foreign actors in the elections. Re Kenya specifically, see Patrick Mutahi, 'Fake News and the 2017 Kenyan Elections' (2020) 46(4) *Communication: South African Journal of Communication Theory and Research* 31.

123 See Kingsley Ngange and Moki S. Mokondo, 'Understanding Social Media's Role in Propagating Falsehood in Conflict Situations: Case of the Cameroon Anglophone Crisis' (2019) 7(2) *Studies in Media and Communication* 55. In 2017 the Cameroon government blamed social media for spreading false news, and aggravating tensions between different sections of the population. See also Christian Nounkeu, 'Facebook and Fake News in the "Anglophone Crisis" in Cameroon' (2020) 41(3) *African Journalism Studies* 20.

124 Iginio Gagliardone, Nicole Stremlau and Gerawork Aynekulu, 'A Tale of Two Publics? Online Politics in Ethiopia's Elections' (2019) 13(1) *Journal of Eastern African Studies* 191; the authors monitored the 2005 and 2015 election cycles in Ethiopia, and tracked the role of digital networks and the authoritarian state's attempts to influence online public spaces. Professional election campaign consultants were used to enable bloggers, influencers and bots to shape public opinion.

125 Rydzak, Karanja and Opiyo, 'Dissent Does Not Die'. Although Guinea's first shutdown was in 2007, the 2011 Arab Spring revolutions resulted in many state authorities implementing shutdowns. By June 2019, twenty-six countries had implemented shutdowns. The shutdown orders usually emanated from the highest government authorities.

126 Siri Lamoureaux and Timm Sureau, 'Knowledge and Legitimacy: The Fragility of Digital Mobilization in Sudan' (2019) 13(1) *Journal of Eastern African Studies* 34. The Sudanese government used digital mechanisms, supplemented by a call to morality, to preserve national security and to silence critics.

127 Re sub-Saharan African countries, see Freyburg and Garbe, 'Blocking the Bottleneck', reporting a strong connection between state ownership of internet service providers and internet shutdowns over thirty-three presidential and parliamentary elections in sub-Saharan Africa between 2014 and 2016.

defamation and libel to punish the dissemination of information considered misleading or false.[128] Unfortunately, African false news laws are also usually framed in broad terms and criminalize, inter alia, the spreading of false rumours, insults and complaints against government or public authorities; the fostering of dissent and unrest between sections of the community through the publication of false news; and the uttering of hate speech designed to incite hatred, violence or any type of disturbance on grounds such as race, religion and ethnicity.[129] Most of these laws are justified to protect national security and social harmony.

The irony of such regulation, however, is that the targets are usually journalists and those critical of authoritarian governments, the real aim being to silence opposition and to enable existing regimes to maintain political control. The consequence is a severe impact on democratic principles in African states,[130] which Charles Fombad has labelled the 'crisis of democracy in Africa'.[131] Fombad claims that

> Many recent elections ... have degenerated into little more than competitive authoritarianism. This is because democratic reforms and periodic elections of the past two decades have come to be increasingly used as a 'survival strategy' by Africa's autocratic rulers. Elections ... come in handy to keep opposition parties in the political game, lest the regimes lose their democratic façade while incumbents perpetuate their rule.[132]

There are some African states, however, which have adopted freedom of information laws that enhance expression, press freedom and democratic principles. These include Namibia, Botswana and Zambia.[133] But, as demonstrated in Section 12.6, South Africa is the outlier, with the Constitutional Court using the Bill of Rights in South Africa's Constitution, 1996, to protect and promote freedom of expression, political rights and democratic governance, even in the face of

[128] See generally Simiyu, 'Freedom of Expression' (n 4), at 76; Wasserman and Madrid-Morales, 'Exploratory Study' (n 4); Fombad, 'Democracy and Fake News in Africa' (n 121), at 145–47.

[129] The COVID-19 pandemic aggravated the situation, with many states using fake news laws to overcome the disquiet caused by vaccination rumourmongering, undermining the measures governments were taking to control the pandemic.

[130] See Max Grömping and Ferran Martínez i Coma, 'Electoral Integrity in Africa', Electoral Integrity Project, 2015, www.electoralintegrityproject.com/electoral-integrity-in-africa, reporting that the Electoral Integrity Project has conducted research which demonstrates that Africa scores very low on the Perception of Electoral Integrity index, well below the global average. Grömping has conducted ongoing research in this field. See also Nicholas Kerr and Anna Lührmann, 'Public Trust in Elections: The Role of Media Freedom and Election Management Autonomy', Afrobarometer, 2017, www.afrobarometer.org/wp-content/uploads/migrated/files/publications/Working%20papers/afropaperno170_public_trust_in_elections.pdf.

[131] Fombad, 'Democracy and Fake News in Africa' (n 121), at 133.

[132] Ibid. at 133–34.

[133] Namibia passed the Access to Information Bill into law in 2022. In December 2014, a Zambian High Court declared s. 67 of the Penal Code unconstitutional because it prohibited the publication of false news.

attempts to silence the press and state condemnation of the courts for interfering in executive matters.

12.6 THE SOUTH AFRICAN LAW

This section will address the way in which freedom of expression and the right to free and fair elections are protected in South African law. Starting with the constitutional framework setting the normative benchmarks for the relevant rights and their legitimate restriction, how South Africa regulates false news is then explained. It will be shown that despite many attempts by the state to stifle media freedom, the South African judiciary has consistently endorsed and promoted a free flow of information and debate (both generally and during elections). This approach is informed by the need to protect the status of the constitutional democracy and open and accountable governance, which underpins the Constitution, and stands in stark contrast to the apartheid approach, where state censorship was rife.

12.6.1 *The Constitutional Protection of Freedom of Expression*

Section 16 of the South African Constitution entrenches the right to freedom of expression. It provides:

16. Freedom of Expression

(1) Everyone has the right to freedom of expression, which includes –
- a) freedom of the press and other media;
- b) freedom to receive or impart information or ideas;
- c) freedom of artistic creativity;
- d) academic freedom and freedom of scientific research.

(2) The right in sub-section (1) does not extend to –
- a) propaganda for war;
- b) incitement of imminent violence;
- c) advocacy of hatred that is based on race, ethnicity, gender or religion, and that constitutes incitement to cause harm.

The South African courts have confirmed the value of freedom of expression in a democratic society on many occasions. For example, in *South African National Defence Force Union* v. *Minister of Defence*[134] Judge O'Regan held that expression plays a significant role as 'a guarantor of democracy' and facilitates the 'moral agency' of society, permitting individuals to form and express opinions and ideas.[135] Nevertheless, freedom of expression is not an absolute guarantee; nor is it a paramount value.[136] It is one of a 'web of mutually supporting

[134] *South African National Defence Force Union* v. *Minister of Defence* 1999 (4) SA 469 (CC), [7].
[135] See also *Print Media SA* v. *Films and Publications Board* [53].
[136] *S* v. *Mamabolo (E-tv Intervening)* [41]; *Khumalo* v. *Holomisa* [25].

rights',[137] and must be interpreted in accordance with constitutional values[138] and other constitutionally protected rights, including the rights to human dignity[139] and to participate in free and fair elections.[140] It should also be exercised with 'due deference' to 'the pursuit of national unity and reconciliation'.[141]

The ambit of Section 16(1) is broad. The word 'everyone' includes natural and juristic persons,[142] citizens and non-citizens.[143] 'Expression' is protected, which is a wider concept than 'speech'.[144] The Constitutional Court's approach to freedom of expression cases is to define expression widely at the threshold stage, deferring the adjudication of the value of the expressive act in question to the limitation analysis in terms of Section 36 of the Constitution.[145] Therefore, in *De Reuck* v. *Director of Public Prosecutions (WLD)*,[146] finding that child pornography was included within the ambit of expression, the Court held that the right 'does not warrant a narrow reading' and that any limitation 'must satisfy the rigours of the limitation analysis'.[147] Confirming *Handyside* v. *United Kingdom*,[148] the Court found that the right to express oneself and the corresponding right to receive information and ideas extends 'not only to "information" or "ideas" that are favourably received or regarded as inoffensive or as a matter of indifference but also to those that offend, shock or disturb'.[149] The wide interpretation of 'expression' means that the right has many components.[150] So, expressive acts such as flag burning, nude dancing,[151] the publication of photographs, the display of posters and works of art, dress[152] and

[137] *Case* v. *Minister of Safety and Security; Curtis* v. *Minister of Safety and Security* 1996 (3) SA 617 (CC), [27].
[138] Constitution, S1. South Africa is declared to be a sovereign and democratic state based on various founding values including human dignity, equality, non-racialism, non-sexism and the advancement of human rights and freedoms and the rule of law.
[139] Constitution, s. 10.
[140] Constitution s. 19.
[141] *The Citizen 1978 (Pty) Ltd* v. *McBride* 2011 (4) SA 191 (CC), [233]; *Qwelane* v. *SAHRC* 2021 (6) SA 579 (CC).
[142] *Ex Parte Chairperson of Constitutional Assembly: In re Certification of Constitution of the RSA* 1996 (4) SA 744 (CC), [57].
[143] *Khosa* v. *Minister of Social Development; Mahlaule* v. *Minister of Social Development* 2004 (6) SA 505 (CC), [47].
[144] Interim Constitution, s. 15(1), provided that every person had a right to 'freedom of speech and expression'.
[145] The General Limitation Clause.
[146] *De Reuck* v. *Director of Public Prosecutions (WLD)* 2004 (1) SA 406 (CC).
[147] Ibid. [48]–[50].
[148] *Handyside* v. *United Kingdom*.
[149] *De Reuck* v. *Director of Public Prosecutions (WLD)* [49], quoting *Handyside* v. *United Kingdom*.
[150] *Phillips* v. *Director of Public Prosecutions (WLD)* 2003 (3) SA 345 (CC), [23].
[151] Ibid. [15].
[152] *MEC for Education: KwaZulu-Natal* v. *Pillay* 2008 (1) SA 474 (CC), [94] – prohibition of a nose stud limited the right to express one's religion and culture.

symbolic gestures (such as salutes)[153] are included within expression and are prima facie worthy of constitutional protection.

It is only during the later proportionality enquiry that the value of the expression in issue is considered to determine the justifiable limitation of the right to free expression. Here, the Court must assess whether the expressive act promotes the rationales underpinning the right and distinguishes between expression that lies at the 'periphery' of the right as opposed to expression which unworthy of protection. In *De Reuck*, for example, the Court had no difficulty in holding that child pornography was 'expression of little value'.[154]

Section 16(1) enumerates four types of expression which are specifically listed. Whilst these are positioned at the core of the right (as opposed to its periphery), they should not be interpreted as being more valuable than other forms of unspecified expression. The listed categories simply expand upon the meaning of expression. They do not fix the scope of constitutionally protected expression. Other types of expression can also bear equal weight, even though not listed textually. The role played by political expression is clearly important given the emphasis on how free expression protects the democracy.

Freedom of the press and other media is specifically mentioned in Section 16(1)(a) because of the significant role that the media play in ensuring the promotion of a democracy. The South African courts have unfailingly confirmed the media's role in a democratic society.[155] As indicated earlier, in *Print Media* the Court linked press freedom to a functioning democracy. The Court also confirmed that laws limiting press freedom must be closely monitored so as not to undermine the public's right to a strong media. Similarly, in *Mail and Guardian Media Ltd* v. *MJ Chipu NO (Chairperson of the Refugee Appeal Board)*, the Court held that the media is a 'key facilitator' of freedom of expression.[156] There is thus no doubt that media and press freedom is positioned at the core of the right and that laws restricting it will face a stiff challenge in the limitation analysis.

The role of the press and the media, however, is two-dimensional – their right is protected by Section 16(1)(a), but they must also fulfil their duty to society. The Court addressed this in *Khumalo* v. *Holomisa*,[157] holding that the media should not only rely on freedom of expression, but must also 'foster' it, and that people's ability to function effectively in society depends on how the media fulfils its obligations. The media are thus both right bearers and 'bearers of constitutional obligations'.[158]

[153] *Afri-forum* v. *Malema* 2010 (5) SA 235 (GNP), [56] – gestures informed the meaning of the struggle song in issue.

[154] *De Reuck* v. *Director of Public Prosecutions (WLD)* [59].

[155] See *SABC* v. *NDPP* 2007 (1) SA 523 (CC); *Independent Newspapers (Pty) Ltd* v. *Minister for Intelligent Services* 2008 (5) SA 31 (CC).

[156] *Mail and Guardian Media Ltd* v. *MJ Chipu NO (Chairperson of the Refugee Appeal Board* 2013 (6) SA 367 (CC), [52].

[157] *Khumalo* v. *Holomisa*.

[158] Ibid. [22]. But see re the issue of false news reporting ibid. [35] and [108].

Section 16(1)(b) protects the right to receive and impart information and ideas – the dual aspect of expression.[159] This is an integral component of freedom of expression as the reception of information and ideas enables individuals to participate fully in public society, buttressing the constitutional values which envisage a responsive, accountable and open democratic state.[160] Accordingly, in *Islamic Unity Convention* v. *Independent Broadcasting Authority*,[161] the Court found that the Broadcasting Code in issue infringed not only the right of broadcasters to disseminate information, but also deprived the public of the right to receive diverse views.[162]

The distinction between ideas and information is interesting, especially in the context of false news laws. The types of expressive acts classified as 'information' must clearly be distinguished from 'ideas', which term is usually widely defined to include opinions, thoughts, plans, creative works and so on. In *The Citizen 1978 (Pty) Ltd* v. *McBride*,[163] the Court held that 'information' includes 'only factual statements', as opposed to opinions and comments,[164] but this conclusion is debatable, as discussed below. The textual inclusion of 'artistic creativity' as a form of protected expression in Section 16(1)(c) is a consequence of strict censorship during apartheid.[165] The same is true for academic freedom. All forms of art are protected, including music, books, paintings and theatre productions.[166]

An interesting question that the Court may have to determine when dealing with potential 'fake news' cases is whether manipulated photos and their ilk could be classed as artistic expression and thus be positioned at the core of the right. This is because the courts acknowledge that artists play a significant role in society by contributing to the existing dialogue and social debate, usually because their views can be controversial and are critical for the development of a vibrant culture in a

[159] Not to be confused with the right to access to information, protected by s. 32 of the Constitution.

[160] *SABC Ltd* v. *NDPP* [28].

[161] *Islamic Unity Convention* v. *Independent Broadcasting Authority* 2002 (4) SA 294 (CC).

[162] Ibid. [47] and [50].

[163] *The Citizen 1978 (Pty) Ltd* v. *McBride* 2011 (4) SA191 (CC).

[164] Information is usually defined as 'facts provided or learnt' about a 'situation, person or event' and is a 'constituent of knowledge'. See also *Democratic Alliance* v. *African National Congress* 2015 (2) SA 232 (CC), [114] – information means only factual statements and not comments or opinions.

[165] *Islamic Unity Convention* v. *Independent Broadcasting Authority*, [27] – expression was censored in the pre-constitutional era, which is incompatible with South Africa's commitment to the protection of human rights in an open and democratic society. Re academic freedom, see s. 25 of the Universities Act 1995, which permitted the state to impose conditions on the grant of university subsidies. A factor considered was how a university controlled revolutionary and political student activities. See *UCT* v. *Ministers of Education and Culture (House of Assemblies and House of Representatives)* 1988 (3) SA 203 (C), the Court later setting aside the regulations promulgated.

[166] *The Citizen 1978 (Pty) Ltd* v. *McBride*, 27.

democratic and functioning society.[167] Also, artists are often at risk of censorship, probably because their work is displayed in the public domain, engaging society and eliciting diverse reactions.[168]

Section 16(2) lists the types of freedom of expression which are not constitutionally protected, namely propaganda for war, incitement of imminent violence and hate speech (which is strictly defined). The boundaries of the categories of expression excluded from constitutional protection are important, because Section 16(2) is definitional, and the Court has held that legislative measures which restrict expression beyond the scope of constitutional exclusion must be justified in terms of the general limitation clause. However, limitations falling within the strict parameters of Section 16(2) will not limit freedom of expression.[169] Plus, all limitations must be restrictively interpreted.

None of the listed exclusions to protected expression in Section 16(2) include false news regulation. This means that any law enacted to restrict the dissemination of information, whether false or not, will be treated as limiting freedom of expression and require justification in terms of the limitation clause, which is introduced in Section 12.6.3, following an examination of the protection of political rights in the Constitution.

12.6.2 *Political Rights*

Section 19 of the Constitution, headed political rights, reads as follows:

(1) Every citizen is free to make political choices which includes:
  a) the right to form a political party;
  b) to participate in the activities of, or recruit members for, a political party; and
  c) to campaign for a political party or cause.

(2) Every citizen has the right to free, fair and regular elections for any legislative body established in terms of the Constitution.

(3) Every adult citizen has the right:
  a) to vote in elections for any legislative body established in terms of the Constitution, and to do so in secret; and
  b) to stand for public office, and if elected, to hold office.

[167] Report of the Special Rapporteur in the Field of Cultural Rights: The Right to Freedom of Artistic Expression and Creativity, United Nations, 14 March 2013, www.ohchr.org/en/documents/thematic-reports/ahrc2334-report-right-freedom-artistic-expression-and-creation.

[168] The debacle concerned Brett Murray's painting, *The Spear*, exhibited at the Goodman Art Gallery in Johannesburg, depicting President Zuma with exposed genitals, as a satirical parody of the Soviet poster featuring Lenin. It is an excellent example of the role that art plays in the promotion of public debate and critical dialogue. See the Films and Publication Appeal Tribunal judgment in *Goodman Gallery and the Film and Publication Board* (case number 8/2012). For further discussion, see Jaco Barnard-Naude and Pierre De Vos, 'Die politiek van die estetiese in 'n postkoloniale konteks: menswaardigheid en vryheid van uitdrukking in die debat rondom Brett Murray se skildery *The Spear*: regte' (2012) 9(2) *LitNet Akademies* 176.

[169] *Islamic Unity Convention* v. *Independent Broadcasting Authority*, [33] and [34].

This section is complemented by Section 1(d) of the Constitution – which guarantees a multi-party system of democratic government, to ensure accountability, responsiveness and openness.[170] These values were stressed in *My Vote Counts NPC* v. *Minister of Justice and Correctional Services (My Vote Counts 11)*,[171] and arise by virtue of South Africa's history under apartheid, where the majority of South Africans were denied the right to vote.[172]

The political right is cast in generous and unqualified terms. Thus, the Court in *Ramakatsa* v. *Magashule*[173] held that 'the section means what it says … It guarantees freedom to make political choices and … safeguards a member's participation in the activities of the [political] party concerned … It protects the exercise of the right not only against external interference but also against interference arising from within the party'. The right to vote thus upholds the democracy and is linked to human dignity – it is a 'badge of dignity and of personhood'.[174]

Section 19 must be applied and interpreted in its entirety. The Constitutional Court in *NNP* v. *Government of South Africa*[175] held that the right to vote will echo a hollow ring without the right to free, fair and regular elections. As to the meaning of free and fair elections, in *Kham* v. *Electoral Commission*,[176] the Court held that the 'free and fair' requirement is singular and not a conjunction of two disparate elements. The term includes 'both the freedom to participate in the electoral processes and the ability of the political parties and candidates, both aligned and non-aligned, to compete with one another on relatively equal terms'.[177]

In the main, elections in South Africa are contested by political parties – they occupy centre stage and play a vital role in facilitating citizens' political rights.[178] But although political parties have been described as 'the engine of democracy in South Africa', there is little regulation of their internal functioning. Nonetheless, as outlined in *Ramakatsa*, political parties must comply with the Constitution, their

170 Democratic values are stressed through the Constitution, with even the traditional libertarian rights of equality and dignity labelled as 'democratic values'.

171 *My Vote Counts NPC* v. *Minister of Justice and Correctional Services (My Vote Counts 11)* 2018 (5) SA 380 (CC), [31].

172 *Minister of Home Affairs* v. *NICRO* 2005 (3) SA 280 (CC), [47].

173 *Ramakatsa* v. *Magashule* 2013 (2) BCLR 202 (CC), [171].

174 *August* v. *Electoral Commission* 1999 (3) SA 1 (CC), [17] – voting rights were extended to prisoners. Their disqualification from voting because they had been imprisoned without the option of a fine was declared unconstitutional. The Court held that '[i]n a country of great disparities of wealth and power … whoever we are, whether rich or poor, exalted or disgraced, we all belong to the same democratic South African nation'. See also *Ramakatsa* v. *Magashule*, [64] and [65].

175 *NNP* v. *Government of South Africa* 2013 (2) BCLR 202 (CC), [12].

176 *Kham* v. *Electoral Commission* 1999 (3) SA 191 (CC).

177 Ibid. [34].

178 But see *New Nation Movement* v. *President of the RSA* SA 2020 (6) 257 (CC), where the Court permitted an individual to stand as a candidate and declared the Electoral Act 1998 unconstitutional for permitting only political parties to contest elections.

own rules, the Electoral Code of Conduct[179] and the Electoral Commission Act.[180] Most importantly, rules of political parties must be consistent with the Constitution. As discussed in Section 12.6.6. , the Electoral Act regulates the dissemination of false news during elections, the legitimacy of which was raised in the important case of *Democratic Alliance* v. *African National Congress*.[181]

In *My Votes Counts NPC* v. *Minister of Justice and Correctional Services*,[182] the Court had to consider whether voters have a right to know who funds political parties and whether a right to vote includes an 'informed vote'. A related but key question was whether political parties and the state have a duty to record, preserve and disclose the sources of their private funding. This issue required an analysis of whether South Africa's Promotion of Access to Information Act (PAIA)[183] was unconstitutional because it failed to oblige political parties to record and disclose their private funding sources. The Court held that people are entitled to information held by political parties because such information is critical to the fulfilment of the political right, especially the right to vote. The Court gave three reasons. Firstly, citizens are entitled to make informed choices when voting so that their vote is an expression of their genuine will.[184] Secondly, the duty of disclosure helps to combat corruption and ensures that elected representatives serve the public interest, rather than the agendas of private entities or foreign governments.[185] Thirdly, this interpretation aligns with that in international law.[186] The Court added that it is not only voters who are entitled to disclosure but also the media and other agents that are obliged to educate the voting public.

The PAIA was thus declared unconstitutional to the extent that it excluded political parties from its ambit and did not require parties to preserve and record information about private funding and make it readily accessible to the public. Parliament was ordered to amend the PAIA or to enact new legislation to promote the effective exercise of the right to make political choices and to participate in elections. The PAIA has since been amended,[187] and the Political Party Funding Act[188] has been enacted to give effect to the Court's order. It is clear that the South African Constitutional Court has aligned the rights to freedom of expression, access

[179] Electoral Act, Sch. 1.

[180] Electoral Commission Act, Act 51 of 1996.

[181] *Democratic Alliance* v. *African National Congress* 2015 (2) SA 232 (CC). The African National Congress and the Democratic Alliance are both dominant political parties in South Africa and ironically, these are the two major players forming the Government of National Unity after the 2024 general election.

[182] *My Votes Counts NPC* v. *Minister of Justice and Correctional Services*.

[183] South Africa's Promotion of Access to Information Act, Act 2 of 2000, giving effect to s. 32 of the Constitution.

[184] *My Votes Counts NPC* v. *Minister of Justice and Correctional Services*, [32]–[34].

[185] Ibid. [40]–[48], which the Court linked to s. 1(d) of the Constitution.

[186] Ibid. [49]–[51].

[187] The PAIA Amendment Act, 2019.

[188] Political Party Funding Act, Act 6 of 2018.

to information and free and fair elections to the founding constitutional values of democracy, freedom, responsiveness, transparency and accountability.

12.6.3 *The General Limitation Clause*

Section 36(1) provides as follows:

36 **Limitation of Rights**

(1) The rights in the Bill of Rights may be limited only in terms of law of general application to the extent that the limitation is reasonable and justifiable in an open and democratic society based on human dignity, equality and freedom, taking into account all relevant factors including –

(a) the nature of the right;
(b) the importance of the purpose of the limitation;
(c) the nature and extent of the limitation;
(d) the relationship between the limitation and its purpose; and
(e) less restrictive means to achieve the purpose.

Section 36(1) permits the justifiable infringement of a protected right if the limitation is both rational and proportional. The limitation must serve a 'compellingly important' purpose. A right can only be limited if the limitation will achieve its purpose and there is no other realistic way to achieve that purpose.[189]

A two-stage analysis is adopted when rights are limited. In the first stage, the ambit of the right in issue is determined by way of an interpretative process – the 'threshold stage'.[190] The right is usually interpreted generously, it being considered unnecessary 'to shape the contours of the right in order to accommodate pressing social interests'.[191] Should a law of general application violate the protected scope of the right; then a second-stage justification evaluation must be conducted. Here, a broad assessment utilizing the Section 36(1) factors is undertaken to determine whether the infringement of the right is justifiable in an open and democratic society, based on human dignity, equality and freedom. The party arguing for the limitation (usually the state) bears the onus to discharge the 'burden of justification' by demonstrating that the rights infringement is justifiable.[192]

To date, the South African courts have been very reluctant to permit the introduction of laws that limit press and media freedom. This is not only because of the impact of past censorship during the apartheid era[193] but also because the courts

[189] S v. *Manamela* 2000 (3) SA 1 (CC) [32].
[190] *Prinsloo* v. *Van der Linde* 1997 (3) SA 1012 (CC).
[191] Halton Cheadle, 'Limitation of Rights' in Halton Cheadle, Dennis Davis and Nicholas Haysom (eds.), *South African Constitutional Law: The Bill of Rights* (Durban: Butterworths, 2002) pp. 698–99.
[192] S v. *Makwanyane* 1995 (3) SA 391 (CC), [102].
[193] *Khumalo* v. *Holomisa*, [22].

have recognized the crucial role that the press play when it comes to protecting accountable and transparent governance, a key component of an open and democratic society based on human dignity, equality and freedom.[194] Laws that limit both freedom of expression and the right to vote will thus be strictly scrutinized by the courts during the Section 36 proportionality analysis.[195] The state will have to show that there is a legitimate need for any such law, with the law's purpose being rationally connected to the outcome it aims to achieve.

South Africa does not have a specifically enacted legislated false news restriction. However, the dissemination of disinformation could be regulated via the common law of defamation and other pieces of legislation regulating cybercrimes, films and publications and elections. Some of these laws and how they have been interpreted and applied by the courts are now briefly introduced.

12.6.4 *Defamation: The Common Law Civil Remedy and a Criminal Offence*

Most of South African defamation cases are civil in nature,[196] aimed at protecting the good name or reputation of both natural and juristic persons.[197] Very few cases of criminal defamation are reported and there have been many calls to repeal the common law crime of defamation.[198] Civil defamation is addressed first, followed by criminal defamation. It will be shown that neither remedy has been used to address false news types of cases and moreover that the courts have developed the law of

[194] In addition to the cases already cited, see *SABC* v. *NDPP*; *Independent Newspapers (Pty) Ltd* v. *Minister for Intelligence Services* 2008 (5) SA 31 (CC), [40]; *Government of the RSA* v. *Sunday Times* 1995 (2) SA 221 (T) at 227I–228A, holding that 'the press is in the frontline of the battle to maintain democracy'; *Midi Television (Pty)* v. *DPP* 2007 (5) SA 540 (SCA), [6]; *Johncom Media Investments Ltd* v. *M* 2009 (4) SA (CC), [28] and [29].

[195] S v. *Mamabolo (E-tv Intervening)*; *My Vote Counts NPC* v. *Minister of Justice and Correctional Services (My Vote Counts 11)*.

[196] Regulated as a delict (tort in English law).

[197] *O'Keefe* v. *Argus Printing and Publishing Company Ltd and Another* 1954 (3) SA 244 (C), but see *Reddell* v. *Mineral Sands Resources (Pty) Ltd* 2023 (2) SA 404 (CC), discussed below. This remedy should be compared to cases of *injuria*, which concern a claim for injuries to feelings, as opposed to an injury to one's reputation or *fama* (good name). *Injuria* is both civil and criminal in nature. There are many reported *crimen injuria* cases dealing with issues such as the use of racial slurs, hate speech and the like. This is because South Africa does not have a legislated hate speech offence. Note though that the President signed the Prevention and Combating of Hate Speech Crimes Bill in May 2024. The date of promulgation is yet to be confirmed. see Joanna Botha, 'A Hate-Crime Model for the South African Context' in Hennie Strydom and Joanna Botha (eds.), *Select Essays on Governance and Accountability Issues in Public Law* (Stellenbosch: African Sun Media, 2020).

[198] The last prominent reported case of criminal defamation is S v. *Hoho* 2009 (1) SACR 276 (SCA), where the accused was acquitted. Here, an issue was whether the crime had fallen into disuse and thus no longer existed. See generally Shannon Hoctor, 'The Crime of Defamation – Still Defensible in a Modern Constitutional Democracy?' (2013) 34(1) *Obiter* 125.

defamation to balance freedom of expression (of the media particularly) and the right to human dignity.

12.6.4.1 Defamation

A person whose reputation has been damaged by the publication of an intentional and unlawful (or wrongful) defamatory statement may claim damages from the wrongdoer, alternatively a so-called take-down order, often coupled with an order that the wrongdoer retract the statement and/or apologize.[199] Once the plaintiff proves that there has been publication of a defamatory statement,[200] the elements of wrongfulness and intention are presumed to have been met. The defendant must then prove a ground of justification (a defence) to rebut the presumptions.[201]

In the constitutional era, the courts have taken active steps to develop the law of defamation, by balancing the rights to freedom of expression and human dignity.[202] Media freedom has benefited especially,[203] with the courts creating special grounds of justification for the media. So, in *Holomisa* v. *Argus Newspapers*,[204] the Court held that 'a defamatory statement which relates to free and fair political activity is constitutionally protected, even if false, unless the plaintiff shows that, in all the circumstances of its publication, it was unreasonably made'. This created an exception to the rule that the defence of truth and public interest could be used only where a statement is factually true. Known as the reasonableness defence, the exception was introduced to protect press freedom to create leeway for false statements around free and fair political activity.

The defence was confirmed in *National Media Ltd* v. *Bogoshi*.[205] The Supreme Court of Appeal[206] held that a publisher could avoid liability for defamation where, even if it could not prove that the statement was true, it could establish that publication was reasonable. The Court held that: '[T]he publication in the press of false defamatory allegations of fact will not be regarded as unlawful if, upon a consideration of all the circumstances of the case, it is found to have been reasonable to publish the particular facts in the particular way and at the particular time.'[207] Relevant factors include: whether the statement related to political discussion; the tone in which the report was written; the nature of the information on which the allegations were based; the reliability of their source; and steps taken to

[199] *Dikoko* v. *Mokhatla* 2006 (6) SA 235 (CC) [62]; *Khumalo* v. *Holomisa*, [26].

[200] A publication is defamatory if it has the tendency or is calculated to undermine the status, good name or reputation of the plaintiff.

[201] *Khumalo* v. *Holomisa*, [18].

[202] Constitution, s. 10.

[203] In terms of s. 39(2) of the Constitution, the courts are obliged to develop all law to ensure that it is aligned with the values which the Constitution enshrines.

[204] *Holomisa* v. *Argus Newspapers* 1996 (2) SA 588 (W).

[205] *National Media Ltd* v. *Bogoshi* 1998 (4) SA 1196 (SCA).

[206] The previous apex court, but now lower in hierarchy than the Constitutional Court.

[207] *National Media Ltd* v. *Bogoshi*, at 1212 F – 1212 G.

verify the information. The defence of reasonable publication was confirmed in *Khumalo*, where the Constitutional Court stressed that the mass media play a significant role in the protection of freedom of expression to enable individuals to receive and impart information and ideas.[208]

The *Khumalo* court did, however, warn that 'while a person cannot claim a strong constitutional interest in protecting their reputation against the publication of truthful but damaging statements, neither do publishers have a strong constitutional speech interest in the publication of false material'.[209] As shown below, this caution did not deter the Court from refusing to enforce a ban on the publication of false information during elections.

Most recently, in 2022, in *Reddell* v. *Mineral Sands Resources (Pty) Ltd*[210] the Constitutional Court took further steps to protect freedom of expression, but in relation to whether trading companies could sue environmental activists for reputational loss.[211] The statements in issue (distributed on multiple platforms, including YouTube, as an e-book and on online news sites) accused the plaintiff mining companies of harming the environment. The environmentalists (as defendants) challenged the constitutionality of the common law defamation rule permitting trading companies to sue for non-patrimonial damages for reputational loss. They claimed that the existing law undermined their right to freedom of expression and that the companies, as juristic persons, could not rely on the right to inherent human dignity to justify a claim for reputational damage.[212]

The majority of the Court agreed, holding that a claim for general damages 'to a trading corporation for harm to its reputation infringes the ... right to freedom of speech, specifically in relation to speech which is of public importance or which requires public debate and participation'.[213] The Court confirmed that the speech in issue was in the public interest (environmental harm) and was of considerable value in an open and democratic society. The Court stressed that the activists created a platform for public participation about environmental compliance by large mining companies and that such speech 'warrant[s] a high standard of protection'.[214] It added that 'discourse about matters that affect all or many of us are of grave public concern ... must be encouraged and not stifled in a vibrant democracy like ours'.[215] This did not mean that the companies had no alternative relief: if necessary,

[208] *Khumalo* v. *Holomisa*, [18], [19], [28], [33], [42], [43] [48], [49].
[209] Ibid. [201].
[210] *Reddell* v. *Mineral Sands Resources (Pty) Ltd*. To be distinguished from a judgment delivered on the same day, involving the same parties, and considering the constitutionality of SLAPP suits. See *Mineral Sands Resources (Pty) Ltd* v. *Reddell* 2023 (2) SA 68 (CC).
[211] To be distinguished from trading losses caused by injurious falsehoods, an unlawful competition claim.
[212] *Reddell* v. *Mineral Sands Resources (Pty) Ltd*, [37] and [94].
[213] Ibid. [100].
[214] Ibid. [105].
[215] Ibid. [112].

they could apply for an interdict (in the form of a takedown order),[216] a declarator, a retraction or an apology.

The minority in *Reddell*, however, was not prepared to develop the common law of defamation to this extent. Whilst the minority's focus was on the interpretation of the right to human dignity, it echoed *Khumalo*'s warning about the limited value of false information, especially in the digital age, given the reach of social media platforms.[217] It added that '[p]ublic discourse is speech that takes place in public. Social media is the town square writ large. It is pre-eminently the platform of public discourse. Issues of legitimate debate is a concept of bountiful elasticity. But a subject may be one of legitimate debate and yet what is said may be false, even hateful, and reputationally ruinous.'[218] Thus, the extent to which freedom of expression can be relied upon in defamation cases must consider 'what speech is used, how it is used, and with what consequences'. Where a defamatory statement is a 'blatant falsehood that does great reputational harm', expression should not prevail.[219] It is noteworthy, of course, that the majority disagreed and protected critical expression where public participation is crucial.

It is thus clear that whilst the South African courts have not had to deal directly with a 'false news' type of case under the realm of defamation, the courts are aware that such a case would require careful consideration given the value placed on freedom of expression. Whatever the future outcome, it is certainly highly unlikely that the courts would permit a criminal sanction for defamatory speech, as is now demonstrated.

12.6.4.2 Criminal Defamation

The crime of defamation is defined as the unlawful and intentional publication of a matter concerning another person which tends to injure their reputation. In 2008 in *Hoho* v. S[220] the Supreme Court of Appeal had to consider whether the crime of defamation still exists in South African law and whether it is constitutionally legitimate. The accused, Luzuko Hoho, had been convicted of twenty-two counts of criminal defamation and was sentenced to three years' imprisonment suspended for five years and, in addition, to three years' correctional supervision. Hoho was a researcher employed by a Provincial Legislature and had published various leaflets in which he defamed the Premier, the Speaker and various other politicians.

[216] Note that the South African courts are reluctant to grant prior restraint orders. See *Midi Television (Pty)* v. *DPP*.

[217] *Reddell* v. *Mineral Sands Resources (Pty) Ltd* [195]. The Court stressed that the defences to wrongfulness include truth and the public interest and fair comment (which requires that the statement upon which the comment is based be true).

[218] Ibid. [202].

[219] Ibid. [205].

[220] *Hoho* v. S [2009] 1 All SA 103 (SCA).

He accused them of corruption, bribery, financial embezzlement, sexual impropriety, illegal abortion and fraud.

Hoho raised various defences, including that the crime of defamation no longer existed in South African law and that, even if it did, it was unconstitutional. The Supreme Court of Appeal disagreed. It held that the crime had not been abrogated by disuse and that it did not unjustifiably infringe the right to freedom of expression.[221] The Court reasoned that whilst a criminal sanction is a drastic measure, the limitation to freedom of expression was balanced by the onerous burden of proof borne by the state in criminal cases, the parallel between the need to protect physical integrity (assault) and injury to reputation, and the fact that there was still a need for a criminal sanction to protect a person's reputation.[222]

Despite this, it is anticipated that legislation may be passed soon to decriminalize defamation in South Africa. Indeed, as far back as September 2015, the state announced that it would introduce legislation to decriminalize defamation on the grounds that it unjustifiably infringes the right to freedom of expression.[223] Whilst the legislation is yet to be tabled, it is highly likely that the current Constitutional Court would have no difficulty in declaring criminal defamation unconstitutional, especially given the calls by the African Commission to decriminalize defamation and the added protection the Court has given to freedom of expression in civil defamation cases.

12.6.5 *The Cybercrimes Act 2020*

The Cybercrimes Act, which criminalizes unlawful activities in cyberspace, commenced on 1 December 2021.[224] The Act was introduced because it was recognized that the existing common law crimes were incapable of regulating criminal conduct committed online.[225] Advances in digital technology amplified the need for the Act,

[221] Ibid. [32] and [33] – the Court rejected the views of academics that the crime should be declared unconstitutional.

[222] Ibid. [33]–[35] – the Court held that the need for a criminal offence was illustrated by the facts of the case. Furthermore, the paucity of prosecutions may be evidence that the existence of the offence serves as deterrence. See also Hoctor, 'The Crime of Defamation' (n 198), at 131, who reviews the arguments concerning the need to retain the crime of defamation when an effective civil remedy is available.

[223] See 'The Case against Criminal Defamation', *Mail and Guardian*, 23 September 2015, http://mg.co.za/article/2015-09-23-the-case-against-criminal-defamation.

[224] There was partial implementation of the Act. Part IV of Chapter 2 is still to be implemented.

[225] The Electronic Communications and Transactions Act 2000 (the ECTA) focused on the regulation of the commercial aspects of online transactions and only created a few cybercrimes. Other laws regulated organized crime (the Prevention of Organised Crimes Act, Act 121 of 1998, and the Financial Intelligence Centre Act, Act 38 of 2001). Only ss. 85–90 of the ECTA created criminal offences: unauthorized access to data; interception of, or interference with data or denial of a service attack; computer-related extortion, fraud and forgery; and attempt, aiding and abetting a cybercrime. For the application of cyber law to a common law crime, see S

aggravated by the ease with which cybercrimes such as fraud, extortion, forgery, child pornography[226] and hacking could be committed. As these crimes became more prevalent, it was obvious that legislated criminal offences, with a specifically adapted procedural framework, were needed to regulate unlawful conduct committed online.[227]

The long title to the Act states that it was enacted to create and penalize cybercrimes.[228] Chapter 2 of the Act contains five substantive criminal law segments. Part I regulates cybercrimes recodified from existing common law crimes,[229] and adds new offences. These include disclosure of an electronic data message that causes damage to property or violence against a person or group of persons,[230] the unlawful and intentional disclosure of a data message of an intimate image of a person[231] and the so-called malicious communication crimes.[232] Part III creates offences in the context of various cybercrime activities, such as attempting, aiding, inducing, inciting or instigating a person to commit a specified offence. Part IV deals with competent verdicts and Part V permits the grant of court orders to protect complainants from the harmful effects of malicious communications. Provisions are also created to regulate the obligations of electronic communications service providers and financial institutions to report cybercrime offences and to preserve information relevant to an investigation.

From a disinformation perspective, it is interesting that the Act does not contain a specific provision criminalizing the dissemination of false data (or news) intended to cause harm. Instead, such conduct would have to be addressed in terms of either cyber fraud[233] or cyber forgery and uttering

v. *Howard* unreported case No. 41/258/02, Johannesburg Regional Magistrates' Court (malicious code loaded onto an employer's network).

226 Child pornography was criminalized in terms of the Films and Publications Act, Act 65 of 1996.

227 See generally Sizwe Snail ka Mtuze and Melody Musoni, 'An Overview of Cybercrime Law in South Africa' (2023) 4(3) *International Cybersecurity Law Review* 299.

228 The Act does not define cybercrimes. An acceptable definition is 'the commission of a crime using a computer, a computer network or a networked device'. A computer would be the 'object' of a crime when theft of hardware or software occurs. It is more likely though to be used as an instrument to commit crimes such as fraud, theft, identity theft, cyberbullying or cyber defamation. See generally Nombulelo Q. Mabeka and Fawzia Cassim, 'Interpreting the Provisions of the Cybercrimes Act 19 of 2020 in the Context of Civil Procedure: A Future Journey' (2023) 44(1) *Obiter* 19.

229 The existing common law crimes, such as *crimen injuria*, or malicious damage to property, where a perpetrator disseminates a virus into another's computer system.

230 This conduct is criminalized based on a person's intention to incite the causing of damage or violence, but also includes a threat to cause such damage or violence; or the unlawful and intentional conduct in attempting or conspiring to aid, instigate or instruct another person to commit an offence in terms of the Act.

231 Section 16.

232 Sections 13–16.

233 Section 8. To address cases such as phishing, spoofing and banking scams. See too Murdoch Watney, 'The Evolution of Internet Legal Regulation in Addressing Crime and Terrorism' (2007) 2(2) *Journal of Digital Forensics, Security and Law* 41, at 49; Fawzia Cassim, 'Addressing

offences,[234] which criminalize, inter alia, the unlawful use/passing off of false data or a misrepresentation with the intention of defrauding another person to cause harm, or the malicious communications provisions. The latter offences are intended to capture within their ambit the electronic communication of data messages which are published with the intention of inciting damage to persons or their property based on identifiable group characteristics.[235] It is thus clear that the Cybercrimes Act was not enacted to regulate false news or disinformation, a conclusion which is supported by the fact that such a purpose is not included in the Act's objectives.[236]

12.6.6 *The Electoral Act 78 of 1993*

The Electoral Act is the domestic legislation that regulates and gives normative content to the right to free and fair elections and the right to vote. The Act contains various provisions which prohibit certain types of conduct by political parties and other actors during elections. The aim is to ensure the achievement of free and fair elections. There are seven main prohibitions. One of these is Section 89(2)(c) of the Act which prohibits the publication of intentionally false statements, with the intention of influencing the conduct or outcome of an election. Any person who contravenes the section is guilty of a criminal offence and may be fined or imprisoned for up to ten years.

Schedule 1 to the Electoral Act contains the Electoral Code of Conduct.[237] Like the Act, it prohibits certain types of conduct to promote '(a) tolerance of democratic political activity, and (b) free political campaigning and open public debate'. Item 9 of the Electoral Code of Conduct provides that no registered party or candidate may publish false or defamatory allegations in connection with an election. This part of the Code must be read with Item 4 thereof, which records that freedom of political expression is a core component of a free and fair election.

These provisions were interpreted by the Constitutional Court in *Democratic Alliance* v. *African National Congress*.[238] The case concerned an SMS sent by the

the Challenges Posed by Cybercrime: A South African Perspective' (2010) (3) *Journal of International Commercial Law and Technology* 118.

[234] Section 9.

[235] See ss. 13–16.

[236] As listed in the Act's long title. It does not have a preamble or objectives section. The Act aims to address money laundering, fraud, harassment and hate speech, committed online.

[237] Section 99(1) of the Act provides that the Code of Conduct requires that all registered political parties and candidates must be subscribed to contest an election. Section 94 of the Act provides that all political parties and candidates are bound by the Act's provisions, including the Code of Conduct.

[238] *Democratic Alliance* v. *African National Congress* 2015 (2) SA 232 (CC). For an excellent analysis of this case, see Gautam Bhatia, 'Autonomy, Fairness, Pragmatism, and False Electoral Speech: An Analysis of *Democratic Alliance v. African National Congress*' (2016) 8(1) *Constitutional Court Review* 23.

Democratic Alliance (DA)[239] to 1,593,682 persons in the Gauteng province, approximately six weeks before the date set for the 2014 national elections. The SMS read: 'The Nkandla report shows how Zuma stole your money to build his R246m[240] home. Vote DA on 7 May to beat corruption. Together for change.' The SMS was based on the Nkandla Report, penned by the Public Protector,[241] released a day before the SMS was sent and reporting that President Zuma had improperly used public finances for security upgrades to his private residence (Nkandla). The African National Congress (the ANC – and Zuma's party) launched an application asking for a declaration that the SMS violated the Electoral Act and the Code. The ANC requested an order restraining the DA from re-disseminating the message and a retraction. The ANC argued that the SMS alleged that the Nkandla Report stated that President Zuma had committed theft, but that this was not the case, and that the SMS therefore contained false information published with the intention of influencing an election in breach of the Electoral Act.

In response, whilst accepting the constitutional validity of the Electoral Act provisions, the DA denied that the SMS was false. It argued that the SMS meant that the Nkandla Report merely demonstrated how Zuma had misused public funds and that 'read in light of the Nkandla Report, the SMS express[ed] an opinion that a fair person might honestly and genuinely hold in light of the facts in the Report, and the Report must be understood and read in its totality'.[242] A key issue therefore was whether the SMS amounted to an expression of comment or opinion as opposed to a statement of fact.

To address this question, the Court had to interpret Section 89(2)(c) of the Act, as read with the Code. The Court opted for a restrictive interpretation because of the principle that legislation limiting a right (here freedom of expression) should not be interpreted broadly, especially when cast as a criminal sanction.[243] Recognizing that freedom of expression serves many purposes, including individual autonomy and the promotion of a vibrant democracy, the Court stressed the need for active participation by informed voters during elections. Linking the right to the apartheid struggle and the censorship that existed then, the Court held that '[i]n celebrating the democracy we have created, we rejoice as much in the right to vote as in the freedom to speak that makes that right meaningful. An election without as much freedom to speak as is constitutionally permissible would be stunted and inefficient'.[244]

[239] The official opposition party to the African National Congress.
[240] Two hundred and forty-six million Rand. In today's money this would be approximately €123,000.
[241] At that time, Prof. Thuli Madonsela.
[242] *Democratic Alliance* v. *African National Congress*, [16].
[243] Ibid. [129].
[244] Ibid. [124].

Another important factor was that the right to freedom of expression underpins many of the other constitutionally protected rights, which together:

> protect the rights of . . . like-minded people to foster and propagate their views. They confirm the importance, both for a democracy and the individuals who comprise it, of being able to form and express opinions – particularly controversial or unpopular views, or those that inconvenience the powerful. The corollary is tolerance. We have to put up with views we don't like . . . It means the public airing of disagreements. And it means refusing to silence unpopular views.[245]

In the electoral context, public debate is especially valuable because it contributes to 'opinion-forming and holds public office-bearers and candidates for public office accountable'.[246] Importantly, for open and transparent governance, the Court added that:

> Political life in democratic South Africa has seldom been polite, orderly and restrained. It has always been loud, rowdy and fractious. That is no bad thing. Within the boundaries the Constitution sets, it is good for democracy, good for social life and good for individuals to permit as much open and vigorous discussion of public affairs as possible.[247]

Having reached this conclusion, the next question was 'what kinds of 'information' and 'allegations' were included in the prohibition in Section 89(2)'. In other words, were both factually incorrect statements and expressions of opinion prohibited or only the former?[248] The answer, according to the majority, was that only false statements or information were prohibited,[249] and that the SMS was clearly an opinion, alternatively a comment, as it appeared in the Report, to which it directly referred for its authority. Thus, the DA had not violated the Act.[250] This decision, whilst controversial at the time, demonstrates that the South African courts take their constitutional mandate in Section 165 of the Constitution seriously – that is, the duty to uphold the Constitution and to apply it, without fear or favour. The consequence is that laws regulating false news or information, especially when cast as penal measures, are unlikely to be condoned by the courts.

12.6.7 *COVID Regulations under the Disaster Management Act 2002*

The first false news laws in South Africa were prompted by the COVID-19 pandemic, under the Disaster Management Act 2002 (DMA), giving the

[245] Ibid. [125]–[126].
[246] Ibid. [132].
[247] Ibid. [135].
[248] Ibid. [119]–[120].
[249] Ibid. [139]–[141].
[250] The minority, on the other hand, held that the SMS alleged that the Report had made a finding that President Zuma had stolen taxpayers' money to build his home. This was a statement of fact, and not a comment, because it was made 'without reference . . . to other antecedent or surrounding circumstances notorious to the speaker'.

executive extensive powers, including the power to implement legislation forthwith and without consultation. South Africa declared a national state of disaster[251] in terms of the DMA in March 2020 in response to the pandemic.[252] A mandatory twenty-one-day lockdown commenced on 25 March 2020.[253] This resulted in the closure of schools, universities, churches and businesses, with freedom of movement being severely restricted.[254] The lockdown was extended repeatedly through regulations authorized by the DMA and operated at different levels, depending on the rise in the number of COVID-19 cases,[255] but officially ended on 4 April 2022.[256]

Disasters in terms of the DMA are classified according to whether they are local, provincial or national. A disaster is treated as a national disaster if it affects more than one province (Section 26(1)), which was clearly the case during the pandemic. The consequence was that the national executive became primarily responsible for the coordination and management of the crisis. A minister designated by the President was given the power to make regulations or issue directions concerning a wide range of matters,[257] including, inter alia, 'other steps that may be necessary to prevent an escalation of the disaster, or to alleviate, contain and minimize the effects of the disaster'. Whilst there were numerous challenges to the constitutionality of the Act and the regulations issued thereunder, most of these challenges were ineffective, the courts deferring to the state's prerogative to manage the pandemic and justifying the

[251] Sections 27(1)(a) and 27(1)(b). See generally, Geo Quinot, 'Justification, Integration, and Expertise: South Africa's Regulatory Response to Covid-19' (2020) 73(1) *Administrative Law Review* 105.

[252] GN 318 in GG 43107 of 2020-03-18. A state of disaster is not a state of emergency. The distinction was explained in *Freedom Front Plus* v. *President of the Republic of South Africa* [2020] 3 All SA 762 (GP). A state of emergency, regulated by s. 37 of the Constitution, may only be declared when the 'life of the nation' is under threat or in cases such as 'armed conflicts, civil wars, insurrections, severe economic shocks, natural disasters, and similar threats'. Another significant difference between a state of disaster and a state of emergency is that rights may only be derogated during a state of emergency, as opposed to the less severe limitation of rights under a state of disaster. See also Pierre De Vos, 'South Africa Is in a State and There Is an Emergency, but Declaring a State of Emergency Is not the Magic Bullet', *Daily Maverick*, 14 July 2021, www.dailymaverick.co.za/article/2021-07-14-south-africa-is-in-a-state-and-there-is-an-emergency-but-declaring-a-state-of-emergency-is-not-the-magic-bullet.

[253] GN 398 in GG 43148 of 25 2020-03-25.

[254] Later all public gatherings were banned, plus all forms of physical commercial activity, except for the sale of food and medicine, and interprovincial travel.

[255] A national disaster lapses three months after it has been declared, but may be extended for one month at a time. The lockdown was extended on numerous occasions.

[256] Coronavirus COVID-19 Alert Level 1, South African Government, www.gov.za/covid-19/about/coronavirus-covid-19-alert-level-1.

[257] In terms of s. 27(2) of the Act. See *Helen Suzman Foundation* v. *Speaker of the National Assembly and Others* (32858/2020) [2020] ZAGPPHC 700 (4 December 2020). This was the minister for cooperative governance and traditional affairs.

restriction of rights on the basis that the lockdown regulations were a legitimate and rational response to both a national and international crisis.[258]

From a freedom of expression perspective, of particular concern was a regulation which made it an offence to 'publish a statement through any medium with the intention to deceive about a narrow range of information related to the transmission of the virus, personal infection status and government measures to address the pandemic'. As a criminal sanction, if convicted, an accused could be penalized by a fine or imprisonment for six months (or both).[259] This prohibition was introduced as soon as the lockdown was announced and was intended to protect public health and prevent the spread of rumours about the virus, the impact of vaccines and so on. The regulation was in fact implemented, with arrests reported (an accused was alleged to have disseminated false news about test kits) and the government operating a reporting system, which it named Real411.[260] People were encouraged to report 'disinformation' via a mobile app, website or a WhatsApp number, and alleged false news incidents were then published on the government website, while awaiting verification by a Digital Complaints Committee, run by a non-governmental organization called Media Monitoring Africa.[261] Whilst monitoring independent of government was welcomed, the regulation attracted extensive critique, particularly because the government actively encouraged whistleblowing.[262]

When the lockdown ended in April 2022 the regulations issued under the DMA were set aside and no longer applied. It is a serious worry, however, that the government has since attempted to use the DMA as a tool to manage other national emergencies, including Eskom loadshedding. The problem with this approach is that it permits governmental overreach, does not provide for parliamentary oversight

[258] Ibid.; *Freedom Front Plus* v. *President of the Republic of South Africa*; *South African Breweries Proprietary Limited* v. *President of the Republic of South Africa* [2022] ZAWCHC 102; *Esau* v. *Minister of Co-Operative Governance and Traditional Affairs* 2021 (3) SA 593 (SCA); *Democratic Alliance* v. *Minister of Co-operative Governance and Traditional Affairs* (22311/2020) [2021] ZAGPPHC 168 (24 March 2021); *British American Tobacco South Africa (Pty) Ltd* v. *Minister of Co-operative Governance and Traditional Affairs* 2021 (7) BCLR 735 (WCC).

[259] Regulation 11(5), issued in terms of s. 27(2) of the Act. See also Fake News – Coronavirus COVID-19, South African Government, www.gov.za/covid-19/resources/fake-news-coronavirus-covid-19.

[260] Ibid. The website remained active as of October 2023.

[261] See 'South Africa: Prohibitions of False COVID-19 Information Must Be Amended', Article 19, 23 April 2021, www.article19.org/resources/prohibitions-of-false-covid-information-must-be-amended.

[262] Ntokozo Sobikwa and Moses R. Phooko, 'An Assessment of the Constitutionality of the COVID-19 Regulations against the Requirement to Facilitate Public Participation in the Law-Making and/or Administrative Processes in South Africa' (2022) 25(1) *Law, Democracy & Development* 309; Bernard K. Sebak and Joseph Mudau, 'Revisiting Whistleblowing Amid COVID-19 Pandemic in South Africa: An *ad nauseam* Problem' (2020) 55(3–1) *Journal of Public Administration* 490.

and results in the introduction of legislation without following the ordinary constitutional rules for law-making.[263]

12.7 CONCLUSION

The aim of this chapter was to present an analysis of the regulation of disinformation in Africa, focusing on African regional law and domestic false news laws in various African states, but with an emphasis on the South African law. The chapter revealed the tension between the need to protect freedom of expression and the right to free and fair elections in the context of a continent which is regularly subjected to disinformation campaigns aimed at undermining public participation in democratic governance and extending political control. Despite commendable efforts at the regional and sub-regional levels to promote the importance of a free press and media for the advancement of accountable and transparent governance in the digital age, the reality is that the dissemination of fake news in African states remains prevalent and poses a severe risk to democracy, especially as digital technology becomes more sophisticated. The harm caused by disinformation cannot be ignored given the fragile state of democracy in most African states. The commitment of the South African courts to the balancing of freedom of expression with the right to an informed vote, as a component of democratic governance, provides some hope, but a more sustained and globally integrated effort encompassing regulatory reform and promotional measures, including international partnerships, is needed if Africa is to withstand the threat of disinformation.

[263] *Helen Suzman Foundation* v. *Speaker of the National Assembly and Others*, [103]. The Court held that the minister acted within her powers. The applicants had argued that the disaster should have been a short-term measure and that new legislation should have been drafted to deal with the COVID-19 situation, as opposed to the continuous reliance on regulations passed by the minister. This gives the executive the power to legislate disasters perpetually and undermines the low hierarchy of delegated legislation. See also *Freedom Front Plus* v. *President of the Republic of South Africa*, [64].

13

Navigating the Nexus of Elections, Technology and Democracy amid Escalating Disinformation and Misinformation Challenges in Kenya

Victoria Miyandazi and Lucianna Thuo

13.1 INTRODUCTION

Despite Kenya's transformative and progressive 2010 Constitution, it is still grappling with a hybrid democracy, displaying both authoritarian and democratic traits. Scholars attribute this status to several factors, with a prominent one being the domination of the political order and wielding of political power by a few individuals and families with historical ties to patronage networks and informal power structures.[1] The persisting issues of electoral fraud, widespread corruption, media harassment, weak rule of law and governance challenges further contribute to the hybrid democracy status.[2] While the 2010 Constitution aims to restructure the state and enhance democratic institutions, the transition process is considered incomplete, especially since the judiciary's role of judicial review is mostly faced with the difficult task of countering democratic regression.[3] Moreover, critical institutions such as the Independent Electoral and Boundaries Commission (IEBC) have faced criticism due to corruption scandals and perceptions of partisanship, eroding public trust in their ability to oversee fair elections effectively.[4]

In the context of Kenya's hybrid democracy, the new challenge posed by disinformation and misinformation has become a pressing concern, particularly in relation to elections. The selective use of information to manipulate political outcomes has led to a detrimental impact on the democratic process, contributing to issues such as voter apathy, ethnic polarisation and a sense of disorientation caused by the rise of

[1] Duncan Okubasu Munabi, 'Real Constitutional Change in Sub-Saharan Africa after the Third Wave of Democratisation: A Comparative Historical Inquiry', PhD thesis, University of Utrecht (2021), p. 205.

[2] See www.populismstudies.org/Vocabulary/hybrid-regime.

[3] Munabi, 'Real Constitutional Change', p. 205.

[4] Richard Stacey and Victoria Miyandazi, 'Constituting and Regulating Democracy: Kenya's Electoral Commission and the Courts in the 2010s' (2021) 16 *Asian Journal of Comparative Law* 193, at 194, 207–8.

misinformation. As this chapter highlights, technology can indeed serve as a tool to enhance democratic legitimacy and combat election rigging when properly implemented and managed. However, it is crucial to recognise that technology, especially digital information technology and social media, has become a double-edged sword. On the one hand, these platforms play a significant role in bolstering democracy by facilitating broader public participation, a fundamental aspect for any democratic society to thrive. Yet, on the other hand, the increased accessibility of the Internet has given rise to a new challenge: the spread of disinformation and misinformation.[5]

This phenomenon poses a serious threat to the integrity of elections and democratic processes. As the overwhelming levels of disinformation and misinformation in Kenya's 2022 General Election illustrate, misleading information can easily circulate, influencing public opinion and undermining the trust that citizens place in democratic institutions. The proliferation of false narratives skews the democratic playing field, making it difficult for voters to make informed decisions based on accurate and reliable information. Therefore, it is essential for the government, the election management body, civil society, tech companies and other stakeholders to tackle this issue collaboratively. As this chapter discusses, striking the right balance between the benefits of technology in enhancing democracy and countering its potentially negative effects requires concerted efforts to promote fact-checking, media literacy and responsible digital citizenship. By equipping citizens with the skills to distinguish accurate information from disinformation and misinformation, Kenya can safeguard the democratic ideals upon which the society is built and ensure that technology remains a tool for progress rather than a source of division. As Kenya prepares for future elections, addressing the challenges posed by disinformation and misinformation and their impact on the democratic process will be crucial in preserving the fairness and credibility of elections.

This chapter is organised as follows: Section 13.2 delves into the historical context of Kenya's hybrid democracy and analyses the prevailing challenges in the electoral landscape. It investigates the complexities arising from ethnic politics and election rigging that have hindered the democratic process. Section 13.3 examines the role of technology in enhancing electoral integrity and legitimacy, particularly in relation to the role of technology in Kenya's 2013 and 2017 general elections. It explores how the IEBC endeavours to leverage technology to administer elections effectively, aiming to curb election illegalities and irregularities. Section 13.4 sheds light on the growing challenge of disinformation and misinformation, particularly during the 2022 general election. It examines the weaponisation of fake news by politicians seeking electoral advantages, and the issues around technology and reliance on false

5 Aderomola Adeola and Makau W. Mutua (eds.), *The Palgrave Handbook of Democracy, Governance and Justice in Africa* (Cham: Palgrave Macmillan, 2022), p. 2; Charles Manga Fombad, 'Democracy and Fake News in Africa' (2022) 9(1) *Journal of International and Comparative Law* 131, at 131–32.

information that arose in the 2022 presidential election petition. Section 13.5 looks at legal, institutional and non-legal measures for detecting and combating disinformation and misinformation. It discusses the pivotal roles various stakeholders such as the IEBC, tech companies and civil society actors play in detecting and combating false information. Further, it emphasises the importance of empowering citizens with media literacy and critical thinking skills to enable individuals to distinguish accurate information from misinformation. Section 13.6 then concludes. It offers a recapitulation of the findings and implications for Kenya's electoral system.

13.2 LAYING THE FOUNDATION: HISTORY OF KENYA'S HYBRID DEMOCRACY AND CHALLENGES IN THE ELECTORAL LANDSCAPE

The high stakes and divisiveness of elections is at the centre of Kenya's woes and resultant cycle of ethnic voting and violence that follows every election.[6] Ethnic politics in Kenya dates back as early as the pre-colonial era, to colonisation and upon independence. The British colonisation of Kenya employed a 'divide and rule' policy that played ethnic groups against each other to prevent a unified nationalist opposition. This strategy was later adopted by post-colonial political elites who saw their ethnic group as their crucial asset when negotiating for 'a seat at the national table'.[7] At the time of independence, Kenya, like many other newly independent African states, prioritised nation-building and socio-economic development. With a limited number of schools, scarcity of hospitals and inadequate infrastructure, the political leaders of the era directed their efforts towards addressing pressing challenges such as high levels of illiteracy, poverty and disease.[8]

The authoritarian model, which provided the President and executive with significant authority to regulate the allocation and distribution of resources, was seen as best to tackle these issues.[9] However, to remove it from its colonial origins to fit the post-colonial agenda, its mission was changed and repackaged as being necessitated by the 'development first' agenda:[10] to win the war against poverty, ignorance and disease, 'the development plan trumped the Constitution as the most important economic and political document of the state' and hence a 'worthy trade-off'.[11] In addition, one-party politics was preferred to multi-party politics due to the fear that the latter would encourage partisan mobilisation of subnational identities

6 Douglas L. Kivoi, 'Ethnicity and Democracy: A Case Study of Kenya' (2010) 2(2) *OIDA International Journal of Sustainable Development* 43, at 43.

7 John Lonsdale, 'Race and Ethnicity in Colonial Kenya' in Nic Cheeseman, Karuti Kanyinga and Gabriel Lynch (eds.), *The Oxford Handbook of Kenyan Politics* (Oxford: Oxford University Press, 2020), pp. 124–25.

8 H. Kwasi Prempeh, 'Africa's Constitutionalism Revival: False Start or New Dawn' (2007) 5 *International Journal of Constitutional Law* 469, at 475.

9 Ibid. at 469.

10 Ibid. at 475–80.

11 Ibid.

and loyalties manipulated by colonialism, ultimately undermining national unity and hindering the post-colonial development project's success.[12] However, despite the ambitious development project, several challenges arose, including rampant corruption, stagnant or negative growth rates, worsening income inequality and a rise in absolute poverty.[13] As a result, the 'development first' initiative ultimately proved unsuccessful.

As public trust in the ruling elite waned, a troubling practice used during the colonial era re-emerged, where certain ethnically aligned sections of the citizenry, particularly those offering strong political support to the ruling elite, received preferential treatment and benefits in exchange for their loyalty.[14] This strategy was used by the ruling elite to maintain their grip on power and retain political support. It marked the inception of divisive ethnic politics in independent Kenya, characterised by election rigging through means such as ballot box stuffing, state-sponsored ethnic violence and a blatant disregard for the rule of law. Incumbents resorted to desperate measures to cling to power, turning elections into a zero-sum 'winner takes all' game. Those in control of the political order wielded significant influence, becoming the primary dispensers of favours and socio-economic benefits, leading to a system where loyalty to the ruling party was rewarded while dissenting voices faced marginalisation.[15] The emergence of ethnicised politics gave rise to profound and enduring ethno-regional inequalities, as politically dissident ethnic groups and their respective regions faced socio-economic marginalisation.[16] It also fuelled ethnic hatred and divisions.

Compounding this problem, a series of amendments to the 1963 Constitution exacerbated the establishment of an authoritarian governmental structure, concentrating power within the presidency and the executive under one-party rule.[17] This concentration of power disrupted the equilibrium between the executive and legislative branches, severely curtailing parliament's ability to effectively supervise the actions of the executive.[18] Concurrently, the independence of the judiciary also suffered. Particularly noteworthy was the removal of judicial security of tenure for High Court and Court of Appeal judges in 1988, which rendered judges susceptible to removal at the discretion of the President.[19] Although this amendment was later

[12] Ibid. at 475–76.

[13] Ibid. at 472 and 482; Richard Sandbrook and Judith Barker, *The Politics of Africa's Economic Stagnation* (Cambridge: Cambridge University Press, 1985), p. 2.

[14] Prempeh, 'Africa's Constitutionalism Revival' (n 8) 482–83.

[15] Godfrey Musila, 'A Preliminary Assessment of the Kenyan Truth, Justice and Reconciliation Commission Bill, 2008' (2008) 5 *African Renaissance* 40, at 40–41.

[16] Victoria Miyandazi, *Equality in Kenya's 2010 Constitution: Understanding the Competing and Interrelated Conceptions* (Oxford: Hart, 2021), pp. 27–28.

[17] Stephen Ndegwa et al. (eds.), *History of Constitution Making in Kenya* (Nairobi: Konrad Adenauer Foundation, 2012), pp. 23 and 30.

[18] Daniel Branch and Nicholas Cheeseman, 'The Politics of Control in Kenya: Undermining the Bureaucratic-Executive State, 1952–78' (2006) 33(107) *Review of African Political Economy* 11.

[19] Constitution of Kenya (Amendment) Act Number 4 of 1988.

repealed, its initial intention was to further consolidate executive power. The amendment weakened the judiciary's credibility, subjected judges to the executive's whims, and eroded the essential 'safeguards necessary for maintaining fair administration, neutrality of public institutions, accountability of government, and the protection of rights in general'.[20] Consequently, the essential system of checks and balances necessary to uphold democracy within the three governmental branches was largely deficient, leading to adverse implications for the overall preservation of democratic principles.

The push for electoral reforms in Kenya took root in the 1990s when there was a growing demand for the repeal of section 2A from the 1963 independence Constitution. This section, introduced through a constitutional amendment in 1982, had transformed Kenya from a *de facto* to a *de jure* one-party state, leaving only the ruling party, the Kenya African National Union (KANU), in existence and outlawing political opposition.[21] This meant that individuals could only vie for political office if they were members of and nominated by KANU. The repeal of section 2A in 1991 and the subsequent restoration of multi-party politics was a significant milestone.[22] However, it soon became evident to the reform movement that this alone was 'insufficient to democratise politics, usher in accountability and ensure responsive political policies'.[23] The 1963 Constitution, along with its various amendments, was deemed undemocratic, solidifying an authoritarian system of government, which made it difficult to challenge the ruling party's political power.[24]

The electoral landscape remained contentious, marred by ethnic hate-speech, violence and persistent allegations of rigging. This environment provided incumbents with a clear advantage, undermining the democratic process, and perpetuating their stay in power.[25] One of the key contributing factors to this situation was the partisan appointment of commissioners to the Electoral Commission of Kenya (ECK), which eroded public trust and raised questions about the Commission's competence.[26] As a result of these challenges, there was an urgent need to establish mechanisms that would ensure transparent, inclusive, and credible elections. This

20 Committee of Experts, 'Final Report of the Committee of Experts on Constitutional Review' (2011), pp. 33–34. See also Miyandazi, *Equality in Kenya's 2010 Constitution*, p. 11.

21 Constitution of Kenya (Amendment) Act Number 7 of 1982; Ndegwa et al., *History of Constitution Making in Kenya*, p. 19.

22 Constitution of Kenya (Amendment) Act Number 12 of 1991.

23 Civic Education for the Referendum: CKRC Curriculum. Constitution of Kenya Review Commission, 2005, p. 7.

24 Ndegwa et al., *History of Constitution Making in Kenya* (n 17) pp. 23 and 30.

25 Godfrey Musila, 'The State of Constitutionalism in Kenya in 2012: Embarking on a Journey to Reestablish a New Order' in Christopher Mbazira (ed.), *Annual State of Constitutionalism in East Africa* (Bukoto: Kituo Cha Katiba, 2013), p. 10; Report of the Independent Review Commission on the General Elections held in Kenya on 27 December 2007, Independent Review Commission (IREC), 2008, p. 1.

26 Musila, 'The State of Constitutionalism in Kenya in 2012'; Report of the Independent Review Commission on the General Elections.

imperative became a central agenda in the pursuit of constitutional reforms. The aim was to foster a system that could guarantee the integrity of the electoral process, promote fair representation, and restore public confidence in the democratic foundations of the country. The ECK made efforts to introduce technology before the 2002 and 2007 elections to support transparent and efficient administration of election processes, but it was generally slow in adopting the use of technology.[27] There was no clear strategy for technology integration and the process lacked statutory and regulatory backing. Moreover, stakeholders were not consulted, and staff were not properly trained on the use of technology in election administration.[28] The result was that technology had limited impact in results management, and a failure to report preliminary results in the December 2007 elections contributed to the widespread suspicion that the ECK lacked transparency and possibly manipulated the results.

After facing several challenges and false starts in the journey towards constitutional reform,[29] Kenya finally achieved a major milestone with the promulgation of a new constitution in 2010. This significant achievement followed a constitutional referendum, in which an overwhelming 67 per cent of Kenyans voted in favour of the Constitution. The success of the referendum can be attributed, in part, to the profound impact of the devastating 2007/2008 post-election violence that left a death toll of over 1,000 people and thousands more wounded and internally displaced.[30] This served as a wake-up call, highlighting the critical need for inclusivity and governance based on the rule of law rather than allegiance to a ruling elite or ethnic favouritism.

To further understand the changes Kenyans sought in the constitutional review process regarding elections, insights from the 2008 Independent Review Commission Report, commonly known as the 'Kriegler Report', which emerged following the 2007/2008 post-election violence, are valuable.[31] The Kriegler Report highlighted severe weaknesses in the ECK, leading to a loss of public confidence and institutional legitimacy. It thus recommended an overhaul of the electoral management process.[32] Consequently, the ECK was disbanded and replaced by the Interim Independent Electoral Commission (IIEC) and Interim Independent Boundaries Review Commission (IIBRC). These interim bodies were tasked with revamping the electoral management system, introducing technology in elections,

[27] *Election Technology and Election Justice in Kenya* (International Commission of Jurists, 2022), p. 18

[28] Ibid. p. 19.

[29] Ndegwa et al., *History of Constitution Making in Kenya* (n 17) pp. 24–34; Civic Education for the Referendum, pp. 5–10.

[30] Truth Justice and Reconciliation Commission (TJRC), 'Report of the Truth, Justice and Reconciliation Commission', Volume IIB (2013), p. 312.

[31] Report of the Independent Review Commission (n 25).

[32] Ibid. pp. ix and 49.

creating a new voters' register and proposing boundary delimitation reforms.[33] It is the IIEC that successfully conducted the constitutional referendum that led to the enactment of the 2010 Constitution.

13.3 HARNESSING TECHNOLOGY FOR ELECTORAL INTEGRITY AND LEGITIMACY: THE ROLE OF TECHNOLOGY IN KENYA'S 2013 AND 2017 GENERAL ELECTIONS

The history of Kenya's elections has been marred by human interference through election rigging, voter bribery, state-sponsored ethnic violence and media blackouts during the announcement of presidential election results.[34] These issues continue to exacerbate the divisiveness of elections in Kenya. As highlighted in the previous section, the Kriegler Commission Report noted the reluctance and indifference of the ECK to take steps to integrate technology and develop systems for results transmission and procurement. This Commission considered various proposals, including one from the International Foundation for Electoral Systems, advocating the integration of technology to streamline and facilitate electoral processes.[35] While acknowledging the efforts made between the 2002 and 2007 elections, the Kriegler Commission concluded that the introduction of technology in elections was inevitable to address existing challenges and enhance the integrity and legitimacy of the electoral process.[36] Notably, scholars perceived the adoption of technology in elections as a means to improve 'the administration of elections and increase voter confidence because of its perceived levels of accuracy, verifiability and efficiency as compared to manual systems'.[37] Consequently, the Kriegler Commission recommended that there be established 'without delay . . . an integrated and secure tallying and data transmission system'.[38]

The aim was to revamp the electoral management system and use technology as a key tool in election management processes, including the creation of a new voters' register. Subsequently, the IEBC was established upon the promulgation of the 2010 Constitution and took over the mandate of the IIEC and the IIBRC.[39] The

[33] Collins Odote and Linda Musumba (eds.), *Balancing the Scales of Electoral Justice: 2013 Kenyan Election Dispute Resolution and Emerging Jurisprudence* (Rome: International Development Law Organization and Judiciary Training Institute, 2016), pp. 4–5; Report of the Independent Review Commission (n 25) p. 102.

[34] Odote and Musumba, *Balancing the Scales*, pp. 2, 22 and 95.

[35] Report of the Independent Review Commission (n 25) p. 102.

[36] 36 Ibid.

[37] Marystella Simiyu, 'Election Technology as a Means of Enhancing Democratic Legitimacy: A Case of Kenya' in Aderomola Adeola and Makau W. Mutua (eds.), *The Palgrave Handbook of Democracy, Governance and Justice in Africa* (London: Palgrave Macmillan, 2022), p. 12; Nic Cheeseman, Gabrielle Lynch and Justin Willis, 'Digital Dilemmas: The Unintended Consequences of Election Technology' (2018) 25(8) *Democratization* 1397, at 1397–400.

[38] Kriegler and Waki Reports Summarised Version Revised Edition 2009, p. 30.

[39] Constitution of Kenya 2010, Ch 7; Regulation 82 of the Elections (General) Regulations 2012.

Independent Electoral and Boundaries Commission Act 2011 was then enacted as the first statute dedicated to the management and conduct of elections, outlining the Commission's additional functions, including the use of appropriate technology in its activities.[40]

Section 44(1) of the 2011 Elections Act provides for the use of technology in election processes. For the presidential election, the IEBC is required to transmit results electronically from polling stations to the constituency tallying centres (CTCs) and national tallying centres (NTCs) through the Results Transmission System (RTS). In addition, the IEBC is obligated to livestream and maintain a public portal for transparency and accountability.[41] By embracing technology in the electoral process and adhering to regulations that promote accessibility and inclusivity, the IEBC seeks to restore public trust and confidence in the electoral system, fostering a fair and credible electoral process in Kenya.

13.3.1 *The 2013 General Election*

The Kenyan public's hope for credible elections was evident in the 2013 general election, where a record 12 million Kenyans, accounting for 85.9 per cent of registered voters, turned out to vote – the highest turnout since the reintroduction of multi-party politics in Kenya.[42] The election marked the first use of the Biometric Voter Registration (BVR) System, an electronically based national register, replacing the manual register known as the Green Book for voter identification. The BVR System was accompanied by the Electronic Voter Identification System (EVID) to verify voters' identities.[43] The 2013 general election witnessed a closely contested race between two presidential candidates, Uhuru Kenyatta and Raila Odinga. After the election, Uhuru Kenyatta was declared the winner with 50.5 per cent of the votes. However, the outcome was quickly challenged in the consolidated petition of *Raila Odinga and 5 Others* v. *Independent Electoral and Boundaries Commission and 3 Others*.[44]

A significant point of contention in the petition was the failure of the RTS and the BVR, which led to multiple variations in the electronic data generated.[45] In its judgment, the Supreme Court acknowledged the irregularities in data and information capture during the registration process, but deemed them insufficient to affect the credibility of the electoral process.[46] Despite acknowledging various

[40] Independent Electoral and Boundaries Commission Act No. 9 of 2011, s. 4(l)(m).

[41] Elections Act 2011, ss. 39 and 44.

[42] Odote and Musumba, *Balancing the Scales* (n 33) p. 5; Simiyu, 'Election Technology', p. 18.

[43] Odote and Musumba, *Balancing the Scales* (n 33) p. 249.

[44] *Raila Odinga and 5 Others* v. *Independent Electoral and Boundaries Commission and 3 Others*, [2013] eKLR (2013 *Raila Odinga* case).

[45] Ibid. [246], [246], [253], [254] and [256]; Simiyu, 'Election Technology'(n 37) p. 18.

[46] 2013 *Raila Odinga* case.

irregularities, the Court found that the evidence did not demonstrate profound irregularities in the presidential election's conduct that would invalidate the final result.[47] Thus, the petition was disallowed, and the Supreme Court upheld the election's outcome.

In response to the discrepancies identified in the 2013 presidential election petition regarding the use of technology in managing and conducting elections, the Election Laws (Amendment) Act of 2016 was enacted to introduce legislative reforms related to election technology to address the issues. One crucial change was made to Section 39 of the Elections Act, requiring the mandatory electronic transmission of presidential election results from each polling station to both the CTCs and NTCs). The Act also mandated the IEBC to publish polling results forms on a publicly accessible online portal maintained by the Commission.[48]

Another significant amendment was made to Section 44 of the Elections Act, which established an integrated electronic electoral system, the Kenya Integrated Elections Management System (KIEMS). This system was designed to facilitate various functions, including biometric voter registration, electronic voter identification and electronic transmission of election results. To ensure the integrity of the technology used, the amendment stipulated that the electoral system must be simple, accurate, verifiable, secure, accountable and transparent.[49] These amendments were aimed at enhancing the reliability and credibility of election processes by leveraging technology.

13.3.2 *The 2017 General Election*

The challenges faced by IEBC in ensuring the proper conduct of elections and curbing illegalities and irregularities during the 2013 general election resulted in a significant decline in voter turnout, from 85.9 per cent in 2013 to 77.5 per cent in the 2017 general election.[50] This reflects a growing sense of voter apathy. The 2017 general election was held on 8 August 2017, and it was anticipated that the IEBC would address the technological issues encountered in the 2013 election. To achieve this, the IEBC implemented the KIEMS for the first time.[51] While the electoral technology performed better than it did in 2013, technological challenges were still encountered, affecting the perceived credibility and legitimacy of election results.[52]

47 Ibid. at [306].

48 Elections Act 2011, s. 39(1C).

49 Elections Act 2011, ss. 44(1), 44(2) and 44A.

50 Simiyu, 'Election Technology' (n 37) p. 22; Final Report Republic of Kenya General Elections 2017, European Union Election Observer Mission, 2018, p. 6.

51 The changes brought about by the KIEMS were reflected in the Elections Act through Election Laws (Amendment) Act 2016 and the Election Laws (Amendment) Act 2017.

52 Simiyu, 'Election Technology' (n 37) pp. 22 and 28; IEBC, Independent Audit of the Register of Voters, KPMG, 2017, p. 106.

Following the declaration of the incumbent president, Uhuru Kenyatta, as the winner by the IEBC returning officer for the presidential election on 11 August 2017, the opposition filed a petition, *Raila Amolo Odinga and Another* v. *Independent Electoral and Boundaries Commission and 2 Others*,[53] challenging the election's fairness and legality. Numerous election irregularities and illegalities were cited, particularly in relation to election technology. The petitioners sought an audit and scrutiny of all presidential election forms and the election system, including Forms 34A, 34B, 34C, and the KIEMS kits, server(s) and website/portal.[54]

In relation to the functions of Forms 34A, 34B and 34C, as per section 39(1C) of the Elections Act, upon tallying presidential election results at a polling station, the presiding election officer is to fill in the results in Form 34A and electronically transmit the scanned Form 34A to the CTC using the KIEMS kits. The returning officer at the CTC is then to verify and tabulate the results from the various polling stations in the constituency and then, using these, generate form 34B. The results are then to be sent to the NTC, where the chairperson of the IEBC is to follow the same process of verification and tabulation in generating Form 34C. Physical Forms 34A are then delivered to the NTC by the returning officers for comparison with the scanned forms.

The audit, supervised by the Supreme Court Registrar, ICT experts and agents of the parties, confirmed various discrepancies.[55] These include the fact that a significant number of the electronically transmitted election results were not accompanied by scanned images of Form 34A, contrary to Section 39(IC) of the Elections Act.[56] This illegality was said to be compounded by various issues: the fact that the results were announced on the basis of Forms 34B before receiving all the necessary Forms 34A; the results on the IEBC portal differed from those on the Forms 34B provided to the Court; there were variations between results displayed on the IEBC portal and those in Forms 34A and 34B; and manipulation of the IEBC electronic system by third parties that generated numbers for transmission to the NTC.[57] Indeed, the IEBC admitted that it had declared the election results before receiving results from 11,883 polling stations, 17 constituency tallying centres and authentic Forms 34A from 5,015 polling stations, which represented more than 3.5 million voters.[58] It was, therefore, the petitioners' contention that the transmission of unverified results flouted the principles of free and fair elections provided for in Article 81(e) of the

53 *Raila Amolo Odinga and Another* v. *Independent Electoral and Boundaries Commission and 2 Others*, [2017] eKLR (2017 *Raila Odinga* case).

54 Ibid. Order of 28 August 2017, [5].

55 Ibid. [73].

56 Ibid. [24]; Alvin Atallo, 'The Kenyan Supreme Court Overturns Presidential Election Results: Of Forms 34As, Bs and Cs', Oxford Human Rights Hub Blog, 26 October 2017.

57 2017 *Raila Odinga* case, [29].

58 Ibid. [273].

Constitution as read together with various provisions of the Elections Act, the Elections (General) Regulations and Section 25 of the IEBC Act.[59]

These discrepancies cast doubt on the integrity of the electoral process and raised questions about whether the election truly represented the free expression of the people's will, as envisioned in Article 38 of the Constitution.[60] Consequently, the Supreme Court made an unprecedented decision on 1 September 2017 to nullify the presidential election. Despite the efforts to improve the electoral process through technology, these discrepancies and irregularities raised concerns about the credibility and integrity of the election results. These issues further contributed to the prevailing sense of voter apathy, as citizens became more sceptical about the electoral process and its ability to reflect the true will of the people. As noted by political scientist Nic Cheeseman, misinformation in relation to the 2022 general election results appeared credible due to a history of failure of technology in 2013 and 2017, as it played into public expectations.[61]

13.4 THE EMERGENCE OF DISINFORMATION AND MISINFORMATION: IMPACT ON THE 2022 GENERAL ELECTION

In the lead-up to the 2022 general election, the IEBC worked diligently to address the challenges related to the use of technology in administering elections. But, at the same time, a concerning trend emerged, as politicians began adopting new strategies to influence political outcomes, capitalising on the rise of disinformation and misinformation. False narratives were strategically disseminated online by politicians with the intention of discrediting opposing candidates and gaining an advantage in the election. An example of this includes the spread of false claims, such as alleged defections or fabricated news of a candidate's demise, often strategically timed on the day of the election or in the days leading up to it.[62] This development aligns with Cheeseman's and political scientist Brian Klaas' observation that it has become increasingly difficult to detect election rigging. This is because whenever monitors devise new strategies to counter tried and true rigging tactics – in the case of Kenya, leveraging technology to prevent election rigging – dictators and despots continue to innovate.[63]

59 Ibid. [19].

60 Ibid. [292] and [378].

61 The Kenyan Elections 2022: The Role and Impact of Misinformation, Democracy in Africa, www.youtube.com/watch?v=_SGduMlo4EU.

62 The Reality of Fake News in Kenya, Portland–GeoPoll, 2018, https://portland-communications.com/pdf/The-Reality-of-Fake-News-in-Kenya.pdf, pp. 4–5.

63 Nic Cheeseman and Brian Klaas, 'How Autocrats Rig Elections to Stay in Power – and Get Away with It', *The Conversation*, 23 April 2018.

13.4.1 *Examining the Phenomenon of Disinformation and Misinformation in Kenya*

Beata Martin-Rozumiłowicz and Rasťo Kužel proffer an apt definition of disinformation as deliberately 'false or misleading information that is created or disseminated with the intent to cause harm or to benefit the perpetrator' and misinformation as 'false or misleading information that is shared without the intent to cause harm or realization that it is incorrect'.[64] In the context of elections, deliberately false information is spread to achieve political or financial gains and is usually directed towards either individuals, or groups, institutions and processes.[65] This section places its central emphasis on the utilisation of disinformation and misinformation, used interchangeably with the term fake news – defined as 'purposefully crafted, sensational, emotionally charged, misleading or totally fabricated information that mimics the form of mainstream news'[66] – as a strategic tool wielded by politicians and various stakeholders to manipulate and shape the political narratives and results within Kenya's electoral landscape. The discussion also covers instances where credible news is illegitimately labelled as 'fake news'.

Misinformation is 'one of the greatest challenges facing democracy in our time'.[67] In democratic societies, information is a powerful tool, especially during election campaigns. Kenyan elections exemplify this phenomenon, with a significant rise in digital campaigning across popular social media platforms such as Twitter and Facebook, messaging apps such as WhatsApp, and the video-sharing app, TikTok, during general elections.[68] At one end of the spectrum, this increases opportunities for the participation of women and youth, coordination by civil society and opposition, and undermines governmental control of information flow.[69] Social media has become an inseparable part of African politics, where politicians leverage influential bloggers to bypass mainstream media and directly reach voters with their campaign messages.[70] However, at the other end of the divide, this approach often involves collaborating with global firms, alongside local tech-savvy teams that engage in disinformation campaigns against election opponents.[71]

64 Beata Martin-Rozumiłowicz and Rasťo Kužel, *Social Media, Disinformation and Electoral Integrity*, IFES Working Paper, International Foundation for Electoral Systems, August 2019, p. 10. See also Fombad, 'Democracy and Fake News in Africa', p. 137.

65 Martin-Rozumiłowicz and Kužel, *Social Media*; Gillian McKay, 'Disinformation and Democratic Transition: A Kenyan Case Study', Human Rights and IHL, 22 June 2022.

66 See https://guides.lib.uw.edu/bothell/news/misinfo.

67 Nic Cheeseman, 'Kenya 2022: Lies, Damn Lies, and Statistics', *The Africa Report*, 2 September 2022.

68 Benjamin Imende, 'Uhuru, Raila Teams Take Campaign Wars Online', *The Star*, 6 June 2017.

69 Nic Cheeseman et al., 'Social Media Disruption: Nigeria's WhatsApp Politics' (2020) 31(3) *Journal of Democracy* 145, at 145–47.

70 The Kenyan Elections 2022 (n 61).

71 Imende, 'Uhuru, Raila Teams'.

The potency of misinformation relies heavily on the extent of internet penetration within a country. As of 2022, reports indicated that internet penetration in Kenya stood at approximately 85 per cent according to Reuters, while Article 19, a human rights organisation, estimated it to be even higher at 93.7 per cent.[72] In addition, there were around 11 million social media users, and this number continues to grow daily.[73] Unfortunately, Kenya's low literacy rate means that internet users can be susceptible to believing and sharing fake news, turning 'uninformed voters' into 'misinformed voters'.[74]

The prevalence of big data in this digital landscape opens the door for foreign companies to engage in user profiling and targeted election campaigns online, exploiting the ease with which individuals can be tracked through social media platforms. The utilisation of information in elections is not a novel concept, and some argue it is akin to 'traditional media advertising', which employs surveys and focus groups to identify the most effective approaches for pitching newspaper and TV advertisements to voters.[75] The use of data in elections and political campaigns is also likened to the data practices used in marketing and commercial advertising.[76] Data companies often claim that the collection of information for profiling purposes is solely aimed at tailoring campaign messaging to suit individual voters, but this assurance raises apprehensions regarding the extent to which voters' actions and beliefs are recorded and manipulated to achieve specific outcomes for particular candidates. This concern is particularly pronounced in authoritarian contexts, where the ruling elite benefit more from such practices due to their greater access to campaign resources and the government's ability to restrict the entry of employees from companies supporting the opposition by denying them visas.[77]

Modern autocrats increasingly find digital manipulation of data and information to be a useful tool, not only because it offers distinct advantages but also because it falls into a legal grey area, escaping strict regulation as election rigging.[78] This makes it an appealing option for those seeking to influence elections discreetly. As Charles

[72] Digital News Report 2022, Reuters Institute, 2022, https://reutersinstitute.politics.ox.ac.uk/digital-news-report/2022, p. 154; Content Moderation and Local Stakeholders in Kenya. Article 19, 2022, www.article19.org/wp-content/uploads/2022/06/Kenya-country-report.pdf, p. 15.

[73] Article 19, 'Content Moderation'.

[74] Fombad, 'Democracy and Fake News in Africa' (n 5) pp. 139–40.

[75] Nic Cheeseman and Brian Klaas, *How to Rig an Election* (London: Yale University Press, 2018), p. 148.

[76] 'Texas Media Company Hired by Trump Created Kenyan President's Viral "Anonymous" Attack Campaign against Rival, New Investigation Reveals', *Privacy International*, 15 December 2017, https://privacyinternational.org/long-read/954/texas-media-company-hired-trump-created-kenyan-presidents-viral-anonymous-attack.

[77] Cheeseman and Klaas, *How to Rig an Election*, p. 148. See also 'Kenya's Social Media Election: Attack Ads and Data Mining', *The Independent*, 27 July 2017, www.independent.co.ug/kenyas-social-media-election-attack-ads-data-mining.

[78] Cheeseman and Klaas, *How to Rig an Election* (n 75) p. 132.

Fombad aptly observes, this strategy makes 'old techniques such as vote-buying, ballot-box-stuffing and double-voting seem positively crude and outdated'.[79]

Mounting concerns surround the increasingly sophisticated methods data companies use to collaborate with candidates in engineering electoral victories through leveraging information to their advantage.[80] In Kenya, Cambridge Analytica, known for its data-driven approach to 'changing audience behaviour', was reported to have been involved in President Uhuru Kenyatta's 2013 and 2017 general election campaigns.[81] The company engages in mining user data from social platforms to target specific messages at individuals, based on profiles created from their internet usage, with the aim to encourage supporters to vote and discourage opponents from showing up to polling stations.[82] These tactics provide a significant electoral advantage to a party, yet they are not explicitly prohibited by electoral law in Kenya, and they are not typically categorised as election rigging in election observation reports such as the IEBC's Post-election Evaluation Report.[83] This raises concerns about the lack of regulation and oversight regarding such practices, and the potential impact on the democratic process and the integrity of elections.

There has been a significant growth in the complexity of disinformation campaigns, in terms of both the content disseminated and the channels used for distribution. Much misinformation is hard to prove or disprove as the information appears highly plausible to a broad range of people. Studies have shown that misinformation is more effective where it plays into existing prejudices or assumptions about a candidate, for example where it involves claims of corruption, incompetence, moral bankruptcy or failures as a spouse.[84]

In Kenya's 2022 general election, TikTok emerged as a major purveyor of false information.[85] Other studies reveal that Facebook was predominantly used for spreading campaign messages, while WhatsApp proved highly effective for mobilisation due to its extensive user base.[86] Aside from these, so-called political keyboard warriors emerged. These are bloggers who strategically position themselves during political campaigns to either create a favourable image of a candidate or decampaign their opponents by spreading misinformation, often in exchange for

79 Fombad, 'Democracy and Fake News in Africa' (n 5) p. 141.

80 Cheeseman and Klaas, *How to Rig an Election* (n 75) p. 148.

81 See 'After Trump, "Big Data" Firm Cambridge Analytica Is Now Working in Kenya', BBC, 3 August 2017, www.bbc.com/news/blogs-trending-40792078.

82 Cheeseman and Klaas, *How to Rig an Election* (n 75) p. 133.

83 'Post-Election Evaluation Report for the 9th August, 2022 General Election: Moving Kenya towards a Stronger Democracy', Independent Electoral and Boundaries Commission, 2022, www.iebc.or.ke/uploads/resources/pabjKTV6Xa.pdf.

84 Cheeseman, 'Social Media Disruption', p. 152; The Kenyan Elections 2022 (n 61).

85 Seth Smalley, 'Kenya's Presidential Election a Hotbed of False Information ahead of and during Voting', *Poynter*, 17 August 2022.

86 The Kenyan Elections 2022 (n 61).

payment.[87] Bloggers also spread misinformation to motivate candidates to hire them to rewrite the narrative and frame them in a positive light.[88]

The combination of these tactics raises legitimate concerns about the manipulation of information and its impact on the democratic process, particularly considering that research indicates at least 75 per cent of Kenyan news consumers struggle to discern between real and fake news.[89] Further, a survey conducted in connection with the 2017 general election uncovered that approximately 90 per cent of respondents reported encountering content they suspected to be fake news, while around 80 per cent had come across information that they believed was intentionally fabricated or false.[90]

Unlike other rigging tactics commonly used in hybrid democracies like Kenya, disinformation stands out as a strategy available to both the government and the opposition to manipulate electoral outcomes.[91] Notably, there have been reports indicating that a group of Twitter influencers were allegedly paid by 'shadowy financers' in May and June 2021 to spread disinformation in favour of the government-backed Constitution of Kenya (Amendment) Bill 2020.[92] This Bill was developed by the Building Bridges Initiative (BBI) Steering Committee and was famously held to be an unconstitutional attempt at constitutional amendment by the Kenyan Supreme Court, having been initiated by the President rather than being citizen-driven, which is what a popular initiative ought to be.[93] The disinformation campaign involved the harassment and discrediting of journalists, judges and civil society activists on Twitter, harming the individuals targeted and also undermining the credibility of the institutions they represent, which are important pillars of democracy.[94] The disinformation campaign had a clear objective: to promote the BBI process and falsely portray the aforementioned group of people (journalists, judges and so on) as villains opposed to development, and as being funded by William Ruto, the then Deputy President, who opposed the amendment. The aim was to deceive people, through hashtags and photoshopped images, into believing

87 Ibid.; Cheeseman, 'Kenya 2022'; Lilian Olivia, 'Disinformation Was Rife in Kenya's 2022 Election', LSE, 5 January 2023 https://blogs.lse.ac.uk/africaatlse/2023/01/05/disinformation-was-rife-in-kenyas-2022-election.

88 The Kenyan Elections 2022 (n 61).

89 *Digital News Report 2021*, Reuters Institute, 10th ed., 2021, p. 154.

90 The Reality of Fake News in Kenya (n 62) pp. 6–7.

91 Cheeseman and Klaas, *How to Rig an Election* (n 75) p. 129. Other strategies discussed include gerrymandering, vote buying, repression, ballot stuffing, and playing the international community.

92 Emmanuel Onyango, 'Kenyan Influencers Paid to Take "Guerrilla Warfare" Online', BBC News, 13 September 2021.

93 *Attorney General and 2 Others* v. *David Ndii and 79 Others*, [2022] eKLR, [238]–[239].

94 Onyango, 'Kenyan Influencers Paid'; 'Inside the Shadowy World of Disinformation for Hire in Kenya', Mozilla Foundation, https://assets.mofoprod.net/network/documents/Report_Inside_the_shadowy_world_of_disinformation_for_hire_in_Kenya_5._hcc.pdf.

that the trending opinions were widely popular, and to create a false narrative surrounding the BBI process.[95]

Commentators emphasise that the utilisation of data in elections and political campaigns is highly intrusive to individuals' privacy and gives rise to significant security questions. Moreover, such practices have the potential to erode trust in the democratic process, as citizens may question the authenticity and legitimacy of election outcomes when data manipulation is at play.[96] As the use of data and digital tactics in elections continues to evolve, it is crucial to strike a balance between the legitimate use of voter information for campaign messaging and safeguarding citizens' privacy and democratic values.

Concern has also been raised about the lack of accountability of global companies that engage in political campaigns within local contexts. A notable example of this occurred during Kenya's 2017 general elections, where campaigns conducted by Harris Media LLC insinuated that presidential aspirant Raila Odinga would be involved in forcibly displacing 'whole tribes from their homes'.[97] In a country with a history of electoral violence and deep ethnic divisions like Kenya, such online campaigns have the potential to stoke the embers of ethnic hatred and exacerbate social tensions.[98]

13.4.2 *Disinformation and Misinformation in the 2022 General Election*

The 2022 general election witnessed the lowest voter turnout in fifteen years, with a mere 65.4 per cent of the registered 22.12 million voters participating, signalling an alarming surge in voter apathy.[99] The deployment of the KIEMS technology played a pivotal role in BVR and, during election day, in voter identification and results transmission. Notably, this system was successfully deployed and showcased improvements compared to prior elections.[100] However, the overarching technological concern during this electoral cycle revolved around the proliferation of disinformation and misinformation across online platforms.

During the election period, a deluge of misinformation plagued social media platforms, including false claims of victory, alleged political kidnappings, conspiracy

95 'Inside the Shadowy World of Disinformation' (n 94) pp. 6–10.

96 'Texas Media Company Hired' (n 76).

97 See 'Kenya in 2020 if Raila Odinga Is Elected President', The Real Raila, www.youtube.com/watch?v=045NlqZXDXw.

98 'Kenya's Social Media Election' (n 77).

99 '2022 General Election Voter Turnout is 65.4pc, Chebukati Says', *Nation*, 10 August 2022, https://nation.africa/kenya/news/politics/2022-general-election-voter-turnout-is-65-4pc-chebukati-says-3909866; Roundtable – Kenya Post-Election 2022 Review, Kofi Annan Foundation, www.kofiannanfoundation.org/supporting-democracy-and-elections-with-integrity/kenya-post-election-roundtable-2022.

100 'Post-Election Evaluation Report' (n 83) p. xii.

theories and targeted attacks.[101] A deeply concerning facet of the misinformation campaigns was the prevalence of sexualised gender attacks, particularly targeting female political aspirants, through platforms including Twitter, WhatsApp and TikTok. The disproportionately frequent attacks against women candidates further compounded the existing challenges they already grapple with during electoral campaigns.[102] This situation was exacerbated by a critical factor: although the IEBC had posted images of Forms 34A illustrating results from approximately 99 per cent of the 46,663 polling stations across Kenya, the Commission had refrained from tabulating the cumulative figures on its public portal. The physical Forms 34A were being transported to the national tallying centre situated in the capital city, Nairobi, for comprehensive verification and tabulation of the grand totals before the official results were slated to be announced by the IEBC chairperson.[103]

This informational gap engendered a confusing tallying process, as different media platforms broadcast conflicting figures based on their individual tabulation of Forms 34A. For example, on 10 August 2022, Citizen TV showcased presidential candidate Odinga leading with 51.3 per cent of the vote, with William Ruto in close pursuit at 47.3 per cent. Concurrently, the Nation Media Group displayed Ruto in the lead with 50.7 per cent, followed by Odinga at 48.6 per cent. This scenario sowed confusion and provided fertile soil for the proliferation of false news narratives. As recent studies show, the spread of misinformation is also problematic when it is sustained in and through traditional media, where traditional media fails to challenge misinformation.[104]

A Mozilla Foundation study highlights that the spread of misinformation was further amplified by tech platforms, contributing to the uncertainty surrounding election results. Despite assurances from these tech companies that they would address problematic content in the run-up to the elections, the proliferation of misinformation remained a significant issue.[105] This failure to effectively combat the dissemination of false information on their platforms contributed to public confusion and distrust, as voters struggled to distinguish accurate information from misleading claims. On this issue, Cheeseman aptly observes:

[101] Odanga Madung, 'Opaque and Overstretched, Part II: How Platforms Failed to Curb Misinformation during the Kenyan 2022 Election', Mozilla Foundation, https://foundation.mozilla.org/en/campaigns/opaque-and-overstretched-part-ii.

[102] '"Fake News" in Kenya's 2022 Elections: What Has Gender Got to Do with It?', *Fumbua*, 3 August 2022, https://fumbua.ke/2022/08/03/fake-news-in-kenyas-2022-elections-what-has-gender-got-to-do-with-it.

[103] Duncan Miriri and Ayenat Mersie, 'Early Signs Show Right Kenyan Presidential Election', Reuters, 10 August 2022.

[104] Ibid.

[105] 'Fellow Research: Platforms Failed to Curb Misinformation after Kenyan Election', Mozilla Foundation, 3 November 2022, https://foundation.mozilla.org/en/blog/fellow-research-platforms-failed-to-curb-misinformation-after-kenyan-election.

> Even those of us well seasoned in analysing rigging claims have struggled to cope with the bewildering monsoon of misinformation that has rained down on social media. When you wake up every morning to a new set of messages about how the process was manipulated, it can be hard not to believe there must be something in them – even as every claim you investigate turns out to be unconvincing.[106]

After the announcement of Ruto as President-elect by then IEBC Chairperson Wafula Chebukati on 15 August 2022, with a margin of 50.49 per cent in the presidential vote compared to the runner-up Odinga's 48.85 per cent, numerous parties contested the result of the presidential race. This situation became more pronounced following a last-minute announcement by four IEBC commissioners who disavowed the verification and tallying process, asserting that the actual results diverged from those about to be declared by the chairperson.[107] This dramatic turn of events occurred just prior to the chairperson's planned announcement of the results, and was replayed on social media by prominent political leaders, causing a heightened state of agitation among Kenyans, and fuelling a surge of conspiracy theories online. As noted by a recent study, misinformation in relation to election results in 2022 appeared credible not only due to a history of failure of technology, which played into public expectations, but also due to its perpetuation by authority figures.[108] Where senior political leaders repeated what was not true, it gave false reports a second life by giving the misinformation political legitimacy.[109]

The consolidated presidential election petitions were titled *Raila Odinga and 16 Others* v. *William Ruto and 10 Others; Law Society of Kenya and 4 Others* (amicus curiae).[110] Similar to the preceding two post-2010 presidential election petitions, the contention arose that the deployment and utilisation of technology did not align with the prescribed constitutional and statutory standards.[111] In response, the IEBC asserted that the electronic election management system conformed to the constitutional criteria and that only authorised individuals could access the essential information, ensuring accuracy, completeness and protection against tampering, from both authorised and unauthorised sources.[112] Upon an order from the Supreme Court, the IEBC granted all petitioners supervised access to servers once the petition commenced. The Court also allowed for a thorough examination, recounting and scrutiny of the ballot boxes from the polling stations in question.[113]

[106] Cheeseman, 'Kenya 2022' (n 67).
[107] *Raila Odinga and 16 Others* v. *William Ruto and 10 Others; Law Society of Kenya and 4 Others* (amicus curiae) [2022] eKLR, [61]–[62] (2022 *Raila Odinga* case).
[108] Cheeseman et al., 'Social Media Disruption' (n 69) p. 152.
[109] The Kenyan Elections 2022 (n 61).
[110] 2022 *Raila Odinga* case.
[111] Ibid at 4.
[112] Ibid.
[113] Ibid. at 9, 22 and 48.

The Court found that there was insufficient evidence to support the assertion that the technology deployed in the election administration failed to meet the prescribed standard set out in Article 86(a) of the Constitution, which encompasses transparency, security, integrity and verifiability.[114] While acknowledging instances of KIEMS kit failures, the Court noted that manual verification successfully took place for the 235 polling stations where the KIEMS kits malfunctioned. It emphasised that Kenya's election process is a blend of technology and manual methods, rendering the resort to manual voting for 86,889 voters compliant and not a disenfranchisement.[115]

It was held that the petitioners did not present any evidence that met the requisite standard of proof to demonstrate unauthorised access to the electronic election management system. The Registrar of the Supreme Court's report likewise failed to indicate any security breaches in the Results Transmission System by unauthorised individuals.[116] Addressing the petitioners' claim of manipulation involving 11,000 Forms 34A before being uploaded onto the IEBC's online public portal within eight minutes, the Court termed this assertion as practically implausible, as it would necessitate intricate coordination of people and alteration by individuals and machines across all 11,000 polling stations in question.[117]

In addition, the claim that certain Forms 34A presented to agents differed from those on the public portal was dismissed for lack of credible evidence. The Court disallowed the use of Forms 34A provided in affidavits by two advocates representing the first petitioner, which deviated significantly from the originals and certified copies on the public portal.[118] The Court reprimanded the advocates for presenting misleading or fabricated evidence in the judicial process. The Court also noted instances of false and misleading information in the affidavit of prominent Kenyan corruption whistle-blower, John Githongo, including forgeries and inadmissible hearsays. Githongo's application to withdraw the affidavit was denied by the Court.[119] The Court's frustration with the petitioners' assertions, which ultimately held no evidential weight despite a rigorous trial process and thorough investigation, prompted the Court to label these claims as mere 'hot air' and liken their pursuit to a 'wild goose chase'.[120] Concluding that the evidence was insufficient to warrant the annulment of the presidential election, the seven-judge Supreme Court bench unanimously dismissed the consolidated petition, thereby upholding the IEBC's declaration of Ruto as the president-elect.[121]

[114] Ibid.
[115] Ibid at 7–8.
[116] Ibid. at 9.
[117] Ibid. at 9–10.
[118] Ibid. at 10.
[119] Ibid. at 11 and 97.
[120] Ibid. at 54.
[121] Ibid. at 19.

As discussed, a concerning increase in the use of misinformation was observed after voting and during the hearing of the petition. It was argued that this increase was attributed to the fact that since voting was over, the potential for backlash from this misinformation affecting voting behaviour was reduced.[122] Even more alarming was the alleged verification of the misinformation by trusted interlocutors such as Githongo, which made the misinformation more likely to be believed by Kenyans. However, little attention was paid to the potential impact of this misleading content on voter sentiment and behaviour, as well as the legitimacy of the new government and credibility of the IEBC.[123] The unchecked dissemination of misinformation can have serious consequences for the democratic process and the extent to which Kenyans can trust future electoral processes to be credible, warranting a closer examination of its implications on voter decision-making and the overall electoral landscape.

13.4.3 *Impact of Disinformation and Misinformation during the 2022 General Election*

With the rise in disinformation and unjustified labelling of credible news sources as 'fake news', there has been a concerning decline in public trust, affecting key institutions such as the traditional media (TV, radio and newspapers) and the IEBC. Kenya is already categorised as a low-trust society, with both political and social trust being at low levels.[124] Trust is a crucial element in the functioning of a democracy, and its absence poses a significant barrier to the consolidation of democratic values and principles.[125]

The erosion of trust can be traced back to the aftermath of the 2007/2008 post-election violence and the subsequent disputed elections in the following electoral cycles, as earlier discussed. These events shook public confidence in the electoral process and raised doubts about the credibility of election outcomes. In particular, the nullification of the 2017 elections, which was overseen by the same chairperson as the 2022 elections, Wafula Chebukati, further contributed to the diminished trust in the IEBC. On this, it has been argued that:

[122] The Kenyan Elections 2022 (n 61).

[123] Ibid.

[124] Matias Bargsted et al. assert that 'social (or generalized) trust refers to the belief that the actions of others will affect positively our own wellbeing, and that others will refrain from selfish, opportunistic, and hostile behavior. Political trust, in turn, refers to our positive expectations regarding the behavior of institutions such as the parliament, government, political parties and courts, and of those individuals leading these institutions, which are perceived as competent, credible, and fair'. Matias Bargsted et al., 'Social and Political Trust in a Low Trust Society' (2023) 45(4) *Political Behavior* 1401, at 1403.

[125] Nic Cheeseman, 'The Lack of Trust at the Heart of Kenya's Democracy', OxPol, 29 October 2013.

> Misinformation thrives, of course, when key institutions cannot be trusted and when it is repeated by respected figures. In the context of the Kenyan elections, many citizens went into the campaign with limited trust in Chebukati because he had presided over the 2017 elections that was nullified by the Supreme Court. Their trust was further eroded – some might say exploded – when, just as he was about to read out the result, four 'rebel' commissioners gave a rival 'presser' saying they could not stand behind the results. It did not matter that when the four commissioners subsequently provided details of their concerns it transpired that they rested, in part, on a mathematical misunderstanding so basic that it called into question both their capacity and their motivations. The sight of the IEBC once again at war with itself was enough to give credence to the claims the Commission had been politically captured and had fabricated the entire process.[126]

The growing distrust of Kenya's traditional media has created an environment conducive to disinformation and misinformation. Studies reveal a decline in public trust in mainstream media, which can be attributed to its perceived affiliation with ethnic and class interests.[127] When media outlets display discernible bias towards a particular candidate or political agenda, it further erodes public trust.[128] The concentration of media ownership in the hands of the political elite has strengthened the perception that the media is captured, prioritising the interests of political and corporate elites over its role in serving the public interest.[129] The media's portrayal of varied election results following the 2022 elections only reinforced this perception of capture by political elites. The contradictory reporting by different media outlets contributed to the growing scepticism among the public, as they struggled to determine the accuracy and impartiality of the information presented.

Dubbed as '*githeri* media' in a derogatory manner after its coverage of the 2017 elections, traditional media has lost its position as the primary agenda setter in the country, yielding ground to social media.[130] The term '*githeri*' refers to a simple local dish made of maize and beans boiled or fried together. The label '*githeri* media' is considered a symbol of disapproval, highlighting mainstream media's fixation on trivial matters. This was evident during the 2017 general election when traditional media incessantly covered a man eating '*githeri*' while overlooking more critical issues related to electoral irregularities and malpractices that were being discussed on social media platforms.[131] This focus on the trivial over substantive electoral

[126] Cheeseman, 'Kenya 2022' (n 67).

[127] Abdullahi Boru Halakhe, 'R2P in Practice': Ethnic Violence, Elections and Atrocity Prevention in Kenya, Global Centre for the Responsibility to Protect Occasional Paper Series No. 4, December 2013, pp. 9–11.

[128] Ibid. p. 11.

[129] Reuters Institute, *Digital News Report* 2021 p. 154; Fombad, 'Democracy and Fake News in Africa' (n 5) p. 133.

[130] George Ogola, 'Kenya's 2017 Elections: How New Media Stole the Mainstream's Thunder', *The Conversation*, 14 December 2017; The Kenyan Elections 2022 (n 61).

[131] Ibid.

matters further eroded public trust in traditional media. However, the decline in public trust in media is an Africa-wide phenomenon.[132]

With the public's increasing scepticism towards traditional media, authoritarian figures and ruling elites find it easier to maintain their grip on power. They capitalise on discrediting independent media outlets that challenge the official state narrative. By undermining the credibility of those who question their authority, these elites can control the flow of information and shape the public perception in their favour.[133] Alongside the credibility deficit caused by the weakened trust in traditional media is the creation of a stratified society in terms of believability of information. As George Ogola correctly posits:

> Significant too are the hierarchies that have emerged online. Those with the largest following tend to be politicians, celebrities, media personalities and those familiar with the digital literacy necessary to build a following. What these people say dominate conversations. The nature of agenda setting is thus personality driven. This is one of the most fundamental flaws of the online communication economy, and one that demands that we develop a deep circumspection.[134]

Moreover, the rise of fake news and digitally manipulated information has given rise to what is known as a 'post-truth' world,[135] where objective facts are heavily contested, and voters may be swayed more by emotions than by verifiable information when making decisions on certain issues or leaders. In this environment, all information can be subject to doubt and scrutiny, allowing election-rigging claims to be disputed and enabling rigged elections to be falsely portrayed as legitimate.[136]

In the past, authoritarian leaders had to exert significant effort to suppress information to maintain control. However, researchers now observe that many voters seem content with only receiving information provided by the government, effectively granting the government complete authority over defining truth and falsehood. This control over information empowers governments to manipulate facts at will, leading citizens to accept blatantly false statements.[137] As a result, the flow of information becomes so controlled by authoritarian regimes that they may no longer need to engage in overt rigging at the ballot box. Instead, they rely on indoctrination and fear tactics to achieve the same desired outcomes from the electorate.[138] In such a post-truth landscape, the erosion of public trust in reliable sources of information

[132] 'Protecting Electoral Integrity in the Digital Age: The Report of the Kofi Annan Commission on Elections and Democracy in the Digital Age', Kofi Annan Foundation, 2020, p. 33.

[133] Cheeseman and Klaas, *How to Rig an Election* (n 75) p. 134.

[134] Ogola, 'Kenya's 2017 Elections'.

[135] Steve Tesich, 'A Government of Lies', *The Nation*, 6 January 1992; Fombad, 'Democracy and Fake News in Africa' (n 5) pp. 132–33.

[136] Cheeseman and Klaas, *How to Rig an Election* (n 75) p. 139.

[137] Ibid. p. 140.

[138] Ibid. p. 141.

and the dissemination of disinformation create challenges for democratic processes. The acceptance of false narratives and the rejection of objective facts may hinder the ability of citizens to make informed choices, leading to the entrenchment of authoritarian rule and undermining the principles of free and fair elections.

Nevertheless, while fake news and misinformation remain challenges for democracies globally, misinformation did not reach the heightened levels many had feared in the 2022 Kenyan elections. Save for one doctored video of Ruto apparently attacking non-Kalenjin communities, which was quickly discredited by mainstream media,[139] the harder elements of misinformation such as use of deep fakes were absent. Kenya's 2022 elections demonstrated that social media, through which a large portion of misinformation is spread, has not entirely changed the nature of elections in Kenya. Success in elections requires great investment in interpersonal campaigns, meaning that a candidate cannot rely exclusively on digital campaigns to sway the voting population. Nevertheless, it is unclear how much digital conversations affect behaviour offline or influence voting decisions.[140] Therefore, the intersection between digital media and pavement media in influencing opinions is an area that requires further investigation.

13.5 DETECTING AND COMBATING DISINFORMATION AND MISINFORMATION: LEGAL LANDSCAPE AND ENGAGING STAKEHOLDERS FOR ELECTORAL INTEGRITY

Given the detrimental impact of disinformation and misinformation on the foundations of democracy and the exercise of political rights, there is an urgent need to implement robust strategies for detecting and combating this pervasive problem. This urgency is underscored by Kenya's historical context, marked by instances of election-related violence and manipulation, where the amplification of misinformation exacerbates the issues of voter disengagement, ethnic divisions and a general sense of bewilderment among the populace. In this section, we explore various recommendations that have been proposed, including legal, policy and institutional measures. Education and media literacy initiatives are also crucial to empowering citizens to discern accurate information from fake news and are discussed here. The section also highlights the significance of transparency, accountability and responsible use of technology to safeguard the legitimacy of elections and democratic processes. It thus emphasises the need to balance the use of technology, freedom of speech and media regulation.

139 Bosco Marita, 'Viral Video of Ruto Allegedly Attacking Communities Fake', *The Star*, 2 August 2022.

140 The Kenyan Elections 2022 (n 61).

13.5.1 *Legal and Legislative Approaches to Combating Disinformation and Misinformation*

In examining the legal and legislative measures to address fake news, it is essential to begin with Kenya's Constitution. Article 33(1) of the 2010 Constitution guarantees the right to freedom of expression, including seeking, receiving and imparting information. However, this right is not absolute, as Article 33(2) clarifies that it does not protect expression that spreads propaganda for war, incites violence, constitutes hate speech, advocates ethnic incitement leading to harm or vilification of others, or promotes discrimination based on protected characteristics. In the context of Kenya's elections, this would specifically involve combating the spread of ethnic hate speech, incitement to violence and defamatory statements that damage the reputation of others (Article 33(3)). Thus, a delicate balance is required between the right to freedom of expression, which includes freedom of speech, and protecting individuals from the harmful effects of misinformation and disinformation. In addition, Article 31 on the right to privacy also places limitations on freedom of expression by safeguarding individuals' right to protect information about their families, private affairs and private communications.

Mainly applicable to journalists, Article 34(1) of the Constitution further guarantees the freedom of the media and the independence of electronic, print and other types of media. However, the limits set out in Articles 31, 33(2) and 33(3) also apply to the media. Article 34(3) allows for necessary regulation of the media to strike a balance between media freedom and preventing the dissemination of harmful information. The limits set in the aforementioned articles have, at times, been exploited to enable the unjust regulation of the media under the pretext of curbing unprotected forms of expression. Nonetheless, the courts have periodically struck down such provisions based on constitutional grounds.[141]

An additional constraint on freedom of expression and the media is encapsulated in Article 24 of the Bill of Rights, which constitutes the general limitation clause. Article 24(1) provides that fundamental rights 'shall not be limited except by law, and then only to the extent that the limitation is reasonable and justifiable in an open and democratic society based on human dignity, equality, and freedom'. Subsequently, the latter part of the limitation clause (Articles 24(1)(a)–(e)) introduces a proportionality test, delineating five factors that must be considered to determine the appropriateness of limiting a particular right. These factors encompass 'the nature of the fundamental right or freedom', 'the significance of the purpose of the limitation', 'the character and scope of the limitation', 'the necessity to ensure that an individual's enjoyment of rights and fundamental freedoms does not impair the rights and freedoms of others' and 'the connection between the

[141] See 'Kenya: Freedom on the Net 2022', Freedom House, https://freedomhouse.org/country/kenya/freedom-net/2022#footnote1_2u96e24.

limitation and its purpose, along with the presence of less restrictive means to achieve the intended goal'. These constitutional provisions are reinforced by Article 27(4), which essentially prohibits misinformation and disinformation directly or indirectly discriminating against individuals based on various grounds, 'including race, sex, pregnancy, marital status, health status, ethnic or social origin, colour, age, disability, religion, conscience, belief, culture, dress, language or birth'.

In addition to the constitutional measures, various statutes penalise the dissemination of certain kinds of fake news. One such is the Data Protection Act of 2019, which in section 2 defines data as any processed and recorded information by means of equipment operating automatically in response to instructions or as part of a relevant filing system. Section 25 of the Act sets out the principles and obligations of data protection, emphasising the respect for the right to privacy of the data subject and that personal data should be 'collected for explicit, specified and legitimate purposes and not further processed in a manner incompatible with those purposes'.[142] The Act also requires data controllers or processors to ensure that personal data is accurate and kept up-to-date, with measures taken to promptly erase or rectify any false or misleading data.[143] These provisions serve to protect against fake news that violates individuals' privacy through the dissemination of personal data and the use of altered photos and videos, commonly known as deepfakes, to spread misinformation and disinformation.[144] As noted above, however, the use of deepfakes in the 2022 general elections was limited.

Section 26 of the Act further provides for the rights of erasure, correction or deletion of false or misleading data, as well as the right to be informed and consent to the collection and use of personal data. Meanwhile, section 28 permits the collection of data from public records when the same has been made public or with the data subject's consent from another source. However, sections 28 and 29 also mandate that reasonable steps must be taken to notify the data subject that their data is being processed, and failure to do so is considered an offence. These provisions aim to address the spread of fake news that involves the manipulation of personal data and provide individuals with the right to manage their data, ensuring accuracy and protection from misuse.

Second, the Computer Misuse and Cybercrimes Act of 2018 addresses the intentional publication of falsehoods and misinformation. In section 22(1) of the Act, the deliberate dissemination of false information is criminalised, and those found guilty can face a fine of 5 million shillings (Ksh; $50,000) or a maximum of two years' imprisonment, or both. Furthermore, section 22(2) of the Act limits freedom of expression, in accordance with Articles 24 and 33 of the Constitution,

[142] Data Protection Act No. 24 of 2019, ss. 25(a) and 25(c).

[143] Ibid., s. 25(f),

[144] See Faith Amatika-Omondi, 'Regulation of Deep Fakes in Kenya' (2022) 2(1) *Journal of Intellectual Property and Information Technology Law* 145, at 170.

with regard to intentional publication of falsehoods and misinformation. The Act specifically targets content that is likely to incite violence, promote war, propagate ethnic hate speech or discrimination, and negatively affect the rights or reputations of others. Section 23 further addresses the intentional publication of false information with the specific intention of causing panic and chaos, or inciting violence. Those found guilty of spreading such false information can face severe penalties, including a fine of Ksh 5 million or a maximum of ten years' imprisonment, or both. These legal measures serve to deter the spread of fake news and misinformation in the digital realm, ensuring accountability for those who intentionally disseminate harmful false information.

The constitutionality of the Computer Misuse and Cybercrimes Act was contested in the case of *Bloggers Association of Kenya (BAKE)* v. *Attorney General and 3 Others; Article 19 East Africa and Another (Interested Parties)*.[145] With regard to sections 22 and 23 of the Act, which criminalise the dissemination of false information, the petitioners argued that truth was not a prerequisite for free speech. They further contended that these laws, which aimed to regulate truth using terms such as 'false, misleading or fictitious data or information', could infringe upon the freedom of expression.[146] In response, the Court reasoned that 'the state has a legitimate interest in ensuring the safety and integrity of information and the protection of its citizens against cybercrimes', especially when the freedom of expression impacts not just individual rights but also the broader public.[147]

Considering the rapid dissemination of misinformation or fake news on the Internet, leading to fear, panic and even potential threats to national security, the limitations imposed by sections 22 and 23 of the Act in the form of the offence of publishing false information over a computer system were found to be reasonable, justifiable and in line with the constraints set out in Articles 24, 31, 33(2) and 33(3) of the Constitution.[148] These provisions permit publishers to express themselves as long as their expression does not harm others and avoids constituting cyber libel.

Addressing the claim that the terms 'false, misleading or fictitious data or information' are vague, overbroad and would have a chilling effect on speech by, inter alia, journalists, activists, academics and politicians, Justice Makau held that the language used in sections 22 and 23 is precise and clear when interpreted contextually according to statutory interpretation principles.[149] He further noted that the term 'false' is readily understood in plain English, and does not necessitate a legal definition. Its application in section 23 was said to be evident – to criminalise the dissemination of false information with the intention to induce panic, chaos,

[145] *Bloggers Association of Kenya (BAKE)* v. *Attorney General and 3 Others; Article 19 East Africa and Another (Interested Parties)* [2020] eKLR.

[146] Ibid. at [31].

[147] Ibid. at [39] and [40].

[148] Ibid. at [40]–[47].

[149] Ibid. at [49]–[50] and [62]–[65].

violence or tarnish an individual's reputation.[150] As a result, the Court upheld the constitutionality of these two provisions.[151] However, civil society actors continue to call for the repeal of sections 22 and 23 of the Act. They argue that 'The vague prohibition of "false", "misleading" and "fictitious" data is highly subjective, and this law has been used to harass journalists, bloggers and activists in the past'.[152] They thus recommend the removal and replacement of these sections with less intrusive measures to combat disinformation.[153]

Third, the Defamation Act offers civil remedies in cases where fake news qualifies as libel, as outlined in Section 7(3).[154] It is also important to note that Section 7(3) specifies that the Act does not protect the publication of any matter that is not of public concern and that does not serve the public benefit. The Act ensures that the law supports the freedom of expression regarding matters of public interest, while also holding individuals accountable for spreading false information that can harm others or undermine public trust in the media.

Fourth, Section 66(1) of the Penal Code criminalises the publication of false statements, rumours or reports that could potentially induce fear, alarm or disrupt public peace.[155] This section designates such actions as misdemeanours and assigned guilt to those perpetrating them. Nonetheless, if the accused person can demonstrate that they took reasonable measures to verify the accuracy of the news before publication, believing it to be true, Section 66(2) provides them with a legal defence.

In the case of *Cyprian Andama* v. *Director of Public Prosecutions & 2 Others; Article 19 East Africa (Interested Party)*, the petitioner challenged the constitutionality of section 66(1).[156] The petitioner argued that the wording of this section, which states, 'likely to cause fear and alarm to the public or to disturb public peace', was overly vague and its coverage too broad, thus allowing for subjective interpretations and potential misuse in charging individuals. This, the petitioner contended, violated their Article 33 right to freedom of expression.[157] Furthermore, it was asserted that the provision was so unclear and uncertain that individuals could not discern the boundaries of permissible communication, potentially ensnaring both innocent individuals and those who were not.[158] The central issue before the High Court revolved around whether the limitations on freedom of expression outlined in

150 Ibid.
151 Ibid. at [150].
152 Final Report of 9 August 2022, European Union Election Observer Mission in Kenya General Elections, 2022, p. 29.
153 Ibid.
154 Defamation Act, Cap 36 of the Laws of Kenya, 1970.
155 Penal Code, Cap 63 of the Laws of Kenya, 1930.
156 *Cyprian Andama* v. *Director of Public Prosecutions & 2 Others; Article 19 East Africa (Interested Party)* [2021] eKLR.
157 Ibid. [1]–[5].
158 Ibid. [12].

Section 66 of the Penal Code could be deemed reasonable and justifiable in a free and democratic society, as mandated by Article 24 of the Constitution, which sets conditions for limiting fundamental rights and freedoms.[159]

Justice Korir's judgment established that Section 66 allowed for the conviction of individuals merely for making statements that were considered untrue, without placing the burden on the prosecutor to demonstrate the statement's falsehood. This, in turn, created an atmosphere of trepidation surrounding the exercise of freedom of expression.[160] Moreover, the section was deemed excessively broad as it could potentially prohibit not only the publication of false statements but also opinions that were honestly believed to be truthful, violating the rule that legal provisions establishing criminal offences are to be clear, concise and unambiguous.[161] The Court also noted that the Defamation Act offered a less restrictive means of safeguarding the reputation of individuals who had been unfairly defamed. It provided a civil remedy to restrain those intending to damage others' reputations by inflicting monetary penalties through the award of damages.[162] Consequently, the Court ruled that Section 66 was an unjustified violation of Article 33 and, therefore, unconstitutional.[163] A cautious approach is thus necessary, as the aforementioned laws, which ostensibly limit freedom of expression and speech, have sometimes been exploited by the government to suppress critics and impede the open discourse of political matters, especially in the context of elections.[164]

While Kenya leads the region in the regulation of data protection and abuse of social media platforms, it is apparent that electoral law, as currently formulated, does not regulate the increased use of social media in elections. While election laws prohibit campaigning two days before a general election, there is no law that bans candidates from purchasing advertising on social media platforms up until election day.[165] Also of concern, online advertising is not adequately regulated as the Electoral Code of Conduct does not cover online activities. Since the IEBC has proposed to undertake a review of its Electoral Code of Conduct following several court challenges arising from the 2022 elections,[166] we propose that the IEBC engage stakeholders in the development of specific regulations for online campaigns, with attendant sanctions also included in the Election Offences Act.[167]

159 Ibid. [35].
160 Ibid. [42] and [59].
161 Ibid. [45]–[46].
162 Ibid. [58].
163 Ibid. [68].
164 See, e.g., *Robert Alai* v. *Attorney General & Another*, [2017] eKLR; *Andare* v. *Attorney General*, [2015] eKLR.
165 Madung, 'Opaque and Overstretched, Part II' (n 101).
166 'Post-Election Evaluation Report' (n 83) p. 31.
167 Election Offences Act Number 37 of 2016.

The Kofi Annan Foundation similarly recommends signing of the Digital Pledge by all political actors to stop the spread of misinformation.[168]

13.5.2 *Institutional Measures to Combat Disinformation and Misinformation*

Institutional measures are equally important in tackling disinformation and misinformation. Social media sites and tech companies have an obligation to moderate content to reduce misinformation and disinformation. However, platforms such as Facebook have been criticised on the basis that the allocation of resources towards misinformation (estimated at 87 per cent in 2021) is disproportionately allocated to English-language content, yet only 9 per cent of its users actually speak English.[169] Odanga Madung attributes this to an unwillingness by tech platforms to 'devote time and resources to an electoral process outside their cultural context'.[170]

Furthermore, Article 19 has expressed concern over the lack of feedback incorporation from local communities in the content moderation strategies of social media companies. As a result, these strategies often fail to consider the cultural, social, historical, economic and political contexts of the communities they affect.[171] Most language moderation tools primarily cater to English, rendering them ineffective in instances where local slang or a mixture of multiple languages like Kiswahili and English are used. Further, these tools struggle to interpret statements involving derogatory metaphors or those heavily dependent on contextual understanding.[172] The absence of comprehensive content moderation facilitates the spread of misinformation and exacerbates its impact on electoral processes.

In 2022, the IEBC entered into memorandums of understanding with the Media Council of Kenya and tech companies, such as Facebook, on regulating online content. It may be necessary to create a coalition of actors to address concerns in this area. Having successfully convened political actors under the Political Parties Liaison Committee, IEBC can use existing goodwill to convene social media platforms to address digital threats to electoral integrity. As proposed by the 2020 study by the Kofi Annan Foundation, having such a coalition would allow for the creation of 'cross-platform strategies for detecting and limiting the reach of weaponized disinformation and hate speech'.[173] Collaboration between the IEBC, online platforms, such as Meta and Twitter, along with local information fact-checking organisations, presents an effective strategy to combat disinformation and

[168] See www.kofiannanfoundation.org/foundation-news/digital-pledge-kenya-elections.

[169] See Kari Paul, 'Climate Misinformation on Facebook "Increasing Substantially", Study Says', *The Guardian*, 4 November 2021.

[170] Madung, 'Opaque and Overstretched, Part II' (n 101).

[171] Article 19, 'Content Moderation' (n 72) p. 39.

[172] The Kenyan Elections 2022 (n 61).

[173] 'Protecting Electoral Integrity in the Digital Age'(n 132) p. 65.

misinformation using both reactive and proactive measures. This can involve actions like suspending accounts linked to disinformation campaigns. In addition, implementing measures such as Twitter's suspension of the trending feature during elections, as observed in Ethiopia during a period of rising disinformation and hate speech, can contribute significantly to countering the issue.[174]

13.5.3 *Non-Legal Initiatives to Combat Misinformation and Disinformation*

Several initiatives have been undertaken to address the question of fake news. Africa Check is a civil society initiative that works across Africa to verify news content and political statements and is part of the International Fact Checking Network (IFCN) which brings together fact-checkers and advocates for factual information, working globally to combat fake news.[175] However, these sites get less visibility than those that spread false information. This limits their reach in addressing disinformation and misinformation.[176] Moreover, a 'tidal wave of misinformation' makes it difficult to keep up with fact-checking and challenge fake news.[177] Therefore, a collaborative approach aimed at enhancing the capacity of organisations already engaged in real-time information fact-checking, particularly in the context of elections and crucial political matters, becomes essential.[178]

Further, the use of artificial intelligence (AI) tools to track misinformation in relation to elections has been demonstrated to be ineffective due to the language settings of these tools as well as their inability to identify context-specific misleading information. Existing tools have been criticised for not being tailor-made to local contexts. It is recommended to find ways of refining AI tools to make them better able to address local languages, in collaboration with local actors. However, since it is difficult to recall misinformation once it achieves virality, it is recommended to increase human review for accounts or posts that threaten the integrity of elections.[179]

Education and media literacy initiatives are also crucial to empowering citizens to distinguish accurate information from misinformation, thereby addressing the human vulnerability that enables the propagation of fake news. As an example, the cooperative effort among stakeholders to provide educational initiatives aimed at fostering critical thinking in the digital realm can be exemplified by Meta's 'trusted

[174] McKay, 'Disinformation and Democratic Transition' (n 65).

[175] Africa Check, https://africacheck.org/; International Fact Checking Network, www.poynter.org/ifcn.

[176] Cheeseman and Klaas, *How to Rig an Election* (n 75) p. 155.

[177] Cheeseman, 'Kenya 2022' (n 67).

[178] 'McKay, 'Disinformation and Democratic Transition' (n 65).

[179] 'Protecting Electoral Integrity in the Digital Age'(n 132), p. 50; Olivia, 'Disinformation Was Rife (n 87)'.

partner' programme. This programme serves to assist civil society in mitigating online and offline risks by offering expert insights and recommendations.[180] Increasing critical thinking and media literacy can make individuals more resilient to the influence of false information and less susceptible to manipulation. Importantly, it is reported that voters who spend more time on social media platforms tend to have a higher capacity for fact-checking and display a greater level of scepticism.[181] This heightened awareness makes them less susceptible to disinformation and misinformation campaigns.

In addition, debunking of misinformation related to the 2022 elections also limited its spread on digital platforms and vastly reduced its effect. Even as more work is done in retraining AI models to make them suitable for local contexts, where political actors, traditional media and other influential personalities call out misinformation frequently, it increases the level of scepticism among the voting population, making it harder for them to be deceived.[182]

13.5.4 *The Need for a Balancing Exercise*

A key aspect to consider is the balance between the effective use of technology in elections and the regulation of abusive behaviour. As this chapter has discussed, technology has the potential to enhance the integrity and credibility of elections, but it can also be exploited to spread disinformation and manipulate public opinion. Striking a balance between leveraging technology for democratic advancement and curbing its misuse is essential. Furthermore, there is a delicate balance to be struck between upholding privacy and security rights and protecting freedom of expression and political rights. Any regulatory measures should carefully navigate these contrasting rights to avoid unnecessary restrictions on freedom of speech while safeguarding against the misuse of data for disinformation and misinformation campaigns.

13.6 CONCLUSION

As noted, technology can serve as a tool to enhance democratic legitimacy and combat election rigging when properly implemented and managed. While social media is now an integral part of our elections, and cannot be disregarded, the dark side of the use of technology to spread disinformation and misinformation remains a threat to democratic trust and legitimacy, and its effects are yet to be fully appreciated. To restore public trust in key institutions protecting democracy, and in the integrity and legitimacy of elections, a comprehensive and multifaceted approach is

[180] McKay, 'Disinformation and Democratic Transition' (n 65).
[181] The Kenyan Elections 2022 (n 61).
[182] Ibid.

necessary to combat disinformation and misinformation. Legal, policy, institutional and educational measures should work in harmony to preserve the integrity of elections, and protect democratic values. Striking the right balance will be key to fostering an informed and engaged citizenry, ultimately strengthening democratic processes and rights, and preserving the democratic values of open debate, informed decision-making and the safeguarding of public trust in the democratic process.

PART V

Civil Society and Tackling Disinformation

14

Knowledge Institutions and Resisting 'Truth Decay'

Vicki C. Jackson

14.1 INTRODUCTION

Today is a time of retrogression in sustaining rights-protecting democracies, and of high levels of distrust in institutions.[1] Of particular concern are threats to the institutions, including universities and the press, that help provide the information base for successful democracies. Attacks on universities, and university faculties, are rising. In Poland over the last four years, a world-renowned constitutional law theorist, Wojciech Sadurski, has been subject to civil and criminal prosecutions for defamation of the governing party.[2] In Hungary, the Central European University (CEU) was ejected by the government, and had to partly relocate to Vienna,[3] and other attacks on academic freedom followed.[4] Faculty members in a number of countries have needed to relocate to other countries for their own safety.[5]

With thanks to Martha Minow, Ron Krotoszynski, Mark Tushnet and Bob Taylor for their generous and helpful comments and to Harvard Law students Jesse Lin and Sergey Smirnov for very able research assistance. On the term used in the title of this chapter, see Jennifer Kavanagh and Michael D. Rich, *Truth Decay* (Santa Monica, CA: RAND, 2018).

1 See generally the 2022 Fall special issue of *Deadalus*, 'Institutions, Experts and the Loss of Trust'.

2 Max Shanahan, 'USyd Professor Sadurski Acquitted of Criminal Defamation', *Honi Soit*, 26 September 2021 https://honisoit.com/2021/09/usyd-professor-sadurski-acquitted-of-criminal-defamation (reporting his acquittal in 2021 of the criminal defamation charge but noting plans of the party to appeal).

3 CEU, at the time headed by Michael Ignatieff, was forced out in 2019; see https://thepienews.com/news/ceu-forced-to-move-to-vienna.

4 See Lydia Gall, 'Hungary Continues Attacks on Academic Freedom: EU Should Attack to Ensure Autonomy of Universities', Human Rights Watch, 3 September 2020, www.hrw.org/news/2020/09/03/hungary-continues-attacks-academic-freedom.

5 See Scholars at Risk, 2022 Annual Report, 7 (noting that Scholars at Risk arranged for 171 positions for at-risk scholars and that the organization received 1,770 applications for assistance). According to the New University in Exile Consortium, on 23 July 2023, Azerbaijan wrongfully arrested an internationally well-regarded economist who is also head of a dissident political party, and was holding him in cruel and health-threatening conditions.

Governments attack what subjects can be taught – in Hungary bans on gender studies;[6] in Poland, a government minister issued a call to ban gender studies and 'LGBT ideology'.[7] Attacks on academics and universities, through government restrictions and public or private violence, are not limited to Poland and Hungary, but are of concern in Brazil, India, Turkey and a range of other countries.[8] Attacks on journalists are similarly rising.[9] These developments are deeply concerning. The proliferation of 'fake news', doctored photos and false claims on social media has

See 'Consortium Scholar, Dr. Gubad Ibadoghlu, Arrested and Detained in Azerbaijan', New University in Exile, 24 July 2023, https://newuniversityinexileconsortium.org/news/in-the-press/consortium-scholar-dr-gubad-ibadoghlu-arrested-and-detained-in-azerbaijan.

6 Becky Prager, 'The Hungarian Gender Studies Ban, and Its Implication for Democratic Freedom', *Harvard Journal of Law & Gender (online)*, 2019, https://journals.law.harvard.edu/jlg/2019/01/the-hungarian-ban-on-gender-studies-and-its-implications-for-democratic-freedom; Lauren Kent and Samantha Tapfumaneyi, 'Hungary's PM Bans Gender Study at Colleges Saying "People Are Born either Male or Female"', CNN, 19 October 2018, www.cnn.com/2018/10/19/europe/hungary-bans-gender-study-at-colleges-trnd/index.html.

7 See 'Minister Calls for Ban on "LGBT Ideology" and Gender Studies at Polish Universities and Schools', Notes from Poland, 10 September 2020, https://notesfrompoland.com/2020/09/10/minister-calls-for-ban-on-lgbt-ideology-and-gender-studies-at-polish-universities-and-schools; 'Poland: Rule of Law Erosion Harms Women, LGBT People', Human Rights Watch, 15 December 2022, www.hrw.org/news/2022/12/15/poland-rule-law-erosion-harms-women-lgbt-people (describing 'a government-supported Family Charter, calling for the exclusion of LGBT people from Polish society', and stating that '[m]ore than 90 regional and municipal authorities have now declared themselves "LGBT ideology free" or signed the charter').

8 See, e.g., Jack Grove, 'Deans Fired at Turkish Universities', *Inside Higher Ed*, 4 February 2022, www.insidehighered.com/news/2022/02/04/firing-deans-raises-academic-freedom-concerns-turkey; Suzy Hansen, '"The Era of People Like You Is Over": How Turkey Purged Its Intellectuals', *New York Times Magazine*, 29 July 2019, www.nytimes.com/2019/07/24/magazine/the-era-of-people-like-you-is-over-how-turkey-purged-its-intellectuals.html; Report on Wojciech Sadurski, of Warsaw University, Poland, Scholars at Risk, 2019, www.scholarsatrisk.org/report/2019-01-20-university-of-warsaw; Emilio Peluso Neder Meyer and Thomas Bustamante, 'Academic Freedom under Attack in Brazil', Verfassungsblog, 19 May 2021, https://verfassungsblog.de/academic-freedom-under-attack-in-brazil; 'PB Mehta Row: Over 150 International Scholars Slam "Attack on Academic Freedom"', *The Week Magazine*, 20 March 2021, www.theweek.in/news/india/2021/03/20/pb-mehta-row-over-150-international-scholars-slam-attack-on-academic-freedom.html; Susi Meret, 'Attacks on Academic Freedom Escalate in France and Denmark', Open Democracy, 31 July 2021, www.opendemocracy.net/en/countering-radical-right/attacks-academic-freedom-escalate-france-and-denmark (describing French education minister's warnings of dangers of 'Islamo-leftism' in universities); Jesus Velasco, 'AMLO's Attacks on Mexico's Higher Education Institutions May Accelerate the Country's Scholarly Exodus to the US', LSE, 9 July 2020, https://blogs.lse.ac.uk/usappblog/2020/07/09/amlos-attacks-on-mexicos-higher-education-institutions-may-accelerate-the-countrys-scholarly-exodus-to-the-us. See generally, Academic Freedom Monitoring Project, Free to Think 2022, Scholars at Risk, www.scholarsatrisk.org/resources/free-to-think-2022 (reporting on '391 attacks on higher education communities' that year in 65 countries and territories in the world, including bomb attacks against historically black colleges and universities (HBCUs) in the United States; up from 332 attacks reported in 2021).

9 'Killings of Journalists up 50 per cent in 2022', UNESCO, 17 January 2023, https://news.un.org/en/story/2023/01/1132507.

been widely documented.[10] Constitutional democracy cannot long be sustained in an 'age of lies', where truth and knowledge no longer matter.[11]

Turning from the world to the United States of America, the position of the USA in rankings of respect for political and civil liberties has suffered a marked decline.[12] Likewise, the USA has seen a decline in its ranking for academic freedoms.[13] Waning confidence in the value of a college education has been accompanied by a pronounced partisan skew in evaluating the value of higher education.[14] Suspicion

[10] See, e.g., Rob Dobi, 'Study: False News Spreads Faster than the Truth', MIT Management Sloan School, 8 March 2018, https://mitsloan.mit.edu/ideas-made-to-matter/study-false-news-spreads-faster-truth (summarizing study by Soroush Vosoughi, Deb Roy and Sinan Aral, 'The Spread of True and False News Online' (2018) 359 *Science* 1146) (research shows that lies spread faster than truth on Twitter); Elizabeth Dwoskin, 'Misinformation on Facebook Got Six Times More Clicks than Factual News during the 2020 Election, Study Says', *The Washington Post*, 4 September 2021, www.washingtonpost.com/technology/2021/09/03/facebook-misinformation-nyu-study (summarizing study by New York University and University of Grenoble).

[11] See Sophia Rosenfeld, *Democracy and Truth: A Short History* (Philadelphia: University of Pennsylvania Press, 2019) 137. Cf. Tom Nichols, *The Death of Expertise: The Campaign against Established Knowledge and Why It Matters* (Oxford: Oxford University Press, 2017) ('No longer do we hold these truths to be self-evident, we hold all truths to be self-evident, even the ones that aren't true').

[12] Compare, e.g., the global rankings of Freedom House, 2023, https://freedomhouse.org/countries/freedom-world/scores?sort=asc&order=Total%20Score%20and%20Status (showing the US score of 83 and ranking 58th among 210 countries and territories rated in overall scores for political rights and civil liberties) with the 2017 global rankings, https://freedomhouse.org/country/united-states/freedom-world/2017 (showing US score of 89) and https://freedomhouse.org/report/freedom-world/2017/scores?sort=asc&order=Total%20Score%20and%20Status (showing the USA ranked forty-third in the world, along with other countries scoring 89) and Freedom House global rankings (2013), www.freedomhouse.org/sites/default/files/FIW%202013%20Booklet.pdf (using a different methodology, showing the USA achieved the highest ranking possible (1 in political rights, and 1 in civil liberties), along with 47 other countries; V-Dem Democracy Report 2022, https://v-dem.net/media/publications/dr_2022.pdf, 46, table 2 (showing decline in US score on liberal democracy index over last ten years).

[13] See Katrin Kinzelbach et al., 'Academic Freedom Index 2023 Update', FAU Erlangen-Nürnberg and V-Dem Institute, https://academic-freedom-index.net/research/Academic_Freedom_Index_Update.pdf ('After a long period of relatively high academic freedom levels, four out of five indicators visibly declined in 2021', and noting both President Trump's 'statements critical of science and academia' and actions by a number of state governments; chart showing the USA in a group of countries in a tier of the top 40–50 percent of countries on its academic freedom index, with countries in the top 10 percent tier including, e.g., Estonia, Belgium, Germany, Israel, Italy, Finland, Spain and Nigeria); ibid. at 5 (showing in figure 4 that the USA has lost ground in protecting academic freedoms since 2012); see also Reporters Without Borders, https://rsf.org/en/country/united-states (noting a 'sharp rise' in violations of press freedoms in 2020 but some improvement since, with the USA ranking 45 out of 170 countries in the 2023 World Press Freedom Index; in the 2020 World Press Freedom Index, the US was ranked 32, https://rsf.org/en/ranking); Erin C. Caroll, 'Obstruction of Journalism' (2022) 99 *Denver Law Review* 407.

[14] See 'America's Hidden Common Ground on Public Higher Education: What's Wrong and How to Fix It', Report, Public Agenda, 2022, https://publicagenda.org/resource/americas-hidden-common-ground-on-public-higher-education-whats-wrong-and-how-to-fix-it; 'The Growing Partisan Divide in Views of Higher Education', Pew Research Center,

of expertise, along with tolerance by significant parts of the public and by leading political figures for outright fabrications, have increased.[15] Bans on teaching Critical Race Theory were encouraged initially by an executive order in 2020 banning the teaching of 'divisive topics'.[16] Tracking language from this executive order, a number of states enacted bans, including Iowa's 2021 law banning institutions of higher education from promoting 'specific defined concepts' including 'race or sex scapegoating' and teaching that 'that the United States of America and the state of Iowa are fundamentally or systemically racist or sexist'.[17] Whether or not the federal courts ultimately will uphold this law, its enactment is plainly inconsistent with basic ideas of pursuing truth through academic freedoms.[18]

This chapter argues that constitutional democracies need 'knowledge institutions', in part because of the role they can play as intermediary organizations for the public in sorting out genuine claims of knowledge from false claims and in checking false claims by those with power. These 'knowledge institutions' should be recognized in comparative constitutional studies as essential elements of a constitutional infrastructure. Section 14.2 introduces a general claim about knowledge

19 August 2019, www.pewresearch.org/social-trends/2019/08/19/the-growing-partisan-divide-in-views-of-higher-education-2.

[15] See Rosenfeld, *Democracy and Truth* (n 11); Vittorio Bufacchi, 'What's the Difference between Lies and Post-Truth in Politics? A Philosopher Explains', The Conversation, 24 January 2020, https://theconversation.com/whats-the-difference-between-lies-and-post-truth-in-politics-a-philosopher-explains-130442; Lee McIntyre, *Post-Truth* (Cambridge, MA: MIT Press, 2018). See also, Atul Gawande, 'The Mistrust of Science', *The New Yorker*, 10 June 2016.

[16] Executive Order on Combatting Race and Sex Stereotyping, US, 22 September 2020 (applying to federal government and its grantees and banning teaching of 'divisive concepts', including, e.g., the concepts that '(2) the United States is fundamentally racist or sexist; (3) an individual, by virtue of his or her race or sex, is inherently racist, sexist, or oppressive, whether consciously or unconsciously; (4) an individual should be discriminated against or receive adverse treatment solely or partly because of his or her race or sex; ... (8) any individual should feel discomfort, guilt, anguish, or any other form of psychological distress on account of his or her race or sex').

[17] House File 802 (Iowa). 'Race or sex scapegoating' is defined in the law as 'assigning fault, blame, or bias to a race or sex, or to members of a race or sex because of their race or sex, or claiming that, consciously or unconsciously, and by virtue of persons' race or sex, members of any race are inherently racist or are inherently inclined to oppress others, or that members of a sex are inherently sexist or inclined to oppress others'.

[18] If a conclusion, a view, is based on sound research within the expertise of the professor, then its expression is consistent with the pursuit of knowledge even if competing views based on research exist; the development of 'justified true beliefs' can be a process of contestation. On the role and limits of consensus in science, see Mark Tushnet, 'Trust the Science but Do Your Research: A Comment on the Unfortunate Revival of the Progressive Case for the Administrative State' (2023) 98(2) *Indiana Law Journal* 335. On the impact of the 2020 Executive Order (n 16) in encouraging state enactments, see, 'CRT Forward: Tracking the Attack on Critical Race Studies', UCLA Law School, 2023, https://crtforward.law.ucla.edu/wp-content/uploads/2023/04/UCLA-Law_CRT-Report_Final.pdf (reflecting enactment of twenty-nine measures targeting institutions of higher learning, though many more target K-12 instruction); see also 'Educational Gag Orders: Legislative Restrictions on the Freedom to Read, Learn, and Teach', PEN America, https://pen.org/report/educational-gag-orders.

institutions in constitutional democracies.[19] Section 14.3 raises a set of concerns about the implications of some recent US Supreme Court case law for the knowledge functions of public universities. It argues that these decisions reflect a fundamental failure to appreciate the role of these and other knowledge institutions in the infrastructure necessary for constitutional democracies to sustain themselves.

14.2 KNOWLEDGE INSTITUTIONS IN CONSTITUTIONAL DEMOCRACIES

Justice Felix Frankfurter once suggested that government-employed college 'teachers' are vital in developing public views that are 'disciplined and responsible', it being their 'special task to foster those habits of open-mindedness and of critical inquiry, which ... make possible an enlightened and effective public opinion'.[20] Knowledge institutions are central to these goals. This section will discuss some definitional questions about knowledge institutions, and explain the need to focus on those institutions in democracies..

14.2.1 *A Simple Definition*

Knowledge institutions are ongoing entities that have, as a central purpose, the dissemination, preservation or production of knowledge.[21] They aspire to some degree of objectivity, reliability or accuracy in evaluating claims and evidence, including the consideration of opposing evidence or views. In doing so they apply distinct disciplinary methodologies designed to enhance the search for better understandings of the world;[22] they seek to maintain an epistemic openness, consistent with commitments to knowledge based on evidence and disciplinary methodologies that, over time, may lead to changed or expanded understandings.[23] In order to aspire to objectivity in the pursuit of knowledge, *independence* in the application of disciplinary methods and openness to having one's beliefs dis-verified through those

[19] See generally, Vicki C. Jackson, 'Knowledge Institutions in Constitutional Democracy: Preliminary Reflections' (2021) 7 *Canadian Journal of Comparative and Contemporary Law* 156. Some of the ideas in this chapter were set forth in this earlier 2021 paper.

[20] *Wieman* v. *Updegraff*, 344 US 183, 196–97 (1952) (Frankfurter J, concurring); see also *Keyishian* v. *Board of Regents of the University of State of New York*, 385 US 589 (1967).

[21] See Jackson, 'Preliminary Reflections' (n 19), at 165–66.

[22] See Carolyn Evans and Adrienne Stone, *Open Minds: Academic Freedom and Freedom of Speech of Australia* Kindle ed. (Melbourne: La Trobe University Press, 2021) p. 85 ('disciplinary methods require researchers to support their theories with evidence and justification, expose them to systematic testing capable of invalidating them and submit them to peer review prior to publication as well as to subsequent criticism and contradiction').

[23] The search for knowledge according to independent disciplinary standards exists not only in the sciences but also in the social sciences and in the humanities; improved understandings of older literary texts, or of a philosophical problem, are a form of knowledge, tested by different methods than those of physics.

methods are required. To be sure, what is accepted as true may vary over time; scientific findings may be based in part on assumptions that are matters of legitimate public debate;[24] but the processes of knowledge development allow for correction and improvement and, over the long run, real lives of real people have thereby improved.[25]

Knowledge institutions include ongoing entities that are public and private – universities, the free truth-seeking press,[26] courts and some government offices (such as the Census Bureau or other government offices charged with collecting and disseminating accurate, reliable data).[27] They are not a 'branch' of government but an essential part of the infrastructure of democratic constitutionalism. Knowledge institutions act as informational intermediaries for the public, helping to navigate among the many claims (some false, some true, some uncertain) now being disseminated.[28] A diverse group of knowledge institutions populated by diverse professionals is a valuable part of the knowledge infrastructure, providing different perspectives and cross-checks on developing understandings of knowledge.

14.2.2 *Knowledge*

The concept of knowledge is a contested one. There are important philosophical disagreements about the nature of epistemic claims; but there is fairly wide agreement on the proposition that knowledge should be understood to mean 'justified true beliefs', or that truth alone does not establish knowledge without something like some further grounds or account for why something is true.[29] Yet, I claim,

[24] See, e.g., Sandra Harding, *The Science Question in Feminism* (Ithaca, NY: Cornell University Press, 1986); Sheila Jasanoff, 'Perspective: Back from the Brink: Truth and Trust in the Public Sphere' (2017) 33(4) *Issues in Science and Technology* 25, at 28 (discussing the multi-participant process of establishing 'public truths').

[25] See, e.g., Gawande, 'The Mistrust of Science' (n 15).

[26] See Vicki C. Jackson, 'Knowledge Institutions in Constitutional Democracy: Reflections on the Press' (2022) 14 *Journal of Media Law* 275.

[27] Vicki C. Jackson, 'Knowledge at Risk: Democratic Constitutionalism and the Administrative State' (unpublished ms., September 2022).

[28] Cf. Brian Leiter, 'The Epistemology of the Internet and the Regulation of Speech in America' (2022) 20 *Georgetown Journal of Law & Public Policy* 903 (discussing the role of knowledge 'gatekeepers' including in academia); Robert Post, 'The Internet, Democracy and Misinformation' (Chapter 2 in this volume, arguing that the absence of professional 'gatekeepers who vouched for the authenticity and epistemological value of distributed information' poses a threat to democracy's public sphere).

[29] See generally, Jonathan Jenkins Ichikawa and Matthias Steup, 'The Analysis of Knowledge' in Edward N. Zalta (ed.), *The Stanford Encyclopedia of Philosophy*, Summer 2018, https://plato.stanford.edu/archives/sum2018/entries/knowledge-analysis. For helpful discussion by a legal academic, see Joseph Blocher, 'Free Speech and Justified True Belief' (2019) 133 *Harvard Law Review* 439, 459–64; see also Jackson, 'Preliminary Reflections' (n 19), at 163–64. For competing perspectives, see David Rabban, 'Can Academic Freedom Survive Postmodernism' (1998) 86 *California Law Review* 1377 (reviewing *The Future of Academic Freedom*, ed. by Louis Menand in 1996, discussing arguments for political rather than epistemological

attempting to govern based on knowledge is likely to yield better outcomes than not doing so, even though 'knowledge' is in some respects socially constructed and subject to change as scientific paradigms shift or new evidence is discovered challenging orthodox beliefs.[30] 'Knowledge' here is understood not in absolute terms but rather, as referring to the best current understanding of descriptive and causal realities, reflecting justified current beliefs about what is true, based on reliable evidence.[31] To recognize this kind of role for 'knowledge' is to embrace the distinction between facts and opinions, to accept that there are understandings of the world about which, for practical purposes, there is a truth of the matter.[32] But it also embraces the idea that knowledge must remain open to being corrected or displaced by new, verifiable, knowledge claims.[33]

grounding of scholars' roles); Carlotta Pavese, 'Knowledge How' in Edward N. Zalta and Uri Nodelman (eds.), *The Stanford Encyclopedia of Philosophy*, Fall 2022, https://plato.stanford.edu/archives/fall2022/entries/knowledge-how (discussing 'anti-intellectualism' claims about 'knowledge how' to do things and whether a 'belief' is necessary to have 'how' knowledge).

30 On epistemological debates about how knowledge changes, see, e.g., Thomas Kuhn, *The Structure of Scientific Revolutions* 3rd ed. (Chicago: University of Chicago Press, 1996) (emphasizing discovery of anomalies leading to new paradigms); Karin Knorr Cetins, *Epistemic Cultures: How the Sciences Make Knowledge* (Cambridge, MA: Harvard University Press, 1999) pp. 3–5, 8–11 (emphasizing how different disciplines use different tools); Robert K. Merton, 'The Normative Structure of Science' in Norman W. Storer (ed.), *The Sociology of Science: Theoretical and Empirical Investigations* (Chicago: University of Chicago Press, 1973) p. 270 (emphasizing the role of empirical confirmation of predictions and goals of disinterestedness and skepticism); Karl Popper, *The Logic of Scientific Discovery* 2nd ed. (London: Routledge, 2002) (emphasizing the role of falsifiability).

31 See Ichikawa and Steup, 'The Analysis of Knowledge' (n 29) (knowledge as a belief that is true and justified); Jasanoff, 'Perspective' (n 24), at 28 ('in democratic societies, public truths are precious collective achievements, arrived at … through slow sifting of alternative interpretations based on careful observation and argument and painstaking deliberation among trustworthy experts'); 'In Defense of Knowledge and Higher Education', American Association of University Professors, 2019, www.aaup.org/report/defense-knowledge-and-higher-education (defining 'knowledge' as 'those understandings of the world upon which we rely because they are produced by the best methods at our disposal' and arguing that '[n]o state can organize effective government policy except on the basis of informed … investigation').

32 See Vicki C. Jackson, 'Thayer, Holmes, Brandeis: Conceptions of Judicial Review, Factfinding, Proportionality' (2017) 130 *Harvard Law Review* 2348, at 2379–80; see also Edward J. Lowe, 'Fact' in Ted Honderich (ed.), *The Oxford Companion to Philosophy* (Oxford: Oxford University Press, 2005) p. 287; Henry P. Monaghan, 'Constitutional Fact Review' (1985) 85 *Columbia Law Review* 229, at 233. This view is in some tension with those of scholars like Richard Rorty, see Bjørn Ramberg and Susan Dieleman, 'Richard Rorty' in Edward N. Zalta and Uri Nodelman (eds.), *The Stanford Encyclopedia of Philosophy*, Fall 2023, https://plato.stanford.edu/archives/fall2023/entries/rorty/ (elaborating on Rorty's challenge to the idea that 'knowledge' corresponds to external realities).

33 How one knows what 'truth' or 'knowledge' is, of course, presents a large question. On some issues (we could call them issues of fact) truth must bear a correspondence to a phenomenon in the world that is capable of intersubjective verification. Other kinds of knowledge may reflect more social or interpretive understandings. To constitute knowledge, these claims must be capable of being grounded in arguments or sources that others can look at or reflect upon. Institutions, applying their own disciplinary mechanisms oriented towards establishing truth,

14.2.3 *Why Focus on Institutions?*

Many constitutional rights provisions – including those of expression, of association, and of the press – serve both democracy-enhancing and knowledge-producing functions, as argued by Alexander Meiklejohn and Justice Oliver Wendell Holmes.[34] Given the robust presence, in the USA and many other constitutional democracies, of judicially enforced protections for freedoms of speech, association and the press, why focus on institutions? Some excellent scholarly work has recently argued that the meaning of freedom of expression must be analyzed differently within different institutional contexts.[35] My own view is in great sympathy with these, but focuses on the institutions as objects of protection as well as the individual speech or speakers within the institutions.[36]

To be sure, individual freedoms are of great importance. They can and do promote the goal of developing and diffusing knowledge. But knowledge institutions – with their aspirations towards objectivity, their role as disciplinary gatekeepers to review the soundness of what is being taken as reliable information, and their epistemic openness to new evidence – offer some distinct advantages in the protection of rights and advancement of knowledge not served as well by a focus that looks solely to individual rights claimants.[37] This is so for several reasons. Institutions can

play a central role in enabling societies to determine when a truth about a matter is – or multiple truths are – established as knowledge. See notes 22 and 23.

34 See Alexander Meiklejohn, *Free Speech and Its Relation to Self-Government* (New York: Harper & Brothers, 1948) pp. 105–7; *Abrams* v. *United States*, 250 US 616, 630 (1919), Holmes J, dissenting. The capacity of 'more speech' to help produce better knowledge has come under question, however, as new technologies on the Internet reduce the likelihood that false speech will be corrected where its viewers see it. See generally Tim Wu, 'Is the First Amendment Obsolete?' (2018) 117 *Michigan Law Review* 547.

35 See Paul Horwitz, *First Amendment Institutions* (Cambridge, MA: Harvard University Press, 2013); Frederick Schauer, 'Towards an Institutional First Amendment' (2005) 89 *Minnesota Law Review* 1256, at 1250 and 1275; see also Joseph Blocher, 'Institutions in the Marketplace of Ideas' (2008) 57 *Duke Law Journal* 821.

36 Various government interventions in college and university autonomy – even if not directly related to speech – may threaten their ability as institutions to sustain knowledge functions, just like government taxes on the use of paper and ink, see *Minneapolis Star & Tribune Co.* v. *Minnesota*, 460 US 575 (1983), may interfere with the constitutional freedoms of the press.

37 On the importance of considering the institutions within which speech occurs, see, e.g., Horwitz, *First Amendment Institutions* (n 35); Schauer, 'Towards an Institutional First Amendment' (n 35), at 1260 (arguing for more recognition of differences among institutions in developing First Amendment doctrine); Frederick Schauer, 'Institutions as Legal and Constitutional Categories' (2007) 54 *UCLA Law Review* 1747, at 1753–54 (noting a 'pattern of treating First Amendment doctrine as institutionally blind', bemoaning 'how insignificant a role [institutions] appear to play in constitutional categorization'); Frederick Schauer, 'Principles, Institutions, and the First Amendment' (1998) 112 *Harvard Law Review* 84, at 86 ('the refusal to draw doctrinal distinctions among culturally distinct institutions is simply unworkable in the context of the vast and increasing domain of free speech claims').

provide focal points for organized action by knowledge producers or disseminators.[38] Ongoing institutions can, moreover, also enhance and reinforce disciplinary cultures of independence and knowledge-seeking. The existence of institutions may offer legal protection for their members when their professional knowledge products lead to liability claims. Such institutions serve as much-needed intermediaries, helping to sort out genuine knowledge from the gushers of information that are now available to so many through social media. And knowledge institutions perform their truth-seeking/dissemination roles non-coercively, unlike regulatory arms of government that may seek to prohibit and punish speech. Although institutions may come under conflicting pressures, it is important that their role as knowledge producers and disseminators, and their independence in that role, be reinforced. An elaboration of these points follows.

14.2.3.1 On Focal Points for Collective Action

Adam Chilton and Mila Versteeg's research discloses an interesting relationship between the presence of written constitutional rights and actual levels of being able to exercise those rights. A positive relationship did not hold for all of the rights they investigated; the presence of rights to be free from torture, or to free speech, typically asserted by individuals, had no association with actual levels of respect for those rights. But for those rights held or exercised by *collective entities* – religious groups, trade unions or political parties – written protections were associated with greater levels of respect for those rights. Chilton and Versteeg suggest an explanation for the difference might be that the collective entities in which certain rights are exercised provide focal points for coordinated, collective action (such as organized protests) that may result in the protection of the rights, even without intervention of courts. That is, ongoing entities can facilitate coordination and collective action to protect those rights whose exercise is necessary to the core functions of the entity.[39] Particular universities and press institutions may provide a powerful focal point for the protection of academic and journalistic speech, research and investigation. Similarly, some government offices may provide powerful focal points for the preservation of the integrity of their own work, including knowledge production. Consider, for example, the collective efforts of Department of Justice officials to prevent the Attorney General from being persuaded by White House pressures to an erroneous legal interpretation as the basis for unlawful action,[40] or the concerted efforts by former members of the Department of Justice Office of Legal Counsel

[38] See Adam Chilton and Mila Versteeg, *How Constitutional Rights Matter* (Oxford: Oxford University Press, 2020). For a critique, see Madhav Khosla, 'Is a Science of Constitutionalism Possible' (2022) 135 *Harvard Law Review* 2110 (reviewing Chilton's and Versteeg's book).

[39] See Chilton and Versteeg, *How Constitutional Rights Matter* (n 38) p. 8.

[40] See Benjamin Wittes, 'James Comey's Damning Testimony', Brookings, 17 May 2007, www.brookings.edu/opinions/james-comeys-damning-testimony (describing how DOJ officials.

(OLC) to uphold or re-envision the legal integrity and knowledge practices of that office in the face of apparent egregious departures.[41]

14.2.3.2 On Disciplinary Cultures

Institutions have institutional cultures, which include habits and norms about valid methods of producing and testing knowledge. Institutions help sustain and pass on these cultures, shared assumptions and codes of behaviors.[42] Institutions sustain their cultures in a variety of ways, including unconscious imitation, reward structures,[43] mission statements and codes of ethics.[44] Many opportunities exist to promote the

Comey, Goldsmith and Philbin coordinated action to prevent what they viewed as an illegal act being urged on the (then-hospitalized) Attorney General by the White House).

41 See, e.g., Dawn Johnsen, 'Foreword' (to War, Terrorism, and Torture: Limits on Presidential Power in the 21st Century Symposium) (2006) 81 *Indiana Law Journal* 1139; Trevor Morrison, 'Stare Decisis in the Office of Legal Counsel' (2010) 110 *Columbia Law Review* 1448; Dawn Johnsen and Neil Kinkopf, 'How to Prevent Another "Torture Memo"', *The Wall Street Journal*, 21 January 2005 ('A group of 19 former OLC lawyers recently reviewed the practices that in the past have promoted high professional standards and prepared a set of 10 principles that, we believe, should continue to serve as the foundation for OLC's legal rulings').

42 See generally, Edgar Schein, *Organizational Culture and Leadership* (Hoboken, NJ: Jossey-Bass, 1985) p. 9 (defining organizational culture as 'a pattern of basic assumptions – invented, discovered, or developed by a given group as it learns to cope with its problems of external adaptation and internal integration – that has worked well enough to be considered valid and, therefore, to be taught to new members as the correct way to perceive, think, and feel in relation to those problems'); Edgar Schein with Peter Schein, *Organizational Culture and Leadership* 5th ed. (Hoboken, NJ: Wiley, 2017) pp. 6–7 (defining 'the culture of a group as the accumulated shared learning of that group . . . to be taught to new members as the correct way to perceive, think, feel and behave in relation to those problems'); see also Don Hellriegel and John W. Slocum, *Organizational Behavior* (Cincinnati, OH: South-Western College, 2007) p. 418 (describing organizational culture as a 'collection of unspoken rules and traditions that play a part in determining the quality and nature of organizational life'); Davide Ravasi and Majken Schultz, 'Responding to Organizational Identity Threats: Exploring the Role of Organizational Culture' (2006) 49 *Academy of Management Journal* 433, at 437 (defining organizational culture as a set of assumptions that help 'defin[e] appropriate behavior for various situations'); cf. Barbara E. Armacost, 'Organizational Culture and Police Misconduct' (2004) 72 *George Washington Law Review* 453, at 521 and 546 (arguing that organizational culture is sustained and changed not only by leaders but also by the group as a whole, posing a challenge, for example, to efforts to change adverse cultures in policing units).

43 Consider here the role of Pulitzer Prizes, awarded by Columbia University, and other awards in journalism. See 'About Us', https://journalism.columbia.edu/about; 'History of the Pulitzer Prize', www.pulitzer.org/page/history-pulitzer-prizes.

44 On the professional culture of truth-seeking news media, see Jackson, 'Reflections on the Press' (n 26), at 284 (noting, for example, the recent creation at *The New York Times* of an office of 'Newsroom Cultures and Careers'). A professional culture of factual integrity is also asserted at the level of policy (and in fact is found) in many government offices. See, e.g., US Census Bureau, 'Scientific Integrity' (last revised 16 December 2021), www.census.gov/about/policies/quality/scientific_integrity.html (asserting its commitment, with other federal statistical agencies, to a 'common set of professional standards and operational practices designed to ensure the quality, integrity, and credibility of our statistical activities'); Emily Bazelon and Michael

truth-seeking mission of universities and colleges and their faculties, including in hiring, promotion and tenure review; mission statements of universities, public and private, emphasize their role in knowledge production, preservation and transmission.[45] At a high level of generality, many in the sciences would agree with the National Academies of Science, Engineering and Medicine in the USA that 'the values of objectivity, honesty, openness, accountability, [and] fairness' are essential.[46] A more general statement, cognizant of the variation in some standards among disciplines, is found in Cambridge University's statement of good research practices, that 'the highest standards of integrity, honesty and professionalism in respect of their own actions in research and in their responses to the actions of others' is necessary, as is 'openness' about research and its availability.[47] Tenure standards of particular schools and departments cast further light on how particular schools talk about research quality.[48] Academic cultures are passed on in various ways – including, inter alia, through policy statements, tenure requirements, formal reviews, informal reviews, academic mentoring and professional associations in the various academic disciplines. So institutions matter because, in part by bringing together people with similar professional commitments over time, they can reinforce disciplinary cultures for the production of different kinds of knowledge.[49]

Wines, 'How the Census Bureau Stood Up to Trump', *New York Times Sunday Review*, 15 August 2021, p. 3; Michael Wines, 'Census Memo Cites "Unprecedented" Meddling by Trump Officials', *The New York Times*, 16 January 2022, p. 21; see also Stephen Skowronek, John A. Dearborn and Desmond King, *Phantoms of a Beleaguered Republic* (Oxford: Oxford University Press, 2021) p. 106 (discussing federal civil servant weather scientists resisting unscientific political interventions).

45 See, e.g., University of Michigan's 'Mission Statement', https://president.umich.edu/about/mission (asserting a mission 'to serve the people of Michigan and the world through preeminence in creating, communicating, preserving and applying knowledge, art, and academic values'); Harvard College's 'Mission, Vision, & History', https://college.harvard.edu/about/mission-vision-history ('The mission of Harvard College is to educate the citizens and citizen-leaders for our society … with exposure to new ideas, new ways of understanding, and new ways of knowing').

46 'Fostering Integrity in Research', National Academies of Sciences, Engineering, and Medicine, 2017, https://nap.nationalacademies.org/read/21896/chapter/14, 9.

47 'Good Research Practice Guidelines', University of Cambridge, www.research-integrity.admin.cam.ac.uk/files/good_research_practice_guidelines_jan_2021.pdf.

48 See, e.g., 'Standards for Tenure and Promotion' (2014), Georgetown University Law Center, www.law.georgetown.edu/wp-content/uploads/2018/05/A.-Tenure-Standards.pdf (describing tenurable qualities of legal scholarship as showing 'wide and critical command of the field of his or her study', stating that the 'highest indication of scholarship is the ability to make original contributions in one's field of knowledge', and '[e]xcellence in legal scholarship is characterized by clear and compelling argument that relies on relevant evidence or authority, by ideas or results that are both original and important, and by the author's attention to method').

49 Although professionals or experts unaffiliated with any institution may apply disciplinary standards, institutions help define and uphold the disciplinary norms by which to assess the validity and reliability of truth claims. I thank Martha Minow, again, for pressing me on this point.

14.2.3.3 Material Resources for Discipline-Conforming Knowledge Work

As discussed elsewhere, institutions matter because they are likely to have material capacities and incentives to protect the rights of their members, at least where their members are seeking to produce or identify knowledge in accordance with the relevant disciplinary norms.[50] Constitutional rights, of course, also provide protection, but that protection can be supported – or supplemented – by aspects of the institutional presence. This protection may take different forms. Institutions will, typically, have more money and access to legal expertise than any individual member. If a *New York Times* journalist or a Harvard scholar is sued or subject to investigation for their journalistic or academic work, their employers may be able to assist in their defense;[51] government employees are often able to have government support for their defense unless the employee's conduct 'does not reasonably appear to have been performed within the scope of his employment with the federal government ... [or] is otherwise determined ... not [to be] in the interest of the United States to provide'.[52] Of course, the interests of institutions and their employees may diverge,[53] but the presence of an institution whose goals generally overlap with those of its employees may provide added support against attacks on those employees for doing their jobs. If institutions fail to support employees in their knowledge production or disseminating capacities, the consequences for an epistemically sound system may be quite adverse.

14.2.3.4 Intermediaries and Massive Misinformation Flows

Another reason to give special attention to knowledge institutions as such arises from the profusion of communications sources that now exist in the world. This profusion of communications sources, including through social media, facilitate very quick and widespread diffusion of claims that may have little foundation or be completely

[50] See Jackson, 'Reflections on the Press' (n 26), at 284.

[51] Moreover, compliance with institutional norms of a knowledge institution may help insulate scholars or journalists from legal liability for their publications. See Horwitz, *First Amendment Institutions* (n 35), pp. 152–53 (noting that journalists' compliance with journalistic norms or customs can rebut claims of legal malice, an element required in the US for a public figure to win a defamation action).

[52] 28 CFR 50.15.

[53] Although there are possibilities for conflicts of interest between employing organizations and employees, in universities and news outlets there is some alignment in the dominant purposes of the institution and its professional staff. With respect to government institutions, the potential conflicts between government as employer and the professional knowledge workers it employs are perhaps greater. Scientific or statistical offices within government work within an overarching institution whose central purpose is to govern. Reconciling the need for independence and impartiality in the development of knowledge with the range of government purposes is a particular challenge, perhaps calling for more internal separation of powers.

untrue.[54] Major sources of information flow on social media such as Facebook, YouTube or Twitter do not generally purport to screen what they disseminate for truthfulness;[55] their principal purposes do not include the creation or dissemination of knowledge, but rather the flow of communications. University communities and those of other intermediary institutions can often sort out true from false knowledge claims in a more authoritative way than any isolated individual acting on their own.

Knowledge institutions serve this function generally by applying appropriate disciplinary standards to determine what counts as 'knowledge', including the credentialing of experts and the identification of areas of epistemic uncertainty.[56] Moreover, a number of knowledge institutions (some independent non-governmental organizations, some universities) have in recent years supported scholarly work and established knowledge-disseminating projects specifically

[54] See Leiter, 'Epistemology' (n 28), at 918–19; cf. Luís Roberto Barroso, 'Populism, Authoritarianism, and Institutional Resistance' (2022) 57 *Texas International Law Journal* 259 (arguing that extremist, authoritarian movements seek to by-pass intermediary institutions, including the press and civil society, to gain power through direct social media appeals to supporters); Luís Roberto Barroso and Luna van Brussel Barroso, 'Democracy, Social Media, and Freedom of Expression: Hate, Lies, and the Search for the Possible Truth' (2023) 24 *Chicago Journal of International Law* 51 (discussing social media's effects on increased public participation and communication and at the same time increased 'disinformation campaigns, hate speech, slander, lies, and conspiracy theories used to advance antidemocratic goals').

[55] Wikipedia might be considered a knowledge institution insofar as its purpose is to disseminate knowledge; it is debatable whether it has a 'disciplinary method', other than relying on transparency, publicity, encouragement of supporting documentation and notation where it is in doubt.

[56] Many questions exist about whether particular institutions – for-profit universities, particular foundations or institutes – are 'knowledge institutions'. Sometimes an entity's mission statement will make clear that developing, preserving or disseminating knowledge is not central to its mission, even if it may be an incidental product. Sometimes an entity will claim to be oriented to knowledge production, but will be viewed by others as incapable of performing this role because commitment to an existing worldview prevents it from the kind of open-mindedness that knowledge institutions should have. A non-governmental organization (NGO), like the RAND Corporation – which describes itself as 'dedicated to furthering and promoting scientific, educational, and charitable purposes for the public welfare and security of the United States', blending 'scrupulous nonpartisanship with rigorous, fact-based analysis to tackle society's most pressing problems' – could be a knowledge institution to the extent it adheres to this self-description. 'A Brief History of RAND', RAND, www.rand.org/about/history.html. Other NGOs with more advocacy, or lobbying goals, might not be: an NGO such as the Tobacco Institute that used to exist in the USA, at least as described by Bath University Tobacco Tactics project, would probably not be. See https://tobaccotactics.org/article/tobacco-institute (describing an internal memo characterizing the institute's work in part as being about '[c]reating doubt about the health charge without actually denying it'). Many associations that play quite valuable (and constitutionally protected) democratic roles – including political parties or advocacy groups – may not be 'knowledge institutions' if one looks at what their central or primary purposes are, as well as whether they apply disciplinary process oriented towards identifying knowledge. In a work-in-progress (a book for Cambridge University Press), I plan to consider such questions.

designed to understand, and to help check, the flow of misinformation online.[57] These projects directly seek to play an intermediary and knowledge-preserving role.

14.2.3.5 Knowledge Institutions as Less Coercive than Government Regulation

Knowledge institutions rely on less coercive measures in promoting knowledge than government regulation. Allowing the coercive powers of government to be used intrusively to regulate knowledge production, testing and dissemination poses acute risks to constitutional democracy. As current events have shown, some governments have invoked the COVID pandemic as a pretext to suppress and punish criticism of the incumbents by asserting coercive control over purportedly 'fake news'.[58] Although knowledge institutions may refuse to reward work that is deemed below par, or may impose employment-related sanctions, they do not have the coercive powers of government to prohibit speech or jail dissidents. Such milder forms of influence exercised by knowledge institutions offer a less threatening alternative to

[57] See, e.g., 'Research, Truth Decay, Fighting Disinformation', RAND, www.rand.org/research/projects/truth-decay/fighting-disinformation/search.html; 'Center for an Informed Public University of Washington', www.cip.uw.edu ('The Center for an Informed Public … is a multidisciplinary research center at the University of Washington … that has a mission to resist strategic misinformation, promote an informed society and strengthen democratic discourse'); 'Science of Science Communication Area of Study', Annenberg Public Policy Center, University of Pennsylvania, www.annenbergpublicpolicycenter.org/science-communication (designed to address 'gaps between expert knowledge of science and public perception'); Annenberg Public Policy Center with Factcheck: www.annenbergpublicpolicycenter.org/appc-in-new-collaboration-to-counter-misinformation-online; Pitt Disinformation Center at Pittsburg University, www.cyber.pitt.edu/disinformation ('creat[ing] a new, community-centered system for warning, understanding, and response to malign influence'); 'Knowledge Enterprise Center on Narrative, Disinformation and Strategic Influence', Arizona State University, https://globalsecurity.asu.edu/expertise/narrative-disinformation-and-strategic-influence (using research to 'support efforts to safeguard the United States, its allies, and democratic principles against malign influence campaigns'); 'Assembly: Disinformation', Berkman Klein Center, Harvard University, https://cyber.harvard.edu/research/assembly ('brings together participants from academia, industry, government, and civil society from across disciplines to explore and make progress on disinformation in the digital public sphere'); MIT Initiative on the Digital Economy, https://ide.mit.edu/research-group/misinformation-fake-news ('shed light on the basic science of how people decide what to believe and share, and leverage these insights to design anti-misinformation interventions').

[58] See Gabrielle Lim and Samantha Bradshaw, 'Chilling Legislation: Tracking the Impact of "Fake News" Laws on Press Freedom Internationally', Center for Media Assistance, 19 July 2023, www.cima.ned.org/publication/chilling-legislation ('[M]any misinformation, disinformation, and mal-information … laws chill press freedom, rather than enhance it'); 'Censorious Governments Are Abusing "Fake News" Laws', *The Economist*, 13 February 2021. In the USA, where there is aggressive First Amendment protection even for deliberately false statements in some contexts, increasingly state statutes have targeted false communications involving the Internet and social media. See Leslie Gielow Jacobs, 'Freedom of Speech and Regulation of Fake News' (2022) 70 (Issue Supplement_1) *American Journal of Comparative Law* i278, at i294.

government efforts directly to sanction or suppress speech and the dissemination of knowledge.[59]

14.2.4 *Why Focus on Democracies?*[60]

All governments need knowledge in order to be able effectively to govern; even the most authoritarian of governments will need knowledge to maintain their own power.[61] But democracies are particularly dependent on knowledge institutions for their own legitimacy and effectiveness. *Democratic* constitutionalism requires at least to some degree the active involvement of knowledgeable citizens, even if only to participate in elections where public approval or displeasure with the performance of office holders can be expressed.[62] On more demanding understandings of democracy, elected representatives must deliberate seriously over issues of policy or, on some accounts, citizens must participate actively in influencing government bodies' agendas and policy outcomes.[63] Elections legitimize government insofar as they reflect the views of the voters who have access to information (about choices of candidates and policies) and access to voting without obstruction or coercion.[64]

[59] Cf. Mary Flug Handlin and Oscar Handlin, *The Dimensions of Liberty* (Cambridge, MA: Belknap, 1961), p. 111 ('The capacity to act through noncoercive means remained a critical element in American liberty. It preserved the latitude of choice available to the individual. By sustaining the conviction that desirable ends could be attained without calling upon the state, it helped set limits upon the use of political power without depriving society of services considered essential to its welfare').

[60] These paragraphs are largely drawn from Jackson, 'Preliminary Reflections' (n 19), at 199–201.

[61] See, e.g., Melissa M. Lee and Nan Zhang, 'Legibility and Informational Foundations of State Capacity' (2016) 79 *Journal of Politics* 118 (suggesting that all governments need knowledge and that, with better knowledge of local practices, views and persons, the state will have improved ability to assess and collect taxes and produce or encourage the production of goods); Stephen Holmes, *Passions and Constraint* (Chicago: University of Chicago Press, 1995) p. 119 (describing Jean Bodin's theory for why even monarchs benefit from some freedom of speech, enabling them to have access to vital information for maintaining their realm); cf. George Washington, 'First Address to Congress', 1790 ('Knowledge is in every country the surest basis of publick happiness. In one in which the measures of government receive their impression so immediately from the sense of the community, as in ours, it is proportionately essential').

[62] See, e.g., Joseph A. Schumpeter, *Capitalism, Socialism, and Democracy* (New York: Harper & Brothers, 1942) p. 250.

[63] See, e.g., Jürgen Habermas, *Between Facts and Norms: Contributions to a Discourse Theory of Law and Democracy* (Cambridge, MA: MIT Press, 1996) pp. 118–31; Hélène Landemore, *Open Democracy: Reinventing Popular Rule for the Twenty-first Century* (Princeton, NJ: Princeton University Press, 2020).

[64] Cf. Meiklejohn, *Free Speech* (n 34) pp. 45–46. Meiklejohn's argument for free speech on public issues rests on the assumption that free speech is the best way to provide a sound informational base for democratic decisions. His argument predates more recent technologies that, for many, have undermined some of the foundations for trusting wholly unimpeded speech.

Thus legitimate elections depend on ample sources of information,[65] as well as unobstructed access to voting. On any version of a real democracy, knowledge relevant to evaluating issues and representatives must be available to voters.[66]

Second, *constitutional* democracies require knowledge institutions to sustain their constitutionalist character. A core idea of constitutionalism is that the rule of law applies to the government itself so as to constrain the government from arbitrary action.[67] Central elements of the rule of law require that the laws, and what they prohibit or authorize, be knowable, and that the enforcement of the law be characterized by some degree of consistency and reliability.[68] Thus, in order to secure the 'constitutionalist' aspect of constitutional democracy, knowledge of the law, about what it is, how it is being applied and how it can be improved, is necessary.

Third, knowledge is essential to the effective policy development and implementation that is necessary for government to respond to the needs and preferences of the public. Democratic constitutions must enable elected governments to work effectively in meeting the material needs of their societies, while at the same time protecting the individual rights that are central to human liberty and equality.[69] Constitutions not only impose constraints on governments but also empower

[65] To be sure, knowledge institutions may fail actually to pursue knowledge. See, e.g., 'Yellow Journalism', Public Broadcasting Service, www.pbs.org/crucible/frames/_journalism.html (describing how 'the Hearst newspapers, with no evidence, unequivocally blamed the Spanish' for the sinking of the Maine, encouraging the USA to intervene militarily in Cuba). Later studies reached divergent conclusions on whether the sinking was caused by an external bomb or by an internal coal bunker near a reserve magazine. See 'A Special Report: What Really Sank the Maine?', US Naval Institute, www.usni.org/magazines/naval-history-magazine/1998/april/special-report-what-really-sank-maine. This and other controversies emphasize the importance of pluralism in the existence and control of knowledge institutions.

[66] Knowledge institutions may play another role in fostering democracy: providing shelter for political dissidents, from their own countries or others, incubating the possibility of political challenge. See, e.g., Linda Colley, *The Gun, the Ship and the Pen: Warfare, Constitutions and the Making of the Modern World* (New York: Liveright, 2021) p. 230 (describing the British Museum as 'the temple of political exiles' in the nineteenth century).

[67] Cf. Charles McIlwain, *Constitutionalism: Ancient and Modern* 3rd ed. (Ithaca, NY: Cornell University Press, 1975) p. 21 (constitutionalism 'is a legal limitation on government; … the antithesis of arbitrary rule; its opposite is despotic government, the government of will instead of law'); see also András Sajó and Renáta Uitz, *The Constitution of Freedom: An Introduction to Legal Constitutionalism* (Oxford: Oxford University Press, 2019) p. 13.

[68] See generally Lon Fuller, *The Morality of Law* (New Haven, CT: Yale University Press, 1964); Jeremy Waldron, 'The Rule of Law' in Edward N. Zalta and Uri Nodelman (eds.), *The Stanford Encyclopedia of Philosophy* (Fall 2023 ed.), https://plato.stanford.edu/entries/rule-of-law (characterizing Fuller as arguing that rule of law principles require that laws be 'general, public, prospective, coherent, clear, stable, and practicable').

[69] See Vicki C. Jackson and Yasmin Dawood, 'Constitutionalism and Effective Government: Rights, Institutions, and Values' in Vicki C. Jackson and Yasmin Dawood (eds.), *Constitutionalism and a Right to Effective Government?* (Cambridge: Cambridge University Press, 2022).

governments to act for the benefit of their people.[70] The democratic and constitutionalist pillars of constitutional democracy must be accompanied by a pillar of effective government.[71] Effective government requires competency in decision-making.[72]

Democratic elections mean less if elected officials are incompetent or lack access to knowledge that forms the basis for competent decisions. Incompetent government cannot effectively respond to and provide for the material needs of the people; constitutional democracies cannot long survive if their governments are not seen as effective in advancing the welfare of the people. Even the protection of individual rights rests on the ability of government to have an effective system that works to promote the protection of rights, including well-trained police, prosecutors, lawyers, judges and courts. Competency, in turn, rests on decision-makers having reliable knowledge of the world.

Constitutional democracies, then, rest on multiple pillars – of democracy and public consent, of respect for rule-of-law protections from arbitrary government conduct, of protection of individual rights and of competent, 'workable' governance.[73] To secure 'democratic', 'constitutionalist' and 'competency' forms of

70 See N. W. Barber, *The Principles of Constitutionalism* (Oxford: Oxford University Press, 2018) p. 19; Sotirios A. Barber, 'Fallacies of Negative Constitutionalism' (2006) 75(2) *Fordham Law Review* 651; Sotirios A. Barber and James E. Fleming, *Constitutional Interpretation: The Basic Questions* (Oxford: Oxford University Press, 2007) ch. 4.

71 See Jackson and Dawood, 'Constitutionalism' (n 69); see also Gillian E. Metzger, 'Foreword: 1930s Redux: The Administrative State under Siege' (2017) 131(1) *Harvard Law Review* 74 (noting the agreement of Brownlow and Landis, who had otherwise largely opposed positions on issues of presidential control in federal administrative law, that a democratic government had to have effective public administration). It is not coincidental that Landis and Brownlow were writing against the backdrop of fascism's rise in Europe.

72 See Elizabeth Fisher and Sidney A. Shapiro, *Administrative Competence: Reimagining Administrative Law* (Cambridge: Cambridge University Press, 2020); Cass R. Sunstein, 'The Most Knowledgeable Branch' (2016) 164(7) *University of Pennsylvania Law Review* 1607; Robert C. Post, *Democracy, Expertise and Academic Freedom: A First Amendment Jurisprudence for the Modern State* (New Haven, CT: Yale University Press, 2012) (distinguishing legitimation by democracy and by competency, and arguing both are needed); cf. Bruce Ackerman, 'The New Separation of Powers' (2000) 113(3) *Harvard Law Review* 633, at 696–97 (discussing need for an 'integrity branch' and a 'regulatory branch' to provide competent and non-corrupt execution of the laws). For an argument that truth must be seen as central to democracy, see Michael Lynch, 'Truth as a Democratic Value' in Melissa Schwartzberg and Philip Kitcher (eds.), *Truth and Evidence* (New York: NYU Press, 2021) (arguing that protecting the means to pursue knowledge in democracy advances values of 'promoting deliberative decision-making procedures such as rational legislative processes and participatory politics' which rest on basic respect for each person and the existence of a 'common currency of reasons' for democratic contestation).

73 See generally, Ackerman, 'The New Separation of Powers' (n 72), at 688–97; Post, *Democracy, Expertise and Academic Freedom* (n 72), p. 34; see also Sunstein, 'The Most Knowledgeable Branch' (n 72), at 1612; *Youngstown Sheet & Tube Co.* v. *Sawyer*, 343 US 579, 635 (1952) (Jackson J, concurring) ('While the Constitution diffuses power the better to secure liberty, it also contemplates that practice will integrate the dispersed powers into a *workable* government') (emphasis added).

legitimation, constitutional democracies require what Ginsburg and Huq call a 'shared epistemic' foundation.[74] A shared epistemic foundation is one that is rooted in verifiable knowledge about the world and a reasoned and open process for interpreting what that knowledge means for policymaking. To this end, democratic constitutionalism requires vibrant 'knowledge institutions', both within and outside of government, to help secure this shared epistemic foundation.

For the reasons discussed above, institutions devoted to knowledge production or dissemination deserve special attention in the field of constitutional studies; their role is a distinctive one in securing the freedoms and epistemological grounding necessary in constitutional democracies. Yet the role of knowledge institutions in constitutional democracy has gone underappreciated, both in US constitutional discourse and in comparative constitutional studies. Shoring up appreciation of and protections for knowledge institutions is thus urgently important.

14.3 BRIEF EXAMPLES: OF PUBLIC UNIVERSITIES AND GOVERNMENT OFFICES

Both government offices and universities, public and private, can be 'knowledge institutions'. Some government offices exist for the principal purpose of compiling and creating knowledge – about different sectors of the economy, about the population as a whole, about natural phenomena.[75] Many government offices also have other purposes to be pursued through the exercise of professionally informed knowledge, as in criminal prosecutors' offices, or in offices of health and safety regulation. In carrying out their knowledge-related functions, ongoing organizations in government, like academic departments, require commitments to the pursuit of truth or knowledge; the application of appropriate disciplinary standards designed to identify reliable knowledge claims; and the ability independently to apply those disciplinary criteria. In the sections that follow, I discuss case law that threatens that independence, in both government offices and public universities.

14.3.1 Garcetti *and Government Employees*

In *Garcetti* v. *Ceballos*,[76] the Court held that criminal prosecutors, and government employees generally, are not protected by the First Amendment from adverse employment action for statements made pursuant to the government employees' official duties – apparently even if the statements address matters of public concern,

[74] Aziz Huq and Tom Ginsburg, 'How to Lose a Constitutional Democracy' (2018) 65 *UCLA Law Review* 78, at 130–31.
[75] See Jackson, 'Knowledge at Risk' (n 27) (identifying several statutes imposing such duties).
[76] *Garcetti* v. *Ceballos*, 547 US 410 (2006).

or of professional ethics and constitutional responsibility.[77] It explained that: 'Restricting speech that owes its existence to a public employee's professional responsibilities does not infringe any liberties the employee might have enjoyed as a private citizen. It simply reflects the exercise of employer control over what the employer itself has commissioned or created.'[78] The implications for faculty at public universities aroused considerable concern,[79] although the Court reserved that question.[80]

Government offices no doubt have 'managerial' needs that warrant control over employee speech that would be unconstitutional if extended by the government as regulator to the citizenry as a whole.[81] But *Garcetti*'s prioritization of bureaucratic control over other public values of truth and legality remains a significant deterrent to expressions of professional disagreement within government offices, including those that are knowledge institutions, even when expressing those disagreements may be in the public interest. Government employees may develop specialized expert knowledge, making their observations and concerns of high value to the public as well as the government.[82] And government officials, like other employers, have incentives to avoid acknowledging or redressing their own mistakes,[83] a tendency that could be mitigated, or deterred, by recognizing that government employees doing 'knowledge' work for the government require, by virtue of the function of their office, greater protection for their speech in the course of official duties. In denying that a government employee has *any* First Amendment interest in

77 See 'Leading Cases, Supreme Court 2005 Term, Public Employee Speech' (2006) 120 *Harvard Law Review* 273 (describing *Garcetti*'s factual allegations that the government prosecutor was professionally and constitutionally obligated to send a memo to his supervisor detailing concerns about an affidavit used to procure a search warrant and to disclose those concerns to defense counsel, he nonetheless suffered adverse employment action as a result). See also n. 89.

78 *Garcetti* v. *Ceballos*, at 421–22. In other cases the Court has taken a categorical approach, treating 'government speech' as outside the concerns of the free speech clause of the First Amendment. See, e.g., *Pleasant Grove City* v. *Summum*, 555 US 460 (2009).

79 See, e.g., Judith Areen, 'Government as Educator: A New Understanding of First Amendment Protection of Academic Freedom and Governance' (2009) 97 *Georgetown Law Journal* 945.

80 *Garcetti* v. *Ceballos*, at 423. The Court narrowed the sweep of *Garcetti* in *Lane* v. *Franks*, 573 US 228 (2014), with respect to sworn testimony by a government employee subpoenaed to testify about matters within his knowledge as a government employee. It distinguished *Garcetti* as resting on the fact that the speech in question – a memo written by the plaintiff to his supervisor – was within the scope of his official duties. Ibid. at 237–38.

81 See generally Robert C. Post, *Constitutional Domains: Democracy, Community, Management* (Cambridge, MA: Harvard University Press, 1995).

82 See Jackson, 'Knowledge at Risk' (n 27); see also Heidi Kitrosser, 'The Special Value of Public Employee Speech' (2015) *Supreme Court Review* 301; Helen Norton, *The Government's Speech and the Constitution* (Cambridge: Cambridge University Press, 2019) p. 11.

83 In addition to counteracting existing incentives to avoid correcting errors, affording some protection to internal speech would recognize the special informational value such speech may have to government decisions, see Kitrosser, 'The Special Value' (n 82), a value that may be central to the protection of professional and constitutional responsibilities, and help deter future mistakes that could arise from dismissing internally raised concerns.

speech made as part of their official duties as a government employee, *Garcetti* also undervalues the role of such speech in serving knowledge-related interests vital in a democracy, including checking or disclosing misinformation and breaches of constitutional requirements.

Although categorical rules have important advantages of clarity, and error avoidance,[84] when deployed to strip all constitutional protections from government employee speech in their official duties, that approach goes too far in cutting off potentially valuable information. At the same time, governments as employers have undoubted interests in being able to manage their workforce, including the ability to discipline employees for errors, incompetence or disruptive behavior at work.[85] And the constitutional system as a whole, and all of its members, have an interest in effective government that requires acknowledging the hierarchical authority in heads of offices to manage their staff.[86]

Those legitimate interests can be accommodated through doctrine that does less harm to the interests of the First Amendment and the public in the kind of information government employees can and should be able to provide,[87] while at the same time recognizing the knowledge-producing roles of government offices. Fred Schauer, among others, has criticized the Court for too rigid an application of legal categories that are insufficiently attentive to contextual differences between institutional settings.[88] As such work suggests, 'government speech' should not be deployed as a category to preclude careful attention to the competing values at stake in conflicts between managerial authority for work-related errors, on the one hand, and the professional judgment of professional employees exercised on behalf of public values, on the other.[89]

84 See generally Frederick Schauer, 'Formalism' (1988) 97(4) *Yale Law Journal* 509; Kathleen Sullivan, 'Foreword: The Justices of Rules and Standards' (1992) 106(1) *Harvard Law Review* 22.

85 See Robert C. Post, 'Subsidized Speech' (1996) 106(1) *Yale Law Journal* 151, at 164.

86 See Post, *Constitutional Domains* (n 81) pp. 234–37 (on the role of hierarchy in organizations).

87 See, e.g., Kitrosser, 'The Special Value' (n 82), at 303 and 333–36 (arguing for inquiry whether competency based claims for disciplining an employee were pretextual and distinguishing scripted and unscripted public employee jobs).

88 See Schauer, 'Towards an Institutional First Amendment' (n 35); Schauer, 'Principles, Institutions and the First Amendment' (n 37), at 100–1.

89 In *Garcetti*, a supervising deputy district attorney believed that an affidavit submitted in connection with a search warrant was misleading; he conveyed his views first, within his office, to his supervisor, and then to a court, in a hearing requested by defense counsel to suppress the evidence seized but in a redacted form as requested by his supervisor. See 'Leading Cases, Supreme Court 2005 Term' (n 77), at 274. The Court rejected the defense motion. Given the role of professional lawyers in prosecutors' offices, one would think that there was a powerful argument that the employee's behavior should not have been subject to sanction because of the value of expert knowledge in protecting the rights secured by constitutional criminal procedure rules.

These arguments warrant significant modification of *Garcetti*, notwithstanding its concern for managerial prerogatives.[90] The US approach severs too completely the public employees' constitutional accountability to the public from its bureaucratically focused conception of the hierarchical responsibility of a public servant.[91] The question of government employee speech highlights one of the benefits of seeing knowledge institutions as a category in constitutionalism, because the benefits to be achieved by protecting the professionally informed, expert speech of some government workers overlap with the benefits to be derived from protecting academic and press freedoms, in ways that separate treatment may obscure.

14.3.2 *Universities as a Special Case?*

As noted, *Garcetti* did not rule on whether its holding – that government employees had no First Amendment protection for speech that was part of their official duties – would apply to professors at public universities. This unanswered question of *Garcetti* has assumed increasing importance, as attacks on basic elements of American academic freedom traditions mount while the Court has seemingly retreated from its prior support for the constitutional status of academic freedom in the context of student admissions. As Paul Horwitz argues, the law of free speech protection 'should be responsive to context, specifically including institutional context', and 'should be built from the perspective of important speech institutions, not imposed upon them'.[92] Academic freedom is central to sustaining constitutional democracy.[93] The central functions of universities as institutions – whether public or private – are to advance knowledge through research and teaching. Similar protections of academic freedoms should be accorded to those operating as public as well as those operating as private universities.

[90] For alternative approaches, see 'Guide on Article 10 of the European Convention on Human Rights: Freedom of Expression', European Court of Human Rights, 2021 (identifying six factors that bear on whether particular actions of whistleblowing or reporting irregularities by public officials are protected under Article 10), www.echr.coe.int/documents/guide_art_10_eng.pdf. Without necessarily adopting their specific criteria, I suggest that the European Court's work suggests that judicially developed criteria for balancing interests in managerial control against interests in truth are possible.

[91] For an incisive analysis of 'public knowledge producers' and the Court's First Amendment jurisprudence across a range of areas, see Heidi Kitrosser, 'Protecting Public Knowledge Producers' (Northwestern University Pritzker School of Law Public Law and Legal Theory Series, No. 22–36, 2022). On the adverse effects of the Court's declining protection of the free speech rights of government employees, especially in state and local governments, see Adam Shinar, 'Public Employee Speech and the Privatization of the First Amendment' (2013) 46 *Connecticut Law Review* 1.

[92] Horwitz, *First Amendment Institutions* (n 35) at 69.

[93] See generally Tom Ginsburg, 'Academic Freedom and Democratic Backsliding' (2022) 71(2) *Journal of Legal Education* 238.

14.3.2.1 Student Admissions

In *Sweezy* v. *New Hampshire*,[94] Chief Justice Earl Warren's plurality opinion noted the 'essentiality of freedom in the community of American universities' as a 'self-evident' feature of the First Amendment, and cautioned against 'imposing any strait jacket upon the intellectual leaders in our colleges and universities'. In a concurrence, Justice Felix Frankfurter famously described the constitutional scope of academic freedom in explaining what freedoms of universities were necessary to maintaining a 'free society'.[95] Drawing from a statement by South African academics, his opinion stated that

> [i]t is the business of a university to provide that atmosphere which is most conducive to speculation, experiment and creation. It is an atmosphere in which there prevail 'the four essential freedoms' of a university – to determine for itself on academic grounds who may teach, what may be taught, how it shall be taught, and who may be admitted to study.[96]

Widely cited,[97] this statement of a US idea of academic freedom proved central to supporting decisions in subsequent cases upholding the use of race in university admissions to promote the diversity of the student body: Justice Lewis Powell's opinion in *Regents of University of California* v. *Bakke* quoted and relied on Justice Frankfurter's *Sweezy* discussion of academic freedom,[98] and this rationale was relied on as well in *Grutter* v. *Bollinger*.[99]

However, in *Students for Fair Admissions* v. *Harvard College*,[100] the Supreme Court in effect disavowed the reasoning in *Bakke* and *Grutter*, holding that consideration of race as such in university admissions violates the Equal Protection Clause; the Court invalidated the Harvard College plan (whose predecessor had been specifically approved by Justice Powell in *Bakke*). Contrary to the reasoning in prior

94 *Sweezy* v. *New Hampshire*, 354 US 234, 250 (1957).

95 Ibid. at 261–62 (Frankfurter J, concurring in the result, joined by Harlan J) (explaining 'the dependence of a free society on free universities [which] means the exclusion of governmental intervention in the intellectual life of a university').

96 Ibid. at 263 (quoting and citing *The Open Universities in South Africa* (Johannesburg: Witwatersrand University Press, 1957) 10–12).

97 See, e.g., *Board of Regents of University of Wisconsin System* v. *Southworth*, 529 US 217, 239 (2000) (Souter J, concurring in the judgment) (quoting Frankfurter's 'four essential freedoms' statement and concluding that 'protecting a university's discretion to shape its educational mission may prove to be an important consideration in First Amendment analysis of objections to student fees'); Post, *Democracy, Expertise and Academic Freedom* (n 72) p. 72; Peter Byrne, 'Academic Freedom: A Special Concern of the First Amendment' (1989) 99 *Yale Law Journal* 251, at 289–90.

98 See *Regents of University of California* v. *Bakke*, 438 US 265, 312 (1978) (Powell J, delivering the judgment of the Court and concurring).

99 *Grutter* v. *Bollinger*, 539 US 306, 329 (2003); *Grutter* was treated as no longer controlling in *Students for Fair Admissions* v. *Harvard College*, 143 S.Ct. 2141 (2023).

100 Ibid. at 2166.

cases, the Court treated the university's aims – including 'better educating its students through diversity' and 'producing new knowledge stemming from diverse outlooks' – as 'commendable goals, [but] not sufficiently coherent for purposes of strict scrutiny', 'worthy', but not enough to justify the use of race[101] – notwithstanding their acceptance in prior cases. The lack of respect for universities' academic decisions is manifest in the evident hostility with which strict scrutiny is applied (for example, the Court's claim that the educational benefits of student body diversity are not 'sufficiently coherent').

Students for Fair Admissions was a major case, with long majority, concurring and dissenting opinions. Of further concern, then, is that in this major case, in which universities defended an admissions program on academic freedom grounds,[102] not one opinion cites *Sweezy*. Why not? Should the majority in *Students for Fair Admissions* be understood as rejecting Frankfurter's formulation of academic freedom, at least as it applies to the admission of students? How concerned should one be about universities' capacities to remain independent 'knowledge institutions' if their academic freedom does not extend, generally, to selection of students? Even more concerning is the possibility that the Court's silence in *Students for Fair Admissions* implies skepticism that 'academic freedom' has any constitutional foundation whatsoever, for in that case, university faculty would be in the same position as government employees under *Garcetti*. *Garcetti*'s unanswered question about its application to public colleges and universities thus looms even larger in light of *Students for Fair Admissions*.

How central to universities is the ability to develop and apply selection criteria for choosing their students? One could perhaps argue – not very. One could argue that the core, or most central, reason to protect universities as knowledge institutions is

[101] See ibid. at 2166–67. Although this language accepts the university's judgment, it does so grudgingly and without calling these 'worthy' goals 'compelling'. In *Fisher* v. *University of Texas at Austin*, 570 US 297, 308 (2013), the Court, in ruling on the constitutionality of an affirmative action plan, recognized the importance of *Sweezy* and of academic freedom in student admissions. But the Court emphasized that race could be used in admissions only if its use survived 'strict scrutiny', and said that while, under *Grutter*, courts would defer to a university's conclusion that racial diversity was 'essential to its educational admission', the school still 'must prove that the means chosen by the University to attain diversity are narrowly tailored to that goal', and held that on that 'point, the University receives no deference'. Ibid. at 311. After remand and further findings in the lower courts, in *Fisher II*, 579 US 365, 381–82 (2016), the Supreme Court upheld the Texas approach, using the language of compelling interests. In *Students for Fair Admissions*, the Court gave no deference at all to the universities' decisions, including on the importance of racial diversity to educational goals, see ibid. at 2190 (Thomas J, concurring) (noting the Court's refusal to defer to the universities' own assessments of the educational benefits).

[102] See Harvard Respondent's brief in *Students for Fair Admissions*, at 30 (citing and quoting *Sweezy*); University of North Carolina Respondent's brief in *Students for Fair Admissions*, at 39 (quoting and citing *Sweezy*, and quoting and citing *Bakke* on the importance of safeguarding academic freedom). For a reference to 'academic freedom', but not to *Sweezy*, see *Students for Fair Admissions*, at 2234 (Sotomayor J, dissenting).

for the production of knowledge that comes from faculty who are relatively untrammeled by the limits of conventional wisdom, and for teaching students both current knowledge and to open their minds to further learning as they go on in life. These core functions, it could further be argued, are not much influenced by the admission of those students – at least at the undergraduate level – who are primarily there to learn from their professors, rather than to assist professors in their research. Or one could argue that the reasons for active selection in the past, rather than, say, accepting as many students as the university had room for, had more to do with maintaining elite status or membership in a particular religion, considerations that are no longer persuasive in a more egalitarian society.

But is this really persuasive? In the context of modern colleges and universities – especially contemporary research universities – does the quality and diversity of one's students not affect the quality of faculty research? Do admissions decisions not reflect profoundly academic judgments about how to achieve a quality education? Such claims seem wholly implausible as applied to graduate students, who are often employed as teaching or research assistants to faculty members. But even undergraduate students may help faculty with their research. And classroom interactions with adult students of all ages, whose diverse experiences lead them to ask different kinds of questions that in turn lead faculty to see materials in new lights, have the potential to sharpen faculty minds and expand their horizons.[103] Thus, the autonomy of faculties over whom to admit seems closely related to core reasons for recognizing academic freedoms in universities and their faculties. Moreover, the qualities of mind and range of experiences that their classmate students have will affect the quality of student learning experience.[104] If research, teaching and learning are the core elements of universities as knowledge institutions, these favor considerable autonomy for universities in selecting their students. And if universities that have adopted affirmative action programs have made deliberate academic judgments about their educational mission (perhaps relying on academic studies to support their educational conclusions),[105] values of academic freedom are, at least arguably, seriously at risk when a court declares their program is invalid.

In this light, the absence of discussion of universities' academic freedoms in *Students for Fair Admissions* is troubling. True, the issue of racial justice/injustice under the equal protection clause dominated, under the standards of strict scrutiny established in *Grutter* and *Bakke*, and is of surpassing importance; constitutional

[103] How many faculty can say that they have not been inspired or provoked to new thoughts, reflected in later scholarship, by questions from their students?

[104] See William C. Kirby, *Empires of Ideas: Creating the Modern University from Germany to America to China* (Cambridge, MA: Belknap, 2022) p. 13.

[105] Cf., e.g., *Students for Fair Admissions*, at 2255–56 (Sotomayor J, dissenting) (noting that Harvard had consulted data to shape and decide whether to continue its program; arguing that data relied on by Justice Thomas was 'unreliable' and advanced an academically 'discredited' 'mismatch' thesis).

interests in equality clearly support general rules prohibiting invidious discrimination against students based on race, sex or religion.[106] Moreover, it is not uncommon for public universities to experience external pressures or constraints to admit, for example, students from their own state,[107] and/or for financial reasons to admit other categories of students (including out-of-state) who can pay higher or full tuition fees.[108] But it was significant that these affirmative action programs reflected exercises of academic judgment, and the Court's decision interfered with those judgments and resulting programs. There are sound reasons to include the right to decide on selection criteria for students as part of a university's academic freedom. Had the protection of academic freedom been seen as of higher constitutional value, then a different balance might well have been struck between presumptive rules against considering race and the universities considered, non-invidious reasons for doing so as a method for building a more inclusive, more diverse student body.

14.3.2.2 Curriculum

The questions of what and how to teach are often said to be at the core, along with freedom of research, of the academic freedom of universities.[109] True, there is often some degree of shared control: it is not uncommon for governments to decide to support particular fields of study – such as medicine, veterinary medicine,

[106] See, e.g., Title VI, 42 U.S.C. § 2000d; Title IX, 20 U.S.C. §1681; *United States* v. *Virginia*, 518 US 515 (1996). Concerns for remedying past societal racial injustices might appear a powerful argument in favor of affirmative action plans, but the case law rejected this argument (except where a particular institution was officially determined to have engaged in unlawful discrimination). See *Bakke*, at 310 (Powell J, delivering the judgment of the Court and concurring); *City of Richmond* v. *Croson*, 488 U.S. 469, 496–97 (1989) (O'Connor J, announcing the judgment of the Court).

[107] See Jessica Callahan, 'Research Report: States with Automatic or Guaranteed College Admissions Policies', Connecticut General Assembly Office of Legislative Research, 3 March 2021, www.cga.ct.gov/2021/rpt/pdf/2021-R-0077.pdf (describing twelve universities with such externally imposed policies for guaranteed admissions); for more detail, see '50-State Comparison, State-Wide Admissions Policies, Does the State Have a Guaranteed Admissions Policy?', Education Commission of the States, May 2022, https://reports.ecs.org/comparisons/statewide-admissions-policies-2022-04.

[108] See, e.g., David Leonhardt, 'Econ 101', *New York Times Magazine*, 10 September 2023, 42, at 46 (noting that as government financial support for public universities has declined, incentives to admit students who pay full tuition have increased).

[109] See, e.g., 'How Academic Freedom Is Monitored', European Parliament, Panel for the Future of Science and Technology, March 2023, p. 6 (noting many different definitions of academic freedom and identifying at the common core the concepts of freedom of research and freedom of teaching); cf. ibid. at IV (providing a more detailed list of what is encompassed in the concept of academic freedom, noting that freedom to teach includes, within certain limits, freedom to choose students).

mechanical arts or agriculture[110] – and to provide funds to be used towards that purpose,[111] and curriculum decisions are often made for universities based on a consensus among faculty and academic staff.[112] But as a matter of academic freedom, it must be up to academic faculty to determine the content of a course and how it should be taught.[113] In this way, the academic expertise of faculty is deployed to advance the field of knowledge that has attracted the government's interest; faculty are not required to speak or teach or write in ways that misrepresent their academically informed views. For governments to offer funds for the study of particular areas is not necessarily incompatible with leading understandings of academic freedom; for governments to require universities to offer specific courses of study may raise questions of academic freedom, perhaps depending on the degree

[110] In the USA, the federal Morrill Act, 2 July 1862, 12 Stat. 503, provided that monies it was enabling the states to obtain should support an endowment 'and maintenance of at least one college where the leading object shall be, without excluding other scientific and classical studies and including military tactics, to teach such branches of learning as are related to *agriculture and the mechanic arts*, in such manner as the legislatures of the States may respectively prescribe' (emphasis added).

[111] On controversy in the United Kingdom whether the government has gone too far in its new funding scheme for higher education in insisting on external, non-faculty direction of universities as to what fields of study to concentrate on, see Eric Barendt, *Academic Freedom and the Law: A Comparative Study* (Oxford: Hart, 2010) pp. 91–92. On threats by US state legislatures to penalize public universities over curricular decisions, see Adrienne Lu, 'State Lawmakers Frequently Try to Tell Public Colleges and Universities What To Do through the Power of the Budget', *Governing*, 24 April 2014, www.governing.com/news/headlines/how-state-lawmakers-control-state-universities.html.

[112] The idea that any constitutional protection of academic freedom beyond ordinary First Amendment freedoms is enjoyed only by universities as institutions (and not by faculty members), see, e.g., *Urofsky* v. *Gilmore*, 216 F3d 401, 411–15 (4th Cir. 2000), is not fully persuasive if universities are to function well as knowledge institutions. For example, while curricular development may be shared within the umbrella of academic freedoms, and research protections established at the university level, the nature and quality of the research and writing that ensues should be largely a matter of the individual faculty members' academic freedom. Whether that freedom should be protected entirely though autonomous within-university methods, such as peer review for tenure, is a different issue. Although some scholars would categorically protect the university's claims of academic freedom over those of individual scholars, academic freedom for universities need not exclude entirely constitutional protection for individuals where it can be shown that a particular institution's purportedly academic judgments are pretextual. Compare David Rabban, 'Functional Analysis of Individual and Institutional Academic Freedom' (1990) 53 *Law & Contemporary Problems* 227, at 283 (arguing that courts can review whether purported academic grounds are pretextual) with Byrne, 'Academic Freedom' (n 97), at 288 (arguing that courts should not review university decisions on academic grounds). And individual faculty members have other constitutional rights, including to be free from invidious discrimination, that can be externally enforced.

[113] See, e.g., 'Statement of Principles on Academic Freedom and Tenure', American Association of University Professors, 1940 ('Teachers are entitled to freedom in the classroom in discussing their subject'); the European Parliament's 'How Academic Freedom Is Monitored' (n 109) (distinguishing between faculty members' freedom to determine content and teaching methods of a course, on one hand, and the development of curriculum (in which faculty should play a role)); Evans and Stone, *Open Minds* (n 22) p. 145 (control over appointments, curriculum and teaching central to academic freedoms of universities).

of faculty involvement in defining the curriculum;[114] but for governments to prohibit the study or teaching of particular topics or content plainly is wholly incompatible with the spirit of free inquiry in prevailing conceptions of academic freedom. Recent events in the USA and in other countries, including Poland and Hungary, challenge this basic aspect of academic freedom and of universities as knowledge institutions.

As noted earlier, the State of Iowa's House Bill 802 applies to public institutions of higher learning. Benignly, it states clearly that it does *not* prohibit teaching about the 'topics of sexism, slavery, racial oppression, racial segregation, or racial discrimination including topics related to the enactment and enforcement of laws resulting in sexism, racial oppression, segregation and discrimination'.[115] Yet it provides that any 'mandatory staff or student training' must not 'teach, advocate, act upon or promote specific defined concepts'. 'Specific defined concepts' include 'that the United States or State of Iowa are fundamentally or systematically racist or sexist'. The law also says that public employees are not 'prohibited from discussing such specific defined topics as part of a larger course of academic instruction'. So it would appear that faculty can *discuss* whether the USA or Iowa are fundamentally racist, but cannot *argue* – even if based on their academic expertise – that they are, at least if they are teaching something that could be regarded as 'mandatory student training' (whose application to, for example, a required history class is on its face unclear).[116]

[114] Compare Rabban, 'Functional Analysis' (n 112), at 278–29 and n 251 (noting Texas requirements that every state-supported university offer a course in government, and history, including that of Texas, and questioning whether the Court would view state control of higher education curriculum in the same light as its control of public school curriculum) with Byrne, 'Academic Freedom' (n 97), at 331 (suggesting that state compulsion of a particular liberal arts curriculum would surely be unconstitutional). Texas's requirements for American history and government at public universities are quite specific. See Texas Education Code, s. 51.301 (specifying that an 'American Way' course of specific content (though not viewpoint) be required of foreign students, and that at least six credits of coursework on government, including study of the USA and state constitutions, be generally required for graduation from universities receiving public funds). For a mandate that a 'core curriculum be developed by public boards with appropriate consultation with the Academic Senates', see California Education Code § 66720. Cf. Thomas I. Emerson, *The System of Freedom of Expression* (New York: Random House, 1970) p. 624 ('[T]he government can prescribe the [broad] character of the curriculum for a particular institution, provide what general areas are to be emphasized or omitted, even require the offering of certain courses', but not 'more immediate details of course content, methods of presentation ... and similar matters ... of academic competence').

[115] Iowa House Bill 802, s. 1.d.

[116] An even more aggressive intrusion on academic freedom in teaching is found in a 2022 Florida law, CS/HB 7, Ch. 2022-72. It prohibits 'training or instruction, that espouses, promotes, advances, [or] inculcates' support for affirmative action programs (that is, that someone 'by virtue of his or her race, color, national origin, or sex should ... receive adverse treatment to achieve diversity, equity, or inclusion') and prohibits instruction 'that [a person] must feel guilt ... [or] psychological distress for actions, in which he or she played no part, committed in the past by other members of the same race or sex'. Such prohibitions have the potential to cut deeply into faculty classroom speech and faculty-student exchange of ideas.

The law is a clear violation of basic principles of academic freedom.[117] And if it were applied to private colleges and universities, it is reasonably clear that the law would be found to violate the First Amendment: it is a content- and viewpoint-based distinction, and it is difficult to imagine any argument that such a restriction would pass muster under the decided cases.[118] But the Iowa law applies only to public employees. As such, it raises the question reserved in *Garcetti* – whether the holding applies to faculty at public universities – which is now of critical importance.[119] Will *Students for Fair Admissions*' failure to endorse the constitutional concept of academic freedoms affect resolution of this question?

Allowing government to dictate what positions faculty can take in teaching university students, as the Iowa law appears to do, is incompatible with the independence necessary for a knowledge institution to function. It is a form of censorship with all of censorship's well-known potentials for harm; it prevents the free deployment of academic expertise for the benefit of student learners; and it can function as a form of government propaganda, anathema to a free society.[120] Seeing

[117] See notes 112 and 113.

[118] See, e.g., *R.A.V.* v. *City of St Paul*, 505 US 377 (1992) (holding that a statute prohibiting certain hateful speech was an unconstitutional viewpoint discrimination); *Brandenburg* v. *Ohio*, 395 US 444, 449 (1969) (holding that unless a speech urging violence constituted an incitement to imminent violence it could not constitutionally be punished); *Boos* v. *Barry*, 485 US 312 (1988) (holding that a law prohibiting signs outside an embassy critical of that embassy's government was unconstitutional because content-based restrictions on speech must be narrowly tailored to serve a compelling government interest and this law was not narrowly tailored).

[119] Although for some scholars criticism of university governance is central to the protection of academic freedom, see Evans and Stone, *Open Minds* (n 22) p. 17, a number of US lower courts have held, in reliance on *Garcetti*, that faculty members with official involvement in policymaking for their universities can be sanctioned for their speech about colleagues or university policy. See, e.g., *Porter* v. *Board of Trustees of Northern Carolina State University*, 72 F.4th 573 (4th Cir. 2023) (holding that a professor ridiculing his colleagues via email and challenging them in faculty meetings was not protected speech); *Renken* v. *Gregory*, 541 F.3d 769 (7th Cir. 2008) (holding that a professor's complaints about the university's use of grant funds was not protected speech); cf. Adrienne Stone, 'The Meaning of Academic Freedom: The Significance of *Ridd* v. *James Cook University*' (2021) 43(2) *Sydney Law Review* 241 (criticizing decision upholding dismissal of professor for breach of code requiring courtesy and decorum). But see *Demers* v. *Austin*, 746 F.3d 402 (9th Cir. 2014) (holding that a professor's proposed administrative reform plan was protected speech). For argument that *Garcetti* should not extend to public university faculty, see Areen, 'Government as Educator' (n 79) at 948–49; 'Case Note' (2014) 127 *Harvard Law Review* 1823 (case comment on 9th Cir. *Demers* decision). For an example of a European approach, see *Sorguç* v. *Turkey*, Application No. 17089/03, European Court of Human Rights, judgment of 23 June 2009 (finding a violation of European Convention speech rights where a professor was assessed damages for defaming a junior colleague in having made a general critique of faculty hiring practices at his institution, the Court emphasizing 'the importance of academic freedom, which comprises the academics' freedom to express freely their opinion about the institution or system in which they work'), http://hudoc.echr.coe.int/eng?i=001-93161.

[120] On the complications of government propaganda, see Hannah Arendt, 'Lying in Politics: Reflections on the Pentagon Papers', *New York Review of Books*, 18 November 1971; cf.

universities (whether public or private) as knowledge institutions should make this clear.

As noted, careful attention must be given to the competing values at stake when the managerial authority of government as employer is countered by a claim that the professional judgment of professional employees be exercised on behalf of public values. In the academic setting, the balance tilts decisively in favor of providing autonomy for the professional judgments of academics, taken in academic contexts; it is the very function of faculty in these institutions to question, dissent and take sides – supported by evidence – on all kinds of subjects, notably including difficult issues. If *Garcetti*'s categorical exclusion of government employees from First Amendment protection when they are speaking within their official capacity survives (it should not), a categorical exception should be applied for academic staff in institutions of higher education. As the Court said in *Keyishian* v. *Board of Regents of the University of State of New York*, 'academic freedom ... is of transcendent value to all of us and not merely to the teachers concerned. That freedom is therefore a special concern of the First Amendment, which does not tolerate laws that cast a pall of orthodoxy over the classroom'.[121] A 'pall of orthodoxy' is precisely what the Iowa law purports to prescribe – and the fact that it was proposed and enacted into law should raise deep concerns.

Freedom of research and freedom of teaching within areas of expertise, according to disciplinary standards of the field, is at the core of academic freedoms. As many scholars note, academic freedom is quite distinct from freedom of speech entitled to constitutional protection; academic freedoms require content-based distinctions to be drawn, and require viewpoints expressed in the classroom and in writing to be adequately supported in an academic way. As Adrienne Stone and Carolyn Evans put it: 'Freedom of speech is a political freedom that should be enjoyed by all people in democratic nations. Academic freedom has a more specific purpose. It protects the pursuit and dissemination of knowledge through free inquiry and ensures that university research and teaching is authoritative and unbiased.'[122] Academic freedoms are necessary in a constitutional democracy because without those freedoms, we stand on less certain ground about what is true knowledge; genuine inquiry requires space to test, explore and try out arguments for what may not yet be known to be true (and for what on further inquiry may not survive the disciplinary processes

Seanna Shiffrin, 'Unfit to Print: Government Speech and the First Amendment', 2022, https://papers.ssrn.com/sol3/papers.cfm?abstract_id=4201762 (arguing that some government speech violates the First Amendment); Helen Norton, 'Government Lies and the Press Clause' (2018) 89 *University of Colorado Law Review* 453 (government lies as impairing democratic function of press to hold government to account); Carolina Mala Corbin, 'The Unconstitutionality of Government Propaganda' (2020) 81 *Ohio State Law Journal* 815 (describing government propaganda as the 'deliberate dissemination of false claims on a matter of public interest').

[121] *Keyishian* v. *Board of Regents of the University of State of New York* at 603.

[122] Evans and Stone, *Open Minds* (n 22), p. 79.

of justification and critique). The pursuit of knowledge is a good in itself and is also a good for society and for democracy, because of the valuable function the institution serves in developing and applying standards for the pursuit and verification of truth. Without independent knowledge institutions as important parts of our constitutional infrastructure, finally, the intermediary role in helping to sort out and check misinformation will go unfulfilled.[123]

[123] A book-in-progress (see n. 56) will seek to address both (i) how to identify knowledge institutions, some difficulties of which are suggested by *Big Mama Rag* v. *United States*, 631 F.2d 1030 (D.C. Cir. 1980) (discussing constitutionality of definition of an 'educational' organization for tax exemption purposes) and (ii) how to protect and improve knowledge institutions (considering the roles of courts, legislatures, public officials, media companies and civic groups, as well as knowledge institutions themselves).

15

Freeing Speech at Work

Journalists' Unions, Workplace Democracy and Political Democracy

Charlotte Garden

15.1 INTRODUCTION

The 'marketplace of ideas' metaphor tends to dominate US discourse about the First Amendment and free speech more generally. The metaphor is often deployed to argue that the remedy for harmful speech ought to be counterspeech, not censorship; listeners are to be trusted to sort the wheat from the chaff. This deep skepticism about the regulation of even harmful speech in the USA raises several follow-on questions, including: How will trustworthy sources of information fare in the marketplace of ideas? And how will participants know whom to trust? Both questions implicate non-regulatory, civil-society responses to mis- and disinformation.[1] This chapter takes on these questions, considering groups and institutions that deal with information and misinformation. Civil society groups cannot stop the creation of misinformation – but they can decrease its potential to proliferate and to do harm. For example, advocacy groups might be directly involved with fact-checking and debunking misinformation, or with advancing truthful or properly contextualized counter-narratives. And civil society groups can also help strengthen social solidarity and reduce the social divisions that often serve as fodder for and drivers of misinformation.

In this chapter, I focus specifically on the role of labor unions in countering misinformation in the US context. US labor unions negotiate on behalf of groups of workers, and also advance workers' interests writ large in political contexts. Both roles can involve countering mis- or disinformation in various forms. First, misinformation is a common weapon in employers' arsenals during union-organizing drives. Among other misleading messages, employers often try to paint union organizers as outside agitators, isolated malcontents, or incompetents looking for protection from

[1] The remainder of the chapter uses the term 'misinformation' as an umbrella term to capture various kinds of untruthful or misleading statements, images, and narratives, whether or not they were deliberately propagated.

rightful accountability. This sort of messaging is so routine as to have become unremarkable – though it can also be difficult to counter effectively, given that employers have vastly more access to employees than do union organizers.[2] Second, employers can be a source of misleading political claims. As political scientists have documented, it is relatively common for US employers to urge employees to adopt the employer's preferred political views, sometimes by creating the impression that the future of the company (and the employees' jobs) is on the line.[3] But would workers be likely to know if their employer lied (or stretched the truth) in making political pitches? The answer is more likely to be 'yes' if the workers are unionized.[4]

The foregoing is true for US workers in general – but some workers, such as journalists, teachers and librarians, have jobs that inherently involve countering (or spreading) misinformation. Here, labor unions can play more specific roles in strengthening the organizations for which their members work. As an illustration, this chapter considers journalists' unions. At one level, these unions fight for the same working conditions as any other union, such as better pay and benefits, stronger worker autonomy and freedom from arbitrary discipline, and the preservation of bargaining-unit work.[5] But in the context of news organizations, these terms can take on special significance. For example, a more diverse set of people will pursue careers in journalism if they can earn a decent living while doing so, which is important because varied perspectives and knowledge within a newsroom can lead to better and more thorough reporting. And protections against arbitrary or inconsistent discipline are important to workers whose jobs involve 'speaking truth to power' – ultimately benefiting both covered workers and the integrity of organizations themselves against individual failings of managers or owners.

In addition, journalists' unions are often able to negotiate contract protections that specifically relate to journalists' integrity.[6] For example, some collective bargaining agreements provide for a degree of independence in the editing process, such as by allowing reporters to withhold their bylines from stories that they believe

[2] There are two things to notice about how this sort of anti-union message relates to the larger misinformation picture. First, this playbook, honed in part in the labor context, is frequently deployed in other contexts, such as when governments portray civil rights protesters as destructive outside agitators. Second, one reason employers often succeed at convincing workers to vote against unionization is their ability to exclude the union and its counter-messaging from the workplace – capturing in microcosm the intersection between speech rights and property rights that repeats in countless other US contexts, including speech on social media and the regulation of campaign spending.

[3] Alex Hertel-Fernandez, *Politics at Work: How Companies Turn Their Workers into Lobbyists* (New York: Oxford University Press, 2018).

[4] John S. Ahlquist, 'Labor Unions, Political Representation, and Economic Inequality' (2017) 20(1) *Annual Review of Political Science* 409–32; David Macdonald, 'How Labor Unions Increase Political Knowledge: Evidence from the United States' (2021) 43(1) *Political Behavior* 1–24.

[5] E.g., Pro Publica Guild, 'Our Mission', www.propublicaguild.org (discussing the union's goals, including 'pay transparency and a raise pool that stays ahead of inflation').

[6] Section 15.3.2.

have been edited in an inaccurate or misleading fashion. Others guarantee that reporters will have input and an opportunity to respond if the accuracy of their reporting is challenged by the subject of that reporting and promise that the news organization will pay for legal representation if a journalist is sued. And still others implement general codes of ethical conduct as part of the collective bargaining agreement (CBA) itself, creating protections for journalists who insubordinately refuse to engage in unethical conduct.

My argument is that journalists' unions (and, similarly, unions of other groups of information workers) can protect free speech values – and the most specific way they do this is by giving workers leverage to demand that their employers live up to their institutional values. Ironically, though, the First Amendment weakens unions' abilities to do this. Although the Supreme Court has held since 1937 that the National Labor Relations Act of 1935 (NLRA) applies to employers that are in the speech business, news organizations have successfully argued to US Courts of Appeals that they cannot be compelled to bargain over editorial policies.[7] This is so even though unions themselves are not state entities, and even though US labor law includes no mechanism to compel a private-sector employer to reach an agreement.[8] In other words, although the First Amendment is crucial to journalists' abilities to do their jobs, it can also benefit employers when journalists exercise collective power to protect the integrity of their work.

The chapter begins with a brief discussion of social scientists' findings on the kinds of traits that make individuals and societies vulnerable to mis- and disinformation. These findings background the chapter's discussion of why strong unions can harden American society against misinformation, including by decreasing social cleavages, increasing government's responsiveness to poor and working class citizens' concerns, and connecting unionized workers to the political process. Then, the chapter turns to unions of information workers, particularly teachers and journalists, and argues that unionization allows these workers to pressure their employers to stay true to their institutional missions. Finally, it shows that already weak labor law is further weakened by courts' understanding of how the First Amendment interacts with labor law in this context.

15.2 CIVIL SOCIETY AND MISINFORMATION

Misinformation researchers have focused primarily on questions such as how to identify and map misinformation, and whether or how to regulate the spread of misinformation by government officials or on social media platforms. But there is

[7] Section 15.3.3.

[8] *H. K. Porter Co.* v. *NLRB*, 397 US 99 (1970) (holding that NLRB does not have power to order contract concessions as a remedy for bad-faith bargaining); see also *Noah's Ark Processors*, LLC, 372 NLRB No. 80 (2023) (discussing remedies for failure to bargain in good faith).

less research focused on civil society's role in fighting misinformation. Still, these groups have a role to play. First, civil society groups will often be trusted by their own members as sources of accurate information.[9] Further, they can bring people together, engaging them on social and political issues and building social connections; this function is important because engaged and connected communities are better able to resist misinformation than more atomized communities.[10] Second, civil society groups can pressure social media platforms or news outlets to take down misinformation without triggering government censorship concerns. Third, they can advance accurate narratives in the press. For example, a news outlet might seek comment from a local civil rights group before publishing a story on a school board candidate's untrue claim that critical race theory is taught in elementary schools.[11]

Civil society groups have a range of purposes and goals, and of course they are also differently situated with respect to political disinformation. Some groups view fighting disinformation – either in general or on a specific topic or platform – as a central purpose; on the other end of the spectrum, others avoid all discussion of political or divisive topics. But many groups fall in between, including labor unions – this chapter's focus. Unions generally have explicit political priorities, but they do not exist only to participate in electoral politics, or specifically to fight misinformation. And while they sometimes address misinformation head-on, they likely also have more indirect effects. Accordingly, this chapter begins with a generalized

[9] See, e.g., Myrto Pantazi, Scott Hale and Olivier Klein, 'Social and Cognitive Aspects of the Vulnerability to Political Misinformation' (2021) 42(1) *Political Psychology* 267–304; Ullrich K. H. Ecker et al., 'The Psychological Drivers of Misinformation Belief and Its Resistance to Correction' (2022) 1(1) *Nature Reviews Psychology* 13–29 (explaining that for information sources other than media outlets, 'source credibility' and trustworthiness affect acceptance of misinformation or corrections).

[10] Joan Donovan, 'How Civil Society Can Combat Misinformation and Hate Speech without Making It Worse', *The Media Manipulation Casebook 2020*, https://mediamanipulation.org/sites/default/files/media-files/TSC002_HateSpeech_TS_fnl.pdf. Many of the chapters in this volume consider the proliferation of misinformation via social media platforms. However, social media can also be a source of community and meaningful discussion that can counter the effectiveness of misinformation.

[11] While this chapter focuses on civil society's role in fighting misinformation, I also acknowledge that these groups can be vectors of misinformation. For example, during protests against police violence in Philadelphia, Pennsylvania, the Fraternal Order of Police posted on Twitter and Facebook a photograph of a White police officer holding a Black toddler. The accompanying text read 'This child was lost during the violent riots in Philadelphia, wandering around barefoot in an area that was experiencing complete lawlessness. The only thing this Philadelphia police officer cared about in that moment was protecting this child.' But the boy's mother filed a lawsuit alleging that this was a lie. She credibly asserted that she was driving home with her children when she took a wrong turn onto a street where police and protesters were confronting each other. Then, she alleged, police surrounded her car, breaking its windows and pulling the mother, her teenage nephew and her toddler son from the car – injuring and terrorizing them, and then separating the family for hours. Katie Shepherd, 'Police Took a Black Toddler from His Family's SUV. Then, the Union Used His Photo as "Propaganda", Attorneys Say', *The Washington Post*, 30 October 2020, www.washingtonpost.com/nation/2020/10/30/philadelphia-fop-posts-toddler.

discussion of how labor unions can strengthen democracy and make US society more resistant to disinformation, before turning to an important subset of unions: those that are comprised of information workers, particularly journalists.

Why focus on labor unions rather than media literacy organizations, civil rights organizations, political parties or advocacy groups? To be clear, my answer is not that unions are more important than these other groups. Instead, it is that unions are *also* important, but frequently overlooked. Most of the remainder of this chapter explains why that is, beginning with unions in general, and then turning to unions of information workers.

15.3 UNIONS AND MISINFORMATION

One reason unions are an important part of this story is that – perhaps counter-intuitively – workplaces can offer opportunities for sustained cooperation and the development of social ties between people of different backgrounds, which can have positive spillover effects for democratic life.[12] Moreover, because three-quarters of US adults aged 25–54 work,[13] and workplaces tend to be more diverse than other American institutions, these opportunities may be more likely to arise at work than in other (relatively segregated) spaces in which people regularly spend time.[14] For that reason, Cynthia Estlund argued more than twenty years ago that the workplace is 'a uniquely important site within a diverse democratic society that aspires to achieve integration and equality among the citizens but that recognizes limitations on the proper scope of regulation'.[15]

But, as Estlund also observed, the story is not entirely rosy, and workplaces' potential to give rise to social bonds that help protect communities from misinformation can easily go unfulfilled. First, as in many other US contexts, racial diversity has been declining in US workplaces over recent decades,[16] and the US Supreme Court's growing hostility towards remedial affirmative action increases the likelihood that this trend will continue.[17] Moreover, most workplaces are autocratic; the philosopher Elizabeth Anderson rightly calls most workplaces 'dictatorships … in

[12] Cynthia L. Estlund, 'Working Together: The Workplace, Civil Society, and the Law' (2000) 89 *Georgetown Law Journal* 1–96.

[13] David H Montgomery, 'Who's Not Working in the U.S.? Learn the Basics', Federal Reserve Bank of Minneapolis, 1 September 2022, www.minneapolisfed.org/article/2022/whos-not-working-in-the-us-learn-the-basics.

[14] Estlund, 'Working Together' (n 12).

[15] Ibid.

[16] Although the population of the USA, and by extension the labor pool as a whole, has become more racially diverse over the decades, a recent study found that individual workplaces were becoming less racially diverse. John-Paul Ferguson and Rembrand Koning, 'Firm Turnover and the Return of Racial Establishment Segregation', SocArXiv, 8 January 2018, https://osf.io/preprints/socarxiv/c6hsd.

[17] See, e.g., *Students for Fair Admissions* v. *President and Fellows of Harvard College*, 143 S.Ct. 2141 (2023) (imposing new limits on the use of race in higher-education admissions).

which bosses govern in ways that are largely unaccountable to those who are governed'.[18] This means that even though workplaces can facilitate or require respectful interactions among employees, US employers are also generally free to insist on a pace of work that precludes community-building interactions among workers.[19] Employers may also rely on pools of high-turnover-contingent workers.[20] And whereas yesterday's employers may have been unable to monitor their workforces closely enough to notice short breaks or side conversations, today's employers have increasingly sophisticated workplace surveillance technology that monitors workers' precise activities, including whether they are 'on task' at any given moment.[21] In addition, many low-wage workers need multiple jobs to make ends meet – leaving little or no time for civil or political engagement outside of work.[22]

Rather than giving up on workplaces' potential to strengthen our social ties, it is worth considering whether there are institutions or practices that can make work more democratic. One obvious candidate: labor unions, which may bargain on behalf of a group of workers only if democratically elected.[23] In turn, a successful union election compels employers to come to the table to attempt to hash out an agreement on wages and working conditions, rather than setting working conditions autocratically.[24]

Collective bargaining (and workplace collective action more generally) allows workers to push back against some of the workplace trends discussed above. For example, pay, scheduling, the pace of work and workplace discipline are the bread-and-butter of collective bargaining agreements.[25] (This is also one reason that unionized workers vote and otherwise participate in politics at greater rates than

[18] Elizabeth Anderson, *Private Government: How Employers Rule Our Lives (and Why We Don't Talk about It)* (Princeton, NJ: Princeton University Press, 2017).

[19] For example, Amazon warehouses famously use surveillance technology to track workers' 'time-off-task', a metric that includes time spent traversing long distances in search of a bathroom, see Emily Guendelsberger, *On the Clock: What Low-Wage Work Did to Me and How It Drives America Insane* (Boston: Little, Brown, 2019).

[20] See generally David Weil, *The Fissured Workplace: Why Work became So Bad for So Many and What Can Be Done to Improve It* (Cambridge, MA: Harvard University Press, 2017).

[21] See, e.g., Jodi Kantor and Arya Sundaram, 'The Rise of the Worker Productivity Score', *The New York Times*, 14 August 2022, www.nytimes.com/interactive/2022/08/14/business/worker-productivity-tracking.html.

[22] This dynamic's significance is underscored in new workplace ethnographies that emphasize time – both that low-wage workplaces can be Taylorist nightmares, and that workers have less time outside of work, and less control over the time they do have. E.g., ibid.; Jamie McCallum, *Worked Over: How Round-the-Clock Work Is Killing the American Dream* (New York: Basic Books, 2020).

[23] 29 U.S.C. § 159 (setting forth the standard union election process for private sector workplaces that are covered by the National Labor Relations Act).

[24] 29 U.S.C. §§ 158(a)(5) and 158(d) (establishing the obligation to engage in good-faith collective bargaining).

[25] 29 U.S.C. § 159(d).

their non-union counterparts.)[26] Beyond that, unions are also active in politics in ways that range from member-to-member conversations, to programs that help union members run for office, to candidate endorsements and related spending. Much of this advocacy involves union leaders or members conveying their own affirmative messages about which party or candidate will be better for workers – but, of relevance to this chapter, it can also involve rebutting misinformation from other sources, including workers' own employers.

Private-sector employers in the USA are mostly free to 'talk politics' to their employees, and a large number of them take advantage of their captive audiences.[27] Some stick to non-partisan messages, such as reminders about when Election Day is or how to register to vote – but others actively advocate for candidates or political parties in ways that can pressure workers, and that can involve misinformation.[28] For example, an employer may 'nudge … people away from thinking about issues in particular ways',[29] or falsely or misleadingly blame government policies as the cause of its own unpopular decisions. More alarmingly, some employers have said or implied if the employer's disfavored candidate wins, it could be forced to cut jobs.[30] When this happens – or even when misinformation circulates in a workplace on a more ad hoc basis – unions may be a trusted source for both facts and alternative policy viewpoints. Thus, researchers have found that unionized workers are rela-

[26] Tova Wang, 'Union Impact on Voter Participation – and How to Expand It', Ash Center for Democratic Governance and Innovation, 2020 (surveying literature), https://ash.harvard.edu/files/ash/files/300871_hvd_ash_union_impact_v2.pdf.

[27] Alex Hertel-Fernandez, *Politics at Work: How Companies Turn Their Workers into Lobbyists* (New York: Oxford University Press, 2018). Government employers, by contrast, are constrained by the First Amendment. They may not, for example, reserve non-policy-making jobs for members of a preferred political party. See *O'Hare Truck Service, Inc.* v. *City of Northlake*, 518 US 712 (1996); see also *Heffernan* v. *City of Paterson, NJ*, 578 US 266 (2016). Further, governmental employers often go beyond constitutional requirements, limiting their employees' abilities to engage in certain kinds of political advocacy to avoid public concern about political favoritism in the provision of public services, e.g., 5 U.S.C. § 7323.

[28] Ibid.

[29] Claire Wardle and Hossein Derakhshan, *Information Disorder: Toward an Interdisciplinary Framework for Research and Policymaking*, Council of Europe, 2017, https://edoc.coe.int/en/media/7495-information-disorder-toward-an-interdisciplinary-framework-for-research-and-policy-making.html, p. 10.

[30] Mitt Romney famously told business owners to 'make it very clear to your employees what you believe is in the best interest of your enterprise and therefore their job and their future in the upcoming elections'. He noted that there was 'nothing illegal about you talking to your employees about what you believe is best for the business, because I think that will figure into their election decision, their voting decision, and of course doing that with your family and your kids as well'. Harry Bradford, 'Murray Energy Miners Allege They Had to Give Up Pay to Attend "Mandatory" Romney Rally', *HuffPost*, 6 December 2017, www.huffpost.com/entry/century-mine-romney-ohio-mandatory_n_1836674.

tively well-informed about politics,[31] and that this is especially true for workers with the least formal education.[32]

In addition, social inequality seems to play a role in making societies susceptible to misinformation, and unions reduce various forms of inequality. To be clear, the premise – that more unequal societies are more vulnerable to misinformation – seems intuitive, but the supporting research is sparse, especially compared to research on characteristics that make individuals vulnerable to misinformation.[33] Still, good reasons exist to believe high levels of social inequality are an important part of the puzzle. For example, one group of researchers has posited that it will be relatively easy to manipulate members of socially segregated societies in which an advantaged group hoards knowledge resources from a disadvantaged group, though the less advantaged group is especially likely to be harmed.[34] Other research specifically focused on public-health messaging in the USA has identified 'inequality-driven mistrust' as an important reason that members of historically and currently oppressed groups may be willing to accept misinformation.[35] Moreover, the content of concerted misinformation campaigns often exploits and attempts to heighten existing social divisions and prejudices, such as racism and/or sexism in the USA;[36] it stands to reason that this material would be less effective in more solidaristic societies.

If this is right, then more widespread unionization would help 'harden' a society against the effects of misinformation because unions both strengthen American democracy and, relatedly, decrease inequality. For example, because US unions are required to operate in a democratic fashion, they can be a kind of training ground (and source of material support) for their members' greater participation in electoral politics. And, in addition to reducing economic inequality (including the

[31] Ahlquist, 'Labor Unions, Political Representation, and Economic Inequality' (n 4); Macdonald, 'How Labor Unions Increase Political Knowledge' (n 4).

[32] Macdonald, 'How Labor Unions Increase Political Knowledge' (n 4), at 120.

[33] For example, a substantial body of work discusses psychological states that might make an individual more or less susceptible to believing misinformation, or that might make a source of information seem more or less trustworthy (e.g., Ecker, 'The Psychological Drivers' (n 9)). Other work focuses on social-psychological factors, explaining that misinformation can be particularly difficult to combat when it successfully taps into the consumer's moral beliefs of worldview (e.g., Wardle and Derakhshan, *Information Disorder* (n 29)).

[34] Mohamed Mostagir and James Siderius, 'Social Inequality and the Spread of Misinformation' (2023) 69(2) *Management Science* 968–95.

[35] Jessica Jaiswal, Caleb LoSchiavo, and David C. Perlman, 'Disinformation, Misinformation and Inequality-Driven Mistrust in the Time of COVID-19: Lessons Unlearned from AIDS Denialism' (2020) 24(10) *AIDS and Behavior* 2776–80.

[36] Craig Timberg and Isaac Stanley-Becker, 'Fake Twitter Accounts Posing as Black Trump Supporters Appear, Reach Thousands, Then Vanish', *The Washington Post*, 20 October 2020 www.washingtonpost.com/technology/2020/10/13/black-fake-twitter-accounts-for-trump; Rachelle Hampton, 'The Black Feminists Who Saw the Alt-Right Threat Coming', SLATE, 23 April 2019, https://slate.com/technology/2019/04/black-feminists-alt-right-twitter-gamergate.html.

racial wage gap),[37] there is also evidence that today's unions reduce racial resentment among their white members – a finding that makes sense when one considers that, to be successful in racially diverse workforces, unions will often have to convince workers to unite to achieve shared goals.[38]

This section has argued that unions in general have a salutary effect on members' vulnerability to misinformation. The next section turns to a subset of unions: those comprised of workers whose jobs involve informing or educating the public.

15.3 INFORMATION WORKPLACES AND WORKERS

Some workplaces have special relationships to information and misinformation.[39] Many news outlets, libraries and schools would reasonably characterize themselves as carrying out a public-facing mission – producing knowledge, educating and informing segments of the public, and inculcating skills to help protect their audiences against misinformation.[40] (Social media companies might also characterize themselves this way, but the major platforms have at best a complicated relationship to information and misinformation that is beyond the scope of this chapter.)

[37] Ahlquist, 'Labor Unions' (n 4).

[38] Paul Frymer and Jacob M. Grumbach, 'Labor Unions and White Racial Politics' (2021) 65(1) *American Journal of Political Science* 225–40.

[39] See Vicki Jackson, 'Knowledge Institutions and Resisting "Truth Decay"', Chapter 14 in this volume. Jackson defines knowledge institutions as 'entities that have, as a central purpose, the dissemination, preservation, or production of knowledge'. Perhaps unions of knowledge workers – including teachers, librarians, journalists and university faculty – could qualify as knowledge institutions under this definition if they conceive of their role broadly. At a minimum, though, unions of knowledge workers often protect and strengthen knowledge workers' (and, by extension, knowledge institutions') abilities to carry out their roles. For example, a key function of the American Association of University Professors has been to define and protect academic freedom. See 'History of the AAUP', www.aaup.org/about/history-aaup (discussing AAUP's 'major contributions to the establishment of academic freedom and tenure throughout higher education in the United States'). Similarly, teachers' unions often frame their advocacy around topics such as staffing levels and teacher training using the pithy phrase 'students' learning conditions are educators working conditions'. '9 Ways to Improve Educator Working Conditions', National Education Association, 30 September 2022, www.nea.org/resource-library/9-ways-improve-educator-working-conditions#:~:text=Students'%20learning%20conditions%20are%20educators'%20working%20conditions.&text=Studies%20have%20found%20that%20the,leave%20and%20impact%20student%20learning.

[40] This chapter's focus is on institutions that would agree their mission is to accurately inform the public, and that genuinely aim to achieve that mission by acting consistently with ethical guidelines and other parameters that are generally accepted within the industry. It does not discuss entities that have other stated or unstated goals, such as organizations that present themselves as news outlets, but that are actually disguised entertainers, manipulators or propagandists. With respect to this latter group, it is perhaps conceivable that empowered workers could exert a counterweight – fighting to bring balance to a propagandist network, for example – but I see no reason to believe this is likely to happen. Instead, it strikes me as at least equally likely that these entities successfully hire employees who share their 'true' mission, even if that mission is unstated.

But organizations that genuinely try to fulfill this mission-driven role can become targets for misinformation spreaders, meaning that both the organization as a whole and its various employees and managers may need to contend with mis- and disinformation. Specifically, they may need to resist targeted campaigns intended to manipulate or coerce them into spreading misinformation, while also retaining their credibility with the public.[41]

How well these institutions resist cooptation by spreaders of misinformation will depend on a range of factors. But I argue that one important factor is the extent to which their workforces are organized and empowered to defend themselves (and, by extension, the institution as a whole) against misinformation. The basic argument is intuitive: most people who become journalists or teachers or professors do so at least in part for mission-driven reasons,[42] and they are singularly well-placed to know how well their employers are doing at carrying out their stated missions and stewarding their institutions.[43] This makes organized and empowered employees a potential first line of defense against organizational decisions or practices that open the door to misinformation, or that erode earned public trust.

The remainder of this section turns to one industry – journalism – as an illustration of the thesis. It begins by briefly describing some of the pressures bearing down on US media outlets, emphasizing that one possible response is for outlets to fall back on practices that tend to erode trust in media. Next, it describes how journalists have unionized and otherwise acted collectively in response, fighting with varying degrees of success to preserve institution-sustaining employment conditions and standards. To be clear, I am not arguing that unionization is 'one weird trick' that will solve the industry's various problems – but unionizing allows journalists to push back with more force than they could muster individually.

[41] Joel R. Malin and Christopher Lubienski, 'Information Pollution in an Age of Populist Politics' (2022) 30 *Education Policy Analysis Archives* 1–23. Malin and Lubienski focus on this phenomenon in the context of US education, but note its existence across the 'modern information landscape' (at 4).

[42] This chapter focuses on journalists in the USA, and a 2022 Pew poll bears out that they mostly feel passionate about and committed to their work, and very concerned about their and their industry's ability to get the facts right and meaningfully inform the public, see Sara Atske, 'Journalists Sense Turmoil in Their Industry amid Continued Passion for Their Work. Report', Pew Research Center, 14 June 2022, www.pewresearch.org/journalism/2022/06/14/journalists-sense-turmoil-in-their-industry-amid-continued-passion-for-their-work. In addition, nearly all of the journalists surveyed said that 'made-up news and information' was either a 'very big' or 'moderately big' problem. Finally, majorities expressed concern about both the industry's ability to handle misinformation, and the degree of public trust in the industry generally.

[43] Analogously, the US Supreme Court has grounded public employees' limited First Amendment right to be protected against termination when they speak on a matter of public concern in institutional governance concerns. *Pickering* v. *Board of Education*, 391 US 563 (1968) (writing that 'Teachers are, as a class, the members of a community most likely to have informed and definite opinions as to how funds allotted to the operation of the schools should be spent. Accordingly, it is essential that they be able to speak out freely on such questions without fear of retaliatory dismissal').

15.3.1 The Changing Media Environment

As Shannon Poulson and Dannagal Young have described, '[t]he quality of journalism and the pursuit of truth depend largely on the commercial, social, and technological changes of the times'.[44] Financialization, the rise of 'both-sides' journalism following a prolonged campaign to label certain kinds of (accurate) reporting as having 'liberal bias', the increasing popularity of 'fake news' or 'alternative facts' rhetoric on the political right,[45] and the shift to online news consumption (especially on social media platforms) all pose significant threats to 'mainstream' journalism and journalists. This subsection briefly (and necessarily incompletely) surveys these trends.[46]

Technological evolution has presented a series of challenges to traditional newsrooms.[47] Widespread adoption of the Internet left print newspapers scrambling to compete with online entertainment of all sorts, and to convince the public to pay for online news content. Then, the rise of platforms like Facebook again changed the way many individuals consumed news, diverting them from news organizations' homepages and towards stories that appear individually in their content feeds. One large, international survey recently found that nearly 80 percent of respondents preferred to access news via a platform or other aggregator (and that Facebook is now being supplanted by other platforms) – but also that fewer people are consuming news at all.[48] This shift has created several misinformation-related problems. Some of these challenges are content-moderation problems, over which platforms have control. For example, legitimate news outlets can report on the existence of sham stories formatted by malevolent actors to closely resemble real news sites – but only platforms can take these posts down and ban their originators, or at least try to.

Similarly, news outlets have had to adapt to the role of algorithmic amplification in determining the reach of individual stories or an organization's collective output.

[44] Shannon Poulsen and Dannagal G. Young, 'A History of Fact Checking in U.S. Politics and Election Contexts' in Brian G. Southwell, Emily A. Thorson and Laura Sheble (eds.), *Misinformation and Mass Audiences* (Austin: University of Texas Press, 2018) pp. 232–48, p. 244.

[45] Eric Bradner, 'Conway: Trump White House Offered "Alternative Facts" on Crowd Size', CNN, 23 January 2017, www.cnn.com/2017/01/22/politics/kellyanne-conway-alternative-facts/index.html.

[46] For further discussion of these topics see, e.g., Martha Minow, *Saving the News: Why the Constitution Calls for Government Action to Preserve Freedom of Speech* (New York: Oxford University Press, 2021).

[47] Nic Newman et al., 'Digital News Report 2023', Reuters Institute, 2023, https://reutersinstitute.politics.ox.ac.uk/digital-news-report/2023; Erin C Carroll, 'Promoting Journalism as a Method' (2020) 12 *Drexel Law Review* 691.

[48] The same survey reflected that the public's interest in consuming any news is higher during times of crisis or political turmoil, such as the COVID-19 pandemic or (in the USA) the election of Trump. Although 67 percent of US respondents said they were 'very' or 'extremely' interested in news in 2015, that number had fallen to 49 per cent in 2023, see Newman, 'Digital News Report 2023' (n 47) p. 21.

This would be challenging and at least potentially harmful even if the algorithms were unchanging and publicly well-understood, because algorithmic amplification often rewards 'clickbait'[49] or 'infotainment'.[50] But the reality is that platforms change their algorithms unpredictably and often without notice. Worse, platforms may provide incorrect information about their own algorithms. The leading example is Facebook's significant overestimation of the amount of time individual users spent viewing video content, leading many news organizations to undertake a doomed 'pivot to video' – sometimes laying off print journalists in the process.[51]

These and other technological changes have led to plummeting advertising revenue, particularly for local newspapers.[52] This has been catastrophic: 'Since 2005, the [United States] has lost more than a fourth of its newspapers (2,500) and is on track to lose a third by 2025.'[53] The result is a growing number of 'news deserts' where no credible local newspaper exists.[54] And although people living in news deserts may be able to access some kinds of local information from other sources,[55] they lose the benefits of reporting by journalists with the skills and deep local expertise required to unearth information that has been deliberately concealed or that is simply difficult to access or understand.[56] Further, local news outlets enjoy considerably more public trust than do national news organizations, especially among Republicans and independents[57] – suggesting that news deserts may leave

49 Clickbait refers to stories accompanied by headlines written to arouse readers' interest, often by provoking a strong emotional reaction.

50 Keach Hagey and Jeff Horowitz, 'Facebook Tried to Make Its Platform a Healthier Place. It Got Angrier Instead', *The Wall Street Journal*, 15 September 2021; see also Helen L. Norton, 'Getting to Trustworthiness (But Not Necessarily to Trust)' (2023) 3 *Journal of Free Speech Law* 7 (discussing how the 'media's need to do whatever it takes to survive financially' can dampen readers' trust).

51 Laura Hazard Owen, 'Facebook's Pivot to Video Didn't Just Burn Publishers. It Didn't Even Work for Facebook', Nieman Lab, 15 September 2021, www.niemanlab.org/2021/09/well-this-puts-a-nail-in-the-news-video-on-facebook-coffin.

52 Sara Fischer, 'U.S. Digital Newspaper Ad Revenue Expected to Surpass Print by 2026', Axios, 21 June 2022, www.axios.com/2022/06/21/digital-newspaper-ad-revenue-print.

53 Penny Abernathy, 'The State of Local News. Report', Local News Initiative, 29 June 2022, https://localnewsinitiative.northwestern.edu/research/state-of-local-news/report.

54 Troublingly, news deserts tend to have lower median household income, graduation rates and broadband access than the national average, and a higher poverty rate. 'Life in a News Desert', *Columbia Journalism Review*, 2019, www.cjr.org/special_report/life-in-a-news-desert.php.

55 Jessica Collier and Emily Graham, 'Even in "News Deserts" People Still Get News', Center for Media Engagement, 14 December 2022, https://mediaengagement.org/research/people-still-get-news-in-news-deserts; but see Nick Mathews, 'Life in a News Desert: The Perceived Impact of a Newspaper Closure on Community Members' (2022) 23(6) *Journalism* 1250–65, (concluding based on nineteen in-depth interviews with residents of a news desert in rural Virginia that loss of a local paper harmed their sense of community and left them uninformed about local events).

56 Lili Levi, 'Social Media and the Press' (2012) 90 *North Carolina Law Review* 1531.

57 Jeffrey Gottfried and Jacob Liedke, 'Partisan Divides in Media Trust Widen, Driven by a Decline among Republicans', Pew Research Center, 30 August 2021, www.pewresearch.org/

large numbers of disproportionately right-leaning Americans with few news sources that are credible and that they also trust.

Outlets that have managed to avoid closure still face budget pressures, which can lead to layoffs of journalists and editors, and create incentives for news organizations to underinvest both in time-consuming accountability or investigative journalism, and in critical behind-the-scenes functions like fact-checking and copy-editing. Outlets may substitute access journalism or stories that simply rehash prepackaged material; in the future, outlets may even turn to stories generated in whole or part by predictive-text applications.[58] Local control of newspapers has also become less common in recent years: as of 2021, 'half of all daily newspapers in the U.S. [were] controlled by financial firms'[59] – often 'vulture' funds that, in the words of writer McKay Coppins, aim to '[g]ut the staff, sell the real estate, jack up subscription prices, and wring as much cash as possible out of the enterprise until eventually enough readers cancel their subscriptions that the paper folds, or is reduced to a desiccated husk of its former self'.[60]

Finally, news organizations have to decide how to deal with misinformation. This might seem straightforward: every credible news outlet strives to uncover the truth, and publicly getting it wrong – especially on a high-profile story – is the stuff of nightmares. But the topic quickly becomes knotty, especially when misinformation and accusations of newsroom bias intersect. For example, consider a journalist who reports the overwhelming scientific consensus that climate change is occurring, that it is caused by human activity, and that it will lead to devastating consequences.[61] In response, powerful industry groups and aligned politicians vociferously accuse the reporter and the outlet for which they work of bias. When this scenario replays itself enough times, the effect can be to pressure editors and reporters to adopt 'both sides' or 'false balance' reporting. In this example, that might look like producing stories that wrongly imply the existence of meaningful scientific doubt about climate change.[62] In other words, news outlets legitimately strive for (some version of) neutrality, but also of its appearance – and so when it comes to hotly contested

short-reads/2021/08/30/partisan-divides-in-media-trust-widen-driven-by-a-decline-among-republicans.

[58] Benjamin Mullin and Nico Grant, 'Google Tests A.I. Tool That Is Able to Write News Articles', *The New York Times*, 20 July 2023, www.nytimes.com/2023/07/19/business/google-artificial-intelligence-news-articles.html.

[59] McKay Coppins, 'A Secretive Hedge Fund Is Gutting Newsrooms', *The Atlantic*, 14 October 2021, www.theatlantic.com/magazine/archive/2021/11/alden-global-capital-killing-americas-news papers/620171.

[60] Ibid.

[61] See Scientific Consensus: Earth's Climate Is Warming. Climate Change: Vital Signs of the Planet, https://climate.nasa.gov/scientific-consensus.

[62] Maxwell T. Boykoff and S. Ravi Rajan, 'Signals and Noise. Mass-Media Coverage of Climate Change in the USA and the UK' (2007) 8(3) *EMBO Reports*, 207–11. As the authors of the article describe, this dynamic is exacerbated when 'generalist' journalists have difficulty getting their arms around scientific literature while also working to a tight timeline.

policy and political issues, they may decide to repeat misinformation in order to appear 'fair'.[63]

As the climate change example illustrates, this dynamic long predates Donald Trump, but Trump's candidacy and presidency presented an especially acute challenge. Trump coupled a disregard for the truth with near-constant accusations of media bias ('fake news'), and he frequently characterized the mainstream media as the 'Enemy of the People', sometimes even celebrating violence against reporters.[64] This left reporters and news outlets with a dilemma – how to handle statements that are false, but also newsworthy because of their source? Early in Trump's presidency, outlets seemed to struggle with this question. For example, many outlets were at least initially reluctant to use the word 'lie' to describe Trump's statements.[65] Similarly, journalists and academics alike grappled with how to report on the propagation of disinformation without inadvertently serving the purposes of its creators.[66]

Whether or not news organizations succumb to the bad incentives created by the confluence of these pressures has consequences for the organizations' public legitimacy. In turn, public trust in media plays a role in determining a society's susceptibility to misinformation. Unsurprisingly, researchers studying the European context found that journalism scandals decrease trust in mainstream media, as does public perception that media is pervasively biased, clickbait-y or of poor quality.[67] And, one might add, if this perception is accurate, this loss of legitimacy is deserved – media that suffers from these flaws is failing to convey useful and accurate information to the public.

Misinformation may fill the void left by an absence of trusted news organizations, though the picture is complex: Carlos Rodríguez-Pérez and María Canel also found that countries characterized by *lower* public trust in media tended to have greater resilience to misinformation. But the finding that healthy skepticism is better than blind trust is not a vindication of poor-quality journalism. Instead, the researchers recommend a two-pronged approach in which government warns the public of the risk of misinformation and develops media literacy through education, while media

[63] See Yochai Bencher, Robert Paris and Hal Roberts, *Network Propaganda: Manipulation, Disinformation, and Radicalization in American Politics* (New York: Oxford University Press, 2018), pp. 358–59.

[64] 'Donald Trump Celebrates Violence against Journalists', *The New Yorker*, 19 October 2018, www.newyorker.com/news/current/donald-trump-celebrates-violence-against-journalists.

[65] Paul Farhi, 'Lies? The News Media Is Starting to Describe Trump's "Falsehoods" That Way', *The Washington Post*, 6 June 2019, www.washingtonpost.com/lifestyle/style/lies-the-news-media-is-starting-to-describe-trumps-falsehoods-that-way/2019/06/05/413cc2a0-8626-11e9-a491-25df61c78dc4_story.html.

[66] Wardle and Derakhshan, *Information Disorder* (n 29) p. 13 ('getting the mainstream media to amplify rumour and disinformation is the ultimate goal of those who seek to manipulate').

[67] Carlos Rodríguez-Pérez and María J. Canel, 'Exploring European Citizens' Resilience to Misinformation: Media Legitimacy and Media Trust as Predictive Variables' (2023) 11(2) *Media and Communication* 30–41.

outlets foster their own legitimacy through transparency, accuracy and fact-checking, and stepped-up 'watchdog' journalism[68] – precisely the functions that are most at risk in today's media environment. The challenges confronting news outlets and journalists today are shaping the news and reporting available to the public, and journalists' working conditions. The next subsection discusses how journalists' unions can respond.

15.3.2 *Journalism Unions and Misinformation*

The dynamics discussed in the previous section have propelled a recent wave of successful union drives at US news organizations. Beginning with the unionization of Gawker Media in 2015, union drives quickly sprang up at other web outlets, legacy newspapers, magazines and public radio stations.[69] Steven Greenhouse, a highly regarded journalist who spent three decades at the *New York Times*, including twenty years covering labor,[70] explained that '[t]wo major forces have propelled the unionization wave: the industry's financial crisis and the wave of acquisitions, wiping out thousands of jobs and clamping down on salaries'.[71] In addition, Greenhouse saw the COVID-19 pandemic as a factor, both because increased remote work led to a desire to build community, and because the pandemic prompted new questions about working conditions, such as COVID-related workplace safety protocols and work-from-home policies.[72]

As Greenhouse explained, union drives are often precipitated by planned acquisitions, as journalists see an acute need for negotiated contractual protections against downgrading of their working conditions. For example, *Los Angeles Times* journalists decided to unionize after the paper was purchased by a news conglomerate, which then unilaterally changed working conditions for the worse and fired newsroom leadership.[73] It turns out this was a smart move: the union successfully negotiated a three-year contract guaranteeing raises each year, as well as instituting

[68] Ibid.; see also Wardle and Derakhshan, *Information Disorder* (n 29) making similar recommendations; Bencher, Paris and Roberts, *Network Propaganda* (n 63) p. 359.

[69] Still, most journalists are not unionized – though a majority of non-union journalists in a 2022 poll said they would join a union if they could. Atske, 'Journalists Sense Turmoil' (n 42).

[70] Michael Calderone, 'Steven Greenhouse Leaves the *New York Times*, as Newspapers' Labor Beat Keeps Shrinking', *HuffPost*, 3 December 2014, www.huffpost.com/entry/steven-greenhouse-labor-beat_n_6262046.

[71] Steven Greenhouse, 'Newsrooms are Unionizing Pretty Much "Nonstop". Here's Why', Nieman Reports, 19 January 2022, https://niemanreports.org/articles/newsrooms-labor-unions; see also Steven Greenhouse, 'More Secure Jobs, Bigger Paychecks', *Columbia Journalism Review*, 2018, www.cjr.org/special_report/media-unions-history.php.

[72] Greenhouse, 'Newsrooms are Unionizing'; Greenhouse, 'More Secure Jobs, Bigger Paychecks'.

[73] Sydney Ember, '*Los Angeles Times* Newsroom, Challenging Tronc, Goes Public with Union Push', *The New York Times*, 4 October 2017, www.nytimes.com/2017/10/04/business/media/los-angeles-times-tronc-union.html.

protections against arbitrary terminations and measures to increase newsroom diversity.[74]

Of course, unions do not always win improvements, and they cannot usually forestall closures of news outlets. The NLRA does not require employers to negotiate with unionized employees over decisions to shut down an entire enterprise – but it does require bargaining with unionized employees over the effects of decisions to shut down, including on topics such as severance payments and the timing of layoffs.[75] This means that even in a worst-case scenario, unionizing gives journalists a better shot at a good outcome, or at least at the best outcome available under the circumstances. For example, after writers working at The Appeal, a web-based outlet devoted to covering the criminal justice system, announced they were unionizing, the site's owner announced a decision to shut the site down altogether.[76] But the union was first able to negotiate severance packages – and better yet, the unionized employees then announced their intention to relaunch The Appeal as a worker cooperative. Today, the outlet still exists as a 'worker-led nonprofit newsroom'.[77]

Unions such as the NewsGuild advocate against harmful acquisitions in other ways as well. For example, the NewsGuild launched a project called 'SaveLocalNews' as a hub for reporting on hedge fund acquisitions of newsrooms,[78] as well as a place to coordinate political, shareholder- and public-facing advocacy when a new acquisition is in the works.[79] Journalists' unions also advocate for regulatory bodies to halt acquisitions of news outlets,[80] and for legislatures to pass

74 Meg James, '*Los Angeles Times* Reaches Historic Agreement with Its Newsroom Union', *Los Angeles Times*, 16 October 2019, www.latimes.com/california/story/2019-10-16/los-angeles-times-first-guild-contract.

75 *First National Maintenance Corp.* v. *NLRB*, 452 US 666, 681–82 (1981).

76 Sally Davidow, 'Good News/Bad News: The Appeal Shuts Down, Staffers Relaunch It as a "Worker-Led News Outlet"', The NewsGuild, 1 July 2021, https://newsguild.org/good-news-bad-news-the-appeal-shuts-down-staffers-relaunch-it-as-a-worker-led-news-outlet-2.

77 See https://theappeal.org/about-us.

78 For example, the project published a report showing that Alden-acquired outlets downsized twice as fast as the national rate; this statistic has been cited in other coverage of Alden's acquisition of news outlets. Julie Reynolds, 'Working under a Hedge Fund: How Billionaires Made the Crisis at America's Newspapers Even Worse', #Save Local News, https://dfmworkers.org/working-under-a-hedge-fund-how-billionaires-made-the-crisis-at-americas-newspapers-even-worse.

79 See generally, #SaveLocalNews at https://dfmworkers.org.

80 For example, Sally Davidow, 'Guild Calls on Biden to Stop TEGNA Merger and Save Journalism Jobs', The NewsGuild, 2 June 2022, https://newsguild.org/guild-calls-on-biden-to-stop-tegna-merger-and-save-journalism-jobs; 'CWA, NewsGuild-CWA, NABET-CWA Recommit to Fighting Hedge Fund Takeover of Local News', Communication Workers of America, 28 February 2022, https://cwa-union.org/news/releases/cwa-newsguild-cwa-nabet-cwa-recommit-fighting-hedge-fund-takeover-local-news; Date Hayes, 'CWA Leads Guilds' FCC Petition Seeking to Block Sinclair–Tribune Merger', *Deadline*, 20 June 2018, https://deadline.com/2018/06/communications-workers-of-america-fcc-petition-seeks-to-block-sinclair-tribune-merger-1202414599; Dan Papscun, 'NewsGuild Asks DOJ to Probe Block's Pittsburgh City Paper Deal', *BloombergLaw*, 25 January 2023, https://news.bloomberglaw.com/antitrust/newsguild-asks-doj-to-probe-blocks-pittsburgh-city-paper-deal.

laws aimed at preserving local news.[81] One important function of this advocacy is to point out where the interests of news organizations' owners diverge from those of journalists. For example, the NewsGuild has warned that iterations of the Journalism Competition and Preservation Act, a bill that would allow news companies to bargain collectively with platforms like Google and Facebook, will be counterproductive if it is not packaged with measures designed to channel increased revenues towards employing more journalists.[82]

Other US newsrooms have unionized precisely because they see a negotiated CBA as a way to protect the integrity of their work. For example, when ProPublica journalists unionized in 2023, they signed a mission statement focused primarily on journalistic standards and workplace equity: 'We want to maintain the organization's focus on ambitious, impact-focused journalism. We want to strengthen existing internal efforts, like those of the diversity committee, that address inequities within our own staff and across our industry.'[83] (As of when this chapter went to print, ProPublica and its journalists had not yet negotiated a CBA, although ProPublica agreed to voluntarily recognize the union as the collective bargaining representative of its employees.[84])

Collective bargaining agreements covering journalists at other outlets reflect a range of terms that help protect journalists' professional integrity. Some of these are terms that are common to collective bargaining agreements across industries. For example, CBAs that cover journalists usually contain protections against termination or other discipline without 'just cause'[85] – an important backstop for journalists who, for example, report on or otherwise criticize their own employers, or who become targets of coordinated, bad-faith attacks.[86] Importantly, just-cause protections

81 For example, Sally Davidow, 'NewsGuild Applauds Local Journalism Sustainability Act', The NewsGuild, 22 July 2021, https://newsguild.org/newsguild-applauds-local-journalism-sustainability-act (listing organizations belonging to 'Rebuild Local News' coalition); Diane Kennedy and Jon Schleuss, 'Commentary: How New York Can Save Local News', Times Union, 19 March 2023, www.timesunion.com/opinion/article/commentary-new-york-save-local-news-17844068.php.

82 For example, Sally Davidow, 'Bargaining Bill for News Companies Still Needs Improvements', The NewsGuild, 23 August 2022, https://newsguild.org/bargaining-bill-for-news-companies-still-needs-improvements.

83 'Our Mission', ProPublica Guild, www.propublicaguild.org.

84 Jon Schleuss, 'ProPublica Guild Wins Voluntary Recognition', The NewsGuild, 4 August 2023, https://newsguild.org/propublica-guild-wins-voluntary-recognition.

85 The CBA negotiated between Gawker Media and its employees' union was a notable exception; the union chose not to seek just-cause protections. Noah Kulwin, 'Gawker Media's Union Officially Has a Contract. Now What?', Vox, 29 February 2016, www.vox.com/2016/2/29/11588348/gawker-medias-union-officially-has-a-contract-now-what.

86 For example, after *The Washington Post* fired reporter Felicia Sonmez for tweeting criticism of a colleague and then of *Post* management, her union filed a grievance seeking reinstatement, and then later a charge with the National Labor Relations Board. Corbin Bolies, 'Felicia Sonmez Takes Her WaPo Fight to the Feds', *The Daily Beast*, 29 September 2022, www.thedailybeast.com/felicia-sonmez-takes-her-washington-post-fight-to-the-national-labor-relations-board. Previously, the union had pressured *The Post* to both provide Sonmez a personal

typically put the burden on the employer to prove it had a sufficient reason to impose discipline or termination; moreover, the union litigates the grievance on behalf of the employee, meaning that the employee need not pay a lawyer themselves. Thus, unionized journalists typically have workplace protections that are much closer to academic tenure than to the presumption of at-will employment that otherwise applies to most private sector workers in the USA.

Additionally, journalists' unions often negotiate contract terms that are either aimed at increasing the diversity of their newsrooms, or that can have that effect; this can increase public trust in reporting by those outlets, especially among marginalized communities.[87] For example, some contracts require news outlets to interview at least one or two members of underrepresented groups for each open position.[88] And CBAs that reflect new pay floors, coupled with predictable raises for more senior journalists, can make careers in reporting more feasible for members of marginalized communities. Finally, journalists' unions have pressured a list of high-profile outlets to respond to racial disparities in hiring, pay or performance evaluations by conducting and releasing surveys of newsroom staff.[89]

Next, many news outlet CBAs contain provisions that are specifically aimed at protecting and operationalizing journalistic standards. For example, the contract that covers US journalists working at *The Guardian* provides for employee representation on 'any editorial boards or internal news committee teams by a Guild-appointed employee', and also states that employees cannot be required to undertake 'any practice which in the employee's judgment compromises the employee's integrity', including by writing in a way that distorts facts or creates wrong impressions[90] – a provision that a journalist could rely on if pressured to imply the existence of a scientific debate over a matter that was actually settled.[91] This CBA also specifically protects covered employees against discipline based on 'the communications of another person on social media' – which means that journalists cannot be

security detail, and reverse its decision to suspend her, after she tweeted about the sexual assault charge that had previously been filed against Kobe Bryant shortly after his death, https://docs.google.com/document/d/1ErQ7bN352jQZoKa8kCzAW8CWr2zEnUIvms5BG2Kdt1E/edit.

87 See 'Hard News: Journalists and the Threat of Disinformation', PEN America, 2022, https://pen.org/report/hard-news-journalists-and-the-threat-of-disinformation.

88 See 'Pay Equity', The NewsGuild, 2020, https://newsguild.org/pay-equity (listing example contracts that contain these terms).

89 Ibid.

90 Collective Bargaining Agreement between Guardian News and Media LLC and New Media Guild, Local 31222, Oct. 6, 2017–Oct. 5, 2020, at 13 and 26.

91 In addition, US labor law protects unionized workers who refuse to follow a management directive because they reasonably believe that, under their CBA, they cannot be required to follow the directive. Thus, if *The Guardian* fired a journalist who reasonably believed they had a right to refuse a directive under this provision, it could be subject to both a grievance and an unfair labor practice charge. See *NLRB* v. *City Disposal Systems*, 465 US 822 (1984) (holding NLRA protects employees who reasonably stand on their rights under a CBA).

suspended or terminated simply because they become a target of online criticism.[92] CBAs are not always this protective or detailed – but they often contain some degree of shared labor–management recognition of and protection for journalistic independence. Thus, some CBAs specify that journalists can withhold their bylines from stories to which they have editorial objections, and some create joint labor–management committees to deal with conflicts of interest of breaches of ethical standards.[93]

In the near future, journalists' unions might negotiate over the deployment of artificial intelligence (AI) in their newsrooms.[94] (The deployment of new workplace technology is typically a mandatory subject of bargaining.) This is an example of a larger issue over which unions negotiate frequently: how labor-saving technology will be used, and how the resulting cost savings will be distributed. Those questions can be existentially important for workers in any context – but this context will have consequences for the broader public as well. A best-case scenario might involve cautious deployment of AI for specific routine tasks, subject to careful checking by humans, in ways that free up journalists to concentrate on investigative reporting. But the worst-case scenario would involve increasing reliance on AI for substance, perhaps triggering a vicious cycle of poor-quality output and fall-offs in subscribers and advertisers.

US news outlets seem to be at an inflection point, and the danger is that publishers will continue to respond by prioritizing short-term fixes at the long-term cost of both public trust and public access to reliable news sources. Journalists may not be able to prevent this outcome – but their odds are better if they act collectively. But how does US labor law shape the leverage that journalists bring to bear on news outlets? The next section turns to that question.

15.3.3 *Labor Law, the First Amendment and Journalists' Unions*

The previous section made the case that journalists' unions can help resist misinformation, including because they provide a way for journalists to pressure news outlets to adopt and maintain strong journalistic standards, and to enforce those standards in individual situations. But one barrier to unions' effectiveness is the weakness of US labor law.[95] First, as I have described elsewhere, labor law preserves a very broad

[92] Ibid. at 13.

[93] See, e.g., Agreement between Foreign Policy and Washington-Baltimore New Guild, Local 32035, Oct. 18, 2017–Oct. 18, 2019, at 10; Collective Bargaining Agreement between The Real News Network and The NewsGuild-CWA, Aug. 1, 2021–July 31, 2023, at 30 and 34.

[94] 'AP Releases New Report on AI in Local News', Associated Press, 29 March 2022, www.ap.org/press-releases/2022/ap-releases-new-report-on-ai-in-local-news (summarizing findings, including that some news outlets are already using AI for certain functions).

[95] Charlotte Garden, 'Tactical Mismatch in Union Organizing Drives' in Richard Bales and Charlotte Garden (eds.), *The Cambridge Handbook of US Labor Law for the Twenty-First Century* (Cambridge: Cambridge University Press, 2020) pp. 199–207.

scope for employers to fight organizing drives,[96] including by making serious 'misrepresentations' about the likely effects of unionization.[97] As a result, it can be very difficult for workers to unionize in the first place, making the recent string of successful union drives among journalists all the more remarkable. In addition, US labor law does very little to compel employers to agree a contract. The NLRA requires employers (and unions) to bargain in 'good faith', but provides no governmental mechanism to resolve bargaining impasses;[98] instead, it assumes that parties will use their 'economic weapons', such as strikes or lockouts, to pressure the other side to reach a deal. And although the NLRA confers legal protection on most strikes[99] – meaning that employers cannot retaliate against strikers by firing them – workers striking over economic issues can be 'permanently replaced'.[100] Moreover, labor law generally requires employers to hold working conditions constant while bargaining, but then allows them to make certain unilateral changes to working conditions upon reaching impasse.[101] This set of principles tends to give employers the upper hand during bargaining, no matter their industry. But at least two US Courts of Appeals, including the US Court of Appeals for the District of Columbia Circuit, have held that the rules should be even more employer-friendly when unions seek to bargain over issues of editorial policy.[102] This is because they see a bargaining requirement – even under these employer-friendly set of rules related to impasse and unilateral changes – as raising First Amendment concerns.

News outlets have been raising First Amendment objections to labor law since the NLRA was enacted in 1935, and the Supreme Court considered this argument in the 1937 case *Associated Press* v. *NLRB*.[103] This decision was issued as part of a trio of cases in which the Court upheld the NLRA as a valid exercise of Congress's

96 Ibid.

97 *Midland National Life Insurance Co.*, 263 N.L.R.B. 127 (1982) (holding that an employer's 'misrepresentations' do not provide cause to set aside the results of a union election). Interestingly, the National Labor Relations Board has at times applied the opposite rule, and held that one side's misrepresentations could merit a rerun election if the misrepresentation was highly salient, and if the other side did not have a meaningful opportunity to reply. Ibid. at 130.

98 *H. K. Porter Co., Inc.* v. *National Labor Relations Board*, 397 US 99 (1970).

99 29 U.S.C. §§ 157 and 158(a)(1).

100 *National Labor Relations Board* v. *Mackay Radio & Telegraph Co.*, 304 US 333 (1938). There are some technical differences between being 'fired' and being 'permanently replaced', but these differences are very unlikely to be consequential for a replaced worker.

101 *National Labor Relations Board* v. *Katz*, 369 US 736 (1962).

102 *Ampersand Publishing* v. *National Labor Relations Board*, 702 F.3d 51, 54 (D.C. Cir. 2012); *McDermott* v. *Ampersand Publishing*, 593 F.3d 950 (9th Cir. 2010). The DC Circuit is especially important in this context because any NLRB decision may be appealed to that court. 29 U.S.C. § 160(f).

103 *Associated Press* v. *National Labor Relations Board*, 301 US 103 (1937).

Commerce Clause authority.[104] The case began when the Associated Press (AP) fired one of its reporters who was active with the American Newspaper Guild. Arguing that it could not be compelled to reinstate the reporter, the AP argued before the Supreme Court that '[t]o name the men who shall choose and write the news for publication is no different either in principle or in result from naming what shall be written or published. Here the author and the product are one and inseparable. If one is to be free, so must the other'.[105] In other words, because the AP had a First Amendment right to choose what to publish, it also had an absolute right to decide whom to (or not to) employ.[106] The Court rejected this argument, correctly observing that the NLRA 'does not compel the petitioner to employ any one; it does not require that the petitioner retain in its employ an incompetent editor or one who fails faithfully to edit the news to reflect the facts without bias or prejudice'.[107] However, the Court did not preclude the possibility of future First Amendment challenges to specific aspects of labor law.[108]

Subsequently, news outlets have had some success in arguing that certain applications of labor law infringe their First Amendment rights. For example, consider *Passaic Daily News* v. *NLRB*, in which the employer-newspaper cancelled a bureau chief's regular column in retaliation for his support for a unionization effort.[109] Normally, the remedy for this sort of anti-union retaliation would be an order for the employer to restore the status quo ante by reinstating the union supporter's duties – but in this case, the Court held that it would be inconsistent with the First Amendment to order the employer to publish the bureau chief's column.[110] Unfortunately, the discussion of the First Amendment issue was quite limited – rather than considering the government interests at stake and possible alternative ways to achieve them, the Court seemed to assume that because the order to

[104] See *NLRB* v. *Jones & Laughlin Steel Corp.*, 301 US 1 (1937); see also US Constitution, Art. I, § 8, cl. 3 (providing that '[t]he Congress shall have Power … [t]o regulate Commerce with foreign Nations, and among the several States, and with the Indian Tribes').

[105] '*Associated Press* v. *NLRB*', AP Brief at *102.

[106] US readers may recognize the parallel to the ministerial exception, which effectively exempts religious entities from the application of many aspects of employment law when they hire employees who qualify as 'ministerial'. See *Hosanna-Tabor Evangelical Lutheran Church* v. *EEOC*, 565 US 171 (2012).

[107] *Associated Press* v. *National Labor Relations Board* at 132. Four dissenting justices (who also thought Congress lacked the authority to enact the NLRA) agreed with the AP that the First Amendment barred the statute's application to the press. They accepted the premise that unionized journalists had a conflict of interest when they covered labor disputes, which they concluded meant that news organizations had to be able to fire journalists on the basis of their union affiliation. Ibid. at 138.

[108] Ibid. at 132–33.

[109] *Passaic Daily News* v. *National Labor Relations Board*, 736 F.2d 1543 (D.C. Cir. 1984).

[110] Ibid. at 1559 ('we find that the remedy mandating resumption of Stoddard's column must yield to the Company's First Amendment interest in retaining control over prospective editorial decisions').

reinstate the column *implicated* the First Amendment, it also *violated* the First Amendment.[111]

The District of Columbia Circuit reached a similar conclusion in *Ampersand Publishing* v. *NLRB*, a case that arose after the owner and publisher of the Santa Barbara News-Press fired or otherwise disciplined several union supporters. Here, the core of the dispute centered on journalistic ethics: reporters and editors employed on the paper's news-gathering side became concerned about how the paper's owner, along with an editorial writer who was promoted to publisher, exercised influence over news-gathering and reporting. The reporters unionized, and sought to bargain over these issues as well as bread-and-butter topics.[112] When the paper's leadership resisted, the journalists held a rally calling for readers to cancel their subscriptions, and the paper responded by firing a group of journalists who supported the union.[113] The NLRB ordered the paper to reinstate the fired reporters, but the DC Circuit reversed on First Amendment grounds, writing that '[g]iven the publisher's First Amendment rights, issues of what is published and not published are not generally a "legitimate employee concern"', because 'The First Amendment affords a publisher – not a reporter – absolute authority to shape a newspaper's content'.[114]

Two important legal implications flow from this approach. The first is that editorial policies would be at most a 'permissive' subject of bargaining, meaning that employers would remain free to change those policies throughout the bargaining process, and they would not bear on whether impasse was reached. The second, more consequential, implication is that an employer could fire or otherwise discipline employees who struck over either a news outlet's refusal to bargain over editorial policies, or the substance of those policies. In other words, journalists could not rely on the NLRA's bargaining requirement or its anti-retaliation provision with respect to editorial policies. My view is that this approach is seriously flawed because it conflates labor law – a mechanism to provide limited protections for employees to exercise voice vis-á-vis their employers – with direct government control of the press.

[111] The DC Circuit analogized the case to the Supreme Court's decision in *Miami Herald Publishing Co.* v. *Tornillo*, 418 US 241 (1971). But *Tornillo* concerned a 'right of reply' statute that would have required the *Herald* to run candidate rebuttals to the paper's criticism. In contrast, the order in this case would have required reinstatement of a column that the paper had already decided to run, and it would not have prohibited the paper from discontinuing the column for any reason other than an anti-union one.

[112] *Ampersand Publishing* v. *National Labor Relations Board* at 54; see also James Rainey, 'Santa Barbara News-Press Bankruptcy Brings Uneasy End to an Owner's Bitter Tenure', *Los Angeles Times*, 29 July 2023, www.latimes.com/california/story/2023-07-29/santa-barbara-news-press-bankruptcy-closure-newspaper-owner-wendy-mccaw (providing a more detailed account of the problems that led to the labor dispute).

[113] *Ampersand Publishing* v. *National Labor Relations Board* at 54.

[114] Ibid. at 56; see also *McDermott* v. *Ampersand Publishing*, 593 F.3d 950 (9th Cir. 2010) (refusing to issue injunction against an employer in the same labor dispute because of 'First Amendment right to editorial discretion').

Unfortunately, the current Supreme Court's highly formalistic approach to First Amendment cases means that it would likely uphold the DC Circuit's approach, were it to decide a similar case.[115]

But even assuming that these courts' understanding of the First Amendment's interplay with labor law is doctrinally correct, journalists' unions will still likely succeed in influencing mainstream outlets' editorial policies. Unions that lack legal rights can still appeal to the public, and editorial integrity is an appealing message. Moreover, many individual journalists have substantial presences on social media platforms, making it relatively easy to reach both the public and other journalists, and news outlets within the same media market report on each other, as illustrated by coverage in the *Los Angeles Times* of labor conflicts at the Santa Barbara News-Press.[116] Finally, once an outlet commits to be bound by a CBA provision related to editorial integrity, that provision is likely to be enforceable through the usual channels without raising a First Amendment problem.[117]

As a result, journalists' unions will have greater prospects for success when they organize and seek to bargain over editorial integrity *before* there is an integrity problem at their outlet. Once the train has left the station – as was seemingly the case at the Santa Barbara News-Press – the outlet may simply double down and fire complaining journalists.[118] But in the absence of a current conflict, outlets should be willing to agree to general integrity commitments along with specific mechanisms to make them real, particularly because these provisions do not generally come with attached price-tags. Thus, although labor law's weakness is a drawback – and an especially significant one in this context – organizing and collective bargaining still have promise as mechanisms to protect journalistic integrity.

15.4 CONCLUSION

This chapter has argued that labor unions are important to the fight against misinformation, both in the near term and on a longer time horizon. Already, unions can inoculate their members against misinformation through member-to-member education, and counter-narratives advanced in the media. In the longer run, higher levels of unionization could decrease the social inequality and resentment that make a society more vulnerable to misinformation.

[115] For an insightful discussion of the Supreme Court's First Amendment formalism, see Genevieve Lakier, 'Imagining an Antisubordinating First Amendment' (2018) 118 *Columbia Law Review* 2117.

[116] See Rainey, 'Santa Barbara News-Press Bankruptcy' (n 112).

[117] See *Cohen* v. *Cowles Media Co.*, 501 US 663 (1991) (holding that generally applicable contract principles applied to newspaper's promise of confidentiality, and rejecting paper's First Amendment argument).

[118] Notes 112–114 and accompanying text.

Further, unions of information workers can play an important role in maintaining the integrity of their own workplaces. (This chapter has focused on journalists, though similar arguments could be made about other groups, including teachers and librarians.) First, collective bargaining between journalists' unions and news outlets can improve bread-and-butter labor standards so that journalism will remain a realistic and attractive career option for people from a diverse range of backgrounds – an important predicate for public trust. Second, collective bargaining is an opportunity to establish meaningful protections for ethical journalistic practices, which unions can then monitor and enforce through grievance procedures. These labor standards and protections are likely to be especially important as news outlets continue to grapple with the serious challenges posed by technology, changing business models and financialization, and threats posed by authoritarian politics.

Unfortunately, union density in the USA has been declining since the mid-1950s.[119] Today, private sector union density hovers at around 6 percent; public sector union density is much higher, but it also varies tremendously among different regions of the country. Moreover, although labor unions enjoy widespread and relatively bipartisan public support,[120] the Republican Party is mostly hostile to organized labor, making pro-union labor law reform very unlikely, especially at the federal level. This means a resurgence in union strength will have to come despite labor law, not because of it. There is a ray of hope, however: young workers have a remarkably favorable view of unions and unionizing, and are driving a new wave of organizing, especially among service workers.[121] Whether young workers will be able to unionize in sufficient numbers to move the needle is unclear – but there is more reason for optimism on this topic today than at any point in the last three decades.

119 'Union Membership Rate Fell by 0.2 Percentage Point to 10.1 Percent in 2022', US Bureau of Labor Statistics, 24 January 2023, www.bls.gov/opub/ted/2023/union-membership-rate-fell-by-0-2-percentage-point-to-10-1-percent-in-2022.htm. In 2022, the private sector union density rate was 6 per cent, and the public sector union density rate was 33 per cent.

120 Megan Brenan, 'Approval of Labor Unions at Highest Point since 1965', Gallup, 2 September 2021, https://news.gallup.com/poll/354455/approval-labor-unions-highest-point-1965.aspx.

121 Aurelia Glass, 'What You Need to Know about Gen Z's Support for Unions', Center for American Progress, 9 August 2023, www.americanprogress.org/article/what-you-need-to-know-about-gen-zs-support-for-unions.

Afterword

For Whose Benefit Is the Freedom of Speech?

Vincent Blasi

United States v. *Alvarez*, oral argument of Jonathan D. Libby on behalf of the respondent, 22 February 2012:

CHIEF JUSTICE ROBERTS:	What is – what is the First Amendment value in a lie, a pure lie?
MR. LIBBY:	Just a pure lie? There can be a number of values. There's the value of personal autonomy.
CHIEF JUSTICE ROBERTS:	The value of what?
MR. LIBBY:	Personal autonomy.
CHIEF JUSTICE ROBERTS:	What does that mean?
MR. LIBBY:	Well, that we get to – we get to exaggerate and create.
CHIEF JUSTICE ROBERTS:	No, not exaggerate – lie.

In *United States* v. *Alvarez*,[1] the US Supreme Court ruled that an official of a water district who introduced himself to his constituents by falsely stating in a public meeting that he had earned the Congressional Medal of Honor had a First Amendment right to make that demonstrably untrue claim. Audience members misled by the statement might well be considered to have a First Amendment interest in not being directly and knowingly lied to in that way. Other members of the community might be thought to have a First Amendment interest in public officials such as Xavier Alvarez telling the truth about their credentials and experiences. Nevertheless, as both the plurality and the concurring justices who together formed the majority in *Alvarez* viewed the case, it was the liar's interest in saying what he wished that carried the day. Why is that? Crucial to answering this question is whether 'the freedom of speech' that the First Amendment tolerates 'no law abridging' is understood to be primarily speaker-centered, audience-centered, or society-centered.

[1] *United States* v. *Alvarez*, 567 US 709 (2012).

I maintain that up until the last fifty years the freedom of speech that is the subject of First Amendment protection had been understood to be primarily for the benefit of audiences and the society beyond. Only as a result of modern Supreme Court interpretations has a speaker-centered understanding of that freedom become dominant. One of the consequences of this shift has been that today liars are more able than ever before to cause harm, and not only because of the way that digital technology amplifies their misbegotten communicative power. Constitutional interpretation is also part of the problem. At least that is so in the USA.

Other societies that have maintained a less speaker-centered approach to the freedom of speech have more capability on that account to punish lying. That capability might become more and more important as digital technology vastly increases the means, the incidence and the reach of lying. For that reason, as well as many others, it is important to realize that the current speaker-centered understanding of the freedom of speech that makes the USA an outlier is something of an aberration – not only by comparison to how other countries view the matter but also by comparison to how the First Amendment itself was conceived in earlier eras.

***

The principal author of the provision that eventually became the First Amendment was James Madison. He also was probably the most influential advocate in securing its passage by Congress and ratification by the states. Earlier, in a fascinating exchange of letters with Thomas Jefferson,[2] Madison had wondered how efficacious 'parchment barriers' protecting the freedoms of speech and press can be in a government that takes the form of a republic. He conceded that declaring rights in a charter can serve as a rallying standard for arousing popular resistance to corrupt or oppressive *monarchical* rule – Jefferson was receiving Madison's ruminations while residing in Paris on the eve of the French Revolution – but surmised that the situation must be different in a *republic*, where the chief danger lies in the wrongful exercise of majority will itself. Nevertheless, Madison concluded that such a declaration could conceivably have a constructive role to play in a republic by means of influencing public opinion: 'The political truths declared in that solemn manner acquire by degrees the character of fundamental maxims of free Government, and as they become incorporated with the National sentiment, counteract the impulses of interest and passion.'[3] Moreover,

> although it be generally true, as above stated, that the danger of oppression lies in the interested majorities of the people rather than usurped acts of the Government, yet there may be occasions on which the evil may spring from the latter source, and

[2] James Madison, 'Letter to Thomas Jefferson', 17 October 1788, in James Madison, *Writings* (Ed. by Jack N. Rakove, New York: Library of America, 1999) pp. 420–21.

[3] Ibid. pp 421–22.

> on such, a bill of rights will be a good ground for an appeal to the sense of the community.[4]

This exchange with Jefferson was echoed on 8 June 1789, when as a member of the House of Representatives Madison spoke in favor adopting a bill of rights which he had drafted, including what became the First Amendment.[5] He addressed head-on the objection that declaring such rights might be ineffectual:

> It may be thought all paper barriers against the power of the community are too weak to be worthy of attention ... [Y]et, as they have a tendency to impress some degree of respect for them, to establish the public opinion in their favor, and rouse the attention of the whole community, it may be one means to control the majority from those acts to which they might be otherwise inclined.[6]

Ten years later, in response to the passage by his political opponents of the Sedition Act of 1798 prohibiting 'any false, scandalous, and malicious writing or writings against the government of the United States',[7] Madison published his most detailed account of the meaning of the First Amendment, and once again he made public opinion the touchstone. The *Report on the Virginia Resolutions*,[8] written by Madison on behalf of the Virginia Legislature, argued that the federal Sedition Act was unconstitutional under the First Amendment for violating 'that right of freely examining public characters and measures, and of free communication among the people thereon, which has ever been justly deemed, the only effectual guardian of every other right'.[9] Madison noted that the Constitution supposes that 'the President, the Congress, and each of its houses, may not discharge their trusts'.[10] Whenever that happens, he reasoned, 'it is the duty as well as right of intelligent and faithful citizens' to control such abuses by means of 'the censorship [i.e., censure] of the public opinion'.[11] He made no mention of an individual right of self-expression. His focus was entirely on the role that an informed public opinion must play as a check on official conduct.

In 1964, the *Virginia Report* was made the centerpiece of the Supreme Court's landmark opinion in *New York Times* v. *Sullivan*,[12] which ruled invalid under the First Amendment a state court defamation judgment against a national newspaper for some factual errors in a story about abusive treatment of civil rights protesters by

4 Ibid. p. 422.
5 James Madison, 'Speech in Congress Proposing Constitutional Amendments', 8 June 1789, in Madison, *Writings* (n 2) pp. 446–47.
6 Ibid. pp. 446–47.
7 Sedition Act, ch. 74, § 2, 1 Stat. 596 (1798).
8 James Madison, 'Report on the Alien and Sedition Acts' (The Virginia Report), 7 January 1800, in Madison, *Writings* (n 2) pp. 651–52.
9 Ibid. p. 651.
10 Ibid. p. 652.
11 Ibid.
12 *The New York Times* v. *Sullivan*, 376 US 254, 270–76 and n 19 (1964).

local officials in Montgomery, Alabama. Justice Brennan's opinion for the Court invoked Madison for the proposition that 'breathing space' for unintentional factual error is requisite under the First Amendment because of 'a profound national commitment that debate on public issues should be uninhibited, robust and wide-open'.[13] It was 'the great controversy over the Sedition Act of 1798', said Justice Brennan, 'which first crystallized a national awareness of the central meaning of the First Amendment'.[14] Not only Madison's writing on the subject but also that of John Milton (*Areopagitica*),[15] John Stuart Mill (*On Liberty*)[16] and Oliver Wendell Holmes (dissenting opinion in *Abrams* v. *United States*)[17] were invoked by Justice Brennan in his opinion for the Court majority in *Sullivan*. Like Madison, each of these thinkers had developed a well-known and distinctly audience-centered account of the freedom of speech.

***

In the early 1930s, when the US Supreme Court first began to rule in favor of First Amendment claimants, the majority opinions, usually written by Chief Justice Charles Evans Hughes, emphasized the interests of audiences and the society beyond rather than the interests of speakers. In *Stromberg* v. *California*,[18] vindicating the right to display a red flag as a symbol of opposition to government, Chief Justice Hughes said: 'The maintenance of the opportunity for free political discussion to the end that government may be responsive to the will of the people and that changes may be obtained by lawful means, an opportunity essential to the security of the Republic, is a fundamental principle of our constitutional system.'[19] In *Near* v. *Minnesota*,[20] holding that judicial enjoining of a publication is as problematic under the First Amendment as requiring a license for the privilege of printing, Hughes quoted Madison's *Virginia Report* for the proposition that 'to the press alone, chequered as it is with abuses, the world is indebted for all the triumphs which have been gained by reason and humanity over error and oppression'.[21] Hughes also invoked the following passage about the freedom of the press contained in a letter written in 1774 by the Continental Congress to the inhabitants of Quebec urging them to join in resisting British colonial rule:

> The importance of [freedom of the press] consists, besides the advancement of truth, science, morality, and arts in general, in its diffusion of liberal sentiments on

[13] Ibid. at 270–72.
[14] Ibid. at 273.
[15] John Milton, *Areopagitica* (London, 1644).
[16] John Stuart Mill, *On Liberty* (London: John W. Parker and Son, 1859).
[17] *Abrams* v. *United States*, 250 US 616 (1919) (Holmes J, dissenting).
[18] *Stromberg* v. *California*, 283 US 359, 369 (1931).
[19] Ibid.
[20] *Near* v. *Minnesota*, 283 US 697, 717–20 (1931).
[21] Ibid. at 718.

> the administration of Government, its ready communication of thoughts between subjects, and its consequential promotion of union among them, whereby oppressive officers are shamed or intimidated, into more honourable and just modes of conducting affairs.[22]

Not only founding-era history but also twentieth-century developments informed the Chief Justice's understanding in *Near* of the audience- and society-centered justification for freedom of the press:

> [T]he administration of government has become more complex, the opportunities for malfeasance and corruption have multiplied, crime has grown to most serious proportions, and the danger of its protection by unfaithful officials and of the impairment of the fundamental security of life and property by criminal alliances and official neglect, emphasizes the primary need of a vigilant and courageous press, especially in great cities.[23]

Further evidence of how the First Amendment was viewed by the Court that first gave it life is the opinion Hughes wrote for a unanimous Court in *Semler* v. *Oregon State Board of Dental Examiners*,[24] a case about the constitutionality of a state law that prohibited dentists from 'advertising to guarantee any dental service, or to perform any dental operation painlessly'.[25] His explanation for upholding the law focused on audience well-being:

> It is no answer to say, as regards appellant's claim of right to advertise his 'professional superiority' or his 'performance of professional services in a superior manner', that he is telling the truth. In framing its policy, the legislature was not bound to provide for determinations of the relative proficiency of particular practitioners. The legislature was entitled to consider the general effects of the practices which it described, and if these effects were injurious in facilitating unwarranted and misleading claims, to counteract them by a general rule even though, in particular instances, there might be no actual deception or misstatement.[26]

Hughes treated the case as raising only an unpersuasive liberty-of-contract objection. No Justice, and not even the dentists asserting a right to advertise, even considered the possibility that a speaker-centered First Amendment had anything to do with the dispute.

Two landmark cases decided in the early 1940s, after Chief Justice Hughes had retired, continued the emphasis on audience and societal interests. In *Chaplinsky* v. *New Hampshire*,[27] the Court ruled that the First Amendment does not protect a speaker's right to utter face-to-face epithets, even to assert a political point. One day

22 Ibid. at 717.
23 Ibid. at 719–20.
24 *Semler* v. *Oregon State Board of Dental Examiners*, 294 US 608, 609, 612–13 (1935).
25 Ibid. at 609.
26 Ibid. at 612–13.
27 *Chaplinsky* v. *New Hampshire*, 315 US 568, 572 (1942).

in Rochester, New Hampshire, a Jehovah's Witness named Walter Chaplinsky offended local citizens in front of the town hall by denouncing all religion as a 'racket'. The City Marshall, one Bowering, came upon the scene, only to be derided by Chaplinsky in the following terms: 'You are a God damned racketeer and a damned Fascist and the whole government of Rochester are Fascists or agents of Fascists.'[28] The US Supreme Court unanimously agreed that Chaplinsky's outburst directed to a government official was not protected under the First Amendment: '[S]uch utterances are no essential part of any exposition of ideas, and are of such slight social value as a step to truth that any benefit that may be derived from them is clearly outweighed by the social interest in order and morality.'[29] Chaplinsky's personal interest in having his say in his own biting way was given short shrift. What determined the outcome of the case was the lack of value to any audience of the speech at issue.

In *West Virginia State Board of Education* v. *Barnette*,[30] the Court held that a schoolchild cannot be required to recite the Pledge of Allegiance in a classroom ceremony. Although the case was largely argued in terms of an asserted individual right to abstain grounded in religious freedom, the majority opinion by Justice Robert Jackson based the holding on a broader freedom derived from the political principle of popular sovereignty: 'We set up government by the consent of the governed, and the Bill of Rights denies those in power any legal opportunity to coerce that consent. Authority here is to be controlled by public opinion, not public opinion by authority.'[31] Although the hardships of the expelled young Witnesses and their parents made for appealing individual claims, the Court's interpretation of the First Amendment focused on the various ways that the pledge requirement corrupted public opinion: "Probably no deeper division of our people could proceed from any provocation than from finding it necessary to choose what doctrine and whose program public educational officials shall compel youth to unite in embracing".[32]

***

Since the 1930s and 1940s, the Court's understanding of the freedom of speech has become much more speaker-centered. This is not the place to trace the complicated history of that evolution, but a few representative cases decided within the last fifty years well illustrate the contrast. In *Miami Herald Publishing Co.* v. *Tornillo*,[33] the Court interpreted the Press Clause of the First Amendment to disallow 'a state statute granting a political candidate a right to equal space to reply to criticism and

28 Ibid. at 569 (internal quotation marks omitted).

29 Ibid. at 572.

30 *West Virginia State Board of Education* v. *Barnette*, 319 US 624, 641 (1943).

31 Ibid.

32 Ibid.

33 *Miami Herald Publishing Co.* v. *Tornillo*, 418 US 241, 248–49, 258 (1974).

attacks on his record by a newspaper'.[34] The Court's analysis began by focusing on audience interests:

> It is urged that at the time the First Amendment to the Constitution was ratified in 1791 as part of our Bill of Rights the press was broadly representative of the people it was serving. While many of the newspapers were intensely partisan and narrow in their views, the press collectively presented a broad range of opinions to readers.[35]

In contrast, by the latter part of the twentieth century, 'chains of newspapers, national newspapers, national wire and news services, and one-newspaper towns, are the dominant features of a press that has become noncompetitive and enormously powerful and influential in its capacity to manipulate popular opinion and change the course of events'.[36] Despite this asserted and never disputed development, the Court ruled that:

> the Florida statute fails to clear the barriers of the First Amendment because of its intrusion into the function of editors … The choice of material to go into a newspaper, and the decisions made as to limitations on the size and content of the paper, and treatment of public issues and public officials – whether fair or unfair – constitute the exercise of editorial control and judgment.[37]

In terms of classifying the various First Amendment interests in play in *Tornillo*, the candidate's claim to have access to the newspaper's readers can be viewed as either speaker-centered for the benefit of the candidate, or audience-centered in that granting him such access might give the newspaper's readers additional information and advocacy that would help them decide how to vote in the forthcoming election. By the same token, the newspaper's claim of a right to exercise maximum control over the content of its pages might be seen as benefiting the newspaper qua speaker or as benefiting its readers who might wish to defer to the judgment of professional journalists regarding what content would best serve their interests.

An additional understanding of the *Tornillo* ruling at the time might have been that audiences and the society beyond have a strong interest in media entities controlling their published content because of the role such powerful actors can play in holding government accountable due to their local knowledge, expertise, resources and professional credibility. Recall the way that Madison placed such accountability at the center of his argument in the *Virginia Report*. Such a notion of instrumental journalistic autonomy would resonate with the Court's talk in *Tornillo* of the distinctive 'function of editors'. In sum, *Tornillo* was a case of apparently rich but uncertain import regarding how the First Amendment would be understood going forward regarding its intended beneficiaries.

34 Ibid. at 243.
35 Ibid. at 248.
36 Ibid. at 249.
37 Ibid. at 258.

Just three years later, the Court invoked the *Tornillo* holding in support of its ruling that a New Hampshire driver had a First Amendment right to cover up the state's motto 'Live Free or Die' on his license plate.[38] Whatever else that case was about, it had nothing to do with journalistic autonomy and very little to do with audience interests. Similarly, a decade later the Court relied heavily upon *Tornillo* to strike down a law requiring solicitors of charitable donations to disclose to their addressees what percentage of their donations would be passed along to needy recipients rather than used by the solicitors to cover operating expenses or for other purposes.[39] Once again, speaker interests dictated the result, on this occasion in the face of a significant audience interest in disclosure. Since then, *Tornillo* has become a favored precedent for a robust speaker-centered right against 'compelled speech', a right enjoyed by almost all targets of regulation, not just journalists, and one that is seldom derived from a comparison of speaker and audience interests.

Arizona Free Enterprise Club's Freedom Club PAC v. *Bennett* (2011)[40] involved a challenge to a public financing scheme for elections which had been adopted by referendum. A candidate for office agreeing to cap her spending from private contributions was granted an initial public subsidy, which would then be supplemented by a second-stage subsidy if her privately financed opponent spent over a specified amount. The law was challenged by a group of privately financed candidates who claimed that the scheme punished them by making their spending for speaking a trigger for extra public funding being directed to their opponents' campaigns. The law was defended on the ground that it enabled more and different candidates to run competitive campaigns, thereby giving voters more choices and more information while still not prohibiting privately financed candidates from spending as much as they wished.

In an opinion by Chief Justice Roberts, the Court majority ruled, citing *Tornillo*, that making a privately financed candidate an instrument for triggering public subsidization of his opponent's campaign was an encroachment on that candidate's liberty under the First Amendment even if the overall result was more total speech available to the electorate, and indeed even if the privately financed candidate was still able to outspend the two-stage-subsidized publicly financed candidate.[41] This logic left the four dissenters aghast. As Justice Kagan put it: 'Except in a world gone topsy-turvy, additional campaign speech and electoral competition is not a First Amendment injury.'[42]

It is possible, of course, that in certain campaigns the mechanism of the triggered subsidy might cause a privately financed candidate to conclude that his best tactic would be to spend less than he could in order to prevent his opponent from getting

[38] *Wooley* v. *Maynard*, 430 US 705 (1977).

[39] *Riley* v. *National Federation of the Blind*, 487 US 781 (1988).

[40] *Arizona Free Enterprise Club's Freedom Club PAC* v. *Bennett*, 564 US 721 (2011).

[41] Ibid. at 740–43, 755.

[42] Ibid. at 763 (Kagan J, dissenting).

the second-stage supplemental subsidy. If so, voters would receive less speech overall. But the majority opinion made no claim that this scenario would ensue more often than the more-spending-by-both-sides scenario. Its ruling was focused exclusively on the burden the law placed on the privately financed candidate. *Arizona Free Enterprise Club's Freedom Club PAC* is a speaker-centered, not an audience-centered or system-centered opinion.

A different kind of speaker-centered understanding of the First Amendment drove the Court's ruling in *National Institute of Family and Life Advocates* v. *Becerra* (2018).[43] California required clinics that primarily serve pregnant women to inform their potential patients that the state 'has public programs that provide immediate free or low-cost access to comprehensive family planning services including … contraception, prenatal care, and abortion for eligible women', and to give them a phone number to call to learn more about such programs.[44] Private clinics that offered pregnancy testing, prenatal care and moral counseling opposed to abortion argued that it violated their freedom of speech to be required to post the mandated message informing patients of their alternatives.

A closely divided Supreme Court held that the state's disclosure requirement violated the First Amendment because of its potential adverse effect on the messaging of the private clinics that considered abortion to be immoral. The Court majority treated a service provider's responsibility to disclose accurate information regarding the availability of alternative services to be as problematic under the First Amendment as would be a requirement that the service provider convey an opinion contrary to its own about the morality of services it declined to provide. In that respect, the *National Institute of Family and Life Advocates* (*NIFLA*) holding went well beyond *Tornillo*, which it cited. Furthermore, the fact that the speech of the clinics was integrated with the act of providing medical services did not reduce the speaker's claim to exercise full control over what patients heard and read within its walls. The Court never considered any possible First Amendment interest of the patients of the private clinic in learning about the full range of alternatives available to them or in understanding at the outset what services were and were not being made available to them at the private clinic.

The problem with the *NIFLA* decision lies not with its premise that a speaker, even one taking on the responsibilities of a service provider, has a First Amendment interest of a sort in exercising full control over what accurate information it conveys or chooses not to convey to the persons it seeks to serve. At least when the choice of what to convey might be perceived by an audience as carrying normative implications, a speaker's interest in not participating in the transmission of certain information might well have First Amendment valence. The problem is that such a conceivable interest was not the only one related to the freedom of speech in play in

[43] *National Institute of Family and Life Advocates* v. *Becerra*, 138 S.Ct. 2361 (2018).
[44] Ibid. at 2369.

the case, and the Court majority reasoned as if it was. Regarding the relative importance of speaker interests and listener or societal interests, *NIFLA* reads nothing like the opinion of Justice Jackson in the foundational compelled speech case, *Barnette*, involving the compulsory flag salute. Rather, *NIFLA* represents the modern triumph of the speaker-centered understanding of the freedom of speech.

All of which brings us back to where we began: the Court's decision in *Alvarez*, recognizing a speaker's First Amendment right to claim in a formal public setting that he had earned the Congressional Medal of Honor when he knew that he had not. This was not a case about punishing falsity in the realm of opinion or delusional assertion. All the Justices read the statute to cover only situations in which there could be no doubt that the speaker knew perfectly well that his statements about specific facts were false. Moreover, although the plurality opinion noted that the statute read literally would apply to 'personal, whispered conversations within a home', such an application was all but inconceivable. The reasoning of both the plurality and the concurring opinions made it clear that the First Amendment concerns that led to overturning Alvarez's conviction would have prevailed even if the statute had been confined to lying in a public setting, or even more narrowly in a formal public meeting.

What exactly was the speaker's legal interest, grounded in the freedom of speech, in being able to tell a deliberate, self-aggrandizing lie to his constituents? It could not have been simply in saying whatever he wished. Had Alvarez issued a 'true' threat or directed a face-to-face epithet to a member of his audience, Supreme Court precedent makes clear that he would have had no First Amendment claim whatsoever.[45] Such communications are not considered to be part of the freedom of speech. So if there is no comprehensive First Amendment right to say what you wish, what was Alvarez's claim to lie the way he did? How does protecting his lying advance the objectives of the freedom of speech? There would be a First Amendment concern if a speaker's being vulnerable to prosecution for lying created a risk of being convicted for telling the truth. Some would-be spreaders of truth surely would opt for silence in the face of that risk. But so long as the prohibition is limited, as was the Stolen Valor Act, to knowingly spreading a falsehood about a hard fact concerning oneself, the chilling effect on, or risk of wrongful conviction of, truthful speakers is bound to be minimal.

The plurality and concurring opinions in the case appeared to find it relevant that many persons knowingly lie, not only to burnish their credentials but also to embellish a story or exaggerate a point, and often are indulged in doing so. In that respect, it might seem to be more problematic for a representative government to criminalize the activity than it is to punish threats or face-to-face epithets, which are forms of speech that may or may not be as common as lying but are more universally

[45] See *Chaplinsky* v. *New Hampshire*, at 571–72; *Watts* v. *United States*, 394 US 705, 708 (1969); *Virginia* v. *Black*, 538 US 343, 359 (2003).

condemned. A different speaker-based interest was thought by the plurality and concurring opinions to be a reason not to uphold the criminalization of deliberate lying. Precisely because the activity is common, prosecutorial discretion not to press charges is bound to play a large role in enforcement practices.

Justice Kennedy for the plurality, and Justice Breyer for himself and Justice Kagan, worried that prosecutorial discretion could be improperly based on disapproval of a speaker's ideas. Such selectivity would violate a speaker-based interest not to be discriminated against on the basis of one's beliefs. However, that risk is not limited to the selective prosecution of communicative crimes. A regime inclined to punish beliefs could do so by selectively enforcing housing codes, tax filing requirements or speed limits. Were that to occur, the objects of such selective prosecutions would be punished for their beliefs just as much as when the underlying crime is lying. The Stolen Valor Act presented no unusual risk of being selectively enforced.

The receptivity of the plurality and concurring Justices in *Alvarez* to these less-than-compelling speaker-centered interests was noteworthy. Equally noteworthy was the lack of receptivity exhibited by the prevailing Justices to the audience- and society-centered interests grounded in the freedom of speech that might support regulating the type of lying at issue in the case. Those could include autonomy interests of listeners not to be manipulated, as well as audience and societal interests in fact-based political accountability and productive public discourse. Justice Kennedy said nothing at all about the wrong done to individual audience members by their being lied to. He said a lot about public discourse, however. He discovered in the Stolen Valor Act the seeds of the most notorious regime of comprehensive thought control ever devised by the human imagination:

> Permitting the government to decree this speech to be a criminal offense, whether shouted from the rooftops or made in a barely audible whisper, would endorse government authority to compile a list of subjects about which false statements are punishable. That governmental power has no clear limiting principle. Our constitutional tradition stands against the idea that we need Oceania's Ministry of Truth. See G. Orwell, *Nineteen Eighty-Four* (1949).[46]

This analogy is dramatic but its drama is of the fictional sort. Oceania's infamous 'Ministry of Truth' existed to decree official truth and punish deviants from that 'truth'. It was about policing heresy. The Stolen Valor Act punished dishonesty not heresy. The only 'truth' it enforced was the understanding the speaker himself had developed before venturing out to mislead others regarding what he believed. A government that punishes deliberate lying regarding hard facts is not thereby enforcing its own truth.

Later in his opinion, Justice Kennedy continued to operate at a very high level of generality: '[S]uppression of speech by the government can make exposure of falsity

[46] *United States* v. *Alvarez*, at 723 (plurality opinion).

more difficult, not less so. Society has the right and civic duty to engage in open, dynamic, rational discourse. These ends are not well served when the government seeks to orchestrate public discussion through content-based mandates.'[47] It is a stretch to characterize what was done to Alvarez as 'suppression of speech' by a government seeking to 'orchestrate public discussion through content-based mandates'. He was convicted of making a deliberate lie about a hard fact concerning an important matter singled out by statute and on the basis of proof beyond a reasonable doubt that he understood the falsity of his statement. His conviction was a discrete event, not part of a wide-ranging, 'list'-driven effort by government to control the thought of its citizens.

There is a place in legal analysis for slippery slope arguments, but they lose credibility when they are employed indiscriminately. Flat-out lying about one's receipt of a specific award falls into a category of communicative activity that is notable for its boundedness. No questions of characterization, intention or degree complicate the classification. Any doctrine devised to address the dangers and transgressions of that activity can be contained. To equate the punishment of deliberate lying about a hard fact concerning the speaker's own experience with comprehensive, dogmatic Orwellian thought control is not to take seriously the distinctive audience and societal interests that are jeopardized by such lying.

That said, some observers who understand the freedom of speech to be at least partly about audience and societal truth-seeking might believe, with Justice Kennedy, that those objectives would be better served if liars were regulated exclusively by refutation. In fact, a preference for private refutation had an honored place in the free speech tradition of yore that gave considerable weight to audience and societal interests. Justice Brandeis memorably argued in *Whitney* v. *California* that, when time permits, 'falsehood and fallacies' are corrected better by 'more speech' than by 'enforced silence', and that 'the fitting remedy for evil counsels is good ones'.[48] Justice Brandeis's favoring of private correction was prompted by what he took to be the benefit of giving audience members informal civic responsibilities. '[T]he greatest menace to freedom', he said in *Whitney*, 'is an inert people'.[49] Justice Kennedy's concern that authoritative legal correction might be obtuse or sought for ulterior purposes was not mentioned by Justice Brandeis in *Whitney*. As a legendary reformer, he did not share Justice Kennedy's comprehensive distrust of government regulation. Indeed, it is not at all clear from the case context whether the 'falsehood and fallacies' and 'evil counsels' that Justice Brandeis believed were better corrected by 'more speech' than by regulation included knowing lies about hard facts

47 Ibid. at 728.
48 *Whitney* v. *California*, 274 US 357, 375, 377 (1927), quoted by Justice Kennedy in *United States* v. *Alvarez*, 727–28.
49 *Whitney* v. *California*, at 375.

concerning the speaker's own personal experience. The defendant in *Whitney* was not prosecuted for lying.

The older free speech tradition also counseled that the circulation of false ideas can have heuristic value for audiences. In his concurring opinion in *Alvarez*, Justice Breyer invoked Mill's famous observation that one good reason to protect 'the liberty of thought and discussion' is that when audiences confront falsity they can develop a deeper understanding of truth and a better capacity to apply and defend it.[50] Mill made that point in a chapter of *On Liberty* in which he discussed how false opinions about values and objectives and matters such as historical causation and political efficacy should be fairly considered and turned to constructive heuristic use. He did not take up the subject of deliberate lies in that chapter. Perhaps Mill thought that discrediting a knowing lie about a hard fact such as whether a specific person had actually been awarded a particular medal does not require or lead to the depth of understanding he took to be the benefit to audiences of engaging with false moral or interpretative opinions.

It is a serious question whether the regulation of specific lies should be governed by the same principles that govern the regulation of unorthodox opinions relating to objectives, or best means, or norms, or predicted effects. The motives of liars are fundamentally different from the motives of ideological provocateurs and other kinds of contrarians. The value to audiences of being exposed to untrue factual assertions regarding the speaker's personal experiences is of a lesser order than the value to audiences of being exposed to aspirational, explanatory and critical ideas that lack current public acceptance. The difficulty of defining and proving violations is much greater when the legally consequential behavior consists of assertions of value or efficacy rather than assertions of specific hard facts. The reasons to distrust regulators are better validated by history when they assert control over heresy, extremism or foolishness than when they assert control over dishonesty. These are differences that the prevailing opinions in *Alvarez* might have addressed directly. Instead, the possible distinctiveness of disputes over deliberate lies regarding hard facts concerning the speaker's personal experience was glossed over.

The current Court's speaker-centered approach to interpreting the First Amendment is in consonance with its conflating of deliberate lies with provocative opinions. When the interests of speakers is the primary concern and when distrust of regulators is a large part of the constitutional tradition, courts might understandably be in search of formal, relatively mechanistic, not overly refined or subdivided criteria of categorization. Reading the First Amendment to protect 'the freedom of speech' rather than 'the freedom of sincere speech' or 'the freedom of speech that is

[50] *United States* v. *Alvarez*, at 733 (Breyer J, concurring). For Mill's discussion in *On Liberty* of the value of engaging with falsehood, see Mill, *On Liberty* (n 16) 64–82.

useful to audiences' is tempting. (An audience-centered approach might protect something more akin to Mill's 'freedom of thought and discussion'.)

A textualist might think it is self-evident that the proper unit of reference is 'the freedom of speech' simpliciter, but that only raises the interpretative question of what 'the' freedom specified in the text of the First Amendment refers to. Is it a nearly all-inclusive freedom of speaking, as the current Court would have it? Or is the reference instead to a less encompassing, more determinate set consisting of the modern analogs of certain historical claims to communicative liberty that were thought at the time of the Amendment's ratification to serve especially important functions?

The recent Court's practice of interpreting the First Amendment expansively in the spirit of conflation with small regard for function has not been confined to the question of how to think about lying. Commercial speech, for example, has been brought within the coverage of the First Amendment in an increasingly indiscriminate manner, with the justification no longer limited to the protection of audience interests.[51] Chief Justice Hughes' assumption in 1935 that dental advertising had nothing to do with the freedom of speech now seems doctrinally anachronistic, even as he certainly qualifies as the better 'originalist' on this point.[52]

The contemporary turn in First Amendment doctrine toward privileging speaker interests is ahistorical and theoretically problematic, but it might be defensible on practical grounds. It could be the case that speaker interests can be turned into operational legal rights in a more disciplined, less politicized, way than is true for audience and societal interests, which are harder to evaluate because the frame of reference is necessarily broader and more drawn out chronologically. That is a plausible theory, but whether experience confirms it is open to question. The Court's recent performance in finding case-dispositive speaker interests in the *Arizona Free Enterprise Club's Freedom Club PAC* and *NIFLA* decisions discussed above hardly inspires confidence on this point.

The Justices who made up the majority in *Alvarez* declined to disable government entirely from the punishing of lies. Longstanding laws against perjury and either impersonating a government official or lying to one are not imperiled by the Court's ruling, they specified.[53] More generally, both Justice Kennedy's plurality opinion and that of the concurring Justices appeared to signal a willingness to uphold public regulatory authority over knowing lies that cause material harm to specific individuals.[54] Thus, *some* interests other than those of speakers were recognized, but those were not the regulatory interests that carry First Amendment valence. To permit

[51] See, e.g., *Sorrell* v. *IMS Health, Inc.*, 564 US 552 (2011) (extending 'the freedom of speech' to include private sales pitches to doctors by representatives of drug companies).

[52] See text at n. 25.

[53] *United States* v. *Alvarez*, 720–21 (plurality opinion).

[54] Ibid. at 723 and 734 (Breyer J, concurring).

individuated material interests to justify the punishment of lying but not the regulatory interest in preventing the general public from being deceived about a matter of common concern is perverse from a First Amendment standpoint. It means that the liars who have the most freedom to practice their craft are those whose principal victim is public understanding.

One argument for limiting the power to punish lying to cases of individuated material harm might be the supposition that those kinds of harms are the most serious. Both the plurality and the concurring Justices in *Alvarez* appear to have embraced that view. But such an evaluation would certainly have surprised the generation that gave us the First Amendment. To conclude that it is a lower-level harm to cause the public at large to be misinformed about such a matter as the credentials and truthfulness of a public official is, to put it mildly, in some tension with the founding generation's preoccupation with public opinion as the single most important object of institutional design. As Madison observed in an essay published four days after the ratification of the First Amendment: 'Public opinion sets bounds to every government, and is the real sovereign in every free one.'[55]

Over a century ago, Judge Learned Hand identified a procedural incongruity that helps to explain why audience and societal interests in the freedom of speech tend to be undervalued in the United States. In a letter to the great First Amendment scholar Zechariah Chafee, Jr., Judge Hand said: 'while the justification for freedom of speech is public enlightenment, historically the "right" – though I join you in hating the word – is vested in the speaker constitutionally'.[56] Usually, the First Amendment interests of speakers and their audiences are aligned, so it does not matter greatly that audience and societal interests in public enlightenment find their expression through speakers who are resisting being regulated. But there is no such alignment when lies are at issue. In that situation, the First Amendment interests of audiences and the broader public typically are served rather than threatened by laws punishing lying. When that is the dynamic, it is important that those interests not lose their special First Amendment salience simply because they are being asserted to justify rather than invalidate a regulation. That, I claim, is what happened in *Alvarez*, at least in the plurality and concurring opinions. As a result, the way that liars not only exercise the freedom of speech but also undercut it did not influence the outcome of the case as much as it should have.

In the United States courts have played an outsized role in giving meaning and efficacy to the freedom of speech. In other countries, that responsibility has been divided more widely among various government actors. As digital technology increases the incidence, extends the range, and magnifies the consequences of

55 James Madison, 'Public Opinion', *National Gazette*, 19 December, 1791, in Madison, *Writings* (n 2) pp. 446–47.

56 Letter from Learned Hand to Zechariah Chafee, Jr., 2 January 1921, reprinted in (1975) 27 *Stanford Law Review* 769, at 771.

deliberate lying, governments and citizens worldwide can be expected to look beyond their own borders for assistance in trying to fashion a regulatory response that addresses the problem but still does justice to the freedom of speech. In doing so, they should keep in mind that the juriscentric way that constitutional rights have been elaborated in the USA has led to an unfortunate understanding of the freedom of speech that privileges speaker interests over audience and societal interests relating to the acquisition of knowledge, thereby giving liars more than their due.

For EU product safety concerns, contact us at Calle de José Abascal, 56–1°,
28003 Madrid, Spain or eugpsr@cambridge.org.

www.ingramcontent.com/pod-product-compliance
Lightning Source LLC
Chambersburg PA
CBHW062133200625
28534CB00004B/33
* 9 7 8 1 0 0 9 3 7 3 2 8 9 *